HERESY IN THE LATER MIDDLE AGES

Heresy in the Later Middle Ages

THE RELATION OF HETERODOXY TO DISSENT c. 1250–c. 1450

by

GORDON LEFF

VOL. II

MANCHESTER UNIVERSITY PRESS
BARNES & NOBLE, INC., NEW YORK

Manchester University Press
316–324 Oxford Road
Manchester 13, England

U.S.A.

Barnes & Noble, inc.
105 Fifth Avenue, New York, N.Y. 10003

Printed in Great Britain by Butler & Tanner Ltd, Frome and London

Contents

PART THREE: THE TRUE CHURCH

PART THREE

The True Church

V

The Doctrinal Background

The convergence between heresy and non-heresy is nowhere closer than in the political and ecclesiological doctrines of the later middle ages. Thinkers like Marsilius of Padua, William of Ockham, Dietrich of Niem, Pierre d'Ailly, and John Gerson shared the same preoccupation over the state of the church as Wyclif and Hus. Reform was the focus of their attention, and prolonged crisis, extending throughout the whole of the fourteenth century into the first half of the fifteenth, their background. Whilst there were plenty of thinkers like Giles of Rome, James of Viterbo, Alvarus Pelagius and Augustinus Triumphus willing to press papal claims to extremes, there were also many like those mentioned above who were for different reasons concerned to redefine the relation between spiritual and secular authority: if in the case of Marsilius, and to a lesser extent Ockham, this was done to the church's detriment, it was also for men like Henry of Langenstein, Dietrich of Niem, d'Ailly, Zarabella, Gerson, sheer necessity if the church was to be saved from the complete degradation and paralysis of schism. Consideration of their different notions would take us far beyond the bounds of our subject; but something must be said of the point at which they impinged upon the ideas of Wyclif and the Hussites in order to see the relation between them and the climate in which they were formed.

Its exceptional nature hardly needs stressing. In the first place, it witnessed a period of renewed struggle between pope and secular ruler, first that between Boniface VIII and Philip the Fair of France (1285–1314) and then between John XXII (1316–1334) and Louis of Bavaria (1314–47). Both conflicts gave rise to a rash of new polemics on each side;[1] but in the case of John XXII these coalesced with his involvement against Michael of Cesena and his followers, and his condemnation of John of Jandun and Marsilius of Padua in 1327,[2] all of whom sought refuge at the court of Louis of Bavaria. Accordingly political theory (in

[1] See R. Scholz, *Die Publizistik zur Zeit Philipps des Schönen und Bonifaz VIII* (Stuttgart 1903); and *Unbekannte kirchenpolitischen Streitschriften aus der Zeit Ludwigs des Bayern 1327–1354* (Rome 1911–14).

[2] MGH *Constitutiones*, vol. VI, pt. I, no. 361, 265 ff.

Marsilius's *Defensor pacis*), the doctrine of poverty, and the personal sins of the pope, mingled with imperialist polemic, often—as in the writings of Ockham—in the same treatise. In that sense the pope's position was probably more seriously impugned than at any previous time; for in addition to the traditional arguments over the limitations of his office and his subordination to the emperor, there was a whole new range of questions which derived from Franciscan sources: notably the concepts of apostolic poverty, simplicity and equality in the primitive church, and the pope's violation of them in claiming legal jurisdictions which had no apostolic foundation. To this was added the unremitting personal campaign of Michael of Cesena, and especially Ockham, against the pope personally; Ockham's compendia of the errors of John XXII and Benedict XII and his repeated charges of heresy against them became common currency by the later fourteenth century. Not only Wyclif and the Hussites spoke of deposing heretical popes; the Council of Constance took the final step of doing so when it deprived John XXIII of his office on seventy-one counts of scandalous and heretical conduct, on 6 April 1415.[1] This, however, was to give practical expression to a doctrine which had received its initial impetus from the Franciscan attacks on John XXII. Lastly, there was the growing crisis within the church, partly through the impact of the developments just mentioned and partly through its own evolution. The permanent establishment of the papal curia at Avignon, next to France, involved it not only more closely with French policies but led to an almost equally permanent papal Italian policy designed to further the pope's return to Rome. It involved John XXII's embroilment with Louis of Bavaria and constant expenditure on financing military campaigns. This in turn accentuated the growing system of papal reservations which became the (no doubt exaggerated) focus of such resentment. At the same time, the coming of the Hundred Years' War between France and England not only hardened the divisions in western Christendom but involved the papacy in them: the English tendency to regard the pope as pro-French was expressed in the hostile anti-papal legislation of the 1350s.[2] National resentment at papal taxation and patronage was a powerful factor in both the Lollard and Hussite movements as we shall see. But undoubtedly the most cataclysmic event from the point of view of the church was the Great Schism, above all the fact that it lasted for nearly forty years. It crystallized what had as

[1] H. Finke, *Acta Concilii Constantiensis* III, 156–209.

[2] See Prologue, p. 24 above.

yet been a series of inchoate ideas and aspirations into something like a coherent movement based upon the common premise that if the papacy could not reform itself the church in the form of a general council must do it instead.[1] The direct contraposition of pope to council and the faithful, however much it may have been foreshadowed in the writings of the earlier canonists,[2] is one of great new facts of later medieval ecclesiology. All the qualifications of its advocates must be set against its actual realization at the Council of Constance. For the first time a general council took it upon itself to depose the reigning pope and his rivals and appoint a new one instead. Although the conciliar movement failed to retain its impetus and gradually came to a standstill in the ten indecisive years of the Council of Basel (1431–41) enough had been said and done to destroy the idea of papal ecumenicality. Wyclif and Hus had not been alone in their challenge to the pope.

* * * *

So far as their bearing upon Wyclif and the Hussites is concerned, we may divide later political and ecclesiological doctrines into two groups: those which directly influenced Wyclif and the Hussites; and those with which there was a parallelism. In neither case was there a complete correlation. Both in his premises and his conclusions Wyclif remained distinct from any other fourteenth-century thinker; while Hus can hardly be credited with a system as opposed to a set of tenets. It is rather that their ideas were part of the currency of the fourteenth and fifteenth centuries even if the stamp which they gave to some of them was distinctive.

Of those who directly influenced the political thinking of Wyclif and his followers, Marsilius of Padua and William of Ockham are the most important. While the first provided the very substance of their attitude towards the church, the latter, frequently cited by name, gave the personal example of anti-papal defiance. With Marsilius, the practical affinities with Wyclif are *prima facie* so striking that it is easy to forget that they began from entirely different premises. Wyclif, as we shall

[1] On the conciliar movement see E. F. Jacob, *Essays in the Conciliar Epoch* (Manchester, 3rd edn., 1962); J. B. Morrall, *Gerson and the Great Schism* (Manchester 1959); H. Heimpel, *Dietrich von Niem* (Münster 1932); M. Creighton, *History of the Papacy*, vols. I and II (London 1907–9); L. Salembier, *Le Grand Schisme de l'Occident* (Paris 1922); W. Ullmann, *The Origins of the Great Schism* (London 1948); N. Valois, *La France et le Grand Schisme d'Occident*, 4 vols, (Paris 1896–1902).

[2] See B. Tierney, *The Foundations of Conciliar Theory* (Cambridge 1955).

see, derived his outlook on the church from an extreme and deformed Augustinianism which was essentially metaphysical. Marsilius, on the other hand, based his upon a denial of the independent existence of the church. Wyclif made the true church so exclusively the preserve of the elect that it bore no immediate relation to ordinary believers or the visible hierarchy. Marsilius went to the other extreme of making the church so comprehensive—as the *communitas fidelium*—that there could be no juridical distinction between it and the rest of the community.[1] It thereby became merely a part of the state with no independent standing. Wyclif in his doctrine of dominion and grace—derived ultimately from the arch-papalist Giles of Rome—treated all power in supernatural terms; Marsilius in his conception of a human legislator did not look beyond the community.

These extremes met in a common denial of church autonomy. Marsilius has often been called an Averroist.[2] If the term means anything at all it denotes the irreconcilability of faith and reason so that each must be allowed to go its own way. What this is supposed to connote in political terms, other than the separation of church from state is not clear; but it can hardly be said to be of relevance to Marsilius who, far from wanting to see the separation of the secular and the spiritual powers, advocated the rigid subservience of the latter to the former. Moreover, whatever Marsilius's philosophical and theological views, and these are not known, politically he certainly did not deny the church its spiritual attributes. He was anti-sacerdotal but not anti-ecclesiastical in the wider sense of rejecting the church's role. His Aristotelianism was directed to bringing everything within the community's purview, which is quite the opposite of excluding the church. To call Marsilius an Averroist therefore seems unapt.

This said, however, it would be hard to gainsay the revolutionary implications of Marsilius's doctrines, which far from falling into oblivion until the Renaissance,[3] were to a large extent incorporated by Dietrich of Niem as well as by Wyclif and to a lesser degree the Hussites. The nature of the *Defensor pacis*, Marsilius's main work,

[1] Lagarde, *La naissance de l'esprit laique*, II, 204 ff., sees this conception of the church as responsible for Marsilius's attitude towards it. But it derived from St. Augustine and was common to the majority of thinkers.

[2] See A. Gewirth, *Marsilius of Padua*, I (New York 1951) 39 ff. for details.

[3] The implication for instance in C. W. Previté-Orton's, Marsilius of Padua, (*Proceedings of the British Academy*, vol. XXI, 1935) and A. P. D'Entrèves, *The Medieval Contribution to Political Thought* (Oxford 1939) 44–87.

has often been described.[1] Briefly, it was designed to establish on Aristotelian lines the secular organization of the state and the subordination of the church to it. The first and shorter part (dictio I) is concerned with the source and the division of political power, which springing ultimately from the entire community (*legislator*), is vested in the ruling part or executive (*pars principans*) by the weightier part of the community (*valentior pars*). If most of Marsilius's discussion of these matters is faithfully Aristotelian and largely based upon the Italian city, it is not confined to these sources. It is also, he says, necessary to look beyond demonstrable experience to the community's final cause or purpose. For this a priesthood and a church are necessary.[2] Moreover, even while immersed in Aristotelian categories, Marsilius shows a flash of true Augustinianism when he asserts that had Adam not sinned there would have been no need for civil authority.[3] If the people is the first efficient cause of the laws by which the *pars principans* regulates society,[4] God's will is their formal or ultimate cause.[5] Accordingly, even within the confines of the community, the church is necessary. For this reason it is false to attribute to Marsilius an exclusively lay attitude or to see him as the forerunner of the modern secular state. Where the latter has absolute sovereignty, Marsilius's rulers were bound by divine law to which they must always submit; in the event of any conflict between human and divine precepts, the divine must be obeyed,[6] even though Marsilius did not specify how. This was essentially a Christocentric conception of society; indeed its anti-sacerdotalism derives its force precisely from this very fact. Had the church not been an integral part of society it could have been simply cast aside. Because it was necessary, Marsilius was able to devise its greatest discomfiture at the hands of a society from which there was no escape. This occupies the second part (dictio II) of the *Defensor*, which is over four times the length of the first part, and which from our point of view is where the interest of the

[1] E.g., A. Gerwith, *Marsilius of Padua*, 2 vols. (New York 1951–5), C. H. McIlwain, *The growth of political thought in the West* (New York 1932) 297–313, J. B. Morrall, *Political Thought in Medieval Times* (London 1958) 104 ff. There are two editions of the *Defensor Pacis*, by C. W. Previté-Orton (Cambridge 1928) and R. Scholz (Hannover 1932). That by Scholz has been used here.

[2] *Defensor Pacis*, dictio I, ch. 4, 19; ch. 5, 25.

[3] Ibid., x, ch. 5, 29.

[4] Ibid., ch. 11, 63–4.

[5] Ibid., ch. 9, 39.

[6] Dictio II, ch. 5, v absque dubitatione aliqua tenendum est, omnes homines . . . personaliter subesse debere iurisdictioni principum seculi, et eisdem obedire in hiis omnibus que non contradicunt legi salutis eterne . . . (188).

work lies. We shall discuss it in those aspects which were later to be significant for Wyclif and the Hussites.

In the first place, and in many ways the foundation of all that followed, Marsilius denied the church an independent coercive authority; just as Christ and the apostles had submitted to the lay power, so must the church. When Christ said before Pilate, 'My Kingdom is not of this world' (John 18: 36) he was speaking for all his successors.[1] It proved that Christ had come into the world to wield not temporal but spiritual power.[2] The distinction between Caesar and God must never be blurred.[3]

In the second place, and inseparable from what has just been said, Marsilius took the example of the primitive church as his model for what the present church should be. Like Ockham he turned away from the canonists, whom he detested, to scripture and also to history for his authority: the sayings of Christ, the apostles, and the *sancti*, together with a critical use of historical sources, such as the chronicle of popes and emperors by Martinus Polonus and the—since proved—pseudo-Isidorian collection of letters and decretals. This historical awareness was shared in a marked degree by Wyclif and to some extent Ockham. It owed much to the prevailing Franciscan emphasis upon apostolic perfection in the disputes over poverty; but, in Marsilius's and Wyclif's hands, it took on a new importance as critique of the entire claim to Petrine and Roman hegemony of the church. This had two facets. One was the denial of hierarchy: Marsilius seems to have been the first to make it a serious argument against the power of the pope and cardinals that in the primitive church there had only been two orders—those of priests and deacons; bishop and priest had been synonymous,[4] and correspondingly pope and cardinals non-existent. They had no coercive power over bishops and priests.[5]

The second facet was more far-reaching and of incalculable influence upon Wyclif and Hus: namely a denial of the primacy of Rome. Here Marsilius called upon historical and textual criticism to show, first, that Peter's position among the apostles was purely personal to himself: two, that it had never been transmitted to the pope as Christ's vicar;

[1] *Defensor Pacis*, dictio II, ch 4, 3, 160–1.

[2] Apparet igitur ex predictis quod de carnali seu temporali regimine vel iudicio coacivo Christus in mundum disponere non venit, sed de spirituali regno sive celesti (ibid., 164).

[3] Ibid., 169–70.

[4] Dictio II, ch. 15, 5, 329.

[5] Ibid., II, ch. 1, 3–5, 140–1.

three, that there was only one head of the church—Christ; and four that to be bishop of Rome was merely what the title said and did not entail universal headship of the church. All the apostles, Marsilius averred, had been under the authority of Christ;[1] they had all been equal with one another;[2] and Peter had never tried to make himself pre-eminent or exercised coercive authority over them.[3] Far from the pope's having been Peter's appointed successor as head of the church, any bishop was indifferently the successor of the apostles and had his power immediately from Christ.[4] The only way in which anyone could be said to be in the apostolic succession was by conforming to the apostles' way of life.[5] This was the distinguishing mark, not difference of status. Undoubtedly the most audacious part of Marsilius's attack on the primacy of the pope was his denial of its Petrine origins. This took two forms, scriptural and historical. Scripturally, for centuries the *locus classicus* for Petrine primacy had been Matthew 16: 18: 'Tu es Petrus, et super hanc petram edificabo ecclesiam meam.' As interpreted from Augustine onwards, Peter had been identified with the rock on which the church was built. He was its foundation, designated by Christ as his vicar on earth. Those who had succeeded him —the popes—had inherited his primacy. Hence their position derived from Peter's. Marsilius rejected this interpretation. The rock, he said, referred to Christ, not Peter; Christ alone was the head of the church and remained so eternally. He alone was inerrable and impeccable.[6] The church as God's temple embraced the multitude of the faithful;[7] with Christ ever at its head it had no need of a vicar for he alone was its universal pastor.[8] Historically, Marsilius was equally far-reaching. To begin with, there was no evidence that Peter had ever been bishop of Rome;[9] none of the apostles had been associated with any special area.[10] If, however, Peter was to be connected with any city it was Antioch, and Paul should be regarded as bishop of Rome.[11]

Reliance, then, upon Peter, provided no support for papal primacy; he was not chief of the apostles in the sense of having had authority over them; he had not been endowed by Christ with headship of the church and so had no vicariate to transmit; and he had not been bishop of Rome, so that the popes could not be his successors. On these grounds Marsilius denied a divine source for papal authority. It was, he averred,

[1] Ibid., II, ch. 16, 10, 346.
[2] Ibid., ch. 15–16, 336–7.
[3] Ibid., ch. 16, 4, 11, 340, 347.
[4] Ibid., 347.
[5] Ibid., 349.
[6] Ibid., II, ch. 28, 532–4.
[7] Ibid., 549.
[8] Ibid., 547.
[9] Ibid., II, ch. 16, 352.
[10] Ibid., 349 ff.
[11] Ibid., 351 ff.

a purely human institution,[1] and he sought to establish its human origins by substituting for the traditional Petrine claims an historical account of how the church at Rome came to have authority over the other churches.[2] It derived initially from the pre-eminent virtues of Peter and Paul which made all other churches wish to submit to them. This desire, at first a voluntary and spontaneous one, with time gradually took on the force of election; but it had never sprung from any words uttered by Christ or the apostles. With the Synod of Nicea, Constantine had confirmed the pope's primacy by decree. Upon this foundation succeeding popes had asserted their authority over the rest of the church.

Accordingly the pope enjoyed no more power than any other bishop, since he was not God's vice-gerent;[3] nor by God's ordinance was any bishop inferior or subject to the pope.[4] Similarly, the pope had no special spiritual prerogatives denied to the rest of the priesthood. In particular, Marsilius denounced the papal claim to the keys, namely, the power of binding and loosing which Peter was held to have conferred upon his successors. When Christ said to Peter, 'I give you the keys to the Kingdom of Heaven' (Matthew 16: 19), he did not thereby confer absolute power (*plenitudo potestatis*) solely upon the so-called vicar of Christ; it was given to all priests as successors of the apostles and represented in the person of Peter.[5] The same denial of special privileges applied also to the cardinals;[6] it extended not only to things spiritual but also to dominion over material goods. In his arguments against ecclesiastical possessions[7] which he traced to Constantine's endowment of Pope Sylvester I—the commonly accepted beginning of the Church's decline[8]—Marsilius leaned heavily upon the Franciscan Spirituals; in particular he accepted their distinction between use and possession[9] and drew the same conclusion that faithfulness to Christ's poverty meant renunciation of all property and rights of litigation.[10]

The third main feature of Marsilius's outlook was the accompaniment of what has just been said: his contraposition of the bible to papal decrees. Here again he anticipated Wyclif although he did not approach the latter's fundamentalism which, as we shall see, derived from his distinctive metaphysics. The bible, he declared, was the basis of all

[1] Dictio II, ch. 28, 558; also 544.
[2] Ibid., and 378 ff., 427 ff., 468 ff.
[3] Ibid., II, 553.
[4] Ibid., 552, 562.
[5] Ibid., II, ch. 6., 198–200; ch. 28, 534.
[6] E.g., II, ch. 20, 396 ff.
[7] II, chs. 11–14.
[8] E.g., 262.
[9] Ibid., 263 ff.
[10] Ibid.

canonical truth; only that which was contained within it or which necessarily followed from it must be believed.[1] In this Marsilius was not saying anything which had not been said many times before; the scriptural basis of all truth was universally accepted. Where he parted from the accepted path was in directly opposing the infallibility of the bible historically interpreted to the uncertainty of human traditions. There was no obligation to adhere to any writings of human invention just because they were liable to be false.[2] Scripture, on the other hand, in being directly inspired by God, must always be true.[3] The former included all the decretals and decrees of popes and cardinals and all human statutes and canons. None of these need be observed.[4] Significantly, the only qualification to this otherwise inflexible distinction was the interpretation of a general council of the church which in case of doubt had the power to determine what constituted an article of faith.[5] The reason for this lay in Marsilius's conception of the church as the *congregatio fidelium* in the broadest sense of embracing all believers; for a general council as representing the whole body of believers had the power to determine what was canonical.[6] Thus Marsilius was prepared to entrust a general council with the very authority which he denied the pope and cardinals; but he must not for this reason be regarded as a conciliarist in the real sense of the word. Not only did his interest not lie in that direction; but he never seriously concerned himself with the circumstances or machinery of a general council, fifty years before the real need for it arose with the outbreak of the Great Schism. Nevertheless he had already laid it down that the decisions of a general council were to be piously upheld by the human legislator, namely the community.[7] Elsewhere Marsilius described the general council as the supreme authority regulating the church;[8] its jurisdiction, besides covering doubtful matters of faith, extended to all matters of worship. The power to call such a council, however, rested with the legislator; he alone could employ coercion against transgressors,[9] unlike the pope. The most that could be said for papal devices was that they might be useful; but they carried no obligation to obedience.[10] Marsilius thus extended anti-papalism into the very heart of church doctrine; from the traditional attack upon papal claims to supremacy it became a

[1] Dictio II, ch. 19, 384–5.
[2] Ibid., 386.
[3] Ibid.
[4] Ibid., 388–9.
[5] Ibid., 384.
[6] Ibid., 384–6.
[7] Ibid., 386.
[8] Dictio II, ch. 21, 410.
[9] Ibid., 410–13.
[10] Dictio II, ch. 28, 574.

denial of the pope's own jurisdiction within the church. For what appears to have been the first time, the hitherto accepted foundations of papal authority were called into question, and rejected on historical grounds. In Marsilius's hands the church became a house divided against itself: Wyclif was to make the division even wider.

In the fourth place, just as Marsilius limited the temporal power of the church, so he restricted its spiritual ramifications. Here, too, he owed as much to non-Aristotelian as to Aristotelian elements. If the very authority of the human legislator brought much, hitherto accepted as coming under the church, within the purview of the state, the reasons were not entirely from the secular side. Nor were they Averroist. On the contrary, they derived far more from the current Augustinian conception of God's omnipotence. Starting from Augustine's notion of the church as the *congregatio fidelium*, Marsilius sought to minimize the distinction between the priesthood, as an order, and the rest of the faithful. Spiritually, he did so by reaffirming God's immediate involvement in all individual actions such as penitence and contrition. Although the priesthood as a whole—and not just the pope and hierarchy—could exercise the power of binding and loosing, theirs was only a declaratory role. The necessary dispositions for inner contrition and confession—the conditions of absolution—were worked by God in the soul before the priest's act of hearing confession. God alone was responsible for the soul's reformation through grace and the remission of sin.[1] The independence of God's operations from anything a priest might do was, said Marsilius, testified by the canonical authorities, like Augustine, Jerome, Chrisostom, Peter Lombard, Richard of St. Victor, as well as in scripture. God's justice depended upon neither the church nor the priesthood.[2] Conversely, if a priest should mistakenly or unknowingly give absolution for pretended repentance, this likewise could have no effect upon God's judgement.[3]

In the case of excommunication the limitations on the priesthood were of another kind; but they sprang nevertheless from the same divergence between God's will and that of the priesthood: God, says Marsilius, does not always follow a priest's judgement if, for example, it is unjust. Hence the action of the church is not necessarily God's. Since, moreover, the decision to excommunicate someone affects the whole of society, it must be decided by the whole of society, that is the whole body of believers. It belongs to the priesthood to promulgate the

[1] Dictio II, ch. 6., 201–2.

[2] Ibid., 206–7.

[3] Ibid., 207.

sentence or absolution from it, but not to arrive at it or to execute it for this entails the exercise of coercive and juridical power, which the priesthood does not possess.[1] Like doctors diagnosing leprosy the priests may take part in the examination of a suspect against faith, but it is not for them to decide the penalty. This is the function of the community or its *valentior pars*.[2] Even then, Marsilius acknowledged that while the punishment of heretics belonged to secular rulers,[3] judging them belonged to Christ, who would do so in the next world, not in this.[4] Once again we are far removed from a concept of absolute secular sovereignty. We are equally distant from any Averroist notion of God as a remote or indirect influence, oblivious of all individual beings which as *generabilia* and *corruptibilia* have no place in the divine mind but are subject to the determinism of the spheres.

Finally, there was the secular position of the church, or more strictly the relation of spiritual to temporal authority. Here all Marsilius's hostility against the church, and especially the papacy, was given free rein. His catalogue of papal enormities, far from showing him as a calculating exponent of *raison d'état*, reveals him as another Christian moralist outraged by the abuses within the church.[5] The usual ones are to be found. The lust for power, ever-increasing; the presumption to issue edicts which all should obey; the pretensions to worldly authority; the pomp and secular ambitions; the dispensing of benefices and the appointing of officials. Marsilius saw the roots of these evils in the corrupting effect of false claims to absolute power (*plenitudo potestatis*)—which in none of its different forms belonged to the pope[6]—and the betrayal of Christ's precepts of poverty and simplicity.[7] They had led to false claims of hegemony over the emperor,[8] to the sowing of tares and schism,[9] and to the excesses which had rendered the papacy into a deformed monster.[10] The true bride of Christ was the multitude of the faithful, not the modern Roman pontiffs.[11]

It is not too much to see this anger as the motive force behind Marsilius's measures against the church. In effect, they amounted to its complete submission to the secular power in all matters other than the purely spiritual functions of worship and the administration of the

[1] Ibid., 209–10. [2] Ibid., 210–11.
[3] Dictio II, ch. 10, 244–5. [4] Ibid., 246–7.
[5] Dictio II, ch. 23, 24, 447–51.
[6] Ibid., ch. 23, 441–5; ch. 24, 459–61.
[7] Ibid., ch. 24, 454; ch. 25, 467. [8] Ibid., ch. 26, 489.
[9] Ibid. [10] Ibid., ch. 24, 459. [11] Ibid., ch. 26, 489.

sacraments. To use his own expression ecclesiastics should be as 'slaves' (*in forma servi existens*) to be judged by the coercive power of others.[1] More specifically this put into secular hands the passing of all judgements and sentences;[2] the correction[3] and regulation of the priesthood, such as compelling them to confer the sacraments;[4] their material provision;[5] the withdrawal of benefices and the imposition of taxes;[6] and the summoning of a general council[7] by whose authority alone a ruler could be excommunicated.[8] Accordingly it was to him alone that full authority—superior to anything enjoyed by the church—pertained.[9] He could, as the ruler over all temporalities, even go so far as to compel the cession to him of a church building (*basilica*), since the church had no right (*ius*) to any temporal ownership.[10]

We return, then, to our starting point: the church's lack of any separate juridical standing as a distinct institution. This was to revert to the pattern of the primitive church, enjoying neither possessions nor legal rights, but firm in the faith of Christ from which all its authority sprang. No one can deny that it was extreme; if followed it would have taken the church back not only to Christ but to its pre-reformed state of subservience to lay power. Yet it was also a moral concept which served to inspire Wyclif and the Hussites. To forget this and to treat Marsilius as an anti-ecclesiastical Aristotelian is at once to remain outside his thought and to fail to recognize his vast influence upon other reformers. How great it was will be apparent when we come to examine Wyclif and Hus.

When we turn to William of Ockham we are dealing with a very different kind of political thinker; as Scholz has truly remarked[11] he is less a political thinker than a theologian concerned with questions of right. In one sense much the same might be said of Marsilius; or, at least, that he was scarcely less a theologian than a political writer. But beyond any such formal similarity, they are quite distinctive in approach. Marsilius, though repetitious, was systematic and direct, dominated by a central theme. There are no nuances and few enigmas in his work. Ockham's political writings are copious, and the work of contrasting moods. Some of them are open and unrestrained polemics

[1] Dictio II, ch. 9, 238. [2] Ibid., ch. 10, 252. [3] Ibid., ch. 30, 596.
[4] Ibid., ch. 17, 368. [5] Ibid., 371. [6] Ibid., 373–4.
[7] Ibid., ch. 18, 382. [8] Ibid. [9] Ibid., ch. 21, 402.
[10] Ibid., ch. 28, 549–50.
[11] R. Scholz, *Wilhelm von Ockham als politischer Denker* (Leipzig 1944), Introduction 27.

against papal power and the popes John XXII and Benedict XII, more outspokenly personal than anything Marsilius wrote; others like the enormous *Dialogus* are deliberately elusive and impersonal, almost extended private games in which one has to guess who believes what. Ockham's work was seminal in the literal sense; unlike Marsilius he did not pass on full-fledged an entire anti-ecclesiastical armoury; he scattered the germs of future concepts, so that it is possible to see his influence among a diversity of thinkers and ideas. Possible but not always fruitful; for Ockham is best judged not by the half-formed suggestions that can be traced to him, but to those ideas that he stood by and openly made his own.

When these are examined it is difficult to see why he should have been so long bracketed with Marsilius and impossible to treat him as a representative of the lay spirit. Compared with Marsilius, Ockham was traditional; compared with himself as a speculative theologian, Ockham the political thinker was conservative. He neither created a new set of concepts nor combined existing ones into a new outlook. Most of his polemics repeated existing—mainly Franciscan—arguments which, even when applied dispassionately, as in the *Opus nonaginta dierum*, added little that was novel. Yet if we cannot look for the revolutionary iconoclasm of Ockham's philosophical ideas in his political writings, they remain none the less indispensable. The reason lies in his preoccupation with certain central themes which recurred throughout the fourteenth and earlier fifteenth centuries. These centred on the relation of spiritual to secular power and the necessary limitations upon each. More specifically, they raised the question of the extent of papal and imperial jurisdiction and the measures to be taken in the event of a pope becoming ineligible or his office vacant. The greatest difference between Ockham and Marsilius is that whereas Marsilius's doctrine was designed to the single end of subordinating the pope and *sacerdotium* to the secular power, Ockham was concerned for each to have its due authority. Hence, although he pilloried the abuses of the curia and arraigned John XXII and Benedict XII as heretics, his attitude towards the papacy was essentially moderate; it was far from being anti-sacerdotal or imperialist as might appear *prima facie* from one who was the emperor's chief apologist. Yet even in his most unrestrainedly anti-papal tracts, like the *Breviloquium* or *De imperatorum et pontificum potestate*, Ockham never went beyond rebutting excessive papal claims to spiritual and secular jurisdiction; he denied not the pope's traditional spiritual *potestas*, but the assertion of a *plenitudo potestatis* covering all things secular and spiritual. He sought to restore the balance between the two in, largely, traditional terms. It was this which marked him off from Marsilius even when he seems to come closest to him, as in their common assertion of Christ's headship of the church and the denial of ecclesiastical jurisdiction or dominion. In fact they were arguing for different things: Marsilius total subservience of ecclesiastical to temporal power; Ockham freedom from total ecclesiastical power. Marsilius looked for unconditional submission; Ockham for mutual rights. In that sense he was a constitutionalist who regarded the exercise of power as conditional upon observing its limitations. Most of his discussion was concerned with adumbrating what these were and what was to be done when they were not fulfilled. Much of this was to be of relevance to the notions of the conciliarists, especially Pierre d'Ailly, although Ockham himself cannot be called one.

Indeed it is otiose to try to classify Ockham in such terms because his concern was with the right exercise of power as such rather than with asserting the prerogatives of any one group. For that reason, his attack on the papal claims to a *plenitudo potestatis* was far more an advocacy of freedom than of an imperialist or conciliarist viewpoint. This affirmation of freedom was as distinctive to Ockham as its denial was characteristic of Marsilius: in that sense they were at opposite poles. For Ockham, Christ's law meant freedom: namely to do what God—the fount of freedom—had willed, as given through his word in the bible.[1] Ockham, like Marsilius, based himself upon scripture and the truths which could be deduced from it. In this case he enunciated five different levels of Catholic truth. First came all that was to be found explicitly or was necessarily implicit in scripture: this had to be believed. Second were the subsequent accounts of the Apostles by their disciples as distinct from what was contained in the bible. Third the histories of chronicles. Fourth legitimate inferences from any of the above sources. Fifth a

[1] E.g., Christus dedit legem tam perfecte libertatis quod revocatis ceremonialibus veteris legis papa super Christianos nullam habet potestatem nisi quod ad illa que precepta sunt vel prohibita a deo (*Dialogus* in Goldast, *Monarchia* II, pt. III, tract II, Bk. III, ch. VII, 935). See also *Breviloquium*, 58; *De imperatorum et pontificum potestate* in Scholz, *Unbekannte kirchenpolitischen Streitschriften* II, 456, 468, 474.

A great deal of play has been made with the difficulty of distinguishing Ockham's own beliefs in the *Dialogus* because all the arguments are framed in the third person. But this is often more apparent than real, since they can be either directly correlated with Ockham's avowed views in his polemical works or deduced from his outlook as a whole. Although these methods do not fully solve all the enigmas they reduce them in the main to marginal matters rather than problems of substance.

special revelation from God.[1] There was therefore the same combination of scriptural authority, rational deduction and historical evidence as in Marsilius, and, in a modified form, Wyclif. Once again, papal decrees and human laws were excluded; Ockham, like both Marsilius and Wyclif, denied them any independent validity. If they accorded with Catholic truth they were to be believed; if they did not, they were to be rejected.[2] So far there was community between the three thinkers in narrowing the sources of canonical truth to scripture, reason and history. Whatever the qualifications that can be made, their exclusion of many papal and ecclesiastical enactments breached the union between the bible and tradition—certainly the tradition of the church in any meaningful sense since the time of Constantine.

It was Wyclif who was to carry the opposition between the 'modern' church and scriptural and apostolic tradition to its furthest point; but he had ample precedents in Marsilius and Ockham. That said, however, Ockham never employed the distinction beyond the limited aim of exposing as false the pope's claims to a plenitude of power. He thereby differed from both Wyclif and Marsilius. Freedom for Ockham meant guaranteeing the balance between secular and spiritual powers as ordained by God; he invoked God's law to affirm for each the rights which God had given them. The divergence here from Marsilius's conception, and use, of God's law hardly needs to be stressed; it outweighs any affinities of method or argument.

We may accordingly consider Ockham's discussion under the three main heads of spiritual power, temporal power, and the means necessary to ensure their right-ordering. Its point of departure was that both derived from God, and, though distinct, they were also complementary. They both therefore had certain inviolable rights, to infringe which was to violate God's law. In the case of the spiritual power Ockham from the outset parted company from Marsilius in his assumption, made explicit in one of the fiercest of his anti-papal tracts, the *Breviloquium*, that the pope's authority was in part from God.[3] It was therefore limited by the precepts and prohibitions contained in God's law, which was designed to ensure perfect liberty.[4] The pope was bound

[1] *Dialogus* (pt. I, Bk. II, ch. 5, 415–16). In the *Tractatus contra Joannem* (*Opera politica* II) Ockham distinguishes between implicit and explicit truths; all Catholics, whether literate or illiterate, are bound to believe all explicitly given Catholic truths (ibid., 47).

[2] E.g., *Octo questiones de potestate pape* (*Opera politica* I, 26–67).

[3] *Breviloquium* (ed. R. Scholz in *Wm. von Ockham als politischer Denker*, 47).

[4] See p. 424 note 1 (*Dialogus* 935).

to respect the rights and liberties of all who enjoyed them, priests no less than temporal rulers;[1] Peter had received no power from Christ which was not necessary for the regulation of faith or was prejudicial to the rights of others.[2] The pope accordingly had no right to judge the emperor, who had had temporal jurisdiction over all the faithful before there had been a pope.[3] But, in deference to the pope's greater spiritual authority, the emperor did not exercise this right over the pope's own temporalities[4]—a sign of Ockham's essential moderation. From this he concluded that neither pope nor emperor was judge of the other or supreme judge of all the faithful.[5] The arguments against the pope's claim to a plenitude of power were drawn from both divine and natural law, submission to which was the foundation of Ockham's political thinking. Many of Ockham's reasons against papal supremacy were the same as those employed by Marsilius; but as we shall see they were directed to the different end of asserting the evangelical law of liberty. To begin with, Christ had not enjoyed any temporal jurisdiction or servants; therefore the pope, as Christ's vicar, could not have more power than Christ had had.[6] Secondly, Christ had not even conferred his own full spiritual authority upon Peter[7] and certainly not any power to impair the rights and liberties of others.[8] Thirdly, this power had been purely spiritual for the well-being of the faithful. Here Ockham sharply diverged from Marsilius. The words 'Tu es Petrus' signified Christ's spiritual commission to Peter; it gave him power over repentance of sins and for ministering to the faithful, but not full spiritual, and certainly not temporal, jurisdiction.[9] Ockham, therefore, in contradistinction to Marsilius, interpreted Christ's words, as signifying Peter's primacy over the church, restricted though it was. It did not make Peter the head of the church: that was Christ's position; but it did give him secondary headship as applied to this world.[10] More

[1] *Octo questiones*, 35.

[2] Ibid., 41. [3] Ibid., 85. [4] Ibid., 86.

[5] Iuri congruit quodammodo naturali ut imperator non sit ordinarius iudex pape, et papa non est in temporalibus ordinarius iudex imperatoris; ideo in huiusmodi nemo est iudex supremus cunctorum fidelium, nemine excepto (ibid.); see also *Dialogus* 787.

[6] *Octo questiones* (ibid., 31, 57). *Dialogus* 509, 781; *An princeps* (*Opera politica* I, 238, 242).

[7] *Octo questiones* (ibid., 57); *An princeps* (ibid., 243).

[8] *Octo questiones* (ibid., 35); *An princeps* (ibid., 247).

[9] *An princeps* (ibid., 248).

[10] *Dialogus*, pt. I, Bk. IV, 862; also 818.

specifically it meant that the pope's role was that of minister not ruler;[1] his *raison d'être* was the common good, not private interest.[2] His function was exclusively spiritual as it affected the cult of God, reading the bible, praying, preaching, administering the sacraments, and the other prerequisites of salvation.[3]

Ockham's recognition of Peter's primacy made his conception of the papacy radically different from Marsilius's. He did not deny the pope's divine sanction,[4] just as he accepted the traditional interpretation of Peter as chief among the Apostles and in the church.[5] Peter was the rock upon which Christ had built his church and from whom spiritual authority was exercised.[6] The pope was Peter's successor and Christ's vicar, although Ockham concurred in Marsilius's view that Rome itself had no primacy over the other churches: there had been churches before Rome, notably Antioch.[7] But this did not lead Ockham to use the fact as evidence against the pope, any more than he exploited the absence of the pope's name from the bible. He was content to rest his case upon Christ's word and the example of the apostolic church which had possessed neither coercive power nor jurisdiction over temporalities. The power of the keys was for the deletion of sins not the acquisition of possessions; it could not be used coercively[8]—which in another context led him to attack John XXII for trying to impose property upon those (the Franciscans) who had taken the vow of poverty.[9] How strongly Ockham felt towards evangelical poverty can be seen from the treatises he devoted to its defence,[10] and the fact that its denial by John XXII constituted one of Ockham's main charges of heresy against him.[11] In the present context we may refer, for brevity, to Ockham's indictment of the papal court at Avignon in *De imperatorum et pontificum potestate*: namely its desertion of God's law by suppressing freedom to discuss the

[1] *An princeps* (ibid., 243, 251).

[2] Ibid., 233; *De imperatorum et pontificum potestate* in Scholz, *Unbekannte kirchenpolitischen Streitschriften* II, 453–480.

[3] Ibid., 466; *Octo questiones* 104.

[4] *Breviloquium* 47.

[5] E.g., *De imperatorum et pontificum potestate*, 455; *Dialogus* 786–8, 859 ff.

[6] Ibid.

[7] *Octo questiones* (ibid., 82–3).

[8] *An princeps* (ibid., 244).

[9] *Opus nonaginta dierum*, passim; *Contra Joannem* (*Opera politica* III, 110 ff); *Dialogus* 778.

[10] E.g., *Opus nonaginta dierum*, *Contra Joannem*, *Epistola ad fratres minores*, as well as references in most of his other political writings such as *De imperatorum et pontificum potestate*.

[11] The other was on the beatific vision which, John said, the blessed did not receive until the Last Judgement; and this was afterwards declared erroneous.

pope's power, by an abundance of possessions instead of the mere necessities of life, and by intervening in the secular affairs of the emperor and doing him injury.[1] Coercive power, dominion and temporal involvement had been prohibited to his disciples by Christ: they were at once the limitation on a plenitude of power and the condition of spiritual power. In betraying them the pope had betrayed Christ's behests and the apostolic church.

From the point of view of reason and natural experience the case against the papal plenitude of power was correspondingly clear. If the pope were absolute everyone would be subject to him as his slaves; freedom would then be destroyed in violation of God's law.[2] The pope would be able to depose kings and emperors which he could in fact do only exceptionally (*casualiter*) not as a regular occurrence (*regulariter*).[3] Moreover, the pope was a fallible man and, like all men, liable to sin;[4] his office did not confer immunity from these failings. He could therefore be deposed for heresy or other cause of scandal, as we shall see more fully.[5] Finally the pope was subject to the law, both divine and natural. Nor indeed could he make new law, unlike secular rulers; for, as we have seen, his was a purely spiritual and non-coercive role as Christ's minister, not their ruler. The three principles of apostolic rule were the superiority of *spiritualia* to *temporalia*; the divine law of freedom from which no pope could derogate; and the pope's obligation by divine law to do all that was necessary for the spiritual well-being of the faithful within the prescribed limits.[6]

This emphasis upon the pope's obligation to observe the divine law was the source of Ockham's radicalism; it was also one of the main elements in Wyclif's extremism. Ockham did not stop at a general injunction, but repeatedly belittled the pope's own juridical power; so that, as we have seen, a papal decree taken by itself was worthless. If it violated God's law it was to be denounced and disobeyed with impunity.[7] Here Ockham set the example in his attacks upon John XXII as a heretic; and it could be argued that both by precept and practice

[1] *De imperatorum et pontificum potestate* 473 ff.

[2] *Octo questiones* (*Opera politica* I, 28, 32); *An princeps* (ibid., 233); *Dialogus* 776–7.

[3] *Octo questiones* (ibid., 31, 91); *An princeps*, 233. Ockham gives the example of Philip Le Bel who he denies was deposed by Boniface VIII.

[4] *Tractatus contra Joannem* (*Opera politica* III, 72).

[5] *Dialogus* 470–1.

[6] *De imperatorum et pontificum potestate*, 468.

[7] Ibid., 81; *Dialogus*, pt. I, 471 ff., 562 ff. *Contra Benedictum* (*Opera Politica* III, 14, 261–3, 320–2). *Octo Questiones* (ibid., 63, 111–12).

this was where Ockham was subversive. Although with him the church retained its independence, with Wyclif, as with Marsilius, it came near to complete subjugation.

These differences are real, and the reasons for them will be perhaps more apparent when we consider the place of the secular power, and especially the emperor. In the first place, it was complementary to the spiritual power, equally ordained of God, not just permitted by him.[1] The emperor (or lay ruler) was to be obeyed in all temporal matters as the pope was—within accepted limits—in spiritual matters.[2] But with this difference: that lay power was of its nature coercive; its purpose was the punishment of delinquents,[3] and to this end it could, in extreme cases, be used against the pope,[4] as we shall mention shortly. Far from deriving from the pope, the right to temporal possessions and jurisdiction could be granted by God to infidels, as to Constantine before his conversion.[5] It was therefore independent of papal authority.[6] Nor did the emperor need papal consecration, as was shown from the fact that there were emperors before there were popes[7]—an argument used also by Marsilius and Wyclif. For all these reasons secular rulers had jurisdiction over all temporalities including those held by ecclesiastics; and they were able to assert it over the latter.[8] Ecclesiastics were thus bound to obey secular rulers in temporal matters.[9] This did not, however, put lay rulers above the law: like the pope they were subject to its divine and natural dictates;[10] but they also enjoyed the positive jurisdiction which came from upholding the temporal order, and which was denied to the spiritual power.[11] As Ockham put it, what pleased the prince had the force of law, provided it was rationally and justly directed to the common good; if it was not, and was actuated by private interest, it

[1] *Octo questiones* (Ibid., 43); *Dialogus*, pt. III, tract II, Bk. I, chs. 26 and 27, 898–900.

[2] *Octo questiones* (*Opera politica* I, 26); *Dialogus*, Bk. II, ch. 20, 918.

[3] *Octo questiones* (*Opera politica* I, 113); *Dialogus* 911.

[4] *Dialogus*, pt. I, Bk. VI, chs. 92, 93, 610–14; and ch. 97, 619.

[5] *Octo questiones* (*Opera politica* I, 43, 85); *Breviloquium* 124–5.

[6] *An princeps* (*Opera politica* I, 236).

[7] Ibid., 237–8; see also *Octo questiones* (ibid., 91, 97, 165); *Contra Benedictum* (ibid., 277).

[8] *Contra Benedictum* (*Opera politica* I, 277); *Contra Benedictum* (ibid., 277).

[9] *Octo questiones* (*Opera politica* I, 120); *Dialogus* 918, 920, 956.

[10] *Dialogus*, Bk. II, ch. 28, 920.

[11] Here Ockham in *De imperatorum et pontificum potestate* 474, went so far as to say that the emperor was above his own edicts: Amplius imperator solutus est legibus quod precipue veritatem habet de legibus positivis imperialibus; quare consimiliter solutus est consuetudinibus que vim legis habere non possunt, nisi imperiali auctoritate.

was then unjust and wrong and became void.[1] In that sense the lay ruler was no more entitled to claim a *plenitudo potestatis* than the pope; it was rather that his power was of a different kind.

With the nature of both powers thus divinely prescribed it now remains to see how they were to be regulated, and what role each played in the affairs of the other. The key to Ockham's treatment of this problem, which was largely the theme of his *Dialogus*, is to be found in his conception of the church. In that work he defined it as the mass (*multitudo*) of all Catholics from the time of the Apostles until now.[2] It was Christ's mystical body, the dead as well as the living. This view approximates to Augustine's view of the church as the *congregatio fidelium*, which was also, as we have seen, that of Marsilius. Here of course, Wyclif owed nothing to the two fourteenth-century thinkers, since his own notion was derived from extreme realist assumptions which were antithetical to Ockham's way of thinking. Nevertheless, it is possible to see in Ockham a not totally unconnected distinction between the church as a whole, embracing all believers, and the hierarchy or the clergy which were only a part of it. Where the former could never err—however many of its members might do so—the latter could, whether pope, cardinals, the majority of the priesthood, or the mass of ordinary believers.[3] Hence even if in its visible form it could be reduced to perhaps one solitary individual, this still did not derogate from its infallibility since, like an iceberg, it represented only a small part of the unseen whole: a fact which seems to have been ignored by the majority of commentators who tend to see Ockham's suggestion that it could be represented by one woman as a sign of irreverence or dialectical extravagance. The most immediate practical consequence of this view is that, although distinct, spiritual and temporal jurisdiction overlapped.[4] Laymen were members of the church and so, as Christians, were involved in its affairs.[5] But where Marsilius made this community the occasion to submit the whole of the church to secular

[1] Ad illam dicitur quod illud quod placet principi, scilicet imperatori, rationabiliter et iuste propter bonum communem legis habet vigorem quando hoc explicat manifeste. Si autem aliquid placet non propter bonum commune propter sed privatum, non propter hoc legis habet vigorem, scilicet iuste, sed inique et iniuste (*Dialogus* Pt. III, tract. II, Bk. I, ch. 28, 924).

[2] *Dialogus*, pt. I, Bk. I, ch. v., 402.

[3] Ibid., 494–5, 498–9, 502–3.

[4] E.g., *Octo questiones* (*Opera politica* I, 26) where Ockham posits the possibility that the two could come under the same man. See also *Dialogus* 930.

[5] *Dialogus* 602–5, 610–18, 621–7, 631.

oversight, Ockham made it reciprocal—to ecclesiastics as well as secular rulers. Normally (*regulariter*) neither had the right to intervene in the affairs of the other: but they could do so in exceptional cases (*casualiter*).[1] This is what Ockham meant when in reply to Innocent IV he said that the church possessed neither sword—of secular or spiritual jurisdiction; but that it could on occasion take hold of both and depose an emperor should circumstances require it.[2] So could the emperor, in the case of an erring pope to whose regulation his authority did not ordinarily extend. This fluidity in relations between the two led Ockham into an almost endless realm of possibilities; the nuances and distinctions which they engendered make the *Dialogus* a quarry for political concepts and help to explain the elusiveness of Ockham's influence. It contrasts strongly with Marsilius's single-mindedness.

Let us begin with the church. Here the main issue was the role of its members in the event of the pope's defection. As we have earlier remarked, this could be due to his falling into heresy or some other cause of scandal which made it necessary to depose him.[3] For Ockham, heresy automatically disqualified a man from being pope since it excluded him from membership of the church. In being a heretic he therefore deposed himself.[4] In the event of this happening, it rested with the faithful to appoint a successor, since the pope had no power to provide for one.[5] It was over how this was to be done that much of Ockham's discussion revolved. His problem arose from his lack of conviction in any substitute for the universal church. Although he accepted the solution of the calling of a general council, because it was superior to a pope,[6] his qualifications gave it only a limited efficacy. As less than the whole of the church it could not be identical with it.[7] Moreover it could err because, unlike the universal church, it was not the repository of canonical truth. In addition to this inherent inability of any representative—group or person—fully to enjoy the prerogatives of that for

[1] *Octo questiones* (*Opera politica* I, 90, 142); *Dialogus* 929–30, 935–6.

[2] *Octo questiones* (*Opera politica* I, 94); he could also in extreme cases institute a king, as for example Pippin (ibid., 132).

[3] Ibid., 61, 123. *Dialogus* 465, 562, 573.

[4] *Octo questiones* (*Opera politica* I, 81); *Dialogus* 572, 573, 585, 587, 599, 709.

[5] *Dialogus*, ibid., 935.

[6] Ibid., 571.

[7] *Tractatus contra Ioannem* (*Opera politica* III, 54). On Ockham's attitude to a general council see J. B. Morrall's 'Ockham and Ecclesiology' in *Medieval Studies presented to Aubrey Gwynn, S.J.* (Dublin 1961) 481–91. He shows convincingly the essentially anti-conciliar bias of Ockham's thought, especially his 'nominalist' rejection of the notion of corporations as fictitious persons.

which it stood, a general council could be dissolved by human action. The universal church on the other hand would endure to the end of time as Christ had promised. Moreover, all the members of a general council could err; their gathering together in a certain place did not of itself confirm them in faith.[1] The same arguments applied to any group and every person within the visible church, as we have already remarked.[2]

These inherent imperfections in a general council meant that it could only command assent if its decisions were in harmony with the Christian tenets; otherwise, like the pope, it was not to be believed.[3] Only the universal church commanded certainty and its canons completely accorded with revealed truth.[4] Here we revert to Ockham's definition of the church as existing in both time and space. For its continuity through the ages made its own history, in the sayings and practices of the faithful, part of Catholic faith. These, like reason and the deductions from scripture, together with a special revelation, made up the five sources from which authentic doctrine was drawn. They all shared in the certainty belonging to the universal church in contradistinction to the uncertainty inherent in the Roman church and the priesthood.[5] For this reason, a gulf divided Ockham from the conciliarists. The very characteristics which gave the church its sanctity—namely its universality in both time and space—was the one thing for which there could be no substitute. Persons, colleges and councils were, by definition, less than the whole for which they stood. No one was immune from this limitation, even the individual evangelists in comparison with the church as a whole.[6] If it derogated from the pope's claims to unlimited authority it did so no less from those of a general council.

[1] *Dialogus*, pt. I, Bk. v, ch. 25, 494–5. Morrall, art. cit., cites the same passage (481–2).

[2] E.g., *Dialogus* 478 ff. Ockham extends this possibility to the defection of all the living faithful (ibid., 495 ff).

[3] Ibid., 826–7.

[4] *Contra Benedictum*, (*Opera politica* III, 72); *Dialogus*, loc. cit.

[5] *Dialogus* 841. See also the passages taken from *Contra Ioannem* (*Opera politica* III, 64, 65, 67) by Morrall, art. cit., 488–90. This leads him to declare that Ockham 'appeals, we might almost say, to the Universal Church in time as against the Universal Church in space' (ibid., 488). But this is to disregard the fact that for Ockham the church is only universal when it is considered in time. It is not therefore a question of contraposing time to place but of stressing the non-universality of the church when taken merely in its visible form.

[6] *Dialogus* 841–3; *Contra Ioannem* (*Opera politica* III, 66 cited in Morrall, art. cit., 489).

This also helps to explain the other aspect of Ockham's outlook—the role of laymen in the church—and the points at which Ockham and conciliar theory met. For laymen, as members of the church, were involved in its affairs. They could therefore intervene should its spiritual part fail. This could arise from the whole priesthood falling into error,[1] or from its refusal to act against an heretical pope. Temporal rulers could then enquire into his errors although not themselves degrade him.[2] In this sense, certain spiritual matters came within lay purview, such as the case of someone denying the truth of the Incarnation. It could be exercised whenever faith was in danger and needed defending.[3] It was in this sense, also, that the emperor and other laymen could participate in a general council or other measures needed for the deposition and/or election of a pope. Since, by definition, a general council did not stand for the whole church, its actions pertained to all the faithful, women included.[4] They therefore had the right to participate.

In the case of the emperor, he was present as a Christian and as one of the Romans to whom election of a pope ultimately belonged.[5] His right to do so therefore sprang from a common interest in maintaining the due laws and customs of the church, not as a divine mission.[6] It was here, in elaborating the relation between head and members, that Ockham was to influence conciliarists like d'Ailly.

The emperor in common with other Romans had the right of electing (*ius eligendi*) a new pope, if the electors could not agree.[7] This could be done in a number of ways:[8] by a general council, although the right of electing belonged to the Romans, or through kings and other laymen whom the pope could allow. Or again, the emperor could have the right either from the pope and the Romans, or from the pope alone, if the Romans transferred their right to the pope or acted to the detriment of the church. On the other hand, should the pope and the cardinal electors be killed or become heretics, the power of election reverted once more to the Romans. They could, moreover, act without the emperor should the latter try to impede election.[9] In all these different combinations the thread was the same; namely that in the event of the failure of those with power, its exercise reverted to those who, as members of the community, had the right to intervene—whether of

[1] *Dialogus* 489 ff. [2] Ibid., 627. [3] Ibid., 631.
[4] *Epistola ad fratres minores* (*Opera politica* III, 10).
[5] *Dialogus* 930. [6] Ibid., 929. [7] Ibid.
[8] Ibid., 936–8. [9] Ibid., 944.

electing or being elected. Ultimately this came near to a doctrine of popular sovereignty, undeveloped though it was. Indeed Ockham in one passage maintained that the emperor's power was from God by means of popular election.[1] So far as the pope was concerned his fallibility and removability had been repeatedly demonstrated. Not only was he not head of the church, but inferiors, to say nothing of superiors in the form of a general council, could supplant him.[2] There was enough here to influence defenders of the church as well as its detractors, as we shall see. For that reason, Ockham was less a source than a presence which superseded the normal boundaries.

This is apparent when we turn to the second group of thinkers, Pierre d'Ailly, John Gerson and Dietrich of Niem. Their choice, although restricted, is not entirely arbitrary. They were all conciliarists, and all, in their different ways, influential both in the development of conciliar theory and its application at the Council of Constance, the zenith of the conciliar movement. They were also sufficiently distinctive to reflect some of the different elements which comprised its doctrines. Of the three d'Ailly has the greatest affinity with Ockham; and it seems clear that he owed his constitutional approach to him.[3] To say this is not to imply that their outlooks were the same. D'Ailly became a cardinal; Ockham ended his days as a rebel. The difference is reflected in d'Ailly's respect for the ecclesiastical hierarchy, especially the cardinals. In addition, d'Ailly believed that a general council represented the whole church and shared its authority and infallibility;[4] d'Ailly, however, followed Ockham in regarding the pope only as the church's first minister, who, if he erred, could be deposed,[5] as indeed he was at Constance. This was Ockham's nearest point of contact with the conciliar movement; it was also the one at which constitutionalism and subversion merged. Gerson and d'Ailly, Dietrich of Niem and Henry of Langenstein, Hus and Wyclif, met here; the first three helped to depose

[1] *An princeps* (*Opera politica* I, 243).

[2] *Dialogus* 955.

[3] For a comparison between the two thinkers see Miss A. E. Roberts 'Pierre d'Ailly and the Council of Constance' (*T.R.H.S.* 1935, 4th series, vol. 18, 123–42) upon which I have drawn freely. I cannot, however, agree with her view of Ockham as an arch-heretic. On d'Ailly see F. Oakley, *The political thought of Pierre d'Ailly* (Yale 1964) which shows d'Ailly's outlook in a new light. See also E. F. Jacob, 'Conciliar thought' in *Essays in the Conciliar Epoch*, 1–23.

[4] The main source of these ideas is *De ecclesie et cardinalium auctoritate* in Gerson's *Opera* (Antwerp 1706) II, 125–60. Cf. the summary in Jacob, op. cit., 24–5.

[5] Gerson, *Opera* II, 942–3.

a pope and remained within the church; the last two advocated his deposition and were excluded from it. The difference between them was in their means as it was to some extent between Ockham and Marsilius. The conciliarists were prepared to use the mechanisms of the church to effect the change; Marsilius, Wyclif and the Hussites looked outside it to forcible lay intervention: Ockham, as so often, stood between the two, and his legacy extended to both. As taken up by d'Ailly it also included his views on the election of a pope, the right of which belonged to the Romans, but which they could delegate to one or more representatives: on a pope's defection it reverted to the Romans again.[1] The same prerogative to elect its ruler belonged to each community. It applied equally to the cardinals of whom there should be seventy-two from each of the church's provinces.[2] Together pope and cardinals normally ruled the Roman church, as one of a number of individual churches.[3] Like Ockham and Marsilius, d'Ailly accepted Antioch's greater antiquity than Rome; but the latter city had gained primacy.[4] The pope, then, owed his position to election by the community's representatives, who could also revoke it. He was constitutionally circumscribed in much the same way as Ockham had envisaged; nevertheless, d'Ailly's conception of the church was far more hierarchical than Ockham's by the time he wrote his *De ecclesie et cardinalium auctoritate* in 1416. By then he had accepted the church's right to temporal jurisdiction and possessions, as well as the pope's to a plenitude of power so far as canon law was concerned;[5] indeed his express intent was to defend the church's rights in these respects against the Waldensian error—which was also Ockham's—that the church had none.[6] This contrasted with his earlier writings such as *Utrum Petri ecclesie lege reguletur*, where he followed Ockham much more closely; while advancing the claim to a general council's infallibility,[7] he allowed the possibility that all the faithful could err without implicating the whole church in error.[8] Nevertheless, enough of Ockham's influence remained to make d'Ailly reserve the full plenitude of power for the church alone, with consequences we have just enumerated.[9]

It would be wrong to draw any sharp antithesis between d'Ailly and Gerson; they were close confrères for over twenty-five years, and from

[1] Gerson, *Opera* II, 931–2.
[2] Ibid., 135 ff., Jacob, op. cit., 15.
[3] Gerson, *Opera* II, 136–7.
[4] Ibid., 128.
[5] Gerson, *Opera* II, 949–5.
[6] Ibid., II, 926.
[7] Ibid., I, 670.
[8] Ibid., 689–90.
[9] Ibid., 951.

the Council of Pisa onwards among the leaders of the conciliar movement. Both were by then conservatives forced to radicalism through the pressure of events; but both remained firm adherents to hierarchy (*ordo*) even if they differed in emphasizing the role of pope and cardinals. Nevertheless there was a difference.[1] D'Ailly had his roots in Ockhamism and enough survived to influence his conciliarism, as we have seen. Gerson, on the other hand, was never an Ockhamist, and though he took over certain of Ockham's tenets—for example on the will and law[2]—they were of different schools. As both philosopher and ecclesiologist Gerson, unlike Ockham, believed in the independent existence of universal concepts. Whereas for Ockham the church was the totality of its members, and nothing less would do, for Gerson it was the mystical body of Christ as it stood. He accepted it in its visible form, through its orders and sacraments, as the bride of Christ.[3] As such its hierarchy enjoyed the full spiritual power with which Christ had endowed Peter, as well as the temporal authority and possessions which came from its canonical power, natural law, and its temporal needs.[4] The two thinkers therefore diverged over their very conceptions of the church, and also the ways to reform it. Ockham sought them in the renunciation of the pope's claims to a *plenitudo potestatis*, if necessary through lay intervention and coercion; the machinery of a general council was secondary. Gerson looked to the church, i.e. the hierarchy, to reform itself; laymen could not interfere and indeed had no part in its decisions beyond the right to be heard.[5] Nor was a denial of the *plenitudo potestatis* involved. What was required was internal readjustment to correct—or depose—an erring pope; the instrument was a general council, which had all the attributes, which Ockham had reserved for the universal church, of infallibility and fullness of power.[6] Accordingly Gerson's interest centred upon the relations between pope and general council within the existing hierarchy. How to assert the power of the latter without impairing the authority of the former was a conflict which he never completely resolved and indeed he had long sought to avoid.[7]

Gerson's mature conciliar thinking is contained in *De auferibilitate*

[1] A brief comparison can be found in J. B. Morrall, *Gerson and the Great Schism* 112 ff. See also Jacob, op. cit., 12 ff.

[2] Ibid.

[3] E.g., *De auferibilitate pape ab ecclesia* (*Opera* II, 212).

[4] Jacob, op. cit., 24–5; *De potestate ecclesiastica*, consideratio 12.

[5] *De potestate ecclesiastica*, consideratio 12 (ibid., 249).

[6] Ibid., consideratio 10, 239.

[7] Morrall, op. cit., 110 f.

pape.[1] At the centre of it was his conviction in the spiritual *plenitudo potestatis*[2] of the visible church through its hierarchy and sacraments[3]—the opposite of Wyclif as well as Ockham.[4] The church, he said, had received its power from Christ through the apostles and their disciples to whom it had been supernaturally granted.[5] It differed from secular power in being confined to the baptized; and baptism, not grace, as the Waldensians and Wyclifites held, was the condition of its exercise. To say otherwise was to undermine ecclesiastical authority by making it dependent upon unverifiable criteria.[6] This power was twofold: the power of orders, concerned with the sacraments;[7] and the power of jurisdiction, which was both external and internal.[8] Internally, it was through the sacraments and the priesthood as the expression of Christ's mystical body.[9] Externally it was coercive and could be applied to all members of the faithful for their spiritual well-being by means of excommunication, interdict and so on. This was the source of the church's plenitude of power, which could also be turned against the pope.[10] It had been expressed by the decree *Sacrosancta*, passed at the Council of Constance on 6 April 1415, which declared that a general council held its power immediately from Christ, and, as representing the whole of the church, even the pope was subject to it in all that concerned matters of faith and the reform of the church.[11] A general council thus legitimately enjoyed the full powers which had been given to Peter as monarch; it was greater than the pope's, who could be judged by it, but not judge it.[12]

To say this was not to deny the pope's authority; it was rather to make it conditional upon observance of God's law and the laws of the church. This was one of Gerson's most constant themes, pre-dating his conciliar phase of thought. In his *Liber de vita spirituali anime*, written between 1398–1402,[13] Gerson, who here came close to Ockham in holding that Christ's law was the law of liberty,[14] stressed the pope's obligation to abide by the truth of natural and divine law.[15] Failure to do so

[1] *Opera* II, 209–24. [2] Ibid., 225–60.

[3] Morrall, op. cit., 88, 100.

[4] He opposed Ockham's suggestion that only one member of the faithful could remain, on the grounds that its sacramental life and hierarchy were indispensable (*De auferibilitate*, ibid., 212–13).

[5] Ibid., 227. [6] Ibid., consideratio 2.

[7] Ibid., 227–230. [8] Ibid. [9] Ibid., 232.

[10] Ibid. [11] Ibid., 231. [12] Ibid.

[13] Morrall, op. cit., 46. [14] Ibid., 47.

[15] Ibid., 34. Morrall, op. cit., 53 f., to whom I am indebted for these remarks.

warranted resistance to him.[1] Nor, for the same reason, could he change the law as given in scripture or the primitive church.[2] As developed in his later writings, Gerson elaborated the general concept of opposition to an unlawful pope into the positive mechanism of a general council, representing the whole church. Even then he did not conceive it as a permanent state. Ideally the pope as head of the church was *ipso facto* part of a general council which by definition included all its members.[3] But if necessary it could proceed without him on the grounds of the need to observe Christ's law. This appeal over the strict letter of the law to its underlying spirit in order to preserve the law—*epikieia*[4]—was one of the distinctive features of conciliar thought. Ockham had mentioned it in the case of an heretical pope.[5] So had Marsilius. But it was Conrad of Gelnhausen, provost of Worms, who had first put it into a conciliarist context in his *Epistola concordie*, written in 1381.[6] As expressed there its purpose was to 'set aside the letter of the law and follow the law's just reasoning which tends towards the good'.[7] The legislator's intention, which was virtue (*epikieia*), was thereby put first. By its agency, the legal obstacle of the pope's supreme jurisdiction was overcome by moral means. Gerson adopted it, but with caution.[8] In his *De potestate ecclesiastica*, he was principally concerned to show that a pope's authority depended upon keeping to the law. Only if he offended against it could a general council override him. The fact that the latter was infallible, where pope and cardinals were not, did not, however, detract from the pope's own position. His power was integral to the whole church.[9] It derived, absolutely speaking, from God, but was conferred by human agency, through which the power originally conferred on all the apostles by Christ gradually came to be concentrated in the pope as monarch of the church.[10] Unlike Marsilius, Gerson upheld the legitimacy of the pope's power: it was neither purely human, nor was it through spurious claims to Petrine descent. Peter had received full spiritual power from Christ and it had eventually been transferred, with the consent of the whole church, to the pope.[11] It therefore formally resided in the pope;[12] but not exclusively. If he was

[1] Ibid. [2] Ibid., 50.

[3] Gerson, *Opera* II, 235, 243.

[4] For a discussion of it see Morrall, op. cit., 121, and *passim*; and Jacob, op. cit., 9 ff.

[5] *Octo questiones* (*Opera politica* I, 62).

[6] In Martène and Durand, *Thesaurus* II, 1200–26.

[7] Quoted from Morrall, op. cit., 121.

[8] Ibid., 106. [9] Gerson, *Opera* II, 243.

[10] Ibid., 238. [11] Ibid. [12] Ibid., 239.

its fount, it extended throughout the entire church of which he was but a member. For that reason, a general council was his superior, although individually he was superior to any other member.[1]

The pope, then, retained his personal supremacy which, through God's dispensation, could not be permanently superseded by a general council.[2] Even the worst pope, as pope, could be adored, have his feet kissed, and be called 'most holy' (*sanctissimus*).[3] Hus's denial of this constituted one of Gerson's twenty charges against him.[4] Except for a general council, the pope's power was greater than any other, ecclesiastical or lay; it was bound only by the law and the right of a general council to invoke it.[5] In that eventuality, although an individual pope could be deposed, his power continued unimpaired.[6] For Gerson the sooner it could be exercised by a rightful pope, the better.

Doctrinally the gulf between Dietrich of Niem[7] and the two French ecclesiastics was greater than anything which divided them from Ockham. With the latter there was at least some resonance; but with Dietrich, Marsilius of Padua was resurrected in conciliarist form: their ends, certainly, were not the same, but Dietrich drew heavily on Marsilius for the means. At the same time, where Gerson and d'Ailly turned to Ockham's constitutionalism, Dietrich's one point of affinity with Ockham—and there is no evidence that it was direct—was to make still more radical Ockham's radical conception of the universal church. When harnessed to Marsilius's ecclesiology it becomes almost indistinguishable from the ecclesiology of Wyclif and Hus. Hence, once again, we are presented with the paradox that doctrinally, Dietrich of Niem was far closer to Hus and Wyclif, whom he helped to condemn at Constance and to whose followers he advocated no mercy,[8] than to their judges of which he was one. It was a further instance among the many we have already encountered of the convergence of heterodoxy and orthodoxy upon the same issues.

Dietrich of Niem's main conciliarist writing was *De modis uniendi et reformandi ecclesiam in concilio*, first written in 1410 and in a second

[1] Ibid., 243.

[2] Ibid., 245. The words *stante lege* were a set form to express this. Morrall, op. cit., 107 appears to attach another unspecified meaning to them.

[3] Gerson, *Opera* II, 246.

[4] See pp. 644, 649 below.

[5] Gerson, *Opera* II, 248.

[6] Ibid., consideratio II.

[7] H. Heimpel, *Dietrich von Niem* (Münster in W., 1932). E. F. Jacob, *Essays in the Conciliar Epoch*, 'Dietrich of Niem', 24–43.

[8] See p. 644 below.

version in 1415.[1] It is the work of a lawyer turned moralist, not a theologian. Dietrich had been an important member of the papal chancery at Rome, having migrated there from Avignon with Gregory XI. He served under Urban VI, Boniface IX, Innocent VII and Gregory XII with growing revulsion against the abuses in the curia and the continuance of the schism. He finally broke away in 1408 and joined the conciliar ranks, although he was not at the Council of Pisa. His *De modis* formulates as a programme his remedy for the evils which he described in his history of his years at the papal court, in *De schismate*.[2] His disillusionment at the whole system of papal preferments to benefices came with Boniface IX, of whose venality he gives a damning picture.[3] Accordingly when he came to write *De modis* he saw reform of the church as inseparable from reunion. Unlike any of the other writers with whom we are concerned he wrote from inside knowledge of, and disenchantment with, a system in which he had had an important part. This gave his hostility an edge, and makes him perhaps the most effective of all papal critics, from whichever side.

Undoubtedly the most interesting part of *De modis* is Dietrich's conception of two churches, which he called the catholic and the apostolic.[4] The first was universal, embracing all who believed in Christ—Greeks, Latins, barbarians, high and low. Christ was its sole head; the pope was only his vicar for this world provided he did not err.[5] All who belonged to it could be saved,[6] so that, as Dietrich said elsewhere in the work, it constituted the church of the saints.[7] As such a pope was not necessary for their salvation; and the universal church never suffered from schism, sin or error, but remained united in Christ, faith in whom was the one condition of membership.[8]

The apostolic church, on the other hand, was a particular and private church within the universal church. It consisted of the ecclesiastical hierarchy, popes and prelates. Thus the Roman church was under the pope and cardinals who were the heads of the other particular churches. Unlike the catholic church, the apostolic church could err and fall into heresy and schism. It was therefore of secondary authority which consisted in administering the keys of binding and loosing for the universal church.[9] The two churches thus differed as genus and species: every

[1] Ed. H. Heimpel, *Dialog über Union und Reform* (Leipzig 1933).
[2] Ed. G. Erler, *De Schismate* (Leipzig 1890).
[3] Ibid., Bk. II.
[4] *De modis* 7.
[5] Ibid.
[6] Ibid.
[7] Ibid., 35.
[8] Ibid., 7–8.
[9] Ibid., 8.

apostolic church was catholic, but the catholic church was not apostolic.[1] Up to this point the parallel between Dietrich and Wyclif and Hus is striking; but Dietrich was not a metaphysician or a theologian. He was concerned with reform, not immutable concepts. We must accordingly beware of pressing Dietrich too far towards his opponents. Having stated these propositions he went on to declare the need to reintegrate the faithful into the universal catholic church.[2] Thus, even if it meant turning away from the erring hierarchy who were responsible for the separation, this did not entail, as it tended to with Wyclif and Hus, questioning the authority of the visible church in itself. It meant rather restoring its unity and eliminating its abuses.[3] Dietrich's was essentially a constructive attitude conceived within the framework of the present church. It took it as given, whereas for Wyclif the true church and the visible church had no necessary correlation.

Nevertheless despite this difference in assumptions Dietrich came very close to his opponents in his practical arguments. Or more accurately they had Marsilius's arguments in common. Dietrich openly invoked him, calling him the 'great theologian'.[4] He took over from Marsilius the notion that the church should be without temporal power or possessions, and the right of laymen to regulate the church if the need arose. Christ had not had civil dominion or engaged in litigation; nor had he conferred such powers on Peter. He had only given him those of binding and loosing for the treatment of sin.[5] It was an exclusively spiritual authority and carried with it no rights over benefices, castles, cities, emperors or kings.[6] Nor did the emperor owe his position to the pope's power.[7] The pope should relinquish all such claims and return to the ancient law of the church.[8] For Dietrich this entailed stripping away all the accretions since the time of the primitive church, and following Christ's example.[9] To begin with, it meant dispensing with all forms of coercion and temporal jurisdiction. Christ had said, 'My kingdom is not of this world', which meant that he did not rule as temporal kings rule. Coercion belonged to the temporal world of corrupted humanity: it could have no place in true spiritual power.[10]

In the second place the pope did not have absolute spiritual power. In the time of the Apostles, Peter, although pope (a departure from Marsilius), did not rule the whole church alone, but only as bishop of

[1] Ibid., 9. [2] Ibid., 9–10. [3] Ibid.
[4] Ibid., 61. [5] Ibid., 46. [6] Ibid.
[7] Ibid., 47. [8] Ibid.
[9] Ibid., 22. [10] Ibid., 23–4.

Antioch, before transferring to Rome. He could not therefore, as one member, possess the full power of the entire body: and if the latter could function properly of itself without a head, its head could be dispensed with.[1] Furthermore, papal decrees to the detriment of the church, and its true nature as Christ's mystical body, were void. They infringed every order of justice and spiritual good.[2] Since the donation of Constantine there had been many such fraudulent decrees, which should be swept away, including those of Gregory IX, Boniface VIII and Clement V.[3] Over the relation of the bible to canon law and human traditions, Dietrich affirmed that a pope's decrees could not contradict scripture.[4] He fully echoed Marsilius in restricting the pope's spiritual role to administering the sacraments, preaching, and correcting sins,[5] which only God could remit.[6] Thirdly, in keeping with the life of the primitive church, the pope should live in poverty.[7] This, together with his return to his spiritual ministrations, should be the object of reform.[8] It therefore entailed renouncing all claims to benefices, dispensations, reservations and the other abuses with which Dietrich's work resounds. He was drawing upon his own experience under Boniface IX when he said that if there were ten candidates for one benefice all would receive it;[9] or that the popes had a thousand ways of extracting money, by which they despoiled the church.[10] No wonder, he declared, that so few had ever wished to relinquish their office, even if it should mean bringing peace to the church.[11]

He accordingly looked away from the popes to a general council, on the one hand, and lay rulers, on the other, to achieve what the papal curia seemed incapable of doing. In justifying action against the pope Dietrich went beyond d'Ailly and Gerson in two respects. Firstly, he held that a pope who committed simony had sinned mortally and so need not be obeyed—positions adopted by Wyclif and Hus for whom, like Dietrich, simony was a universal affliction. Anyone implicated in evil works was himself evil.[12] Living became the test of sanctity—or at least probity—and so of authority. Here Dietrich was saying what both Wyclif and Hus were condemned for. The only difference was that the two heretics put this notion into a theological context and made the evil-doer also one of the *presciti*, the eternally damned. But in practi-

[1] *De modis* 75–6.
[2] Ibid., 13, 82.
[3] Ibid., 19.
[4] Ibid., 25, 89, 22.
[5] Ibid., 115.
[6] Ibid.
[7] Ibid., 113.
[8] Ibid., 53.
[9] Ibid., 94.
[10] Ibid., 37–8.
[11] Ibid., 106; Jacob, op. cit., 37.
[12] Jacob, 25–6.

cal—and ecclesiological terms—there was no real difference. The pope was to be judged by his deeds: if he was found wanting he automatically forfeited his authority and the obedience due to him. Dietrich also added Ockham's argument that the office did not sanctify the holder, who could not thereby claim immunity.[1] Indeed he went farther and committed another of the errors of which Gerson accused Hus: namely that not to be in grace was to be in sin:[2] and no pope making reservations or appointing to benefices could be in grace.[3] Even if canonically elected he became uncanonical through sinning.[4]

Dietrich's second divergence from his conciliarist confrères was in his recourse to lay intervention—shared by Marsilius, Ockham, Wyclif, and Hus as well as Henry of Langenstein. Here his arguments were more pragmatic. What pertained to matters of faith concerned laymen as well as ecclesiastics, and demanded their participation, as in the early church.[5] In time of stress such as the present, it fell to the emperor to act, and intervene, as Henry II and Henry III had done in the past.[6] It was to the emperor that Dietrich now looked to summon a general council. If he was unable to, then let the kings and princes; and failing them the communities and lay lords. As a last resort the duty devolved upon the ordinary citizens and peasants, for it concerned all the faithful.[7] We are a long way from Gerson's belief in the exclusiveness of the ecclesiastical hierarchy: in practice, of course, both Gerson and Dietrich accepted the emperor Sigismund's hegemony at Constance. The difference was that Dietrich's outlook was formed from the lessons of the past rather than a set of theological tenets. It seems also to have been coloured by Marsilius whose conciliarist tendencies have been underrated as Ockham's have been exaggerated.[8] Marsilius, as we saw, not only accepted the principle of an assembly of the faithful drawn from different nations; he also put it under the aegis of the lay ruler and advocated the participation of laymen.[9]

Nor did Dietrich display any of Gerson's hesitations over its sovereignty. Just as it did not pertain to a pope to summon a general council, so the pope had to obey it in every respect; it could limit his power; it

[1] Ibid., 25.
[2] Ibid., 108.
[3] Ibid.
[4] Ibid., 25–6.
[5] Ibid., 36–7.
[6] Ibid., 71, 72, 90.
[7] Ibid., 100.
[8] The affinities with conciliar doctrine have been clearly shown by Gewirth, *Marsilius of Padua*, vol. I, 286 ff. But he goes too far in calling Marsilius the founder of conciliar theory. See Tierney, *Foundations of Conciliar Theory*.
[9] *Defensor Pacis* II, chs. 20, 21.

could depose him and elect his successor; it could make new laws and abrogate existing ones. Its decisions were immutable—subject only to a future general council; as representing the whole church it had the power of binding and loosing. What it decreed was Christ's law.[1] It must therefore use its power to restore unity and return the church to its ancient laws.[2] This reform must extend to every branch of the church, cardinals, prelates, priests, monks and friars.[3] Dietrich was, like Wyclif, particularly scathing about the last-named. In a city like Cologne, he said, only five among a community of seventy could preach.[4] They should have their liberties and immunities withdrawn.[5] Dietrich also employed the analogy of monarchy as an argument for only one pope; it was the form of government best suited to keep the peace[6]—another echo of Marsilius for whom this was the prime function of government. But just as a king could be deposed for the salvation of his kingdom, how much more did this apply to the well-being of the church.[7] The pope was a man—not an angel—fallible and ever liable to sinfulness and scandal.[8] There must be an authority which could be invoked to make him observe God's law. The need to do so there and then constituted Dietrich's case for a general council. He urged it as a matter of practical necessity; and when it came at last at Constance he was foremost in seeking to give it effect.

Wyclif and Hus, then, were not lone voices. Many others besides those we have just mentioned shared their revulsion at the existing state of the church: some, like Matthew of Cracow in his *De squaloribus*, by denouncing them, others like Zarabella by recourse to the idea of a general council. It was a preoccupation common to the age—or rather its articulate sections. If Wyclif and Hus ultimately went too far, for much of their journey they were of a numerous and distinguished company. The reasons why they became isolated from it form the subject of the final three chapters.

[1] *De modis*, 39–40. [2] Ibid., 46–8, 73–4.
[3] Ibid., 48–9. [4] Ibid., 49. [5] Ibid.
[6] Ibid., 26. [7] Ibid., 16. [8] Ibid., 21.

VI

The Older Heresies and the Flagellants

The traffic between heterodoxy and heresy was not solely one-way. If it is true that most of the heretical beliefs of the later middle ages derived from non-heretical sources, it is equally true that existing heresies—particularly those of the Cathars and the Waldensians—affected later heresy. The Waldensians especially were a pervasive presence which not only left no heretical sect untouched but entered into the very intellectual and spiritual climate of the time. Marsilius, Wyclif and the Hussites all show striking affinities with the Waldensians in some of their most important concepts about the church. Although these were probably not consciously due to Waldensian ideas, the latter almost certainly contributed to the stock from which they were drawn. This should not be surprising. Ideas cannot be compartmentalized. If there are different currents in a society they will certainly meet and often intermingle. Moreover, the process was reciprocal. Just as the older heresies of the Cathars and the Waldensians helped to nurture the newer ones, so they were in turn modified. This applies above all to the Cathars, who, starting from an essentially non-Christian body of belief, came during the thirteenth century to display many Christian traits.

Of the older heresies whose origins lay outside the circumstances which we have been considering,[1] Catharism was the great anomaly.

[1] What follows does not pretend to be an exhaustive treatment of the Waldensians and the Cathars. Both have been the subject of a considerable corpus of work of which the most immediately relevant are cited in the notes to this chapter. Sources for the later middle ages are extremely fragmentary.

For the Waldensians in general see: C. Thouzellier, *Catharisme et Valdéisme en Languedoc* (Paris 1966); K. Müller, *Die Waldenser und ihre einzelnen Gruppen bis zum Anfang des 14 Jahrhunderts* (Gotha 1886); G. Volpe, *Movimenti religiosi e sette ereticali nella società medievale Italiana, sec. XI–XIV* (Florence 1961); R. Manselli, *Studi sulle Eresie del secolo* XII (*Istituto storico per il medio evo, Studi Storici*, Fasc. 5) Rome 1953, ch. IV; A. Dondaine, 'Aux origines du Valdéisme', in AFP 16 (1946) 190–235; G. Gonnet, H. Haupt, W. Preger works cited below.

For the Cathars see: A. Borst, *Die Katharer* (and bibliography) (Stuttgart 1953); A. Dondaine, *Un traité néo-manichéen: Liber de duobus principiis* (Rome 1939); R. Manselli *L'eresia del male* (Naples 1963); A. Dondaine, 'Nouvelles sources de l'histoire doctrinale du néomanichéisme au moyen âge', *Revue des sciences philosophiques et*

Unlike the others, which were Christian in inspiration and aspiration, Catharism was a body of non-Christian belief. It is now generally accepted that it came through the Bogomils in Bulgaria, but whether during the eleventh or twelfth centuries is disputed.[1] Its central tenet was that all being was a dualism between spirit, which was good, and matter which was evil. As developed by the Bogomils in the tenth century, it conceived a radical conflict between the soul and creation; the one was from God, the rest from the devil. Accordingly man's true spirit was not engendered in this world and remained alien to it; he was a fallen spirit[2] imprisoned in an evil body and surrounded by an evil world. The problem was how to extricate himself from it: of preserving the good isolated amidst evil. Envisaging the world as the devil's work meant denying satisfaction of all physical needs since to fulfil them led to the perpetuation of existence and so of evil. It need hardly be stressed how diametrically opposite this was to the Christian conception of providence, as well as rejecting the sacramental life of the church as traditionally conceived. In its stead was an independent hierarchy, which owed no allegiance to Christian authority or practices. In particular the great Cathar division was between the elect (*perfecti*) and the mass of believers (*credentes*) subservient to them. The elect practised to the full the basic Cathar tenets of self-abnegation as the path away from evil. They remained celibate; they abstained from meat; and they led a life of austerity. For the ordinary believers who were not capable of such rigours, a normal life of marriage and the satisfaction of natural needs was permitted, provided that they received the special absolution of the *consolamentum* before death. Since this raised the recipient into the ranks of the elect it was administered only when he seemed beyond recovery. In the event of his survival, however, he was prevented

théologiques 28 (1939) 465–88; 'L'Hiérarchie cathare en Italie' AFP 19 (1949) 280 ff.; 'L'origine de l'hérésie médiévale', *Rivista di Storia della Chiesa in Italia* 6 (1952) 47–78, and works cited subsequently.

[1] See especially Borst, *Die Katharer* 143 ff. Dondaine, op. cit., argues for the eleventh century in opposition to R. Morghern, *Medioevo Christiano* (Bari 1951) esp. 256 ff.; 'Movimenti religiosi populari' in *x Congresso Int. di Scienzi Storiche* (Rome 1955), *Relazioni*, III, 335–56; and 'Le origini dell'eresia medioevale in Occidente' *Ricerche di Storia Religiosa* I (1954) 1–24. He has now been joined by J. B. Russell, *Dissent and Reform in the Early Middle Ages* (California 1965), who, like Morghern, regards most of the known cases of so-called dualism until the 1140s as indigenous manifestations of reform doctrine. There is much force in these arguments, though the inadequacy of the sources robs them of decisiveness.

[2] The expression used at Cologne in 1163. Borst, ibid., 145.

from the perils of relapsing into his fallen state by undergoing voluntary asphixiation or fasting (the *endura*).[1]

The ordinary Christian concepts thus originally had no place in Cathar belief. In the course of time, however, Catharism became modified through the impact of Christianity. During the twelfth century a mitigated[2] form of Catharism grew up alongside its original, more extreme, version. Starting from the assumption common to both, that creation was subject to an evil spirit, the fallen angel Lucifer, the moderate Cathars confined his lordship only to sensible things in species and individuals. God was responsible for the elements and Lucifer for their division into actual material beings.[3] It was in this state that they were evil. There was thus something like a distinction common to the Christian belief between an intelligible archetypal world and its created manifestation.[4] Similarly the moderates, instead of making all souls come from the good God, to which this world was alien, confined the process to the first soul (i.e. the first man). In punishment for his sin he had been imprisoned in a body; but subsequent souls had been engendered naturally thereby giving them a relation to the material world and their own bodies.[5] Terrestrial life, however, remained as a state of punishment; and liberation from it could only come by renouncing material things which were used as a temptation by the devil to keep the soul chained to his domain.[6]

The effects of this modification are also to be seen in the Cathar attitude towards Christian concepts. Thus the Old Testament had been originally denounced by the Bogomils as the work of Satan, depicting him in his evil role as creator of the world. By the thirteenth century the moderates had come to treat the Prophets and the Sapiential Books as divinely inspired, although Rainier Saccone said that the extremists still rejected these.[7] The New Testament was taken as the gospel, although the Apocrypha came to be revered more.[8] Christ likewise began as merely a good angel, the counterpart of Satan, the fallen angel: he was

[1] Ibid., 194 ff.

[2] For this and what immediately follows, see A. Dondaine, *Le liber de duobus principiis* 17 ff.

[3] Ibid., 28–9. Lucifer received permission to establish his rule from God.

[4] This is the theme of John of Lugio (vicar to the bishop of the moderate party of the church of Desenzano), whose system (c. 1250) is described by Dondaine as at once a reaffirmation of dualism and its integration into a system with Christian parallels. Ibid., 51.

[5] Ibid., 29.

[6] Ibid., 29–30.

[7] Ibid., 29.

[8] Borst, *Katharer* 156 ff.

a preacher, not a redeemer. But in the thirteenth century he became transformed into the son of God,[1] although the previous view continued also to be held.[2] In *toto*, however, Catharism constituted a standing challenge not just to the church but to Christian belief. This is where it differed from the other heresies. Its priests (*perfecti*) did not simply perform their own rights and exercise the power of priests; their denial of the worthiness of Christian priests and the Christian sacraments was also a denial of Christian tenets. As a foreign body within the mystical body of Christ, they suffered the near-annihilation of the Albigensian Crusade from which they never recovered.

The Waldensians, on the other hand, are the classic example of Christian piety turning into heresy.[3] They originated as a band of wandering preachers, concerned, like St. Francis and his followers thirty years later, to follow Christ's example and propagate his word. Even Peter Valdes's[4] sudden conversion at Lyons c. 1176, and his decision to sell what he had and give all to the poor, was echoed in Francis's similar resolution at Assisi in 1206. As such they were but one of a number of groups of pious laymen who sought a return to Christ's precepts through a life of poverty and preaching. At first they were accepted by the church for such, in the same way as the Humiliati were. At the Third Lateran Council of 1179, Alexander III approved their vow of poverty, but made their freedom to preach subject to the local clergy's approval. From the outset, they displayed the two most basic characteristics of all heretical movements, a veneration of poverty and the bible; and, more specifically, the desire to emulate Christ in precept and practice. Both aims soon led them into conflict with the church; for in exalting poverty Valdes and his followers were also decrying the luxury and laxity of the lives of the priesthood;[5] and in taking it upon themselves to speak for Christ, they were usurping their role. They were therefore challenging the church in the very process of affirming their own ideals. It was not long before the two clashed. In 1181 the bishop of Lyons prohibited them from expounding scripture. This only inflamed the sect's ardour 'to obey God before man'.[6] Three years later they were condemned by pope Lucius III together with the Cathars,

[1] Borst, *Katharer* 163 ff. [2] See pp. 465 ff. below.

[3] See especially H. Grundmann, *Religiöse Bewegungen* 91 ff.

[4] A. Dondaine in 'Aux origines du Valdéisme' has shown that Peter did not have a surname in his own day and that Valdes, not Waldo, is the correct usage.

[5] Dondaine, 'Aux origines', has pointed to the anti-sacerdotal element in Valdes's exaltation of poverty. [6] F. Tocco, *L'Eresia nel medio evo* (Florence 1884) 172 ff.

the Patarines of Lombardy, and the Arnoldists, at the Council of Verona and a ban put upon all unauthorized preaching.[1] Steps were also taken to track down these sects; as we have seen earlier, archbishops and bishops were ordered to conduct inquisitions in their localities and make inhabitants declare their beliefs on oath, and if necessary purge themselves. The guilty, and especially relapsed heretics, were to be handed over to the lay authorities. This predatory role of the archbishops and bishops marked a new active stage in the fight against heretics which had effectively been inaugurated at the Third Lateran Council in 1179. In acting as apostolic delegates they were in fact carrying out the role of inquisitors; and these measures may be regarded as the beginning of the process which led up to the creation of the papal inquisition under Gregory IX.[2]

The excommunication of the Waldensians and their expulsion from Lyons was the beginning of their evolution into a full-fledged heretical sect. It did not come about at once. Valdes's followers dispersed into Provence and Lombardy, where at Milan they merged with some of the Humiliati, becoming a separate group known as the Poor Men of Lombardy. The same occurred elsewhere. In the course of the thirteenth century the Waldensians spread to most parts of Western and Central Europe, except for England; there can be little doubt that they were numerically the greatest as well as the most widespread of any heresy. Valdes himself may have at first attempted to get a reversal of the ban against him. But he and his followers were irrevocably anathematized. What had originally been a group of pious unlettered laymen, not intrinsically different from the early followers of St. Francis, had by 1215 developed into a recalcitrant sect claiming to be the one true apostolic church and denouncing the Roman church as the *congregatio malignantium* and the whore of Babylon. Whereas Innocent III recognized the piety of the Humiliati in 1199 and constituted them as an order of the church, as he was also to do with St. Francis and his band, the Waldensians were anathematized. Innocent's attitude is understandable. Faced by the intractable Cathars who infested Southern France, the danger of allowing disaffection to spread outweighed every other consideration. As he wrote to the clergy of the province of Bremen in 1214, Valdes was a 'son of perdition, a heretic and schismatic' for denying the power of the keys and presuming to exercise priestly office himself, although excommunicated and deposed.[3] The Fourth Lateran Council

[1] Mansi, 22, 477.

[2] See pp. 41 ff. above.

[3] *Opera Omnia*, PL vol. 217, 280.

in 1215, repeated in general terms the previous constitutions of the Council of Verona, that all heretics were to be delivered to the secular arm for punishment, and their goods confiscated.[1] Its preoccupation with heresy can be seen from Innocent's opening address and the seventeen different canons devoted to the state of the church and the need to reform the life of the priesthood.[2] The path of the Waldensians thus lay outside the church. As we shall see, they came closest to constituting, if not an ecumenical, at least a Europeanwide, counter-church, which outlasted the middle ages and became part of the Reformation.

The Cathars

As we have already mentioned, the Cathars, as the result of the Albigensian Crusade, were dealt an irreparable blow. By the time they become relevant to our study—i.e. from the second half of the thirteenth century—they had long been on the wane, confined mainly to isolated pockets in Languedoc and Lombardy.[3] In Languedoc the coming of the Dominican inquisitors put an effective end to their groups after 1244; in Lombardy they fled in terror from them. Only a few *perfecti* remained in hiding, and by 1275 no Cathar bishops survived; around Albi a few heretics were to be found in cottages. After 1295 there seems to have been a revival and there was mention of some hundred and twenty-five new groups in Provence, totalling a thousand people. But this was shortlived; by 1310 the inquisiton had once again asserted control. The leader of the heretics, Autier, was burned; while others fled to North Spain. In 1326 at Carcassonne the last Cathar in France, Limosus Niger, was burned.[4]

In Lombardy the movement lingered long into the fifteenth century; but south of the Po, in Apulia, Orvieto, Spoleto, Viterbo, Ancona, most of it was at an end by 1280. The large towns, like Milan, Genoa, Verona, Venice and Florence, became Cathar hiding places, and until the 1320s the inquisition was active there.[5] For a time, from about 1300 to 1340, Sicily, under Frederick II, king of Aragon, proved to be an

[1] Canon 3. Hefele et Leclercq, *Histoire des Conciles V*, pt. II, 1329–30; Mansi, 22, 986 ff.

[2] The point was made by Guiraud, *Histoire de l'Inquisition* II, 431 ff. The canons include 3, 7, 8, 10, 11, 14, 15, 16, 17, 30, 43, 44, 46, 63, 64, 65, 66.

[3] For a résumé of their history from c. 1250–1400 see Borst, op. cit., 135–42.

[4] Ibid., 136.

[5] See R. Manselli, 'Per la storia dell' eresia catara nella Firenze del tempo di Dante', in *Bulletino dell' Istituto storico Italiano per medio evo*, no. 62 (1950) Rome, 123–38.

asylum, as we saw for the Fraticelli. But the best hiding places were the mountain fastnesses of Piedmont, where the Waldensians were also strong in number. In the later fourteenth century, outbreaks of Catharism seem to have been few and far between. It appeared at Siena in 1387 to have disappeared by 1388.[1] In Chieri, to the west of Turin, in 1412 fifteen Cathars were exhumed and burned[2]—as symbolic of the moribundity of the movement as of its erstwhile adherents. As it declined so it increasingly drew its support from the lower orders.[3] There were few wealthy townsmen or large landowners among them. From about 1280 its mainstay became butchers, innkeepers, barbers, manual workers, shepherds, wandering artisans and prostitutes. These continued to belong after the doctors, writers and notaries, who had until the end of the thirteenth century been such a strong element, vanished. If in its last phase the Cathars' heresy was now truly a movement of the poor, they paradoxically did not embrace the doctrine of evangelical poverty.[4] Indeed it was a common belief that failure to repay a loan, whether by a believer or one of the *perfecti*, endangered the soul.[5] There are also examples of its members' preoccupation with breadwinning to the exclusion of their devotions.[6] In other respects, however, the core of their teaching remained basically unaltered. Dualism still dominated their outlook, as Bernard Gui tells us; this was reflected not only in the dichotomy between the spiritual and the material but also between the good and true church, which was Cathar, and the evil church, variously called the synagogue of Satan and the whore of Babylon.[7] The fundamental anti-Christian character of their belief was still in evidence: the denial of the sacraments, the Incarnation, Christ's passion and his—or any other—bodily resurrection, and Mary's motherhood.[8] They also rejected all oaths, lies,[9] Christian prayers, and the adoration of the cross, relics and so on[10]—which were also Waldensian traits.[11] Yet at the same time there had been permeation by Christian concepts. The Cathars had their own form of eucharist with their own bread; they denied Christian baptism but gave the *consolamen-*

[1] Borst, op. cit., 137, who cites a range of sources, notably Döllinger, *Beiträge* II, Limborch, *Liber Inquisitionis*, Guiraud, Douais, Molinier, on the inquisition.

[2] Ibid. [3] Ibid., 138 f. [4] Ibid., 139. [5] Ibid.

[6] Ibid. [7] *Manuel* I, 10. [8] Ibid., 12–14.

[9] Christians, of course, did so as well; but both the Cathars and the Waldensians made it an explicit tenet. [10] Ibid., 24.

[11] J. B. Russell, *Dissent and Reform* 211 ff. has argued convincingly that these were the traits of enthusiasts who had come to reject the authority of the church and were not specific to the Cathars.

tum the same regenerative power—even if for the mass of believers it was at the end of life. Penitence came with joining their sect.[1] As for marriage, although Bernard Gui said that they damned it as carnality,[2] there is plenty of evidence to show that they accepted it fully among their own members, only prohibiting it with outsiders.[3] If they in turn had, as we shall see, an influence upon the Waldensians, they had long lost any direct impact by 1300. As they slipped further and further into a few clandestine corners, they also lost much of their own earlier character: literacy (still taken as a sign of Catharism) among the *perfecti* waned; they seem to have become infected with apocalypticism: on the one hand, they were persecuted by their four devils of pope, king, inquisitors and bishops; on the other they would be delivered by the coming of a future Frederick III who would make them rulers of the world.[4] This eschatological sense was little different from that of the Provençal Beguins, and testifies to the eroding effect of constant persecution. What identity they had sought refuge in the Joachite dreams common to most of the hunted sects of Italy and Southern France in the fourteenth century.

Thus the Cathars, as we find them, were a broken movement. Their direct influence upon society or the church at large—beyond the inquisitors and local clergy concerned with hunting them—was by 1300 negligible. Indirectly, they had helped to shape the very forces which had displaced them. Their presence in Languedoc had been the catalyst which transformed heresy-hunting from one among many clerical activities into a full-fledged war, waged first by the so-called crusaders of Northern France, and then by a permanent army of inquisitors from the 1230s onwards. At the same time, many of their own beliefs were taken up by Waldensianism whence they radiated into most parts of Western Christendom. Thus their presence remained even when they themselves had ceased to animate it.

The Waldensians

To turn to the Waldensians is not, however, to see the reflexion of the Cathars. Throughout, the two movements remained not only distinct but fundamentally opposite. Their affinities were the result of circumstances, not nature: as Guiraud has said, together they opposed the

[1] *Manuel* I, 12. [2] Ibid. [3] Borst, *Katharer* 140.

[4] Dicebant quod Fridericus tertius surgeret et ampliaret eorum ecclesiam et manuteneret eos et opprimeret clericos, et tunc ipsi predicarent et essent in honore et ecclesia deprimeretur (Döllinger, *Beiträge* II, 247) quoted by Borst, loc. cit.

church and together they were combated by it—not as a combined operation but as the two main heretical movements.[1] Inevitably, therefore, they took on, at once to their opponents and to themselves, certain common characteristics. Inquisitors, like Bernard Gui, described the Waldensian initiation into the ranks of the *perfecti* as the *consolamentum*, though it rested upon quite different principles from those of the Cathars. Similarly both movements, in setting themselves in opposition to the Roman church, became in the process independent churches with their own priesthoods, each known as the *perfecti*. Moreover, because they both suffered at the hands of authority, they both came to hold similar beliefs on the impermissibility of oaths, of temporal jurisdiction, the taking of life for breaking the law, as well as the general rejection of the sacramental authority of the church and its rites. Most of these were initially Cathar tenets; for Catharism, unlike Waldensianism, reached the West as a self-contained outlook, whereas the Waldensians in the main were illiterates[2] as well as being poor. But, at the same time, these were essentially the responses of persecuted sects towards their persecutors. As sufferers from an alien law they rejected both the law and its coercive machinery. In doing so, of course, they were striking at the very root of society, above all feudal society, the cornerstone of whose existence was the honouring and enforcement of oaths. Thus, a social doctrine insensibly grew out of their spiritual beliefs, as the result of their experiences in society; since these were broadly the same for both sects so were many of their tenets.

But this did not mean that they shared the same dispensation. The Cathars for all their claims were non-Christians who began and ended outside the church. The Waldensians were Christians who evolved into an independent Christian church. Thus where the Cathars challenged the basic tenets of Christian belief the Waldensians appropriated them to themselves. Where the Cathars claimed to be the one true church, the Waldensians asserted that they were the only true Christian church. This difference in inspiration was more fundamental than any similarities, and needs constantly to be borne in mind in any comparison between them.[3] It may well account for the other great difference between the two sects: namely, that while the Cathars as a movement never spread beyond Northern Italy and Southern France, the Waldensians were to be found throughout the length and breadth of Western,

[1] Guiraud, *Histoire de l'Inquisition* I, 256. [2] Guiraud's point, ibid., 243.

[3] E.g., Valdes's profession of faith, which Dondaine, 'Aux Origines du Valdéisme' (AFP 16, 1946) says was made to show that he was not a dualist, ibid., 197.

Southern and Central Europe, except for England. They were the one sect which was multi-regional. The reasons are not far to seek. To begin with, they very soon became a missionary church. The famous Council at Bergamo in 1218,[1] called to mend the schism between the Lombard and Ultramontane groups, shows clearly that, despite their differences, they regarded themselves as one church. As such they were always treated by their opponents. The Council of Bergamo is interesting less for the actual questions at issue—which ultimately faded into insignificance—than for showing that, even in this comparatively early phase, the Waldensians were not either a pure creed or a monolithic body. In this case there were five main points of contention: election of heads and bishops, manual work, marriage, baptism and consecration of the host. The Ultramontanes showed themselves to be the more rigid and hierarchical on each of them. They upheld baptism and work, disapproved (as far as one can judge) of marriage for the elect and wanted bishops to pass through the gradations of deacon and priest first. Over the eucharist they believed that any priest—of their own sect—could consecrate it whereas the Lombards said that any just man, but no sinner—priest or not—could do so. Within these broad areas of disagreement there seems to have been a further number of conflicting views: on the eucharist, for instance, the same *Rescriptum* mentions three other opinions held among the Ultramontanes.[2] The divergences themselves were never of lasting importance: the Lombard view on the inefficaciousness of sinful priests came, within a generation, to be one of the distinguishing features of Waldensianism, while the Ultramontane attitudes to hierarchy, baptism, and marriage, tended to prevail; manual labour never became an issue: beyond general agreement that it was not performed by the *perfecti*, it was practised more generally north of the Alps than in Italy.[3]

[1] *Rescriptum heresiarcharum Lombardie ad Leonistas in Alemaniam* in Döllinger II, 42–52; and the *Liber supra stella*, by Salvo Burci of Placento, ibid., 52–84, and W. Preger in ABAW 13 (1875) 232–42. *The Rescriptum* was a letter by the Lombard Waldensians to their brethren in Germany giving an account of the proceedings at Bergamo. For a discussion of Waldensian sources see G. Gonnet, 'Waldensia' in *Revue d'histoire et de philosophie religieuses* 33 (1953) 202–54. Also A. Hugon and Gonnet, *Bibliografia Valdese* and Gonnet, *Enchiridion Valdensium* for a critical discussion of Waldensian sources.

[2] Döllinger, *Beiträge* II, 47 ff.

[3] E. Werner, 'Ideologische Aspekte des deutsch-österreichen Waldensertums im 14 Jahrhundert' (*Studi Medievali*, 3rd ser. IV, 1963) 225 seems to put a misplaced emphasis upon this difference.

Contemporaries all showed themselves aware of these divergences between the Ultramontane and Lombard Waldensians. Some of them, like the inquisitor Anselm of Alexandria in his *Tractatus de hereticis*, c. 1260,[1] emphasized those on the powers of sinful priests, baptism, and work.[2] Rainier of Saccone merely divided them into these two main groups of north and south of the Alps.[3] Most writers treated them, together with the Cathars, as one of the two main heretical sects; as we have said, this conjunction had its effect both upon the doctrines attributed to the two sects and their own beliefs. Yet their different origins were not always forgotten. Salvo Burci of Placento in his *Liber supra stella*[4] (1235) exclaimed to them: 'You were first of the Roman church';[5] while virtually all the inquisitors' manuals emphasize their claim to be the only true Christians and in the direct line of apostolic descent.[6] Thus David of Augsburg—or more strictly the pseudo-David of Augsburg[7]—in his *Tractatus de heresi pauperum de Lugduno* (c. 1250–60)[8] reported that 'they say they are the Apostles' successors and have apostolic authority and the keys of binding and loosing'.[9] He also stated that, while they rejected the Old Testament, they used the books of the Evangelists to attack the Roman church and defend themselves, and likewise with the writings of the Fathers from which they excerpted for their own ends.[10] There was a widely accepted consensus among all the main writings on Waldensian beliefs from the time of Alan of Lille's and Bernard of Fontcaude's polemics against them, at the end of the twelfth century, to Bernard Gui's *Manual of the Inquisitor*,

1 Text in A. Dondaine, 'La hiérarchie cathare en Italie', AFP 20 (1950) 234–324. Most of it is devoted to the Cathars; but a few pages (317 ff.) treat the Waldensians.

2 Ibid., 317 ff.

3 Rainier Saccone, *Contra sectam Waldensium* in *Maxima Bibliotheca Veterum Patrum* (*Lyons* 1677), vol. 25, 262–77.

4 In Döllinger, *Beiträge* II, 52–84. See Ilarino da Milano, 'Il *Liber supra Stella* del piacentino Salvo Burce' in *Aevum* 16 (1942) 272–320; 17 (1943) 90–146; 19 (1945) 281–341, including partial edition of the text 307–41.

5 Döllinger, ibid., 74: Ilarino da Milano, art. cit., 17, 95, and 19, 328.

6 For a survey of these manuals for the hundred years from 1230–1330, see A. Dondaine, 'Le manuel de l'inquisiteur' AFP 17 (1947) 85–194.

7 Esposito, 'Quelques écrits concernant l'hérésie et les hérétiques au 12e et 13e siècles' in RHE 36 (1940) 158–62.

8 In W. Preger, *Der Tractat des Davids von Augsburg* (in ABAW 14, 1878), 181–235. Also in Martène and Durand, *Thesaurus* v (Paris 1717) cols. 1777–94, where the author is given as anonymous.

9 Preger, ibid., 207; Martène and Durand 1779.

10 Preger, ibid., 208; Martène and Durand 1780.

written c. 1320.[1] Since our main concern with them lies rather more towards the end of this span, and because of Bernard Gui's own qualities of mind and grasp, we may take his account as the starting point.[2]

The Waldensians were, he wrote, ignorant and unlettered men who read the New Testament and the Fathers in the vernacular, and preached upon them travelling from village to village. They presumed to imitate the life of the Apostles by pretending to live in poverty and sanctity, saying it was more important to obey God than man.[3] Like David of Augsburg, whom he followed very closely, Bernard Gui put foremost among the Waldensians' errors their contempt for the power of the Roman church. It was for this that they had been excommunicated, and from it their numerous errors had sprung.[4] More specifically, they denied they were subject to the pope's authority, or that, in refusing obedience to him and the prelates, they could be excommunicated.[5] They rejected all oaths as without exception prohibited by God—although they reserved the right to swear in order to escape death;[6] and one of the common means of detecting a member of the sect was to insist that he swore an oath. Similarly they denied all power of judgement—i.e. exercising jurisdiction—and especially condemnation to death, which was in no circumstances permissible.[7]

So far as the church was concerned, the Waldensians dismissed all ecclesiastical decrees and sanctions as worthless, as well as denying any authority to ecclesiastical laws of fasting, feast days, and so on. They rejected all the sacraments of the Roman church. The power of the keys (remission of sins) came direct from God; and it was granted to them, as it had been to the Apostles, to hear the confessions of those wishing to make them, and to absolve. The eucharist could only be performed by one not in sin; and since all not of their sect were sinners, this power was reserved to the Waldensians alone. It could be carried out by any just person, even a layman or a woman.[8] Their own ritual was reduced to a minimum. Communion was made only once every year.[9] They denied purgatory which, with true penitence, they held belonged to this life.[10] This rendered otiose all prayers and alms for the dead and the intercession of saints who could not hear their prayers in heaven.[11] The

[1] For a survey of these anti-Waldensian works see G. Gonnet, 'Waldensiana'.
[2] *Manuel* I, 34 ff.
[3] Ibid., 34–36.
[4] Ibid., 38.
[5] Ibid.
[6] Ibid.
[7] Ibid.
[8] Ibid., 42.
[9] Ibid., 44.
[10] Ibid., 46, 62.
[11] Ibid., 46.

soul went immediately to heaven or hell.[1] In the same way, they observed only Sundays and the Virgin's feast day. In their way of life they constituted a separate church, divided between simple believers and superiors, whom they were bound to obey as if they were Catholics: acceptance into the sect entailed the promise to obey. Their superiors had to observe evangelical poverty, chastity, and the absence of individual possessions. They lived from alms and abstained from manual work.[2] They would sometimes enter Catholic churches. They would recite the Lord's prayer thirty or forty times each day; it was their only prayer because they averred that all the others, including the *credo*, had been composed by the church, not God.[3] These superiors (or *perfecti*), as the Apostles' successors, were pledged to a life of missionary wandering, taking the word of the evangel to the villages and holding conventicles in houses. To be received into this elect, they had to undertake a special oath.[4]

These outlines are to be found repeatedly during the thirteenth and fourteenth centuries. There were variations, as we shall see; but on the main points they agreed: namely that the Waldensians set themselves up as an alternative church with their own lore and hierarchy; that they rejected the sacraments and ritual of the Roman church; and that what they put in its stead was the bare minimum of Sunday observance, the Lord's prayer, annual communion and their own form of initiation and baptism. Above all, purity of life was the condition of spiritual authority; hence any just man could administer the sacraments.[5] If this did not make the Waldensians quietists, they tended towards spiritual simplicity which, with anti-sacerdotalism, was their hallmark, as it was of the Lollards later. This can be seen from other statements about the Waldensians. In David of Augsburg's treatise we find a deep-seated sense of their apostlehood; there is here, as elsewhere, a hint of apocalyptic feeling in the not uncommon designation of the Roman church as the whore of Babylon and all obeying her as damned.[6] Moreover, it is given a characteristically historical setting, reminiscent of the Joachism we examined in part one of this book: the source of Rome's degeneration was its endowment by Constantine; since the time of pope Sylvester I, who accepted the emperor's donation, it had ceased

[1] Ibid., 62. [2] Ibid., 50, 52, 58.
[3] Ibid., 52, 54. [4] Ibid., 58.
[5] Guiraud, *Inquisition* I, 243, speaks of anarchy; but this cannot be applied to a group which had its own obligatory obedience.
[6] Preger, *David von Augsburg* 207; Martène and Durand, *Thesaurus* V, 1779.

to be the true church; all its statutes and laws were of no value and were not to be observed.[1] There was thus the distinction, so prominent in fourteenth-century thinking from Marsilius to Wyclif and Hus, between the apostolic age (which for the Waldensians appeared to end with the resurrection of Christ), and that of the subsequent church, when Christ's teachings were betrayed. This historical awareness was one of the motive forces of thirteenth- and fourteenth-century anti-sacerdotalism. It was interpreted more comprehensively by the Waldensians than any other sect. In one sweep they damned the whole array of feasts, fasts, offices, and benedictions which made up the life of the church; churches and cemeteries were declared to be of no greater value than unconsecrated buildings and fields. They were the work of priestly avarice, not God.[2] The sacraments equally were dismissed, the eucharist, according to David, being treated merely as consecrated bread and wine, not Christ's body and blood.[3] The same happened, as we have seen, with purgatory and prayers for the dead and to the saints.[4] In place of all these outward human forms was the apostolic devotion to the *perfecti* who lived without homes, possessions, or wives (whom they had to relinquish upon entering their new state).[5] David of Augsburg distinguished among them those who were masters (*magistri*), and heard confessions, and their disciples who were apprentices to the masters. Their time was spent in overseeing the faithful, preaching and ministering; they lived as paupers on alms collected for them.[6]

Much the same picture emerges from the account of the so-called Anonymous of Passau, formerly mistaken for Rainier of Saccone.[7] But besides enumerating the ways in which they derogated from the sacraments, he makes the hard statement that from his own experience as

[1] Omnes clericos et eis obedientes a tempore B. Silvestri pape dicunt esse damnatos. . . . Omnia statuta post ascensionem Christi dicunt non esse servanda, nec alicuius esse valoris (Preger, ibid.; Martène and Durand, ibid.).

[2] Ibid. [3] Preger, 208; Martène and Durand, 1780. [4] Ibid.

[5] Preger, 210. He also describes the Waldensian attitude to marriage as legalized fornication: Matrimonium dicunt fornicationem juratam nisi continenter vivant; Preger, 207; Martène and Durand, 1779.

[6] Ibid.

[7] To be found in Jacob Gretser, *Scriptores contra sectam Waldensium*, in *Maxima Bibliotheca Veterum Patrum* (Lyon 1677) vol. 25, 262–77, and Gretser *Opera*, vol. 12 (Ingoldstadt 1612), 48–99; and edited by W. Preger, *Beiträge zur Geschichte der Waldesier*, ABAW 13, (1877) 242–5. See also A. Dondaine, 'Le manuel de l'inquisiteur', appendix 1, 170–2; also his *Liber de duobus principiis* (Rome 1939) 57 ff.

inquisitor he had computed forty-one[1] Waldensian churches in the diocese of Passau. The figure does not seem exaggerated, for, as we shall mention, this region lying between Germany, Austria and Bohemia remained a hotbed of Waldensianism well into the fifteenth century. He also mentions their apocalyptic tendencies, calling the Roman church the beast and the whore of the Apocalypse and once again dating its declension from pope Sylvester;[2] he in turn damned all heretics as Antichrist.[3] We hear once again of the Waldensians' convictions in their apostolic descent: they alone lived justly while the church was the repository of all sin; they were the guardians of Christ's evangelical teaching, the true *pauperes spiritu* suffering persecution for justice and faith. In addition to rejecting all ecclesiastical authority, they condemned the pope and prelates as murderers for supporting wars—not specified, but which probably referred to the conflicts between the popes and the Hohenstaufen in Italy, Sicily and Germany. They disavowed any obedience to the church, reserving it exclusively for God. We are also given a series of practical forms which their insubordination took, very reminiscent of Wyclif's and the English Lollards' programme almost 150 years later: these included non-payment of tithes, the rejection of any ecclesiastical right to possessions (which with Wyclif became open advocacy of disendowment), jurisdiction, endowments, privileges, or immunities and the decrees of all councils and synods. The anonymous author makes their views on the sacraments equally uncompromising: only those not in sin could consecrate the eucharist (which in effect confined it to the Waldensians, since all not of their sect were in sin); moreover, its efficacy depended upon the words of a worthy man, which could be spoken in the vernacular: a challenge to the ritual of the church. It need only take place once a year, and—in direct contrast to the Hussites—its daily performance was reproved. Marriage likewise they damned, if there was no issue, together with unction, indulgences and excommunication. They themselves heard confessions which were made in the vernacular. In their desire for austerity, they condemned all vigils, singing, hours, miracles and

[1] *Max Bib. Vet. Pat.* 265; Gretser, *Opera* 12, 53: Inquisitioni examinationi hereticorum frequenter interfui, et computate sunt schole hereticorum in diocesi Patiensi 41. Preger, *Beiträge* 185 taking the text from MS. CLM 311 gives the number as 42; he also enumerates the individual locations, 241–2.

[2] *Max Bib. Vet.*, 265.

[3] Ibid., 262. For what follows, ibid., 265–6, where the Anonymous's accusations are drawn up as a series of articles.

legends associated with Christ's cross, fastings, feast days, burials, funerals, processions, rogations—a further foretaste of the Lollards and Hussites. They also denied purgatory and the existence of any but mortal sins. Perhaps most significant of all—in the light of the future—in casting off all ecclesiastical authority they asserted that the doctrine of Christ and the Apostles sufficed in itself, and opposed it to the tradition of the church which they called of the Pharisees.[1] Together with this—again of the first importance for the future—they insisted upon their own interpretation of the bible, scorning the church's claim to interpret it.[2]

The essentials of this outlook continued for another century and a half; it recurs time and again both in the writings of opponents like John of Pilichdorf (c. 1395)[3] and John of Jesenice (in 1417),[4] as well as in lists drawn up by inquisitors and confessions made before them. John of Jesenic's testimony is particularly apposite, for as chancellor of the university of Prague he was rebutting Waldensian teaching in the first flood of Hussite revolt: his nine propositions are in the form of re-affirmations of what the Waldensians denied: namely, that purgatory existed; that prayers should be said for those who were there; that images should be worshipped; that the pope should be adored; that councils should be believed; that the customs of the church should be observed; that the kissing of images was not idolatry; that decoration of images increased the fervour of devotion; and that no images should be destroyed. Their practical—almost disciplinary—nature is perhaps the best testimony to the threat from Waldensian anti-sacerdotalism which, there can be no doubt, inspired the radicals of Tabor.[5] It was a declaration of authority, an order to keep discipline. The need to assert it was the outcome of Waldensian teachings in the actual challenge which they presented to the sacramental life of the church.

The judgement of Peter Zwicker, of the Celestinian order, who together with Martin of Prague conducted the inquisition against the Waldensians in South and East Germany, Bohemia and Austria, in the

[1] Item nullum sanctum credunt, nisi Apostolos; nullum sanctum invocant nisi deum. . . . Item dicunt quod doctrina Christi et Apostolorum sine statutis ecclesie sufficiat ad salutem. Quod traditio ecclesie sit traditio Phariseorum (ibid., 265).

[2] Ibid.

[3] *Max. Bib. Vet.* 25, 277–99, 299–307; there is also an anonymous treatise of the same period 275–7, which Preger, *Beiträge* 189, associates with the inquisitorial activity of that time.

[4] Printed in E. Werner, 'Ideologische Aspekte', 237.

last decade of the fourteenth century,[1] confirms John Jesenice's emphasis. Written in 1398, on the evidence of his encounters with the Austrian Waldensians, it runs to 92 articles.[2] If it is naturally far fuller, the tenor is similar: the Waldensians' repudiation of church ritual and teaching to the point where belief becomes virtually invisible, needing not even consecrated buildings or ground. A church was no better than any house, nor a cemetery than the fields, nor an altar than any other stone.[3] The whole impedimenta of worship was discarded, including baptismal water and the other traditional elements. All religious, monks, cathedrals, colleges and university privileges were condemned; so were church and secular laws and jurisdictions alike. The efficacy of the mass was reduced to merely the words of consecration, and—a novelty—a priest celebrating it sinned every time he invoked the name of a saint.[4] All those not mentioned in the bible were also sinners, including Saints Benedict, Francis and Dominic.[5] For the rest there was the full array of stock positions on the saints, purgatory, prayers for the dead, the sinfulness of those not of their sect, oaths, and their own apostolic claims. How deep-rooted this belief in their mission was can be seen from a Waldensian letter of the same period (c. 1368). Written from Italy to brethren who had been convicted of heresy,[6] it was clearly intended to raise their morale by reminding them that they were the true apostles. In style reminiscent of the apocalypticism of the Spirituals, they were enjoined to recognize that it was their role as apostles to be persecuted until the world's end; though judgement was passed upon them it was from men, not God.[7] Here, too, there is evidence of the same insistence upon spiritual rather than visible signs: it was untrue, the letter averred, that many of them did without communion because they did not receive the sacraments; just as men could receive the host spiritually, so those in accord with Christ had no need to eat and drink

[1] See pp. 478 ff. below.

[2] Given in Preger, *Beiträge* 246–9.

[3] E.g., articles 17, 18, 19 and 20.

[4] Arts. 83 and 84.

[5] Art. 92.

[6] In Döllinger, *Beiträge* II, 355–62. G. Gonnet, 'Waldensia' 230, has pointed out that Döllinger has wrongly called the previous document, 351 ff., a confession, which it is not. See also G. Gonnet, 'I Valdesi d'Austria nella seconda del sec. XIV' (*Boll. di Soc. della studi Valdesi*, No. 111 (1962) 3–41, 11); G. Gonnet, 'Casi di sincretismo ereticale in Piemonte nei secoli XIV et XV' (BSSV 108 (1960) 3–36); T. Kappaelli and T. Zaninovik, 'Traités anti-Vaudois dans le ms. 30 des Dominicains de Dubrovnik (AFP. 24, 1954, 297–305).

[7] Döllinger, *Beiträge* II 357–8.

him.[1] This depreciation of the sacraments, especially the eucharist, was again one of the most prominent traits of the Taborites and a prime source of their conflict with the orthodox Hussites.[2]

Similar propositions are to be found throughout the fourteenth century: a list of twenty Waldensian errors drawn up by Master Jacob of Petrikau c. 1395[3] shows this combination of extreme simplicity, anti-sacerdotalism and apostolic conviction: they alone were the just men and to them alone confession could be made; children of sinful parents were damned because of the sins of their parents.[4] With Sylvester I the church had defected from God, and in their order lay all salvation.[5]

The progression towards total rejection of all ritual, and visible forms—including music, singing, buildings and cemeteries—becomes apparent by the second half of the fourteenth century. It seems to have been mainly a Central European phenomenon; but that may be because of the paucity of inquisitorial records for Lombardy. Its prevalence in the area bounding Bohemia can hardly have failed to have influenced the religious groups there, above all the Taborites, as Preger observed over seventy years ago.[6] This will become clear when we consider them in chapter nine. What is equally of interest is that the Hussites also had their impact upon the Waldensians. A group of 443 in Pomerania and the Mark of Brandenburg, examined by Peter Zwicker from January 1393 to February 1394, showed fully developed the traits just enumerated:[7] they made confessions to their own priests; did not pray for the dead; did not believe in purgatory, baptism, benedictions or the elements used for them; they opposed indulgences, pilgrimages, excommunication, singing in church, lying, passing judgement, images, pictures.[8] They particularly disavowed oaths saying that it was easier for anyone who swore to pass through the eye of a needle than enter the kingdom of heaven.[9] Despite the hostility towards the church engendered by the

[1] Döllinger, *Beiträge* II, 359.

[2] See pp. 690 ff. below.

[3] In Werner, 'Ideologische Aspekte' 236.

[4] Articles 7 and 8.

[5] Articles 15 and 20.

[6] W. Preger, 'Über das Verhältnis der Taboriten zu den Waldensiern des 14 Jahrhunderts' ABAW 18 (1899) 3–111.

[7] W. Wattenbach, 'Über die Inquisition gegen die Waldenser in Pommern und der Mark Brandenburg' (*Philosophische und historische Abhandlungen der königlichen Akademie der Wissenschaft zu Berlin* (1886) III, 1–102.

[8] Ibid., 30–1, 33, 34, 38, 42–4, 59–67.

[9] 'quod ita possibile est iuratorem possidere regnum celorum, sicut unus camelus posset transire foramen alicuius acus' (ibid., 64).

inquisition—one of them, Sybert Curaw, called the inquisitor Antichrist's precursor[1]—they remained firmly opposed to the taking of life.[2] Nor were they actually against the cult of the Virgin; the 'Ave Maria' was permitted while recognizing that neither she nor the saints had any power.[3] They were convinced of their own salvation as the one true Christian sect outside which all others were damned.[4] Beyond revering their own ministers they looked only to God; he alone knew the heart of man; he alone was omnipotent; and he alone should be invoked.[5] Fifty years later, however, a new inquisition in 1458 discovered that the descendants of the same sect now worshipped Wyclif, Hus and Jerome, who were saints in heaven (*esse in vita beata*). They had also taken over the Hussite tenet of communion in both kinds and so become utraquists.[6] Forty years of Hussite propaganda had left their imprint: the influence had become reciprocal.

In the second place what distinguished Waldensianism from mere piety was its organization as an independent church and the historical justification brought to its authority. It thereby gave cohesion to what might otherwise have been just a protest, and undoubtedly accounts for its remarkable staying power. As Peter Zwicker said of the Austrian Waldensians, 'they had endured there for more than 140 years and in recent times from the year 1395 they continually erupted in the violence and terror of incendiarism and murder'.[7] Allowing for the inevitable overstatement, the fact of their continuance was a major preoccupation for both the church and the secular power. They survived because they were knit into groups which, by meeting clandestinely, could often escape detection indefinitely, as in the case of the Brandenburg and Pomeranian Waldensians who were only uncovered at the end of the fourteenth century and were still in existence in 1458. Much of this was due to their hierarchy, variously called ministers, *barbes*, *perfecti*, according to source and time and place. Generally speaking they seem to have retained their three orders of deacons, priests and bishops; and no doubt they continued to meet in chapters twice yearly or more where they

[1] Ibid., 31. [2] Ibid., 65.

[3] Ibid., 55–8. Many also prayed for souls although they did not believe in purgatory. Ibid., 58.

[4] Credidit alios, qui non sunt de secta sua, non posse salvari (ibid., 66).

[5] Deus solus omnipotens est et solus deus adorandus est et nullus sanctorum . . . quia nullus in celo sciret cor hominis nisi solus deus, et ideo non deberent eos invocare, et quod non scirent invocationes nostras (ibid., 54).

[6] Ibid., 79–80. For utraquism see ch. IX below.

[7] Ibid.

ordained priests and deacons and sent out missions, as described by Bernard Gui[1] and other commentators. But quite as important was their spiritual standing: the fact that they had to live on a different plane of apostolic poverty devoted only to propagating the gospels gave their followers the conviction that they were of Christ's true church. They thus confronted the church of Rome with the cohesion of an organized faith. The difference which it made is best seen in the fate of the Provençal Spirituals and Beguins, who had a like conviction without a comparable organization.

The elaborateness of initiation into the Waldensian hierarchy shows its standing. An extract from an inquisitorial record in Poland for 1391[2] tells of the promise of those becoming *perfecti* to live without labour and on alms, and to go wherever they were sent on mission; the masters then laid their hands upon their heads thereby conferring the power to hear confessions and said: 'Welcome, good brother, now you are ordained in our faith as a major of the apostles.'[3] The same source describes them as calling themselves apostles, masters and brothers, who fasted three or four days a week, one of them on bread and water, and who prayed on the seventh day; they wore vile garments and were illiterate and rustic.[4] In Peter Zwicker's account the Pomeranian and Brandenburg witnesses told of the way in which they would contribute to the upkeep of the preachers and ministers either with money or food and hospitality.[5] The reverence in which they were held was comparable to that in which the Provençal Beguins regarded the Spirituals—except that with the latter it never went beyond being personal. The Waldensians believed that their ministers held power from God and they could help them spiritually and lead them—the simple believers—to eternal life.[6] They taught what was true and could remit sins; they did not need to be ordained as priests by the Roman church for they held their order directly from Christ's Apostles. It was better to hear good and holy men than ordinary priests.[7] They also believed that their ministers received their wisdom 'before heaven' and that every seven years they returned there to renew their under-

[1] *Manuel* I, 52.

[2] Döllinger II, 368–9.

[3] Ibid., 369.

[4] Ibid., 368.

[5] Wattenbach, 'Über die Inquisition', 50–1.

[6] tales qui ipsum possent iuvare ad vitam eternam (ibid., 42).

[7] E.g., a deo habent auctoritatem dimittendi peccata et predicandi verbum dei melius presbiteriis . . . non tamen reputaverit eos presbiteros ordinatos, sed ordines habere ab apostolis Christi (ibid., 42–3).

standing.[1] With such confidence in the power of their elect they had neither to fear from the church nor indulge in apocalyptic dreams, since, for them, they were already living among the chosen in this world. They had only to hold fast to them to be taken along the path of salvation. Such a conviction in the palpability of God's word may well account for the almost complete absence of Joachism among the Waldensians. It certainly helps to explain their strength and resilience.

So far we have taken our examples from Germany and Central Europe. When we turn to Southern France and Italy there are significant differences. These can be accounted for almost entirely by the presence of Cathar influence, which, as we have said, never really penetrated further north. Here the emphasis was far more upon the evils of the flesh, and in one instance at least Cathar and Waldensian ideas were inextricably mingled. This was at trials in Upper Lombardy in 1387 and 1388.[2] Here we encounter a quite distinct network in which the 'supreme pontiff' of the sect lived in Apulia.[3] The doctrines are equally distinctive. On the one hand there are many of the usual tenets on oaths, purgatory and the exclusively apostolic character of the sect compared to the *congregatio peccatorum* which the Roman church had been from the time of Sylvester I.[4] On the other hand dualist influences introduced a new element of non-Waldensian and/or anti-Christian notions. They included the repeated emphasis upon the importance of baptism and their own form of eucharist. These, in contrast to the ultramontane depreciation of the special properties of baptismal water, were variously regarded as the condition of salvation. Only baptism, said one witness of the church's sacraments, was to be accepted; the rest were of human invention and not true sacraments.[5] But it soon becomes clear that they understand it as a rite of initiation into the saved rather than the mere deletion of original sin. As such it came far closer to the Cathar conception. The same applied to the eucharist which was performed with unleavened bread.[6] Moreover, the group seems to have

[1] et quod de septennio ad septennium venirent ante paradisum ad audiendum sapientiam (ibid., 44; see also 43).

[2] G. Amati, 'Processus contra Valdesi in Lombardia superiori, anno 1387', *Archivio Storico Italiano* 1865, ser. 3, I, pts. I and 2, 3–51, 3–61; and in a shortened version in Döllinger, *Beiträge* II, 251–73, principally used here, although it is at times arbitrarily abbreviated.

[3] Döllinger, ibid., 252.

[4] E.g., ibid., 252, 253, 256, 265.

[5] Ibid., 256.

[6] Amati, art. cit., pt. 2, where the bread of the eucharist is held to be superior to the water of baptism (30) or exceeds all other sacraments (57, 17, 20, 23). On the other hand another witness asserts that God cannot be in the host (25).

adopted the Cathar rite of the *consolamentum*, described by one witness as the greatest sacrament (though whether it was identified with baptism is not clear).[1] Certainly, it seems to have been conceived in the Cathar sense, for we learn from another witness that any woman pregnant had the devil within her and could only be saved if she received the *consolamentum* at her death.[2] To die without it entailed traducianism, the passing of one's spirit into another body, either of man or brutes; this transmigration would continue until spiritual benediction had finally been received from one of their own ministers.[3] Abhorrence of the flesh was also evinced in the attitude towards Christ, the traditional view of the eucharist, the Virgin and creation: 'Alexona La Lauriane especially abjured the incarnation, passion, resurrection and ascension of Christ because God would not nor could not so humiliate himself as to assume a carnal human (nature).'[4] 'Martin said Christ is not in the sacrament of the eucharist, as Christians say and think, but is always in heaven.'[5] Brother Anthony denied that Mary was a virgin or the mother of God.[6] The sect as a whole was accused of teaching 'that God did not create or make anything visible; but this world and all others had been created by the devil who fell from heaven. . . . Also that every man and woman consisted not of a rational soul and a body, but one (the body) was from demons who had sinned.'[7] Thus to the Waldensian denial of visible forms was added to the Cathar abomination of the visible world. Several witnesses described it as under the devil's rule and the arena of the war between them.[8] No wonder that the two sects were so frequently confused, even being given the name

[1] Döllinger, ibid., 259.

[2] Ibid., 267. Item quod, si aliquis de eorum secta non recepisset consolamentum in morte, quia non habuit dantem, ille spiritus iterato intrabit aliquod corpus, sive humanum sive brutum usque quod recipiat in morte benedictionem salutarem a patre spirituali ipsorum.

[3] Ibid.

[4] Ibid., 257.

[5] Ibid., 256, though he appears then to go on to contradict himself by asserting that he 'saw Christ in the sacrament of the altar'. See also 267 for similar denials.

[6] Ibid., 262.

[7] Ibid., 266.

[8] Item quod diabolus fecit Adam et Evam. . . . Item quod Moyses fuit maior peccator . . . et quod habuit legem a diabolo (ibid., 267). It is probably no accident that they called the devil the dragon: persecution must have made them receptive to apocalypticism, although they did not express it in Joachist terms. E.g., Item dicebat quod draco debebat adorari, et erat potentior deo in mundo isto (Amati, art. cit., pt. 2, 23). . . . Item quod omnia ista visibilia sunt creata per draconem magnum qui pugnat cum deo, et est fortior in mundo isto et debet adorari pro deo (ibid., 25). Also ibid., 5 and 30.

of *Gazores* by the inquisitors from this combination of beliefs.[1] This syncretism is to be found elsewhere among the southern Waldensian groups. The confession of Raymond de Costa, a Waldensian deacon, made in 1319–20,[2] strongly asserted the superiority of chastity to marriage, which, for all their earlier disapproval, is not given prominence in the later documents of the Ultramontanes. However, he conceded that if chastity was not possible then marriage was preferable. The same emphasis recurs in Lombardy.[3] At a trial held at Chieri, west of Turin, in 1395, for example,[4] transubstantiation was doubted.[5] Nevertheless here as elsewhere these accretions only overlaid—but never drove out—the hard core of Waldensian doctrine: its rejection of ecclesiastical authority and practice for their own apostolic forms; the need of spiritual probity in the administration of the sacraments; the denial of purgatory, most prayers, the intercession of the saints and almost all visible signs in ritual. No doubt this sometimes led to blasphemy as with the group of 16, condemned at Arras and Douai in 1420,[6] for uttering various abuses of the faith. These included denying the Trinity, the eucharist and baptism, insulting the cross, asserting that Mary had had more than one child, rejecting requiem masses and illicitly preaching. Perhaps the decree of Charles VI, king of France, in 1397 complaining of blasphemy against Christ and the Virgin was also the result of Waldensian agitation. If so they were the exceptions. Waldensianism was a fundamentally serious outlook; unlike the Free Spirit its adherents left little room to doubt the sincerity of their convictions. They challenged the church on its own ground, both in principle and in practice, and whatever its exaggerations, for the most part it was professing a recognizably Christian doctrine. The same could hardly be said of the Free Spirit; it is perhaps the measure of the difference between the two sects that whereas Waldensian ideas helped to inspire important sections of the Hussites, the followers of the Free Spirit—the Adamites—were crushed for their irreligiosity.

The almost European-wide extent of the Waldensians has already

[1] J. Marx, *L'Inquisition en Dauphiné du 14e siècle au début du règne de François Ier* (Paris 1914) 23, and G. Amati, art. cit., II, 57, 'Es tu bene Gazeris?'

[2] Döllinger, II, 105 ff.

[3] Ibid., 95.

[4] P. G. Boffito, 'Eretici in Piemonte al tempo del Gran Scisma (1378–1417)' in *Studi et Documenti di Storia e Diritto*, 18 (1897), 381–431.

[5] Ibid., 392, though very probably this was the result of the way the inquisitor's question was framed; see also 398.

[6] P. Fredericq, *Corpus* III, no. 48 (260 bis) 57–8.

been remarked. They were probably strongest in South and East Germany, Bohemia, Austria, Dauphiné, Lombardy, and Apulia; but for Italy, the evidence after the later thirteenth century is sparse. Let us briefly examine each of these main areas.

We may take the central European lands together, for much of the inquisition's activity treated them as a unity and it seems clear that the Waldensians there intermingled, going backwards and forwards between the different countries. Thus among those tried for Waldensianism in Poland in 1391 were Conrad of Saxony, Ulrich of Hardeck, Simon of Galiz in Hungary, John of Dickhartz near Krems in Austria, Conrad of Gemed in Swabia and two others from Bavaria.[1] There was also the case of John Drändorf, a Saxon noble burned in 1425, who had first gone from Dresden to Prague; then from Prague to Leipzig at the time of the exodus of the German masters from the university there in 1409;[2] he had then returned to Prague before going back to Germany to propagate Waldensian doctrines.[3] The links between Dresden and Prague seem to have been strong and went back to at least 1414, where among a group of Waldensian masters were two Hussite radicals, Peter and Nicholas. John of Drändorf was Peter's pupil as was also Bartholomew of Rautenstock, of Franconia, who was tried at Neuhaus in 1421. Although he rejected oaths, indulgences and followed other Waldensian anathemas, he denied that he had ever been a Hussite,[4] which may well have been the truth, since such attitudes would be sufficiently explained by being a Waldensian. Lea in his *History of the Inquisition* also noted the high number of concurrent burnings in Germany at the time of the Hussite revolt:[5] at Regensburg in 1420 a priest, Henry of Grünfeld, for Hussitism; in 1423 another priest, Henry Rathgeber; in 1425[6] John of Drändorf at Heidelberg; in 1426 Peter Turnow[7] at Speier; in 1450 John Müller who had preached Hussite doctrines in Franconia and gained a large following had to flee and 130 of his adherents were captured at Würzburg. The climax to these disturbances came in the

[1] Döllinger, *Beiträge* II, 367 ff.

[2] See pp. 628 ff. below.

[3] H. Haupt, 'Waldenserthum und Inquisition im südöstlichen Deutschland seit der Mitte des 14 Jahrhunderts', in *Deutsche Zeitschrift für Geschichtswissenschaft* III, 1891 (Freiburg i Br.) 357; 'Husitische Propaganda in Deutschland', *Hist. Taschenbuch*, 6 (1888) and 'Johann von Drändorf', *Zschft. für die Gesch. des Oberreins*, 15 (1900).

[4] Ibid., 357–8.

[5] H. C. Lea, *Inquisition* III, 414–15. Haupt, 'Johann von Drändorf'.

[6] Lea gives the date as 1424, but I have followed Haupt.

[7] For Turnow's condemnation see Haupt, 'Husitische Propaganda' 298 ff.

decade from 1466 to 1476 with the successive appearance of the Wirsberger brothers, John and Livin, and then the drummer, Hans of Nicklashausen.

Before discussing them, however, it is necessary to consider the extent and nature of Hussite influence in Germany. The evidence shows that, far from being haphazard, with the outbreak of the Hussite revolt from 1416 onwards it became carefully planned by a section of the Hussite leaders. The affinities between the Hussites and the Waldensians went back considerably earlier, for they both shared the same revulsion against clerical abuses and similar leanings towards simplicity. But, as we shall see in chapter nine, they were not the same; and in neither Hus nor any of his confrères is there the remotest suggestion of Waldensianism;[1] they were separated by their attitude to the sacraments, especially the eucharist; to purgatory; and above all by the basic fact that the Waldensians denied the authority of the Roman church whilst the Hussites accepted it. But there were certainly more radical elements, later to become the Taborites, who saw in the Waldensians allies. Foremost among them were Nicholas and Peter of Dresden already mentioned. Nicholas was the main collaborator of Jacobellus of Misa (or Stříbro), who in turn was one of Hus's closest companions, and after Hus's death the guiding influence in the Hussite—as opposed to the Taborite—reformation in Prague until his own death in 1429.[2] Nicholas's treatise on oaths (*De iuramento*)[3] was strongly Waldensian in tendency; he seems to have transmitted something of his Waldensian sympathies to Jacobellus, who in a sermon on the text *Liber generationis*, preached on 8 September 1415, claimed for them membership of Christ (*certe illi sunt pars Christi*) while blaming them for their denial of purgatory and the suffrages of the saints.[4]

Nicholas of Dresden and Peter Payne, the English Wyclifite who, after his flight from England may have taken shelter with the German

[1] The accusation of Michael de Causis against Hus at Constance 'quod pavet errores, scilicet Leonistas, Runcarios et Waldenses' (F. Palacký, *Documenta* 198) is at best rhetoric, although in view of his discreditable part in Hus's trial—see ch. IX below—it could have been a further attempt to incriminate Hus, in which case Michael de Causis was deliberately lying.

[2] See ch. IX below.

[3] What follows is based mainly on two articles in the *Bolletino della Societa di Studi Valdesi*: A. Molnar, 'Les Vaudois et le réforme tchèque' no. 103 (1958), 37–51; and V. Vinay, 'Friedrich Reiser e la diaspora valdese di lingua tedesca nella XV secolo', no. 109 (1961) 35–61.

[4] Molnar, art. cit., 42.

Waldensians before going to Prague, seemed in 1415 to have conceived the idea of union between the Hussites and the Waldensians. Nicholas disappeared into Germany and never returned, probably taken by the inquisition.[1] Nicholas's path was followed by his friend, Peter of Dresden, who died in Bavaria in 1420. His pupil, John Drändorf, as we have seen, also spent his later years rallying the German Waldensians, and is known to have visited Basel and Speier before being arrested and burned at Heidelberg in February 1425. Peter Turnow, already mentioned, was another of this Prague-Dresden line, although himself from Prussia; he was burned for utraquism—a purely Hussite tenet at this time.[2] But the prince of these Hussite apostles was Frederick Reiser.[3] A Swabian, born c. 1401 or 1402 near Donauwörth, he went to Nuremberg in 1418. His father, a merchant, was a Waldensian, and Frederick became consecrated a master in 1420. He lived in Fribourg (Switzerland) and Vienna before going to Prague in 1428. He became a Hussite, and stayed at Tabor, where he was made a Hussite preacher in 1431. He was included in the Hussite delegation to the Council of Basel in 1432. Some time before 1440 he undertook a mission to Germany, journeying to Strasbourg and the Rhine as well as Neustadt, Nuremberg, and Würzburg, and Uckermark and Neumark in Brandenburg.[4] Shortly before 1450 he returned to Bohemia, having passed through the greater part of the German lands preaching the Hussite gospel to the Waldensian faithful. As the result of this expedition, he proposed that the two groups should unite in Bohemia.[5] The Hussites agreed, and a mission of twelve under four bishops, with Reiser at their head, was appointed; his title expressed his wide province: 'Frederick by God's grace bishop of the faithful in the Roman church who reject Constantine's donation.'[6] Two hundred florins were collected to finance the undertaking. Reiser himself went back to Strasbourg preaching and organizing. Waldensians in danger of arrest from the German inquisition were sent into Bohemia. The leaders of the operation met periodically: in 1453 at Engelsdorf, near Meissen, and in 1456 at Žatec in Bohemia.[7] In 1457 Reiser returned to Strasbourg; but the next year he was discovered there by John of Wengrauf, the inquisitor, and after a trial condemned to burning together with his friend, Anna Wieler of Nuremberg. He seems to have been tortured for information. His confession included

[1] Molnar, ibid., 43. This conjecture seems plausible in the light of subsequent expeditions to succour the German Waldensians.

[2] Molnar, ibid., 44.

[3] For what follows, Vinay, *Friedrich Reiser* 35 ff.

[4] Ibid., 46.

[5] Ibid., 47.

[6] Ibid., 47–8.

[7] Ibid., 48.

adherence to the Taborite tenets of the symbolic—as opposed to real—presence of Christ in the host, and communion in both kinds.[1] He himself had administered the sacraments; the 200 florins found on him were probably for financing his rescue work rather than a sign that he did not embrace a life of poverty.[2]

The cause in which Reiser died was almost realized a generation later. In 1467, ten years after the remainder of the Taborites had formed themselves into the separate church of the Unity of the Czech Brethren, they attempted to come together with the German Waldensians. In that year they made the final break with the orthodox Hussites, which arose over the question of apostolic succession, by consecrating their own ministers.[3] Now in negotiations with Stephen, the Waldensian bishop who had been Frederick Reiser's coadjutor, the two groups failed to agree to merge.[4] Shortly after, Stephen was seized by the inquisition and burned at Vienna.[5] At his trial he confessed to having lived for thirty years in Bohemia (he was born at Basel). He upheld utraquism and denied the real presence: Christ was only in the host *figurative et representative*; in his own being he remained in heaven on the right hand of God the Father, and would only descend to earth at the Last Judgement. In good Hussite style he denied that a pope who was not the most holy (*sanctissimus*) could be true pope: he was then Antichrist, and was to be judged by his works. Stephen also denied that such a pope's sentences of excommunication could be valid. With views like these in common, coalescence between the Waldensians and the Taborites would have been the appropriate outcome of their long association. Although not at that juncture realized, heresy was passing over into reform, foreshadowing the Waldensians' formal adhesion to the new reformed churches at Chanforan in 1532.

It is hardly surprising that these disturbed conditions should have given rise to periodic disturbances. The most notable both occurred in the diocese of Würzburg within a decade or so of one another from 1465 to 1476. In each case Hussite influence is apparent, but it was not

[1] Ibid., 53–6.

[2] The latter is Vinay's interpretation (ibid., 50) but, in view of the operation in which he was engaged this can hardly be taken as a personal testimony.

[3] The Taborites had appointed their own bishop, Nicholas Pelhřimov, as early as 1420. See ch. IX, below.

[4] A. P. de B. Brock, *The political and social doctrines of the Unity of the Czech Brethren* (The Hague 1957) 77–9. According to Brock's account the Unity regarded the Waldensians as having become corrupted.

[5] Molnar, art. cit., 47 ff.

the only element. The first outbreak was associated with the brothers John and Livin Wirsberg.[1] They came to the fore during 1465, in the district of Eger (Cheb), when they were denounced by the bishop of Regensburg. They had been propagating their doctrines for ten years; but it was not until 1466 that they were caught and tried by the bishop, having six months earlier been give a safe-conduct by the king of Bohemia, George Podebrady, which he then revoked.[2] The precise role of the brothers is unclear; John seems to have disappeared before the trial, and it was Livin who confessed and was sentenced in 1466 to life imprisonment. He died within a year. Their beliefs clearly reflect the apocalyptic atmosphere which the Hussite wars had engendered; in their combination of Joachism and Hussite beliefs they came close to the early Taborites. There is nothing startlingly original about them,[3] and they had no lasting impact. If the Wirsbergers had a following it was quickly dissipated. They preached an apocalyptic doctrine of a coming saviour who would usher in the third age.[4] He was called the 'Anointed One', and born of the Virgin. All those believing in him would receive spiritual illumination enabling them to know the true essence of the Trinity and that the pope was Antichrist, together with all prelates, priests and others not believing in the Anointed One. His advent would be preached by a John the Baptist of the East—whom John of Wirsberg presumed to be. The anti-sacerdotal tenor of the message no doubt accounts for the wide response which it was said to have gained.[5] It appealed to the latent desire to throw off the church's

[1] The main sources are Nicholas of Glassberger, *Chronica* in *Analecta Franciscana* II (Quaracchi 1887) 422–6; G. Ritter, *Zur Geschichte des häretischen Pantheismus* in ZKG, 23 (1924) 158–9, which gives the 15 articles condemned by the bishop of Regensburg in 1466: these constitute the second of two groups of articles, and the title technically applies to the first (see pp. 383 ff. above) rather than the second group under consideration here. See also the articles by O. Schiff, 'Die Wirsberger', *Historische Vierteljahresschrift*, 26 (1931) 776–86 for an account of the main events.

[2] R. Kestenberg-Gladstein, 'The Third Reich: a fifteenth century polemic against Joachism and its background' in *Journal of the Warburg and Courtauld Institute* 18 (1955) 256. This contains edited extracts of the polemic, but much of the article itself is of questionable validity and should be treated with reserve, e.g., that with Dolcino Joachism developed the theory of the right of resistance for the first time (p. 252); that Olivi saw Antichrist as the pope (248 ff.); that the Spirituals [*sic*] formed an alliance with Louis of Bavaria (250); and in her assessment of the Wirsbergers' teachings, the originality of which she exaggerates for their combination of Hussite and Joachist doctrines (258).

[3] Ibid., 258.

[4] To be found in Glassberger, *Chronica* 422 ff. and Ritter, ZKG 23, 158–9.

[5] Glassberger, *Chronica* 422.

yoke, instructing the faithful that they could lie to their priests, and ascribing all tribulations to the 'sins of the clergy'. Indulgences, excommunication, and all censures by the church were worthless; the prelates were scribes and pharisees. They and the princes would shortly lead them all into a war which would end in their own speedy destruction. The third age would then begin.

To these Joachite and Hussite tendencies there were distinct overtones of the Free Spirit. Of the fifteen articles for which the Wirsbergers were censured by the bishop of Regensburg in 1466,[1] over half relate to the supernatural attributes of the Anointed One: he was divinely inspired; he was similar to the son of man in the Apocalypse and would address the seven churches; he would lead the whole world to a new faith; he would be followed as 'Caesar imperator and deus'; he alone understood the depths of the bible; he had seen the essence of the Trinity; and only he was of spiritual birth, Christ not excepted, just as he alone was the Lord's anointed. While he did not deny Christ's divinity, he effectively usurped his role: without the coming of the Anointed One, there would be no salvation; and when he came he would recently have drunk of Christ's blood. The megalomaniacal element reached its climax in his statement that he had liberated God from his sufferings.[2] He also deprecated the use of force against his opponents in the manner of Free Spirit quietism. Such an amalgam testifies to the confused atmosphere of the time. It is not the first time that Joachism was found together with doctrines of the Free Spirit, as we saw with the Men of Intelligence.[3] The Joachist element, however, seems to have drawn some attention; for, in 1470, a disputation took place at Erfurt university over the correctness of Joachim's belief in a third era (*status*). Its main opponent, John of Dorsten, in confuting it, referred to *quidam homines pestiferi*.[4] He regarded it as an error of the Waldensians, Wyclifites and Hussites, although he exempted Joachim himself from the charge of heresy.[5] Dorsten probably exaggerated the extent of Joachist influence; but the fact that the year 1471 had been chosen by the Wirsbergers as the date when the third state would begin,[6] may well have prompted his attack as the best

[1] Glassberger, ibid., 423; Ritter, loc. cit.

[2] Glassberger, ibid, 425.

[3] See pp. 395 ff. above.

[4] Kestenberg-Gladstein, art. cit., 261.

[5] Ibid., 270.

[6] Est igitur textus questionis talis. Utrum tertius mundi status quem Joachim abbas ymaginatur et hereticorum conventiculum minatur catholice venturus astruatur postquam annus domini millesimus MCCCCLXXI compleatur (ibid., 267).

means of defence. It shows that the idea of a third age could still act as a dangerous rallying cry.

The story of Hans Böhm, the drummer of Nicklashausen, is a more extreme, and notorious, example of similar happenings.[1] There was the same anti-sacerdotalism, and the same claim to divine intelligence; in this case, however, it came *via* visions of the Virgin, and although the tenor was apocalyptic there was no mention of a third age. The anti-ecclesiastical theme once again suggests Hussite influence in the attack upon the luxury, pride, and avarice of the priesthood, compulsory payment of tithes and ecclesiastical jurisdiction.[2] Böhm himself was a wandering drummer who came to Nicklashausen, near Würzburg, from Bohemia.[3] He was described by Trithemius as 'a simple peasant, absolutely illiterate', who had been a swineherd.[4] In 1476, urged on and abetted by a priest, who kept in the background, he claimed to have had revelations from the Virgin. She told him that God had refused to allow sins of the clergy to continue any longer. Unless they reformed he would bring the world to an end.[5] To placate God, Böhm preached the complete abolition not only of all ecclesiastical dues and privileges but those of secular princes and lords as well; everything, it appears, was to be held in common, 'for the rich as well as the poor, the peasant as well as the bishop and the prince'.[6] He denied the power of priests and called on all those wishing for absolution to come to him at Nicklashausen.[7] With such a message it was not long before crowds, said with doubtless characteristic medieval exaggeration often to have numbered as many as 30,000, were flocking to him. Böhm's claim to divine inspiration coupled with his programme of wholesale expropriation could not fail to carry. People came to Nicklashausen from far and wide—Bavaria, Swabia, Alsace, Thuringia, the Rhineland, Saxony, Meissen. He was worshipped as God's prophet; elaborate offerings were made to him, and because of the clamour to touch him, he needed a fresh suit of clothes daily. He would recount how he had received a vision of the

[1] The sources for what follows are: Trithemius, *Annales Hirsaugiensis* (St. Gall 1640) II, 486–91; *Memoriale thüringisch-erfurtische Chronik von Konrad Stolle*, ed. Richard Thiele, (Halle 1900) in *Geschichtsquellen der Provinz Sachsen* vol. 39, 379–83; K. A. Barack, *Hans Böhm und die Wallfahrt nach Nicklashausen im Jahr* 1476 (Documents 65 ff.).

[2] Trithemius, *Annales* 487 ff., who specifically observed that Böhm 'imitated Hussite errors'.

[3] Lea, *Inquisition* II, 418.

[4] Trithemius, *Annales* II, 486.

[5] Stolle, *Memoriale* 379.

[6] Trithemius, *Annales*, 488; Stolle *Memoriale* 379.

[7] Stolle, *Memoriale*, ibid.

Virgin while pasturing his pigs, and after his message he would give the people his blessing.[1] The authorities soon became alarmed. Bans upon travel to Nicklashausen were issued over a wide area.[2] The archbishop of Mainz addressed a series of letters to the bishop of Würzburg, instructing him to take action. He later charged Böhm with contempt for the church in denying it the power of the keys; rejecting 'the fires of purgatory'; inciting the populace and promising remission of all sins and full indulgence to those making the pilgrimage to his church.[3] The bishop of Würzburg wrote to the count of Würzburg; the count replied to the archbishop of Mainz. But to no effect.[4] People continued to congregate at Nicklashausen; and Böhm announced a special meeting for the feast of St. Kilian, on 8 July 1476. The authorities now acted. Böhm was arrested shortly before the meeting; the throngs which had gathered were ordered to disperse. But convinced that in following Böhm they were following God, they stormed the castle where Böhm was imprisoned, 'crying with one voice, give us back our youth . . . our holy innocent.'[5] They appear to have believed that at their approach the walls would fall down and Böhm would be restored to them. Instead they were met by volleys from the soldiers guarding him; in their shock they fled, leaving according to one source, 38 dead and 127 wounded.[6] The movement was at an end. Böhm was charged; he confessed and was burned.[7] His ashes were thrown into the river to prevent his burial place becoming a martyr's shrine. His accomplices also confessed, but were later released. The church at Nicklashausen was suppressed and demolished and its liberties withdrawn.[8] The path to reform was not to be won by social insurrection.

Even if we ascribe Böhm's outlook to influences other than Waldensian and Hussite reforming ideals, it took on significance through the ferment they had created. In the inflammatory atmosphere of the middle decades of the fifteenth century, to proclaim apocalyptic denunciation of the church as visions was merely to strike the spark which started the conflagration. Like the Jacquerie or the Flagellants such a man was the occasion for latent discontent to become open disturbance. As with those movements it burned itself out without removing the cause of the unrest.

The history of the Waldensians in Germany and these neighbouring

[1] Trithemius, *Annales* 486.
[2] Barack, *Hans Böhm* 59 ff.
[3] Ibid., 98–9.
[4] Ibid., 66 ff.
[5] Trithemius, *Annales* 489.
[6] Stolle, *Memoriale* 383.
[7] Trithemius, *Annales* 490.
[8] Barack, op. cit., 104–5.

areas during the later middle ages is the record of sporadic waves of inquisitorial activity similar to that which we saw in the case of the Free Spirit. As we have mentioned already, when the Anonymous of Passau was writing c. 1260, the Waldensians were credited with forty-one churches in his diocese alone.[1] The first great assault upon them in Austria came in 1266;[2] but, as Peter Zwicker was to observe nearly 130 years later, they continued in being.[3] The beginning of the fourteenth century saw another and fiercer attack upon them in Austria and the adjoining lands. In 1301 at the synod of Prague a list of canons concerning heretics prepared the way for a papal inquisition of the diocese.[4] In 1311 inquisitors were reported in Steyr—one of the hotbeds of Waldensianism—seeking out heretics and forcing them to recant.[5] A number were captured at Schieterhaufen, as well as 16 at Krems, 11 at St. Pölten,[6] and 2 in Vienna.[7] Those at Krems showed traces of the dualism which we have noted previously among the Waldensians.[8]

[1] As will be seen from the references, much of what follows has been based upon Haupt's two articles in the *Deutsche Zeitschrift für Geschichtswissenschaft* I (1889) and III (1891). Those who have had to work in this obscure field will realize the importance of Haupt's pioneering articles. It is the greatest pity that he was not able to synthesize the vast amount of manuscript evidence which lies scattered in numerous periodicals and articles many of which are hard of access. By any standards Haupt stands high in the list of historians of religious movements.

[2] H. Haupt, 'Waldenserthum und Inquisition im südöst Deutschland bis zur Mitte des 14 Jahrhunderts', ibid., I, 285—in future cited as 'Waldenserthum' I.

[3] Döllinger, *Beiträge* II, 305.

[4] Haupt, ibid., 304.

[5] Ibid., 305.

[6] Ibid.

[7] Given groundlessly by Hauck, *Kirchengeschichte*, as 102, as P. P. Bernard in 'Heresy in 14th century Austria', *Medievalia et Humanistica* 10, 55 has pointed out. Pez II, 533.

[8] Text in H. Pez, *Scriptores rerum Austriacarum* II, 533–6. See also P. P. Bernard, 50 ff. G. C. Fries in 'Patariner, Begharden und Waldenser in Österreich während des Mittelalters', *Österreichische Vierteljahresschrift für Katholische Theologie* (Bd. 9, 1872, 209–72) publishes an extract 254–7 of similar articles from an inquisition at Krems in 1335. This time the sect had 12 apostles with a major called Ulrich; they also rejected oaths. Such syncretism has given rise to unduly solemn discussions of the nature of the groups holding them. In view of what we have seen elsewhere it seems most likely that they were Waldensian with Cathar accretions. Lea calls those of 1312 Luciferans (*Inquisition* II, 358) as he does a priest Rudolph who for the second time—at Salzburg Cathedral in 1340—dashed a cup containing Christ's blood to the ground (ibid., 376). This seems altogether far-fetched; and I am inclined to doubt the existence of such sects. The descriptions of nocturnal orgies which accompanied them were stock inquisitorial blackguarding (ibid., 334–5) and point to nothing specifically Luciferan.

They had masses in honour of Lucifer's work and opposed him to the archangel Michael. They also spoke of sixteen apostles who renewed their power of binding and loosing by visits to Enoch and Elias in heaven. They denigrated the Virgin and rejected the sacraments, calling marriage licensed prostitution. As with the Waldensians a church was 'a stone house'; they attacked fasting and claimed they were the only members of the true church; they had a bishop, Neumaister, who claimed he had held the office for 50 years: a combination which, in my view, points conclusively to their being Waldensians.

It was Neumaister, who was said to have given the total number of his adherents as 80,000:[1] a figure as implausible as most such computations in the middle ages. That the number was considerable cannot be doubted. An anonymous heretic named 36 localities between Traiskirchen and St. Pölten where their sect was.[2] Certainly they were not entirely passive towards their persecutors; and in 1318 an inquisitor was murdered at Krems.[3] On 1 April of the same year came John XXII's bull suspending bishop John of Prague[4] who had been denounced to the pope by his provost for allowing heresy to spread in the diocese. In the city alone, the bull reported, the heretics had an archbishop, seven bishops and three hundred followers. From their description—which included the belief that oaths were sinful, that there was no resurrection, and no unity of the divine persons, and their practice of rebaptizing[5]—it is likely that they were Waldensians. The bull was followed on 1 May 1318, by a series of bulls to the secular and ecclesiastical authorities of Olmütz, Meissen, Kracow and Breslau as well as to the king of Bohemia and the lords and magistrates of the towns there. What resulted from the inquisition is not known; but even before this there had been a number of burnings, including 50 at Schweydnitz in 1315 and others at Breslau and Neisse.[6]

Inquisition trials continued over a wide area during the 1320s and 1330s:[7] in Austria, at Klosterneuberg in 1336, and at Eng and Steyr in 1338. In Bohemia and Poland further acts against heretics were promulgated in 1330 while in 1327 there had been a series of papal decrees

[1] H. Pez, *Scriptores rerum Austriacarum* II, 533 ff.

[2] A. Hauck, *Kirchengeschichte* V, 1, 399.

[3] Ibid., 306.

[4] B. Dudik, *Iter Romanum* II (Vienna 1855) 136–41; Haupt 308; G. Mollat (ed.), *Jean XXII, Lettres Communes* II (Paris 1905), no. 6812, 119–20.

[5] Dudik, op. cit.

[6] Haupt, 'Waldenserthum' I, 310.

[7] Ibid., 311–14.

to the archbishop of Gnesen and other bishops. Silesia was also active. In that year Gallus Neuhaus,[1] too, was appointed inquisitor for the Prague diocese; this was accompanied by a drive in the German areas. In 1340 Gallus went to Avignon and returned with authority to conduct a crusade against the heretics.[2] In the following years, in 1343, 1353 and 1355, new measures were taken against them under Ernest of Pardubik, first archbishop of Prague.[3] But, as with the Beguines and Beghards, the heretics survived to provoke repeated offensives against them for another century.

The next great wave came in the 1370s, under the impetus of the emperor Charles IV and pope Gregory XI, who as we saw in an earlier chapter made a similar attempt to stamp out the heretical Beghards and Beguines.[4] On 18 September 1376, a royal edict was issued against the Waldensians in Bohemia, and energetic action ordered.[5] Already in 1371 archbishop Ernest had, at the synod of that year, promulgated a series of statutes on heretics; they were repeated ten years later not only for Bohemia but also for the bishoprics of Bamberg, Meissen and Regensburg. Bohemia seems to have been the Waldensians' centre; it was the home of their bishop, and judging from the reports of contemporaries, like John of Pilichdorf, the numbers apprehended ran into thousands. Pilichdorf, a professor at the university of Vienna, stated in his treatise against the Waldensians that in Bohemia and Moravia alone more than a thousand Waldensians were reconciled to the church.[6] If this is remotely true, it was undoubtedly due mainly to the two inquisitors Peter Zwicker and Martin of Prague, who were the spearhead of the drive against the Waldensians from the 1380s until the first decade of the next century.[7] They were responsible for most of the confessions for that period, some of which we have already encountered in Brandenburg, Pomerania, Poland and Austria.

The alert against the Waldensians had been given at Regensburg in 1377, where, among the other warnings, was one against the offence of

[1] Novo Castro. Its precise reference is unclear: Haupt suggests Nimburg or Neuhaus (ibid. 314).

[2] Ibid.

[3] Ibid., 317; Dudik, *Iter Romanum* II, 15–17 for Benedict XII's 3 bulls of September 1341—to the Gallus Neuhaus, archbishop John of Prague, and the king of Bohemia—on measures to exterminate the Waldensians.

[4] See pp. 343 ff. above.

[5] Haupt 'Waldenserthum' II, 338 ff. for what follows.

[6] Max. Bib. Vet. 25, 281.

[7] Haupt, 'Waldenserthum' II, 346.

upholding the *consolatio* (= *consolamentum*)[1] which as we have seen was to be found among the Waldensians. In July 1378 the dean of Regensburg was appointed inquisitor with extensive powers; it was during his tenure of the office that Martin of Prague absolved a Waldensian weaver, who was later charged at Strasbourg in 1400. Between 1380 and 1400 there were at least two inquisitorial trials at Regensburg; they also took place in other parts of Bavaria and Swabia. The pressure upon the Waldensians in the south east of Germany seems to have led to a series of migrations northwards along the Rhine to Strasbourg—which had its own dénouement in 1400—from towns like Nörlingen, Augsburg, Dischingen and Donauwörth.[2] Peter Zwicker and Martin of Prague are known to have been active first in the bishopric of Eichstädt where 42 were burned.[3] There, over sixty years later, in 1460, a number of what were described as Hussites were imprisoned.[4] All the articles laid against them, except for utraquism, were pure Waldensianism: refusal to invoke the saints, observe the feasts and fasts of the church, offer prayers, masses, or alms for the dead; denial of purgatory and the power of sinful priests; rejection of ecclesiastical censures, images, the bread and wine of the host, killing, the taking of oaths, pilgrimages, divorce except for fornication, obedience to superiors in mortal sin, and tithes to the church. They submitted and confessed to their own masters, who lived in poverty as the priesthood should.

Peter was also concerned with the discovery earlier mentioned of the 400 and more Waldensians in Brandenburg and Pomerania,[5] while Martin was at Würzburg in 1391 and Nuremberg in 1399. Both towns appear to have been centres of sedition. Nuremberg had a heretical past going back to the beginning of the fourteenth century; it had already undergone more than one visitation by inquisitors. There had been a great heresy hunt from 1332 to 1333; in 1354, 24 people had been banished from the city for five years for heresy; in 1378, 39 heretics had had publicly to repent and others had fled. The following year 7 were burned, 11 had to do penance, and 11 fled. Martin's register shows one

[1] Haupt, ibid., 348: item prohibemus consolationem manus impositionem ab hereticis ne aliquis recipiat.

[2] *Chroniken der deutschen Städte*: Augsburg I, 96; II, 45, cited in Haupt 'Waldenserthum' II, 349.

[3] Döllinger, *Beiträge* II, 615; Hauck, V, 401 ff.

[4] MS CLM 17796 165v–166r. Altogether there were 24 articles: no. 23 was on communion in both kinds: quod communicant sub utraque specie. Clearly, it was this which earned them the name of Hussites.

[5] See pp. 462 ff. above.

prosecution for 1400, and there may have been more.[1] Erfurt, Magdeburg and Dresden, as we saw earlier, were other places in which Waldensians were hunted and captured. A synod at Magdeburg in 1370 specifically condemned the Waldensian doctrine that sinful priests could not administer the sacraments.[2] In 1381 and 1391 Bohemian inquisitors were active in other parts of Saxony and in Thuringia, as well as Poland and Hungary. But it was perhaps in Austria, and above all in the district of Steyr that they were most numerous in the decades spanning the fourteenth and the fifteenth centuries.[3] Trials and *auto da fés* took place in 1391, 1397, 1398 and 1401. In 1391, 20 heretics were converted by Peter Zwicker, including both masters and disciples.[4] The Steyr chronicler speaks of a thousand Waldensians in the provinces for 1397; and in the two years, 1397 and 1398, 100 were burned.[5] Vienna, too, still had its heretics; they are reported for at least three different occasions, in 1411, 1430 and 1460, those for the middle date being swollen by Taborites.[6] Their conjunction was the natural outcome of their close rapport. It was also self-interest, since the Waldensians who, as a result of these persecutions fled to Brandenburg rather than Bohemia, faced renewed onslaught from the inquisition in 1480.[7] In Switzerland, essentially part of the German lands, there were inquisitorial processes at Fribourg for the years 1399, 1429 and 1430.[8] That for 1399[9] was especially remarkable in ending with the absolution of all the accused. Whether this was because of local bourgeois influence, as has been suggested,[10] or from a genuine conviction that they were innocent can only be surmised. It certainly did not recur in 1429 and 1430, when three were burned and many condemned to imprisonment. It also marked the end of the Waldensians in this region. In northern and western Germany, the Waldensians seem to have been overshadowed by the Free Spirit. The one big trial was at Strasbourg

[1] Haupt, 'Waldenserthum' II, 350–1.

[2] Hartzheim, *Concilia Germaniae* IV, 412, 413.

[3] Haupt 370 ff.; Döllinger, *Beiträge* II, 305–11, 330, 348 ff., 351 ff.

[4] Döllinger, ibid., 330.

[5] Lea, *Inquisition* II, 399.

[6] Haupt 'Walderserthum' II, 382.

[7] Lea, *Inquisition* II, 415–16; Molnar, 'Vaudois, 49.

[8] Gonnet, *Waldensia* 232.

[9] Gertrude Barnes Fiertz, 'An unusual trial under the inquisition at Friburg, Switzerland' *Speculum*, 18 (1943) 340–57.

[10] Ibid. They were charged on 15 counts, most of which were the standard Waldensian positions on ceremonies and oaths; but article 12 denounced marriage without issue as sinful (ibid., 344).

in 1400, where the accused despite their name of Wincklers were indistinguishable from Waldensians.[1]

In the Low Countries and Northern France there is little evidence of Waldensian activities. In addition to the group at Arras, which we earlier noted, there is the report of the capture and execution of a Waldensian at Douai in 1460.[2] A treatise on the Waldensians, dating from the same time and drawn from inquisitorial reports,[3] suggests by its vehemence[4] that they were of some importance in the region. It also contains references to isolated captures of Waldensians at Douai and Tournai.[5] The one other case, a century earlier in 1355, is of a priest called Jacob who was sentenced by the bishop of Tournai to imprisonment for pertinaciously asserting that 'the saints cannot and will not pray for us'.[6]

There were two other main Waldensian areas which must be considered briefly: Southern France, especially Dauphiné, and Northern Italy. Despite the fact that these regions were near to the original nuclei of the heresy, documentation for the period c. 1250 to 1500 is sparser than for the German lands which we have just been considering. In France, in particular, we do not really encounter Waldensians until the beginning of the fourteenth century, with Bernard Gui's tenure as inquisitor, which, as we have seen, began in 1307. He claimed that altogther more than 1,000 heretics were tracked down and either forced to repent or were punished.[7] But of these the greatest part were Cathars; their virtual extirpation in Languedoc was largely due to him; he gave only passing attention to the Waldensians. The first evidence of this is in 1316 when a number of them confessed to the inquisition. In 1319 three were burned, 18 were condemned to make pilgrimages and 26 sentenced to perpetual imprisonment. In 1321[8] two were burned. In 1322 eight were sent on pilgrimages and two to prison; and the remains of six bodies were exhumed and burned for having been heretics. Compared with his engagements against the

[1] Lea, *Inquisition* II, 400; K. Müller, *Die Waldenser und ihr einzelen Gruppen bis zum Anfang des 14 Jahrhunderts* (Gotha 1888) 169.

[2] Fredericq, *Corpus* III, no. 76 (303 bis) 92.

[3] Ibid., no. 77, 93–109.

[4] It describes them as an association of demons, ibid., 94.

[5] Ibid., 98–9.

[6] Ibid., II, no. 92 (206[4]) 143.

[7] Lea, *Inquisition* II, 104 ff.; and, for the Waldensians in France, 149 ff.

[8] Lea, loc. cit. Limborch, *Liber Inquisitionis* 200–1, 207–8, 216–43, 252–4, 262–5, 289–90, 340–7, 353, 355, 364–6.

Cathars this toll, as Lea remarked, does not suggest over-activity. This could have been, however, because many Waldensians were treated as Cathars in a predominantly Cathar region, just as we saw earlier how Waldensian groups in Lombardy had become permeated by Catharism. Whatever the precise cause, it was in Dauphiné and Burgundy that the main core of French Waldensians was to be found. Their strength is testified by the concern of Benedict XII, who in 1335 appealed to the rulers of the counties of Vienne and Poitou to help the inquisitors to crush them; from 1336 to 1346 there was a series of attacks against them.[1] Benedict's successor, Clement VI, repeated the exhortation to the ruler of Vienne, Humbert II, in 1348, who again responded, but clearly without lasting effect. Gregory XI turned his zeal not only upon the Waldensians in Dauphiné and Lyonnais but also Provence. In letters to the French king, Charles V, in 1372 and 1373,[2] he lamented their widespread existence, and protection by the lay authorities, and urged him to act against them; he did so again in 1375. Charles finally responded. In May 1375, Francis Borel, the inquisitor, is said to have caught many hundreds.[3]

But the inquisition continued to fight an unceasing struggle against them in the valleys of Dauphiné, Freyssnière, Argentière, Valpute, and Valcluson.[4] Nor was the struggle entirely one-sided; under repeated pressure Waldensian opposition to the taking of life weakened; there are records of the murder of inquisitors in 1321, 1332, 1365, 1374 and 1383. In 1332 at Turin, five hundred are said to have risen up against the inquisitor, John Albert Castellazo, obliging him to flee; they then went on to kill a vicar, who had just celebrated mass, on suspicion of his having denounced members of the sect to the inquisition.[5] The attacks on the Waldensians in Dauphiné culminated in the crusade of 1488, following the death of Louis XI who had given them protection. It was directed by Innocent VIII and the number of crusaders ran into thousands.[6] But here, as in Bohemia, they survived—thanks to the hills—to become part of the Reform. Even before this, however, they seem to

[1] Lea, *Inquisition* II, 151 ff.; Raynaldus, ann. 1335, no. 63.

[2] Raynaldus, ad annum 1372, no. 34.

[3] Lea, *Inquisition* 152.

[4] For this region see J. Marx, *L'Inquisition en Dauphiné du 14e siècle* (Paris 1914) 5 ff. He brings out what Lea had already suggested—their identification with sorcerers by the inquisition in the fifteenth century, for which they became a prime object of persecution.

[5] Ibid., 17.

[6] Ibid., 158; Lea, *Inquisition* II, 160 ff.

have had some contact with the Hussites, for the Council of Bourges in 1432 accused the Waldensians of sending money to them.[1]

In Italy, as we have seen, the Waldensians were established in Calabria and Lombardy; there was a third group in Umbria and the Abruzzi extending to the Papal States and Spoleto.[2] The fullest source for them is the inquisition of 1387, previously discussed.[3] There we saw that they were well established in the region of Turin, professing an outlook permeated by Catharism. But there were many persecutions both before and after that date: in 1292, 1313, and 1332, on the occasion just alluded to at Turin when there was a rising against the inquisitor. Further actions took place in 1354 and in 1363–4 under the direction of Urban V. Gregory XI in the 1370s also turned his attention to the Piedmontese Waldensians as well as those in Dauphiné; Francis Borel, the French inquisitor, was called in to attack them. But neither he nor Vincent Ferrier's attempt at their conversion in 1403 succeeded in eliminating them. Fifty years later in 1453, Nicholas V, in a bull to the bishops of Turin and Nice and the inquisitors there, stated that the majority of the inhabitants had been found to be tainted with heresy, with frequent relapses from those who had recanted. An intensive drive against them was made in 1475 and 1476, followed by the crusade of 1488 which resulted in the extermination of large numbers.

* * *

Of the social composition of the Waldensians, there seems little doubt that they appealed to the poorer sections of society. From the outset they were a movement of the poor layman, which makes them distinctive from virtually all the other movements we have considered. The Spirituals were of a religious order, and often until the fourteenth century men of learning; their poverty was spiritual in conception, rather than part of their social state. The Free Spirit, although probably attracting many of the poorer strata, were inextricably involved in a religious movement—the Beguines and Beghards—for which poverty or absence of possessions was a voluntary state, and one not always followed: the distinction between the working and the mendicant Beguines and Beghards, was, as we saw in chapter four, one of the means by which the orthodox were distinguished from the heretical.

[1] Ibid., 157. [2] Marx, op. cit., 14.

[3] See pp. 467 ff. above. For what follows, see Lea, *Inquisition* II, 257 ff. G. Gonnet, 'Casi di sincretismo', BSSV, 108 (1960) 24; G. Amati, 'Processus contra Valdenses in Lombardia superiori, anno 1387'; P. G. Boffito, 'Eretici in Piemonte al tempo del Gran Scisma'; Döllinger, *Beiträge* II, 251 ff.

Again, the Hussite leaders and Wyclif's early followers were academics and religious; only later did the English Lollards become drawn predominantly from the poorer sect, whilst the Hussites became a national movement.

The hallmark of the Waldensians, on the other hand, was that they were *ydiote et illiterati*[1]—simple and unlettered. They never pretended to learning; they knew the bible in the vernacular; and they were the only movement whose tenets did not rest upon some wider theological or philosophical base, whether the Spirituals' doctrine of poverty and prophecy, the debased mysticism of the Free Spirit or the ecclesiology of the Wyclifites and the Hussites. They were simply poor men, claiming to be Christ's true disciples, who put the simplicity of their own practices and the probity of their priests before those of the church of Rome. What wider doctrinal implications their tenets had was the result of Cathar influence. They can be assigned no mentors, direct or indirect; if interaction is to be sought beyond that with their fellow heretics, then, as we suggested before, it must rather be from the side of the Waldensians, certainly upon the Hussites, and perhaps even Wyclif and Marsilius of Padua. It was in the Waldensians' direct appeal to a true church of simple believers that their strength lay; they demanded only obedience to their superiors and loyalty to the principles in which, as Christians, they had been brought up to believe. This entailed for them not a break from the true church but a return to it. Neither habits nor outlook need be changed; members continued to live their normal lives as tailors, weavers, peasants, among their own families;[2] their allegiance to Christ remained: the only difference lay in those to whom they immediately gave it and where. Waldensianism thereby offered an outlet for anti-sacerdotalism within not just a Christian, but an ecclesiastical, framework. This was its foundation: as a poor man's religious movement, doing for the ordinary lay believer what the mendicants, and before them the monks, had done for the religious. As such the Waldensians must be accounted the nearest thing to a popular religious movement, certainly from 1300 onwards, when their own spread was accompanied by the Cathars' decline. They represented a stream of belief which can be discerned in all the other movements, especially the English Lollards and the Hussites, and sometimes in the more anti-ecclesiastical notions of the Free Spirit. They were a self-

[1] E.g., Bernard Gui, *Manuel* I, 34.

[2] E.g., Döllinger, *Beiträge* II, 330 for lists of their occupations: e.g., sartores (2), textor, faber, cerdo, filius rustici.

constituted church within a church whose example inspired the Taborites to a similar course. Like a Trojan horse their presence within Christendom helped to subvert the church's authority until its hold finally broke in the sixteenth century.

The Flagellants

The Flagellants first appeared at Perugia in 1260,[1] the year—according to Joachist prophecy—when the seventh age of the church would begin. They spread throughout Italy, then racked by the struggle of Guelf and Gibelline in the aftermath of the war between Frederick II and the papacy. In the following year they came to Central Europe and the Balkans, Bavaria, Bohemia, Austria, Hungary, Poland, and the Rhineland. Complaints were made of their heretical tendencies; but they died out within a few years, and are only occasionally met—for example, at Strasbourg in 1296, Bergamo in 1334, Cremona in 1340—before the great explosion in 1349.

Before we consider this general outbreak it should be said that flagellation as such was neither new nor heretical. To scourge the flesh was a regular part of the lives of all ascetics, and its practice went back to the beginnings of Christianity. What was new was its organized character and its mass scale, which could soon lead its participants beyond their original aims. Beginning as a form of penance it tended to end as the way of salvation. When it did so, it became a threat to the authority of the church; it was for this that Clement VI banned the Flagellants in 1351. In his bull, *Inter sollicitudines*, the pope distinguished true penance, voluntary or imposed, from the activities of 'the multitude of simple men, calling themselves Flagellants'.[2] He reproved them on two main grounds: first for attacking the church by denying it the power of the keys; second for disobedience in taking a habit—black with crosses both in front and behind—and gathering illegally into groups and conventicles.[3] We have here the two main elements in all

[1] For a general account of the Flagellants see article 'Flagellants' in DTC VI, 12–19; H. Haupt in RPT VI, 432–44; Lea, *Inquisition* II, 380 ff., 406 ff. See also *Il movimento dei disciplinati nel settimo centenario dal suo inizio* (Perugia, 1962) passim.

[2] Fredericq, *Corpus* I, no. 202, 200–1.

[3] . . . claves ecclesie vilependunt ac in contemptum discipline ecclesiastice habitum certum, nigrum videlicet, ante et retro ipsius vivifice crucis impressum habentes signaculum, sine superioris licentia deferentes sub nomine poenitentie gerunt, et alias in causa insolita congregationes, conventicula et coadunationes, que a iure sunt prohibite (ibid.).

later medieval heresy: doctrine and discipline. In Clement VI's insistence upon the unauthorized nature of the Flagellant movement he was echoing the countless attacks upon the Beguines and Beghards as well as John XXII's treatment of the Provençal Beguins. Once again the far-reaching implications of the Fourth Lateran Council's ban upon new orders can be seen in the tendency to associate extra-regular groups with heresy.

The Flagellants, for their part, underwent the characteristic evolution from unofficial piety to heterodoxy. Fear of God's retribution led them to seek forgiveness through self-chastisement. The impulse on each of the main occasions was a sense of calamity: in 1260 on the approaching end of the sixth age; in 1349 on the approaching end of the world as portended by the horrors of the Black Death. Although there were subsequently sporadic outbreaks in 1357, 1369, 1374 and 1400, they never again reached the previous level. Flagellation was essentially a mass movement which arose in time of crisis and engendered an atmosphere akin to hysteria. But it was far from being inchoate or undisciplined. The Flagellants had a very elaborate ritual[1] and a rigorous code of conduct. When they entered a city[2] they formed a procession two by two. Singing in whatever was their native tongue they would make for the church where they would pray to the Virgin. They would then go to the market place, or some other area suitable to their devotions, and, divesting themselves of their outer garments, would stand with covered heads and bare feet in a special garment stretching from their waist to the ground, holding their scourges in their hands. The latter, which, when they walked, hung from a slit in their habit, consisted of three knots each with four sharp points. Together with these they carried their crosses. In prescribed order, they formed a circle: certain among them would lead the singing in their own dialect, the others joining in. They divided into three different orders, the members of each simultaneously prostrating themselves, their arms outstretched to form a cross. When they were all lying thus, they got to their knees and would flagellate themselves, usually until the blood came.[3] Beating and scourging themselves they sang of the Virgin and Christ's sufferings:

[1] The fullest collection of sources for the Flagellants is in Fredericq, *Corpus*, vols. I–III. References in the pages which follow.

[2] The following is based upon Giles Li Muisis's account which is about the fullest, *Corpus* II, no. 61 (194) 100–9, especially 108–9, *De modus veniendi*.

[3] Not specifically stated here, but frequently attested by other writers, e.g., Fredericq, *Corpus* I–III, loc. cit., e.g., I, 200, II, 120, 122.

they would kneel as one of their leaders prayed and preached to them as a priest would in church, all the while lashing themselves until it was time to stop. Then rising and singing of the Virgin they would once more don their clothes. This ritual was performed twice publicly each day and once in private at night. With variations it was repeated over much of Christendom—England excepted—during 1348 and 1349. Beginning in Hungary,[1] the Flagellants moved rapidly westwards through Bohemia, Germany and the Low Countries. They only penetrated France as far as Picardy owing to the French king's prohibition upon them. They seem to have been thickest in Germany, the area of the Lower Rhine and Belgium. The continuator of William of Nangis's chronicle, and others, put them at 80,000—a fantastic figure, but indicative of their impact.[2] Certainly they came to many individual towns in hundreds at a time.[3] Tournai was the main centre in Belgium with numbers reaching over five thousand at their height, from August to October 1349. At Erfurt, in Germany, three thousand were reported to have been refused entry into the town by the magistrates; and the figure for the neighbouring area was put at six thousand.[4] Strasbourg and Magdeburg province were other important centres.[5] At their peak, which was passed by the end of 1349, the total must have run into many thousands.

The Flagellants were a people's crusade, which, of its nature, could not be long sustained. For a few months they generated a fervour which carried all before it, including a pilgrimage to Avignon. Contemporary sources—uniformly hostile—testified to their power over ordinary people, attracted by their fervour and humility.[6] It was this irresistible pull—with all the attendant dangers of its getting out of control—which caused the authorities alarm. Clement VI in his bull spoke of the multitude of simple followers which would spread, if not checked.[7] At first, however, the Flagellants were far from being a

[1] E.g., Trithemius, *Annales*; *Chroniken der deutschen Städte* (Strassburg) I (vol. 8) 116 f.

[2] Fredericq, *Corpus* II, no. 70 (197) 118; III, no. 23 (197) 21.

[3] E.g., 200 in Bruges (ibid., II, 101); Ghent 410 (ibid.); Sluys 300 (ibid.); Dordrecht 400 (ibid.); Tournai 556 (ibid.).

[4] Ibid., II, no. 74 (197[5]) 123; *Monumenta Erphesfurtensia* (Hanover and Leipzig 1899) 380.

[5] *Chroniken der deutschen Städte*, vols. 7 (204–10), 8 (104–20) 9 (767–8).

[6] Fredericq, *Corpus*, II; passim. Strassburg Chronicle II, *Chroniken der deutschen Städte*, vol. 9, 767.

[7] Fredericq, *Corpus* I, 201.

rabble. On the contrary they regarded themselves as a strictly regulated brotherhood; their lives were modelled on those of a crusading order.[1] Every member had to take an oath which pledged him to follow it for $33\frac{1}{2}$ days—symbolizing Christ's years on earth. Before a man could be accepted he had to make restitution of any debts and wrongs, gain permission from his wife, and confess to his new masters from whom he received the cross. During that period all had to obey their masters, who arbitrated in any disputes; they had to enter towns together; never stay in the same place for more than one night; never speak to women or beg or receive anything from them. They were not to seek alms, though not to refuse them; not to wear white—the colour of penitents—over their habit; not to carry arms; they were to say five Paternosters and Ave Marias before each meal, five Paternosters when they left a house where they had received (but must not have sought) hospitality; and five Paternosters and Ave Marias before entering; they could only accept an invitation to dine with their superiors' permission. They were not to sit on cushions or bathe. They were to care for their own sick and never leave them behind. They were to suffer patiently all wrongs and pray for the wrongdoers. Transgressors were to be punished by their masters, and those who had been murderers and adulterers were to lie on the ground separately from the rest. Finally, they were bound to flagellate themselves three times in the day and twice at night for the rest of their lives on each anniversary of Christ's passion.

This sense of vocation became one of divine mission through the publication on Christmas Day 1348 of the so-called letter from heaven.[2] It purported to have been written by God and delivered by an angel upon the altar of St. Peter's, Jerusalem, in the presence of the patriarch. Its appearance had been heralded by a great lightness in the sky, and the people, stupified, had thrown themselves upon the ground crying 'Kyrie Eleison'. The message was simple and apocalyptic. Christians must cease sinning, or God would destroy the world; failure to fast on Fridays and observe Sundays would lead to famine and tribulations, and persecution from the Saracens. Unless God answered the prayers of

[1] For what follows see Fredericq, *Corpus* II, no. 62 (194) 106–7 (Giles li Muisis); no. 62 (194 bis) 111–12; and III, no. 15 (194 bis (*a*)) 14 (extract from William of Nangis); Strassburg and Magdeburg Chronicles, loc. cit.

[2] Fredericq, *Corpus* II, no. 71 (197 bis), 119 (from Kervyn's *Histoire de Flandre*) and *Corpus* III, no. 24 (197 bis) 22–3 (William of Nangis continuation). I have followed the William of Nangis version.

the Virgin and the angels, he contemplated bringing the world to an end on 10 September, the Sunday after the date of the Virgin's birth. Those who refused to believe this letter were excommunicated; those who accepted it and transmitted it would receive God's blessing and enter his kingdom (*domus*).

The directness of the message spoke for itself; it appealed to the basic precepts practised by the simplest believers; it was devoid of all doctrinal undertones or overtones, beyond the need to repent and be saved. As such it served to heighten the sense of urgency which inspired the Flagellants. In performing their rites, said William of Nangis's chronicle, they believed they were doing what God had commanded through the angel; by their penitence they would be purged of all sins as they had been after baptism.[1] The theme of Flagellation as a second baptism recurs, and it was one of the prime causes of ecclesiastical alarm, since it threatened to supplant the sacraments and priestly ministrations. As Meyrerus in his *Annals of Flanders* put it, with probable exaggeration, they revered neither priests, nor gospel, nor the eucharist, but only their own insane practices.[2] Jean le Bel described how at Liège everyone ran to see the Flagellants and gave them money; they were regarded as holy people sent by God to make ordinary believers repent their sins. Among their errors Jean le Bel singled out their belief that, through their effusions, their blood mingled with Christ's.[3] The author of the *Gesta* of the bishopric of Liège likewise spoke of their assertion that Flagellation was a new baptism revealed to them by the angel.[4] To William of Nangis's continuator they were usurping the church's authority by their own (*auctoritate propria*).[5] The most extreme expression of Flagellant beliefs at this time is contained in a sermon reported at Tournai in 1349.[6] Addressed to the populace by one of the brethren it claimed that the blood which flowed from their self-inflicted wounds mingled with Christ's—whether they went to heaven or to hell (!).[7] Moreover, theirs was no less precious than Christ's when

[1] et disoient qu'ils fasoient toutes les choses qu'ils fasoient par la révélacion de l'ange, et tenoient et créoient que leur dicte pénitance faicte par XXXIII jours et demy, ils demouroient purs, netz, quictes et absolz de tous leurs péchiez ainsi comme ils estoient après leur baptesme (ibid., III, no. 23 (197) 21).

[2] Fredericq, *Corpus* I, no. 201, 198.

[3] Fredericq, *Corpus* II, no. 74 (197 bis[5]) 122–3.

[4] Ibid., no. 77 (197[8]) 126.

[5] Ibid., no. 76 (197[7]) 125.

[6] Fredericq, *Corpus* III, no. 19 (194 bis (*e*)) 18.

[7] Si sanguis istorum justus est militum et unitus cum sanguino Christi; et si sanguis Christi est in paradiso et sanguis istorum; et si sanguis istorum in inferno, et sanguis Christi; et si dampnatus est iste sanguis, et alter (ibid.).

he had been crucified. All who shed it, as they did, would be saved. Anyone denying these truths would cause the people to rise up against him for speaking falsely. How representative—or indeed faithful—this account is, must remain conjectural; but it points to the likely way in which untutored fervour could transgress orthodoxy and authority. The very growth of such a movement, even without such doctrinal refinements, was enough to threaten the existing order. As we have seen, it was duly banned.

In a sermon given before Clement VI in 1349, the preacher deplored the spread of the Flagellants throughout Germany, Hungary, Brabant, Flanders, Holland (Frisia) and Northern France, blaming the ineffectualness of both spiritual and lay authorities in not punishing them.[1] He also drew attention to one of the universal consequences of the movement, namely the extermination of the Jews. The latter, as non-Christians, had already been turned upon, accused of having plotted the destruction of Christians by causing the Plague. Charged with having poisoned the wells, many were massacred, especially in Germany.[2] The Flagellants continued the work. Themselves the product of terror, they turned it upon the Jews, slaughtering thousands.[3] The Jews, while sometimes resisting, were also said to have taken these tribulations as the fulfilment of their prophets' words. The coming of the Flagellants presaged their own ascent to paradise. They went to their deaths singing and dancing.[4] Thus the Flagellants' sense of salvation was heightened by the belief that they were engaged in a religious war; it no doubt helped to canalize feelings which otherwise might have been directed against erring members of their own faith, especially ecclesiastics. Anti-sacerdotalism there undoubtedly was, but never on a mass scale. The threats reported by the chronicles seem only occasionally to have been translated into deeds, and then limited ones.[5] The accounts, moreover, do not always ring true, as for example that in the Flanders

[1] Fredericq, *Corpus* III, no. 26 (201 bis) 29–37, 33.

[2] Tertio decimo, nituntur ubique Judeos occidere putantes deo placere in exterminio Judeorum. . . . Si predicti Flagellatores ista diligenter adverterent, non putarent se deo placere in exterminio Judeorum. Verum est autem quod adhuc est una causa quare volunt eos occidere: imponunt enim eis quod huius magne mortalitatis . . . ipsi sunt in causa. Dicunt enim quod aquam, unde maxima pars nutrimenti dependet, infecerunt in fontes et puteos proiciendo venera (ibid., 36–37).

[3] See, Fredericq, *Corpus* II, no. 74, 123, II, no. 79, 130.

[4] Ibid., 123.

[5] E.g., Lea, *Inquisition* II, 383, mentions the stoning to death of one of two Dominicans who tried to reason with a band on the borders of Misnia.

Chronicle, in which the subversion of the old law by their new one included the command not to fast.[1] Not for the last time the Jews drew the fire which might otherwise have been directed elsewhere.

At their height the Flagellants included a diversity of elements, among them both heretics and recalcitrant priests. The latter caused particular concern; and both the pope and the ecclesiastical authorities singled them out for arrest.[2] By the end of 1349, however, the movement was on the wane and declined rapidly. The Flagellants were condemned not only by the church[3] but by the king of France who, acting on the counsel of Paris university, banned them from his kingdom.[4] As we saw they never penetrated France beyond Picardy.

Although the Flagellants did not vanish for another century and a half, they were no longer a mass movement; apart from groups of Dancers, who appeared in North Germany and Flanders between 1373 and 1375,[5] they now tended increasingly to become a clandestine sect. The Dancers, however, were a transitory phenomenon. Composed of both men and women, they descended upon towns, dancing and singing themselves into a frenzy until they collapsed, when they would be revived and continue. They seem to have been much more openly hostile to the church than the Flagellants of 1349 and 1350; various blasphemies, including devil worship, were attributed to them.[6] The Westphalian chronicler described how at Liège they inflamed the people against the clergy, and urged them to capture and kill them.[7] They disappeared, however, within a few years, and do not seem to have spread beyond the middle and lower Rhine.

The most formidable Flagellant outbreaks of later years were those associated with Conrad Schmidt in Thuringia.[8] He was probably

[1] Fredericq, *Corpus* II, no. 80 (197[11]), 132. The other injunction was not to revere the eucharist.

[2] Duplessis d'Argentré, *Collectio* I, 361–8, especially 363.

[3] E.g., the archbishop of Cologne in 1353, Hartzheim *Concilia* IV, 471–2; and 1357, Fredericq, *Corpus* III, no. 28 (207 ter) 38–9; and the bishop of Utrecht 1355, ibid., II, no. 91 (206 ter) 142.

[4] Fredericq, *Corpus* II, no. 64 (194[4]), 113–14; II, 68 (194[8]) 116–17; II, no. 76 (197[7]) 125 (William of Nangis); no. 79 (197[10]) 130.

[5] Fredericq, *Corpus* III, nos. 30–3, 40–6; II, 93 (223 bis) 144.

[6] Fredericq, *Corpus* III, no. 30 (22 bis) 40–1; *Corpus* II, 94 (223 ter) 145–6; 95 (223[4]) 146; 97–102, 147–9.

[7] Fredericq, *Corpus* II, 102 (223[11]) 149.

[8] For what follows see works: A. Stumpf, *Historia Flagellantium, precipue in Thuringia* in *Neue Mitteilungen aus dem Gebiet historisch-antiquarische Forschungen* II (1836), ed. C. E. Förstemann. I have been unable to obtain Förstemann's own *Die christlichen*

burned with a number of his followers at Nordhausen in 1369;[1] but his name and teachings lived on. They inspired an apocalyptic outlook which was a combination of Waldensianism, Joachism and a cult of blood. It came to light at Sangerhausen, Thuringia, in 1414–16. Conrad Schmidt, who had originally prophesied the end of the world for year 1369,[2] had by then become Enoch through the transmigration of his soul; likewise one of his companions was now Elias[3]—echoes of Cathar doctrine, which, as we saw at Krems in 1312, was found among the Waldensians there. Schmidt, it was held, would sit in Christ's place at the last judgement.[4] He was also called king of Thuringia and king Frederick[5]—almost certainly a Joachist allusion to the future world emperor.[6] Such changes were characteristic of a sect's evolution; we have seen similar developments in the growth of the Olivi cult and in the later years of the Fraticelli. Similarly, there were the anti-sacerdotal tenets which accompanied them[7]—denial of the real presence, priestly confession and absolution, and the other sacraments, save marriage, which was not mentioned. The only days to be observed were Fridays and the anniversaries of the birth of Christ and the Virgin: but when Christ's birthday fell on a Friday there could be no dispensation from fasting. With the Waldensians, they also rejected purgatory, the veneration of images and prayers for the dead. To Conrad Schmidt were ascribed the doctrines that churches were just stone buildings, the public places of sinners and thieves; that to baptize with water was to sprinkle 'infernal sparks' from the devil; and that oil, water, salt and the other sacramental appurtenances were worthless: as was the reciting of the divine office, which was no better than shouting.[8] Where the distinctiveness of the sect lay was in their attitude to flagellation. They believed that the letter from the angel sixty years before had inaugurated a new era in which the power of the church had been supplanted by that of the Brothers of the Cross, as Christ had supplanted the

---

Geisslergesellschaften (Halle 1828); H. Haupt, 'Zur Geschichte der Geissler' in ZKG 9 (1888) 114–18; Haupt, 'Geisselung' in RPT, vol. 6 (Leipzig 1889), 432–44, especially 440–2; Raynaldus, *Annales*, ad ann. 1414, no. 14; Trithemius *Annales*, II, 296, Cornerus *Chronicon* in J. G. Eckhart *Corpus historicum medii aevi* (Leipzig 1723), II, 431–1393.

[1] Haupt, RPT 441.

[2] Haupt, 'Zur Geschichte der Geissler', ZKG 9 (1888).

[3] Haupt, ibid., 117; Raynaldus, loc. cit.

[4] Raynaldus, ibid.

[5] Haupt, ZKG 9, 118.

[6] See pp. 195 ff. above.

[7] See Raynaldus, ibid.; Duplessis-d'Argentré, *Collectio* I, 366.

[8] Duplessis d'Argentré, ibid.

Mosaic law with the expulsion of the merchants from the temple. Baptism by blood (the act of flagellation) had replaced all penance and the other sacraments. It was symbolized by the marriage at Cana where Christ had turned water into wine. Henceforth the only true Christian was he who was baptized in his own blood in memory of Christ's sufferings. Without it there could be no salvation. Flagellation had thus become the sign of the new age; if it did not correspond to Joachist numeration, it shared the same belief in a final and distinct era on earth under the aegis of God's elect: the barefooted monks of Joachim's vision had given way to the scourged bodies of the Flagellants; the spiritual import of Christ's teaching and the sacraments was now distilled in blood. Under the inquisitor, Henry of Schönfeld, who was dispatched there, the sect was hunted out at Sangerhausen between 1414 and 1416. His first visitation resulted in well over 100 persons being burned at Sangerhausen and other places in the neighbourhood.[1] But survivors still remained, and Schönfeld returned. This time three hundred were discovered at Sangerhausen. Penances were imposed upon those who repented; the others were handed over to the secular arm. But, after the inquisitor had departed, the princes gathered them together and had them all burned.[2] This horror did not entirely finish the sect. A number survived, and there were further trials and executions at Nordhausen in 1446; Sangerhausen, Aschersleben and Sonderhausen from 1453 to 1456; Quedlinburg in 1461; and Halberstadt in 1481.[3] By then they were of little consequence. The doctrine of Flagellation although not officially condemned at Constance received the disapprobation there of both d'Ailly and Gerson[4] for usurping the place of the sacraments. Once again a genuine religious impulse had been taken too far and imperilled orthodoxy.

[1] Lea, *Inquisition* II, 407–8.

[2] Cornerus, *Chronicon*, Eckhart, *Corpus historicum* II, 1206.

[3] Haupt, RPT VI, 441.

[4] Gerson, *Opera Omnia* II, 652–7, 660–4.

VII

John Wyclif

Life and writings

John Wyclif (c. 1330–84) is the outstanding example in the later middle ages of an heresiarch who inspired heresy on a national—and indeed continental—scale. This sets him apart from all others implicated in heterodoxy with the exception of John Hus. On the one hand, he had nothing in common with the petty heads of local bands like Gerard Segarelli, Dolcino, Walter of Holland or Nicholas of Basel. He was primarily an academic who became for a time involved in politics at the highest level. His agitation never went beyond the lecture hall and the pulpit; his media were words, thousands upon thousands, not action; his audience was the kingdom of England not a clandestine group. He never muffled his voice even if he did not court martyrdom; and however subversive and extreme his views, they were always expressed in terms of reason not a hidden revelation. To the end he remained a communicant member of the church and died hearing mass. On the other hand, the contrast between Wyclif and thinkers like Joachim of Fiore, Olivi and Eckhart is equally marked. They were not the authors of heresy either by accident or design; they were embroiled in it in spite of themselves, and posthumously, through the debasement or misinterpretation of their ideas. The same cannot be said of Wyclif. Although he did not personally instigate heresy and recoiled from the consequences of the Peasants' Revolt in 1381, the Lollard—and up to a point Hussite—heresy was the recognizable, if not always direct, outcome of his own. Wyclif presented a new challenge to the church which others sustained. In doing so, they sought to apply what he had first advocated. If the means of Lollardy were not his, the ends were. He helped to nurture an anti-sacerdotalism which the other authors of heterodoxy would have disavowed. That was his distinctiveness.

John Wyclif was born c. 1330, probably near Richmond in Yorkshire.[1] He spent the greater part of his adult life in the schools at Oxford.

[1] There are many accounts of Wyclif's life. The two main ones are H. B. Workman, *John Wyclif* (Oxford 1926) 2 vols., and K. B. McFarlane, *John Wycliffe and*

He was fellow of Merton in 1356, master of arts at Balliol in 1360, and doctor of divinity in 1372. Apart from an unfortunate interlude as warden of Canterbury College in 1365, which he had to vacate after two years because of its monastic constitutions, Wyclif lived in hired rooms at Queen's College until his final departure from Oxford in 1381. During that time he held a succession of benefices as an absentee before being rewarded in 1374 with Lutterworth in Leicestershire for services to the crown.[1] His connexion with John of Gaunt probably began in 1371. He went on a diplomatic mission to Bruges in July 1374 to negotiate on financial payments to the pope;[2] in 1376 he took a leading part in John of Gaunt's persecution of William of Wykeham by preaching in the London pulpits.[3] For this and other partisan activities and opinions against the church he was summoned by William Courtenay, bishop of London, to St. Paul's in February 1377. But Gaunt's presence in Wyclif's support helped to cause the assembly to break up in disorder.[4] By then Wyclif had already put forward his views on lordship and church wealth, given full expression in *De civili dominio* published between 1376 and 1378. This helped to account for the growing ecclesiastical hostility towards him, culminating in the despatch of extracts from the work to the pope, Gregory XI. It led to the first official condemnation of Wyclif's views in 1377 when the pope censured eighteen articles.[5] We shall discuss these and his subsequent condemnations in the next chapter. For the present it is enough to record that Wyclif was again saved from any action against him by his powerful connexions, together with the outbreak of the Great Schism. When after a delay of several months the papal bull was finally published in England, towards the end of 1377, no attempt was made to arrest Wyclif as the pope had enjoined. By mutual consent between him and the university authorities, he was merely confined to Black Hall in Oxford, while his teachings were investigated. The verdict was

---

the beginnings of English Nonconformity (London 1952), which I have followed here. See also J. A. Robson, *Wyclif and the Oxford Schools* (Cambridge 1961) 9–17, for the years until 1374, and A. B. Emden, *A Biographical Register of the University of Oxford until 1500*, vol. 3.

[1] Workman, I, 209; McFarlane, 63.

[2] Workman, I, 240 ff.; McFarlane, 63 ff.

[3] Workman, I, 279 ff.; McFarlane, 69–70.

[4] Workman, I, 286 ff.; McFarlane, 74–6.

[5] Workman, I, 295 ff.; McFarlane, 79–81. Published in FZ 242–4, Wilkins, *Concilia* III, 116–18; Walsingham, I, 345–53.

that they were true although 'they sounded badly to the ear'.[1] Absolved by the university he refused to answer a first summons by the archbishop of Canterbury to appear at St. Paul's; but finally appeared at Lambeth in March 1378. With his safety virtually guaranteed by the queen mother, he received nothing more than an admonition not to spread false doctrines.[2]

Although it was the last occasion on which Wyclif was formally arraigned it was the beginning of his alienation from the church. 1378 had long been recognized as the watershed in his career. It not only saw the completion of his royal service and *De dominio civili*, the first major work of his new theological and ecclesiological phase, but the shift to extreme anti-sacerdotalism. Beginning with *De veritate sacre scripture*,[3] as yet comparatively moderate, Wyclif made a swift progression from unqualified fundamentalism to an heretical view of the church in his *De ecclesia*.[4] Shortly afterwards he wrote *De officio regis* (November 1378) in which he asserted the king's supremacy over the priesthood and looked to him to reform the church, thereby nullifying what he had said about civil lordship in *De civili dominio*. With the publication of *De potestate pape* in 1379 Wyclif's disavowal of the existing hierarchy was complete. He had already reviled Gregory XI in *De ecclesia*[5] and he continued to deny the pope's right to summon him to Rome.[6] All his subsequent writings on the church, to be found in his *Polemical works, Opera minora, De blasphemia*,[7] *Opus evangelicum*,[8] as well as his *Sermons*, add little or nothing to the doctrines of the bible, church and lay power already formulated. The difference was one of tone, which was becoming increasingly virulent, whereas between him and other critics of the church it was one of kind. The majority of them attacked its abuses but accepted its authority. Wyclif however opposed it on both counts.

He was not just a moralist whose bitterness may have derived from his own lack of preferment;[9] nor did his case stand or fall entirely by his own personal failings of pluralism and absenteeism. Beyond any

[1] Workman, I, 305–6; McFarlane, 81.

[2] Workman, I, 308–9; McFarlane, 81–2.

[3] 1378. [4] 1378. [5] P. 366.

[6] E.g., *Pol. Works* II, 546–64; *Opus evangelicum* I, 20, 434. See also Workman, II, 314–15.

[7] 1382. [8] 1383–4.

[9] For the opposite view see McFarlane, 30, 66–9, 84–5, who also, however, sees his 'frenzied attack upon institutions and doctrines' as partly the result of 'the flattering attentions of the great' and possible physical causes (85).

individual aberrations Wyclif was also a theorist who gave to his hostility to the church a far-reaching theoretical framework. Whether one is to be seen as cause and the other effect can never be more than conjectural and is secondary to the main fact that Wyclif became a heretic not only because he attacked the church but because he denied its authority in the name of the bible and his own conception of the true church. These provided him with the justification for seeking its radical reform at the hands of the king. All the elements of this outlook were already in being by 1379; they only needed a catalyst to fuse them into open dissent. His eucharistic teaching, formulated the same year in *De apostasia*[1] and *De eucharistia*,[2] supplied it.

It was the measure of the distance Wyclif had already travelled from orthodoxy, even if until then he had escaped serious reprisal, that his comparatively innocuous eucharistic tenets[3] should have become one of the focal points of his heresy. The reaction to it was almost immediate. It lost him the support of the friars many of whom had been his allies in the attack upon clerical abuses. Henceforth they became among the most bitter of his enemies and a ceaseless target for his abuse. His last plea to his erstwhile friends among them in *De apostasia*—with *De eucharistia* one of the two main sources for his doctrine of the eucharist—in 1379, testified to the breach it had made.[4] The effect upon his own life at Oxford was no less far-reaching. In 1381 his doctrine was condemned by a twelve-man commission appointed by the chancellor, William Barton, one of Wyclif's academic opponents, and its teaching prohibited on pain of excommunication.[5] Wyclif, surprised, appealed to the king in vain.[6] He then published his *Confessio*,[7] defending his views, in May, and by the end of the summer had left Oxford never to return.[8] While he retired to his Lutterworth rectory, William Courtenay, now archbishop of Canterbury, acted against his doctrine and followers in Oxford. In May 1382 he convened a synod at Blackfriars (the so-called Earthquake Council) where twenty-four

[1] 1379. [2] 1379.

[3] See pp. 549 ff. below for a discussion of the doctrine itself.

[4] *De apostasia* 44. It is also expressed in the amusing action of Adam Stockton who changed the note, describing Wyclif by a passage he had copied from *De potestate pape*, from *venerabilis inceptor* to *execrabilis seductor*. A. Gwynn, *Austin Friars* 238–9.

[5] Workman, II, 141–5; McFarlane, 97–8; text in FZ 105–14.

[6] McFarlane, 98; Workman, II, 145; Wilkins, *Concilia* III, 171.

[7] FZ 116–31. Workman, II, 146–7; McFarlane, 98–9. Whether he was advised against further resistance is uncertain (McFarlane, 98).

[8] Workman, II, 147–8; McFarlane, 99.

propositions from Wyclif's writings were condemned.[1] He then proceeded to enforce the ban at Oxford.

The impact of Courtenay's actions upon Oxford Lollardy belongs to the next chapter. Wyclif's own part in its development ended with his withdrawal to Lutterworth. Although he was not mentioned as the author of the censured propositions, and remained unmolested by Courtenay, his name headed the list of those banned from preaching at Oxford and he may well have been compelled to submit.[2] If so, he did his best to compensate with his pen, or, as he seems to have suffered a stroke, that of his secretary, John Purvey.[3] His last three years at Lutterworth were passed in a frenzy of writing. It was not until 1407 that Arundel, then archbishop of Canterbury, set up a committee to examine all Wyclif's works. This resulted in a comprehensive list of 267 censured as heretical or unsound in 1411.[4] They were also sent to Rome; although not condemned in their entirety some of his works were burned at a Lateran Council in 1413,[5] and finally forty-five articles first banned at Prague in 1403 were again proscribed at the Council of Constance in 1415.[6] Wyclif thus officially became a heretic twenty years after his death. But it was not until 1428 that the other order by the Council of Constance, for his body to be exhumed, was carried out, and his remains thrown into a stream at Lutterworth.[7] By then the ideas he had propagated had long since passed into other hands and produced their own martyrs.

Wyclif's doctrine, for all the attention its author has received, has still not been treated in its entirety.[8] This is hardly surprising not only

[1] Workman, II, 266; McFarlane, 105. Printed in Wilkin's *Concilia* III, 159–60, and translated in Workman, II, appendix T, 416–17.

[2] McFarlane, 115–16.

[3] Ibid., 119–20.

[4] *Snappe's Formulary* 128 ff.

[5] Mansi, vol. 27, 505 ff.

[6] Ibid., 610, 630. Workman II, 273–4, implies that the full 267 articles were condemned. They were not. The forty-five had become the badge of the Wyclifite heresy in Prague, although in fact many of them were not Wyclif's at all. For their history, see ch. IX below.

[7] McFarlane, 120.

[8] The major study on Wyclif to date is Workman's. Although of monumental scale and as comprehensive as he could make it, it suffers from unsystematic arrangement and at times lack of penetration, especially into Wyclif's thinking. He also tends to a certain romanticism, and many of his early conjectures on Wyclif's Oxford are unfounded, as are his later ones on Wyclif as the leader of his band of poor preachers. From the point of view of this study its main lack is of a sustained analysis of Wyclif's outlook, in place of which useful but superficial summaries of his main works are given. McFarlane should be consulted wherever possible both for its own sake in its

in view of his enormous prolixity, but because of the clear division between his earlier metaphysical and his later theological and ecclesiological writings. Yet they remain interdependent; and it is especially important to consider them as a whole if we are to try to locate the source of his heresy. We have to ask whether it is to be found within the system itself, in some tenet or emphasis which threw it out of orthodox gear; or whether it resulted from experiences extraneous to the purely intellectual plane, such as Wyclif's passing over for a prebend at Lincoln in 1373, which gradually engendered a sense of persecution and injustice.[1] To make either the exclusive explanation would not be tenable. We know too little about Wyclif's personality to be able to gauge the likely effects of a setback to his chances of preferment. At the same time it seems unlikely that his progression towards heresy was purely autonomous: the marked change in temper during the last six years of his life from 1378, suggests that his growing extremism was at least aggravated by mounting hostility towards him. This is particularly apparent in his eucharistic teaching: only in this later phase did he draw the heretical conclusions that had been open to him at any time during the past fifteen or so years from metaphysical premises which had remained unaltered. Indeed it is the conjunction of later events, including no doubt the accentuation of his own traits of character, with a fundamentally constant intellectual orientation which offers the most likely explanation of Wyclif's development. While we should not succumb to the temptation to treat the course of Wyclif's ideas as intellectually preordained, they remain nevertheless the one palpable source of explanation. If we can never know Wyclif the man, at least through his writings we can come within distance of knowing him as the heretic.

For this reason, it will be necessary to devote some attention to Wyclif's philosophical assumptions and the character of his thinking. To take the latter first, Wyclif was from the outset an intellectual extremist; he pressed everything to its limits, a trait which became overriding towards the end of his life. Not unexpectedly this was accompanied—whether as causes or effects it would be otiose to say—by rigidity and unsubtlety. Even as hagiography some of the eulogies

mastery of the historical material and as a corrective. For Wyclif's philosophy, see J. A. Robson, *Wyclif and the Oxford Schools*, which unfortunately does not go beyond his metaphysics; and S. H. Thomson, 'The philosophical basis of Wyclif's theology' in *Journal of Religion* 2 (1931) 86–116.

[1] This has been suggested by McFarlane, op. cit., 30, 67–8, 84–5.

by Wyclif's editors of sixty or more years ago to his 'subtle genius' and philosophical daring go too far. Wyclif's originality, like his daring, consisted in stepping in where angels feared to tread. It was not just that most of his concepts were derived from others: that is something common to the greatest thinkers. But where, say, Aquinas gave new significance to Aristotle's categories, Wyclif made whatever he touched unserviceable. His strong preconceptions and his unconstrained evangelical fervour led him invariably to exaggerated notions, whether in metaphysics or scripture. He had something of Bradwardine's one-dimensional outlook but without Bradwardine's intellectual control. Wyclif as a thinker was lacking in both discipline and flexibility. His works are generally without structure; his arguments, rigorous in themselves, do not cohere; development is lost in repetition and order in irrelevance. While his writings add up to more than a series of *pièces d'occasion*, they hardly constitute a system, as his late compendium, the *Trialogus*, shows. For all his words, what can be meaningfully isolated are a half-dozen or so guiding ideas endlessly repeated. But this does not allow us to dismiss them. Wyclif's very intellectual limitations gave his thought an emotional unity and impact. His desire for certainty, and his conviction that he had found it, led him to reduce problems to palpable terms which could be readily seized. Within a metaphysical framework of extreme realism he applied his undoubted logical powers and dialectical eloquence to establishing his version of the truth. Together these attributes made him a formidable teacher and opponent in the Oxford schools. What Wyclif lost as a thinker he gained as an advocate. In the latter role he achieved an ascendancy at Oxford which only the use of force after his departure could dissipate, but not destroy. His influence lived on to inspire generations in England and Christendom. Whatever his intellectual failings they helped to make him a religious force of incalculable effect upon the later middle ages.

Metaphysics

From the point of view of this study Wyclif is a further example of the way in which heresy invariably arose less from a different set of assumptions than from carrying those commonly accepted too far. More than any of the other thinkers we have had to consider Wyclif was an extremist. Whether by temperament or circumstances is of no consequence, since it permeated his whole outlook. Extremism was at once

Wyclif's main failing as a thinker and the prime cause of his heresy; his approach was such that had he started from the other end, and made signs, not being, the foundation of truth, he would still have carried his arguments beyond the bounds of orthodoxy. In fact, however, the concepts in which he dealt, and which he followed—or more correctly pushed—unwaveringly to their end, were those most in harmony with his temperament. Nor were they achieved fortuitously. Wyclif himself seems to suggest that he had once been a terminist, i.e. one who accepted only the reality of individuals, in the manner of the Ockhamists, and who regarded all general categories, such as man and being, as merely mental descriptions.[1] It was later that he came to find truth in the pre-eminence and reality of universal being.[2] Now from that position, as we shall see, much of Wyclif's heterodoxy and heresy flowed; but it should be regarded as the vehicle, rather than the source, of his extremism, which can hardly be contained within a single concept. This is seen from the corresponding havoc that he wreaked upon other orthodox assumptions. Of these the most prominent was his treatment of the church. He took St. Augustine's division between the earthly and heavenly cities to arrive at an exclusive conception of the church which Augustine had never held, and which was turned against its hierarchy. Equally extreme was his employment of the bible to question the church; even if it is accepted that Wyclif provided a new basis for its literal truth this still did not in itself entail utilizing its authority in the way that he did. Accordingly, before we proceed to consider these and other aspects of Wyclif's thought in greater detail, it is worth emphasizing that what unites them is less metaphysics than their application; and what makes them damaging is less the assumptions upon which they were founded than the extremes to which they were pressed. There is little of the deep-seated intellectual unity in Wyclif's outlook which informs the great scholastic systems. If the effect was not wholly irrational, nor was it fully the work of reason; and it is the absence of intellectual balance in Wyclif's works that ultimately makes his outlook unsatisfying.

This is perhaps most clearly to be seen in his doctrine of being, the metaphysical basis of his thinking. As we have said Wyclif became a realist, and one of such extremity that he believed in the self-subsistence of all universal concepts, such as goodness, man and so on, only stopping short of Plato—who had made them autonomous—to locate them eternally in God. The majority of medieval thinkers, with the

[1] Robson, op. cit., 141–70.
[2] Robson, ibid., 145.

exception of the nominalists, or the terminists, of Wyclif's own day, subscribed to some degree of realism, at least to the point of conceding that every recognizable being, dog, cat, man, tree, possessed an essence which made it what it was. The differences came over the status of this common humanity or caninity: did it exist in its own right, independently of and prior to individuals, or only through the medium of particular beings? Those who asserted the self-subsistence of universals were extreme realists and Wyclif was of their number. But characteristically he went beyond the traditional bounds in endowing the divine archetypes of all creatures with being. This he called intelligible being (*esse intelligibile*); it was the highest of the three grades of being which everything created possessed. In contradistinction to the other two—potential being in secondary causes and actual being in individuals—intelligible being inhered eternally in God; it constituted a creature's supreme being and was eternal in the sense that God eternally intended its existence to be realized at a specific time.[1] This threefold division between what God eternally saw, what was possible, and what was actually realized in time was not original to Wyclif; he quoted St. Augustine's *Super Genesim* as his source.[2] Where Wyclif went farther was in attributing eternal being to these eternal archetypes in God;[3] since they were inseparable from God's being they were essentially, though not formally, part of his essence.[4]

Again and again Wyclif returned to the same theme. Every creature, he said, possessed an absolutely necessary intelligible being eternally in God. This in turn gave rise to its essence in things from which its actual existence in time and place could be realized.[5] There was therefore a

[1] cum omni creature simul insunt [illa tria] secundum quemdam ordinem: ut esse intelligibile creature est eius esse supremum; quod esse est eternum in hoc quod deus eternaliter intendit illam creaturam existere tempore suo; et post illud esse sequitur esse possibile creature in causis secundis a deo ad producendum creaturam in tempore suo; et illud est temporale medians inter esse intelligibile et esse existere; 3° vero sequitur esse existere vel esse accidentale creature in suo genere (*De ente* (WS) 101–2).

[2] Patet ista distinctio per beatum Augustinum 6°, Super Genesim ad litteram, 13° . . . (ibid., 102).

[3] Ideo satis est pro sensu philosophorum quod esse generatione productum sive effectum habet suum esse intelligibile pro mensura eternitatis . . . cum sit veritas absolute necessaria, idem essentialiter cum deo (*Miscellanea philosophica* (WS) I, 231).

[4] sicut et quotlibet alie veritates eterne . . . que omnia sunt essentialiter sed non formaliter divina essentia (*De dominio divino* (WS) 179.

[5] sequitur quod omne creatum habet esse intelligibile absolute necessarium quod est esse intelligibile vel esse intellectum adintra in deo . . . et res secumdum esse intelligibile, quod est ultimum sue intelligibilitatis eternaliter intellectum, est ydea

chain of being from the archetype in God to the individual in the material world; so that ultimately, as Wyclif himself was wont to say, the individual's existence was merely accidental to its being which inhered eternally in God.[1] The effect of this attribution of being to the eternal archetype was momentous. Although Wyclif was careful to distinguish its inherence in God from the actual existence of a creature, which could only take place temporally in the created world, not eternally in God,[2] he had nevertheless endowed the archetype with being; or, more strictly, he made it share God's. Now this immediately conferred upon it the same attributes of eternity, necessity and indestructibility as God enjoyed; and since all created being was in turn dependent upon that of the *esse intelligibile* in God, the same attributes were transmitted to the created world. For if a creature's being was merely the temporal realization of its eternal archetype, it was itself antecedently eternal and necessary, and could not be destroyed without the destruction of the archetype whose being made its own existence possible. Wyclif had in fact identified the ideal, or the intelligible, not merely with ultimate reality—the prerogative of all good Platonists—but with being. The result was a system of singular cumbrousness. Everything was tied to everything else in an eternal chain reaction, God included. Although, as we have said pantheism did not arise, the due distance between the divine and the created was blurred, and the latter made to share in the eternity and necessity of God's own movements.

To give him credit Wyclif did not flinch from these consequences, which were soon apparent to Oxford contemporaries like the East Anglian Carmelite, John Kenningham.[3] Their dispute, when Wyclif was incepting in the theological faculty,[4] provides a good introduction to the more obvious implications of Wyclif's metaphysical position. Kenningham was particularly concerned to counter Wyclif's belief in the eternity of scripture and of all future events. He pointed to the wrong order of priorities which Wyclif's use of the *esse intelligibile*

creature vel ratio exemplaris; et eadem res secundum existentiam in genere est effectus (ibid., 61). Also ibid., 194–5; and *Trialogus* 86.

[1] Wyclif sometimes interchanged the terms individual and accidental in this context: e.g., 3° vero sequitur esse existere vel esse accidentale creature in suo genere (*De ente* 102).

[2] E.g., *De dominio divino* 195.

[3] Printed in FZ 4–103 and 453–80.

[4] In J. A. Robson, *Wyclif and the Oxford Schools*, 162–70, who dates them c. 1372–4, ibid., 163.

entailed; to say that archetypes had eternal being in God was to imply that whatever God knew must be; hence Antichrist would already be, since God already knew him.[1] The same applied to everything else; and Kenningham rightly reminded Wyclif of John of Damascene's saying that the order was from what God willed to what was possible, not that God willed whatever was possible:[2] with Wyclif's identification of being with intelligibility, even God could not escape his determinism, however much it was affirmed in God's name. Equally pertinent was the distinction which Kenningham drew between his and Wyclif's conceptions of being: Wyclif distinguished a creature from its being, whereas for Kenningham a creature was his being. As Kenningham put it, 'a creature's being is this creature, intransitively'.[3] This was the fundamental difference between the two disputants. Wyclif regarded a creature's being as existing eternally in God: Kenningham denied that a creature was before it had been created; its being was its individual existence (*in genere proprio*) and this could not be before the creation of time.[4] Similarly Kenningham drew a distinction between God's knowledge of something as an object which was not in itself present, and something which was. By the first mode he knew all archetypes eternally without his knowledge of them denoting their existence.[5] Kenningham employed similar arguments to combat Wyclif's belief in the literal truth of scripture, which he deduced from the same grounds of the eternity of being.[6]

Given their different standpoints Kenningham's advantage over his opponent is scarcely surprising; Wyclif's buoyancy is. Considering that he was labouring under a weight which would have kept most

[1] Consequenter dicit magister in hac materia quod claudit contradictionem formalem deum quicquam cognoscere nisi istud proportionaliter habeat esse. Et distinguit triplex esse, scilicet esse intelligibile in deo; esse possibile in causis secundis; et esse existere in genere proprio. . . . Secundo principaliter arguebam contra positionem sic: si ista consequentia sit bona, deus intuetur .a., ergo .a. est . . . sed certum est quod nunc intuetur, ergo nunc Antichristus est (FZ 33–5).

[2] Ibid., 35.

[3] Et ratio est: ego non distinguo inter creaturam et suum esse, et ideo voco esse intelligibile creature ipsam creaturam intelligibilem, ut sit constructio intransitiva (ibid., 74).

[4] Tertio arguitur sic: nulla creatura existit antequam sit creatura; ergo nulla creatura existit antequam sit facta vel creata. . . . Item existere creature est esse in genere proprio; sed nulla creatura ante initium temporis habuit esse in genere proprio; ergo ante omne tempus, vel initium temporis, nulla creatura habuit existere (ibid., 40).

[5] Ibid., 10.

[6] Ibid., 4–9, 15–27 and passim.

men for ever on the bed of the sea, his dialectical surfacings were remarkable. But it is also a sign of Wyclif's failings as a thinker; he had an inexhaustible supply of logical devices which hid an impoverished and inflexible mode of thought. He became a slave to his concepts and made a virtue of his bondage. This can be seen in the main conclusions which he drew from the eternity of being, resumed in his surviving determinations against Kenningham. These centred on the necessity and eternity of all being, and the consequent ever-presentiality of scripture as God's word. Each followed from the premise that God's knowledge extended to the *esse intelligibile* of all being, including therefore those which were simply possible. Since it would be contradictory for God to know what did not have being, the possibles must have being in proportion to God's knowledge of them—i.e. intelligible being—and so be. From this, Wyclif concluded, all that can be, is.[1] Although under pressure from Kenningham Wyclif distinguished between God's intuition of what existed and his simple apprehension of what was possible, he failed to meet the Carmelite's contention that, according to him, what God knew, was.[2] Despite Wyclif's qualifications, his own position was that all possible non-existents were from eternity, even though, as past and future, sometimes they existed in time, and sometimes they did not.[3] For an object to be present to God, therefore, it must be; and as we have said Wyclif located its being in its *esse intelligibile*.[4]

Wyclif, in effect, was upholding the eternity of all being; throughout his philosophical works he reverted to the proposition that all that is present to God, is,[5] whether past, present or future. Before it could exist in its own time and place it had to have intelligible being in God, through its archetype or exemplar.[6] Wyclif did not hesitate to

[1] quia dico cum S. Thoma quod omnia presentia, preterita et futura deus intuitive cognoscit. Omnia autem possibilia, que non habent existentiam in genere, cognoscit eque perfecte, licet solum notitia simplicis apprehensionis; sed contradictionem claudit deum quicquam cognoscere nisi proportionaliter habeat esse. Ideo instruxerunt nos sancti doctores quomodo creature habeant triplex esse, scilicet esse intelligibile in deo, esse possibile in causis et esse existere in proprio genere. . . . Et sic concesserunt quod omne quod potest esse, est; et quod deus solum possibilia potest cognoscere (ibid., 463–4).

[2] Ibid., 464–5.

[3] cum omnia possibilia non existentia eternaliter sunt et nunquam non sunt, preterita et futura aliquando sunt, et aliquando non sunt . . . (ibid., 465).

[4] Ibid.

[5] Quod tertio pertinenter sic applico. Omne quod est deo presens est; omne quod fuit vel erit est deo presens; igitur omne quod fuit vel erit, est (ibid., 475).

[6] Ibid.

draw the conclusion that being was necessary and eternal, and as such indestructible.[1] In its widest sense, then, being was not just that which existed in the temporal present but all that was possible and intelligible.[2] As Wyclif put it, intelligibility and knowability were categories of being; and conversely whatever could not be known could not be.[3] Every being, therefore, to the extent that it derived from the intelligibility eternally present in God, shared in the necessity and eternity inseparable from God's knowledge. While it was contingent in its actual temporal realization, it was eternally necessary in its capacity to be.[4] It is here that we come to the most distinctive feature of Wyclif's conception of being: namely, its eternity through the *esse intelligibile*.[5] Unlike the vast majority of scholastics, Wyclif not only asserted the ever-presentiality of God's knowledge but extended it to the beings that God knew. The two became inseparable; from their inseparability flowed all the radical consequences of his realism.

In the first place, whatever had been or was to be, past or future, was present sempiternally.[6] As Wyclif put it with exemplary clarity in his reply to Kenningham: all that is present to God, is; all that was or will be is present to God; therefore all that was or will be is.[7] It followed from the assumption that if something is present to God it must be:[8] an assumption which, as Kenningham repeatedly stressed, was due to Wyclif's refusal to distinguish between what God knew as an object

[1] E.g., Ex quo patet quod quelibet essentia est perpetua, quia non posset desinere esse nisi per annihilationem, sed nihil potest annihilari; ergo etc. (*De ente predicamentali*, 43). See also ibid., 1–2; *Miscellanea philosophica* (WS) II, 170–4, *De ente* 62–3, 287–308.

[2] Cum ergo ens non potest una vice esse communius et alia vice minus commune, patet quod semper est commune ad omne possibile, et per consequens ad omne intelligibile (*De ente* 63).

[3] Ibid., 99.

[4] 2° sequitur quod quelibet volutio dei terminata ad volubile in esse intelligibile est absolute necessaria, et quelibet terminata ad contingens secundum non esse, non sit deo accidens, sed contingens (ibid., 116–17).

[5] Et omnis aptitudo presupponit illud cuius esse posse vel possibilitas, non quidem secundum esse existere, sed secundum esse intelligibile, vel saltem esse intentionale. Unde existere non est synononum cum esse, sed longe inferius, quia est existere in proprio genere. Sed prius oportet quod creatura habeat esse intentionale vel intellectuale in deo (ibid., 62).

[6] Ex quo sequitur quod omnia qui erunt vel fuerunt sunt in tempore sempiterno. Nam si deus vult aliquid, ipse eternaliter vult illud ex prima veritate; et si vult aliquid, ipsum est (ibid., 116).

[7] Quod tertio pertinenter sic applico. Omne quod est deo presens est; omne quod fuit vel erit est deo presens; igitur omne quod fuit vel erit, est (FZ 475).

[8] et si est presens tunc est (ibid.).

outside him and what he knew as an idea.[1] For Wyclif all that God knew, including past and future, was present to him as intelligible being.[2]

In the second place, as a consequence, Wyclif's conception of contingency was radically different. On the one hand everything God knew he knew as intelligible being; hence whatever was possible as individual being was at the same time necessary in its aspects of intelligibility:[3] contingency was confined to the realization of particular individuals from an archetypal being which inhered in God eternally.[4] In that sense all creation was conditionally necessary (*ex suppositione*).[5] On the other hand, since God knew all possibles eternally and necessarily, they had to be, the future equally with the past;[6] they were possible only so far as their temporal existence was concerned—in the interval before their appearance as individuals in the created world. Strictly speaking, then, time was at once the individuating factor and the bridge between necessity and contingency.[7] As Wyclif expressed it, the difference between the possible and the necessary lay in the duration of time; they became merged not through the acquisition of any absolute quality but when that which previously need not be, now had to be.[8] Time then for Wyclif was the medium of actual existence; it

[1] See p. 504 above.

[2] Minorem credo doctorem dare indubie; deus nihil intuetur nisi quod est sibi presens; sed omne quod fuit vel erit deus eternaliter intuetur, etiam secundum doctorem; igitur omne tale est sibi presens, et per consequens est (FZ 476).

[3] Ymmo ens communicatur omni existenti in aliquo tempore preterito vel futuro, et hoc absolute necessario, quamvis contingenter secundum esse existere (*De ente* 63).

[4] Nam omnia creata habent esse intelligibile eternum et absolute necessarium . . . et illi superadditur existentia pro tempore suo, que existentia deficit eis pro mensura eternitatis (*Miscellanea philosophica* I, 229).

[5] Sed nego maiorem, cum omne creatum necesse est esse necessitate ex suppositione (FZ 465).

[6] FZ 463–4. Also: Et sic futuritiones rerum ... erant eterne in deo, in quo eternaliter fuit quod ipsa erunt futura (*De ente* 111) An: Tanta ergo est necessitas utrobique in veritate de preterito et de futuro (ibid., 305).

[7] Ideo inter contingens in communi et necessarium in communi est tanta latitudo, et non inter quodcunque contingens et quodcunque necessarium. . . . Non igitur videtur mihi quod inter proprietatem contingentis ad utrumlibet et proprietatem necessarii sit talis magna distantia nisi quoad ad durationem temporis . . . (*Miscellanea philosophica* I, 77).

[8] dicitur quod ex contingenti fit necessarium, non quidem ut ex nocte fit dies, sed idem quod iam est contingens erit alias necessarium, non per absolutum sibi adquiritum, sed per hoc quod oportet ipsum esse postquam fuit possibile ipsum non esse (ibid., 75).

was merely the last stage in an eternal process from archetype to individual. Each could not but be; where they differed was in their mode of being. The archetype, as we have seen, was being, in virtue of being known by God; the individual through being willed. Accordingly, where the former was eternally and absolutely necessary, the latter existed temporally and conditionally: both its contingency and its necessity rested upon God's will. God in willing communicated first the possibility of existence, which once realized, then became necessary and never to be undone.[1] As Wyclif said, the contingent could become necessary, but the necessary never contingent.[2] It hardly need be stressed that the margin between the necessary and the contingent was an ephemeral one. Contingency lay neither in being nor in the creature but in God's will, which, since it was necessary, ultimately communicated the need to be to what he had in the beginning decreed possible: as such contingency was reduced to the first stage in an inexorable process. Moreover, just as God's will eternally determined what was possible he also decided what was impossible by not extending it his power and so denying it the capacity to be.[3] As with Bradwardine, Wyclif reduced contingency to the working of God's will, thereby identifying it with necessity, on the ground that God was both supremely free and absolutely necessary.[4] In effect this was to eliminate contingency from creation and to reduce the existence of God's creatures to the expression of his will.

Nowhere is this more apparent than in the other feature of Wyclif's doctrine of being, namely, its indestructibility. His argument here sprang directly from his tenets of the necessity and the eternity of all being. As inseparable from God's being, to posit the destruction of being in any form was ultimately to threaten God—which was both blasphemous and impossible. Wyclif developed his argument most fully in an extract from a treatise on God's power.[5] It rested upon God as the cause of truth, which, here as elsewhere, Wyclif made synony-

[1] Istis premissis, patet quod tales veritates de preterito sunt simpliciter necessarie, et sua opposita sunt simpliciter impossibilia, hoc est, non possunt esse, sicut ille veritates non possunt non esse (ibid., 74). Also ibid., 66–7.

[2] Nam contingens potest mutari in necessarium, sed non est possibile e contra, quia semper proficit et non desinit quantum ad perpetua (ibid., 75).

[3] Ibid., 114.

[4] Nec sequitur: libere dat prima causa necessitatem isti veritati; igitur potest tollere libertatem ab illa; quia summa libertas est necessitas, et libertas contradictionis est infima (ibid., 78). Also ibid., 148.

[5] Published in *De ente* 287–308.

mous with being.[1] It was a contradiction in terms to posit a non-existent creature, for every creature constituted positive being which could not be annihilated without annihilating all substance of which it was part. Thus to destroy one thing would be to destroy all being.[2] Even at this comparatively early non-theological stage of Wyclif's career he sought confirmation in the bread of the eucharist, the substance of which, he said, must remain together with the accidents after consecration.[3] Wyclif characteristically went further when he argued that annihilation would require the destruction of its corresponding archetype, or idea, in God as the cause of its being; but since this would be essentially God, any creature's destruction would require the destruction of its subject in God: an impossibility. God as pure being cannot be the opposite of being and so cannot cause destruction except by accident.[4] Just as God cannot destroy the past or the future, he cannot destroy the present; for all presuppose being and all are united by the extension of time, which, as we have already seen, was the medium joining the contingent and the necessary.[5] In the same way, he could not annihilate time or space: nor therefore the world as their substance.[6]

Ultimately, then, it was the chain of being which inseparably bound God to all that was, accidents as well as substance, individuals together

[1] Impossibile est ens aut veritatem esse nisi vel deum vel causatum a deo mediate vel immediate; sed annihilatio nec potest esse deus nec causata a deo; igitur non potest esse (ibid., 288). See also *Summa de ente* (ed. Thomson, 2 and 20).

[2] Habito igitur quod annihilatio non sit deus, probatur quod non potest poni creatura vel creature inexistens, quia omnis creatura est ens predicabile positivum, quod non potest annihilationi competere; igitur nec est creatura. Si enim esset creatura, tunc deus de potentia absoluta non posset annihilare nisi succedet universitas annihilationis (*De ente* 288).... igitur annihilata substantia qualibet singulari, annihilaretur genus substantie, et per consequens non maneret post annihilationem existens in aliquo singulari: totum igitur genus substantie destrueretur ad cuiuscunque substantie annihilationem (ibid., 289).

[3] Ibid., 289.

[4] Ymmo ulterius ordinando videtur quod ad simpliciter annihilationem requiritur ydee corruptio, que est idem essentialiter cum causa existente; et cum talis ydea sit essentialiter deus . . . videtur quod ad cuiuslibet creature annihilationem requiritur annihilatio sui subiecti. . . . Et ex hoc capiunt philosophi evidentiam quod deus qui est purum esse, non potest esse contrarium, non potest causare corruptionem nisi forte per accidens . . . (ibid., 290).

[5] Confirmatur tripliciter. Primo sic. Omne fuisse vel fore rei supponit esse eiusdem tamquam prius naturaliter; sed deus non potest annihilare fuisse vel fore; igitur nec esse. . . . Constat autem ex dictis de extensione temporis quod sequitur: si creatura fuit vel erit, ipsa est, et non econtra (ibid., 291).

[6] Ibid., 293.

with their intelligible forms. As such it precluded the destruction of any part of it. To create was to produce an actual being from pure intelligible being; since the latter was essentially part of God, it was indestructible, and so was the actual existence of the individual in which it inhered.[1] This was the essence of Wyclif's position: by identifying the intelligible in God with being, he had made being necessary and eternal and so incapable of not being. As the constituent of all individual existents, the same indestructibility inhered in all creation, so that anything, once in being, could not but be.[2] Although not pantheistic—since actual being was dependent upon an act of creation from God's will—it was to say the least bizarre. It bound God irrevocably to the world he had created no less than it determined the existence of his creatures. Each was encompassed by the eternal order which he had ordained. Wyclif thereby uniquely succeeded in making not only creation subject to God's decrees, but God the prisoner of his own knowledge.

How deeply Wyclif's thinking was permeated by these metaphysical concepts can be seen in nearly every aspect of his thinking. Two assumptions in particular governed it. The first was the identity of truth and being so that whatever the mind conceived as an entity corresponded to a reality outside it. The second was the eternity of all truth and thus of being. They were like magnetic poles; from whichever point he began, he tended always to move in their direction; and certainly in the case of the bible, the church, and the eucharist, his thinking was directly framed in their terms. Whether employed deliberately or otherwise, then, Wyclif's notions of being and eternity had a formative part in his outlook. For our purposes its main aspects were the bible; the church and tradition; dominion and grace; and the eucharist. In each of them what Wyclif said was novel not in the sense that it had never been said or suggested before; it was rather that he went further in his conclusions, which in nearly every case carried him across the boundary separating orthodoxy and heterodoxy from heresy.

[1] Item omnis creatio proprie dicta dicit productionem rei a puro esse intelligibili ad existentiam actualem. Igitur per idem omnis annihilatio, si est, dicit corruptionem rei ab actuali existentia ad purum esse intelligibile . . . et tunc probatur quod deus non potest quicquid annihilare, quia annihilato manet adhuc fuisse eius cum esse intelligibili (ibid., 292).

[2] E.g., Corollarium quintum. Omne quod fuit et quod erit est esse; et omne quod potest esse est (*Misc. philos.* II, 172). See also 173–4, and especially the third corollary of the second conclusion, 174: Quodlibet ens sive creatura habuit esse ab eterno.

The Bible

To take the bible first, Wyclif, in asserting its sovereignty as the foundation of faith, was only echoing a tradition which went back beyond the great scholastics of the thirteenth century and which had become even more pronounced during the fourteenth century.[1] Thinkers as diverse as St. Bonaventure, St. Thomas, William of Ockham, Bradwardine, and Gregory of Rimini, to say nothing of St. Anselm and Hugh of St. Victor, had all seen the bible as the source of Christian revelation, the yardstick by which all that pertained to faith must be judged. Indeed what is most striking in the light of subsequent history, is the lack of attention which they gave to the role of tradition. Certainly they made no attempt to define the relation of one to the other, but assumed that scripture was the basis of faith and as such underlay the sacramental life of the church.[2] Where Wyclif differed was in his notion of the nature, not the relationship, of both bible and church. It sprang in each case from the same realist outlook which governed his metaphysics: namely the conviction that they were timeless and unchanging and independent of the vagaries of the created world. But while this led him to fundamentalism where the bible was concerned, it also caused him to reject the existing order of the church for its archetypal reality. The paradox—that these opposing conclusions were reached from the same premise—is more apparent than real. The bible, as God's word, was true in itself; it therefore literally sufficed. To seek the church in its corresponding essentiality, however, meant going beyond its temporal existence to its eternal being as conceived by God. What was so noteworthy in Wyclif's attitude was not that he made scripture more important than the church; but rather his conception of both as independent of time and place. They were co-eternal in truth. The bible did not displace the church but was invoked in its defence: as God's word it was the criterion of truth and falsity. If it was pre-eminent it was not exclusive. It was not only accessible to reason; a full understanding of its

[1] For a survey of the attitude towards the bible in the thirteenth and fourteenth centuries, see P. de Vooght, *Les sources de la doctrine chrétienne*. As we shall have occasion to remark shortly the undoubted value of Dom de Vooght's study in establishing the cotninuity of biblical authority is marred in Wyclif's case by his failure to distinguish between Wyclif's formal professions and the application which he gave to his beliefs. On Wyclif's biblical writings see B. Smalley's works listed in bibliography, i.e., 'John Wyclif's Postilla super totam bibliam'; 'The Bible and Eternity: John Wyclif's dilemma.'

[2] De Vooght, op. cit., passim.

meaning was often dependent upon the elucidation and explanations of the fathers and the saints. In that sense the question of the bible alone (*scriptura sola*) did not arise. There was too much of the scholastic in Wyclif to dispense with the impedimenta and the authorities of a millennium.

Wyclif's reverence for the bible is a commonplace and does not need reiteration here. Not only did he devote to it an entire work, *De veritate sacre scripture*,[1] to prove its sovereign truth, endlessly repeated in his other works; but he brought to its eulogies a particular intensity, almost lyricism, beyond even his normal fervour: the bible was a jewel, the sole word of perfection, the voice of Christ and so on.[2] Above all, of course, Wyclif gave practical expression to his beliefs in inspiring its first English translations.[3] Not the least remarkable feature of Wyclif's view of the bible is its consistency. From early on, in his disputes with Kenningham, he had already firmly endowed it with the properties of timelessness and literalness. From the metaphysical fact of God's eternity and immensity, in whom all beings were ever-present, followed the literal truth of scripture.[4] Originally Wyclif had made this apply to each word (*vi vocis*); but under pressure from Kenningham, who pointed to the absurdities inherent in making the contradictory statements concurrently true, he modified this to mean the strict sense of the words (*de virtute sermonis*).[5] Even so the difficulty remained of making any statement hold for ever. Thus when Amos said, 'I am not a prophet,' this would mean that he had never been and never would be a prophet—which was palpably at variance with other passages in the bible.[6] Wyclif's reply is revealing. He in effect simply jettisoned his doctrine of the extension of the present to include all time, and took refuge in dialectic: prophecy here meant the gift of prophecy at a particular time.[7] It was the answer of one who argued better than he thought. As Kenningham justly said, to make the past and the future part of the present in this way was not extension, but confusion, of time.[8]

[1] 3 vols., WS 1905–7.

[2] See de Vooght, op. cit., 168–9 for a summary of Wyclif's expressions.

[3] There is no evidence that Wyclif himself took part in the work of translating it. For a study of the subject see M. Deanesly, *The Lollard Bible*.

[4] Tertius nidus est altissimus, ut dicit, est metaphysicus quo cognoscimus eternitatem dei ex eius immensitate coassistere omni tempori preterito vel futuro, et per consequens omnia que fuerunt vel erunt esse deo presentia. 'Et per illam,' inquit, 'veritatem sustinemus scripturam sacram esse veram de virtute sermonis' (FZ 14).

[5] FZ, ibid., 20. [6] Ibid., 20–2. [7] Ibid. [8] Ibid., 27.

Wyclif, however, continued to adhere to it; and his belief in the ever-presentiality of the bible as God's word was the foundation of his scriptural teaching. Like his metaphysics in general it was extremist and tended towards unorthodoxy. Wyclif extended to the bible the necessity by which God knew everything; every part of it had to be taken absolutely and without qualification.[1] This inevitably made it self-sufficient, perfect, and infallible. As the mirror of God it was also the mirror of conduct, providing the norm to which all men must conform.[2] As the voice of Christ it was sacred, the law of the church, and the source of all doctrine and laws.[3] As the truth, it contained all that could be known; and nothing could be added to it or subtracted from it.[4] These assertions recur again and again throughout Wyclif's writings. Although as testimony to the authority of the bible they could hardly have invited dissent, their cumulative effect was an exclusive fundamentalism in which Wyclif made the bible the touchstone of all knowledge and conduct. This did not, as we have said, preclude either the exercise of reason or moral judgement. It rather reduced them to a biblical framework. Here, as Kenningham drily observed, Wyclif indulged his proclivity for intellectual constructions *in excelsis*.[5]

The most succinct statement of Wyclif's biblism is to be found in the *Trialogus*.[6] There Wyclif gives the three connotations of scripture: as the book of Christ's life in which all truth is inscribed; as the truths, both eternal and temporal, which comprise it; and as the books in which God's law is given—its usual meaning.[7] Just as Christ as a man is of infinitely greater worth than any other man, so the bible is infinitely greater than any other book. Even the books of the greatest doctors are apocryphal and only to be believed in so far as they are founded on the

[1] Ibid., 474; See also *De veritate sacre scripture* I, 1–2 and passim; II, 99; *Sermons* IV, 140; *De officio regis* 221.

[2] E.g., *De veritate* I, 20, 80; *De eucharistia* 41; *Sermons* III, 389; IV, 79; *Pol. works* I, 14; *De officio regis* 10, 111; *De potestate pape* 34; *De civili dominio* I, 120–1, 377–9.

[3] E.g., *De veritate* I, 100 passim; *De civili dominio* I, 347–51, 394, 469 where M. Hurley, '"Scriptura sola": Wyclif and his critics', *Traditio* 16 (1960) 288 points out that Wyclif uses the expressions *per se sufficere* and *pure per se sufficere*; *Opus evangelicum* I, 12; *Sermons* I, 376; III, 262; *Opera minora* 75; *De blasphemia* 10; *Dialogus* 94; *De officio regis* 222.

[4] E.g., *De civili dominio* I, 118–24, 391, 427; *De veritate* I, 395, 399, 402, passim; II, 181–4; *Sermons* I, 83; III, 283; *Pol. works* I, 257; *De blasphemia* 44–51.

[5] verumtamen, ut mihi videtur, magister meus nidificat in excelsis (FZ 14).

[6] Bk. III, ch. 31, 238–43.

[7] Ibid., 238–9.

bible.[1] The bible constituted the faith of the church providing it with God's truths and laws. It was completely true in every part, and as the voice of Christ could never deceive.[2] Not all of it was equally accessible. Here Wyclif followed St. Augustine in distinguishing between its implicit and explicit meaning. Since not every truth was of the same moment and God did not want men to be distracted from the central ones, some were not immediately apparent to the senses and had to be deduced by reason. From this aspect, only what was implicitly contained in the bible was to be believed. That applied to all writings, papal decrees included.[3] Thus Wyclif once more pushed his fundamentalism to the farthest point by making conformity with the bible the test of all authenticity. Nor was this a matter of blind faith. Reason, guided by scripture, was an essential element in arriving at the truth. Just as Wyclif's fundamentalism sprang from his metaphysics so his metaphysics served his fundamentalism. Once given the scriptural basis of all truth, itself the product of God's eternal knowledge, its elucidation had to conform to the rules of metaphysics. In asserting their need Wyclif was directly taking up the challenge of the contemporary terminists, who employed logic to show the incompatibilities and inconsistencies in scripture.[4] Those who made such assertions, he said, were of Antichrist, attributing to the bible their own failures to comprehend.

For Wyclif humility towards the truth of the bible was a moral question.[5] Hence the more than intellectual ardour with which he insisted upon its intelligibility. There were five conditions for achieving it: a knowledge of universals; knowledge of the metaphysical nature of time and other accidents inhering in a subject, without which they could not exist; knowledge that both in God and among men all things past and future were ever-present; knowledge that all creatures have intelligible being eternally in God and antecedently to their own individual existence; and knowledge that material essences are perpetual.[6] Thus a decade after Wyclif's disputes with Kenningham the founda-

[1] Bk. III, ch. 31, 239.

[2] Ibid., 239–40.

[3] Ex hinc Augustinus saepe praecipit quod nemo credat scriptis suis vel verbis nisi de quanto se fundaverit in scriptura; et in ipsa, ut dicit, omnis veritas explicite vel implicite continetur. Et indubie idem est iudicium de scriptis aliorum sanctorum et multo magis de scriptis Romanae ecclesiae et doctorum novorum (ibid., 240).

Wyclif also added elsewhere, *De eucharistia* 277, that Augustine and the four doctors were only to be believed in so far as they followed the bible.

[4] Ibid., 241. [5] Ibid., 241–2. [6] Ibid., 242–3.

tions of both his metaphysics and the bible had remained unaltered. Moreover, and in the highest degree significant, Wyclif consciously made the one the basis of the other. The truth of the bible lay in metaphysics not logic. It was reached not by the juxtaposition of words but through an awareness of the nature of being: what existed did so eternally; it was indestructible and always present. So therefore was the bible. As God's word it was both literally true and the source of truth. There could be no truth without it.

Earlier in *De veritate sacre scripture* Wyclif had given five different levels of scriptural truth which corresponded to this metaphysical conception; these followed a similar chain of being from the bible's archetypal reality as the book of life, through its intelligible being, to its actual existence manifested in man's soul and the materials with which it was physically written.[1] They confirm beyond doubt the radical divergence between Wyclif's conception and those of any other known scholastic. Both in his assumptions and conclusions he went beyond normal bounds. We are therefore dealing with a difference in kind, one that consisted in regarding the bible as a metaphysical entity, eternally in being with every word denoting an ever-present reality.[2] Small wonder that Wyclif made no attempt to answer Kenningham, when past and future were essentially unreal.

Had Wyclif stopped there, his doctrine would have remained a somewhat singular attempt to gain certainty in an age when the prevailing intellectual fashion was doubt. But he did not. The same metaphysical outlook, when applied to the church, led him to reject it in its contemporary state as untrue to its real nature; in combating it he increasingly turned to scripture, which from about 1378 onwards, as his theological and polemical activity grew ever more intense,[3] became his main weapon against the church of his day. It was at this point that Wyclif's teaching became explosive, rendering what had been extravagance into subversion. Although this progression from heterodoxy to

[1] *De veritate sacre scripture* I, 107–13.

[2] The failure to so much as mention this is one of the two major factors invalidating the whole of de Vooght's treatment of Wyclif; the other, as we shall mention, is the equally glaring failure to consider what Wyclif understood by the church. Together they reduce his discussion to a merely formal adumbration of Wyclif's words; it is made more unreal by having confined his sources to *De veritate sacre scripture*. For a discussion on this and other points concerning de Vooght's book see M. Hurley, art. cit., 275–352.

[3] All Wyclif's main theological and doctrinal writings appeared from 1376 onwards, as we have seen.

heresy cannot be attributed to metaphysical causes, they certainly provided the impulse; for it was through Wyclif's conception of the ideal church as radically different from its visible form that—unless we are to deny him any vestige of intellectual conviction—he came to reject the latter so decisively. Had he not believed in a distinct archetypal reality he could not have denied the authority of the visible church without having rejected the church altogether. But by positing its true essence independently of its earthly condition he was at once contraposing the ideal to its debased image and justifying opposition to the latter in the name of the former.

The Church

For this reason, Wyclif's doctrine of the bible is inseparable from his notion of the church. The destructive role which Wyclif assigned to the bible in his assault upon the church was not inherent in his fundamentalism. The latter alone could deny the false claims of the hierarchy, but hardly that the church was the true church; its role in doing this can only be explained by taking into account Wyclif's doctrine of the church.[1] Here, as elsewhere, he was strongly under the influence of Augustine; but whereas his metaphysics, beyond giving primacy to the universal or idea, bore no recognizable affinity to St. Augustine's, his ecclesiology was the direct outcome of taking to the limits St. Augustine's own definition of the church.[2] St. Augustine in his *De civitate dei* had distinguished between the heavenly and the earthly cities. The members of the heavenly city were the saved who would enjoy everlasting life; those of the earthly city were the damned. All, however, reprobate as well as elect, while in this world were members of the church; only when they reached the next were they separated. But

[1] This de Vooght failed signally to do. Consequently we are misleadingly presented with a series of eulogies of the bible, abstracted from Wyclif's writings, together with a number of isolated testimonies to the authority to the church. What is omitted is the repeated way in which Wyclif, in his later works, attacked the church hierarchy in the name of the bible and denied any scriptural authority for the office of pope or the majority of the priesthood. The entire purport of Wyclif's use of the bible is thereby ignored and a misleading picture of Wyclif's biblism created. The reason seems to be that Dom de Vooght was so concerned to absolve Wyclif from the charge of denying tradition that he failed to consider how Wyclif understood both the bible and the church whose traditions he was attacking.

[2] Workman's statement (II, 9) that Wyclif inherited his conception of the church from Bradwardine is groundless.

what for Augustine had been a metaphorical division, Wyclif made literal. He foreshortened the entire process by keeping the two apart from the outset. Since only the saved were destined for the heavenly city, they alone were of the church; the damned, called by Wyclif the foreknown (*presciti*), were eternally excluded. The status of each remained what it was eternally. Nowhere is the character of Wyclif's thought more fully exposed than here. His penchant for reducing everything to its archetypal reality led him inexorably to the complete separation of the elect and the damned. Eternally distinct conceptually, they must remain so existentially. Each represented a distinct mode of being; hence neither could merge with the other. Rigidity could scarcely go further, and the far-reaching consequences which resulted cannot be overestimated. In the first place, the church became defined as the community of the elect. If it remained the expression of the saving will of God, both its membership and the efficacy of its ministrations were confined to those already saved.[1] The chasm which Wyclif thereby opened up between himself and tradition was unbridgeable and more than anything else made his teaching heretical.

He seems first to have put this forward in *De civili dominio*;[2] it was elaborated more fully in his treatise on the church, *De ecclesia*. But like all Wyclif's leading ideas, once formulated, it continued to recur in work after work, regardless of the ostensible theme, as part of his general attack upon the church.[3] The true members of the church, he asserted, were bound together eternally by the grace of predestination which enabled them to remain in a state of election until the end.[4] This, too, was an essentially Augustinian concept, which Wyclif again

[1] Quamvis autem ecclesia dicitur multipliciter in scriptura, suppono quod sumatur ad propositum pro famosiori, scilicet congregatione omnium predestinatorum (*De Ecclesia* 2). Eo ipso quod est ecclesia universalis sive catholica, ipsa continet in se omnes predestinatos (ibid., 7). Ideo patet ex fide Christi scripture et multiplici testimonio sanctorum quod nullum est membrum sancte matris ecclesie nisi persona predestinata (*Supplementum Trialogi* 415).

[2] *De civili dominio* I, 288: Tertio vero accipitur propriissime ecclesia pro universitate predestinatorum. In *De dominio divino* 235 he still adhered to Uthred of Boldon's final option (Hurley, art. cit., 84).

[3] E.g., *De potestate pape* 25; *De eucharistia* 98–9; *Supplementum trialogi* 415; *Opus evangelicum* I, 119–20; *Sermons* IV, 42–5, 148; *Opera minora* 100, 118–19, 176.

[4] Sic redeundo ad propositum, patet quod gratia et charitas Jesu Christi que realiter est ipsemet Christus, est terminus communis copulans quodcunque membrum ecclesie cuilibet alteri (*De ecclesia* 107). Et sic omnes predestinati habent continue fidem gratia predestinationis formatam, et sic non cadit a membris ecclesie per mortale (ibid., 111).

took to extremes in granting the elect immunity from the consequences of mortal sin; their grace of predestination could stand with mortal sin without impairing their status.[1] Once more the truth of eternity triumphed over the vagaries of time. Indeed for Wyclif the church was not only timeless but outside space; it was not a physical entity, or, as he put it, a spatial and temporal continuum, but scattered far and wide. It was in being wherever the elect were.[2] They included the three parts of the triumphant church in heaven, the sleeping church in purgatory and the militant church on earth.[3] Wyclif accordingly combated the view that the church had come into existence through the Incarnation; as with any being its *esse intelligibile* was for all time, in its own species, its principles, its individuals and its causes.[4]

In the second place, unity of the damned was no less absolute. Just as the faithful were eternally joined to one another by the grace of predestination, with Christ at their head, so the foreknown shared eternal exclusion from God's company under Antichrist.[5] They therefore constituted a parallel congregation, made up of the three classes of infidels, heretics and those not chosen.[6] Furthermore, in lacking the grace of final perseverance, however great their grace in this world, it did not suffice for salvation. Hence, in contradistinction to the saved, those who were damned remained in mortal sin even though temporally in grace.[7] Each body was constituted eternally, and the destiny of every member irrevocable.

In the third place, these divisions meant that, in practice, the church as a visible body ceased to exist; for, in striking contradiction to Wyclif's insistence upon the sovereignty of every word in the bible, he never ceased to emphasize that in this world neither the damned nor the saved could be known. There were, he said, three mysteries hidden from all men: whether they were predestined to glory or to damnation;

[1] Quo ad secundum dicitur cum nemo dubitat quin multi predestinati peccarunt mortaliter . . . et predestinatio non potest perdi iuxta dicta, manifestum est quod gratia predestinationis stat cum peccato mortali (ibid., 139). See also *Trialogus* 149–50.

[2] Ibid., 99.

[3] Ibid., 8.

[4] Ibid., 106.

[5] . . . manifestum est quod est unum corpus diaboli, sicut est unum corpus Christi . . . Forma autem extrinseca est prescientia dei eterna qua scit et ordinat omnes tales constringi ad penam perpetuam; deformitas autem intrinseca est finalis inobedientia vel superbia (ibid., 102–3).

[6] Ibid., 63.

[7] sicut gratia presciti secundum presentem iustitiam repugnat dampnationi, licet aggregatum ex illa gratia et prescientia inferat necessario dampnationem (ibid., 139).

when they would die; and the day of judgement.[1] Now it was his insistence upon men's ignorance which perhaps more than anything else made Wyclif's doctrine so disruptive; for it undermined the whole of the existing order. If only those who were chosen by God belonged to the church, and they could not be known, there was no reason for accepting any visible authority or for recognizing the claims of those who exercised it. Even more, there was no reason for such authority at all: if those who were predestined to glory remained of the elect, regardless of temporal vicissitudes, nothing could further or detract from their final destiny. And likewise for the damned. The church in its traditional form therefore lost its *raison d'être*.

Nothing is more characteristic of Wyclif than his espousal of these implications; he was not the first thinker to have been confronted with them. But no one else in the whole of the middle ages so completely accepted them as ineluctable and made a virtue of the necessity for doing so. To begin with, it led him in effect to discount the visible church in the name of the invisible church. Here if anywhere the strength of his metaphysical beliefs are to be seen. The church as the body of the predestined existed independently of space and time; it owed allegiance to no one save Christ,[2] who was, to use Wyclif's favourite phrase, its chief abbot.[3] Faith in the authority of any local church was due only in so far as it emanated from Christ, the sole source of its apostolic nature.[4] The church was a universal concept, and antedated the Incarnation.[5] For this reason Wyclif constantly looked beyond the present hierarchy for the true source of Christian doctrine and authority; this led him to question and discard everything and everyone, from pope to parish priest, who did not conform to the precepts and practice of Christ as found in his word in the bible.

Now it was through this invocation of the invisible church that Wyclif's use of the bible became so destructive. Anyone could, and frequently did, point to discrepancies between the precepts of the bible and the practice of the visible church without undermining the latter's *raison d'être*, as for example the Franciscan Spirituals. The challenge was then not to the church as a body but to abuses within it: the call was not to another church but to the revivification of the existing one, which remained the only one. When taken too far it could become indistinguishable from the demand for a new church, as we have seen in

[1] E.g., *Opus evangelicum* III, 216; *De civili dominio* 25, *De ecclesia* 251.

[2] *De ecclesia* 7, 94, 99.

[3] E.g., *De civili dominio* II, 166; III, 5.

[4] *De civili dominio* I, 375.

[5] *De ecclesia* 30.

the case of the Provençal Beguins and Waldensians, but its source remained unaltered. The same cannot be said of Wyclif: for him the true church bore no direct relation to the visible church. Like the Spirituals and Joachites in general he was obsessed by the presence of Antichrist; and he gradually came to identify the endowed church with the forces of Antichrist, as the church of the reprobate. In his later works, such as *De blasphemia* and the *Opus evangelicum*, and in some of the sermons, the presence of Antichrist becomes all-pervasive in every aspect of the visible church.

Whether we care to attribute this to psychic or political factors is incidental to the underlying continuity in Wyclif's attitude. From the outset his metaphysical conception of the two bodies of Christ and Antichrist engendered an ambivalence towards the church which became ultimately irreconcilable. On the one hand, since the church was constituted from the elect, who were unknown, there could be no guarantee of the authority of any pope, prelate or priest; they might all be of the damned (*presciti*), in which case they should not be obeyed.[1] On the other hand, every member of the elect, as alone of the true church, was *ipso facto* more priest than layman, ordained of God, just as any layman could be endowed by him with sacerdotal powers.[2] This was tantamount to a denial of the priesthood as an order. As such it must be accounted the single most destructive and heretical feature of Wyclif's teaching. As he himself expressed it, there was no need to be a cleric in order to be a priest;[3] and conversely to be ordained a priest offered no certainty of God's approval or authority.[4] The way was thus opened for taking God's law into one's own hands; or more exactly for making his word in scripture the sole criterion of truth with the help of reason, the testimony of the saints and fathers and such later authorities as upheld the apostolic tradition. Together these authorities constituted the *sensus catholicus*;[5] although they were to be followed where a literal

[1] E.g., *De ecclesia* 28, 29, 31, 32.

[2] Nullus, inquam, fidelis dubitat quin deus posset dare layco potentiam conficiendi. . . . Ymmo videtur iuxta testimonium Augustini, Crisostomi et aliorum sanctorum quod omnis predestinatus laycus est sacerdos, et multo magis devotus laycus conficiens, cum daret ecclesie sacrum ministerium, haberet rationem sacerdotis (*De eucharistia* 98–9). See also *De veritate* II, 138; *De ecclesia* 577. [3] *De officio regis* 149.

[4] Simpliciter autem maximam potestatem inter viantes habet filius adoptionis qui est excellentius heres regni (ibid., 142).

[5] patet quod necesse est stare concorditer expositioni sensuum quos sancti doctores concorditer elicuerant. Aliter enim liceret extorquere sensum scripture ad votum peccantis, quod hodie incipit in multis (*De veritate sacre scripture* I, 386).

interpretation of the bible failed,[1] they were not the exclusive source of authority. Discrepancies among the fathers called for individual judgement,[2] and, in the absence of other guidance, for belief in whatever the bible contained, no matter how unlikely.[3] Accordingly the individual believer's reason and faith supplemented the authority of the fathers.[4] How equally indispensable each was can be seen from Wyclif's account of St. Augustine's pre-eminence. It was, he said, due to three causes: unqualified acceptance of the bible; his powers of reasoning which were used in harmony with scripture; and his personal holiness.[5] While Augustine was, like all men, fallible, Wyclif had never found an error in his writings;[6] he was to be believed above all others because of his adherence to the bible as the sole criterion of human perfection.[7]

The conjunction of these different elements underlay Wyclif's doctrine of authority. The bible was the foundation of all truth, upon which all knowledge, laws and conduct must be based; reason was

[1] religiosius videtur concedere verba scripture ad sensum catholicum quam impossibilitare illam scripturam concedendo eius nudam sententiam (ibid., 46); see also *De officio regis* 125.

[2] *De veritate* III, 284–5.

[3] *Pace* de Vooght, op. cit., 181–2, who misinterprets the following passage (as well as wrongly referring to it) to mean that the church is the source of evangelical truth: Primo oportet recurrere ad fidem conversationis domini Jesu Christi, quantum in scriptura sacra exprimitur, et ab illo fonte sapientie capere flumina ex hinc scaturiencia de ventre matris ecclesie (ibid., I, 217–18). The truth that flows from scripture into the church is neither said to be that of Rome, nor, in view of all Wyclif says about the true church as the body of the predestined, could it possibly be understood as such; even if such an identification were to be granted, everything that Wyclif says about the Roman church's betrayal of Christ's evangel nullifies a single chance remark. The only other passage in which de Vooght is able to find a reference to the church's interpretative role is in *De dominio divino* 2, an early work, which has little relevance to Wyclif's subsequent ecclesiological thinking. In fact, Wyclif frequently took the bible and the fathers in conjunction as constituting the doctrine of the church. E.g. *De veritate* I, 277, 304. But the bible remained supreme: Ecce, regula huius sancti est ut honoremus scripturam sacram, credentes quod, quandoque falsa de illa concipimus, est ex nostra ignorantia, ipsa manente undique summe autoritatis incorrigibiliter ordinata (ibid., 61).

[4] E.g., *Dialogus* 93.

[5] Debemus ergo acceptare testimonium Augustini specialiter propter tria. Primo propter testimonium scripture; secundo propter fortitudinem rationis, que consonat dictis suis; et tertio topice propter famam sanctitatis sue ab ecclesia approbate (*De veritate* I, 36).

[6] Hinc dico, ut sepius quod locus a testimonio Augustini non est infallibilis, cum Augustinus sit errabilis (ibid., 35).

[7] quia inter omnes doctores scripture sacre citra autores est Augustinus precipuus (ibid., 35). Also ibid., 39.

the instrument in reaching truth; and sanctity its prerequisite. Together they constituted received faith. Ultimately, its attainment was a moral question; for, as Wyclif repeatedly stressed, scriptural understanding was given only to the humble, who in their poverty of spirit, were the true followers of Christ.[1] The bible itself had its own grammar or logic, which could only be grasped, literally and mystically, by understanding it as God conceived it.[2] To achieve this meant turning away from the visible meaning of the senses to what was inscribed in one's heart.[3] For Wyclif, the very need to accept the bible in its own terms, regardless of its obscurities,[4] put the onus for doing so upon the individual believer. Although it had a logic, the nature of which for all his reiteration he never specified—save for the principle of contradiction[5]—belief, not dialectic, mattered.[6] The Christian was bound to its truths by an inner conviction in the same way as he took for granted the facts of the senses.[7] Orthodoxy was the result of applying reason to this faith.[8] It was confirmed and nurtured by the authority of the fathers, but was not exclusive to them for the simple reason that all were equally subject to the authority of the bible.[9] Hence it can be said that true faith was

[1] sic discipulus scripture non acquirit aurum sapientie nisi contritione fuerit humiliatus (ibid., 60). See also *Opus evangelicum* I, 15.

[2] *De veritate*, I, 42–4.

[3] Ibid., 44–5.

[4] Ecce, quod Augustinus reputavit blasfemos qui negarent dicta scripturarum. . . . Unde sepe dicit Augustinus sibi adversantibus: 'quare hoc asseris?' quod hoc, ideo quia scriptura hoc dicit (ibid., 46–7).

[5] Et si queretur ubi scriptura sacra docet logicam, dico, ut supra, quod in illo precepto Christi sit sermo vester est est, non non (ibid., 53).

[6] Christianus debet loqui sub autoritate scripture verba scripture secundum formam qua scriptura ipsa explicat (ibid., 51–2).

[7] Unde sicut vanum est discredere quin loquor vel vigilo, sic vanum est Christiano opinari vel dubitare de quocunque articulo sue fidei, cum videt illum in homine interiori (ibid., 249).

[8] Et sic intelligo Christianum debere reddere rationem de fide cuicunque poscenti, non que quietat omnem protervum vel infidelem poscentem, sed que quietaret vel deberet quietare quemcumque poscentem, quia omnis homo ex hoc argumento debet acquiescere fidei orthodoxe: deus dicit tibi ut credas hoc, igitur debes hoc credere (ibid., 249).

[9] Quoad tertiam partem venerationis scripture in suis testibus et devotis discipulis, dictum est capitulo secundo de beato Augustino et aliis sanctis doctoribus quomodo credendum est eorum testimonia. Si enim legistam oportet credere in causa suspecta testimonia fallaci, multo magis crederet catholicus testimonio sanctorum doctorum in causa non seductiva propter lucrum. . . . Unde videtur michi signum infidelitatis, postquam probatum est sanctorum testimonio, aliquem esse sensum scripture sacre, illi discredere vel defensionem eius gratis omittere . . . (ibid., I, 201). Also ibid., 137.

the outcome of an alliance between the fathers and the saints and the individual, each applying reason to the bible as the foundation of their beliefs. It was *fides querens intellectum* over again, but this time with the bible as the object of understanding and the *sensus catholicus* as its support.

In his approach to the bible Wyclif followed Augustine's postillatory treatment of taking a topic and analysing its meaning rather than commenting a text for its literal or mystical signification; by that means, he said, the arbitrary interpretations and sophisms which were current were obviated.[1] Whilst giving pride of place to St. Augustine, who he believed was inspired by the Holy Spirit[2] and surpassed Aristotle and every other philosopher in logic and metaphysics,[3] he put Ambrose, Jerome, Gregory the Great and St. Bernard close to him;[4] and among more recent doctors he singled out Anselm, Hugh of St. Victor and Grosseteste as the continuators of St. Augustine.[5] At different times, like most scholastics, he drew upon a diversity of names, including Ockham; but it was principally to the fathers and those just mentioned, who represented the platonic and Augustinian tradition, that he looked.

For that reason it is, as we have said, untenable to suggest that Wyclif held a doctrine of *scriptura sola*; quite the contrary. The individual must not only be buttressed by the full weight of apostolic and patristic authority; he must also be himself versed in theology and a proper understanding of metaphysics. What Wyclif did stress was the personal responsibility of each believer to know the bible and to defend it.[6] It was this insistence upon the individual Christian's obligation to be a theologian[7] which was so crucial. It meant the exclusion of the church in its existing state from the dialogue between the individual and tradition; in place of its hierarchy Wyclif put God's word as fittingly interpreted. The latter became the mediator between God and the faithful; as the arbiter of truth it constituted the *sensus catholicus* in

[1] Ibid.

[2] Unde de ipso canit singulariter ecclesia quod deus beatum Augustinum in exponendis scripture sacre mysteriis doctorem catholicum sue ecclesie providebat (ibid., 37–8).

[3] Ibid., 38–9.

[4] Et consimilis quodammodo est consideratio de sanctis Ambrosio, Ieronymo, Gregorio, Bernardo cum sanctis eis similibus et specialiter quoad logicam et sententiam scripturarum (ibid., 39).

[5] Ibid., 38.

[6] Ibid., 136.

[7] Ibid., 378; also II, 141, 145, 166.

contradistinction to the visible church. This was Wyclif's real break with the past. He appealed over the heads of pope and prelates direct to scripture and the apostolic tradition; and in turning to the latter he was disavowing the former. He therefore created an alliance between the individual and the apostolic tradition against the present church hierarchy, with far-reaching results.

In the first place it led to exalting preaching into a position of paramount importance; for in a world where the true church remained unknown, God's word, properly comprehended, offered the one certainty. It therefore became the first duty of the priest, as Christ's disciple, to undertand and expound it.[1] As such it was his *raison d'être* and the test of a true priest;[2] it was more important than the sacraments[3] or the Lord's Prayer.[4] Any ecclesiastic who failed to preach failed as a priest; and the widespread absence of preaching among the lower clergy provided Wyclif with one of his main weapons against the existing hierarchy.[5] It also, as we have just seen, served to minimize the importance of the sacraments. This was the second consequence of Wyclif's attitude to scripture and the church. He never openly disavowed the need for the sacraments; but everything he said tended towards their depreciation. It may well be, as Workman has said, that Wyclif never fully grappled with the problem;[6] certainly he never openly came to a clear-cut judgement. But it seems more than probable that he placed little faith in them for the same reason that he disregarded the visible church. God was the direct source of all spiritual power,[7] and since he had eternally decided who was saved and who was damned

[1] Sexto sequitur quod omnes Christiani et precipue sacerdotes atque episcopi tenentur cognoscere primo omnem legem scripture (ibid., II, 137) . . . secunda conclusio huius sancti pape [Gregorii magni] est quod sacerdotibus, prepositis et specialiter episcopis iniungitur a deo sancte predicationis officium. Patet ex hoc quod ipsi succedunt in ecclesia loco apostolorum ac discipulorum . . . (ibid., 138).

[2] Ibid., 173.

[3] Patet secundo quod predicatio verbi dei est actus solempnior quam confectio sacramenti (ibid., 156). See also *Pol. works* I, 261.

[4] Ibid., 179.

[5] E.g., *De veritate* I, 348; II, 138–9, 141–4, 147, 150, 166, 170–9, 187–94, 207. *Sermons* I, 100, III, 73–5, 266, IV, 115; *Opera minora* 76, 305, 313, *Pol. Works* I, 261. There is absolutely no evidence, however, from Wyclif's writings, especially the sermons, that Wyclif organized a body of poor russet-coated preachers as Workman, II, 201 ff. asserted. See McFarlane, op. cit., 100–1.

[6] Workman, II, 13.

[7] Et per consequens preter potestatem quam deus creat in anima non est dare aliam datam ab homine (*De potestate pape* 14).

nothing remained to the agency of intermediaries, even prayer.[1] This applied equally to the sacraments and to the priests who administered them. God alone remitted sin;[2] baptism and penance conferred grace but not election;[3] God caused contrition before a priest's absolution, a state that in its true sense was exclusive to the elect.[4] Similarly there could be no excommunication without God's preceding punishment;[5] for no true member of the church could ever be severed from it, whatever the ban pronounced upon him.[6] Wyclif decried both annual communion and aural confession as unscriptural and the result of arbitrary human decrees, especially by Innocent III.[7] God could absolve, provided there was true contrition, independently of a priest's absolution:[8] the very words 'I absolve thee' were not to be found in the bible.[9] Wyclif never entirely lost his equivocation over the place of aural confession as indeed he did not over the role of priest. He tended to come down against the former in favour of what he called vocal confession to God; but if the priest were a true one he counselled regular confession to him as the best course. If, however, he was not, then communion with God or confession to a suitable layman sufficed.[10]

Now it was precisely in the relationship of priest to layman that Wyclif came closest to the abyss without ever quite falling over it among the Waldensians. He not only excluded the simoniac and the wrongly ordained from any canonical authority,[11] but also, as we have mentioned, cast doubts upon ordination itself.[12] In the primitive church

[1] Wyclif several times stressed that prayer was efficacious only for the elect. *De ecclesia* 517–20; *Opus evangelicum* III, 222; *De civili dominio* IV, 465–6, where following Augustine's view that lust nullifies prayer, he concluded that the prayers of a sinner were harmful.

[2] E.g., *De civili dominio* I, 260, 281; *Sermons* II, 433; *De ecclesia* 577–8; *Opera minora* 264.

[3] *De civili dominio* I, 371; *Trialogus* 292; *De blasphemia* 288.

[4] *De ecclesia* 28, 31, 353; and *Trialogus* 330–1.

[5] *De civili dominio* I, 265–6, 276, 277, 278–80; *De veritate* III, 39–40; *Sermons* II, 312, III, 147, 152, 158; *De officio regis* 36, 167–76, 231–7; *De potestate pape* 353; *De blasphemia* 70.

[6] *De ecclesia* 111; *De officio regis* 166.

[7] *Trialogus* 327–8; *De blasphemia* 114–15, 127–8; *Sermons* I, 165–6, IV, 56–7, 100, 101; *De eucharistia* 333–7; *Opera minora* 317–18.

[8] *Trialogus* 330–1; *Sermons* III, 67–8; *De blasphemia* 129–33, 134–40, 167; *De potestate pape* 31.

[9] *De blasphemia* 134.

[10] Ibid., 140.

[11] Ibid., 125.

[12] See pp. 519 ff. above. See also *Opera minora* 98–9, 178, where Wyclif said that there could be priestly acts without ordination and ibid., 322 that Christ ordained no form of ordination; also *De blasphemia* 101.

it had consisted in election by Christ, the Apostles and the people;[1] and it could only take place now if the prelate who ordained could confer the Holy Spirit, impressing it into the recipient[2]—to say the least an unrealistic requirement, in view of Wyclif's implication of the majority of the priesthood in sins against both Christ and the Holy Spirit. With this uncertainty towards priestly power went Wyclif's exaltation of the saved layman: he was, as we have seen, a priest in his own right and could exercise the functions of a priest in absolving and hearing confession;[3] he could also be pope:[4] for ultimately he alone was of the true church.[5] Wyclif never resolved these antinomies. At times he denied the sinful priest any power since the only true priest was eternally free from mortal sin;[6] at others he conceded that there could be benefit even from the ministrations of the wicked;[7] sometimes he stressed the need for obedience,[8] but more often he urged disobedience, especially over excommunication.[9] Certainly he tended to derogate from the need for a hierarchy at all.[10]

Thus between the upper millstone of God's omnipotence with whom alone lay the power of excommunication, absolution, grace, salvation and damnation, and the nether millstone of priestly blasphemy, simony and apostasy, which rendered the ministrations of most priests null and void, there was little left for the faithful few other than to follow Christ and preach his word. These, for Wyclif, were the sole criteria of spiritual fitness; according to whether or not they were observed a man was to be obeyed as priest and tithes paid to him. Since, in Wyclif's eyes, the majority of the hierarchy failed to pass this test, he denounced them as usurpers and traitors to Christ.[11] Thus although Wyclif never

[1] *Dialogus* 50; *De simonia* 36, *Opera minora* 286.

[2] Unde dicitur communiter quod non datur ordo clerico nisi quando episcopus dat sibi spiritum sanctum et imprimit in mentem suam characterem (*Trialogus* 296).

[3] *De blasphemia* 10, 140; *De ecclesia* 577, *De veritate* II, 14; III, 100.

[4] *De potestate pape* 226.

[5] E.g., *Opera minora* 98–9, 176; See also *Dialogus* 415–16; *Sermons* III, 428, IV, 42–5, 148; *De eucharistia* 98.

[6] *De veritate* II, 255, III, 67, 93; *Opera minora* 239; *Sermons* III, 69; *Opus evangelicum* III, 175, 177–8; *De ecclesia* 377.

[7] *De potestate pape* 42; *De ecclesia* 442.

[8] E.g., *Opera minora* 241.

[9] Ibid., 158–61; also *De blasphemia* 4–8 and pp. 533 ff. below.

[10] *Sermons* III, 42, 69, 146–7, 158, IV, 144; *Pol. works* I, 257; *Opera minora* 166–9, 291, *De blasphemia* 70. See also pp. 531 ff. below.

[11] Ex quo videtur quod maior pars et specialiter superiorum ecclesia sit heretica (*De simonia*, 4).

launched a general assault upon the sacramental system, nor denied the role of a priest, even at times a bad one, the doubt he cast upon them was inevitably a challenge to their efficacy and *raison d'être*.

Accordingly the third consequence of Wyclif's doctrine of authority was an unceasing attack upon the life and claims of the contemporary church. It took two main directions: against the authority of the pope, cardinals and ecclesiastical hierarchy, especially the Roman curia; and against the material wealth and corruption of the church in general. In each case Wyclif took as his norm the apostolic life of poverty and preaching practised by the early church.

There is a striking affinity between Wyclif's, the Waldensians', and the Franciscan Spirituals' conception of the apostolic tradition and its contrast to the modern church. Each saw in it the direct successor to Christ's evangelical life of poverty, humility and charity; each extolled its freedom from wordly interests and its egalitarianism; each saw the causes of its subsequent decline in the acquisition of wealth, the growth of a 'Caesarian' hierarchy, and civil involvement. They differed in the means by which a return could be made to the true path of Christ. The Waldensians constituted themselves a counter-church; the Spirituals were predominantly quietists who sought voluntary withdrawal from the world and became martyrs in the attempt; Wyclif, for all his professions to the contrary, was a militant moralist who was prepared to use force to reform the church. His open advocacy of its compulsory disendowment and his disavowal of its hierarchy made his ideas a focus of subversion and himself an heresiarch regardless of his own intentions.

For Wyclif the early church had continued unbroken the life of Christ and the Apostles, pledged to poverty, humility and charity. Christ had remained its head, as he was of the true church for ever; and his disciples had ordained others to follow his triple path in his name, not theirs.[1] They had lived without property and on alms, to which their own merits had been their only title.[2] Accordingly the same obligation to observe their example lay upon the entire church, and

[1] . . . cum ipse (Christus) sit summus pontifex manens hic cum sua ecclesia usque ad finem seculi, nec in Petro nec in alio talem dignitatem approbans, sed voluit Petrum, Paulum et ceteros apostolos esse socios, ut patet Gal II, in paupertate, humiliate et caritate ad patiendum usque ad mortem pro Christi nomine si oporteat, et ad hoc ordinavit apostolis multos fideles vicarios ipsos in ista virtute triplici imitantes (*Opera minora* 204). See also *De veritate sacre scripture* I, 70.

[2] *Opera minora*, 23.

every priest, high and low, was bound to a life of evangelical poverty.[1] Its betrayal by the church of his own day formed the gravamen of his charge against it. To the abandonment of poverty he attributed its spiritual degeneration.[2] Desire for goods was the occasion of sin,[3] and priestly avarice the most dangerous of all heresies.[4] The great break had come with pope Sylvester I and the emperor Constantine, who had been responsible for the crime of secularizing the church by permitting its endowment.[5] Wyclif's occasional qualification in praise of the desire to endow, and his admission that it was possible to live meritoriously with possessions,[6] did not detract from his habitual view that they were the root of all evil,[7] and attachment to them the mark of Antichrist.[8] In terms reminiscent of St. Francis and his followers he extolled Christ's poverty as the supreme virtue, the summit of simplicity and purity;[9] it was the foundation of perfect charity[10] and the most perfect of all states.[11] Evangelical poverty was inseparable from Christ's first and truest privileges; it could never therefore be renounced.[12]

[1] Omnes sacerdotes Christi, pape, cardinales, episcopi, abbates, priores vel eius subditi, tenentur sequi Christum in evangelica paupertate (*Opera minora* 20). Also ibid., 292; *Trialogus* 298, 302, 348; *De veritate* III, 5; *De blasphemia* 32–6.

[2] Postquam autem dotata est dotatione sapiente seculum, decrevit continue tam virtute tam quantitate, cuius causa indubie est declinatio ad carnem et seculum (*De civili dominio* III, 217).

[3] *Supplementum trialogi* 411.

[4] *De civili dominio* I, 59.

[5] E.g., . . . crimen Constantini in hoc fuit damnabile et non accipiendum a catholico vel a fidelibus approbandum (*Opera minora* 266) also *De blasphemia* 54–5, 61.

[6] Ibid., 34. But cf. *De ecclesia* 191–2 where he says just the opposite.

[7] E.g., Ideo quoad ad substantiam possessionis temporalium debuit notare regulam Apostoli, I Tim. VI, 7–10: 'Radix omnium malorum cupiditas' (ibid., 292). Also *Trialogus* 303–11, 314; *De eucharistia* 22.

[8] E.g., *De potestate pape* 161–2; *De veritate sacre scripture* I, 71; *De blasphemia* 54–5, *Trialogus* 333; *Opus evangelicum* III, 126.

[9] Ex istis colligitur quod Christus quem oportet esse exemplar cuiuslibet vite laudibilis, qui vixit continue pro statu vitam pauperrimam et oportet primum principium cuiuscunque generis esse simplicissimum, purissimum et virtuosissimum (*De civili dominio* III, 60). Also *Trialogus* 302.

[10] Et inde est quod ad perfectionem caritatis acquirendam primum fundamentum est voluntaria paupertas, ut aliquis absque proprio vivat (ibid., IV, 444).

[11] Ille status est perfectissimus ut patet in VI° decretalium, cap. *Exiit qui seminat.* (*De ecclesia* 177). Note the reference to Nicholas III's bull.

[12] Cum ergo antiquissima et validissima privilegia, instituta a Christo, steterunt in paupertate altissima, sequitur quod non licet cuiquam privilegium illud subtrahere (ibid., 191); see also *De apostasia* 88, 90–1; *Trialogus* 378–83.

On the contrary it was property which must be forsworn for ever.[1] The way back to Christ was through casting off all endowment and appropriations, and living once again in the poverty which he had enjoined.[2]

This was Wyclif's call to his generation, uttered with increasing stridency but unchanging insistence. As time went on the attainment of poverty became for him synonymous with disendowment; but in his earlier more balanced *De civili dominio* his conception of it closely followed the official Franciscan doctrine which Michael of Cesena and his confrères had sustained so obdurately against John XXII. Like them, Wyclif defined it as use without ownership,[3] and the absence of private possessions.[4] Although he did not elaborate his meaning of use into anything approaching the notion of the *usus pauper*, and seemed undecided about the place of tithes,[5] he repeatedly limited it to necessary need as opposed to absolute penury:[6] it should be moderation after the example of Christ.[7] What possessions the church did retain were to be regarded as in trust for the poor.[8] This, in turn, as with the Franciscans, entailed the renunciation of all dominion, another of Wyclif's ceaseless themes.[9] Christ, he said, had been without civil rule and so must his disciples.[10] Even when he had received alms he had not thereby been endowed with new dominion but new use.[11] Similarly Wyclif defended Christ's purse by distinguishing between evangelical buying, which was

[1] E.g., Ex istis videtur quod omnes pure clerici debent esse pauperes evangelii in specie altissime paupertatis, quia debent renunciare omni proprietati pro suo perpetuo (*De civili dominio* III, 242).

[2] Ulterius pro materia argumenti affectarem si deus decreverit quod non foret in regno nostro talis ecclesiarum appropriatio vel redditum temporalium. . . . Primo per hoc quod ecclesia cleri vixit sic exproprietarie ex ordinatione Christi et apostolorum usque ad dotationem cesaream (*De ecclesia* 371–2).

[3] *De civili dominio* III 441. And: stat dominum papam et alios prelatos ecclesie habere licite usum quorumlibet dominiorum sine dominatione civili (*Opera minora* 23).

[4] *De civili dominio* III, 89, 204.

[5] Ibid., I, 311–16, and ch. 41, 377 ff.; also *Trialogus* 292. *Opera minora* 298–9.

[6] Ibid., 219–20, 241; see also *Trialogus* 305; *Dialogus* 70; *De postestate pape* 89.

[7] *De potestate pape* 83.

[8] Ibid., 213.

[9] Ibid., 485.

[10] *De potestate pape* 200–1; *De civili dominio* II, ch. 13, 145 ff., III, ch. 5, 60 ff., IV, ch. 21, 425 ff.; *De ecclesia* 184–7, 365; *Opera minora* 19–71, 159, 166–9, 188–9; *De potestate pape* 83.

[11] *De potestate pape* 285.

necessary, and civil buying which was not.[1] True dominion was from Christ;[2] it was superior to civil dominion and closer to the state of innocence,[3] whereas civil dominion derogated from grace.[4] Always tainted with sin, as practised by the church, and in its dispossession of the poor, it was actively sinful.[5] The only power possessed by priests was for the edification of the faithful; their involvement in civil dominion, imperfect in itself, could only lead to evil. It was in defiance of Christ's law and must therefore be abandoned.[6] The same held for litigation, from which a priest was barred by Christ's precepts to own nothing, and his example of suffering any injustices which befell him.[7]

Together with this insistence upon material poverty went an equally strong emphasis upon humility or spiritual poverty which at times Wyclif was inclined to rate even more highly.[8] If pride and avarice were the marks of Antichrist, humility and poverty were of the kingdom of heaven. Like Christ one should suffer injury rather than look for gain.[9] The growth of ecclesiastical pomp, wealth, civil dominion, and the taking of the law into its own hands were all characteristics of a Caesarian priesthood in its departure from the life of Christ's disciples.[10] To these he contraposed the equality of the primitive church. It was marked not only by the lack of property, civil rights, dominion and litigation but, equally, by a single order of priests and deacons. They had been the only ones instituted by Christ and they alone enjoyed divine authority.[11] Moreover, as we saw, appointment

[1] *De potestate pape* 287; *Opera minora* 298–9. [2] *De potestate pape*, 230.

[3] Istis suppositis quod status huius paupertatis est statui innocentie conformior et per consequens status viandi perfectior. . . . Nam in statu innocentie non fuisset civile dominium (*De civili dominio*, III, 89). Also 53.

[4] Servet itaque clericus illam paupertatem altissimam et non est compossibile civile dominium sibi pro tunc in gratia coequari (ibid., 201).

[5] Ibid., 412.

[6] *De civili dominio* IV, 411; *Trialogus* 306; *Opera minora* 3, 19–71, 159–88.

[7] *De civili dominio* I, 148–58; *De ecclesia* I, 365. See preceding note.

[8] Paupertas autem mentalis, quam dixi sepius esse signatam per hec signa extrinsica, est per se causa religionis Christi (*De civili dominio*, IV, 492). Also ibid., III, 108 ff. *Opera minora* 443; *Opus evangelicum* I, 15, 17.

[9] E.g., *De civili dominio* II, 150.

[10] E.g., *Sermons* II, 58, III, 42–69, 78; *Opera minora* 255.

[11] Item terminus potentie et ministri ecclesie, ne evagetur in devium, est signandus . . . sed nullius si non ille quem Christus instituit. . . . Tunc autem non ordinavit nisi diacones et presbyteros. Idem autem sunt presbyteri et sacerdotes sive episcopi (*De blasphemia* 66). See also ibid., 65; *Opera minora* 142, 143, 305; *De civili dominio* I, 380, *Trialogus* 296.

to their office had been direct from God or by popular election.[1] There had accordingly been no patronage, and no popes, bishops, cardinals or curia to exercise it; they were all unscriptural both in their offices and their abuses of them.

Wyclif's rejection of the ecclesiastical hierarchy was undoubtedly his single most revolutionary step.[2] It constituted an attack upon not simply the pope, cardinals and bishops in the name of God's word, but the very existence of the church in this world. As both a corporation and a congregation it lost its *raison d'être*, being entitled to neither its possessions and privileges nor to its claims to be mediator between God and men. Instead of being the visible expression of God's saving will and the mystical body of Christ, it became Antichrist incarnate, with the pope at its head.[3] This is where Wyclif's opposition to the church hierarchy finally led him; it was crystallized in his treatment of the papacy which he disqualified on the double grounds of contradicting both God's omnipotence and scriptural authority. By the first, since God alone knew and willed who would be saved and who damned, he alone could create a pope;[4] and conversely since no man knew, without a special revelation, whether he was damned or saved, he could not claim a supremacy over others[5]—least of all that obedience to him was necessary for salvation.[6] Already in *De civili dominio*, before he became irrevocably opposed to the papacy, Wyclif had divested the pope of any inherent justification by contraposing his human fallibility and lack of scriptural authority to Christ's divinity. With Christ lay the true headship of the church. He alone was necessary for its governance—its chief abbot[7]—where pope and cardinals could be dispensed with by God, and, if in mortal sin, were already excluded from the church.[8]

[1] Olim enim fuit lex quod vel deus limitaret, vel populus regulandus eligeret sibi sacerdotem sive episcopum (*De simonia* 43).

[2] Wyclif frequently asserted that the humblest priest was the pope's equal. E.g., *De potestate pape* 35, 272.

[3] E.g., *De simonia* 27–8; *De potestate pape* 217. See also pp. 537 ff. below.

[4] . . . videtur quod solus deus eligit hominem in papam vel summum pontificem (*De potestate pape* 176).

[5] sed nemo cui non fit specialis revelatio debet presumere se esse sic electum (*De civili dominio* I, 381); also ibid., 374; *De ecclesia* 31; *De blasphemia* 42.

[6] *De ecclesia* 31.

[7] E.g., *De civili dominio* II, 166; *De ecclesia* 31; *Trialogus* 263; Sermons III, 422, IV 59.

[8] Ex istis colligi potest quod nullum papam cum cetu cardinalium citra Christum sit absolute necessarium capitaliter regere ecclesiam sanctam dei. Primo patet ex hoc quod omnem talem personam sit possibile peccare mortaliter et dampnari, ex proximis dictis, sed tunc non est pars ecclesie, ergo conclusio. Item deus libere

Even at the human level the pope, like any priest, was only to be obeyed if he observed God's law.[1] After his condemnation by Gregory XI in 1377,[2] Wyclif's attitude to the papacy became outspokenly hostile, and lost even those qualifications in favour of accepting his authority to be found earlier.[3] The outbreak of the Great Schism, with the two popes each denouncing the other, served to confirm him in his opposition; his initial partisanship for Urban VI—'our Urban'[4]—gradually gave way to condemnation of both as Antichrists who were fulfilling Christ's prophecy.[5]

De potestate pape, written in 1379 or 1380, was designed to disprove the need for a pope at all. Despite its extremism it was among the best ordered of all Wyclif's writings, with the historical evidence, always one of Wyclif's proclivities, marshalled with academic care. In it he followed Marsilius of Padua's denial of the primacy of Rome, the office of pope or cardinals, or the authority of the latter to elect a pope. While reaffirming his earlier arguments drawn from God's immediate power, he now drew upon scripture to expose the falsity of papal claims both in theory and in practice. Beginning with a discussion of the different kinds of power, he concluded that spiritual power was exclusively from God, conferred directly by him and independently of any creature. As a spiritual quality such power could not lie with a created being like man.[6] Hence no pope could exercise it or bestow it upon others, whether by bull or directly impressing it in the soul;[7] conversely he could not revoke spiritual powers given by God, nor

---

contradictorie dat sua carismata cuilibet Christiano, constituens cum eo tamquam membro suo unum corpus mysticum; ad nullam talem influentiam requiritur persona hominis disparata; ergo nulla persona Romane ecclesie requiritur tamquam mediamen absolute necessarium ad regulandum ecclesiam. Item caput Christi cum sua lege est per se sufficiens ad regulam sponse sue, ergo nullus alius homo requiritur tamquam sponsus (*De civili dominio* I, 380).

[1] Ibid., II, 283–5.

[2] FZ 142–4.

[3] E.g., *De civili dominio* I, 381.

[4] *De eucharistia* 125; *De potestate pape* 247, 255.

[5] *De potestate pape* 185, *Dialogus* 424–5; *Sermons* III, 275–6, IV, 137, 156, 173, 184–5; *Opera minora* 204, 252, 267–72; *Opus evang.* III, 169; *De blasphemia* 42.

[6] Item nulla pura creatura cooperatur cum deo in producendo quantitatem mentis indivisibilem; omnis huiusmodi potestas est qualitas mentis indivisibilis, ergo nulla pura creatura cooperatur cum deo . . . et per consequens preter potestatem quam deus creat in anima non est dare aliam datam ab homine (*De potestate pape* 14).

[7] Ibid., 14–15.

loose what had been already bound. The pope's power consisted simply in promulgating that received from God, a function made necessary as a result of the fall;[1] it could not be altered in its essence but only in its execution.[2] Power was thus not something in its own right, but a grant, from God to minister for him; permission to exercise it came either immediately from God or through the sacraments.[3] God was its sole author, and without his willing there could be none.[4] Spiritual power, of its nature, then, was dependent upon a non-sensory source; hence even when it was in the hands of a creature it belonged not to him but to God and could not be used save as God directed. By making spiritual power totally independent of human agency, Wyclif, like Bradwardine before him, treated God's will as the sole determinant, and conformity to it the sole condition of its possession by a creature. In the case of the pope it enabled Wyclif both to restrict his authority to what had been decreed in the bible and to judge him as true or false according to whether he conformed to it.

From this point of view alone Wyclif's doctrine led to a denial of many of the traditional papal attributes, above all the power of binding and loosing. Since only God could authorize such actions, only God could perform them. Accordingly, the pope could only bind and loose if God had done so previously in heaven—a point which Hus was to make so much of; for the pope to act alone was worthless.[5] The same applied to absolution and excommunication: no man, pope any more than parish priest, could confer the Holy Spirit or the gift of grace or absolve, unless God had already made a sinner contrite;[6] and conversely God had first to punish before the pope could ban.[7] This led Wyclif still further to blur the distinction between priest and layman —just as the pope could be a layman.[8] God gave his power, he said,

[1] Ibid., 16. [2] Ibid.

[3] . . . potestas non est quid absolutum, quod posset per se existere, sed potestas dicitur dari ab autore, quando datum est a deo creature, ut ministero dei . . . et illa licentia est potestas quam deus nunc dat immediate per se, et nunc per sacramentale ministerium ad notificandum populo dei licentiam (ibid., 21).

[4] Ibid., 22.

[5] et sic deus necessario prius absolvit vel ligat personam viantem antequam aliquis eius servus hanc absolvit vel ligat (*Opera minora* 264). See also *De ecclesia* 353; Sermons II, 433, 434, IV, 175, 177; *Trialogus* 329.

[6] *De potestate pape* 26–8.

[7] Ibid., 31–2.

[8] Quoad secundum obiectum de laycis, patet logico quod laycus potest esse papa (ibid., 272).

without visible sign[1] as Christ had ordained his Apostles without outward sacrament.[2] Accordingly there was no means of assessing a priest's powers, which were entirely a matter for God's will. Scripture and reason could be the only guides, not the constitutions of the church.[3]

When Wyclif turned to scripture he took over Marsilius's main arguments: although never mentioning the Paduan by name it is inconceivable that Wyclif was not conversant with his doctrines, which, together with those of the other anti-papalists at the court of Louis of Bavaria, had passed into common currency. Like Marsilius, Wyclif rejected the pope's claim to be vicar of Christ and St. Peter's successor on both exegetical and historical grounds. Where earlier in *De civili dominio* he had been prepared to grant that a pope should be obeyed if true to God,[4] he now turned the bible against him. Not only was there no mention of a pope in the bible,[5] but Christ's commission to Peter in Matthew 16: 18 and 19 ('Thou art Peter . . .') provided no support. The rock of the church referred to Christ; he, not Peter, was its sole head and for ever. Peter's primacy was purely personal to himself; it derived from his own spiritual qualities which had made him preeminent among the other apostles. As such it conferred no authority among his successors as bishops of Rome.[6] But even in the latter capacity Peter had not been supreme; Paul had had more right to the title of bishop, while Rome at least shared her position with Alexandria, Antioch, Constantinople and Jerusalem—a now common argument in fourteenth-century ecclesiology. Each of these had merely represented a local church and none had a jurisdiction which extended to the church

[1] *De potestate pape* 32.

[2] Ibid., 33. Also *Opera minora* 259.

[3] Ulterius videtur incertum quantum potestatem oporteret viantem habere, ad hoc quod sit sacerdos, vel si omnes sacerdotes sunt paris potestatis ordinis, quia certum est quod deus dat vel non dat, ut sibi placuerit, ordinis potestatem. . . . In qua materia vellem nostros solempnizantes constitutiones humanas ad fidem scripture et puram rationem attendere et non amplius fingere ad onus ecclesie (*De potestate pape* 34–5).

[4] E.g., *De civili dominio* I, 377–9, 391–416, 427.

[5] Sed pro nomine pape, notandum quod in scriptura sacra, si bene habeo, non exprimitur (*De potestate pape* 165). See also *Opus evangelicum* I, 5; II, 187; *Opera minora* 101; *Sermons* III, 509.

[6] quia, ut patet in parte ex dictis, propter spiritualem primatum quo ceteris fuit humilior, servitior et ecclesie amantior, et non propter aliquam dignitatem mundanam deus dedit sibi primatum ecclesie (ibid., 97). And: . . . preeminentia Petri in alios non stat in honore in dominatu vel gloria seculari, sed in omnino oppositis (*De potestate pape* 135).

as a whole.[1] Furthermore, a comparison between pope and Apostles showed that the pope was in no way their successor. Just as the Apostles were without Christ's divinity, and hence his power of dying and returning to life and redeeming mankind,[2] so the pope could not work miracles[3] or write canonical books,[4] besides being their inferior sacramentally.[5] How then had the pope's power arisen? From usurpation. The papacy was the result of imperial contrivance. The emperor Constantine had elevated his bishop into head of the church,[6] an action which was no more permissible to him than to any other Christian; none had the right to prescribe new articles of faith beyond those already contained in the bible.[7] Wyclif therefore denied a pope's authority, or the need to obey him for salvation, so long as he had received his office by human election and not from God.[8] Like the bishops he had been no part of the primitive church, and his decretals carried no weight.[9] The same applied to the cardinals for whom Wyclif reserved some of his most violent invective; they were monsters who had usurped the place of the Apostles; their mode of election was a scandal; they amassed and devoured the benefices of the church thereby robbing the poor; they served no purpose except that of Antichrist.[10] Above all just as the pope must first have had a special revelation

[1] *De potestate pape* 97, 111, 140–1, 150, and 165–79. He cited especially the chronicle of Ralph Diceto. See also *Trialogus* 330; *Opus evangelicum* I, 40, III, 109, 188; *Sermons* I 352–3, II, 433, III, 509, IV, 63, 96, 133–6, 172–3, 193, 194; *Pol. Works* I, 1, 35, 101, 256–7, 259, 260, 349, 350, II, 678, 685; *Opera minora* 84, 86, 87–88, 89, 104–5, 109, 113, 129, 132–3, 162–3, 203, 204, 207, 227, 230, 276, 279, 284, 285, 303, 360–2, 367, 368; *De blasphemia*, 4–8, 16, 44, 72; *Dialogus* 25, 49, 73, 82–3; *De apostasia* 68, 69, 171–6, 200–4.

[2] Ibid., 102–4.

[3] Ibid., 106–7.

[4] Ibid., 108–9.

[5] Ibid., 108; *Opera minora* 262.

[6] . . . imperator Constantinus circa annum domini trecentesimum primum hoc censuit et precepit quod suus episcopus ab omnibus papa vocaretur (*De potestate pape* 215). Also ibid., 319; and *De officio regis* 18–19.

[7] Sed ille imperator non habet plus potestatem condendi noves articulos fidei quam quilibet alius Christianus . . . non enim licet vel angelo de celo onerare sanctam ecclesiam novis articulis vel ritibus extra scripturam sacram a spiritu sancto doctam (*De potestate pape* 259).

[8] Unde nichil maius hereticum quam quod tam necessarius est iste ordo Cesarius, ut nemo posset sine papa istius ordinis esse salvus (*De potestate pape* 246), *Opera minora* 132–4, 267–72; *Sermons* IV, 203, 227, 237; *Opus evangelicum* I, 40.

[9] *De potestate pape*; see p. 534 nn. 5 and 6 above.

[10] *De potestate pape* 195–7. Also *Opera minora* 118, 142, 196, 203; *Sermons* IV, 193, 284–6; *Supplementum Trialogi*, 450–2.

from God in order to be its ruler, so must those who made a true pope have first been justified by God. Only he could create the pope.[1] The cardinals merely appointed an official.[2]

At this point Wyclif wavered—no doubt because he did not want an irrevocable rupture with the church—by distinguishing between a true and a false pope. Whereas for the church as a whole it sufficed, for the present, to treat those who followed Christ's precepts of poverty, humility and charity as God's servants to be obeyed, the pope, by definition, was not of divine origin. Nevertheless, Wyclif adopted a similar criterion by which to judge him, thereby committing the double inconsistency of both denying and asserting his divine authority, and making the evidence for it at once exclusively inner revelation[3] and external conformity to Christ's precepts.[4] By doing so, he gave himself the best of two worlds but only by flawing his own structure. Again Wyclif failed to harmonize his different sequences of papal usurpation. In addition to blaming Constantine for inaugurating the office, he elsewhere contrasted human election by bishops, as the consequence of endowment, with divine appointment,[5] implying thereby an originally just form of institution by God.

In the event, however, so far as the practical consequences were concerned, it made little difference; for Wyclif's main ground for disqualifying the pope, cardinals, bishops, and the Caesarian priests as a whole, was precisely their *visible* betrayal of Christ. From this point of view the higher their original status the greater their subsequent crime, a fact which he repeatedly emphasized. Thus the pope who lived on endowments was Antichrist, the 'abomination of desolation' and a usurper.[6] Like Satan and Judas, antichrists in chief, those who had been closest to God fell farthest.

By the same token the clergy, as the continuators of the apostolic

[1] . . . sic dux Christiani exercitus debet ostendi revelatione divina quia nichil falsius quam quod humana electio facit papam, nam solus dominus iustificat hominem. Omnis qui facit papam vel membrum sancte matris ecclesie facit iustum, igitur solus dominus facit papam (*De potestate pape* 195).

[2] *De potestate pape*; see also, *Opus evangelicum* III, 109, 181; *Dialogus* 423; *Pol. Works* I, 101; *De blasphemia* 65–6; *Opera minora* 118, 279, 289.

[3] Ex istis videtur quod nemo sumeret sibi honorem papalem, ut dicit Apostolus, nisi a deo revelatione abscondita sit vocatus (*De potestate pape* 363).

[4] Ex quo patet quod nemo sit papa nisi sit Christi et Petri filius imitando eos in moribus (*De potestate pape* 215).

[5] *De potestate pape* 176; also 362; *Opus evangelicum* I, 40.

[6] *De potestate pape* 321–3; *Opera minora* 101, 207, 349, 678.

tradition, were, in failing to uphold it, Christ's greatest betrayers. Wyclif accordingly sought Antichrist from among them,[1] meaning by the term not, as we have seen earlier, a specific individual but the whole body of the damned: in this case anyone going against Christ.[2] His definition of what this constituted is summed up in the ten signs of Antichrist which he contrasted to the true path of Christ. They were seduction away from Christ's teachings; the making of new laws other than those in scripture; worldliness instead of poverty; palatial splendour instead of missionary preaching; the assertion of authority instead of submission to it; the use of force; hostility to foes; the desire for jurisdiction; arrogance and lack of humility.[3] To these he added a list of twelve abuses of a similar tenor, specific to the pope.[4] Thus Wyclif's attack centred upon the evils associated with endowment and secular power.[5] Time and again, in work after work, he repeated the catalogue of crimes: the taking of first fruits, which was simony; excommunication for the non-payment of tithes, which was uncanonical; litigation; civil jurisdiction; patronage; the desire for honours; robbing the poor; false grants of indulgences.[6] Like the chorus of a Greek tragedy their

[1] Secundo notandum quod de clero necesse est Antichristum trahere suam originem; cum enim non omnes sacerdotes confirmati sunt, necesse est quod aliqui propter status excellentiam cadant profundius. Sic magnus Antichristus fuit Lucifer cum complicibus, sic magnus Antichristus fuit Scarioth cum avaris suis sequentibus (*De potestate pape* 119; also 327).

[2] Quod quicumque est Christo vel legi sue contrarius dicitur Antichristus (ibid., 118); also 217.

[3] Ibid., 120–4.

[4] Ibid., 386–92.

[5] See especially ibid., 237–43.

[6] E.g., *De dominio civili* I, 276–80, 297, 311, 312, 314, 317, 320, 336; II, 15, 21–5, 32, 56, 71, 101–2, 104, 107, 110, 145; III, 37, 60–5, 72, 73, 182, 193–4, 200–1, 204, 206, 209, 212, 213, 217, 219–220, 227–9, 230, 235, 242, 257–62, 351, 382, 385, 400, 402, 405, 411, 412, 413, 435, 454–9, 469, 485;

De ecclesia 184, 187, 191, 195, 258, 274, 292, 294, 300–2, 307, 365, 371, 372, 564–70, 578–87;

De potestate pape 80, 83, 85, 89, 91–2, 93, 101, 129, 150, 153, 170, 237, 238–42, 246, 349, 353;

De veritate sacre scripture I, 71; II, 248 f.; III, 1, 3, 15, 21, 39–40, 51, 56, 58, 59, 62, 85;

De eucharistia 322; *Trialogus* 297, 299, 306, 368 ff., 380 ff.;

Supplementum Trialogi 411 f., 415, 416, 423; *De simonia* 2, 4, 6, 7, 27–8, 33, 38, 40, 44, 48, 54, 56, 58, 61, 63, 67, 93–8, 104;

De blasphemia 4, 32–6, 54–5, 56, 61, 70, 71, 72, 81, 264, 270–1;

Dialogus 14, 58–9, 61–2, 64–8, 76, 79–80, 81, 84, 85, 86–95;

Opus evangelicum I, 18–19, III, 194–5;

repeated invocation was at once a lament upon the ills of the world and a never-ending source of denunciation.

But Wyclif did not stop at denunciation; he openly challenged the authority of the hierarchy and called for its dissolution. Here, above all, in his practical measures, was the real danger from his doctrines to be found. Negatively, they entailed the denial of ecclesiastical power;[1] positively its supersession by the lay power.[2] The bible was the agent ot the first, the king—so far at least as England was concerned—of the second. Taken together, and acted upon, they meant revolution, as a closer examination should make clear.

As we have already suggested, Wyclif was as pragmatic as he was metaphysical. While confining to God not only all power but also all knowledge of who was of the church and who was not, he was yet prepared to judge its priests by their conduct: similarly with the pope, although rebutting his authority he was prepared to accept or reject him on purely palpable grounds of whether or not he lived according to Christ. If he did he could be accepted;[3] if not he stood self-condemned.[4] Now since every pope and most priests belonged to the second category, because of endowment and the secularization of the church, Wyclif treated virtually all its hierarchy and most of its decretals as null and void. In the growing conviction that they were the voice of Antichrist, he came to identify the latter above all with the pope, including even the claim to be pope,[5] since it entailed exalting man's will above God's.[6] The intensity of his feeling against the papal office is well

---

Sermons I, 132, 270–1, 273, 366; II, 312, 313, 442; III, 20, 21–4, 78, 101–3, 158, 159–161, 217, 489–90; IV, 122–3, 136, 143, 145, 155, 173, 187;

Opera minora 3, 19, 20, 21, 22, 23, 24, 27, 28, 32, 37–45, 48, 51, 63, 68, 82, 83, 86, 87, 93, 101, 104, 105, 159, 162–3, 171, 172, 173, 174, 183, 188, 189, 190, 191, 207, 244, 245, 246, 248, 249, 251, 292, 293, 294, 295, 298–9, 301, 302, 317–18, 410, 412, 413, 414, 416, 421.

See also *Polemical Works*, 2 vols., which are largely devoted to attacking the religious orders.

[1] E.g., *Opera minora* 265–7, 279, 282–3, 284, 285; *De blasphemia* 65–6.

[2] *De ecclesia* 337–45; *De veritate* II, 21, 28, III, 86, 93; *Sermons* III, 210–11, 217; *De simonia* 44.

[3] Ibid., 65, 102, 261–2.

[4] Ibid., 120, 148, 218.

[5] *Opera minora* 87, 227; *Opus evangelicum* III, 106–8, 134–8, 181.

[6] Unde per hoc iudicium iustificatum a Christo notatur convertibilitas iuste vite vel operis, querendo voluntatem deitatis et iniustitia vite vel operis querendo propriam voluntatem (*Opus evangelicum* III, 137).

illustrated by his remark that Gregory the Great would have been of still more worth to the church had he not been pope.[1] Wyclif accordingly saw the conflict between Christ and Antichrist primarily as one between the truth of the bible and the pretensions of the modern hierarchy.[2] It increasingly dominated the writings of the last six years of his life, from *De civili dominio* to the unfinished *Opus evangelicum*, the last two books of which were entitled *De Antichristo*. There, with unbridled violence, he demanded the removal of the pope as well as the dissolution of the religious orders.[3] The progression was complete: from denying the pope's sanctity and the need to believe in him, he came to deny him, as Antichrist, his very existence. If not inevitable it was predictable, granted Wyclif's attitude to the church and the bible. The antinomy which he saw between them made their claims irreconcilable. There could, he said, be no comparison between the infallibility of the bible and the decretals of the church; the one was from Christ, the other could and did err:[4] they were subject to constant change, one decretal superseding another, often from the same pope.[5] The bible was divine and had to be believed;[6] the church's laws when wrong had to be repudiated.[7] The bible alone was the standard of truth and all departures and deviation from it heresy.[8] There could therefore be no mingling of divine and human traditions.[9]

[1] Ibid., 306.

[2] *De potestate pape* 111.

[3] *Opus evangelicum* III, 181. See also *De blasphemia* 46, *Pol. Works* I, 3–9; *Supplementum trialogi* 423.

[4] Patet ex hoc quod nemo post Christum potest parificare in autoritate cum ipso. Et sic non oportet parificare omnes decretales epistolas cum evangelio vel dictis sanctorum doctorum, qui per idem crederetur de quibuscunque bullis papalibus, quod vanum est fingere, cum ecclesia nedum in iudicialibus fallit et fallitur vel ignorat, sed in aliis privatis punctis concernentibus statum ecclesie (*De veritate* I, 407). See also *De civili dominio* I, 377–80; *De potestate pape* 67; *De ecclesia* 563.

[5] *De veritate* I, 407.

[6] E.g., *De civili dominio* I, 377–9; *De veritate* I, 268; *Opus evangelicum* II, 91–2; *Sermons* I, 83, 399; III, 262, 263, 264, 283, 398–9, 505; IV, 79; *Pol. works* I, 1, 257; *Dialogus* 21; *De apostasia* 244–6.

[7] Ex quo patet primo quod Romana ecclesia potest errare in articulis fidei cum sic fecit; patet secundo quod non oportet credere quod si Romana ecclesia quidquam catholicat vel hereticat, ergo vere (*De eucharistia* 32). See also *De veritate* I, 407; *Pol. Works* I, 141, 181; *Sermons* I, 376, II, 427, 430–1; *Trialogus* 239–40.

[8] *De veritate* I, 132 and 370; *De civili dominio* II, 58; *Pol. Works* I, 246.

[9] *De veritate* I, 221, 395; II, 129, 148; *De civili dominio* I, 411, 427, 428; *De eucharistia* 126, 172, 289–90; *Sermons* III, 245, 254, IV, 80, 96; *De blasphemia*, 10, 44, 45, 46.

Now it was Wyclif's refusal to allow any part to the present church in interpreting the bible which made for conflict between them. For if, as he ceaselessly repeated, the church owed its authority to the bible this was only to be acknowledged in so far as it conformed to scripture.[1] Nothing remained to its own aegis; its laws, decretals and bulls, taken in themselves, were of purely human invention devoid of divine sanction;[2] to claim otherwise was blasphemy.[3] The pope and the hierarchy could not declare or legislate on matters of faith except to confirm what had been eternally decreed in the bible and so was already law.[4] Above all, they were subject to the arbitrament where accessible of the saints and reason for their understanding of the bible; where these were lacking they were bound by its literal meaning, as we have seen earlier.[5] The hierarchy was therefore effectively denied any standing in its own right; and it was in its attempt to assert it that Wyclif branded the pope above all as Antichrist. Always sensitive to the dangers of confusing human traditions—as he called them—with divine law,[6] he arrived at open rejection of the church's authority in his later works. Thus in *De eucharistia* he declared that not even a thousand times a thousand bishops should be believed before the bible or St. Augustine;[7] for the only true test of authority was pastoral as well as

[1] *De civili dominio* I, 377–80, 399, 409–10; *De veritate* I, 192, 348, 402, 403, 404, II, 135; *De potestate pape* 248, 346; *De eucharistia* 173, 243, 282, 283, 289, 291; *Dialogus* 77, 78, 94; *Sermons* III, 263, 264, 445, 509, IV, 46; *Pol. Works* II, 713–14; *Opera minora* 75, 87, 137, 138, 227, 240, 243, 289; *De officio regis* 191, 222, 223, 224. *De apostasia* 244–6; *Trialogus* 262; *Opus evangelicum* I, 12, 100.

[2] Quarta conclusio . . . quelibet pars scripture sacre est infinitum maioris auctoritatis quam aliqua epistola decretalis, patet sic: quelibet epistola decretalis est condita per aliquem papam . . .; quelibet pars sacre scripture immediate et proxime autorizatur per deum, igitur conclusio (*De veritate* I, 395).

[3] Ideo dicere quod omnes bulle papales sunt paris auctoritatis aut certitudinis veritatis cum scriptura sacra foret blasfeme imponere quod sit Christus (ibid., 408).

[4] E.g., ibid., II, 61–2; *De civili dominio* III, 399.

[5] See especially *De veritate* I, 198–207.

[6] For subsequent references to the subordination of church decretals and canon law to the bible see, *inter alia*; *De eucharistia* 286–91; *Sermons* I, 302, 370; II, 66, 283, 323–5, 388–9, 434–5; III, 58, 81, 158, 245, 262, 392, 447, 505, 509; IV, 63, 66, 79, 80, 96. *Opus evangelicum* I, 12, 29, 91–2, 100; II, 380; III, 189. *De simonia* 25, 64–5; *Dialogus* 21, 25, 27, 49, 77, 94. *De officio regis* 125; *De blasphemia* 128, 159–61. *Opera minora* 75, 87, 138, 240. *Polemical Works* I, 349–50, II, 713–14.

[7] nec solum debet credi cuicunque parti scripture plus quam millies mille episcopis etiam Romanis vel Avinonicis sub ratione qua tales, verum etiam plus beato Augustino et aliis sanctis doctoribus quoad materiam fidei quam papis et cardinalibus qui non sunt in fide scripture adeo approbati (*De eucharistia* 279).

intellectual excellence[1]—which *ipso facto* disqualified the pope and the hierarchy who were guilty of the three great crimes of exalting human traditions, depressing Christ's law, and making evil falsely appear as good.[2] The cause of the church's fall, and of the blasphemy, apostasy and simony which accompanied it, were personified in him who claimed to stand for Christ—the pope.[3] It sprang from the three principles of Antichrist's teaching: that the elected pope was head of the whole church and Christ's supreme vicar on earth; that whatever he decreed on matters of faith was to be accepted as gospel; and that his laws were to be followed above the gospel.[4]

Antichrist, then, came to represent a rival authority to Christ's law; or, as Wyclif put it in his last work, power not founded on the bible was that of Antichrist.[5] It included the pope, the four religious orders—or sects as he called them—and the Caesarian priesthood with their pretence of being able to excommunicate, imprison and take rents.[6] This was where Wyclif's biblism had led him. In its name he had come not only to debar the entire hierarchy of the church, and its orders, from any valid title to speak for Christ but to make them of Antichrist. Opposed to them were those true to the bible and the authentic apostolic tradition, a combination of faith, reason and sanctity, in the face of which the modern church stood condemned.

Even before he had reached this conclusion, however, Wyclif was already advocating the remedy for the evils which had brought him to it: the disendowment of the church, which once more freed from possession and lordship, and the avarice and worldliness they entailed, could return to the apostolic simplicity of its original state. Thus restored to Christ, the priesthood would again follow his example, ministering to

[1] Ibid., 281.

[2] . . . per quos Sathan introducit maiora scelera, ut sunt 1. traditionum humanarum exaltatio, 2. scole legis Christi depressio et 3. in malo sub apparantia boni coniuratio (*De blasphemia* 19). See also *De eucharistia* 328.

[3] Ibid., 41.

[4] Sunt autem huius scole principia ex quibus sequuntur conclusiones Sathane cum quibus populus est cecatus. Primum videtur quod eo ipso quo quis eligitur in Romanum pontificem ipse est caput ecclesie totius militantis et summus vicarius Christi in terris. Secundum principium: quidquid concernens fidem ipsum est ut evangelium acceptandum. Et 3m principium est quod leges sue sunt plus quam evangelium exsequende. Ex ista triplicitate sequuntur blasfemie infinite (ibid.).

[5] Regulariter igitur omnis potestas in fide scripture non fundata est ab Antichristo sive dyabolo false ficta (*Opus evangelicum* I, 97). Also ibid., III, 71, 106.

[6] Ibid.

their flock and preaching God's word.[1] Disendowment and the renunciation of secular ways became the panacea which Wyclif urged without remission from *De civili dominio* until his death. It was the most palpable aspect of his teaching on the church and, as we shall see, his most explosive legacy to his disciples. In the context of the time it constituted a frontal attack upon the very existence of the church as a corporate entity; had it succeeded, it would have meant its material and juridical dissolution.

To achieve his aim Wyclif turned to the king and the lay lords; they were to expropriate the church and withdraw its civil rights.[2] Instead of living on endowments those of its priests who were worthy were to be supported by voluntary offerings and tithes; the rest were

[1] As passages on it are innumerable, the following quotation and select list of references must suffice:

Si autem queritur quid nos sacerdotes debemus facere, dicitur indubie quod debemus in conversatione sequi ipsum quantum sufficimus. Sic quod primo abraderemus quantum sufficimus omnem occupationem mentis aut corporis que fuerit impertinens aut contraria officio sacerdotis. Secundo vero poneremus omnem sacerdotalem potestatem quantum sufficeremus efficaciter in effectum, et omnium istorum exemplar et specula debet esse dominus Jhesus Christus. Ex istis sequerentur tres conclusiones gratiose ecclesie. Primo quod papa non intromitteret se iudicando de negotio seculari, quia est alienum sacerdotali officio. . . . Secundo quod renueret omnem dotationem cesaream, cum ex facto Christi et Petri patet quod foret impertinens papali officio, et per consequens omnes alii episcopi ut sit conformitas ad caput, et revera necessarior foret conformitas paparum sequentium in ista pauperie ad Christum,. . . . Tertio quod papa et omnes alii episcopi debent evangelizatione, oratione, et sancte vite exemplatione assidue pascere oves Christi. . . . Et sic spoliatis superfluis pateret quis episcopus remaneret habilis ex thesaurio domino et quis remaneret vacuus precisso organo et officio laycali (*De potestate pape* 101–2).

Also: *Opera minora* 24, 32, 37, 39, 41, 42, 45, 51, 63, 68, 82–3, 101, 159, 171, 172–4, 183, 188, 189, 191, 207, 246, 293, 295, 410, 412, 414; *De civili dominio* I, 330–1, 450, 469, 470–8, II, 14, 18, 22, 23, 24, 32, 115, III, 25; *De ecclesia* 190–2, 292, 294, 337–45, 372; *De potestate pape* 89, 198, 341; *De veritate sacre scripture* I, 62, 65, 81, III, 16, 21; *De officio regis* 60, 61, 64, 89, 97, 203, 210–13, 224; *De simonia* 67, 93–8; *De blasphemia* 32–6, 56, 70, 81, 264, 270–1; *Dialogus* 50, 58–9, 84, 86, 95; *De eucharistia* 311, 322; *Sermons* I, 132, 376, 435, II, 367, III, 20, IV, 3, 55, 246, 292, 414; *Trialogus* 376–88; *Supplementum Trialogi* 412–22.

[2] Quomodo igitur religiosi nostri susciperent de manu secularium temporalia ecclesie dedicata nisi emendare eorum usum sit licitum? Correspondenter licet dominis et tenentur, viso quod eorum elemosine vergunt ad detrimentum ecclesie et sophisticantur infideliter in furto et rapina earum secundum traditiones et ritus hominum preter evangelicum adinventas . . . (*De officio regis* 210). Also ibid., 211–13; *De veritate sacre scripture* I, 28, 93; *Opus evangelicum* III, 8; *Opera minora* 189, 207.

to be dispossessed.[1] Such in essence was the course which Wyclif, with the inevitable inconsistencies, advocated for the spiritual regeneration of the church. By making its implementation depend upon the lay power he turned an indefinite aspiration into an immediate programme; in place of the prophetic expectations of the Franciscan Spirituals and Joachists, which he explicitly rejected,[2] he put political action. It was this which made him an heresiarch where they remained primarily heterodox. Unlike them, his conception of Antichrist as a palpable presence at work within the church called forth palpable measures for its destruction; where they looked to a new spiritual order and the end of the present age, Wyclif looked to the strength of the secular arm and the consummation of the existing state.

Not surprisingly, then, Wyclif was the champion of royal authority. His treatise *De officio regis* was devoted to exalting the king's supremacy over all mankind, including the priests. Whereas the king's power was fashioned in the image of Christ as God, that of the priest was to be compared with Christ's humanity.[3] The king was God's vicar and he stood apart from the rest of men,[4] who were his servants.[5] To resist him was to sin.[6] Even tyrants were ordained of God and had to be suffered, provided that the evil done was to men and not to God.[7] All men were therefore bound to obey the king, as Christ had enjoined.[8] To Wyclif the principle of kingship was inherent in all forms of human association; it applied in the church before the fall and the coming of endowment, when with a minimum of civil law it had been subject to

[1] *Opera minora* 23, 171, 244, 302; *De officio regis* 59; *De civili dominio* I, 56, 311–13; *Dialogus* 76, 79–80.

[2] Sed licet hunc diem iudicii sit necessarium evenire, tamen plene et ex se *nemo scit illum diem nisi fuerit pater solus*. . . . Istam autem veritatem Christus hic exprimit ne calculatores se vane sollicitent circa precisionem temporis vel instantis quando hic dies domini inchoabit. Unde circa prenosticationem hanc vanam abbas Joachim et multi alii sunt decepti (*Opera minora* 375). Also ibid., 165–6. *Opus evangelicum* III, 102.

[3] Nec est fingendum ministerium huius differentie verborum nisi quod rex gerit ymaginem deitatis Christi sicut episcopus ymaginem deitatis Christi sicut episcopus ymaginem sue humanitatis (*De officio regis*, 13). See also 16, 137, 143, 144, and *Dialogus* 73.

[4] Rex enim est dei vicarius quem proximo dictum est esse timendum, ideo necesse est sibi servari honorificentiam in eius vicario, et per consequens, non obstante quod sit frater noster, differenter ab ab aliis fratribus honorari (*De officio regis* 4); also 246.

[5] *De officio regis* 5; *Sermons* III, 210–11, 217.

[6] Non licet dei ordinationi resistere, sed omnis potestas brachii secularis est ordinata a deo sive in penam sive premium; ergo non licet sibi resistere (ibid., 7–8); also 9, 104, 203.

[7] Ibid., 8.

[8] Ibid., 14.

the king's guidance.[1] Since the church's secularization, it had been dependent upon the king for its temporalities,[2] as indeed in all other respects. From this position of suzerainty, Wyclif, although frequently reiterating the king's obligation to act in conformity with God's decrees, which was his *raison d'être*,[3] attributed to him virtually limitless powers over his kingdom.[4] Because he was of the world, unlike the priesthood whose duty was to stand apart from it,[5] its right ordering fell to him even should it entail sanctions against the church.[6] Thus, as its spiritual overseer,[7] he could ban evil priests;[8] withdraw alms;[9] sequestrate church property;[10] correct the priesthood;[11] demolish churches in an emergency and convert them into towers for the defence of the realm.[12] The contrast between royal and sacerdotal power hardly needs stressing. Not only was the entire church, including the pope in matters such as patronage,[13] subject to the royal power, but so even were the predestined during their sojourn in this world.[14] Whereas Wyclif effectively denuded the church hierarchy of any authority, he insisted upon universal submission to the king and lay lords.[15] A pope could be deposed, disobeyed and corrected;[16] but even a tyrant must ordinarily be obeyed.

Once again Wyclif's pragmatism triumphed over theory. Strictly speaking there was no more means of knowing whether a king or lay lord was damned or saved than a priest. Practically, however, property and power were the yardstick: for the church, their possession was a sin; for the king, his badge of office.[17] The church in enjoying them betrayed Christ;[18] the king was merely being true to his own nature: and the more he excelled in them the truer he was. If the contrast between priest and king was meant to reflect Wyclif's contempt for worldliness,

[1] *De officio regis* 19.
[2] Ibid., 36–7, 139.
[3] Ibid., 55, 57, 78–9, 82, 96, 110, 234–5.
[4] E.g., ibid., 66, 118–20.
[5] Ibid., 96–7.
[6] Ibid., 205.
[7] Ibid., 68–70.
[8] Ibid., 61, 64, 71.
[9] Ibid., 84; See also *De ecclesia* 337–45, *De veritate* II, 28, 21; III, 86, 93; *Sermons* III, 210–11; *De simonia* 44.
[10] *De officio regis*, 97.
[11] Ibid., 207.
[12] Ibid., 188.
[13] Ibid., 192.
[14] Ibid., 133.
[15] This applied to villeins and serfs equally; although Wyclif averred that it was better for men to be free than bond, he believed with Aristotle that some men were naturally fitted for servitude, and lords should never be resisted (*Opera minora* 153–8). There was nothing about him of the social, as opposed to ecclesiastical, revolutionary.
[16] *De civili dominio* II, 114, 123.
[17] E.g., *De civili dominio* I, 188–9, 291, II, 148: *De officio regis* 60.
[18] E.g., *Dialogus* 14, where he said that the pope's temporal possessions made him a heretic.

in elevating the church above the mundane, it resulted in debasing it at the hands of the king, and the king of England in particular. It is a final paradox of Wyclif's thinking that the practical consequence of his universal reverence for being and God's omnipotence was to entrust the king of England with salvation from the pope and the forces of Antichrist.[1]

There remain only to consider the two doctrines of dominion and grace and the eucharist. Although they bore no direct relation to one another, and were both too academic to be of any practical consequence, they were important for a similar reason. They each marked a decisive moment in Wyclif's progression towards heresy. The doctrine of dominion and grace, as expounded in *De civili dominio* provided the majority of the articles for Wyclif's first condemnation in 1377, by Gregory XI. It thereby precipitated Wyclif's breach with the papacy and his own growing antagonism towards the church hierarchy. His eucharistic teaching completed it, and extended it to the friars who, from once being allies, became from about 1380 his most bitter enemies. Under the taunting mnemonic of CAIM (compounded from the initials of the four mendicant orders) Wyclif arraigned the 'sects' for treason to Christ. His former admiration for the Franciscans in particular gave way to a ceaseless stream of abuse of them, their confrères and their founders. They were the devil's sect,[2] locusts who devoured the country's wealth and put an intolerable burden upon the land;[3] their existence was illicit and unauthorized by scripture;[4] and those responsible for founding them, like St. Benedict, St. Dominic and St. Francis, far from being praised, should be blamed.[5] Among their many crimes, the supreme ones concerned the eucharist[6] and mendicancy.[7] Any of

[1] E.g., *Opus evangelicum* III, 138. [2] *Pol. Works* I, 56, 368–9. [3] Ibid., 28 ff.

[4] Ibid., 14, 24, 59, 89, 101, 175, 180, 181; see also *Trialogus* 345 ff., 361–85; *Opera minora* 305, 442.

[5] Ex istis ultra colligitur quod sive Benedictus, sive Dominicus, sive Franciscus vel quivis alius novam sectam supra Christianam collegerit, non in hoc est laudandus nec persona ipsum sequens sectaliter, sed culpanda, et multo magis secte fingentes false se habere patronos vel extravagante superflue sine illis, ut de Augustinensibus et Carmelitis supponitur (*Pol. Works* I, 24).

[6] E.g., especially *Trialogus* 338–41 where it is one of their three errors, the others being mendicancy, ibid., 338, 341–9, and false charters, ibid., 338, 349–56. See also p. 546 n. 1 below.

[7] *Trialogus*, loc. cit., *Pol. works* I, 453–4; *Opera minora* I, 223; *Sermons* I, 226, III, 107, 108, 110–14, IV, 13.

Wyclif's earlier affinities to Franciscan poverty were obliterated by his hatred of its disciples for their denial of the true nature of the sacrament of Christ's body and blood. They became all members of Antichrist.[1]

Dominion

Wyclif owed his doctrine of dominion and grace primarily to FitzRalph's *De pauperie salvatoris* who in return derived its germ from Giles of Rome's *De potestate ecclesiastica*. It is hard not to feel that its importance in Wyclif's teaching has been much exaggerated. While itself of high subversive potential, within Wyclif's system it was largely nullified by his views on the church, the bible and royal authority. Once he had expounded it in the first book of *De civili dominio* it had little formative part in his subsequent thinking. Practically, both the visible church and the pope were disqualified from civil and spiritual jurisdiction on metaphysical and biblical grounds, quite independently of questions of dominion and grace; while the king and secular lords, to whom it could have applied with most force, were explicitly endowed by Wyclif with scripturally sanctioned authority for the purpose of putting down the church. In the process the doctrine of dominion and grace was superseded. Theoretically it was subsumed under Wyclif's definition of the church as the body of the elect, where only those eternally in grace alone enjoyed spiritual power. In this aspect it is best regarded as a transitory stage in Wyclif's evolution of a doctrine of authority.[2]

Briefly its lineage was as follows: Giles of Rome had sought to establish the ecclesiastical basis of all authority by making the church the sole medium of justice. Since this was from Christ alone,[3] and it was inseparable from real authority, only those who had been regenerated

[1] In addition to the citations already given, for a general condemnation of Friars and religious as a whole see especially *Sermons* I, 227, II, 435 ff., III, 38–9, 126–32, 152, 163–5, 219–24, 233–9, 372–3, 416–20, 496–501, IV, 10, 39–41, 50–2, 59, 61–62, 64–5, 109–12, 118–21, 122–3, 184–5; *Pol. works* I, 252, 340; *De blasphemia* 201–72; *Opus evangelicum* III, 63. *De apostasia* 1–46, 60–1, 148–9.

[2] For a different view see M. Wilks 'Predestination, Property and Power: Wyclif's Theory of Dominion and Grace' *Studies in Church History* 2 (1965) 220–36. He rightly sees Wyclif's theory of dominion and grace as 'the reverse of revolutionary', but because it served as 'a smokescreen which enabled him to reconstruct the old lay ideal of a theocratic monarchy and a proprietary church' (ibid., 235). This seems to me to ignore the evolution of Wyclif's thought.

[3] *De potestate ecclesiastica* (ed. Scholz) Weimar 1929, Bk. II, 73.

by the church, i.e. believers, could enjoy dominion.[1] All authority therefore had to be exercised through the church; anyone outside its communion, for whatever reason, was unworthy of goods or rights over others.[2] FitzRalph took up where Giles had left off. Where Giles had emphasized the dependence of all laymen—kings included—upon the church, FitzRalph developed this equation of justice with authority to make dominion exclusively from God. It was a gift which in turn pre-supposed the gift of justice and grace. Only if a man was first justified by God with grace would he rule on God's behalf.[3] Accordingly there could be no dominion without grace as its formal cause;[4] and conversely mortal sin in destroying grace destroyed dominion.[5] These two propositions together with their elaboration said everything which Wyclif was to say and said it more cogently. The central issue for FitzRalph was the independence of original lordship from natural and civil circumstances. Neither civil power nor coercion,[6] possession[7] or use,[8] denoted lordship in the strict meaning of a gift from God; while private property had not existed before Adam's fall,[9] which had entailed the loss of his dominion and its restoration in a modified form.[10] All these were outward signs, of themselves denoting no intrinsic right to lordship which only God could confer.[11] For that reason lordship was not transferable; when a great noble made a donation he was acting not from dominion but from munificence.[12] Possessions held by natural or civil right were not thereby property; this was the exclusive preserve of God's dominion.[13] Thus FitzRalph separated all physical control from true ownership, so that whatever the degree of possession, even consumption, it did not constitute lordship.[14]

FitzRalph had been concerned principally with the issues raised in the debate over Franciscan poverty, namely, what constituted possession.

[1] Ibid., 70, 74. [2] Ibid., 96, 109–10.

[3] *De pauperie salvatoris* Bks. I–IV (ed. R. L. Poole) together with *De dominio divino* (WS London 1890). Istud . . . dominium non sequitur naturam specificam immediate sed mediante iustitia, que sine iustificante gratia non habetur (ibid., 344). See also 348, 352, 441.

[4] Item, supraposite rationes que probant gratam acceptionem istius dominii prevenisse tanquam causam formalem ipsius, satis ostendunt istud dominium in nullo homine posse sine gratia remanere (ibid., 355).

[5] Ibid., 353, 354, 443.

[6] Ibid., 369–70. [7] Ibid., 381–5.

[8] Ibid., 388, 389. [9] Ibid., 437. [10] Ibid., 353, 354, 359, 363.

[11] . . . cum possessio a se nullum ius habeat, scilicet sibi intrinsecum (ibid., 385).

[12] Ibid., 456. [13] Ibid., 438. [14] Ibid., 469.

In one sense he had gone further than Michael of Cesena and his followers in taking it entirely out of the human arena and locating it exclusively with God. On the other hand, in strictly legal terms, he was nearer to John XXII in holding that, while naturally there could be simple use without lordship or other legal entitlement, if a man relied solely upon his natural dominion,[1] civilly the right of use (*ius utendi*) was required to be legally justified.[2] Wyclif, however, in taking over FitzRalph's doctrine of dominion and grace largely changed its import; whilst also touching on use and possession he treated the whole subject as a moral question. Thus, at the work's outset he declared that his aim was to demonstrate two truths: that no one in mortal sin had justice as a gift from God; and that he who enjoyed God's final grace enjoyed, both in right and actuality, all God's goods.[3] Whereas the key word for FitzRalph was lordship, for Wyclif it was justice: lack of justice from God meant not merely lack of lordship, but injustice.[4] Moreover, Wyclif went beyond FitzRalph in drawing an emphatic moral conclusion from the absence of grace: in addition to absence of lordship it denoted continual mortal sin.[5] It is difficult to know how far this should be taken in view of Wyclif's oft-repeated assertion that temporal grace could go with final reprobation, and temporal sin with final election. Is a reprobate's final damnation to be understood as entailing continual mortal sin even though temporally in a state of grace? And does the lapse into sin of a predestinate exclude him from lordship during its duration? It is not clear. What can be said is that absolute justice totally precluded mortal sin, and *vice versa*;[6] and that lordship could only come as a grant from God,[7] while grace alone conferred the right to civil dominion.[8]

Nevertheless, although power derived exclusively from God, Wyclif acknowledged that God could permit tyrants not only to punish

[1] *De pauperie salvatoris*, 472, 473. [2] Ibid., 475–6.

[3] Intendo itaque pro dicendis ostendere duas veritates quibus utar tamquam principiis ad dicenda: prima quod nemo ut est in peccato mortali habet iustitiam simpliciter ad donum dei; secunda quod quilibet existens in gratia gratificante finaliter nedum habet ius, sed in re habet omnia bona dei (*De civili dominio* I, 1).

[4] Ibid., 12. [5] Ibid., 13. Also ibid., 136.

[6] nam nemo est iustus simpliciter nisi sit immunis a peccato mortali (ibid., 62). Hurley, art. cit., 286–7, calls this 'theological dynamite' in its denial of created right, as well as uncreated right. It may well be; but without knowledge of who is in mortal sin it is dynamite without a fuse.

[7] Nulla creatura potest esse dominus alicuius nisi deus ipsum donaverit (ibid., 39).

[8] Ibid., 15.

sins and try the just, but to assert the independence of all civil and administrative authority,[1] an unusual exercise in divine omnipotence. He was also prepared to allow that a sinner might rule well, even though not entitled to true dominion.[2] The purpose of civil law was to preserve the necessities of life;[3] but without God's grace there could be neither right to their use nor dominion over them.[4] All rule must therefore be based upon the gospel;[5] it could not be achieved by conquest or force.[6] Lordship, then, was confined to those who possessed the grace of predestination (i.e. final perseverance) and so were eternally God's adoptive sons.[7] To those who lacked it no authority was given or obedience due.

Wyclif's doctrine of dominion and grace, for all its seeming inexorability, was singularly devoid of immediacy. To begin with, it was a special case of Wyclif's general theory of election and damnation as it concerned human society. But, of decisive importance, its practical consequences were reduced to nullity first by the impossibility of knowing who was damned and who was saved; and second because lay rulers were virtually exempt from it. If the unjust might rule well, if tyrants could be divinely approved, and if kings, as we have seen, were God's vicars who were to be unswervingly obeyed and only deposed by Christ,[8] to whom else was the test of legitimate rule to apply but to the church? And even here Wyclif was able to condemn it by the far more direct expedient of denying it any civil rights. Above all the bible provided him with the one universal and infallible criterion for judging any institution or man. It was one he used to the full. Hence the doctrine's ineffectiveness.

The eucharist

Lastly there was the eucharist. Here Wyclif's teachings, unlike those on dominion and grace, marked the culmination of his later thinking

[1] Ibid., 43–4. [2] Ibid., 24. [3] Ibid., 128–9.

[4] et sic gratia non est impertinens sed fundamentum dominii . . . sic, inquam, gratia requiritur ad usum, et per consequens ad omne verum dominium (ibid., 25); also ibid., 135.

[5] et per idem nemo potest servare dominium, uti divitiis, vel debite exequi ius humanum, sine evangelica lege regulante (ibid., 139).

[6] Ibid., 150.

[7] Iterum omnis existens in caritate predestinationis est, quandocunque habet gratiam dei, filius adoptivus (ibid., I, 47).

[8] *Dialogus* 72.

and the breaking point in his relations with the hierarchy; his withdrawal from Oxford in 1381 was the direct result of the condemnation of his eucharistic doctrine.[1] The question became almost compulsive for him in his last three or four years; in addition to being the subject of almost two complete books—*De eucharistia* and *De apostasia*—it recurred in all his later writings, especially *De blasphemia*, as the supreme test of orthodoxy, and received a special section running to over thirty printed pages in the *Trialogus*.[2] Moreover, again unlike the doctrine of dominion and grace, his final position grew directly out of his metaphysics. It could have been reached at any time within the previous fifteen or more years, from the period of his philosophical writings and his disputes with Kenningham. That it was not, is the sign of Wyclif's reluctance to pass beyond the bounds of orthodoxy; this is shown by his earlier attempts to seek other explanations than the final one. Thus, according to Woodford, he initially defined the substance of the eucharist as a mathematical body; and when this proved unsatisfactory he was prepared to leave it unexplained, merely averring that it had a substance.[3] As he recounted in *De eucharistia*, he had taken the utmost pains 'to explain transubstantiation in agreement with the sense of the early church' until he saw that it was contradicted by the modern church.[4] Or, put another way, Wyclif had subordinated his own doubts to the dogma of the church until he no longer trusted its authority. His change of view was a theological change; but when it came it carried with it the impetus of over fifteen years' delayed metaphysics. Hence the predominantly metaphysical arguments on an essentially theological issue.

The violence with which Wyclif put his case and attacked his enemies, above all in *De blasphemia* and the sermons,[5] tends to obscure the fact that his was but one more contribution to a debate in which all the participants shared the same fundamental belief: that the bread and the wine of the eucharist after consecration were transubstantiated into Christ's real presence. This remained as axiomatic for Wyclif as for his predecessors and opponents. On that point he was never heretical; his challenge was not to its truth but merely the explanation of how it

[1] Workman, II, 141; McFarlane, op. cit., 97–8.

[2] Ibid., 247 ff.

[3] Translated by Workman, II, 35 from FZ xv.

[4] Workman, ibid., from *De eucharistia* 52.

[5] E.g., *De blasphemia* 20–30, 244, 247–50, 252–4, 287, 288; *Sermons* III, 277–83, 286, 392, 445, 471, IV, 14–15; *Opus evangelicum* III, 142–3, 149–53; *Opera minora* 4–5, 210–14, 307–11.

occurred. This centred on the changed status of the bread and wine after they had become Christ's body. On the one hand, they were now of a different nature; on the other they still retained the outward appearance of their previous nature. In scholastic terminology the substance had changed into Christ's body but the accidents remained—those of bread and wine. The problem was how to explain the continuing appearance of the bread and wine with their disappearance as the underlying reality—*panitas* and *vinitas*; and more particularly the nature of these accidents divorced from their original substance.

Wyclif was confronted with two main explanations. That by St. Thomas who had said that these outward manifestations of the sacrament—the form, colour, movement and so on of the bread and wine—were maintained by quantity, through which they received physical extension. Quantity replaced the original substance of the bread as the force which kept the accidents physically in being. Hence after consecration the bread was no longer bread but in substance Christ's body and in appearance quantity.[1] The other explanation, by Duns Scotus and accepted by Ockham and his school, was the one with which Wyclif was principally concerned; it held that the substance of the bread and wine was annihilated to become Christ, the accidents remaining through God's omnipotence. Accordingly, the bread and wine, after being transubstantiated, became simply accidents upheld by God, while their substance was now Christ's body. The host therefore was Christ under the appearance of the bread and wine, which were by a miracle no longer such in reality, and for which there was no natural explanation.[2]

Both these solutions denied the continued existence of the bread as a substance after it had been consecrated. For St. Thomas nothing remained of its outward appearance save quantity; for Duns and Ockham it was an accident in a void. Wyclif denied both. Instead he affirmed the continuance of the bread and wine after consecration. They remained both as substance and as accident; appearance was also reality. In this way he brought the explanation back into accord with the two main tenets of his own metaphysics: namely, that there could be no accident without a substance, since, as we have seen, ultimately all being reflected an archetype or *esse intelligibile* without which nothing could be; and that essence was indestructible. Hence bread once in being could

[1] Summarized in Workman, II, 31–2 from Dziewicki's Introduction to *De apostasia* XV.

[2] Workman, II, 32–3.

not be annihilated; even when transubstantiated its own essence continued to coexist with the new substance which had been engendered. These formed the bases of Wyclif's case which he pressed with a wealth of repetition and citation in a succession of works.

For our purposes we may take as representative the views expressed in *De eucharistia*, *De apostasia* and the *Trialogus*. In the latter work he defined the sacrament as 'the body of Christ in the form of bread and wine'.[1] He thereby asserted the independent existence of the bread and wine as natural elements after consecration. In doing so he was combating two main heresies as he called them: that which said that, naturally, the elements of the host—the bread and wine—were mere accidents; and that which denied them any independent existence because they had been annihilated and replaced by Christ's body.[2] For Wyclif, on the contrary, if the bread and wine stood for Christ's body sacramentally, they must continue to exist as bread and wine naturally.[3] Against the first argument he rested his case upon the metaphysical impossibility of having accidents without substance.[4] An accident by definition belonged to a subject. God, far from being able to override their inherence, must sustain it because he could not permit contradiction.[5] Moreover, no accident could be understood except as part of a subject. As white signified the essence of whiteness so the accidents of the sacrament,[6] quantity, quality, relation, were not of themselves sufficient to stand alone but were sustained by the substance of the bread which they denoted.[7] The whiteness of the host represented the whiteness of the bread.[8] To stop at accidents would be the negation of all knowledge since men would then be at the mercy of their sense-impressions with no means of attaining to the reality beyond them.[9] Morally the case for independent accidents was equally mon-

[1] Et primo quod hoc sacramentum sit corpus Christi in forma panis (*Trialogus* 249). See also *De eucharistia* 29, 199; *De apostasia* 210.

[2] *Trialogus* 249.

[3] Ibid.

[4] E.g., *De apostasia* 48, 49–50, 55–60, 79–80, 84, 85–7, 89–90, 96, 111, 117, 120, 121, 129, 132–48, 151–5, 156–9, 160–3, 163–4, 165–8, 204.

De eucharistia 51, 52, 57, 64, 67, 71, 78, 100, 128, 132, 134, 199, 202, 213, 220–1, 280, 284.

Trialogus 254, 259, 261, 263, 265, 268, 269.

[5] *De apostasia* 111; *De eucharistia* 134.

[6] *De apostasia* 119–20.

[7] *De apostasia* 132–48; *De eucharistia* 133, 150, 199, 202; *Trialogus* 259, 261, 263, 265, 269.

[8] *De eucharistia* 202.

[9] *De apostasia*, 120; *De eucharistia* 78–80.

strous. If the visible signs of the host were accidents, to worship them would be the basest idolatry and the most abominable of all heresies.[1] It would be to make the bread and wine worthless and worse than poison.[2] To the prevalence of this attitude, which he blamed upon the friars, Wyclif attributed many of the current ills among the faithful.[3]

Against the second solution, which sought to subsume the bread entirely under Christ's body, Wyclif deployed a greater variety of arguments. They included the indestructibility of being, already mentioned, which although invoked far less than the subject/accident group was treated as decisive. To posit the annihilation of bread would also entail the annihilation of the world, since to destroy one part of it would be to destroy it all: an unthinkable course for God in whom all being resided.[4] The destruction of the bread being impossible, its assimilation to Christ's body was no more feasible: their incompatibility excluded the conversion of the form and substance of one into the other;[5] Wyclif viewed the attempt to identify them with disgust as well as moral outrage. To begin with, if Christ were physically within the host, the latter would be animated and behave like a man, which it did not.[6] In the second place it would be to commit the blasphemy of associating Christ's body with the corruptibility of the host's physical elements and so subject him to any physical indignities which it might undergo, such as the spilling of his blood through spilling the wine.[7] Thirdly, it would no less sacrilegiously mean that every time the priest broke the bread he would be breaking Christ's body, which he did not any more than an animal would be eating Christ if it were to eat the host.[8] Finally, for the same reason, the priest in celebrating the mass, did not make or consecrate the body of Christ but the sacrament, as the sign or garment of Christ;[9] to say otherwise would again be the height of blasphemy.

For these reasons Wyclif denied the current doctrine of the transubstantiation of the consecrated bread and wine into Christ's body, such that the former were replaced by the latter. He regarded it as a

[1] Quid queso maior abhominatio desolationis quam quod ex institutione Antichristi pendeant venerabiliter supra altare multe hostie consecrate . . . ? (*Trialogus* 268–9). See also, *De apostasia* 129; *Trialogus* 261, 263, 269; *De eucharistia* 14, 63, 284.

[2] *De apostasia* 172.

[3] E.g., *Trialogus* 261.

[4] *De apostasia* 99–100, 144–6; *De eucharistia* 129.

[5] *De eucharistia* 55; see also *Trialogus* 276–8.

[6] *De apostasia* 185–6.

[7] *De eucharistia* 22–4; *De apostasia* 186, *Trialogus* 271.

De eucharistia 11–13; *Trialogus* 272.

[9] *De eucharistia* 16.

violation of the original teaching of the early church; in support he invoked a host of authorities, even if the inferences he drew from their words would not have been theirs.[1] Two sources in particular he regarded as especially important. One was from Matthew 26 : 26 where Christ's words, 'This is my body', were taken by Wyclif as referring to the bread of the host.[2] The other was the decree of Nicholas II *Ego Berengarius*, of 1059, in which Berengarius abjuring his previous error stated: 'I believe that the bread and the wine placed on the altar after consecration are not only a sacrament but also the true body and blood of our Lord Jesus Christ.'[3] For Wyclif this implied that the bread and wine placed on the altar before consecration remained after it, so that it was then both a sacrament and the body of Christ.[4] The modern church had turned its back upon the truth of Berengarius's confession and in doing so had erred from the true path of tradition.[5] In this connexion Wyclif criticized Innocent III although he also sought Innocent's backing for his own view.[6] In taking up his position, then, Wyclif firmly believed that on this matter, as in every other on which he had views, it was he who was on the side of tradition and the present church which had lapsed from it. What, he asked, were the last 100 years compared with the thousand which had preceded them.[7] This conviction not only in the truth of his cause but in its accord with the saints and Apostles was undoubtedly one of the sources of Wyclif's buoyancy.

Granted, then, the independent existence of the bread (and wine) so that it was neither a mere accident nor anything but Christ's body, in what did its changed state lie? Here Wyclif was much more precise than some of his commentators have given him credit for.[8] Tran-

[1] In *De apostasia* chs. 15 and 16 are devoted to citing the testimony of 23 authorities. See his treatment of Hugh of St. Victor, *De eucharistia* 73–6.

[2] E.g., *Trialogus* 250, 251–2, 253, 257; *De apostasia* 48, 49–50, 180–2; *De eucharistia* 98–101, 114–16, 122, 126, 138, 150, 153, 154, 173, 296.

[3] *Decretum*, pt. III De Cons., d. II, ch. 42, Friedberg, I, 1328–9 and Mansi, vol. 19, 900.

[4] E.g., *De eucharistia* 30–1; also ibid., 110, 117, 125, 225, 226, 279, 307; *De apostasia* 68, 79, 108.

[5] *De eucharistia* 34.

[6] *De apostasia* 65, 134, 135, 172, 200, 234; *De eucharistia* 272–6.

[7] *De apostasia* 174.

[8] E.g., Workman, II, 36 and Matthew, quoted ibid. Workman's consideration of Wyclif's eucharistic theory suffers from the same defect which mars his treatments of Wyclif's thinking as a whole. Through lack of sympathy and/or understanding he never comes to grips with the nature of Wyclif's arguments, too often dismissing

substantiation he said was twofold: natural, where it meant the substitution of one form for another, the substance remaining the same, as when water became wine;[1] and supernatural, through a miraculous transformation of the subject, as when Christ, who was also God, became man.[2] Applied to the eucharist both aspects were involved. The bread remained; but to it was now added the body of Christ. The change came not in the destruction of the bread but in its coexistence with Christ.[3] Accordingly, the eucharist, like Christ, had a dual nature. In its earthly aspect it was bread; in its divine aspect it was Christ's body.[4] From this it followed that one could not be identified with the other essentially, substantially, corporeally or dimensionally.[5] Rather Christ was present in the host spiritually, or as he also expressed it in the *Trialogus*, as a habitude (*habitudinaliter*)[6] or an influence. There was no question of his being seen as a figure except in heaven;[7] within the host he was to be discerned spiritually as through a glass darkly, just as his body was to be taken and eaten in a spiritual sense.[8] For it was only through faith that it could be received.[9] Accordingly Christ was present in spirit in every host, throughout the churches of the world, without any physical or corporeal movement on his part; there was no question

---

them as hoary scholasticism. In consequence he does not go beyond superficial summary of his different tenets, which is a pity since he frequently sees their import without examining their structure.

[1] *De apostasia* 170. [2] Ibid.

[3] Corruptum autem non est fingendum nisi essentia panis secundum se totam destruatur . . . sufficit, inquam, ad illum motum miraculosum quod terminus a quo sit exclusio cuiuscunque corporis per datum locum preter nudam existentiam panis, et terminus ad quem sit principalitas existentie corporis Christi per eundem locum vel forma secundum quam panis denominatur formaliter esse corpus Christi (ibid., 210); also ibid., 180.

[4] Supponatur igitur . . . quod sicut Christus est due substantie, scilicet terrena et divina, sic hoc sacramentum est modo suo equivoco corpus panis sensibilis, qui de terra crevit, et corpus Christi quod verbum in Maria suscepit . . . sic quodammodo corpus panis, servando panis substantiam, est miraculose factum cum hoc corpus domini, non audeo dicere ydemptice secundum substantiam vel naturam, sed tropice secundum signantiam vel figuram; non tamen false et improprie dicitur corpus Christi, sed vere et proprie, sicut Christus vere et proprie dicit illum panem esse corpus suum (ibid., 106).

[5] Ibid., 103, 110, 213; *Trialogus* 270–2, 276, 278–9, 280; *De eucharistia* 19, 51–2, 230.

[6] sed corpus Christi non est identice quelibet pars quantitativa panis, sed habitudinaliter (*Trialogus* 276). See also preceding note.

[7] Ibid., 276.

[8] *De eucharistia* 13. [9] Ibid., 17.

of his descending from heaven and entering a church every time the eucharist was celebrated.[1] One host was distinguished from another as individuals of the same species;[2] they differed numerically because of the bread and wine.[3] From this it followed that the sacrament was to be taken at once as a sign for Christ in its natural form, and as other than a sign in its spiritual sense of being Christ's sacramental presence, where it was indiscernible.[4] Beyond saying that the bread became Christ's body sacramentally, while remaining bread naturally, Wyclif did not attempt to explain how the change took place[5] other than by a miracle.[6]

From this it can be seen that transubstantiation for Wyclif consisted not in any change to the bread in its natural state but in its conversion sacramentally, so that it both remained the same and became something new—Christ's body.[7] It was essentially a spiritual transformation which could only be felt as a spiritual, not a physical, presence.[8] That was Wyclif's final position, repeated in a variety of different ways but always returning to the same dual conception of the eucharist as naturally bread and wine and sacramentally Christ's body.[9]

However genuine Wyclif was in regarding this position as meta-

[1] Unde non oportet rem factam a deo secundum talem habituationem suum figuratum requirere ipsum figuratum moveri ad ipsam localiter, vel ex hinc realiter alterari. Ut non est intelligendum corpus Christi descendere ad hostiam in quacumque ecclesia consecratum, sed manet sursum in coelis stabile et immotum, ideo habet esse spirituale in hostia . . . (*Trialogus* 272). Also ibid., 267; *De eucharistia* 271.

[2] Ibid., 273.

[3] *De apostasia* 117.

[4] patet ex hoc quod alius est modus essendi signum corporis Christi et alius modus essendi vere et realiter, virtute verborum domini, corpus Christi (ibid., 223). This distinction explains Wyclif's previous distinction (ibid.) between *in signo* et *ut in signo* which puzzled Dziewicki (Introduction 24) but which Matthew explained without difficulty (Workman, II, 36). See also *De apostasia* 109, 182, 163. *De eucharistia* 109, 121; *Trialogus* 254.

[5] *De apostasia* 118.

[6] Teneamus ergo quod virtute verborum Christi panis ille fit et miraculose corpus Christi ultra possibilitatem signi ad hoc humanitus institui (ibid., 224).

[7] Tertia conclusio est ista: hoc sacramentum ex fide evangelii est naturaliter verus panis, et sacramentaliter ac veraciter corpus Christi . . . quia fideles satis sciunt quod panis virtute benedictionis Christi in melius, quia in corpus domini est conversus, et remanet panis, quia manet sacramentaliter ipsum corpus. Et si dicunt quod transsubstantiatur virtute verborum sacramentalium, placet mihi . . . (*Trialogus* 263–4). See also *De apostasia* 84, 184, 224.

[8] See his *Confession*, FZ 119.

[9] E.g., Ibid., 125.

physically and theologically ineluctable it had also more directly ecclesiological consequences. By locating the change to the host in the spiritual coming of Christ, rather than the physical disappearances of the bread, the role of the priest was correspondingly altered. Where previously his words of consecration had made the bread and wine into Christ's body, these now became the occasion, the efficacious sign (as he called it), of Christ's hidden presence.[1] Although Wyclif denied that it derogated from priestly power,[2] this was the outcome of making Christ's presence independent of human agency and physical change. Not surprisingly, then, his eucharistic teaching became one of the main hallmarks of his heresy, even though in the strict sense it was but another—if unorthodox—explanation of an accepted belief.

* * *

Ultimately, Wyclif's heresy, like any other, must be judged by its impact upon society. The question of what is potentially subversive—as in the case of dominion and grace—has to cede to what was regarded as such by contemporaries and successors. In Wyclif's case the issues were of two main kinds: theological and socio-political. Both were found together in the official condemnations, reflecting the different standpoints from which they considered. Wyclif's opponents being ecclesiastics and theologians, theological matters, like the eucharist, the sacraments and the church hierarchy, were of the first importance, in addition to those with political implications. To his Lollard followers, often semi-literate or illiterate, his message was more direct and concerned the church's wealth and abuse of privileges. Each, however, represented different aspects of the same problem—of the church—which was made the focal point of his doctrine. It was his chief legacy. The myriad topics he had raised, and the scholastic refinements with which he had treated them, became for the wider world distilled into a comprehensive anti-sacerdotalism; whatever the criterion employed—metaphysical, practical, moral or theological—the cumulative effect of Wyclif's teaching was as a condemnation of the visible church in its existing state. This made him not only a heretic, in effectively denying the church as it stood a *raison d'être*, but an heresiarch in inspiring others, however dimly they perceived his theoretical reasons, to demand its disendowment and disestablishment.

Wyclif had begun by investing God with all true being and power; the created world was but the reflexion of the true being in God; its

[1] *De eucharistia* 15–16, 123, 143–4. [2] Ibid., 15.

individuals the transitory realization of their eternal archetypes; and its attributes, time, space, extension and so on, the accidents which accompanied them until they returned once more to the ideas whence God had realized them. The process only escaped being cyclical through the intervention of God's will.[1] Nevertheless the archetype in God became the reality and the actual world a fleeting arena. When applied to the church it transferred its true body to the elect, eternally chosen by God, and left nothing by which they could be recognized here on earth. This passage from heterodoxy to heresy became complete when the visible church, denuded of identity, was systematically divested of authority for failing to conform to the one palpable criterion of God's word expressed in the bible. In the end pope and hierarchy were Antichrist; and Christ, had he returned to earth, would have been burned as a heretic.[2] The true priests were the elect, and, in default of their final revelation, any man inspired by God's word could be considered an Apostle. Scriptural truth and the apostolic tradition had supplanted the visible church; these for Wyclif were the true mediators to which all believers must turn. We must now trace the effects upon those who did so.

[1] See the suggestive article by B. Smalley, 'The Bible and Eternity: John Wyclif's dilemma' *Journal of Warburg and Courtauld Institutes*, vol. 27 (1964) 73–89, where Wyclif's outlook is compared to Plotinus rather than St. Augustine.

[2] In tantum quod si Christus prelatus incognitus visiteret peregrine prelatos istius ecclesie presentia corporali . . . est evidens quod excommunicarent eum in curia Romana et nisi veritatem revocare voluerit, condempnarent eum ad ignem tamquam hereticum et blasfemam (*De blasphemia* 62).

VIII

The Lollards

Lollardy is the outstanding example in the later middle ages of popular heresy as the direct outcome of learned heresy. Wyclif had already travelled the path from heterodoxy to dissent; and what he transmitted to his followers was dissent ready-made. Its subsequent evolution as Lollardy made it more extreme and violent. It moved farther and farther away from Wyclif's outlook so that he would have certainly disowned it by the time of Oldcastle's rising in 1414,[1] if not before, as he had denounced the violence of the Peasants' Revolt in 1381.[2] Nevertheless he was its progenitor, and its inception, though not its subsequent development, was from him.

This is not to say that Wyclif founded the Lollards as a movement; only a social revolutionary, which Wyclif was not, would have done that. The word Lollard, as we have already seen from the Beghards and Beguines, was a term of abuse, meaning originally a mumbler.[3] It was first applied to Wyclif's followers by Henry Crump in 1382, for which he was censured.[4] Since Wyclif's doctrine of the eucharist was at the centre of these charges of heresy against him, it became one of the hallmarks of Lollardy; and at Oxford the Lollard cause was fought and lost over it.[5] But Lollardy also came to comprise Wyclif's fierce anti-sacerdotalism without the nuances of thought with which he had invested it. The emphasis of the Lollards was predominantly moral and practical: upon righteous living, voluntary tithes, and disendowment. The learned advocacy of the Oxford schoolman was translated into the vernacular of the poor preachers who formed the Lollard cadres. How this happened and with what effects we have now to consider.

[1] See pp. 599 ff. below.

[2] *De blasphemia* 189–99, 267–9.

[3] See p. 319 n. 2 above.

[4] FZ 312; McFarlane considers that it was 'in process of slow formation after 1379', after his eucharistic doctrine (100–1). The earliest official use of the word was, according to Mrs. M. E. Aston, 'Lollardy and Sedition, 1381–1431', *Past and Present*, 17 (1960) 36 n.1, by the bishop of Worcester in 1387.

[5] The central part played by the eucharist in Oxford Lollardy no doubt accounts for its over-emphasis by McFarlane, loc. cit., in Wyclif's heresy.

We must begin with Oxford, where the heresy originated under Wyclif's influence. Because Wyclif escaped Hus's fate and died a communicant, of a stroke instead of at the stake, there has been a tendency to magnify his immunity during his own lifetime. In fact, as we have seen, he had to face two prosecutions and three condemnations between 1377 and 1382; and he was probably only saved from more by a unique combination of circumstances which would not recur: his own high-placed connexions and the absence of anti-heretical machinery in England at that time. Even so, had he not retired to Lutterworth but attempted to teach at Oxford what he was writing there in the last three years of his life, he would certainly have been banned and probably imprisoned. Indeed, his very presence would have earned him prosecution in an Oxford by then largely purged of Lollards. Accordingly, the attack upon Wyclif became the prelude to a general offensive against Lollardy by archbishop Courtenay, first at Oxford and then on its strongholds in the country at large.

The condemnations of Wyclif and Oxford Lollardy

Gregory XI's condemnation of nineteen articles taken from *De civili dominio* in 1377 gave the church a legacy upon which it continued to draw long after his death. Five of the censured propositions concerned civil dominion, and in his letters to the English authorities the pope emphasized the subversive implications of Wyclif's doctrines for all government, comparing them with those of Marsilius of Padua and John of Jandun.[1] Since dominion and grace formed the subject of a great part of the work from which the articles were taken, the attention given to it by the pope is not surprising. But it continued to be made a central tenet of Wyclif's teaching after it had been effectively superseded in his own thinking. As we have seen, on the one hand, from *De ecclesia* onwards the disqualification of those in mortal sin from lordship was confined almost exclusively to the church hierarchy. On the other, in *De officio regis* and after, Wyclif expressly exempted the king, and by implication the lay lords, from any challenge to their authority: they were needed to disendow and reform the church. Theory had ceded to pragmatism and had been duly modified. Nevertheless ecclesiastical writers continued to try to haunt the government with the spectre of social revolution first raised by Gregory XI. In the event they appeared to frighten themselves more than laymen. After the Peasants'

[1] FZ 243.

Revolt in 1381, in particular, ecclesiastical writers saw the hand of Wyclif and his followers everywhere. The monastic author of the *Chronicon Angliae* blamed the outbreak upon the failure of the church authorities to curb their eucharistic heresy which had infected the populace; and another anonymous chronicler attributed the cause of the insurrection to Lollard preaching.[1] Moreover John Ball, 'the half-crazed hedge priest',[2] who had helped to instigate it, was widely treated as the disciple of Wyclif whose doctrine he was regarded as having propagated:[3] in fact, there was no connexion between them; Ball had a long record of religious disaffection going back to the time of archbishop Islip who had excommunicated him.[4]

The church's fear of Wyclif's and the Lollards' doctrines was of course well-founded; it was its attempt to extend this fear to the lay power which, for many years, was not. While the Lollards continued for a generation and more after Wyclif to preach church reform and to look upon the state as the indispensable ally in attaining it, ecclesiastics did not cease to give warning lest what had begun as an attack upon the church should end in the destruction of all lordship and wealth. It is significant that in the thirty years from Wyclif's death in 1384 to Oldcastle's rebellion in 1414 mention of civil dominion came from the side of the church, not the Lollards.[5] Only when a combination of despair and adventurism, for which there is no evidence that the main inspiration was even Lollard, finally turned a small group to outright rebellion, did the movement become actually implicated in sedition and some of its adherents a threat to state as well as church.

Accordingly, we have to recognize the exaggerated importance given to Wyclif's doctrine of dominion and grace both in the condemnations

[1] *Chronicon Angliae* 310–11; also FZ 272–3. The question of the political consequences of Lollardy is examined by M. E. Aston, art. cit., 1–44. To her account and that of McFarlane's in *John Wycliffe*, I owe much of what follows in this chapter. Unfortunately J. A. F. Thompson's *The Later Lollards 1414–1520* appeared too late for me to use. But he has now unquestionably established the survival of the Lollards into the sixteenth century, and hence the continuity with Lollardy at the Reformation.

[2] McFarlane, op. cit., 72.

[3] *Chronicon Angliae* 321; FZ 73; T. Walsingham, *Historia Anglicana* II, 32.

[4] Workman, II, 238. See also McFarlane, 100.

[5] E.g., The dominican Roger Dymok's reply to the Lollard Twelve Articles of 1395 in *Rogeri Dymmok Liber contra XII errores et hereses Lollardorum* (ed H. S. Cronin) WS 278; and Woodford's refutation of 18 censured in 1395 in Brown *Fasciculus* I, 231. Aston, art. cit., 9. See also Arundel's reply to William Thorpe in Foxe *Acts and Monuments* I (1684) 612 (quoted in Aston, art. cit., 11).

and denunciations of his own writings and of Lollard teachings. The strongly anti-ecclesiastical bias in Wyclif's thought can be seen clearly, even in Gregory XI's list of nineteen[1] censured articles. Of the five devoted to dominion and grace, the first three rejected perpetual dominion for a man or his heirs on earth;[2] the fourth confined true lordship to those finally in God's grace;[3] and the fifth restricted human authority to acting for God (*ministratorie*).[4] Their tenor was thus to deny true lordship in this world through inheritance or any human agency. The remaining articles were all directed against the church. The sixth empowered lay lords to confiscate its property if it failed to fulfil its spiritual office;[5] and the last three asserted the subjection of all ecclesiastics from the pope downwards to the lay power.[6] The other nine all derogated from papal authority. Eight of them denied the pope the power of excommunication under three main heads: that true power resided with God alone;[7] that a man was only excommunicate if he himself was the principal cause by cutting himself off from Christ's law;[8] and that its ban could not be imposed by the pope independently or for temporal ends.[9] Only God had the power of binding and loosing, which took place in heaven not on earth. Finally, as the obverse to these restrictions on the pope, article fourteen held that any priest, whatever his grade, could administer the sacraments and absolve: a position which Wyclif was later to qualify, and indeed deny, as we have seen.

Five articles qualifying the absoluteness of civil dominion, then, hardly suffice to outweigh fourteen denying ecclesiastical power in theory and practice and setting it under lay control. The discrepancy between them, already considerable, increased as time went on.

From the outset, the charges against Wyclif, despite the pope's admonitions to the king to beware, were essentially theological and ecclesiological. They concerned the fitness of the church to be God's mediator on earth. This element was greatly accentuated by Wyclif's

[1] The articles are printed in Walsingham, I, 353–5, where they number nineteen (the punctuation of the first is faulty), Wilkins, III, 123, which also contains nineteen, and FZ 245–57, where eighteen of them are defended. The last version has been followed here.

[2] FZ 245–7. [3] Ibid., 247. [4] Ibid., 247–8.

[5] Ibid., 248–9. In Walsingham and Wilkins the seventh article (omitted in FZ) is made the corollary to sixth, giving the lay lords power to decide whether the church should be disendowed.

[6] XVI, XVII, XVIII FZ 254–7. [7] IX, X, XIV, ibid., 250–1, 253.

[8] VIII, X, ibid., 250–1. [9] VII, XI, XII, XIII.

two subsequent condemnations, at Oxford in 1381 and Blackfriars in 1382; for the eucharist now came to the forefront, and henceforth remained as one of the badges of Lollardy. Wyclif's censure by Barton's commission at Oxford[1] was concerned exclusively with the eucharist, as we have said. It centred on two points. The first was Wyclif's contention that the bread and wine remained bread and wine after consecration as before; and second that, conversely, Christ's body was only present in the host figuratively and not essentially, substantially or corporeally.[2] The commission reversed this order, to make the bread and wine present only in their species or appearances and Christ's body present in the host truly and corporeally (*ibi veraciter et in sua propria presentia corporali*).[3] Reduced to these essentials, in which it was henceforth to recur, Wyclif's eucharistic teaching was solemnly banned,[4] by a narrow margin of 7 votes to 5,[5] which may well have reflected doubts about its heretical nature.

Between Barton's commission and the Blackfriars synod of 17 May 1382, came the Peasants' Revolt. Its occurrence no doubt accounts for the speed with which Courtenay acted in summoning the council only eleven days after he had become archbishop of Canterbury in succession to Sudbury, murdered by the rebels.[6] Wyclif, although he had left Oxford, was more vociferous than ever. *De blasphemia*, probably published in March 1382, was his most violent outburst yet, with an attack upon the twelve orders of the church.[7] Then on 7 May he addressed a seven-point appeal to parliament calling for resistance to the pope and action against the church, including the taking of church endowments, to save taxing the poor, and the non-employment of ecclesiastics in government.[8] In Oxford tension had been rising between the seculars, who included many of Wyclif's followers, and the religious. In February 1382, the heads of the four mendicant houses appealed to John of Gaunt to take action against Nicholas Hereford,

[1] Printed in FZ 110–14. A list of twelve conclusions by Wyclif, probably drawn from his writings, is printed, ibid., 105–6, together with three publicly preached by him. The first two of these (the third is that there are no accidents without a subject) were those examined and condemned by Barton's commission; there is nothing to say, as Workman, II, 141 does, that the commission had these twelve articles before it, or that the commission was packed, ibid., 142.

[2] Ibid., 110. [3] Ibid., 111. [4] Ibid., 111–12.

[5] According to Wyclif, *De blasphemia* 89.

[6] For the Peasants' Revolt see Workman, II, 221–45.

[7] Workman, II, 249–50.

[8] Walsingham, II, 51–2; McFarlane, 105; Workman, II, 250–1.

one of Wyclif's leading Oxford disciples, whom they accused of stirring up trouble together with his accomplices.[1] There seems to have been no reply; and shortly afterwards, on the first Sunday in Lent, Hereford, preaching before the university in Latin, challenged the right of the religious to take degrees in the university. The protests of two of them, John Wells, a monk, and Peter Stokes, a Carmelite—whose letters to Courtenay are the main source for the subsequent events in Oxford—went unheeded. For, by then, Richard Rigg, a secular, was chancellor of the university, and favoured the Lollards.[2] Hereford does not seem to have confined himself to attacking the friars; he is also reported to have said that Sudbury had been killed justly because he had wished to punish Hereford's master, Wyclif.[3]

Another of Wyclif's Oxford disciples, and the most recent, Philip Repton, or Repingdon, had at about the same time endorsed Wyclif's eucharistic theology in a sermon at Brackley in Northamptonshire.[4] The other prominent member of the group, John Aston, does not appear until after Courtenay began his proceedings.[5] Finally Wyclif himself, despite his retirement to Lutterworth, continued to excite contention. His *Confession* drew a number of replies, of which two, by John Tissingham, a Franciscan and a member of Barton's commission of twelve, and Thomas Winterton,[6] an Augustinian, are extant.[7] Winterton's in particular was of a high intellectual order; but more than arguments were needed if the Lollards were to be checked. The time had come for official action, and Courtenay provided it.

Included among the thirty-six graduates in theology who attended the Blackfriars synod on 17 May were seventeen doctors. Not one of them was a secular; sixteen were friars, and one a monk.[8] This over-

[1] FZ 292. [2] Ibid., 305. [3] Ibid., 296. [4] Ibid.

[5] For a list of them and accounts of their careers see McFarlane, op. cit., 102–3 and passim; Workman, II, 130 ff., and especially A. B. Emden, *A biographical Register of the University of Oxford until A.D. 1500*, 3 vols. John Purvey, Wyclif's secretary and companion of his last years at Lutterworth, has left no trace at Oxford, despite Netter's description of him as a noted doctor (*Doctrinale* I, 619, quoted in Workman, II, 137; McFarlane, 119). His association by Workman (II, 130, 137) with Hereford and Repton as the leaders of the Oxford Lollards should therefore be treated with reserve.

[6] FZ 133–80.

[7] Ibid., 181–238. Two other unnamed monks, one from Durham and one from St. Albans, as well as Barton, are given among Wyclif's other opponents (ibid., 241). There is also an extract from John Wells's *De religione perfectorum* (ibid., 239–41). For an account of Wyclif's earlier opponents see Workman, II, 119 ff.

[8] Names in Wilkins, III, 158; FZ 286–8; Workman, II, 260; McFarlane, 106.

whelming preponderance of religious indicates Courtenay's determination to crush the Lollards. Twenty-four articles from Wyclif's teaching were condemned, ten as heretical and fourteen as erroneous.[1] Of the first group, three concerned the eucharist, two in the form already stated by Barton's commission: namely that after consecration the bread continued to exist substantially and Christ was present only figuratively;[2] the third rejected accidents without a substance.[3] The next three dealt with the sacraments: the fourth denied sacramental power to a priest in mortal sin; the fifth the value of oral confession; the sixth scriptural authority for the mass. The seventh, that 'God should obey the devil', was Wyclif's paradoxical way of stressing the virtue of obedience for itself. Initially in *De civili dominio* it extended to prelates,[4] who whether good or bad, should be obeyed as Christ had obeyed Pilate and Judas. But as employed in *De officio regis* it became the basis for royal supremacy.[5] Hence, apart from the article's blasphemous form, it may well have been condemned also for stressing secular lordship. Propositions eight and nine were directed against the papacy; no one damned or in sin could exercise spiritual power and after Urban VI there should be no further allegiance to a pope.[6] The tenth and last heretical proposition was that the church should not have temporal possessions.

Of the fourteen errors, three were on excommunication, the third of which denounced its use against appeals to the king and government.[7] Two treated the permissibility of unlicensed preaching.[8] The sixteenth proposition said that there could be no civil or ecclesiastical lordship for anyone in mortal sin. The seventeenth and eighteenth empowered lay lords to deprive unworthy priests of their possessions and parishioners to withhold tithes, since they were pure alms. The nineteenth rejected special prayers. The last five denounced the religious orders as unfitting for the worship of God,[9] sinful[10] and unchristian,[11] and condemned begging instead of labouring;[12] to support them with alms was to render both donor and recipient excommunicate.[13]

All Wyclif's[14] most explosive tenets were included here. It will be

[1] Wilkins, III, 157–8; FZ 277–82. [2] I and III.
[3] II. [4] III, 40. [5] *De officio regis* 193. [6] IX.
[7] XIII: that the priest who excommunicated a cleric for appealing to the king was a traitor to God and to the realm. [8] XIV and XV.
[9] XX. [10] XXI. [11] XXII. [12] XXIII. [13] XXIV.
[14] It will be recalled that Wyclif was not mentioned. The articles were not finally ratified until 21 May at the same time as an earth tremor shook England. Hence the name 'Earthquake Council', given ironically by Wyclif, *Trialogus* 274.

seen that those treated as heretical were exclusively theological and ecclesiological, headed by the eucharist, whereas the question of dominion was relegated to the errors. This shift in emphasis away from Gregory XI's list is borne out by what followed. Courtenay, having obtained the comprehensive condemnation of Wyclif's teaching, in fact if not in name, sought royal support to apply it against Lollardy. He first persuaded the king to add an ordinance to the statute just passed by parliament—but too late for it to be debated—for the arrest of Lollards and unlicensed preachers. A month later this was simplified by an order from the king empowering the ecclesiastical authorities to arrest and hold any fautors of Lollardy either in their own prisons or those of the king's officers until such time as they abjured their errors or the Council should itself have acted.[1] But, by then, already armed with the Blackfriars condemnation and royal support, Courtenay had turned his attention to Oxford.

Matters there had come to a head with the summoning of the Blackfriars synod. First Hereford, on Ascension day (16 May), and then Repton on Corpus Christi (5 June), had been chosen by Rigg to preach the university sermon. Both made it the occasion for a full-fledged defence of Wyclif's teachings. Hereford spoke in English before a large gathering of townsfolk and was described as 'inciting them to insurrection'.[2] Repton's sermon was delivered on the very day on which Courtenay had ordered Peter Stokes to promulgate the Blackfriars decrees.[3] Before the chancellor and the proctors he proclaimed the truth of Wyclif's doctrines, especially his eucharistic teaching and the subordination of the pope and prelates to temporal lords. He also claimed that the Lollards had John of Gaunt's support[4]—an assertion soon to be tested and found wanting. According to Stokes, Rigg had not only refused to assist him carry out Courtenay's orders;[5] but on the day when they should have been published he sat and applauded Repton's sermon, and at the end of it had left the church together with him smiling.[6] No wonder the Lollards were pleased.[7]

But it was not for long. Although Rigg continued to prevaricate,

[1] Wilkins, III, 156; Workman, II, 269; McFarlane, 107.

[2] FZ 296, 306. A list of 9 propositions attributed to him shows that he followed Wyclif in all essential points and regarded his teaching as free from heresy or falsehood (ibid., 303–4).

[3] FZ 297. He had also on 30 May written to Rigg enjoining him to assist Stokes and expressing disapproval of the favour shown to Hereford (ibid., 298–9).

[4] FZ 297, 299–300, 307.

[5] Ibid., 306–7. [6] Ibid., 307. [7] Ibid., 300.

the next day telling Stokes that he must first gain the university's assent to the Blackfriars decrees,[1] two days later, on 8 June, he was himself awaiting the archbishop's pleasure in London. Whether he went of his own volition or was summoned is not known;[2] but he, together with Brightwell, suspected of Lollard views, continued to wait for four days until Stokes, who meanwhile claimed to have gone in fear of his life, should arrive to give evidence.[3] On 12 June the synod reconvened to consider seven charges against Rigg of having given comfort to the Lollards.[4] He made no attempt to resist, accepting the synod's decision on the twenty-four condemned articles and begging Courtenay's pardon on his knees for having treated his letters with contempt. In response to Wykeham's plea the archbishop forgave him.[5] He then commanded Rigg to publish the twenty-four articles at Oxford, to protect those like Stokes, who had loyally helped the archbishop, and to ban from preaching and disputation Wyclif, Hereford, Repton, Aston and Bedeman until they should have abjured their heresy, together with any others found harbouring the same opinions.[6] Rigg's protestations of fear at the outcome were overridden.[7] The next day the Council endorsed Courtenay's mandate.[8] The chancellor duly complied, with the results he had foreseen. On Sunday, 15 June, publication of the decrees at Oxford led to renewed dissension between seculars and regulars. Hereford and Repton, on hearing that they were to be suspended, went immediately to seek out Gaunt, whom they found at Tottenhall near London. Any initial success they may have had with the duke was soon counteracted by the arrival the following day of a group of doctors from Oxford. After hearing both sides Gaunt pronounced the Lollards' views on the eucharist detestable.[9]

[1] Ibid., 301.

[2] McFarlane, 108, says Rigg went to forestall Courtenay's resentment.

[3] FZ 304. Stokes was summoned by Courtenay on 8 June (ibid., 302).

[4] FZ 304–8.

[5] Ibid., p. 308. Brightwell took longer before he too accepted the articles, Wilkins, III, 159.

[6] FZ 309–11.

[7] Failure of the university to comply, Courtenay declared, would make it an accomplice of heresy (ibid., 311).

[8] Ibid. The measure of government support for Courtenay can also be seen in a letter from the king to the university at about the same time ordering the reinstatement of Henry Crump, an Irish Cistercian, and a member of the Blackfriars synod, who had been suspended for calling Hereford's party Lollards. It also forbade Stokes or Stephen Patrington to be molested (ibid., 314–17). For Patrington see Workman, II, 247 ff. It was his collection of documents on the Lollards which formed the basis of Netter's history later incorporated into the FZ: ibid., lxxvii.

[9] FZ 318–19.

This was the turning point. Deprived of Gaunt's protection, the Lollards' resistance collapsed. They obeyed him and went to the archbishop; on 18 June they appeared at Blackfriars accompanied by Aston.[1] Presented with the twenty-four condemned propositions, Hereford and Repton asked for a day to deliberate; Aston expressed his willingness to answer at once, but returned the same non-committal reply to all of them. Courtenay accordingly prohibited him from preaching in the Canterbury province and ordered him to appear again together with Hereford and Repton on 20 June.[2] The replies of the latter were heard first.[3] While accepting the heretical nature of all twenty-four condemned propositions, they were sufficiently sophistical for the archbishop to order further examination. This resulted in their replies to four articles—three on transubstantiation and one on Christ's obligation to obey the devil—being pronounced heretical, and three others—on excommunication, special prayers and mendicancy—erroneous.[4] Sentence was deferred for a week. When it came to Aston, he faced the further charge of having circulated copies of his confession devoted to the question of the eucharist—which he and Hereford had both drawn up—among Londoners on the previous day.[5] This did not deter him from attempting once more to rouse them by speaking in English and refusing to keep to the point. His insolence and evasion only gained him immediate imprisonment[6] and his confession a reply from the clergy on the same subject of transubstantiation.[7]

To avoid further disorders Courtenay now transferred the proceedings first to Oxford, on 27 June, and then to Canterbury on 1 July.[8] At Oxford, Hereford and Repton had been joined by a third suspect from Oxford, Thomas Hilman of Merton; but only he answered Courtenay's summons and appeared at Canterbury, where he duly recanted and was absolved. Hereford and Repton, for their disobedience, were excommunicated.[9] They at once appealed to Rome, and, ever playing to the crowd, put up notices of having done so at St. Paul's and Mary le Bow. Courtenay replied by repeating the sentence with bell, book and candle at St. Paul's;[10] numerous mandates to seize them were sent to Oxford and elsewhere.[11] These included letters from the

[1] FZ 289. For what follows see Wilkins, III, 160–4.
[2] Wilkins, III, 161.
[3] Wilkins, III, 161–2; FZ 319–25.
[4] Wilkins, III, 162–3; FZ 327–9, and 290.
[5] FZ 329–30.
[6] Wilkins, III, 163–4; FZ 290.
[7] FZ 331.
[8] Wilkins, III, 164–5; FZ 290–1.
[9] Wilkins, 165.
[10] Ibid.
[11] Ibid., 165–8.

king on 12 July ordering an inquisition into the errors and heresies of Wyclif, Hereford, Repton and Aston to be held throughout the university within seven days. Their adherents were to be expelled and the writings of Wyclif and Hereford confiscated and despatched to the archbishop.[1]

Within a matter of months Repton and Aston, as well as Laurence Steven (*alias* Bedeman), had submitted. Bedeman was the first to do so;[2] and the day after his suspension from Oxford had been lifted by Courtenay, on 21 October, Repton abjured before the archbishop and his council at Blackfriars; he was also restored to Oxford.[3] In the following month Courtenay's victory was complete, when, having called the meeting of the Canterbury convocation for Oxford, Aston also recanted[4] and Repton repeated his previous abjuration.[5] A commission was also set up to investigate the teaching of all members of the university,[6] and a last attempt to charge Stokes and Crump with heresy squashed,[7] as was Lollardy at Oxford. Henceforth Repton rose rapidly in the service of the church to become successively abbot of the Austin canons at Leicester, his own house, in 1393; chancellor of his university in 1404; and bishop of Lincoln shortly after, in which capacity he saved Wyclif's remains from the violation ordered by the Council of Constance.[8] Aston's restless nature soon broke out again, as we shall see, but never within the precincts of Oxford, nor did Hereford, who alone journeyed to Rome and remained at large until 1391,[9] ever again involve Oxford with his heresies.

How earnestly the university had taken Courtenay's lesson to heart can be seen from the case of Henry Crump. Condemned for heresy in Ireland for attacking the friars, he returned to Oxford only to find himself suspended and brought before Courtenay and a council at Stamford where he was made to abjure.[10] Even allowing for a solitary article on the eucharist, described as the mirror of Christ's body,[11] there was nothing of the Lollard about Crump. But pressure to conform tends invariably to make an issue out of any disagreement; differences come to be treated as symptoms of dissent thereby engendering the very disaffection which is feared.

[1] FZ 312–14. [2] Wykeham's Register, II, 343–52; Wilkins, III, 168.
[3] Wilkins, III, 169.
[4] Ibid.; FZ 331–3 for the account of how he was convinced on the eucharist.
[5] Ibid., 172. [6] Ibid. [7] Ibid.
[8] McFarlane, 114, 120. [9] Ibid., 126–9.
[10] FZ 343–59. Summarized in Workman, II, 292–3. [11] FZ 353.

In Oxford, although Lollardy never seriously raised its head again, after 1382, a final crisis occurred in 1411 under Arundel, who succeeded Courtenay as archbishop of Canterbury in 1396. Even so, the issue was not Lollardy but the university's privileges. The trouble dated back to the previous year, 1395, when the university, in answer to its petition to the pope, received from Boniface IX a bull exempting it from all episcopal jurisdiction. This applied even when the archbishop was also the pope's legate.[1] In February 1397, at Arundel's first convocation of Canterbury as archbishop, members of the university representing the faculties of canon and civil law denounced the rights granted by Boniface;[2] but they were not upheld by the university which in the following month sought to keep its new-found gains.[3] Arundel then turned to the king who decreed that the university should renounce the privileges recently obtained, on pain of losing all its others.[4] He then followed this by reaffirming Arundel's right, as archbishop, to visit the university.[5] Arundel had won, although his own impeachment in the same year, and Richard II's subsequent deposition in 1399, for a time put an end to further developments. When they were resumed, under the new dynasty of Henry IV, the archbishop's personal position had been greatly strengthened. The occasion for Arundel's renewed activity was the resurgence of Lollardy. With its larger manifestations we are not immediately concerned, but they included widespread unauthorized preaching. In order to combat this, Arundel in 1407 drew up thirteen constitutions, which he presented first at a provincial synod at Oxford in November 1407[6] and then in the January convocation at St. Paul's, 1408.[7] The first three were directed against unlicensed preaching;[8] the fourth and the fifth concerned false doctrines on the sacraments;[9] the sixth banned the reading and teaching of all Wyclif's works unless previously examined and passed by at least twelve masters of the universities of Oxford and Cambridge and confirmed by the archbishop;[10] the seventh prohibited unauthorized translations of the bible into English.[11] The remainder principally concerned matters of procedure,

[1] Printed in *Snappe's Formulary* (ed. H. E. Salter) Oxford 1924, 144–6; Wilkins III, 227.

[2] Snappe, 146–51.

[3] Ibid., 151–3.

[4] Ibid., 153–5.

[5] Ibid., 155–6.

[6] 6th and 11th constitutions are printed ibid., 115–16. For a résumé of the events at Oxford from 1407 to 1411, ibid., 101–15.

[7] Wilkins, III, 314–19.

[8] Ibid., 315–16.

[9] Ibid., 316–17.

[10] Ibid., 317; Snappe 115.

[11] Wilkins, ibid.

except for the eleventh constitution which was crucial for the university. This provided for a monthly enquiry by all heads of houses, colleges, hostels and halls into the opinions of their inhabitants and for measures to be taken against any scholars or masters suspected of heresy, as well as those negligent in dealing with offenders.[1]

Constitutions six and eleven have usually been read in conjunction with one another, as indeed they should, since they impinged directly upon Oxford's intellectual life. Yet of the two, the eleventh was the more disruptive. Although there is little to choose between the demerits of censorship and inquisition, the former had long been an established element of Oxford, as of Paris, life, going back to at least 1277.[2] Moreover, since the Blackfriars condemnation, Wyclif's works, with those of Hereford, and sometimes Purvey and Aston, had been repeatedly banned. But this was the first time that a regular machinery of enquiry had been set in train; even Arundel seems to have been impressed by the momentousness of the occasion, for he prefaced the constitution with a long apologia stressing the need to defend the true faith from subversion. In the event it became a dead letter just as the commission of twelve did; but the latter, however troublesome an issue it was to prove, did at least leave a monument behind in the list of 267 condemned propositions which it drew up from its enquiry into Wyclif's writings.

The causes of Arundel's suspicions were of long standing. As early as 1395 the king had ordered Oxford to expel all Lollards under Robert Lechlade and for an enquiry to be made into the *Trialogus*;[3] but this was part of the general alert against them, following the publication of the Twelve Conclusions in that year.[4] There is no evidence of an independent Lollard movement in the university. More recently, in 1406, William Taylor, principal of St. Edmund's Hall, Oxford, preaching at St. Paul's Cross, had attacked temporal possessions by religious and upheld the right of lay lords to dispossess them when circumstances warranted.[5] In the same year there had been the notorious case of Peter Payne, who had sent a eulogy of Wyclif, purporting to be from the university and

[1] Ibid., 318–19.

[2] When Robert Kildwardby, archbishop of Canterbury, condemned 30 propositions associated with Aristotle and St. Thomas. See the writer's *Medieval Thought* 230.

[3] *Calendar of Close Rolls*, 1392–6, 434 and 437. For a discussion of the 19 articles taken from the *Trialogus* see p. 585 below.

[4] See pp. 584 ff. below.

[5] A. B. Emden, *An Oxford Hall in Medieval Times* (Oxford 1927) 125–33. Quoted in Aston, art. cit., 18.

bearing its common seal, to Prague.[1] Although Payne was a Lollard he subsequently became principal of St. Edmund's Hall before fleeing the country in 1413 for Prague.[2] These were isolated cases, but they appeared to have been enough to re-ignite Arundel's suspicions. What followed[3] was a much more heavy-handed attempt to repeat Courtenay's triumph of gaining the university's subsmission—this time to the constitutions. But from the first the university was adamant. The committee of twelve to enquire into Wyclif's writings was not appointed until 1409,[4] and its work proceeded slowly; there was opposition to its election, and one of the proctors, John Birch, tried to have it disbanded.[5] Matters were further complicated by charges of heresy against Richard Fleming, one of the twelve:[6] despite Arundel's unsolicited intervention and his citing of four other masters,[7] Fleming was finally cleared by a committee of eight established on the orders of the king to whom Fleming had appealed.[8] Finally, in March 1411, a list of 267 of Wyclif's errors was sent to Arundel and the Canterbury convocation.[9] From there they were forwarded to the pope.[10] In February 1413 Wyclif's writings were condemned at a Lateran Council[11] and it seems probable that previously in 1410 a number of Wyclif's errors had been censured in Oxford and his works burned.[12]

Arundel in order to have the ban on the condemned articles enforced, now appointed five members of the university to administer an oath of loyalty.[13] The university protested to the king[14] and threatened the archbishop with excommunication for breaking his oath taken as a member of the university.[15] But he was not deterred, and in August he advanced on Oxford where he had requisitioned the church of St. Mary for his visitation.[16] He had, however, to break it open before he could enter.[17]

[1] Workman, II, 347–55; McFarlane, 156–8.

[2] where he subsequently took an active part in the Hussite movement. He appeared at the Council of Basel in 1433 when he debated with his old Oxford confrère in Lollardy, William Partridge (Workman, II, 352). According to Workman (ibid., 354) he seems to have died in prison in Prague in 1456 faithful to Wyclif's teachings to the last. See ch. IX, pp. 705 ff. below.

[3] For a general account see Workman, II, 355–73.

[4] *Snappe's Formulary* 117–21.

[5] Ibid., 198. [6] Ibid., 126–8. [7] Ibid., 121–4.

[8] Ibid., 125–8. In 1410 the king himself warned the university against false teaching (ibid., 136–8). [9] Ibid., 128–30; Wilkins, III, 339–49.

[10] Ibid., 133–5. [11] Mansi, 27, 505 ff.

[12] The number of errors is given variously at 61 and 18. *Snappe's Formulary* 100.

[13] Ibid., 156–8. [14] Ibid., 158–9. [15] Ibid., 161–2.

[16] Ibid., 162–3. [17] Ibid., 163–5.

Proceedings were soon cut short by word from the king summoning all parties before him.[1] Arundel left after bolting and barring St. Mary's and putting it under interdict. Although this was defied, the university's resistance was at an end. The king wrote asking the pope, John XXIII, to revoke Boniface IX's bull, which he did.[2] and the university authorities were made to submit to the archbishop's jurisdiction.[3] It only needed its further assertion in 1414 by Repton,[4] as bishop of Lincoln, within whose diocese Oxford fell, to show that the return to obedience by both university and the erstwhile leader of the first Oxford Lollards was complete.

Arundel's actions formed the epilogue to Courtenay's a generation earlier. But where Courtenay had confronted a real adversary, Arundel, so far as heresy was concerned, was largely sparring at a phantom; what he overthrew was not Lollardy but corporate privilege, and for a time philosophy. The effect of his comprehensive censure of all Wyclif's works lived on, even though the machinery to enforce it soon fell into disuse. The failure to discriminate between heresy and realism helped to taint the latter, and must be accounted an important factor in the decline of Oxford philosophy during the fifteenth century. Before Arundel's constitutions, Wyclif's philosophy continued to be discussed; after the archbishop's attempt to impose them it was driven underground and, where Wyclif's writings survived, his name was erased. In the process the ideas which he had drawn upon disappeared from current usage to the detriment of Oxford's intellectual life.[5]

Popular Lollardy

So much for Oxford Lollardy, which after 1382 ceased to be a movement, and where the main opposition to it, apart from Arundel's, took the form of refutations of Wyclif's ideas by religious like Woodford[6]

[1] Ibid., 165–6.
[2] Ibid., 176–9.
[3] Ibid., 179–180.
[4] Ibid., 181–6.

[5] For an account of the disappearance of Wyclif's works see Robson, *Wyclif and the Oxford Schools*, especially 224 ff. and 240–6. He cites a number of instances where Wyclif's name was erased from copies of his writings.

[6] E.g., in 1395, when the king ordered the expulsion from Oxford of Robert Lechlade and all Lollards (*Cal. Close Rolls* 1392–6, 434) and an enquiry into the *Trialogus* (ibid., 437–8). It was in reply to the nineteen articles taken from the work and censured by the Canterbury convocation in 1396 (Wilkins, III, 229–30) that Woodford wrote probably in the same year (*Fasciculus* I, 191–265).

and later Netter.[1] Lollardy as a popular movement, however, continued well into the fifteenth century and beyond. Like most clandestine forms of activity it is hard to penetrate to its underlying nature and form any accurate assessment of it either quantitatively or qualitatively. As with all medieval heresy its numbers elude our grasp: there are the usual wild estimates, sometimes running into tens of thousands,[2] to be unanswerably offset by the pathetic following of Oldcastle estimated at between 200 and 300.[3] But it is equally, if not more, important to know what kind of body the Lollards constituted. That it was tightly-knit or centrally organized can be excluded both on *a priori* grounds—poor communications, illiteracy, localism—and the available evidence.[4] It seems far more to have consisted, as with the Free Spirit, in a number of groups or conventicles, on the one hand, and on the other, of individual evangelizers, who roamed the countryside preaching. Its main areas were the diocese of Lincoln—which included the Midlands—with centres early at Leicester and Northampton, and the west country dioceses of Worcester and Hereford, and the Welsh border.[5] The reasons, as we shall see, were in every case local rather than national and owed nothing to Wyclif or an autonomous body of poor priests. Particularly important is the non- or semi-literate character of the Lollard cadres. This was the direct result of Courtenay's Oxford purge;[6] for after the original Oxford Lollards like Aston and Hereford had died, or made their peace with the church, the movement was fostered not by men who had learned their doctrine from Wyclif, but by unbeneficed semi-literate clerks like William Swinderby and pious laymen of whom William Smith was the forerunner. This helps to explain the nature of Lollardy; for if its inspiration was theological and its ends spiritual, its practices were anti-ecclesiastical and its means secular. That was its paradox as it had been Wyclif's. To the hierarchy and sacraments of the church it opposed Christ's example of poverty and preaching; but it sought to achieve them by lay intervention. The return to the true church of Christ was to be made through the forcible disbandment of

[1] *Doctrinale.*

[2] E.g., a letter to Arundel from poor priests claiming that there were 9,200 Lollards in England among whom 200 were squires, 70 knights and 500 priests. *Snappe's Formulary* 130–3.

[3] McFarlane, 176.

[4] See above all Thompson, *The Later Lollards*, who shows its local fragmentary nature throughout the fifteenth century.

[5] Ibid., 121 f., 126 f., 138.

[6] The point is McFarlane's, 114–15.

the present one. For this reason the Lollards, like the Free Spirit, do not appear to have attempted to set up an independent church in opposition to the existing hierarchy; although there are instances of ordination there is little evidence that it was practised on a large scale;[1] or that, as in the case of the Free Spirit, the Lollards ever distinguished between differing degrees of spiritual fitness, beyond the one test of loyalty to Christ. Certainly nothing is known of comparable initiation ceremonies. For the most part they were content to make true spirituality, based on living and preaching God's word, the alternative to the pomp and worldliness of Antichrist's church.

Lollardy can thus best be described as militant spirituality. On the one hand, it looked to naked force for the physical overthrow of the existing church; on the other it opposed to it not another church but purity of heart and personal example. This attitude or—perhaps more accurately—ambivalence underlies the majority of Lollard writings; it is to be found expressed in innumerable places in the English works formerly ascribed to Wyclif,[2] in the opinions and confessions of prominent Lollards like Swinderby,[3] Purvey,[4] Sawtry,[5] Oldcastle,[6] and Taylor,[7] and in declarations such as the Twenty-five Points[8] and the Twelve Conclusions of 1395.[9] There is often considerable variation between them as is to be expected from their diversity of circumstances and authors. But they have enough affinity to be taken as one, as we shall now discuss.

Among the most comprehensive, and in many ways enlightening, of these documents are the Twenty-five Points. Written in 1388,[10] within four years of Wyclif's death, they are a bridge between Wyclif and

[1] For these see M. Aston, art. cit., 13.

[2] There are two collections of writings in English originally ascribed to Wyclif: *Select English Works of John Wyclif* (ed. T. A. Arnold, 3 vols., Oxford 1869–71) and *The English Works of Wyclif* (ed. F. D. Matthew (EETS) 1880). The first two volumes of Arnold's edition consist of sermons, many of which were English renderings of Wyclif's Latin originals, though not done by him; the third volume consists of Lollard tracts, controversial works, and letters and documents. Matthew's volume consists mainly of longer treatises on the standard Lollard topics, most of which, again, are not by Wyclif. For a discussion of the question see Workman, I, appendix C; also M. Deanesly, *The Lollard Bible* 445 ff.

[3] FZ 334–40. [4] Ibid., 383–407. [5] Ibid., 408–11.

[6] Ibid., 414–50. [7] Ibid., 412–13.

[8] *Select English Works* III, 454–96; also summarized by Knighton, *Chronicon* II, 260–3.

[9] FZ 360–9; Wilkins, III, 221–3.

[10] Knighton, II, 260; Arnold, III, 454; See also Workman, II, 387.

Lollardy as a popular outlook. The differences, as well as the similarities, are apparent. If the framework is Wyclif's many of the emphases are Lollard. All the main Wyclifite tenets are there. The pope is Antichrist;[1] he cannot grant indulgences,[2] make decretals[3] or excommunicate.[4] Aural confession is otiose and contrition alone necessary to delete sin.[5] Priests and deacons are bound to preach.[6] The whole hierarchy of the church was condemned,[7] together with the trading of spiritual ministrations[8] for money, absenteeism,[9] holding secular offices,[10] non-performance of duties[11] and self-indulgence.[12] The church should be disendowed[13] and priests only hold property in common.[14] Tithes should not be paid to bad priests.[15] Elaborate ceremonies,[16] church music,[17] excessive worship of saints[18] and images[19] were all attacked. In the sacrament of the eucharist the bread remained after consecration[20] and sinful priests could not administer the sacraments.[21] Above all scripture was the sole guide for true followers of Christ.[22] Yet there are often notable differences from Wyclif both in the expression of these views and in others not to be found in him. Thus the attack on saints' days is more far-reaching than any made by Wyclif, and included that of Thomas Becket.[23] Likewise the denunciation of images. The dislike of any kind of pomp and excess runs through the articles. At the same time they expressed an essentially moral rather than theological standpoint. There is no trace of Wyclif's theoretical premises: merely his conclusions as they affected spiritual life and the practices of the church. In this connexion the treatment of lordship is particularly significant. The question of dominion

[1] Art. I (Arnold, III, 457–9).
[2] Art. II (ibid., 459–60).
[3] Art. III (ibid., 460–1).
[4] Art. VII (ibid., 465–6).
[5] Art. IV (ibid., 461–2).
[6] Art. VI (ibid., 464–5).
[7] Art. X (ibid., 469–72).
[8] XII (ibid., 473) and XXII (ibid., 492).
[9] XXIII (ibid., 493–4).
[10] XIV (ibid., 476).
[11] XXIV (ibid., 494).
[12] XXV (ibid., 494–5).
[13] Art. XIV (ibid., 474–9).
[14] Art. XIII (ibid., 473–4).
[15] Art. IX (ibid., 468–9).
[16] Art. XV (esp. ibid., 481–2).
[17] XV (ibid., 479–82).
[18] Art. VIII (ibid., 466–8) XX (ibid., 489–91).
[19] V (ibid., 462–4) XXI (ibid., 491–2).
[20] XVII (ibid., 483–5).
[21] XVIII (ibid., 485–6). Workman has misinterpreted the somewhat ambiguous discussion to mean that priests in sin can administer the sacraments. It is true that this is initially stated but it is then qualified out of existence to mean the opposite. I.e., 'If the priest unworthily say mass and receive the sacrament unworthily he receives damnation to him. . . . And if his sin be open the people ought not to receive sacraments of him lest consent to his sin made them partners in pain [suffering]' (ibid., 485–6).
[22] XXV (ibid., 495).
[23] Ibid., 490.

and grace does not arise, as it does not in any important Lollard statement.[1] Instead a clear distinction was drawn between clerical lordship, which was *ipso facto* sinful, and secular lordship which was justified so long as it was conducted in a Christian manner: 'secular men may have wordly goods enough without number, to us [according to our opinion], so that they get them truly and spend them to God's honour and furthering of truth and help of their Christian brethren, and that they suffer not Antichrist's clerks to destroy secular lordships and rob their tenants by feigned jurisdiction of Antichrist'.[2] While the maintenance of secular lordship had become a holy task and opposition to it a sign of Antichrist, priests must 'live in simpleness and forsake the world, and truly teach Christ's gospel and acknowledge them[selves] servants of all men.'[3] One was hallowed; the other denied.[4]

Despite this militancy, the stress on spirituality in the manner of the Waldensians is perhaps even more striking. It is shown indirectly in the revulsion against pomp and images already mentioned, as also in the articles on confession and indulgences; in both the latter the appeal was to the individual, 'to each man to do verey [true] penance for his sins, keep God's behests and do works of charity'.[5] But it is in the nineteenth point on prayer that this attitude can be seen most clearly. Prayer in church, it asserts, is no better than anywhere else: 'in each place where a man is he owes for to pray to God in spirit and truth, that is with will and devotion and cleanness of living'.[6] Moreover 'the place hallows not the man, but a man hallows the place.'[7] The main churches of the day were places of sinning and sin, 'dens of thieves and habitations of fiends', which it behoved true Christians to avoid.[8] After prayer men may say Paternoster 'medefully under the cope of heaven as Christ did'.[9] Affinities with mysticism and quietism should not be sought. There was no inner search for God in the soul or withdrawal from the world in order to reach him. As with the Waldensians, it was rather a moral insistence upon individual responsibility before God. Right living was the sole criterion of righteousness; spiritual probity could only be proved in practice. It is epitomized in the final exhortation that priests

[1] Occasionally there are hints of action to be taken against evil lay lords as in the tract *Of servants and lords,* in *English Works of Wyclif* (ed. F. D. Matthew) 229; cited in Aston, art. cit., 10.

[2] Ibid., XI, 472.

[3] Ibid.

[4] The absence of reference to the king has been taken by Workman II, 390, as showing the Lollards' loss of faith in him.

[5] Arnold, III, 460.

[6] Ibid., 486.

[7] Ibid., 487.

[8] Ibid.

[9] Ibid., 488.

should sell their all and give the proceeds to the poor and then 'go meekly on their feet and preach truly the gospel as Christ and his apostles did'.[1] Their fullness makes the Twenty-five Points one of the most illuminating Lollard documents; in particular they illustrate the singular juxtaposition of militancy and spirituality which was the characteristic of Lollardy, as of Waldensianism, making it at once a political and moral outlook rather than mystical or speculative. Only over the eucharist did the vestiges of its theological origins remain.

There can be little doubt of Purvey's inspiration in helping to form the Lollardy expressed in the Twenty-five Points. Although as Wyclif's disciple and amanuensis he bears many of his master's traces, he went further, crystallizing it into predominantly a protest. Himself probably not the sole author of the Wyclifite translation of the bible into English,[2] he was more than anyone responsible for popularizing Wyclif's ideas in the vernacular; and many of the works formerly attributed to Wyclif were probably Purvey's.[3] From our point of view the most certain and comprehensive statement of his outlook is to be found in his confession and the articles drawn up from his works and brought before him in 1401. From his base at Bristol, where he had gone after Wyclif's death, he had become a noted Lollard preacher. Moving around the dioceses of Hereford and Worcester dressed as a layman, he duly came under the bishop of Worcester's ban in August in 1387, when he was condemned together with Aston, Hereford, John Parker and Swinderby.[4] This was followed by the appointment of royal commissions in 1388 and 1389 for the confiscation of their and Wyclif's works.[5] But for another dozen years Purvey remained at liberty. By the time he was caught the statute *De heretico comburendo*[6] had been recently passed, and its first victim, William Sawtry of Lynn in Norfolk, only just consigned to the flames.[7] Purvey, never having been previously arrested, had not previously recanted and so could not be charged under the new act as a relapsed heretic. But the added threat of a possible future death by burning may well have ensured his compliance; for after abjuring the errors and heresies presented to him he passed the remainder of his life in a benefice at West Hythe, Kent.[8]

Purvey's confession,[9] like the Twenty-five Points, is remarkable for

[1] Arnold, III, 495.

[2] See Deanesly, *The Lollard Bible* passim; Workman, II, 150 ff.

[3] Workman, II, 162 ff., 192 ff.

[4] McFarlane, 127.

[5] Ibid., 128.

[6] See below.

[7] McFarlane, 150–2.

[8] Ibid., 152.

[9] FZ 383–407.

its fullness. Together they provide a comprehensive insight into the foundations of Lollardy, making explicit much that remains unsaid in manifestos like the Twelve Conclusions. In their final form there were seven charges of heresy against Purvey—on the eucharist; confession; holy orders; evil priests; unlicensed preaching; taking of vows; and Innocent III's decrees on the eucharist and annual auricular confession. These had been reduced from a list of some 64 heresies and errors grouped under eleven heads: the eucharist; penance; holy orders; binding and loosing; preaching; marriage; vows; church temporalities; sanctions against the clergy; the laws and decisions of the church; the place of the pope and the priesthood. Running to 17 printed pages they show at once how deeply Purvey had drunk of Wyclif's teaching and yet had on certain points crucial for Lollardy gone beyond him. Thus, to take the different propositions in their order, while adding nothing fresh on the eucharist—always the egregious theological anomaly in the predominantly moral concerns of Lollardy—he damned Innocent III as chief Antichrist for his part in having made a new article of faith out of the falsehood that accidents can exist without a substance.[1] Of interest is the fact that Purvey did not confine himself to castigating heresy; he admonished his followers, when questioned on whether the sacrament was simple bread, to reply openly that it was. Purvey was a propagandist and leader.[2] He likewise stigmatized the canon on the sacrament of penance, passed at the same Fourth Lateran Council, which commanded annual aural confession, as heretical and blasphemous, and the penalties for enforcing it as irrational and unjust.[3] It enabled the priests to oppress ordinary folk and entangled men's consciences in sin, dragging them down to the inferno. Finally it destroyed the freedom of the gospel and prevented men from seeking counsel from God's true priests.[4] Purvey urged men to protest against it.[5]

The most revolutionary part of Purvey's teachings was on the priesthood.[6] With Wyclif he held that all good Christians are predestined, that true priests are ordained of God, and every predestinate, even when

[1] Item quod Innocentius tertius papa fuit capitalis Antichristus ... (FZ 383). Purvey throughout confused the Fourth Lateran Council in 1215, at which Innocent III's decrees were enacted, with the Council of Lyons of 1274.

[2] Item quando Antichristus vel aliquis suorum mundialium clericorum interrogat te, simplex Christiane, numquid hoc sacramentum sit verus panis, concede hoc aperte (ibid., 4, 384–5).

[3] Ibid., 386. [4] Ibid., 386–7. [5] Ibid., 387.

[6] III 'De sacramento ordinis' 387–9.

a layman, is a true priest.[1] But he also at the same time made explicit what Wyclif had only hinted at: namely that God could ordain priests independently of human operation and sacramental signs, their sacerdotal character being recognized from the sanctity of their lives.[2] This had been the case with the first priests before the mosaic law, when God had ordained Moses.[3] Here, again, in making living *tout court* the test of election, Purvey was setting Wyclif's more fluid ideas into a defined mould; the mystery and uncertainty that underlay the master's notion of predestination hardened, in the disciple's, into a new morphology. The identification of purity of life with inner sanctity, and thereby election, lost the nuances it had had for Wyclif. It became a tenet in its own right for Lollardy. As employed by Purvey, it meant the rejection of all priests who did not emulate God;[4] it also meant the nullity of ecclesiastical ordination, from the pope downwards, and the equality of all priests, whatever their office:[5] to be a pope or bishop depended not on the custom of the church but on Christ or popular assent;[6] any saved priest was such without a bishop's hands being laid upon him.[7]

This in turn led Purvey to denounce the hierarchy. The pope was Satan, to be worshipped by no Christian. To accept either his censures or his indulgences was to betray God;[8] and papal interdicts could not harm.[9] As to worldly priests they lived entirely contrary to the example of Christ and his Apostles; they did not teach the gospel but lies and false human traditions.[10] Their keys were to hell not heaven, and they were without power from God.[11] Whatever the pope and cardinals bound on earth was not bound in heaven.[12] In the eleventh and last group of errors Purvey described proud priests as Antichrist, and the pope and all his appointees as simoniacs for accepting first fruits.[13] Rome itself was the great whore of Babylon described in the

[1] Quod omnes boni Christiani sunt predestinati, veri sacerdotes ordinati seu facti a deo . . . Et sic omnes predestinati facit deus sacerdotes (1 and 2 ibid., 387).

[2] 2, ibid. [3] Ibid. [4] Ibid., 387–8.

[5] Item quod presbyteri, si sint sacerdotes dei, sunt episcopi, prelati et curati Christianorum fratrum suorum . . . (ibid., 3, 388).

[6] Item quod licet nullus esset papa secundum consuetudinem ecclesie, adhuc Christus, qui est caput ecclesie, talem ordinat papam ad suum libitum. . . . Et licet nullus [fiat] episcopus per sublimationem super alios secundum consuetudinem ecclesie, tamen omnes sacerdotes bene possunt regere ecclesiam per communem assensum (4 ibid.).

[7] Ibid., 389. [8] IV, 1, 2 ibid. [9] Ibid., 6, 390.

[10] Ibid., 3, 389. [11] Ibid.

[12] Ibid., 7, 390. [13] XI, 1, 2, 399.

Apocalypse.[1] Similarly Purvey rejected all church laws not found in the bible; but once again he went beyond Wyclif in openly advocating rebellion against the pope when he infringed the teachings of scripture. All Christians, he said, 'should practise disobedience' against the pope and his unscriptural decretals.[2] Their refutation was in the interests of all Christians; once rid of them the church could again live securely in God's ordinance, as it had for 1,000 years before their appearance.[3] While papal laws were to be ignored and rejected,[4] the opinions of the doctors of the church were to be treated with reverence so long as they accorded with scripture.[5] If one good book was to be burned because of a single error, then so should all the books of canon law for theirs.[6] Failure of priests to live like Christ and preach his word made them excommunicate, and, even if they committed no evil, Antichrist.[7] Purvey's depression of the priesthood was complemented by his elevation of laymen. They could legitimately administer all the sacraments necessary to salvation, including baptism and marriage, as well as preach; while some sacraments, like the eucharist and unction, could be dispensed with.[8] Moreover receipt of the sacraments depended upon the worthiness of the recipient and so was open to any priest, in contradiction to Clement V's decree *Religiosi*.[9]

But it was when he dealt with the lay power that Purvey surpassed anything that Wyclif had said. Not only could the king reduce all priests to Christ's humble state,[10] and withdraw their laws until they had learned to obey Christ;[11] but kings had the power to ordain priests as Solomon and Josephat had done.[12] They could also depose priests as well as judge them.[13] This was to make them the spiritual superiors of priests, a position in keeping with the most extreme imperialist ideas of the past. Nor did Purvey fail to draw the practical conclusions. More fully than any other Lollard he advocated the unqualified subservience of the church to the lay power. Bishops who claimed independent jurisdiction in ecclesiastical matters were traitors to the king and the bible,[14] as, for that reason, Boniface VIII was.[15] There could

[1] Ibid., 3.
[2] x, 1, 2, ibid., 397–8.
[3] Ibid., 3, 398.
[4] Ibid., 5, 6, 7, 8.
[5] Ibid., 4.
[6] Ibid., 9, 399.
[7] v, 1, 2, 390–1.
[8] iv, 4, 390.
[9] Ibid., 5. Clementines, v, 7, 1.
[10] ix, 1, 395.
[11] Ibid., 5.
[12] Ibid., 7, 396. This idea, together with other Lollard views derived from the bible, is described by Mrs. Aston, art. cit., p. 11, as 'erratic'; but it is very much in keeping with Purvey's outlook which is perhaps most notable for its consistency.
[13] Ibid., 13, 397.
[14] Ibid., 6, 396.
[15] Ibid., 9.

be no ecclesiastical exemption from the king's authority.[1] By both divine law and reason—Purvey's two constant supports—secular lords could arrest and imprison cardinals for crimes like adultery, simony and blasphemy;[2] nor was the pope exempt from judgement;[3] and he destroyed God's ordinances if he failed to appear before his true lords.[4] Secular rulers had an obligation to judge the Roman church, the whore of Babylon.[5]

For their guidance Purvey drew up a blue-print for the church's disendowment, which later became the basis of the notorious petition presented to parliament in 1410 on the same subject.[6] To confiscate all ecclesiastical possessions, he said, would yield the equivalent of creating 15 new earldoms and 15,000 knights, together with an additional £20,000 for the king's treasury. It could also provide for the foundation of fifteen new universities and for the support of fifteen thousand new priests to replace those disendowed, as well as one hundred alms houses each with land worth one hundred marks.[7] This was the bait with which Purvey apparently sought to tempt lay lords to realize their inborn rights to strip the church of its material possessions and secular dominion, and reduce it once more to Christ's simple life of poverty.[8] It was also necessary for the well-being of their own souls; for not to act against 'the great abhomination' of worldly prelates and monks[9] was blasphemy.[10]

Purvey reflects more clearly than anyone else the legacy of Wyclif's teachings; although omitting some Lollard tenets, such as their opposition to image[11] worship, he made a platform out of Wyclif's ecclesiology. The element of moral protest, so prominent in Wyclif, now became autonomous. The appeal was exclusively to conduct. Living and example, according to scripture short-circuited theoretical considerations. On the one hand dominion and grace, long overlaid in Wyclif's own system, had been transcended by a theory of secular sovereignty as far-reaching as any. On the other, the church was deposed spiritually and only awaited its final dismemberment temporally. At the same time, enough of the original impulse to these beliefs remained in Purvey

[1] IX, I, 8. [2] Ibid., 10. [3] Ibid., 11.
[4] Ibid., 12. [5] Ibid., 14, 397.
[6] See pp. 596–7 below. Reported in Walsingham, *Historia* II, 282–3. See Workman, II, appendix Z, for sources. Reference to Purvey's scheme is also made in the corollary to the seventh of the *Twelve Conclusions* (FZ 364).
[7] VIII, I, 393.
[8] Ibid., 2, 3, 394. [9] Ibid., 6. [10] Ibid., 4.
[11] He did, however, oppose the taking of vows, ibid., VII, 392.

to form a connexion with Wyclif's thinking. For that reason he gives a clearer insight than anyone into the way in which Lollardy grew out of Wyclifism.

The essentially practical and moral character that it assumed is illustrated repeatedly in the other known Lollard sources. William Swinderby, who has been called 'perhaps the very greatest of the Lollard evangelists',[1] originally confessed to eleven errors in 1382,[2] before Buckingham, the bishop of Lincoln. He soon relapsed, and nine years later was caught and charged a second time for holding to much the same views. These were all of a severely moral and practical kind. Five were errors:[3] against imprisonment for debt, tithes to a sinful priest, and priestly excommunication independently of God. The six branded as heresies all concerned sinful priests and the sacraments: mortal sin in priest or parents nullified an infant's baptism; evil living disqualified a priest from holy orders; contrition came before absolution, which could be granted by any priest if a sinner was truly contrite; priests who received an annual payment were simoniacs and excommunicate; no priest in mortal sin could perform the sacrament of the eucharist; and all priests entered houses only to seduce the women within.[4] Other Lollards like Richard Wyche[5] attacked the friars and mendicancy[6] as well as images,[7] papal excommunication,[8] payments to priests.[9] Wyche further held that the power of all good priests was equal,[10] and that anyone, even a boy, could bless the bread of the eucharist.[11] All this and more, he asserted, had the authority of the bible; and he declared himself ready to retract whatever could not be found there.[12]

William Sawtrey, the first to be burned as a Lollard in 1401 under the new act of *De heretico comburendo*, was a fair representative of his creed.[13] He opposed the adoration of the cross and worship of relics;[14] took preaching as the foremost duty of priests;[15] attacked vows to go on a pilgrimage;[16] and maintained the standard Lollard heresy of the eucharist,[17] on which he was examined, in vain, by Arundel.[18] Such views as these represented the religious rather than the political face of

[1] McFarlane, 135; and 129 ff. for these happenings. [2] FZ 334–40.
[3] Ibid., 337–8. [4] Ibid., 338–9. [5] Ibid., 370–82.
[6] Ibid., 372–3. [7] Ibid., 370–2. [8] Ibid., 374.
[9] Ibid., 274–6. [10] Ibid., 373.
[11] Ibid., 378. [12] Ibid., 370.
[13] Ibid., 408–12. [14] Ibid., 408–9. [15] Ibid., 409.
[16] Ibid., 409–10, where he expressly mentions journeys to Becket's tomb.
[17] Ibid., 410. [18] Ibid., 411.

Lollardy. They were hardly less subversive of ecclesiastical authority for that; but they did not invoke the supreme sanction of the lay power to administer the *coup de grâce* to the system they condemned.

The supreme instance of the coercive, political aspect are the Twelve Conclusions of 1395. They were formerly thought to have been presented to parliament as a petition; but it now seems firmly established that they were nailed to the doors of Westminster Abbey and St. Paul's when parliament was sitting.[1] The articles were both a condemnation of the church along familiar lines[2]—endowments,[3] the priesthood,[4] vows of chastity,[5] the doctrine of the eucharist,[6] the holding of secular offices by priests,[7] pilgrimages, worshipping of images,[8] oral confession[9] —and a call for action by the king to reform it.[10] Included among its points were several less common ones; against exorcisms and blessings on objects like wine, bread, water, oil, salt and so on, which partook more of necromancy than theology;[11] against war and capital punishment for temporal causes, without a spiritual revelation.[12] They also opposed vows of chastity for women;[13] and the multiplicity of 'unnecessary arts', such as goldworking and weapon making,[14] 'which did nothing but generate curiosity and sin'. With St. Paul men should ask for nothing but food and raiment.

That the Twelve Conclusions were not intended to be more than an incomplete résumé of the Lollard positions, can be seen from their reference to 'another book entirely in our own language' where these matters and many more were fully treated.[15] The articles themselves were simply heads of proposals stripped of the finer points of Lollard doctrine. When read in conjunction with Purvey and the Twenty-five Points the affinities between them are not hard to see: true spirituality

[1] *Liber Rogeri Dymmok* (ed. H. S. Cronin) Introduction, xxxiii ff; Workman, ii, 391 ff.

[2] FZ 360–9.
[3] Ibid., i, 360.
[4] Ibid., ii, 360–1.
[5] Ibid., iii, 361.
[6] Ibid., iv, 361–2.
[7] Ibid., vi, 363.
[8] Ibid., viii, 364–5.
[9] Ibid., ix, 365–6.
[10] 368–9.
[11] Ibid., v, 362.
[12] Ibid., x, 366–7.
[13] Ibid., xi, 367–8.
[14] Ibid., xii, 368.

[15] Ibid., 368–9; see Workman, ii, 392 ff. for a discussion of the identity of this book, which he thinks with some plausibility was Purvey's *Ecclesie regimen* (ed. J. Forshall, 1851, unwarrantably, as *Remonstrance against Romish corruptions in the Church addressed to the People and Parliament of England in 1395*). It seems probable that the basis of the *Ecclesie regimen* was in turn the *Thirty Seven Conclusions* (published by H. F. B. Compston in EHR 26 (1911) 738–49) a much more moderate statement of the same points.

versus sacramentalism and sacerdotalism; simplicity of living in accordance with Christ versus the pomp of Antichrist; lay dominion versus ecclesiastical dominion. Its implications for Lollardy as a whole may perhaps be gauged from the findings of the enquiry into the *Trialogus* which king Richard II ordered Oxford university to undertake[1] in the same year as the publication of the Twelve Conclusions. They issued two years later in the condemnation of eighteen articles taken from the work.[2] Three were on the eucharist;[3] six on the other sacraments;[4] two were devoted to the priesthood confining it to the two orders of priests and deacons, the others being denounced as the twelve 'procurators of the Antichrist';[5] three concerned religious possessions and disendowment;[6] two were on true dominion and election;[7] one stigmatized as heretical all actions by the pope and cardinals not authorized in the bible;[8] and one affirmed the necessity of everything.[9] A comparison of these with the Twelve Conclusions shows how popular Lollardy had fastened upon the more directly moral and practical features of Wyclif's teaching, with little reference to their theoretical foundations: priesthood, sacraments, disendowment, loyalty to Christ, simplicity of living, became the key tenets which, as we have seen, recurred repeatedly. Questions of dominion, election, scriptural versus ecclesiastical authority, were for the most part supplanted by the more immediate issues to which they had given rise. Occasionally they continued to attract attention as in the statement of William Taylor, burned at Smithfield for Lollardy in 1423,[10] that God only permissively willed kings and lay lords to have dominion in all civil matters.[11] But then Taylor was an academic. In essence, however, Lollardy was a movement for a spiritual reformation. Since this could only be realized by the physical overthrow of the existing church hierarchy, its adherents looked to the lay power as an ally. Only when Lollardy ceased to hope for lay support did it become subversive in the wider sense and challenge state as well as church. It is to this development that we must now turn.

[1] Wilkins, III, 227–30.

[2] Ibid., 229–30. [3] 1, 2, 3. [4] 4, 5, 7, 8, 9, 14.

[5] 6, 10. [6] 11, 12, 13. [7] 15, 16.

[8] 18. For a somewhat laboured, but useful, discussion of this proposition, see Hurley, 'Scriptura sola', 321 ff.

[9] 17. [10] FZ 412–13.

[11] Ibid., VI, 413; the same as the principal of St. Edmund Hall who preached against church temporalities in 1406. See also pp. 602–3 below.

The persecution and decline of Lollardy

Even before Courtenay censured Wyclif's teachings at the Blackfriars synod in May 1382, the attack upon the Lollards outside Oxford had begun. In March of that year John Buckingham, bishop of Lincoln, started proceedings at Leicester which, with a large area of the Midlands, came within his diocese. Swinderby had created a Lollard stronghold in the city;[1] and Buckingham, alarmed at its vigour, on 5 March 1382, prohibited Swinderby from preaching, citing him to appear before officers of the diocese. Swinderby took no notice; and, the churches being closed to him, preached in the open drawing large crowds. As with Lollards in other Midland towns, the civic authorities appear to have made no attempt to stop him. But his superiors excommunicated him for disobedience; after various delays, he finally appeared at Lincoln in June 1382 to answer eleven charges which we have earlier discussed.[2] Given a month to gain the witness of twelve worthy priests to his probity, he was only able to produce the seals of the mayor and burgesses of Leicester testifying to his orthodoxy. But they were not enough to save him from having to recant publicly on successive Sundays. As we have seen the complexion of his teachings was predominantly moral; the eucharist,[3] although initially included among the counts against him, did not figure in the final list of charges. Once cleared, Swinderby although he probably perjured himself in the process, moved to Coventry where he remained until episcopal pressure once again forced him to move. This time he went west beyond the Severn where he was soon followed by Aston and other former Oxford Lollards. Henceforth the dioceses of Worcester and Hereford, and the south Welsh marches became their happy hunting-ground. In September 1383, Aston, despite his reconciliation with authority in the previous year, preached at Gloucester against the bishop of Norwich's Flemish crusade.[4] In 1385 Nicholas of Hereford, having escaped from prison at Rome, where he had gone to appeal to Urban VI in person against Courtenay's sentences of excommunication, joined his confrères.[5]

[1] For what follows, see McFarlane, 121 f. See also the account of Swinderby's career in Knighton, II, 189 ff.

[2] p. 583 above.

[3] McFarlane, 124, who says it was probably at first 'thrown in by mistake'.

[4] Knighton, II, 178; McFarlane, 126; Workman, II, 336. The purpose of the crusade was to force the supporters of the anti-pope to change their allegiance. This action became the target of some of Wyclif's bitterest invective.

[5] Knighton, ibid., 172–4; McFarlane, 126–7; Workman, II, 336.

Meanwhile Purvey went to Bristol, which he was to make one of the main Lollard centres.[1] He was described by Knighton as pretending to a greater sanctity than other men. Dressed as a layman he went assiduously to work spreading the doctrines of his master Wyclif.[2] By 1387 they had attracted the attention of the bishop of Worcester, Henry Wakefield, who on 10 August banned Swinderby, Aston, Hereford and Purvey together with John Parker from preaching, and extended this to any other Lollards.[3] The bishop singled out Hereford and Aston, the two doctors, as the leaders.[4] During 1388 and 1389, following the decisions of the parliament of 1388, royal commissions to suppress the works of Wyclif, Hereford, Aston and Purvey were set up at York,[5] Nottingham,[6] Worcester,[7] Leicester,[8] Salisbury[9] and Lincoln.[10] Most of the surviving authors did not remain immune for long. Aston probably died in 1388.[11] Hereford had already been arrested in 1387 at Nottingham and handed over to Courtenay.[12] He recanted some time before December 1391, when he received the king's protection;[13] two years later he was one of the bishop's assessors in the trial of Walter Brute in Herefordshire.[14] Not surprisingly he was denounced for his treachery by an erstwhile fellow.[15] In 1394 he became chancellor of Hereford cathedral;[16] he continued to receive favours from both Richard II and Henry IV until in 1417 he withdrew to the charterhouse of St. Anne at Coventry, where he died.[17]

As for Swinderby the efforts to bring him to book failed after a diverting series of evasions on his part. In 1388 the sheriff of Hereford was ordered to arrest him; but, despite his almost brazenly provoking conduct—preaching without licence; celebrating mass in an unconsecrated chapel; once even confronting the bishop of Hereford, John

1 McFarlane, 127.
2 Knighton, II, 178.
3 Wilkins, II, 202–3.
4 Wilkins, III, 202; McFarlane, 127; Workman, II, 163.
5 *Calendar of Patent Rolls, 1385–9*, 427.
6 Ibid., 430.
7 Ibid., 448.
8 Ibid., 468.
9 Ibid., 536.
10 Ibid., 530.
11 McFarlane, 128.
12 Ibid.
13 Ibid., Workman, II, 336–7.
14 *Registrum Johannis Trefnant* (Canterbury and York Society, London 1916) 359.
15 Ibid., 394–6.
16 Ibid., 178, 193; McFarlane, 128; Workman, II, 337.
17 McFarlane, 129; Workman, II, 337–8.

Trefnant—he remained unmolested until 1391.[1] In June of that year the bishop summoned him to appear at Bodenham church on the last day of the month to answer a series of charges. To ensure his attendance he was granted a safe-conduct.[2] Swinderby duly appeared with a written defence and at once left.[3] His replies concerned two groups of charges: the first that he had relapsed into the errors he had abjured at Lincoln in 1382; the second that he had since then further spread heresy and error which were listed under fifteen counts.[4] Swinderby's replies to both groups consisted in first denying and then explaining what was imputed to him, the explanation serving only to underline the dubiousness of his views. The first group of eleven errors he blamed on the friars' malice; he had, he said, only assented to them for fear of burning.[5] The second group drawn up from what he had been heard to preach at Whitney and Newton went farther than the first.[6] To the disabilities of sinful priests, those of the pope were now added; equality of all priests was stressed; oaths and worship of images were denounced; above all an article on the eucharist was now added to the list: namely, that after the consecration of the host, Christ's true body was not present and the bread remained, since accidents needed a subject. Finally he was accused of celebrating mass in an unhallowed chapel at Derwald's Wood and in Newton Park near Leintwardine.

It was not until October, after a number of attempts to cite him had produced no response, save more written apologies by Swinderby,[7] that he once more appeared. He again produced a long statement in writing and again vanished.[8] He was now pronounced a heretic,[9] and in due course excommunicated. Swinderby, in true Lollard style, appealed not to superior ecclesiastical authority but to the knights of parliament[10]—with no visible result. Trefnant meanwhile submitted the condemned propositions to some Cambridge doctors who not surprisingly endorsed the bishop's anathema.[11] But their verdict can have made no difference to Swinderby who remained at large to the end of his days. He had popularized Lollardy wherever he had gone; the

[1] A good account of Swinderby's confrontations with Trefnant is to be found in McFarlane 129–35. The case is fully documented in Trefnant's *Register* 231–78, 365–94, 408–9.

[2] *Reg. Trefnant* 232.

[3] Ibid., 237.

[4] Ibid., 233–6.

[5] Ibid., 238–9, and 238–43.

[6] Thirteen are listed in the official charge against him in Latin (ibid., 235–6); but Swinderby replied (in English in both cases) to fifteen (ibid., 244–51).

[7] Ibid., 251–61.

[8] Ibid., 262–70.

[9] Ibid., 270–1.

[10] Ibid., 271–8.

[11] Ibid., 365–94.

future rebel leader John Oldcastle was probably one of the many he influenced.[1] Swinderby helped to make Lollardy a popular morality in which preaching God's word was joined to practising Christ's precepts as the test of the true Christian. He brought the evangelical fervour of the simple priest to what might otherwise have remained unleavened academic doctrine.

Another Lollard who gave Trefnant even more trouble was Walter Brute who appeared at Hereford soon after Swinderby's sentence in October 1391. What followed[2] was a much more prolonged repetition of Swinderby's proceedings, except that in this case Brute finally recanted—albeit in meaningless general terms.[3] The charges against him were initially all Lollard errors:[4] that any Christian, including a woman, could perform the sacrament of the eucharist; that the host did not contain Christ's real body but was a sign for it; that tithes and offerings were voluntary; that the bishop of Norwich's crusade was indefensible; that the pope was Antichrist. He then went on to defend all Swinderby's condemned propositions.[5] Subsequent citation led to Brute's expanding his views into a series of apocalyptic treatises of little relevance or interest,[6] which led correspondingly to the expansion of his heresy in every direction. After examination by a group of Cambridge theologists, thirty-seven errors were condemned[7] on 3 October 1393, when Brute made his recantation. He was subsequently killed in Owen Glendower's rising.[8]

Elsewhere the main areas of Lollard activity continued to be the Midlands, especially at Leicester and Northampton. In 1389 Courtenay completed the operation begun by Buckingham in 1382 against Swinderby's following at St. John's chapel, Leicester. The two original inmates had been William Smith, a self-taught layman, and Richard Waytestathe, a chaplain.[9] They had started a conventicle in the deserted chapel and taught Lollard doctrine which before long had attracted Swinderby, at that time a hermit.[10] They and the other inmates had remained after Swinderby had left; and it was upon them that Courtenay descended on 30 October in a visitation of the diocese.[11] He cited

[1] McFarlane, 134.

[2] *Reg. Trefnant*, 278–365. For a résumé see McFarlane, 135–8.

[3] Ibid., 360.

[4] Ibid., 279–80.

[5] Ibid , 280–4.

[6] Ibid., 285–358.

[7] Ibid., 360–5.

[8] McFarlane, 138.

[9] Knighton, II, 181–2; McFarlane, 103–4.

[10] Knighton, II, 182, 191–2.

[11] For an account of what follows, see Knighton, II, 311–13; Wilkins, III, 208–9; McFarlane, 139–141.

eight of them to appear before him on 1 November, including Smith and Waytestathe. The others were predominantly craftsmen—a tailor, scrivener, goldsmith and parchmener.[1] They were accused of errors on the eucharist, tithes, images, venerating the cross, sinful priests, excommunication, indulgences, preaching, the friars, offerings, and aural confession.[2] When they failed to appear Courtenay pronounced a general ban on all who held such errors; but on the next day, having been assured by prominent townsmen that the eight were notorious heretics, he pronounced sentence upon them by name.[3] Within ten days Smith and two others had been arrested and had abjured.[4] They were condemned to appear as penitents in the market place at Leicester.[5] Among Smith's and Waytestathe's earlier offences had been burning an image of St. Catherine.[6]

Northampton came into prominence three years later, in 1392, although it too had been visited by Courtenay at about the same time as he had visited Leicester.[7] The rise of Lollardy in the town was attributed to the aid and comfort which the heretics had received from John Fox, elected mayor in 1392. Lollard demonstrations led to a series of disorders at the end of 1392 and the early part of 1393. But apart from bishop Buckingham's subsequent search for five Lollards in November 1395 the earlier traces of Lollardy are circumstantial.

Thus during the 1380s Lollardy became a full-fledged heresy with a distinctive body of doctrines and its own heresiarchs, condemned alike by ecclesiastical and secular authorities. The persecutions inaugurated by Courtenay and Buckingham assumed nation-wide ramifications; the writings of Wyclif, Hereford, Aston and Purvey were proscribed and their surviving authors hunted as heretics; above all, as we shall shortly discuss, a new machinery was slowly evolved which in a few years put anti-heretical measures on to a permanent and comprehensive footing. For its part, Lollardy became a clandestine sect, its leaders driven into hiding and its adherents formed into conventicles and small groups. Their numbers and extensiveness will almost certainly never be known; but their distinctive doctrines, as we have seen, were already widely diffused in vernacular writings: many of which were crude renderings of Wyclif's sermons and tracts, and others by the first generation of his Lollard followers like Purvey and Hereford.

[1] Wilkins, III, 208. [2] Ibid. [3] Ibid., 209.
[4] Ibid., 210–12. [5] Ibid., 212.
[6] Ibid., 212; Knighton, II, 182, 313.
[7] For what follows see McFarlane, 141–5.

Above all, from the impulse of Wyclif's twin devotion to the bible and preaching, came the Lollard translations of the bible.[1] There were two versions. The first, during Wyclif's lifetime, was a literal translation probably designed to be used as an aid to the Vulgate. No evidence suggests that Wyclif himself had a hand in it, beyond having inspired it. Nicholas of Hereford is usually held to have been responsible for it, until the third chapter of the book of Baruch. Its extreme literalness, however, made it unsuitable for widespread use; and a second translation was undertaken. Probably completed in 1396 it seems to have been a composite effort rather than work of Purvey to whom it has been ascribed;[2] certainly his trial contains no reference to it.[3] This second version was very much more readable; and it became widely diffused, as can be seen from the number of 140 extant manuscripts written within forty years of its first appearance, compared with thirty for the first version.[4] Nor was it confined to the Lollards and their followers; as so often, the poorer manuscripts have not survived, and among the better ones which have there is a number of expensive copies. For the fact is that a vernacular version met a growing need when English, even in the official and upper reaches of society, was replacing French and Latin. It has been truly said that had the Lollards not translated the bible, in the age of Chaucer and Langland it would have come about through other agencies as was already happening in France and Germany.[5] Nevertheless, of unexceptionable orthodoxy as it was, the Lollard bible combined with Lollard preaching was bound to increase the spread of error and heresy and so evoke opposition to unauthorized vernacular renderings. Although these were not prohibited until Arundel's constitutions in 1407, attempts to check them had begun at least a decade before;[6] and the total effect could only be

[1] McFarlane, 118–19, 148–9. On the Lollard bibles see M. Deanesly *The Lollard Bible*, Workman, II, 150–200, McFarlane, 118–19, 148–9. The two versions are printed in the edition by J. Forshall and J. Madden, 4 vols. (Oxford 1850).

[2] E.g., the reference in the general Prologue to the help of 'many good fellows and cunning' (ibid., I, 57). Although quoted by Workman, II, 165, this does not prevent him from making Purvey the translator though without any conclusive evidence.

[3] McFarlane, 149.

[4] Deanesly, op. cit., 381.

[5] Workman, II, 179 ff.

[6] E.g., The oath undertaken by John Croft not to use 'English books publicly or privately evilly taken from the bare text of the bible' (*Reg. Trefnant* 148) cited in Workman, II, 198; and William Butler, Franciscan regent at Oxford, who in 1401 determined there against the translation of the bible into English (Workman, II, 198–9).

to confound translation with subversion and intensify the measures against Lollardy as a whole.

The history of the official attitude towards the Lollards is the record of the growing co-operation between church and lay power to suppress it. That Lollardy found some support among the aristocracy cannot be doubted: Sir Thomas Latimer of Braybrooke, Northamptonshire, from where Wyclif's *De civili dominio* was in 1407 copied and transmitted by two Czechs to Prague; Sir John Montague, earl of Salisbury; Sir Lewis Clifford; and Sir John Cheyne. Each of these is in varying degrees suspect.[1] Furthermore, the ordinary Lollards, like Purvey and Swinderby, long believed in aristocratic support, as the preamble to the English version of the Twelve Conclusions addressed to the lords and commons of parliament makes plain.[2] But neither then nor at the supreme test in 1414 did they come to their aid: and henceforth they faded from Lollard sight.

So far as the government was concerned it became, as we have said, increasingly involved on the side of the church. Its first official measure had, as we saw, been in 1382 when it supplemented the long-standing procedure of the writ *significat*.[3] By this, also known as *De excommunicato capiendo*, a bishop could obtain a writ directing a sheriff to imprison a person excommunicated for heresy by an ecclesiastical court. Once taken the suspect was to be held until he had made his peace with the church. The time and stages involved made the method cumbrous at the best of times and quite unsuitable to coping with numbers of peripatetic heretics who did not obligingly keep to the diocesan and county boundaries, upon the observance of which its effectiveness depended. To meet the need for more summary measures, the king accepted an addition to the parliamentary roll for 7 May 1382.[4] This provided for the issue of commissions to sheriffs and other royal officers to arrest and imprison unauthorized preachers and their accomplices upon certificates received from prelates in chancery. Those arrested were to be held until they justified themselves to the church. The measure was designed specifically against Lollards who preached without licence 'in churches, cemeteries, markets, fairs and other public places where large numbers

[1] W. T. Waugh, 'The Lollard Knights' *Scottish Historical Review* 11 (1914) 55–92; McFarlane, 146–7; Workman, II, 280 ff. The names are given by Walsingham, *Historia* II, 159, 216; see also Knighton, II, 181.

[2] McFarlane, ibid.

[3] For what follows see especially H. G. Richardson, 'Heresy and the Lay Power', EHR 51 (1936) 1–28.

[4] *Rotuli parliamentorum* III, 124–5.

of people congregated'.[1] It had the effect of short-circuiting the earlier channels for a direct junction between the spiritual and secular arms. To give it effect a statute was drawn up in July to arrest and imprison anyone maintaining the Twenty Four articles condemned at Blackfriars in May. They were to remain in gaol until such time as they abjured them or the king's council decided otherwise.[2] Moreover, on this occasion the earlier need for a bishop first to certify the offenders was now omitted.[3] Initially the new method applied only to Canterbury province; but in 1384 it was extended to York,[4] the Commons' protest in November 1382, that they had not assented to the new decrees, having been ignored.[5] It remained in force for six years.

A new stage of secular intervention was reached in 1388. Just as the earlier measures had come in the aftermath of the Peasants' Revolt, so these latest ones followed the upheaval in government by the 'Merciless Parliament'. But they were also doubtless the result of the growth of Lollardy which, we have seen, had been carried westwards to the Welsh Marches. No mention of action against heresy is to be found in the statutes or parliamentary records. But we learn from Knighton[6] that Lords and Commons appealed to the king to act against the spread of Lollard opinions. On their advice he directed the archbishop of Canterbury and the bishops to proceed against heretics and heretical writings in English. Inquisitors were appointed for every county to search them out; this was followed during 1388 and 1389 by the creation of a series of commissions already alluded to.[7] Addressed variously to laymen and/or ecclesiastics they had the effect of now formally identifying Lollard heresy with the works of Wyclif, Hereford, Aston and Purvey and their adherents.[8] Their works were to be seized and brought before the council; 'the maintenance of those opinions, or the keeping, writing or selling of those books' was prohibited under 'pain of imprisonment or forfeiture'; and all who were in possession of the said books were to give them up. The commissioners were empowered to 'summon offenders and examine them, and to commit them, when convicted, to prison until they disavow their heresy or until further action for their

[1] Ibid., 124. [2] Wilkins, III, 156; *Calendar of Patent Rolls, 1381–5*, 150.

[3] Richardson, art. cit., 8.

[4] Ibid., 8–9; *Cal. Pat. Rolls, 1381–5*, 487.

[5] *Rot. parliamentorum* III, 141.

[6] *Chronicon* II, 263–4.

[7] *Cal. Pat. Rolls* 1385–9, 427, 430, 468, 536, 550; Wilkins, III, 204.

[8] Ibid., 468; see also Knighton, II, 264–5.

delivery'.[1] These new measures led to renewed prosecution of the Lollards in their two main haunts of the Welsh border and the Midlands, as we have seen. The campaign against the heretics remained firmly in church hands; initiative was still with the bishops, who continued to use the older methods as well: as for example the instruction to the sheriff of Northampton to arrest John Woodward and 45 Lollard followers;[2] the king's order to the sheriff of Hereford and other royal officers to arrest Swinderby and Stephen Bell after they had fled in 1391; and the application by the bishop of Lincoln in 1394 for writs against six Lollards for not answering his summons.[3] The lay power, for its part, merely retained the right of final appeal, which it occasionally exercised as in the case of four Lollards who abjured before the king's council at York in 1396.[4] But beyond this right of intervention its part was to second the ecclesiastical powers. The fact that it was prepared to take up a supporting role suggests that the main impulse to repression came from the church. Certainly this was true of 1382; and even if it is not so apparent in 1388, the effect was further to strengthen its authority.

Subsequent developments were occasioned by the appearance of the Lollard Twelve Conclusions in 1395. Despite the previous measures taken against them, the Lollards, far from being crushed, in that year issued their appeal to parliament in January 1395. Nailed to the doors of Westminster and St. Paul's its call for disendowment[5] confronted the church with the most direct challenge it had yet received. Even if no aristocratic influence lay behind it,[6] the declaration was an overt invitation to the king and lay lords to despoil the church; it seems, circumstantially, more than likely that it was then, in the book that he had already presented to the king,[7] that Purvey's proposals for the redistribution of the church's wealth were made.[8] The reaction on the

[1] *Reg. Trefnant* 408–9. Richardson, art. cit., 15–16. See also *Reg. Trefnant* 410–11, for the king's commission to Sir John Chandos and other laymen to prevent interference with the trial of Brute. Richardson, art. cit., 14.

[2] *Cal. Close Rolls*, 1385–9 (London 1921) 667–8; Richardson, art. cit., 16.

[3] *Cal. Close Rolls* 1392–6 (London 1925) 260.

[4] Wilkins, III, 225; *Cal. Close Rolls* 1392–6, 487.

[5] For its provisions, see pp. 584–5 above.

[6] Walsingham's account of events *Historia* II, 216 makes the Lollard knights responsible for it, without any foundation.

[7] FZ 364: quia fuit probatum in uno libro quem rex habuit quod centum domus eleemosynarum sufficiunt in toto regno.

[8] See p. 582 above.

latter's part was immediate. The Canterbury convocation, in February 1395, petitioned the king as its 'gracious lord and protector' to extend the death penalty to the Lollards as heretics.[1] Copies of the Twelve Conclusions were forwarded to Boniface IX who replied on 17 September 1395 in letters to the king, the archbishops of Canterbury and York, and other bishops—and later the mayor and sheriffs of London—urging them to suppress 'the cunning and bold sect of pseudo-Christians' and invoking the aid of the lay power.[2] The pope also took the opportunity to remind the secular lords, in good ecclesiastical style, of the threat in such doctrines to their own authority and possessions; if unchecked, it could only lead to their subversion and ruin.[3] Beyond ordering the expulsion of all Lollards from Oxford[4] and an examination of the *Trialogus*[5] the government appears to have done little; and two years later a renewed appeal to the king through parliament for the introduction of the death penalty,[6] was thwarted by the exile of Arundel and the subsequent abdication of Richard II.[7]

Even so, the delay was not for long. In 1401, within two years of Henry IV's accession and the restoration of Arundel as archbishop of Canterbury, came the statute *De heretico comburendo*.[8] It decreed that all those found guilty of heresy or the possession of heretical writings, by due canonical process, who refused to abjure their errors, or having done so, relapsed into them, were to be handed over to the lay power and burned. It was accompanied by renewed restrictions on Lollard preaching, against which the new king had already acted in May 1400;[9] and it was followed by a further statute directly empowering the bishops to arrest and imprison suspects.[10] This, too, had come from the clergy, who expressed alarm at the spread of Lollard ideas through preaching and private conventicles.[11]

De heretico comburendo marked a new stage in the official attitude

[1] Wilkins, III, 223.

[2] *Calendar of Papal Letters IV*, 1363–1404 (London 1902) 515–16; *Reg. Trefnant*, 405–7.

[3] *Reg. Trefnant*, 407.

[4] *Cal. Close Rolls, 1392–6*, 437.

[5] Ibid., 434.

[6] For these events see M. McKisack, *The Fourteenth Century* (Oxford 1959) 378 ff., 392 ff.

[7] Richardson, art. cit., 22.

[8] *Rotuli parliamentorum* III, 466–7; Wilkins, III, 252–4.

[9] *Calendar Close Rolls, 1399–1402*, 185.

[10] *Statutes of the Realm* II, 125–8.

[11] Wilkins, III, 254; *Rot. parl.* III, 473–4.

towards Lollardy. Hitherto reprisal had lain almost entirely with the spiritual power; it had merely had the co-operation of the secular arm in apprehending and handing over suspects. Now, however, the final sanction passed to the king's officers. Forfeiture, fining, and ultimately burning became the penalties for heresy. Lollardy had passed from being a periodic irritant to an endemic crime. This change, reached after twenty years of heresy-hunting, finally brought England into line with the rest of Christendom. But it did more: in treating Lollardy as a crime it came to regard Lollards as criminals as well as heretics. From this time forward, although Lollards continued to be arraigned for spiritual depravity, as Sawtry, the first victim of the new statute, and Thorpe, the first to escape its application, were, they now also appeared as felons against the law. Secular measures brought with them secular attitudes. To the sin of heresy was now added the crime of subversion: if not treason in so many words, those convicted of it suffered a like fate. From being merely policeman the state had become executioner.

How this affected its conception of Lollardy can be seen from parliament's enactments of 1406 and 1414. On each occasion the background was one of social unrest. The new dynasty of Henry IV had had to face a series of external invasion and internal disorders; the legend that Richard II, murdered in 1400, was still alive, acted as a rallying point for opposition to the present king. Much of this is reflected in the 1406 act passed against the Lollards.[1] For the first time laymen now took up the alarm, long sounded by theologians, that to confiscate the temporal possessions of the church was ultimately to threaten the very existence of all lordship, secular as well as spiritual. The Lollards by teaching these ideas in their conventicles and 'secret places called schools' were, they warned the king, inciting the people into 'open commotion . . . and the final destruction of your kingdom for all time'.[2] They were also spreading rumours that Richard II still lived, as well as engaging in false prophecies. In order to put them down it was decreed that anyone found propagating such opinions was to be arrested and imprisoned without bail and brought before the chancellor for judgement by king and lords in the next parliament. Both secular and spiritual powers were authorized to seize all suspects without further commissions.[3] Civil and ecclesiastical offences had thus become one in the eyes of the law. It is true that the 1410 parliament tried unsuccessfully to get it modified,[4] when also Purvey's proposals were supposed to have been presented in

[1] *Rot. parl.* III, 583–4. [2] Ibid., 583. [3] Ibid., 584.
[4] *Rot. parl.* III, 623; McFarlane, 155.

a petition to disendow the church.[1] Neither, however, came to anything. The first was decisively rejected by the king; the second, if it was ever made, met its nemesis in the defeat of Oldcastle's rising four years later.[2]

This entailed more than the destruction of a band of desperadoes; it meant the end of any hopes of aristocratic support of Lollardy: the sympathies for it which had periodically found expression both in parliament and in rumours, such as those of proposals made by a number of knights at Worcester in 1402 and 1405 to strip the bishops of their possessions,[3] may or may not have had serious intent; but that they indicated a tendency there can be little doubt. After 1414 it was irrevocably overthrown by the rival tendency which had gathered increasing strength in the disturbed atmosphere of Henry IV's reign: namely to regard Lollardy as sedition. The parliament which met at Leicester on 30 April 1414, barely three months after Oldcastle's *débâcle*, enshrined it in law. The statute which it passed[4] laid it down that henceforth the chancellor, treasurer, justices, sheriffs, bailiffs and all other royal officers were responsible for suppressing heresy as part of their duties. The obligation to do so was to be included in their oaths of office; they were empowered to investigate any suspected source of heresy—sermons, conventicles, schools, congregations and writings. Those accused could be charged in royal courts, and hearing such cases now came within their purview.

By this legislation the lay power, for its part, had created an anti-heretical machinery which had been building since 1382. It only needed complementing by similar ecclesiastical measures for the process to be complete. That was done two years later in 1416, when the archbishop of Canterbury, Henry Chichele, provided for a parallel system of twice-yearly visitations of every rural deanery.[5] Thus in little over thirty years after Wyclif's death the impulse begun by his teachings had carried Lollardy to open insurrection and the state to systematic repression. By 1416 England had joined the rest of Christendom in putting heresy-hunting upon a permanent footing.

That in all essentials it was an inquisition is rarely acknowledged. Perhaps this is because it remained under royal aegis and not the holy office. But if it was free from papal direction and mendicant control

[1] Walsingham, II, 282–3. [2] See pp. 601 ff. below.
[3] *Annales Henrici Quarti*, 373, 414, quoted in Aston, art. cit., 18.
[4] *Rot. parl.* IV, 24–5; Wilkins, III, 358–60; *Statutes of the Realm* II, 181–4.
[5] Wilkins, III, 378.

it had a comparable judicial standing: it employed the same methods of hunting suspects by enquiry, arrest and trial; and made similar efforts to gain abjuration before imposing the now accepted penalty of death by burning if these failed. Regular visitation; support from the secular arm; special legal proceedings leading to imprisonment, forfeiture and death. These were the elements of all anti-heretical activity. By 1416 England possessed them in full measure. Whatever the name assigned them, they were also those of the continental inquisition.

It now only remains to consider briefly the Lollard movement in its later subversive phase. As with all the heretical groups we have examined this was as much the result of interaction between it and the established authorities as of its own evolution. Nor did the change to which it led destroy its original characteristics, but rather overlaid them. Thus if at one level Lollardy became increasingly identified with political subversion and plotting, it also remained true to its theological inspiration. Lollards like Badby, Oldcastle, Claydon and Wyche, held to the basic tenets of their creed while being arraigned for rebellion; and all the time simple adherents continued to look to the observance of God's word and right living as the road to election without giving political vent to their beliefs. For this reason Lollardy continued as a spiritual and religious outlook, surviving into the Reformation,[1] despite its failure politically by 1431.

The passing of *De heretico comburendo* in 1401 led inevitably to renewed activity against the Lollards. It was not long before the act claimed Sawtry as its first victim, burned for having relapsed into the stock heresies, mentioned earlier.[2] His example was enough to lead Purvey, captured in the very week of Sawtry's death, to recant[3] and end his life in a benefice. It may well have sufficed for others as well; for in spite of further anti-heretical measures by the 1406 parliament and the publication of Arundel's constitutions, which as we saw[4] imposed a censorship as well as a ban upon vernacular translations of the bible in 1409, only one other person was burned during Henry IV's reign. He was John Badby, a tailor from Evesham,[5] and he was said only to have

[1] For Lollardy in the fifteenth century see A. G. Dickens, 'Heresy and the origins of English Protestantism' in *Britain and the Netherlands* (ed. J. S. Bromley and E. H. Kossmann) II (1964) 47–66, and now above all Thompson, *Later Lollards*.

[2] See above pp. 583–4.

[3] See above p. 578.

[4] See pp. 570 ff. above.

[5] John Foxe, *Acts and Monuments*, London 1684, I, 593–5; also Wilkins, III, 326.

been finally consigned to the flames after the Prince of Wales, the future Henry V, had vainly entreated him to abjure. Nor was the attempt to save him an isolated one. Arundel, in spite of his uncompromising hostility towards the Lollards, more than once showed that concern for a man's soul which to some degree mitigated the harshnesses of the inquisition. However abhorrent the notion of regulating men's beliefs must be, the compassion which often accompanied it must also be recognized.

An example of Arundel's scrupulousness is the trial of William Thorpe in 1407. It was given lasting fame by John Foxe, who in his *Acts and Monuments*, put Thorpe among the forerunners of the English Reformers who suffered at the hands of the Catholic church.[1] Arundel was worsted in argument, if we are to believe Thorpe's account, which may be the reason why there is no record of the trial. Certainly he was not burned and he did not recant. He had been a preacher for thirty years and had been arrested previously in 1397 without having been made to confess. Hence he had not relapsed. Cases like these help to show how Lollardy in its theological, as opposed to its political, aspect suffered no wholesale decimation. Despite the growing paraphernalia of repression, and the increasing tendency to identify it with other subversive movements, the two Lollard martyrs burned for heresy in Henry IV's reign reflect its predominantly theological and individual mode of activity. It also indicates how clandestine they were.

Their momentary eruption into the open under Oldcastle in 1414, however, changed all this.[2] Oldcastle was born in Herefordshire in 1378 and was attached to Henry V's household. He was made Lord Cobham in 1408. His Lollardy was of long standing and probably went back to the days of Swinderby whose preaching he had heard when a boy. By 1413, when Henry V succeeded to the throne, there was a growing body of evidence against him. One of his chaplains had been cited for heresy in 1410; Oldcastle had written to support the Hussites in 1410 and again to Wenceslas in 1411.[3] In March 1413 suspicions were aired in convocation;[4] and when some heretical works belonging to him were

[1] *J. Foxe's Acts and Monuments*, ibid., 600–18. Accounts of most of the important trials—Swinderby, Brute, Repingdon, etc.—and condemnations are to be found here.

[2] No attempt here has been made to recount the events of the rising. It is described by McFarlane, 160–182, and W. T. Waugh, 'Sir John Oldcastle' in EHR xx (1905), 434–56, 637–58.

[3] McFarlane, 161–2.

[4] The account of Oldcastle's indictment and subsequent examination leading to his imprisonment and excommunication is in FZ 433–50; Wilkins, III, 353–8.

found in an illuminator's shop the king was told.[1] Despite Oldcastle's disclaimer[2] that he had not examined their contents properly, convocation expressed alarm at aristocratic support for the Lollards and singled out Oldcastle as their 'chief harbourer, accomplice and protector in the dioceses of London, Rochester, and Hereford'. He was also accused of holding Lollard opinions on the eucharist, penance, pilgrimages, images and absolution. Accordingly appeal was made to the king to proceed against him.[3] The king tried, but failed, to persuade Oldcastle to submit. Arundel was then allowed to proceed against him. Oldcastle was summoned but refused to appear before the archbishop, and was finally arrested and put in the Tower on 23 September.[4]

At his trial which followed Oldcastle rejected Arundel's offer to absolve him and proceeded to read a statement of his views on the eucharist and other matters with which he had been charged. These did not satisfy the archbishop who pressed him about his eucharistic opinions. Oldcastle would not explain further, beyond denying that it was a question for the pope and the prelates to decide.[5] He was then given the week-end to ponder a statement of the church's teaching on the eucharist, confessions, the authority of the pope and the priesthood, and pilgrimages.

At the trial's resumption, Oldcastle again rejected absolution from any but God. He next gave his own replies to the four articles: of the eucharist he said the bread remained after consecration; of confession he said that it was advisable to obtain it but not necessary for salvation; of the adoration of the cross he averred that only Christ's body should be venerated. As to the power of the pope and the hierarchy he declared that the pope was the true Antichrist and its head; the prelates were its members; and the friars its tail:[6] a similar division to that maintained by John Claydon, one of Oldcastle's followers, burned after the rising.[7] Oldcastle then denounced the assembled judges and refused to answer more.[8] He was duly excommunicated and made over to the secular arm.[9]

The king gave Oldcastle forty days in which to abjure. Over half his time had passed when, on 19 October, Oldcastle with the help of friends escaped and went into hiding near Smithfield.[10] He now set

[1] Wilkins, III, 351.
[2] Ibid., 352.
[3] FZ 434; Wilkins, III, 352.
[4] FZ 435–7.
[5] Ibid., 437–41.
[6] Ibid., 443–45.
[7] See below p. 602.
[8] Ibid., 445.
[9] Ibid., 445–9.
[10] For what follows see McFarlane, 167 f.; Waugh, art. cit., 639 ff.

about plotting to seize the king and overthrow the government. His object was later stated as

> wholly to annul the royal estate as well as the estate and office of prelates and religious orders in England, and to kill the king, his brothers, the prelates and the other magnates of the kingdom, and to turn men of religion, after they had abandoned divine worship and religious observances, to secular occupations: totally to despoil cathedrals and other churches and religious houses of their relics and other ecclesiastical goods, and to level them completely to the ground.[1]

November and December were spent in mustering his followers who, to the number of 20,000 men, were to converge on St. Giles's Fields, London. The coup was planned for the night of 9/10 January; but it was betrayed shortly before. Oldcastle was deserted and his provincial adherents trapped and overwhelmed. He himself escaped, but sixty-nine of those captured were condemned to death. Most of them had come from the Midlands, with Leicester again one of their chief centres; some were also from Essex; but hardly any from Kent and East Anglia. Probably the total number did not reach three hundred, justly termed 'a miserably small response'.[2] Of these only a minority were genuine Lollards as the figure of seven burned to thirty-eight hanged indicates.[3] Their execution on 13 January signalized Lollardy's entry, as a political movement, upon the collision course of conspiracy and treason. It was now reduced to rebellion as the only hope of attaining its ends.

Inevitably Lollards now came to be implicated in plots against the realm, such as that of Southampton in 1415, and the Scottish raids on Berwick and Roxborough.[4] Complicity with foreigners to overthrow the king figured prominently in charges against Lollards like Thomas Payne and Thomas Lucas. Payne of Glamorgan, described as Oldcastle's 'chief counsellor', was, when captured in 1418 or 1419, accused of being about to release the king of Scotland then imprisoned at Windsor.[5] Lucas, a fellow of Merton College, Oxford, was charged in 1417 with having planned the king's downfall; this included writing to the emperor Sigismund, then in England, that Richard II was still alive in Edinburgh, and scattering bills to the same effect in London, Canterbury and other places.[6] Others accused with him were Richard Benet and John Whitlock whom Lucas, 'acting with, counselling and

[1] *Rot. parl.* IV, 107–10. Quoted from Aston, art. cit., 18–19.

[2] McFarlane, 176.

[3] McFarlane, 177. Many probably joined for gain. See Aston, art. cit., 20.

[4] Aston, art. cit., 20–2. [5] Ibid., 21. [6] Ibid.

abetting the works of John Oldcastle, both his opinions of Lollardy and all his other evil deeds', incited with others to kill the king.[1] Lucas repented and was acquitted; but the other two were punished for conspiracy, Benet by hanging. So also was Thomas of Beckering, Lincolnshire, who died in prison.[2] Whitlock's sedition in Richard II's cause dated back to 1406.[3]

At the same time an element of apocalypticism had entered into Lollardy. Wyclif's later identification of the pope and church hierarchy with Antichrist had been taken a stage further by Oldcastle in his elaboration of their correspondence to the different parts of the beast. John Claydon, burned in September 1415, for his part in Oldcastle's rising, did the same.[4] Arraigned for heresy on fifteen counts he called the pope chief Antichrist, the archbishop and bishops its seat, and the source of all error by which the faithful were misled, and the religious its poisonous tail.[5] Licences for preaching were 'the true sign of the beast'.[6] Other of his opinions were that only the elect belonged to the church;[7] that Christ had not founded private religious orders, which were useless and should be extirpated;[8] that possessions and begging were the two causes of Christian tribulation;[9] and that prelates should not be obeyed unless they cared for souls and preached.[10] There were also the usual Lollard articles on the eucharist, indulgences, image worship, and 'elaborate arts'.

Oldcastle was caught and burned in 1417,[11] but the movement he had fashioned went on. During the next decade Lollards of all colours continued periodically to be caught. The record of some was chequered, like that of William Taylor who had preached against endowment as long ago as 1406[12] and was finally burned at Smithfield in 1423: it was perhaps a sign of the times that, as well as denouncing clerical dominion, he gave only qualified authority to secular lordship. God allowed it permissively but did not actively will or approve it:[13] it was the same argument as that which the scholastics took to explain sin. If this was not a resurrection of the doctrine of dominion and grace, neither was

[1] Aston, art. cit., 21. [2] Ibid., 22. [3] Ibid., 21–2.

[4] *Register of Henry Chichele* (ed. E. F. Jacob) 4 vols., Canterbury and York Society (1937–47) IV, 132–7.

[5] Arts. 1, 2, 4 (ibid., 136).

[6] Ibid., 3. [7] Ibid., 5. [8] Ibid., 6.

[9] Ibid., 7, 8. [10] Ibid., 14. [11] McFarlane, 182.

[12] See p. 585 above.

[13] FZ 413. A full account of his trial is in *Reg. Chichele* 157–73. It took place in the presence of Humphrey, duke of Gloucester, and the earls of Warwick and Vendôme.

it an avowal of the rights of lay lordship. Oldcastle's accomplices continued to be prominent among those brought to light. They included John Prest, vicar of Chesterton, Warwickshire, who had given Oldcastle shelter for two years, and John Reynold, a tailor, both in 1421 bound over to renounce Oldcastle's opinions;[1] also Robert Hook, rector of Braybrooke (Northants), one of Oldcastle's propaganda centres,[2] and Thomas Drayton, rector of Snave (Kent), an associate of William Taylor,[3] who were afterwards discovered and tried before convocation in 1425.

Kent, where Oldcastle's Cobham estates lay, seems to have been one of the main centres of Lollardy during the 1420s, and included priests like William White, tried at Norwich in September 1428,[4] and Richard Wyche who was burned in 1440.[5] White, who migrated to Norwich from Canterbury diocese, following his citation, with seventeen others, for heresy by the archbishop in July 1428,[6] held to nearly everything that Purvey had said. On ecclesiastical disendowment he regarded lay lords as bound, under pain of mortal sin, to take away the church's lands.[7] The remaining Lollards named with White seem to have escaped, though it is possible that the archbishop was more successful with others: a contemporary account of his drive against the Lollards speaks of 30 being imprisoned.[8] Among those condemned in 1428 was Ralph Mungyn, brought before the Canterbury convocation on 26 December[9] and sentenced to perpetual imprisonment for refusing to abjure his two errors: that no one should fight against the heretics in Bohemia and that no goods should be held in common;[10] he was said also to have come under the influence of Peter Payne, the Oxford Lollard who had fled to Prague and who had preached Wyclif's errors at Oxford and London. Mungyn, when he left Oxford for London, disseminated English translations of Wyclif's and Payne's writings and had in his possession a copy of the *Trialogus*.[11] He had also had dealings with Bartholomew Cornmonger and Nicholas Hoper, one of Oldcastle's servants.[12] Others tried for heresy at the same convocation included Robert, rector of Hedgerley, Bucks, who showed dubious

[1] Aston, art. cit., 23.
[2] Aston, art. cit., 23–4; *Reg. Chichele* III, 111.
[3] Aston, ibid., 24.
[4] FZ 417–32. See p. 583 above.
[5] Aston, *art. cit.*, 23.
[6] *Reg. Chichele* IV, 297–301.
[7] FZ. 431.
[8] *Reg. Chichele* I, cxxxvii; cited by Aston, art. cit., note 112.
[9] *Reg. Chichele* III, 197–205; Aston, art. cit., 23.
[10] *Reg. Chichele* III, 197, 204.
[11] Ibid., 198.
[12] Ibid., 199.

opinions on the eucharist, pilgrimages, adoration of the cross, and church temporalities;[1] Thomas Garntner, or Garenter, chaplain to Nicholas Shadworth of London,[2] and Richard Monk, a priest born at Melton Mowbray, Leicester, and formerly vicar of Chesham.[3] Both the latter recanted.[4]

These cases show enough continuity with Oldcastle's cause for us to be not altogether surprised at a further attempt to revive it. In the spring of 1431 a new insurrection, led by William Perkins alias 'Jack Sharpe of Wigmoreland', was discovered at Salisbury and nipped in the bud.[5] Its aims, besides disendowment of the church—again based upon Purvey's proposals presented in 1410—this time included a comprehensive plan to replace the royal family and leading members of the nobility by the victorious insurgents: the royal uncles, regents for the minor Henry VI, were to be killed, as well as nine abbots, three priors, the dukes of Norfolk and York and the earl of Huntingdon.[6] A score or more of 'certain poor people', unknown to themselves, were to replace them; and a number of others were selected for important offices including 'the mysterious posts of *regis controrotulator, embasiator, custos London*', and *capitalis hered*''.[7] This time, in order to avoid the fiasco of 1414, the assembly point was to be at the village of East Hendred, Berkshire, in a field called Gyldynmylle, with Abingdon Abbey the first target.[8]

The reactions of the government show how seriously it treated the plot. A special commissioner was sent to Coventry, and the duke of Gloucester himself twice visited the Midlands. Perkins was executed at Abingdon and other measures taken in Wiltshire and Somerset. These areas, with London, seem to have been the chief centres of the rising; Perhaps the greatest difference between 1414 and 1431 was the absence of gentry from the later rising. Only Sir John and Thomas Cheyne were arrested; and their association with heresy went back to Oldcastle with whom their father had been involved.[9] But in the main it was a pre-

[1] *Reg. Chichele* III, 188.
[2] Ibid., 200–1, 205–7, 210.
[3] Ibid., 197–9, 201–2, 205–8.
[4] Ibid., 205–8.
[5] It is described by Mrs. Aston, art. cit., 24–30, whose account has been followed here.
[6] Ibid., 27.
[7] Ibid., 28.
[8] Ibid. Perkins was executed at Abingdon (ibid., 29). For John Long and William Russell, other leaders of the rebellion, ibid., 25 ff., especially Russell's connexions with John Claydon and Richard Gurmyn, both executed in 1415 and 1416 (ibid., 25–6).
[9] Ibid.

dominantly artisan movement as its location in both the urban centres and the rural areas of the woollen industry suggests. Lollard suspects were drawn mainly, as we have seen, from such trades as weavers, wool men, dyers, girdle-makers, shoemakers, wire-drawers and so on.[1] These together with its poorer priests, for the most part unbeneficed, appear to have formed the core of Lollardy, giving it its at once theological and practical character.

1431 marked the extinction of Lollardy as a political force, even though it continued as an outlook. No doubt individual Lollards participated in such events as Jack Cade's rebellion in 1450, and a group of them, sworn to overthrow Antichrist, was to be found as late as 1457 in Lincoln.[2] Yet it was as a current of beliefs that it passed into the age of the Reformation, with its emphasis upon simplicity of worship and righteous living which was later to form such a strong element in Puritanism. It is not our purpose here to follow it further. In the context of this study it has been shown how Wyclif's ideas were harnessed to an ideal, at once spiritual and political, which, in challenging the church, ultimately came to challenge the state. As so often the desire for reform led to revolution, and the quest for the true church to the rejection of the present order.

[1] For example ibid., 15.

[2] Ibid., 30. For further examples in the second half of the fifteenth century, see Thompson, *The Later Lollards*.

IX

The Hussite Reformation

Even today, when the independent character of the Hussite movement has long since been generally acknowledged, there remains a lingering tendency to treat it as an extension of Lollardy. This is understandable. Wyclif did have a strong influence upon Hus and his contemporaries; both Lollardy and Hussitism were moral protests against the abuses in the church, which they were both united in ascribing to its departure from Christ's precepts and the ways of the primitive church. For both the path of reform lay in the renunciation of worldliness and wealth and the return to apostolic poverty, humility and simplicity. Both made the bible the sole criterion of truth, and conformity to its tenets the test of righteousness; and, perhaps most characteristic of all, both went beyond the bounds of orthodoxy in denying much of the authority of the existing hierarchy in the name of the invisible church of the elect, which alone constituted the mystical body of Christ. The importance of these common convictions should not be underestimated; but nor should they obscure the very real differences in character between the two groups which held them.

Wyclif, for all the intensity of his beliefs and his intellectual eminence among his contemporaries, was an essentially solitary figure, with no real forerunners and few disciples worthy of the name. He spent most of his life in academic seclusion at Oxford and died in isolation at Lutterworth. Nor did his system survive him, if it ever lived. His heirs were a handful of Oxford scholars, who either abjured their errors or took to the wilderness, and an assortment of unbeneficed priests and semi-literate laymen, together with perhaps a few gentry. Their influence was never more than peripheral; and when they attempted to make themselves felt at the centre of affairs it was by characteristically clandestine devices like nailing anonymous manifestos to church doors or the abortive insurrections of 1414 and 1431. English Lollardy was from the outset deformed by Wyclif's extremism; it remained to the end a cripple with all the bitterness of ineffectuality. At most it can be regarded as a forerunner of the Reformation, a straw in the wind rather than an agent in its attainment. It is difficult to believe that English or continental history would have been very different for absence of Lollardy.

The same cannot be said of Hussitism. It represented the turning point from heresy to reformation. With it for the first time protest against the church took the form of national revolt; in the process it crystallized the main positions of subsequent Protestantism. What began as heresy towards the Catholic church ended in the creation of an independent Christian church. This was the achievement of the Hussite revolution, which in all essentials anticipated Luther's of a century later. The burning of Hus, far from marking the failure of one more movement of protest, signalized its transformation into the beginning of a European-wide movement for reform.

This profound difference between the two groups is not fortuitous. It sprang from the very discrepant backgrounds of English Lollardy and Czech Hussitism. To begin with, the latter had its source not in any single individual but in a succession of reformers dating back to at least 1360 when Charles IV (1347–78) the emperor, and also king of Bohemia, called in Conrad of Waldhausen to preach against the prevailing abuses in the church.[1] Waldhausen was the beginning of a line of preachers which reached right through into the fifteenth century and helped to give the Czech reforming movement its distinctive moral and practical outlook. The Czech reformers evinced little of Wyclif's metaphysical and speculative interests; for that reason alone Hus was never a Wyclifite in the real sense of the term, despite all his reverence for the English scholastic. It also accounts for their different roles. Wyclif's connexion with Lollardy was an indirect one; he was an heresiarch without being a leader. Hus, on the contrary, followed in the steps of two generations of Czech reformers and became a leader without being a heretic, let alone heresiarch. He was not an original thinker or a doctrinal innovator but a reformer and preacher, who through circumstances came to take up an increasingly uncompromising attitude towards authority. His writings, except for academic exercises like his Commentary on the *Sentences*, reflected the day-to-day struggle in which he was engaged. They are predominantly concerned with the abuses within the church, above all simony and the false pretensions of the hierarchy over excommunication, absolution and the sacraments, as we shall later discuss.

The second important discrepancy between the English and Czech

[1] P. de Vooght, *L'hérésie*, F. Palacký, *Geschichte von Böhmen* III, and Count Lützow, *Master John Hus*.

movements lay in the different positions of the church in the two countries. England, for all the irritations caused by papal preferment, enjoyed a degree of detachment because of its geographical position; and the papacy's long established deference to royal wishes in matters of patronage enabled the king to do much as he liked towards the church. By the time of Wyclif royal control of the clergy in England had long been established in most spheres. Wyclif's denunciations of papal interference, for all their truth, have in comparison with the king's power, an air of unreality. Bohemia, however, enjoyed neither this relative immunity from the papacy nor the relative subordination of the church.[1] It has been estimated that the church and monasteries together owned one half of all the land; the king was the next greatest landowner with a sixth of the total, leaving the remaining third to be shared among the entire lay population, noble and ignoble alike. There was accordingly a very real sense of grievance towards the church, which was accentuated by the undoubtedly corrupting effect of wealth upon ecclesiastics and the religious orders. Although indictments of clerical immorality are as old as the church, and the same charges of idleness, sexual licence, avarice and spiritual depravity can be found no less in the time of St. Bernard than in the fourteenth and fifteenth centuries, this does not make them any less probable. It does not require explanations of moral decline to accept the endemic existence of such abuses in the later middle ages; they sprang from the very tensions between spiritual aspirations and the material and corporate privileges which had evolved to support them. Those guilty of the standard charges levelled against the church were probably never more than a minority; but in fourteenth-century Bohemia they seem to have been particularly prevalent no doubt just because of the excessive wealth which the church and monasteries enjoyed. Hus himself wrote bitterly of them in his work *On Simony*, where he referred scathingly to 'priests who shamefully squander pay for requiem masses in fornication, in adorning their concubines, priestesses, or prostitutes more sumptuously than the church altars and pictures, purchasing for them skirts, capes, and fur coats from their tithes and offerings of the poor'.[2] He also spoke of the self-indulgence of the religious and their hypocrisy as shown in their double standards of brewing different

[1] For what follows see F. G. Heymann, *John Žižka and the Hussite Revolution* (Princeton 1955) ch. 3, 36 ff.

[2] *On Simony* translated by M. Spinka in *Advocates of Reform* (London 1953) (Library of Christian Classics, vol. XIV) 251.

kinds of beer, weak for visitors and strong for themselves and their intimates.[1]

The contrast between the materialism among the hierarchy, and the religious, and the impoverishment of the lower orders, both clerical and lay, was accentuated at Prague by Charles IV's rich adornment of many of the churches there: hostility to images and relics was one of the hallmarks of the reform movement. Resentment against the hierarchy was also nourished by the papal monopoly of preferments, which increased greatly after Prague became an independent See in 1347. The power of the Roman curia to appoint to benefices and the consequent obligation of the new incumbent to pay to it his first year's stipend, annates, was, as we have observed, a source of universal hostility. Bohemia—or perhaps more accurately Prague—was no exception. Revulsion at having obtained his canonry by such means led Milíč of Kroměříž—one of the Hussite forerunners—to renounce the path of preferment and office and devote himself to furthering reform.[2] For Hus, as we shall see, the system was unadulterated simony, which he regarded as the worst and most deep-seated evil of the contemporary church. Its denunciation was one of the main planks in the reformer's platform.

Finally to this must be added what may be called the German question. The Germans had played a leading part in the colonization of Bohemia and had come to occupy most of the leading positions in the kingdom. Even Prague university, founded by Charles IV in 1348, was dominated by German masters until their secession to Leipzig in 1409; the government of the city was likewise in German hands. Inevitably, the desire for the reform of the Bohemian church and its independence from outside interference helped to stimulate latent nationalist feeling against the Germans, which was of long standing.[3] One of the recurrent charges made by the Czech clergy against Hus was that he had stirred up anti-German feeling. But the consequences of this friction between Czechs and Germans went beyond anything Hus might have said or done. In 1409 the German masters at Prague university seceded *en bloc* to Leipzig, after the king, Wenceslas (Václav) IV, had reversed their majority of three votes to one Czech vote.[4] The German exodus changed the university into a Czech body. In due course, under mounting pressure, the Germans were also forced out of their positions of control in other sectors, making possible the alliance

[1] Ibid., 238. [2] See pp. 611 ff. below.
[3] See Cosmas of Prague: quoted in Heymann, op. cit., 50.
[4] See pp. 628 ff. below.

between the university and the capital in what was to become a struggle for Bohemian independence.

The leadership of Prague was one of the most remarkable aspects of the Hussite Movement; a city for the first time replaced king and nobles not only in the government of a kingdom but in directing resistance against foreign attacks and ultimately obtaining imperial and papal recognition. Its hegemony was in no small measure due to the Czech reformers, who, as masters and preachers, fused doctrine and popular ideals into what was both a religious and national struggle. This is where their strength lay; they were at once advocates of reform and spokesmen for a people.

Seen in this light the disparity between the Lollards and the Hussites could hardly have been greater. It was the result at once of different national circumstances and the different status of the Czech reformers. Unlike their English counterparts, they neither acted, nor were treated, as heretics in their own land. True, the charge of heresy was repeatedly made against Hus in particular; but to the end he enjoyed the support of much of the university, usually of the king and queen, and probably always of the people. Had he stayed in Bohemia, it is inconceivable that he would ever have been burned, just as his followers were not. Nor was his position in any way unique; it was rather their final penalty which set Hus and Jerome of Prague[1] apart from their confrères. The reformers in their roles as theologians and preachers were an accepted part of Czech religious life. They spoke not just for themselves, or a small sect, but for the majority. For that reason, they succeeded where the Lollards failed.

The Hussite tradition: the forerunners

The coming of Conrad of Waldhausen to Prague in 1360,[2] was an event of the first importance. Not only did it inaugurate a new line of religious criticism culminating in Hus and his successors; it also influenced its nature. Waldhausen was a preacher and a moralist; although little of what he said has survived, there is enough to show how closely he anticipated some of the main lines of Hussite thought in the next

[1] For Jerome see R. R. Betts, 'Jerome of Prague' in *University of Birmingham Historical Journal* I (1947) 1–91.

[2] The best general account is still to be found in F. Palacký, *Geschichte von Böhmen*, vol. III, 161–4; the same book V, ch. 3, treats the beginnings of the reform movement down to Hus and Jerome.

century.[1] Like the Hussites, he was above all concerned with the contemporary state of religious life. His outspoken denunciations of its abuses in Prague, especially by the monks and friars, brought down upon his head false charges of heresy and defamation which he just as outspokenly rebutted. In particular he inveighed against simony, which he saw as the worst and most widespread of all the heresies;[2] the veneration of relics which exposed simple believers to deception such as the pretence that the truffa carried on St. Barbara's day in Prague belonged to the saint, whereas it could only be in Prussia;[3] and the general laxity of the religious orders through their avarice and excessive wealth.[4] He also sounded the apocalyptic note so common to the Prague reformers, warning against the multitude of pseudo-prophets who like wolves in lambs' clothing attempted to beguile the faithful. Although he did not mention Antichrist in so many words, he implicitly identified it with those who put love of the world before love of God[5]—again one of the hallmarks of his successors. Waldhausen was not, however, a systematic thinker; it was in his attitude rather than any set of tenets that he was influential.

How considerable this was can be seen from Milíč of Kroměříž (or Kremser) usually called the father of the Czech reformers.[6] Milíč inherited from Waldhausen the same repugnance against clerical immorality and a missionary zeal to preach a return to the apostolic purity of the primitive church. Unlike Waldhausen Milíč was a native of Bohemia. The call that he answered came from within as a result of hearing Waldhausen preach. He had been secretary to Charles IV's court and the emperor had obtained a canonry for him when in 1363 the combined effect of reading the bible and hearing Waldhausen caused his conversion. He renounced his offices and embraced a life of ascetism and preaching. His main theme was the coming of Antichrist.[7] For the next ten years he tirelessly delivered his message. He became the foremost preacher in Prague speaking not only in Latin but German

[1] The following is based upon the reports of Waldhausen's preaching together with his replies to over twenty charges made against him, in K. Höfler, *Geschichtsschreiber der Hussitischen Bewegung*, (*Fontes Rerum Austriacarum Abt. I, Scriptores*, Bd. VI, Vienna 1865) 17–39.

[2] Ibid., 18, 20, 21, 22–3, 30, 32.

[3] Ibid., 27.

[4] Ibid., 17, 18–19, 20.

[5] Ibid., 22–3.

[6] For Milíč see *Fontes rerum Bohemicarum* I ed. J. Emler (Prague 1873) 403, 431–36; also Palacký, *Geschichte von Böhmen*, Bk. V, ch. 3; De Vooght, *L'hérésie*, 17–21.

[7] His *Libellus de Antichristo* is published in vol. III of Matthew of Janov's *Regulae veteris et novi testamenti* (Prague 1908–26) 368–81. Janov's *Narratio de Milicio* is also to be found there, 333–57.

and Czech; his audiences included Charles IV himself whom for a time he came to identify with Antichrist, putting his advent for 1365 or 1367: although arrested for this Milíč was soon released; and in 1367 he went to Rome to announce his revelation to the pope. He was arrested again, but freed on Charles IV's arrival in the city in 1368. By then his conception of Antichrist had finally evolved from that of an individual into the evils within the church at large. Although obsessed by its imminence there was no trace of the Joachist about Milíč, save perhaps for his belief that Antichrist had his beginning in about the year 1200.[1] In his last years he founded the house of Jerusalem in Prague for restoring fallen women. It attracted the derision of his enemies and did not survive him. He died in 1374 on his way to the papal court at Avignon.

Milíč, like Waldhausen, was not a theologian or thinker. Apart from his book on Antichrist he left only letters and three collections of sermons, still unedited.[2] The twelve articles drawn up against him by the Prague clergy and sent to the Roman curia are probably the best indication of what he thought, although Milíč denied them.[3] They were mostly of a moral and practical nature.[4] In addition to his preaching the imminent advent of Antichrist he was belaboured for his attacks on scholasticism (9), religious possessions (12), the abuses in the church (7), and for his foundation of Jerusalem (6). He was also said to have advocated frequent communion, if possible daily, but otherwise twice a week (4 and 5), and to have minimized the importance of contrition, penance (6) and excommunication (8). Of interest, too, was his condemnation of usury (1 and 2).

However distorted these charges may have been in point of detail, their affinity with the reforming outlook of his successors cannot be in doubt. In addition to his views on the eucharist and religious wealth, his criticism of scholasticism, even if he did not put it in the form attributed to him—that to study the liberal arts is sinful—expresses their common emphasis upon conforming to God's precepts and participating in his life rather than engaging in abstract speculation about him.

This attitude was given systematic expression by Milíč's disciple, Matthew of Janov.[5] If Milíč was the spiritual father of the reformers, then Janov was their theorist. His five-volume *Regulae veteris et novi*

[1] *Regulae* III, 372.

[2] De Vooght, *L'hérésie*, 14.

[3] *Fontes rerum Bohemicarum* I, 424–6.

[4] Palacký, *Geschichte* III, 171; De Vooght, *L'hérésie* 15–19.

[5] For Janov see Palacký, *Geschichte* III, 173–82.

testamenti (not complete) is the one major intellectual monument to its only original thinker. Janov himself was the opposite of Milíč; he was not a preacher or a man of action; and his own clash with authority ended in somewhat ignominious submission. Having been fired by Milíč's preaching, he went to Paris in 1379 where he studied for two years. On his return to Prague he became a canon of the cathedral. In 1388 the Prague synod passed a decree against laymen receiving communion more than once a month; in 1389 it prohibited preaching against the veneration of images. Both were aimed at Janov among others:[1] and he submitted. In 1392 he made a further promise of obedience to the archbishop. Janov died in 1394.

The twin foundations of Matthew of Janov's outlook were the bible and the sacrament of the eucharist. The one contained all truth and provided the rules by which Christ's precepts could be obeyed and his detractors exposed. The other enabled the believer to become joined with Christ through sacramental participation in his nature. Just as the bible allowed a true believer to return to Christ's law, so frequent communion enabled him to renew contact with Christ as a person and so transcend the false blandishments of images and relics mistakenly venerated in his name. Thus Janov was actuated by similar moral and reforming impulses to those of Milíč and Waldhausen. Where he went beyond them was in systematically seeking biblical and sacramental support for his ideals. So far as the bible was concerned, Janov contraposed it to human laws and traditions; in strictly theoretical terms, he relied upon it more completely than even Wyclif; for in his own words, 'I have in my writing throughout used the bible to the utmost and the words of the doctors a little.'[2] But in practice, both in his numerous citations from the doctors in his *Regulae* and in his submission to his superiors mentioned above, he accepted tradition and the authority of the church. The bible, said Janov, contained 'all the most divine truths by which we can clearly and patently confirm all our opinions'.[3] He had treated it as his friend and bride, indeed mother, from the time of his youth; it was his resort in all uncertainty and the consolation of his soul in tribulation. For these reasons he had followed the bible rather than the words of the doctors who could be read in their own books.[4]

[1] Palacký, *Documenta*, 699–702. See also the treatise by an anonymous Augustinian against Janov's three errors concerning the veneration of the relics of Christ, images, and daily communion for the laity. J. Sedlak, *M. Jan Hus*, appendix 21*–33*.

[2] Quapropter in his scriptis meis per totum usus sum maxime biblia . . . et modicum de dictis doctorum . . . (*Regulae*, vol. I 12). [3] Ibid. [4] Ibid., 12–14.

Janov's object in writing the *Regulae* was no mere scholastic exercise; indeed he stressed his disapproval for the dominance of the study of canon law and other human arts over the bible.[1] His own system was scholastic in neither form nor content. It was designed to confute Antichrist, whose presence dominated his pages just as he believed that it dominated the world of his day. By Antichrist he understood all those false Christians who put self-love and the world before Christ.[2] He described them as hypocrites, psuedo-prophets and carnal Christians,[3] and gave five signs for their recognition; all concerned their attempts to beguile the faithful away from Christ's law.[4] To counter these efforts he enunciated twelve rules of Christian conduct (four drawn from the Old Testament and eight from the New Testament).[5] Based upon submission to divine precepts and the sacraments, he saw their propagation as the best counter to the forces of evil.

While Janov, like Milíč, was obsessed by Antichrist's omnipresence, he differed from his master in regarding it in almost Manichaean terms. The world, he declared, was divided into the spirit of Christ's truth and the spirit of satanic falsity.[6] At the present time the latter was in the ascendant. Its disciples were to be found particularly among the worldly priests and religious, whose pomp and ignorance Janov flayed.[7] He treated non-scriptural innovations and what he called human traditions as the abomination of desolation,[8] especially the refusal of priests to administer the sacraments without payment.[9] He denounced papal provisions, excessive veneration of images, and like Wyclif he held that all religious orders were contrary to faith and a source of superstition which should be suppressed.[10]

[1] *Regulae*, vol. I 13–14.

[2] E.g., Ille ergo amor sui est radix totius vite ypocritarum (ibid., I, 185); see also ibid., I, 181–2, II, 216–20, III, 1–5, IV, 235–8.

[3] E.g., I, 3 ff., 19–50, 166–311; III, 1–251.

[4] Vol. I, 37–42.

[5] Ibid., 30 ff.

[6] Ex hiis manifeste sequitur quod spiritus Jesu et spiritus Belial, spiritus mendacii ab initio creature mox inceperunt operari (ibid., 21).

[7] E.g., I, 3, 194, II, 161–2, IV passim.

[8] Et principaliter abhominatio in desolationem existit, videlicet iustificationes reputare sibi et querere in quibusdam novis recentibus observanciis ac advertentionibus nominum et interim non reputare vel minus curare saluberrima divina sacramenta . . . (ibid., 83).

[9] Ibid., 84.

[10] Ex istis evidenter potest colligi quod videtur repugnare in christiano populo esse multas regulas et religiones. . . . Omnis talis multiplicatio videtur esse superstitiosa et nociva communitati ecclesie, et ergo esse diminuenda aut extirpanda a dei populo (ibid., II, 142–3).

On the other hand, their attitudes to the pope had nothing in common. Janov neither denied his title nor singled him out as chief Antichrist; he was to be judged by the same canons as any other Christian, true if he followed Christ, false if he was of Antichrist. If the latter, like Clement VII who had set himself up against Urban VI, he was not only an abomination but, *ipso facto*, not true pope.[1] At the same time, Janov, like so many of his contemporaries, had been profoundly affected by the Great Schism. It reflected, he said, the spiritual division within the church;[2] as such, it was a necessary means of bringing evil into the open. He therefore came to see the Great Schism as living evidence of Antichrist's presence. It undoubtedly helped to stimulate his apocalyptic sense just as it did that of the Fraticelli. Nevertheless its members were not confined to the priesthood. As comprising all those actuated by self-love, it also included the Beghards and the Turlupins who, in the guise of mysticism, sought their own gratification:[3] Janov followed Milíč in seeing the year 1200 as the beginning of Antichrist's tribulations. He also put the date of his appearance as after the year 1335;[4] he would be the worst Christian of all—*pessimus Christianus*—'fraudulently contrary to the truth of Christ's life and teaching'.[5] This did not, however, prevent Janov from most of the time concentrating upon the wider meaning of Antichrist as connoting all false Christians. He stressed its similarity with the beast of the Apocalypse,[6] even though only those infused with Christ's spirit could discern it.[7] Hypocrisy and worldliness were its distinguishing marks, and its presence among Christians the cause of all their troubles.

Janov's apocalyptic sense was central to his outlook. It was also, like so much else in it, distinctly individual. He neither shared the Joachist belief in a third era nor the traditional view of a single Antichrist. For him first Gog and Magog, whom he identified with the false Christians, would be exposed;[8] then the mystic Antichrist which he called the great whore, and elsewhere defined as the multitude of hypocrites,[9] would be revealed and killed by the spirit of Christ.[10] The tribulations leading to this dénouement had begun within the church some years

[1] Ibid., III, 29–34. [2] Ibid., II, 161, 186.

[3] Ibid., I, 199, III, 378.

[4] Ibid., III, 13–16, 21–2.

[5] Est vel erit Antichristus homo veritati vite Christi et doctrine fraudulenter contrarius, Christianus pessimus (ibid., 10).

[6] Ibid., 68 ff. [7] Ibid., 102.

[8] Ibid., II, 162–3. [9] Ibid., 159. [10] Ibid., 163.

ago and were still continuing.[1] Thus Janov regarded himself as being in the midst of the struggle and the measures he put forward as directly contributing to its outcome. These, as we have said, were a return to the bible and frequent—if possible daily—communion for all believers. Accordingly while many of his contemporaries looked to a constitutional mechanism, like a general council, for the reform of the church, Janov turned to its existing spiritual resources. These as instituted by Christ were the way of return to him.

If the bible provided the precepts for following Christ, the eucharist consummated the union between the believer and Christ. The importance which Janov attached to the eucharist was the most striking and original part of his outlook. He alone of the reformers of his era gave first place to a sacrament, elevating it above even poverty and preaching, although he stressed the necessity for both of these. This emphasis in turn became one of the hallmarks of the Czech reformation. It need hardly be said that Janov's—and subsequently the Czech reformers'—attitude towards the eucharist was at the opposite pole from Wyclif's.[2] Where the English scholastic had been concerned with the metaphysical and sacerdotal implications of transubstantiation, Janov treated it entirely for its sacramental properties, namely as a means of grace. It was just because it possessed this capacity in the fullest degree that Janov saw in the eucharist the panacea to Christendom's ills. His own accounts of its effects make up some of the most eloquent passages in his vast work. He devoted large parts of the first two volumes of the *Regulae* to it and it takes up the whole of the fifth volume.[3] Briefly, Janov held that the eucharist represented God's gift to man of his only son in sacrifice. In eating his body and drinking his blood through the

[1] Hec vero omnia tunc fieri inceperunt quando plage generales prefate in dei ecclesia inceperunt . . . que inceperunt fieri ab annis iam LX vel citra vel fiunt omni die usque modo (ibid.).

[2] McFarlane *John Wycliffe* 158–9 makes the puzzling statement that 'Those who regard the Lollard denial of transubstantiation as growing inevitably out of Wycliffe's ultra-realism will find their refutation in the school of Prague. The Hussites saw no difficulty in stopping half-way along that route, in adopting realism without discarding what are regarded as its logical consequences.' If this means that the Czech reformers were realists without being remanists, it is untenable, for leading masters like Jakoubek of Stříbro and Stanislaus of Znojmo (and probably Stephen Páleč) in their earlier years, and irrelevant to the majority of Hussites whose interest in the eucharist was for its efficacy as a *sacrament*. For these, Hus included, realism never had the central part in their outlook that it had had for Wyclif.

[3] E.g., vol. I, 51–165; vol. II, 1–139.

transfigured bread and wine, a man reached the most intimate contact with Christ attainable; for he was possessing him in himself. Accordingly, such communion should be repeated as frequently as possible and certainly every day.[1] To do so was to renew the union between God and man in an intimacy which surpassed all others. It was therefore the surest and best way of bringing man to God. This was the essence of Janov's message repeated again and again.[2] Its corollary was summed up in three points: communion should be for all, laymen as well as priests; it should be daily; and to impede its celebration was to do the greatest injury to Christ.[3] Communion was man's spiritual food, as necessary to the life of his soul as material food was for his bodily existence.[4] To support his plea, Janov quoted chapter and verse not only from the bible but from the fathers despite his earlier declaration.[5]

It is sometimes suggested that one of the Czech reformers' motives for including the laity in daily communion was a desire for democracy and egalitarianism. If this is meant in a social and political sense then it is nonsense: even the most radical elements of the movement—the Taborites and the Orebites—did not practise such ideals. These men were religious reformers motivated by religious conceptions. The prominence they gave to the eucharist sprang from a twofold belief: first that as a sacrament it constituted the closest means of approaching God; and second that as symbolizing the communion between God and man it must include all the faithful and not simply the priesthood. Here, too, Janov set the course for the reformers. In his case it followed from the distinction which he made between the church as the body of all believers, good and bad, and God's communion of the saints. Unlike Hus, however, he did not contrapose one to the other, so that the visible church bore no relation to the true church. Every member of the true

[1] Delectatur homo in eo quod deus pater dat unicum filium suum eidem in sacrificium et tali modo quod esset eius cibus vite et potus, et per consequens quod esset hominis intima et proprissima possessio nihil penes differens a seipso; nichil etenim magis proprie et intimius cedit in possessionem cuiusquam quam eius cibus et potus, que in corpus et sanguinem proprium transfigurantur. Delectatur insuper quod deus pater sic sibimet dignificavit hominem ut filium suum unigenitum posset suaviter et in veritate omni die in hoc sacrificio offere (ibid., I, 66).

[2] E.g., Ibid., 67–9, 73, 164; II, 37–9; V passim.

[3] Ibid., I, 73.

[4] Ibid., 54.

[5] The third treatise of Bk. II (vol. II, 68–139) is devoted to the 'Determinationes sanctorum doctorum pro cottidiana vel crebra communione sacramenti altaris a plebibus christanis'.

church had also to belong to the church on earth.[1] Accordingly, they all—good and bad—had to participate in its sacramental life, even though only the good Christians would do so worthily:[2] this again contained the germ of Hus's later belief that the priest in sin could only administer the sacraments unworthily. The church at large was therefore only loosely a communion since it could and did include the false and carnal Christians.[3] God's communion, on the other hand, in containing only the saints, was free from schism and sin and remained for ever true to the life and spirit of Christ.[4]

Now it was precisely Janov's awareness of the false Christians—the body of Antichrist—which made him reject the division between the priesthood and the laity; for foremost amongst them were the sinful priests. To confine to them exclusively the right of frequent communion was to permit the worst members of Antichrist to enjoy unworthily what was denied to many true Christians, for whom alone it could be efficacious. Thus Janov, although in very different terms from Wyclif and later Hus, illustrated the far-reaching consequences which came from looking beyond the visible hierarchy. The concept of a communion of Christians which transcended the failings of the present church was at the least bound to introduce two standards, even when, as in Janov's case, it did not posit two churches. The emphasis put upon personal spiritual probity was the most revolutionary aspect of both Hussitism and Lollardy and perhaps the one most destructive of Catholic unity.

Finally there is the question whether Janov was an utraquist: that is, did he advocate the taking of communion by the laity in both kinds, the wine as well as the bread? Or did he adhere to the traditional conception of the western Church by which only the priest took both, the congregation receiving but the bread? The generally held view that Janov was not an utraquist is true in the literal sense that he never expressly advocated communion in both kinds. But neither did he ever deny it. Nor is this entirely an argument *ex silentio*; for he almost invariably referred to both the bread *and* the wine whenever he spoke of communion by the laity: 'The frequent eating and drinking of this most sweet sacrifice,' he said, '. . . must be common to everyone, in-

[1] E.g., ibid., II, 269–70. [2] Ibid., V, 73. [3] Ibid., II, 290.

[4] Per nullam scismam ecclesia sanctorum est divisa que semper manet unita suo capiti domino Jhesu Christo, sed multitudo yppocritarum prius divisa a Christo Jhesu in spiritu et veritate et facta difformis Christo et sanctis Christianis, postea inter se est divisa et facta difformis (II, 166).

cluding the people, and not simply the priests.'[1] Again Janov spoke of the daily offering by God of himself to man through the act of eating and drinking:[2] 'to eat and drink by offering, and to offer by eating and drinking'. These and other passages suggest that Janov envisaged the two as inseparable and not confined to the priest. How far Janov directly contributed to the adoption of utraquism a generation and more after his death, and how far it was due also to the Greek origins of the Bohemian church,[3] cannot be known for certain. But Janov had said enough to make it a comparatively short step to be taken.

Janov's place among the early reformers was less that of theorist—since theory played little part in what was a practical and moral outlook—than of guide; he undoubtedly helped to orientate it along the paths of moral and sacramental reform, making the bible and the ancient practices of the church the criterion of conduct in a world beset by Antichrist. He channelled Miiíč's sense of urgency, which he fully shared, into practical and ecclesiastical forms. He was the Fabius of the movement. And the fact that, even in the supreme crisis of the early years of the Hussite war, the Hussite church never became revolutionary owes much to the impulsion it had received from him.

Janov was only one of a number who sought to end the abuses in the church. Among the most prominent were Thomas of Štítný, the first important layman, who wrote in the vernacular;[4] Matthew of Cracow who attacked papal corruption in his work *De squaloribus curiae Romanae*;[5] John of Jenstein; Adalbert Ranconis; and Hus's master Stephen Kolín. Some of them, like Štítný and Ranconis, also advocated frequent communion for laymen. Accordingly, Hus had many forerunners. He was first and foremost their successor and only secondarily Wyclif's disciple: what he added to their achievement was not new doctrine, either on his own or Wyclif's account, but the courage of the convictions which he had gained from them. He translated these from being the property of a small band into becoming the standard of a national movement.

[1] Ibid., I, 73, corollary I. [2] Ibid., 67.

[3] Bohemia was first evangelized by Saints Cyril and Methodius. The Greek church continued to practise communion in two kinds and the Hussite reformers felt a special affinity with it. See F. Dvorník, *Les Slaves, Byzance et Rome au IX siècle* (Paris 1926).

[4] Accounts of the following can be found in Palacký, *Geschichte von Böhmen* vol. III; De Vooght, *L'hérésie*; Lützow, *Master John Hus*; also R. R. Betts, 'English and Czech influences on the Hussite movement' (TRHS vol. XXI, 1939, 71–102), which must, however, be treated with caution in its philosophical judgements.

[5] In *Fasciculus* II, 584–607.

Hus and the struggle for reform at Prague

Hus and the movement which bears his name have been treated so often and so authoritatively that it would be otiose, and presumptuous, to attempt a full account here. Our concern must be twofold: with the nature of Hus's beliefs and the movement they helped to inspire. For both, but especially Hus, a great part of what concerns them centres upon Prague. Apart from Hus's two years of exile and his last eight months spent at Constance, the Bohemian capital was the scene of his entire career. His own development and that of the reforming party, took place within its spectrum and were shaped by its events.[1]

John Hus was born of peasant stock at Husinek in south western Bohemia, c. 1369. He entered Prague university c. 1386, taking his bachelor's degree in 1393 and becoming M.A. in 1396. He was ordained in 1400, and in 1401 made dean of the arts faculty. The following year, already known for his eloquence and reforming zeal, he was appointed rector and preacher of the Bethlehem chapel. It had been founded in 1391 by a wealthy Prague merchant, Wenceslas Kříž, to promote preaching in the vernacular in accordance with the reformers' beliefs. Sermons in Czech were to be preached twice daily. Under Hus Bethlehem became the focus of the reforming spirit just as Jerusalem had been in the days of Milíč. The vast audiences which he drew extended far beyond the immediate vicinity and included a regular following of aristocratic ladies, among them the queen, Sophia. From its pulpit Hus not only propagated the ideas of reform but increasingly fought out his struggle with the hierarchy. It was from there that he denounced unjust papal pretensions, especially over excommunication and indulgences, as well as the abuses of the local clergy. Bethlehem, and with it Prague, thus took on an ecumenical significance; and Hus, in the process, the status of a national religious leader. It was this fact which set him apart from his contemporaries: the difference lay not in his outlook, but in his powerful advocacy of common beliefs. What in 1400 had largely been the concern of a few idealists had by 1414 become a universal issue confronting the whole of Christendom. That it had, was in no small measure due to Hus. That above all was his achievement.

To say this, however, is not to imply that Hus was primarily a popular leader who went his own way. On the contrary the most striking thing about him was his complete identification with the

[1] For details of Hus's early life see De Vooght, *L'hérésie*, Lützow, *Master John Hus*, Palacký, *Geschichte* III.

native reformers. He shared to the full their practical and moral emphasis; and like many of his confrères, he had an accepted place in Prague life, both as preacher and university master. The support that he enjoyed from many of his fellow masters as well as, for much of the time, from Wenceslas and Sophia—whose confessor he was—gave Hus's position a stability which Wyclif lacked. Whether or not it helps to account for his refusal to go to Wyclif's extremes it did enable him to remain firmly integrated in his milieu until his exile in 1412—the years when he wrote his most extreme works, *De ecclesia* and *On simony*. Accordingly if any one thing characterized Hus it was his representativeness. He drew upon a common stock of beliefs to oppose universally felt abuses. His views to the end remained those of a moderate even if he came to assert them with increasing vehemence. Throughout he spoke with the voice of a Czech reformer, even if the words were often Wyclif's. It was this essential bond with his native tradition which enabled Hus to become its spokesman and his martyrdom the signal for a protest of national dimensions.

The stages by which Hus reached this position are bound up closely with events at Prague. After being appointed preacher at Bethlehem, he continued his connexion with the university. In 1402 he became rector for the first time; in 1404 he graduated as bachelor of divinity, and began incepting for his doctorate; his Commentary on the *Sentences* was written from 1407 to 1409 for this purpose, but he never actually took his doctor's degree.

Perhaps the most remarkable thing about Hus's Commentary, as we shall mention again, is its almost startling conventionality; there is hardly a flicker of personal idiosyncracy in it, and certainly not a trace of heterodoxy, whether over the eucharist or the church. Hus is sometimes credited in this work with having had the courage to dismiss some of the more pointless questions, such as whether the angels were capable of paternity or maternity, with a curt 'let it sleep'.[1] But when it is remembered that so many English and French theologians did not even deign to consider more than twenty or thirty questions out of a total of six hundred[2] this is not so striking as it may first appear; indeed if Hus's Commentary displays anything it is want of imagination and freshness as he dutifully proceeded from question to question. Only in what he says about excommunication and unworthy priests do his reforming ideas take control. Their significance, as we shall discuss later,

[1] M. Spinka, *John Hus and the Czech Reform* (Chicago 1941) 23.
[2] See G. Leff, *Bradwardine and the Pelagians* 6 ff.

was essentially practical rather than speculative; in the context of the rest of his Commentary they are the best witness to Hus's cast of mind.

The academic detachment of the Commentary on the *Sentences* is the more noteworthy for having been written at the very time when controversy over Wyclif was reaching a new height and Hus's own orthodoxy was being impugned. Hus's relation to Wyclif is central to an understanding of his outlook and for determining the justice of his sentence at Constance. For both his Prague contemporaries and his accusers at the papal court, and later at the general council, Hus's crime was that he was a Wyclifite, indeed the leading exponent of the English scholastic's heresy. It was around this issue that the main struggle between the reform party and their opponents came to be waged; and it was the main cause of Hus's own involvement in the struggle.

The influence of Wyclif's writings upon the Czech reformers probably dates to at least the last decade of the fourteenth century,[1] by the end of which Hus had copied three of his philosophical works, *De materia et forma*, *De ideis* and *De universalibus*. In the first decade of the fifteenth century more were added. Jerome of Prague, Hus's fellow student and martyr, who had spent probably from 1399 to 1401 in Oxford, was responsible for the *Trialogus*, *De eucharistia*, the *Dialogus* and *De simonia*. But it was from Faulfiš and Kněhnic who visited England in 1406 and 1407 that the main corpus came. They went not only to Oxford but also Braybrooke, the home of the Lollard knight Thomas Latimer, and may have seen other Lollards including Oldcastle. Before long most of Wyclif's theological works were in circulation. But already in 1403 the first move against them had been made by the theological faculty of Prague university.

This may well have been in part due to the conflict between the Czech and the German masters which bulks so large in the early years of the struggle against Wyclif. Doctrinally the Germans, true to the prevailing philosophical vogue which derived from Paris, embraced so-called nominalism. A number of Czech masters, on the other hand, seized upon Wyclif's extreme realism. Stanislaus Znojmo, Hus's teacher and examiner, was the most prominent, together with Stephen Páleč and Jakoubek of Stříbro (Jacobellus of Misa). Among them was also Hus who, as we have just mentioned, had as early as 1398 copied Wyclif's philosophical works. How closely Znojmo followed Wyclif may be gauged from his treatise on universals having been mistaken for Wyclif's, and included in the volumes of his *Miscellanea Philo-*

[1] For a summary of what follows, see Betts, art. cit., 81–2.

sophica.[1] Znojmo's uncompromising realism helped to precipitate the first clash over Wyclif in 1403, when a German master, John Hübner, presented to the university for condemnation forty-five articles which he claimed to have drawn from the English scholastic's writings.[2] In the previous year, Hübner had petitioned the Roman curia for action against Znojmo's treatise. Of the forty-five articles, twenty-four were those which had been censured at Blackfriars in 1381; the remaining twenty-one were selected by Hübner. They added little save invective which, often taken out of context, made Wyclif seem more extreme than he was. The main topics were the papacy—the pope was Antichrist (art. 30) and the papacy Satan's synagogue (37); the religious orders, which were the work of the devil (45) and their founders, Augustine, Benedict and Bernard damned for having endowed them (art. 44); and the universities, which should be suppressed (29). The university was entrusted by the Prague chapter with deciding upon them; with its built-in German majority of three votes—one each for the Bavarian, Silesian and Polish nations, into which the Germans were divided—against one by the Czech nation, they were able to carry the day and ban the teaching of the 45 articles. The Czech masters under Znojmo and Stephen Páleč opposed the measure. They did so mainly on the grounds that they were not all 'heretical, erroneous and scandalous', Páleč going so far as to declare that he was willing to defend every single word of Wyclif's teaching:[3] as so often happens, Páleč was to change round completely to become Hus's bitterest opponent and the man perhaps most responsible for his death.

The condemnation of 1403, far from checking the spread of Wyclif's doctrines, stimulated interest in them. They had not been pronounced heretical; only not to be held. They were thus not out of bounds to study, and Hus, it seems, now seriously applied himself to Wyclif's theological works. He had taken no overt part in the proceedings of 1403; but the following January (1404) he upheld Wyclif at the annual dispute (*Quodlibet*) against Hübner who again sought to brand him as a heretic.[4] Hus's attitude then, as throughout, seems to have been to defend Wyclif from the charge of being heretical, not his doctrine *in toto*:[5] a position which Hus never reached. The best evidence of Hus's

[1] Vol. II (WS) 1–155. [2] Palacký, *Documenta* 327–30, 430.

[3] Spinka, op. cit., 22; Znojmo's letter to Hübner is printed by J. Sedlák, *M. Jan Hus* II, 94*–98*.

[4] See Hus's purported open letter to Hübner defending Wyclif in V. Novotny, *Korespondence a Dokumentý* (Prague 1920) 11–15. Spinka, op. cit., 23. [5] Ibid.

independence is to be seen in his Commentary on the *Sentences*, work on which he was then beginning.

For all Hus's espousal of Wyclif's cause it betrays virtually no sign of his doctrinal influence. This ambivalence towards the English master stayed with Hus throughout the rest of his career: his affinity with Wyclif was ecclesiological and moral rather than theological. He admired him for his outspoken condemnation of the same abuses as the Czech reformers were attacking; for the rest, as we shall see, he was not prepared to sacrifice his own predominantly orthodox beliefs to Wyclif's. It was this refusal to become the indiscriminate partisan of everything that Wyclif had held which shows Hus as a figure in his own right, if intellectually not a particularly original or profound one. To the end he dissociated himself from the greater part of Wyclif's forty-five articles; but he opposed their wholesale condemnation.[1]

Whereas Hus never fundamentally changed his attitude, both Znojmo and Páleč did. Znojmo had defended remanence in his Commentary on the *Sentences* (1402). In 1404 or 1405 he was attacked by a Cistercian monk in the university[2] and denounced to the archbishop of Prague. Since his election as archbishop in 1402 the youthful Zbyněk had shown his sympathies with the reformers; in 1405 he had appointed both Hus and Znojmo preachers to the annual synod of that year. On instruction from the pope Zbyněk now set up a commission to investigate Znojmo's opinions. When confronted by it, Znojmo capitulated. He asserted that he had included remanence for the purposes of discussion and he agreed to complete his treatment by declaring against it.[3] This action was the beginning of Znojmo's gradual retreat from reform, and his supersession as its leader. In July 1406 Zbyněk publicly banned the defence of remanence.[4] Jacobellus at this time also upheld it, though he was never prosecuted and later dropped it. Hus, on the other hand, soon afterwards wrote *De corpore Christi* which at once defended the accepted doctrine of transubstantiation and implicitly criticized the view contained in Zbyněk's decree that nothing of the elements remained after consecration. Both Jacobellus and Hus remained firm in

[1] Novotný, *Korespondence* 124; Spinka, 23.

[2] De Vooght, *L'hérésie* 86.

[3] Ibid.

[4] Palacký, *Documenta* 332. In this decree he himself lapsed into error by asserting that after consecration of the host *nothing* of the elements remained. Hence Hus's emphasis upon the host as bread in *De corpore Christi Op. omnia*, (Prague 1904) I, fasc. 2. In contrast to Spinka, op. cit., 27, who seems to regard this as the main reason for Hus's emphasis, I shall later consider other possible reasons.

their defence of Wyclif; their resoluteness contrasted with Znojmo's wavering.[1] As the latter fell back they increasingly assumed the leadership, Jacobellus following Hus, after the latter's death, until his own death in 1429. Of the two, Jacobellus was the more extreme. In his *De paupertate cleri*,[2] composed in 1407, he adopted Wyclif's—and the Franciscan—position over evangelical poverty; Christ and his apostles had renounced all civil dominion and priests should do likewise. If they did not Jacobellus, like Wyclif, advocated their forcible expropriation by the secular arm.[3] He similarly regarded the king as being bound to defend his poor subjects from clerical rapaciousness.[4] In his sermons of the time Jacobellus followed the tradition of Waldhausen and Janov in his diatribes against the clergy;[5] he also defended Wyclif's Book on the Decalogue.[6]

Meanwhile Hus himself in his sermons at Bethlehem, and especially those preached before the archiepiscopal synods between 1405 and 1407,[7] flayed clerical shortcomings. His attacks were moral rather than doctrinal: his main targets were sexual immorality and financial exactions, which he branded as simony. Within this term he included any form of payment for priestly ministrations, including the custom of paying for the sacraments. Inevitably he gained the hatred of the Prague clergy who duly repaid his charge of simony with interest. Complaints against him were first lodged with archbishop Zbyněk in August 1408.[8] This was the culmination of a series of attacks upon the leading reformers.

In 1407 Znojmo and Páleč had been accused directly to Rome by a Polish Cistercian, a member of the German masters at the university. They were both summoned to appear in person at the curia. They went in the autumn of 1408, but on reaching Bologna were imprisoned by cardinal Baldasarre Cossa, the future John XXIII. They were released by the pope, Gregory XII, on abjuring Wyclif's teaching.[9] They remained true to their oaths. On returning to Prague they moved away from the reformers until they came to oppose Hus and his friends with all the vehemence they had once brought to their common cause and the added bitterness of apostasy. In Prague the signal for the renewed

[1] Jacobellus for a time embraced remanence (Spinka, op. cit., 27).
[2] J. Sedlák, *Studie a texty* I, 449–77.
[3] Ibid., 454–5. [4] Ibid., 461 ff. [5] Ibid., 372 ff. [6] Ibid., 316–28.
[7] *Historia et Monumenta* (henceforth cited as *Mon.*) II, 25v–36v.
[8] Palacký, *Documenta* 155–63.
[9] Spinka, op. cit., 28.

attack on Wyclif came with the imprisonment of a young Czech master, Matthew of Knín, and pupil of Znojmo and Hus, for upholding remanence; he retracted under duress.[1] This incident seems to have convinced Zbyněk, already under pressure from the pope, that Wyclif's doctrines were a danger to the university. He accordingly summoned the Czech masters on 20 May and asked them to renew the ban on Wyclif's forty-five articles. They did so equivocally: the articles were not to be held in their 'heretical, erroneous or scandalous sense'. They did agree, however, that only masters should read the *Trialogus*, *Dialogus* and *De eucharistia*.[2]

For Zbyněk this marked the end of his reforming days and the beginning of his estrangement from Hus.[3] He has often been accused of duplicity towards the reformer; it is true that as his own position became more difficult he acted more deviously. But it must be remembered that he found himself increasingly between the upper and nether millstones of his allegiances to the pope and to the king, at a time when, as we shall see, they were in conflict. At this stage, certainly his actions are fully explicable. Accusations of heresy reaching back to at least 1403 had now culminated in the summons of Znojmo and Páleč to Rome and the charge against Matthew Knín. Both pope and king, not yet at variance, were showing increasing concern.[4] As archbishop of Prague his first duty was to defend the faith. His initial actions were not extreme. The declaration of the Prague masters still enabled Wyclif to be read; and at this stage Zbyněk contented himself with calling in Wyclif's books for examination.[5] Nor was he responsible for the first charges which the Prague clergy brought against Hus: it was only after them that he took his own action.

The first of these were in August 1408, as the outcome of the growing offensive against the reformers. They are remarkable only for their innocuousness.[6] Firstly Hus was said to have declared that any priest performing offices for money was a heretic; secondly that he had ex-

[1] Palacký, *Documenta* 328–40.

[2] Spinka, op. cit., 28.

[3] De Vooght, *L'hérésie* 108 ff. tends to give this estrangement too central a place in Hus's subsequent career. So long as he faced Zbyněk alone he ignored his measures with impunity. It was only when Hus incurred the hostility of the pope, due largely to his opposition to John XXIII's bull on indulgences, that his position radically changed.

[4] Palacký, *Documenta* 392. In June 1408, Zbyněk acceded to the king's demand and declared that there was no heresy in Bohemia (ibid.).

[5] Ibid.

[6] Ibid., 153–5.

pressed the wish for his own soul to be where Wyclif's was; and thirdly that he had defamed the clergy. Hus defended himself without difficulty.[1] In particular he explained that his hope of Wyclif's blessedness lay in precisely the absence of any certain knowledge here on earth of who was saved and who was damned. No one could so condemn a man unless first condemned in scripture or through a special revelation.[2] The nearest the clergy came to an accusation of heresy was in their vague assertion that many in the parish held to the doctrine of remanence.[3] The charges proved one thing: that Hus was being attacked as a reformer, not a heretic. They could hardly be expected to succeed, and they did not. His clerical accusers accordingly changed their tactics. They next enlisted a number of witnesses, one of whom at least—John Protiva—was put amongst Hus's congregation as a spy.[4] These testified to having heard Hus make heretical statements on different occasions going back to 1399. It was at this point that the struggle between Hus and his opponents entered a new phase, one in which debates on fundamental issues were increasingly overlaid by personal innuendo and falsehood. The devices used to trap Hus are the strongest evidence in support of his, and his fellow reformers', charges against the state of the Bohemian church. Like a secret microphone in a room, they record unwittingly the very vices of worldliness, dishonesty—and above all—unscrupulousness for which the reformers arraigned them.

The next attack on Hus came in 1409.[5] He was now accused of charges which were to be repeated until his final trial at Constance, and which he not only never ceased to deny but the evidence of his own writings refutes. The first was reminiscent of Waldensianism: that a priest in mortal sin cannot consecrate the host or administer the sacraments. As attributed to Hus it also implied remanence:[6] for through a sinful priest failing to effect the bread's transubstantiation, it remained but bread. He was also accused of denying the validity of excommunication and regarding the Germans as his enemies.[7] The other charges mainly reiterated those of the previous year, including that on the state of Wyclif's soul. This time Zbyněk referred the charges to the inquisitor who expressed himself satisfied with Hus's denials.[8]

[1] Ibid., 156–63; Novotný, *Korespondence* 30–41.
[2] Palacký, *Documenta* 161. [3] Ibid., 153–5.
[4] Spinka, op. cit., 31; on one occasion Hus called out to him among the congregation at Bethlehem to be sure to take back to his masters report of what he had heard. [5] Palacký, *Documenta* 164–9.
[6] Ibid. [7] Ibid., 168. [8] Spinka, 31.

So far Zbyněk had acted with correctness. But his hand was now forced by circumstances beyond his control and outside Bohemia. It was this greater involvement which henceforth decisively shaped events at Prague, Hus's struggle becoming part of a wider conflict. It centred upon the Great Schism which had now lasted over 30 years. In 1408 a group of the Roman pope's—Gregory XII's—cardinals broke away and sought the calling of a general council to restore the church's unity. The council, so long advocated, met at Pisa. King Wenceslas agreed to be represented. He had a strong personal interest in the election of a new pope. He had been deposed as German emperor in 1403 and Rupert of the Palatinate elected in his stead. Wenceslas now hoped that, in return for supporting a new Pisan pope, the latter would recognize his imperial title. He was to be disappointed just as the new pope—Alexander V—was to be: in 1410 a third emperor, Sigismund, was elected, while both Gregory XII and his Avignonese rival, Benedict XIII, refused to resign and acknowledge the choice of the Pisan council. Thus three popes and three emperors confronted one another and Christendom. But whereas Sigismund succeeded in making himself effective emperor, it required another and much more far-reaching general council, at Constance four years later, before the schism in the church was finally resolved.

The immediate relevance of the Pisan council to Bohemia was that it divided Wenceslas from Zbyněk. The latter had been appointed by Gregory XII and he followed Bohemian tradition in remaining loyal to the Roman pope. He accordingly refused to conform to Wenceslas's demands for the renunciation of Bohemia's allegiance to Gregory XII. The division between king and archbishop had the effect of polarizing the relations between Zbyněk and the Czech reformers in Prague university. The latter, as we should expect, favoured the calling of a general council and the prospect of reform which it gave. But the German masters opposed withdrawing recognition from Gregory XII. Thus Zbyněk found himself on the side of the anti-reformers, against the king and the Czech masters. If it drove the archbishop irrevocably into the arms of Hus's enemies, it drove the German masters from Prague; for Wenceslas, incensed at the latter's flouting of his will, reversed the balance between the Germans and the Czechs. By the decree of Kutná Hora, in January 1409, he now gave, as we mentioned earlier, the Czech masters—always numerically the majority—three votes to one for the combined German nations.[1] The Germans pro-

[1] Palacký, *Documenta* 347–8.

tested in vain;[1] they then left Prague and Bohemia. Most of them went to Leipzig where they founded another university. Their departure, although due to Wenceslas, left its mark upon the Bohemian religious scene. Their claim that they had left because of heresy, while groundless, added to the calumny surrounding Hus and his followers, and helped to poison the atmosphere against him at Constance.[2] Moreover, as we said earlier, it transformed the university into a Czech institution, making it at once the head of the reform movement and standing it in sharper relief to the non-Czech, anti-reform forces outside it.

The immediate effect of the German exodus was a manifestation of Wyclifite feeling, as evidenced in the January *Quodlibet* for 1409. Matthew of Knín, so recently charged with remanence, having upheld the thesis that God was the creator of all beings, Jerome made it the occasion for an all-out declaration of support for realism and Wyclif.[3] But it also led to a hardening of Zbyněk's attitude. In the winter of 1408 he had already suspended Hus as a preacher;[4] he now sought support from Gregory XII for further action against Wyclif and repeated his demand for the surrender of Wyclif's works, on pain of excommunication.[5] But his anathemas had no effect. The truth was that the tide was running too strongly against Zbyněk. On 25 June 1409, Alexander V was elected pope by the Pisan council; he was recognized by Wenceslas, who also confiscated the archiepiscopal estates. The archbishop was powerless so long as he opposed the king. On 2 September he submitted, and agreed to recognize Alexander as pope.[6] He was now restored to his estates and authority. His future actions against the reformers, whom he now treated as Wyclifites, would receive at least papal support.

It was not long in coming. On his reinstatement Zbyněk wrote to the new pope, stressing the danger from the prevalence of Wyclif's doctrines which were being preached throughout the city. In particular he singled out their heresy over the eucharist and their advocacy of clerical dispossession by the lay power.[7] In November he followed this

[1] Ibid., 350–2. For Wenceslas's withdrawal of recognition from Gregory XII, ibid., 348–50.

[2] E.g., the charge at Constance that Hus had instigated anti-German feeling, ibid., 281–2.

[3] Sedlák, *Studie a texty* II, 197–262.

[4] De Vooght, *L'hérésie* 113; Novotný, *Korespondence* 42–4.

[5] Palacký, *Documenta* 374–6; Spinka, op. cit., 34.

[6] Ibid., 372–3.

[7] Novotný, *Korespondence* 226.

up by sending a secret delegation to the curia to press his case. The university did likewise; but without the same success.[1] Alexander, now that Zbyněk had recognized him, showed himself willing to co-operate in putting down the Wyclifites. He issued a bull on 20 December—although it did not reach Prague until 9 March 1410—reaffirming the archbishop's decree against possessing Wyclif's writings. He also went further, due to the prompting of Zbyněk's representatives, and banned all preaching outside cathedral, monastic and parochial churches. This was deliberately aimed at Hus and the Bethlehem chapel, and other such unauthorized places where the reformers were strongest. Finally the pope charged Zbyněk to appoint a commission of six to investigate the spread of heresy, and to take action against those found guilty.[2]

Zbyněk soon gave effect to these mandates. He set up a commission and while it was deliberating renewed his bans upon the holding of Wyclif's works and preaching remanence.[3] The *coup de grâce* came on 16 June 1410, when he published a decree for burning as heretical seventeen books by Wyclif. He condemned the masters who had in the previous year protested to the pope against his earlier order for Wyclif's books to be handed in, and threatened those who still possessed them, or who preached the heresy of remanance, with excommunication. He also renewed the ban on unauthorized preaching.[4]

The reaction was immediate. On 21 June the entire university, masters and students, protested at the archbishop's decision.[5] Hus did likewise in a series of sermons and writings. His argument against banning the works was the same as before. Some of them were purely philosophical; if they were to be prohibited, then why not those of Aristotle who denied creation? or the *Sentences* of Peter Lombard which, according to Hus, 'contained many errors'.[6] But beyond the works of Wyclif, Hus was now himself personally involved in the ban against 'private' preaching. In refusing to be silent Hus for the first time committed himself to the course of deliberate disobedience, which he was to follow for much of his remaining life, and which, more than anything else, led him to Constance. He gave his reasons in his *Exposition of the Decalogue*, written in Czech, during his exile in 1413: 'The word of God says "preach the word to all the world". But theirs [the pope's and the archbishop's] are to the contrary: Do not preach to all the world. . . . Know accordingly that you are not bound to obey

[1] De Vooght, *L'hérésie* 128–9. [2] Palacký, *Documenta* 374–6.
[3] De Vooght, *L'hérésie* 130. [4] Palacký, *Documenta* 378–85.
[5] Ibid., 386. [6] Ibid., 399–400; *Mon.* I, 107; Novotný, *Korespondence.*

except in such matters in which you are bound by obedience to God. . . .'[1] Henceforth Hus increasingly came to see his actions in this light. Loyalty to God came before submission to superiors. Not that Hus had entered on the path of revolt. To the end he remained convinced of his orthodoxy. That was his great difference from Luther: he sought reconciliation and looked to the reform of the church as it stood. He was challenging not institutions or the authority of the hierarchy, as such, but their misuse. He was therefore never an extremist, like Wyclif, nor a rebel like Luther. This can be seen in the appeal which he and his confrères immediately made to John XXIII, who had succeeded Alexander V as pope, on the latter's death in June 1410.[2]

Hus by continuing to preach at Bethlehem openly proclaimed his defiance of Zbyněk; he treated the chapel as his forum, reading out his appeal to the pope there as well as denouncing his opponents. In the middle of July Zbyněk took two steps which made the breach between him and the reformers irrevocable. On the 16th he publicly burned in his courtyard all Wyclif's writings which had been handed in to him;[3] and two days later he excommunicated Hus and his followers for disobedience.[4] For a time there was turmoil in the city; even children went about chanting scurrilous rhymes about the archbishop's illiteracy.[5] The university expressed its disapproval by a marathon defence of Wyclif's works, lasting a week. Among the masters engaged in the operation Hus upheld Wyclif's *De Trinitate* as free from heresy,[6] and Jacobellus did the same for the *Decalogus* though in more outspoken terms. It was not difficult to make the archbishop look foolish for his indiscriminate bonfire, and the reformers did not hesitate to do so. Hus preached a sermon *Vos estis sal terrae* delivered shortly afterwards, which consisted mainly of extracts from a corresponding sermon by Wyclif. This had been taken as having the same purpose of demonstrating Wyclif's orthodoxy.[7] Whatever the reason it shows how Wyclif had become the principal issue between the two sides. Yet to stop there would be misleading. Wyclif's prominence was due in the

[1] Spinka, op. cit., 36.

[2] Palacký, *Documenta*, 387–96.

[3] De Vooght, *L'hérésie* 137.

[4] Ibid., Palacký, *Documenta* 397–9.

[5] Spinka, op. cit., 35. Zbyněk had had no theological training and was probably almost theologically illiterate; he had been appointed archbishop of Prague as a young noble whose previous life had been entirely secular and military.

[6] *Mon.* I, 105 ff.

[7] Spinka, op. cit., 37; Text in PRS 134.

first place to the anti-reformers; it was they who sought to brand their opponents as the champions of his heresy. Hus and his colleagues took up the challenge. In doing so they were inevitably fighting on their opponents' ground. So much of their energy was devoted to defending Wyclif that they give the impression of being more Wyclifite than they really were. Certainly it was as Wyclifites that they appeared to both the papacy and leading ecclesiastics like d'Ailly and Gerson, who prosecuted Hus at Constance. They may also have done so to Zbyněk; but Hus and Jacobellus were above all reformers who admired Wyclif as a reformer, not a heretic. They were also realists; but this was more a philosophical badge than the all-pervading conviction that it had been for Wyclif. Neither Hus nor his contemporaries were deep original thinkers as may be seen from the largely formal debates in which they engaged.[1] It is difficult to believe that Hus's outlook would have been any different for not having known Wyclif's philosophical works, whereas it is inconceivable that it could have been the same without Janov's.

At this stage, moreover, Wyclif, despite the Blackfriars and subsequent English condemnations, had not yet been declared a heretic by the pope; that did not occur until February 1413 in Rome.[2] Accordingly, even in espousing Wyclif's cause, Hus and his confederates were not so far flouting the church.[3] This was confirmed by the pope's own action in appointing a commission drawn from theologians from Paris, Oxford and Bologna universities to pronounce upon Wyclif's works; their verdict was that his works did not warrant burning, although

[1] E.g., The Quodlibet on a first infinite cause (ed. B. Ryba, Prague 1948). A highly tendentious and, in my view, misleading attempt has been made by R. R. Betts in 'The Great Debate about Universals in the Universities of the fourteenth century' (*Prague Essays*, Oxford 1949, 69–80) to argue that the realism was the inspiration behind the fourteenth-century reformers. In the first place, even in the case of Wyclif, the relation between philosophical realism and his moral and political doctrines is to say the least, tenuous. In the case of the Prague reformers it is virtually non-existent, not excepting Janov the most speculative and original of them. The only direct connexion, over the eucharist, has no bearing upon Hus's outlook. In the second place, to oppose the 'progressive' character of realism to the conformist 'passive' nature of nominalism is ridiculous. The author was apparently unaware that it was the Augustinian realists of the thirteenth century who resisted the innovations of Aristotelianism. More important, it makes nonsense of the fourteenth-century transformation in thinking, theological, speculative, and scientific, wrought by Ockham and the so-called nominalists.

[2] Mansi, *Concilia*, 27, 505 ff.

[3] E.g., Hus's defence of Wyclif's *De Trinitate* (*Mon.* I, 105v–107v).

certain of his doctrines should be banned.[1] This was essentially Hus's position; and the king,[2] Hus,[3] and the rector of Prague university, respectively, wrote to the pope for abrogation of Zbyněk's decree.[4] But to no avail. The pope now transferred Hus's case to cardinal Colonna, who, through Zbyněk, requested Hus's appearance at the curia.[5] On Hus's failure to go, he was once again excommunicated by Zbyněk, on 24 September 1410.[6] Hus's reasons, which he later gave, are illuminating for their combination of reforming and hard practical considerations. On the one hand, he felt it would be wrong to deprive his congregation of hearing him preach the word of God. On the other, he distrusted papal justice: his representatives there had been consistently refused a hearing; he objected to the false claims to authority which the pope made for himself; he regarded Alexander V as having been bribed by Zbyněk to issue the bull against his preaching; and finally he did not want to lose his life: 'for the pope and the cardinals are affected by the preaching against pride, avarice and especially against simony'. Distance and expense were also deterrents.[7]

Zbyněk now went further and determined to present Hus as a heretic. To that end he despatched the most odious of all the informers against Hus, known as Michael de Causis (of Německý Brod) to the curia with a list of charges.[8] They numbered about fifteen, and contained the by now stock-accusations of remanence, the disability of sinful priests to consecrate the host, and the invalidity of papal indulgences and excommunication. To these was added a section, under the heading of 'the church', in which the pope was called 'Antichrist' and the curia, Satan's synagogue. Hus was also accused of preaching slanders against the Prague clergy, advocating the secular dispossession of ecclesiastics, inciting the people against the hierarchy, and embracing Wyclif's errors. The testimony of informers was included to support the indictment. Despite Hus's denials and clarifications, these were to be brought forward again at Constance. Hus's position was made worse when in February 1411 he was excommunicated by cardinal Colonna for noncompliance with his summons to Rome.[9] Despite Zbyněk's placing Prague under interdict the decree remained without effect. Hus continued to preach and enjoy the support of the king and the university.

[1] Palacký *Documenta*, 426–8.
[2] Ibid., 410–13.
[3] Novotný, *Korespondence* 82–3.
[4] Sedlák, *M. Jan. Hus* II, 197.
[5] Palacký, *Documenta* 401–8.
[6] Ibid., 191.
[7] Spinka, op. cit., 38–40.
[8] Palacký, *Documenta* 169–85.
[9] Ibid., 190–1, 202.

It was Wenceslas's resentment against Zbyněk's increasing high-handedness which proved to be the archbishop's undoing. It arose largely over the latter's failure to compensate the owners of Wyclif's burned books as had been promised. In reprisal Wenceslas sequestrated the revenues of the clergy and cathedral canons, causing them considerable hardship. Zbyněk in May replied by excommunicating those involved;[1] he had by then retired to Roudnice. Wenceslas next proceeded to seize the cathedral treasure and ordered a general visitation of all churches and religious houses.[2] When Zbyněk put Prague under interdict in June, Wenceslas forbade its observance.[3] Hus supported the king, employing Wyclif's arguments in *De officio regis* that he had his power from God and should be obeyed by all his subjects, including priests.[4] By July, Zbyněk's resolution buckled. He agreed, in return for the restoration of revenues, to lift the interdict and write to the pope, asking him to end proceedings against Hus and declaring that Bohemia was free from heresy.[5] But two months later in September he left Prague for the Emperor Sigismund in Poland, without having performed his undertaking.[6] He died at Bratislava at the end of September.

Hus's position, however, remained substantially the same, and before long it worsened. For all his innate moderation there was also an element of the rhetorician and egotist about him. It betrayed him into the somewhat flamboyant gesture of challenging the seasoned anti-Wyclifite, John Stokes[7] to a disputation, when the latter came to Prague on a diplomatic mission in September 1411. Stokes refused, merely saying that anyone reading Wyclif was a heretic.[8] Hus then proceeded to speak in Wyclif's defence alone.[9] No doubt for Hus the subject was still of burning importance; but from a distance it appears to be flogging an already over-driven horse. Certainly, it could not have commended him to Wenceslas, to whom any suggestion of heresy within his realm was abhorrent. It also served Hus ill at Constance where Stokes testified to having seen a treatise by him defending Wyclif's eucharistic teaching.

But whereas the Stokes affair at most went to swell the final dossier against Hus, his opposition to indulgences made his breach with the papacy irrevocable. It also for a time lost him the king's support and led directly to his exile. Nevertheless, in the then state of the papacy,

[1] Palacký, *Documenta* 429–32. [2] Ibid., 735–6. [3] Ibid., 736.
[4] *Mon.* II, 47v. [5] Palacký, *Documenta* 437–41.
[6] See his letter to Wenceslas, ibid., 443–6.
[7] Novotný, 102–4. [8] Ibid. [9] *Mon.* I, 108v ff.

it is hard to envisage the necessary straightness of purpose, or stability of policy, which would in any circumstances have made reconciliation with Hus possible. On the one hand John XXIII's designs were constantly shifting, including those over Hus. Thus in January 1412 he entrusted Hus's case to cardinal Zarabella, who briefly showed himself more sympathetic to the reformers; but before long Zarabella was replaced by cardinal Brancas, while Hus's representative at the court, John of Jesenice, was imprisoned in May, and, on escaping, excommunicated.[1] Meanwhile cardinal Colonna's original sentence on Hus stood, even though it lay dormant for a time. On Hus's side, equally, the likelihood of some new clash remained as great as ever. So long as the existing abuses were left unreformed sooner or later he and his followers were bound to denounce a particularly flagrant example of them. It so happened that the sale of indulgences in 1412 became the great issue and precipitated the next phase in Hus's struggle with the hierarchy.

The immediate occasion of this development was John XXIII's war against the king of Naples, Ladislas, to finance which he issued a bull for the granting of indulgences, in September 1411.[2] This was accepted practice; when a similar sale had been made in 1393 Hus had himself bought an indulgence, although his master Stephen Kolín had protested.[3] Wenceslas Tiem was now the papal collector appointed for Bohemia. His methods of farming out the kingdom to different subcollectors aroused opposition not only from Hus but a large part of the university. The arts faculty was particularly outspoken, but although the more conservative faculty of theology also disapproved, Stephen Páleč, as its dean, prevented any protest by the university as a whole.[4]

The action Hus now took put him irrevocably on the opposite side to Páleč[5] and Znojmo and, worst of all, the king. Hus had recently, at the beginning of September, addressed to the new pope John XXIII a public protestation of his faith and loyalty to the church before the masters of the university.[6] But within a few months he found himself beyond any hope of reconciliation with the pope. Tiem and his band of collectors reached Prague in May 1412. Hus, like Wyclif, opposed indulgences for pretending to give for money what could only be

[1] De Vooght, *L'hérésie* 156.
[2] *Mon.* I, 171v–172v; 172v–173v.
[3] Spinka, *John Hus*, 43.
[4] Ibid., 43–4.
[5] 'Páleč is my friend; truth is my friend. Of the two it is better to honour truth' (*Mon.* I, 264v).
[6] Palacký, *Documenta* 271–2; text of the letter in Novotný, *Korespondence* 95–8. Hus also wrote a letter to the cardinals, ibid., 101–2.

granted by God. There could be no remission from the penalties of sin except through contrition, which was the work of grace. To confer absolution, regardless of the disposition of the penitent, was fraudulence.[1] Hus also attacked the whole idea of John XXIII's crusade and the warring of Christian against Christian.[2] He did so not only in separate Latin treatises but in sermons preached in Czech to his congregation at Bethlehem. He also attempted to hold a public disputation in the university, but Páleč, who refused to follow Hus in challenging the pope's authority, prohibited bachelors from participating.[3] Since Hus was only a bachelor of divinity the ban was aimed at him; but it did not prevent him from delivering his address before a large audience in early June.[4]

The struggle, however, was already passing beyond the halls of the university and Bethlehem on to the streets. Protests and demonstrations against the sellers of indulgences became widespread; what had been at first a debate between theologians swelled into a popular outcry. It culminated in a procession through the city depicting a prostitute mounted on a cart bearing an imitation bull, which then was ceremonially burned. The king now intervened. He ordered a cessation of such activities and severe penalties against those who refused to accept the bull. He called together a meeting of Hus and eight leading members of the theological faculty at Žebrák in an effort to compose their differences. But Hus refused to be convinced by the theologians, and they attacked him for refusing to submit.[5] In July the king again summoned the eight theologians, but this time separately, to Žebrák. He accepted their proposal to reissue the condemnation of Wyclif's forty-five articles together with six new ones.[6] These all concerned the arguments of Hus and his associates against indulgences: the first was a general censure of heresy against anyone disputing the church's decision on the power of the keys; it in effect affirmed the pope's power to issue indulgences. The other five errors were stigmatized as false: that Antichrist's reign had begun—probably aimed at Jakoubek who at the January *Quodlibet* had called the pope, John XXIII, Antichrist;[7] that the bible alone determined faith; that relics should not be venerated; that a priest did not absolve but merely *declared* a penitent's absolution; and

[1] *Mon.* I, 174r–189r.
[2] Ibid., 190 v.
[3] Palacký, *Documenta* 449–50.
[4] Ibid., 448–50.
[5] Reply to the eight Doctors in *Mon.* I, 302v (292v) ff.
[6] Palacký, *Documenta* 451–7.
[7] De Vooght, *L'hérésie* 182, 200; Palacký, *Documenta* 448–50.

that the pope could not proclaim a crusade or grant indulgences to those who were contrite or prepared to participate in it.[1]

The real division between the two sides was over their attitude to the pope's power. Hus's opposition to indulgences had driven him to a position not dissimilar from Wyclif's where, as we shall discuss below, he refused to accept as valid papal decrees which did not conform to the bible and the teaching of the Apostles. Once reached, he inevitably came to question the authority of a pope who failed to pass this test; and from here it was only a short step to denying him and the Roman curia true headship of the church. This was the difference between Hus's position before 1412 and afterwards; in a distorted form, it was the basis of the final charges on which he was condemned at Constance.

The decree against the Wyclifite articles, old and new, was presented on 16 July before the whole university, assembled on the orders of Wenceslas at the Old Town Hall.[2] By then blood had already flowed in the city. Three youths had been arrested in the previous week and summarily executed the next day (11 July) despite the magistrates' undertaking that they would not be. Hus had tried to intercede for them, offering himself in their place, as the real offender. There can be no doubt that his passionate denunciation of indulgences had inflamed the populace; at this stage of his career he had become a popular leader. Although the bodies of the three martyrs were taken to Bethlehem, Hus later denied having had any part in the burial ceremony, and remained silent for a number of days. Then in a sermon he spoke out against the intimidation being used against the people.[3]

Within the university he went even farther. Immediately after the ban of 16 July on the 45 and 6 articles, a group of masters, under the rector, Mark of Hradec, passed their own resolution that Wyclif's theses could be held in a non-heretical sense.[4] Hus immediately put it to the test by maintaining six of Wyclif's condemned articles:[5] (14) that those who cease to preach, or hear, the word of God because of human excommunication are themselves excommunicated and will be treated as traitors to Christ at the final judgement; (24) that any deacon or priest may preach God's word without authorization from pope or bishop; (17) that secular lords can withdraw the temporal goods of delinquent

[1] Palacký, *Documenta* 155.

[2] De Vooght, *L'hérésie* 205; Spinka, 47; *Documenta* 456.

[3] Spinka, 42; De Vooght, *L'hérésie* 203; see Hus, *De ecclesia* 201.

[4] Sedlák, *Studie a texty* 1, 55–6; De Vooght, *L'hérésie* 206.

[5] Novotný, *Korespondence* 123–5; *Mon.* 1, 111r–134v.

ecclesiastics; (18) that tithes are pure alms; (15) that no one in mortal sin has civil or spiritual lordship.

We shall discuss Hus's views on these questions when we come to consider his doctrine as a whole. Of immediate relevance is Hus's deliberate challenge to the authorities, made the more provocative by his extensive use of Wyclif's own statements.[1] The streak of exhibitionism in Hus led him into gratuitous acts of bravado and not surprisingly still further incensed his enemies. Their numbers at Constance shows that, for all the justice of his cause, he had been more than simply a retiring scholastic. In these articles he succeeded in demonstrating that there was an orthodox meaning to each of them; what he seemed to ignore was that often it was not Wyclif's meaning, and that to infuse another content into the same form, especially when dubiously framed, risked perpetuating the same error rather than correcting it. That was to be Hus's fate at Constance, where he was accused of holding beliefs which he had never held.

In this dialectical defence of the English reformer, Hus was seconded by the young bachelor in canon law, Frederick Epinge, who maintained Wyclif's views on wrongful excommunication,[2] and Jakoubek who argued against clerical riches.[3] Those disputes extended into August, and they hardly improved Hus's standing with the authorities. Among his opponents Znojmo and Páleč both replied with refutations of the articles Hus had defended.[4] Páleč was especially vitriolic and also preached in Latin and Czech in the Prague churches.[5] Others joined in the controversy, including the Carthusian Stephen of Dolnay who attacked Hus in his *Antihussus*[6] and Nicholas of Dresden who replied to Páleč in his *De quadruplici missioni*[7] in which he defended freedom to preach.

Meanwhile the immediate cause of all this dissension—the crusade—had been dissolved with peace between John XXIII and Ladislas on 17 June, the day after the latest decree against Wyclif's preaching; final settlement was reached in October. But even before this the pope had again taken up Hus's affair. In addition to Hus's opposition to the bull

[1] E.g., article 18, 'Nullus est dominus', which, like so many other of Hus's writings and sermons, contains numerous excerpts from Wyclif—in this case, *De civili dominio*. See Spinka, op. cit., 48 and passim.

[2] Included in Hus's *Tractatus responsivus* (ed. S. H. Thomson, 1927) 103–38.

[3] Ibid., 30–53.

[4] De Vooght, *L'hérésie* 217–18.

[5] Ibid., 218–19.

[6] Ibid., 220.

[7] Ibid., 222–3; Sedlák, *Studie a texty* I, 95–117.

on indulgences which, according to an observer at Rome, had made Czech and heretic synonymous,[1] there had been further complaints from the Prague clergy,[2] renewed by Michael de Causis in July.[3] From Rome it appeared that the Wyclifites were in control and that the 'Catholic masters' had been driven from the university.[4] This impression had been strengthened by the death of the three young martyrs.[5] In July 1412 cardinal Stephanesci of St. Angelo took over Hus's case and promptly excommunicated him for non-appearance at the curia; Hus was declared cut off from all Christians who were to refuse him food, drink, or any form of human contact. He was given a month in which to repent; otherwise wherever he resided was to be placed under interdict.[6] The sentence, promulgated on 29 July, reached Prague at the end of September. Hus, deprived of any human arbitrament, appealed direct to Christ.[7] It was the point to which his own actions had been steadily driving him. It is remarkable not for what it contained—a series of remonstrances against his detractors—but for having been made at all. Hus cannot have been the first ever to have felt despair at human injustice. But he was the first of the epoch openly to turn away from all earthly tribunals and publicly address himself to God. In doing so, he gave personal expression to his own—and Wyclif's—rejection of the Roman curia which he elaborated in *De ecclesia*.[8]

The terms of the sentence of major excommunication upon Hus meant that if he remained in Prague he would cause suffering to the city. After heart-searchings between his duty to his flock and his desire to spare them unnecessary hardship[9] he finally accepted the advice of his friends and quitted Prague in October 1412. Before his departure an attempt to storm Bethlehem had been repulsed,[10] and proposals in the city council for its destruction defeated. He left it in the charge of his friends and disciples, Havlík and Nicholas of Miličín.

The next two years, until his departure for Constance in October 1414, Hus spent in southern Bohemia near Tabor. It was during this period that—deprived of pulpit and university—he composed his most

[1] De Vooght, *L'hérésie* 224; *Studie a texty* I, 65–8.
[2] Palacký, *Documenta* 457–60.
[3] De Vooght, *L'hérésie* 224.
[4] Ibid., *Studie a texty* I, 67. [5] Ibid.
[6] Palacký, *Documenta* 461–4; Novotný, *Korespondence* 125–8.
[7] Palacký, ibid., 464–6; Novotný, ibid., 129–33; Sedlák, *M. Jan Hus* II, 198*–201*.
[8] See pp. 662 ff. below.
[9] E.g., Novotný, *Korespondence* 137–9, 159–60.
[10] For these developments see De Vooght, *L'hérésie* 227 ff.

important works. They included *De ecclesia*, his Czech trilogy, *Exposition of the faith*, *Exposition of the decalogue*, and *Exposition of the Lord's Prayer*, and *On Simony*. The Expositions in particular were designed to make the essentials of faith accessible to the ordinary believer; they also, together with his other vernacular writings,[1] had an important influence upon the development of the Czech language.

While Hus was thus engaged, events in Bohemia and the outside world were deciding his future. Not that he was wholly divorced from those in Bohemia. There Wenceslas, in spite of his anger against Hus for opposing the bull of indulgences, was not long in seeking to reconcile the two sides. That had been his desire from the beginning, and his persistence in spite of all the obstacles is not the least remarkable feature of this period. His main concern was with the state of the kingdom and the damaging effect of religious discord, and charges of heresy, upon it, especially so far as the outside world was concerned. That Wenceslas, despite his basic loyalty to Hus, was in no sense a religious reformer can be seen from the appointment of his physician, the wealthy Albík of Uničov, as Zbyněk's successor. After a year in his unaccustomed spiritual role, Albík found it too much for him; and Conrad of Vechta, bishop of Olomouc, was appointed administrator of the diocese, succeeding as archbishop in July 1413.

In January 1413 Wenceslas called a synod of all the Czech clergy to assemble at Český Brod. It was to take measures against heresy.[2] It actually met at Prague in February. But its deliberations came to nothing.[3] From the outset it was riven by the irreconcilable viewpoints of Hus's opponents and supporters. The position of the former had hardened into two main demands:[4] unqualified recognition of John XXIII's authority and rejection of Wyclif's heresy. This meant accepting the ban on the forty-five old and six new articles and the sentence upon Hus, as well as the crusade against Ladislas and papal indulgences. For Páleč and his confrères the pope and the cardinals were the successors of Christ and the Apostles to whom absolute obedience was due.

There could clearly be no agreement on this basis. It assumed, and indeed explicitly stated, that Hus and his followers were heretics who were sowing dissension among the faithful. In particular it was implied that they did not accept the sacraments; and their opponents demanded that they did so, like the majority of priests. They also accused the

[1] De Vooght, *L'hérésie* 232–44.

[2] Palacký. *Documenta* 472–6.

[3] De Vooght, *L'hérésie* 245–63; Palacký, *Documenta* 475–80.

[4] Ibid.

reformers of making the bible their sole arbiter and ignoring the wisdom of the traditional authorities.

Hus himself composed a reply to these allegations which was delivered for him at the meeting.[1] He challenged his calumniators to prove their charges that he was a heretic or that heresy was rife in the kingdom. Among his supporters both Jacobellus[2] and John of Jesenice[3] drew attention to the need to reform the church as the prerequisite of peace. In addition John of Jesenice also denied the charges of not observing the sacraments and sought to refute the theologians' claims for the pope and cardinals; all the faithful constituted the body of the church and the bishops and priests were the true successors to the Apostles. While Hus acknowledged the pope's primacy on earth, Christ was the sole head of the church; moreover not every pope was his servant: some had been heretics, and at present there were three claimants where there should only be one. Whereas the church could be without a pope, the bible was the law to which all must submit, pope included.

It was their blindness to the actual state of the church which made the position of Hus's opponents so unreal. They were demanding unconditional obedience to the very abuses—of simony, fornication, unjust war, false papal pretensions and unjust condemnations—which had caused the reformers' protests. The two sides were, as in the case of John XXII and the Franciscan Spirituals, arguing about two different things: the theologians obedience, the reformers reform. This divergence was clearly expressed by bishop John of Litomyšl, one of Hus's sternest critics, and with Páleč and Michael de Causis, a leading accuser at the Council of Constance. He had supported the king in summoning the synod, and in his reply to the statements by the two parties, addressed to Conrad of Vechta,[4] he insisted that the ban on Hus must stand. Hus was a heretic. To shield him was to disobey the pope. He should go to Rome to answer the charges against him; his followers should be excluded from Bethlehem and neither Hus nor they be allowed to preach.

Hus's reaction to these accusations of heresy against him was a public letter in Czech, in which he again defended himself.[5] Not he but the

[1] Ibid.

[2] Palacký, *Documenta* 493–4. De Vooght, *L'hérésie* 246, thinks that it was probably before the meeting.

[3] Palacký, *Documenta* 495–9.

[4] Ibid., 505.

[5] Novotný, *Korespondence* 161–2.

sinful clergy were the heretics. In another statement written in Latin[1] he gave instances of when a pope should not be obeyed, among them Boniface IX's support for Rupert of the Palatinate against Wenceslas in 1400 over the imperial title. If a pope were one of the damned (he used the same term *prescitus* as Wyclif) or violated Christ's precepts in his actual life, he could not be considered Christ's successor. The real dispute, as Hus himself wrote to Christian of Prachatice,[2] concerned the old questions, of the forty-five articles and indulgences for the pope's self-proclaimed crusade, and the new ones of heresy, obedience to superiors and recognition of the pope and cardinals as heads of the church.

Wyclif and John XXIII were the two poles around which the disputes centred. They raised the two main issues of heresy and obedience, which the synod failed to resolve. These were only solved at Constance by anathematizing the one and deposing the other, as well as burning Hus who was universally—but wrongfully—treated as Wyclif's most important disciple.

Now, however, the Prague synod broke down. The theologians put forward twelve conditions for reconciliation with Hus. In essence they consisted in demands for the rejection of the forty-five articles as heretical, and acceptance of all John XXIII's decrees on the crusade and indulgences. Hus was also to abstain from preaching until such time as he should be absolved.[3] A final attempt to reach agreement was made by a commission of five, one of whom, Christian of Prachatice, was a friend of Hus. But it failed after two days of discussion. Once again the great obstacle was the divergence in attitude to the pope and heresy. Páleč and company made recognition of John XXIII's decrees the prerequisite of agreement. Hus's party, on the other hand, remained firm in opposing the condemnation of the forty-five articles and were only prepared to obey the curia in so far as it was in harmony with every good and faithful Christian.[4] Thus ended the efforts to heal the division within Bohemia. Wenceslas showed his anger at their failure, and the intransigence of the theologians opposed to Hus, by, in April 1413, exiling their leaders, including Páleč and Znojmo: they were deprived of their canonries and university posts.[5]

Hus, as we indicated, had not been inactive during these happenings. But the flight of Páleč and Znojmo was far from being the victory it

[1] Palacký, *Documenta* 499–501. [2] Novotný, *Korespondence* 162–3.

[3] Palacký, *Documenta* 486–8.

[4] See Páleč's *relatio* of the discussion, ibid., 507–10. [5] Ibid., 510.

might at first appear. His own personal position had deteriorated rather than improved in the first months of his exile. On 2 February 1413, the pope before a Roman council at the Lateran had solemnly condemned Wyclif's writings which had then been burned outside St. Peter's.[1] This meant that Hus was now liable to conviction as a heretic for defending Wyclif, and he was correspondingly more vulnerable to attack. It should be remembered that the initial charges of heresy against Hus at Constance were made on the basis of the forty-five articles which it was generally believed that Hus upheld. More immediately nearer home, Hus had found how insuperable a barrier the interdict was to his attempts to return to Prague. The third of them, made in April 1413, led to disorders after the immediate application of restrictions, such as the refusal of religious burial. He left on the entreaty of the king after his presence threatened the annual feast of the showing of the relics on 5 May. It has been justly remarked that this showed the tenuousness of Hus's hold upon the people of the city.[2]

Nor did the attacks on him cease. The flight of Páleč and Znojmo merely served to add to Hus's enemies beyond Bohemia. Both also wrote treatises against him, as did Andrew of Broda and Stephen of Dolnay.[3] Those by Znojmo included a tractate on Antichrist and two on the church. Páleč wrote altogether three works on the church, the last of which was on a large scale,[4] and a vitriolic personal polemic, the *Antihus*.[5] The predominance of the church as the main topic of dispute indicates what the issues between them were: namely the authority of the hierarchy and the obedience due to superiors. For Páleč a priest or pope could only be usurpers if their appointments had been uncanonical. For Hus, as for Wyclif, the test was the moral and practical one, of how they *lived*. Páleč and Znojmo regarded all election to holy office as from Christ.[6] Only afterwards could subsequent misconduct disqualify an ecclesiastic. From this followed the other great divergence between Hus and his two erstwhile allies—over the bible. Hus, like Wyclif, took it as God's law and the ultimate criterion by which everything must be judged; it was this reliance upon it, which, together with his conversion to Wyclif's definition of the church, finally drove him to deny an integral place to the pope in the governance of the church.

[1] Ibid., 467–9; Mansi, 27, 505 ff. [2] De Vooght, *L'hérésie* 262–3.

[3] De Vooght, *Hussiana* 263–81, for an account of contemporary Czech ecclesiology.

[4] Selections in Sedlák, *M. Jan Hus* II, 202*–304*.

[5] Ed. Sedlák, Brno, 1913.

[6] *Responsio ad scriptum Stephani Páleč* in *Mon.* I, 259r.

Páleč and Znojmo, on the other hand, through their extreme papalism, tended to subordinate the role of scripture to the canons of the church. As Hus indignantly put it, Páleč blasphemed in treating the bible as an inanimate being (*res inanimata*).[1] De Vooght has aptly remarked that they remained untouched by the doctrines of the conciliarists; in an age of qualified papalism, they remained full-blooded papalists. If they attacked Hus for not being one, they were at least being consistent. It was his condemnation by conciliarists like d'Ailly and Gerson—who had just deposed a pope for misconduct—for saying that a sinful pope could be deposed that makes an irony of the proceedings at Constance.

During 1413 and 1414 Hus was also becoming increasingly the object of outside attention. Both Gerson and Dietrich of Niem—whose ideas on the position of the pope were as we have seen almost identical with those of Hus—attacked his opinions. Gerson wrote to Conrad of Vechta, now archbishop of Prague, on 27 May 1414, drawing attention to the report of heresies in Bohemia.[2] A month later he sent him a list of twenty articles, taken from *De ecclesia*[3] which he variously designated as imprudent, heretical, scandalous, seditious and pernicious. We shall examine their implications later. Dietrich of Niem, the most extreme of all the conciliarists,[4] in a document written on 6 March 1414, called for the extirpation of the Bohemian Wyclifites. He particularly attacked them for their eucharistic doctrines and for driving out decent masters and students who refused to succumb to their depravities. They should be summarily imprisoned and handed over to the secular arm. As heretics, examination was pointless; it was enough for their condemnation that they were suspected of heresy. All the improvising of Alexander V and John XXIII was mistaken. Enough of hearings and appeals. The time had come to destroy them, if necessary by a crusade.[5] The only extenuation that can be made for Niem is that he was attacking the Hussites for being Wyclifites and not for what Hus and his followers actually held.

Hus at Constance

In December 1413 John XXIII finally yielded to the emperor Sigismund's pressure, and the widespread desire, for a new general council.

[1] *Responsio ad scriptum Stephani Páleč* in *Mon.* I, 262r.
[2] Palacký, *Documenta* 523–6; Conrad's reply, ibid., 526–7.
[3] Ibid., 185–8. [4] See pp. 439 ff. above.
[5] *Concilium Theodorici de Niem ad Wicklefistas reprimendos* in *Studie a texty* I, 45–55.

He endorsed the emperor's decree of 30 October summoning it to convene at Constance on 1 November a year hence.[1] Included among its preparations to reform the church and restore it to unity was an invitation to Hus to appear before it.[2] That Hus welcomed such an occasion for being heard was natural.[3] As a reformer he could only rejoice in the prospect of a long overdue cure to the church's ills. As one unjustly excommunicated without a hearing he could now put his case before the representatives of Christendom. His doubts—which he certainly felt—were outweighed by his hopes; and, even if hind-sight makes them appear naïve, he was justified in holding them. In the first place, Sigismund guaranteed his return to Bohemia under a safe-conduct;[4] nothing can excuse his failure to honour it. The usual attempts to explain it away,[5] on the grounds that Hus as a heretic could look to no form of protection, begs the very question: namely, that Hus went to Constance to defend himself and not to be tried and condemned. It was Sigismund's duplicity—whether its source was from weakness or intent—which allowed Hus, within a few weeks of his arrival there, to be made a prisoner and henceforth treated as a felon. In the second place, it was Hus's very conviction in his innocence, and the baselessness of the sentence against him, which had inspired him in all that he had said and done over the previous three years. His appearance at Constance was only the realization on an ecumenical scale of what he repeatedly offered to do before his accusers in Bohemia. For Hus, Constance presented the long-awaited opportunity to confront Christendom with the truth. This overrode all questions of expediency, and to discuss his acceptance of Sigismund's invitation in terms of gullibility or fallible judgement is to invert Hus's order of priorities, reducing matters of principle to considerations of self-interest. Lastly, Hus went to Constance as more than a solitary individual, even though he suffered and died on his own account; that he voiced the convictions of a movement—albeit not at that time of national proportions—can be seen not only from the support he received on his journey, and during his imprisonment, but above all in the explosive consequences of his death.

Hus had envisaged his appearance at Constance as a mission, as the

[1] L. R. Loomis, *The Council of Constance* (ed. J. H. Mundy and K. M. Wood) 75–8; Delaruelle etc., *L'Église au temps du Grand Schisme*, pt. 1, ch. 7.

[2] Novotný, *Korespondence* 197.

[3] Ibid., 275–6.

[4] Text in Novotný, *Korespondence* 209–10.

[5] E.g., Spinka, op. cit., 51–2.

sermons and statements he had prepared for it show. In his proclamation on the eve of the Prague synod, to be held on 27 August 1414, he announced that he would prove his innocence and defend his faith at Constance.[1] Although John of Jesenice, to whom he entrusted his statement, was not given a hearing, he eventually gained a declaration from the supreme court that he could defend himself at Constance.[2] In addition to defending himself from the accusations brought against him between 1409 and 1411, by the Prague clergy and Michael de Causis, Hus composed a sermon on peace[3] and two statements on the law of Christ[4] and on faith.[5] In both the latter, he adhered to his definition of the church as the community of the elect, which he gave in *De ecclesia*. Hus's departure for Constance on 11 October was not a lone pilgrimage. Altogether a party of about thirty accompanied him. Among them were two men, appointed by the king to defend him on the journey, and three companions, John of Chlum, Wenceslas of Dubá and Henry Lacembok.[6] They reached Constance on 3 November without trouble, and spent the first weeks there undisturbed. Hus received his safe-conduct on 5 November. A few days later the pope (John XXIII) suspended the interdict against him and Hus was allowed to move about freely although not to participate in religious ceremonies. But these first appearances were deceptive. At this time the Council was not yet under way. John XXIII was present but many important dignitaries, like d'Ailly and Gerson, as well as the emperor Sigismund, had still to come. But, behind the scenes, Hus's numerous enemies were already active. Indeed the events at Constance are largely to be seen in terms of the machinations of Michael de Causis, Stephen Páleč and John, bishop of Litomyšl, together with a host of illwishers ranging from Wenceslas of Tiem to the émigré German masters from Prague university.

Michael de Causis set things in train by deposing before the pope a new list of charges against Hus.[7] These were the most far-fetched and scurrilous of any. They were under three heads: the eucharist, the priesthood and the church. Under the first, to the old charge of

[1] De Vooght, *L'hérésie* 305; *Documenta* 75–7.

[2] De Vooght, *L'hérésie* 306; Palacký, *Documents* 531–2.

[3] *Mon.* 52r–56v. [4] *De Sufficientia legis Christi*, in *Mon.* I, 44v–48r.

[5] *De fidei sue elucidatione*, ibid., 48v–51v.

[6] Peter of Mladoňovice's Chronicle, *Documenta*, 237–324; which forms one of the main sources of Hus's trial, also in C. Höfler, *Geschichtsschreiber der Hussitischen Bewegung* (in *Fontes Rerum Austriacarum, Scriptores*, Abt. I, Bd. II, 111–315).

[7] Palacký, *Documenta* 194–9.

remanence was now added communion in both kinds. In the second group the twin to remanence was repeated, namely that a sinful priest could not consecrate the host. Others alleged that laymen could administer the host (4); that the pope was not of the hierarchy (6); that priests in mortal sin were without power (10); that all priests were equal (9); that the church should have no temporal possessions (8); and so on. To complete these predominantly Wyclifite positions, de Causis also asserted that Hus was a Wyclifite who had exacerbated ill-feeling between the Czechs and the Germans in Prague. He had also disobeyed the archbishop and incited others, including the secular lords, to do the same.

On 11 November the Council first gave warning against Wyclifite errors. Matters may well have been made worse by the growth of utraquism in Prague. Jacobellus and Nicholas of Dresden were its leading advocates, and although it had not yet gained general acceptance among the reformers there—Havlík, Hus's successor at Bethlehem, for example—it had already stirred up opposition from conservatives, like Andrew of Broda, who wrote a reply to Jacobellus's treatise in defence of the practice.[1] D'Ailly, who was to take the leading part in Hus's prosecution, reached Constance on 17 November. Then on the 28th, Hus was arrested. He was taken away on pretext of being asked to go to discuss with the representatives of the pope and cardinals,[2] despite the protests of his faithful defender, John of Chlum, who remained at Constance for the whole of Hus's time there. After a week's detention in the house of a canon of Constance, Hus was imprisoned in the Dominican convent; he remained there from 6 December to 24 March.

Michael de Causis now drew up a further list of articles against him,[3] this time recounting Hus's culpability in the events of 1410 and 1411. It was a reply to Hus's own version which he had written before leaving for Constance in 1414.[4] Once again it sought to emphasize Hus's subversive Wyclifism.

From now on Hus was a prisoner; and perhaps the most poignant aspect of his ordeal at Constance was his failure to grasp the fact. Time and again he would recount how he had come to Prague of his own volition; the fact that he need not have done so, but could, as he said

[1] De Vooght, *L'hérésie* 323. Printed in H. von der Hardt, *Rerum Concilii, Oecumenici Constantiensis* IV, 392–415.

[2] Palacký, *Documenta* 253–4.

[3] Ibid., 199–204.

[4] De Vooght, *L'hérésie* 321 ff.; Novotný, *Korespondence* 225–34.

at his trial, have had protection from many Bohemian nobles,[1] increased his sense of equality before his judges. Allied to his unwavering conviction in the truth of his own beliefs, it turned their encounters more into scholastic debates than the cross-examination of a defendant. Only at the end, when Hus still sought a proper hearing to explain himself, did he realize that it would never come. Yet even at the final scene in the cathedral Hus still continued to protest his innocence and to correct the views attributed to him.

These underwent definite modification in the course of six months' interrogation; the change is indicative of the initial belief among the Council that Hus was simply a disciple of Wyclif. Hus was finally condemned on his own opinions, though the false charges of remanence and on sinful priests, which had dogged him since 1410, were also retained in a separate list of witnesses' statements. Thus the wires between Hus and Wyclif remained crossed. Besides the frustration of being misunderstood on his own account he had the most galling experience of all for a sincere man, of being accused of another man's beliefs which he had never held. The alternations in the appearance, disappearance, and reappearance of Wyclifite accusations, especially remanence, were almost Pavlovian, even if they sprang from the conflict between Hus's denials and the testimony of his accusers.

At the beginning of December a commission for the defence of faith against heresy, especially Wyclif's, met under d'Ailly. On 4 December it was replaced by a commission of three.[2] Its first action was to present Hus with a list of Wyclif's 45 condemned articles and to ask for his replies to each. The fact that he unqualifiedly rejected thirty-six of them, and either qualified or remained undecided towards the other nine, caused the commission to turn from Wyclif's to Hus's own writings. The evident surprise of the commission at Hus's denial of Wyclifism might have been decisive had he not had enemies like Páleč, de Causis and John of Litomyšl, who used the statements of witnesses past and present to present Hus as a dangerous heretic.[3] Moreover, much that Hus had said, and done, could be used against him. He had disobeyed his superiors, condemned the pope's actions, and attacked the hierarchy. Although he and the Council fathers were both united on the need to reform the church, their premises were opposed. Hus thought in moral

[1] Palacký, *Documenta* 281.

[2] De Vooght, *L'hérésie* 328, who thinks that d'Ailly was behind Hus's arrest.

[3] E.g., the professors of theology, formerly the German masters of Prague. Palacký, *Documenta* 334.

and religious terms, which transcended the immediate circumstances of schism; those of his accusers were fundamentally juridical in which rightness not goodness was the test of the validity of a pope's—or priest's —standing. Hence for much of the time Hus and his interlocutors were at variance.

Towards the end of the year, Hus's health deteriorated as the effect of the dank subterranean room in which he was confined. His spirits were further reduced by failure to gain any redress from Sigismund on whose safe-conduct he had come to Constance. The emperor, when told of Hus's position, is said at first to have fulminated against the fathers and sworn to release him. He did not arrive at Constance until Christmas Eve, 1414; and early in January recognized the Council's power in matters of faith.[1] Hus's imprisonment was therefore confirmed. His conditions, however, improved through the efforts of his friends, particularly John of Chlum who had done all he could to obtain his release. A change of quarters near to the convent refectory brought about improved health; and he was again able to write. The next stage in his interrogation was a list of 42 articles drawn up by Páleč from Hus's *De ecclesia*.[2] As we shall mention later, these all concerned the church and contained nothing about the eucharist or other Wyclifite doctrines. Hus, in his reply to each of them, showed that, despite their inaccuracies, most of them had been held by him. At the same time witnesses at Constance and at Prague were interrogated in connexion with Zbyněk's complaint of 1410 and Michael de Causis's charges of 1411. The omission of any reference to Hus's opposition to John XXIII and events after 1412 is probably explained by the growing hostility against the pope among the Council: it may well have gone in Hus's favour.[3] Towards the end of January, Hus's health for a time again declined; his position also worsened with the arrival of Gerson who handed his 20 articles to the Council. Gerson was outspoken on the need to punish heretics, not reason with them.[4]

These leisurely proceedings were abruptly interrupted on 20 March by John XXIII's flight from Constance to Schaffhausen in the duke of Austria's lands. It led to Hus's transfer to the house of the bishop of Constance on 24 March, where, though chained to the wall at night, he enjoyed greater freedom during the day. He remained there until early June. For a time the Council was occupied with John XXIII.

[1] Palacký, ibid., 254; De Vooght, *L'hérésie* 334.
[2] De Vooght, *L'hérésie* 363; Palacký, *Documenta* 204–24.
[3] Ibid. [4] Ibid., 364.

He was soon brought back to Constance. On 29 March he was deposed on 72 counts including simony, murder, sodomy and fornication.[1] A week later on 6 April, the superiority of a general council over a pope was proclaimed.[2]

Thus when the fathers came to turn their attention once more to Hus, they had themselves committed the very impiety of rejecting a pope of which they were to accuse the Czech reformer. Different though their respective grounds were for justifying such a step, it remains incontestable that the Council of Constance condemned Hus to death largely for saying what it had done. A new commission of three was named.[3] It included d'Ailly who was henceforth to lead the prosecution. Four others were shortly added to it. It had before it Páleč's 42 articles taken from Hus's *De ecclesia* and the accusations of witnesses. It now drew up a new list of articles numbering 39[4] in all, composed of twenty-six from *De ecclesia* and thirteen taken from Hus's treatises written in exile against Páleč (7) and Znojmo (6). Of the first group of twenty-six articles only eleven of the original list of forty-two articles presented by Páleč remained, testimony to the lack of conviction which Páleč's accusation carried. Hus had qualified the great majority of the original forty-two articles and the commission did him the justice of not bringing them forward again.

The new list still included a few not attributable to Hus[5] but in the main they faithfully expressed his attitude to the church, which was their theme. Hus was interrogated on them during May, but saw no one else. However, clamour was rising in Bohemia against his prolonged imprisonment. Letters were sent from two gatherings of nobles at Brno, on 8 May, and Prague, 12 May,[6] while a combined deputation of Czech and Polish aristocrats appeared before the council to protest on the same day.[7] All demanded an immediate hearing for Hus. They were not assuaged by the replies of John of Litomyšl who admonished them for not treating the danger of heresy with due seriousness.[8] An official letter was also sent on behalf of the Council.[9] It rejected the suggestion that Hus's safe-conduct entailed his liberation, on the grounds, later to be employed by Sigismund, that he had only received it two weeks after being imprisoned. It also asserted that Hus

[1] Von der Hardt, op. cit., IV, 98 ff.; Finke, *Acta Concilii Constantiensis* III, 156–209.
[2] Ibid.
[3] De Vooght, *L'hérésie* 370.
[4] Palacký, *Documenta* 286–308; Sedlák, *M. Jan Hus* II, 318*–21*.
[5] See pp. 680 ff. below.
[6] Palacký, *Documenta* 547–55.
[7] Ibid., 256–8.
[8] Ibid., 259–60.
[9] De Vooght, *L'hérésie* 381.

had been excommunicated by John XXIII but had continued to preach. The exchanges continued.[1] The number of signatories, in some cases over 250, no doubt influenced the Council in bringing Hus to trial. On 31 May the patriarch of Antioch announced that it would take place on 5 June. Hus was now brought from the bishop's house at Gottlieben on the Rhine to the Franciscan house at Constance.

The trial opened in the refectory.[2] A formal condemnation seems to have been envisaged. First a piece of incriminating evidence, said to have been taken from one of Hus's letters, was read out; in it he averred his bad faith.[3] Then the thirty-nine articles drawn up against him were read. The action of John of Chlum and other of Hus's friends, however, in going to Sigismund ensured that he received a hearing. The emperor, not then present, commanded the assembly not to condemn Hus in his, Sigismund's, absence. Hus, who until then had not been present, was now called in; but he had difficulty in being heard. The mood of the Council was for straight replies of yes or no, and exception was taken to his attempts to defend himself. Finally the session was adjourned until 7 June.

This time Sigismund was present; so was Hus from the beginning. The agenda was also different; Wyclif's errors were now the subject of the accusation. It began, as might be expected, with remanence. The charges went back to 1410 and were based on the statements of a number of witnesses, none convincing, and most of them self-contradictory.[4] Hus denied them as he had always done. When d'Ailly, one of the arch-nominalists of the age, tried to bait him into a confession through playing upon Hus's realism, Hus replied that the eucharist was an exception.[5] Stokes then came forward and repaid with interest Hus's reply to him in 1412. He claimed that, while then in Prague, he had seen a treatise by Hus defending remanence.[6] Hus again denied it. D'Ailly next accused Hus directly of defending and preaching Wyclif's errors, and cited his opposition to the ban on Wyclif's forty-five articles.[7] Hus replied, again as he had always done, that his conscience would not permit him to acquiesce in all of them being condemned as wrong. A number of the articles were mentioned, Hus standing firm on tithes (art. 18) as pure alms which could therefore be withdrawn

[1] Palacký, *Documenta* 264–70.

[2] Peter Mladoňovice's account, ibid., 273–315. It has since been translated into German by J. Bujnoch, as *Hus in Konstanz* (Graz, Vienna, Cologne 1963).

[3] Ibid., 274.

[4] Ibid., 174–85; De Vooght, *L'hérésie* 266–89.

[5] Palacký, *Documenta* 276.

[6] Ibid., 277–8.

[7] Ibid., 278.

from habitually delinquent priests. After these more academic exchanges, Hus's past conduct in the Prague disorders was once more revived.[1] He was again accused of fomenting trouble between Czechs and Germans; of wishing his soul to be with Wyclif's; and of inciting people and lords against the church. As in the first session some of his replies, over Wyclif and appealing directly to Christ, caused jeering among his auditors. Before he withdrew he was advised by both d'Ailly and Sigismund to submit to the correction of the Council. The emperor's attitude was hardening. He would not, he said, defend a heretic.[2]

The next day, 8 June, saw the third and final public hearing. Hus was now confronted with the thirty-nine articles from his own works. Since these mainly concerned the nature of the church and the authority of the priesthood, the discussion was principally ecclesiological. It is indicative that, once away from the hearsay statements of witnesses, none of which was substantiated, nothing was said on remanence or sinful priests being unable to administer the sacraments; for nothing on them is to be found in Hus's own works, as we shall shortly see. The pope's headship of the church was one of the main issues. While Hus followed Wyclif in making the pope's position depend upon election by Christ, d'Ailly and the conciliarists made it come from a general council. Both therefore denied him to be the direct successor of St. Peter. Yet it was Hus who was inculpated for a view which was not so startlingly different in its conclusions from that of his accusers.[3] Another vexed question was over the powers of true priests and superiors. Here Hus's moral criterion of following Christ was contraposed to the juridical conception of the conciliarists; for Hus a pope or priest, to be true, had to be good: sins like simony automatically disqualified him; for d'Ailly and his confrères, a pope had to be rightful; hence John XXIII's deposition for, *inter alia*, simony was a legal, rather than a moral, disqualification. He had, at this stage,[4] been a true pope but a bad one.[5] The same applied to what Hus had said about Judas's status. Hus in opposition of Páleč maintained that, in betraying Christ, Judas had never been a true Apostle.[6] It was when Hus was extending this concept to secular authority that Sigismund, who had been talking to two companions, had his attention drawn to Hus's words and made the oft-quoted reply:

[1] Palacký, *Documenta* 280 ff. [2] Ibid., 283–4. [3] Ibid., 306–7.
[4] Afterwards excluded.
[5] Palacký, *Documenta* 300 ff.; de Vooght, *L'hérésie* 403–4.
[6] Palacký, *Documenta* 303–4.

'John Hus, no one lives without sinning.'[1] Other points of dispute concerned virtuous and vicious actions, and Hus's attack upon the cardinals to which d'Ailly, as one of them, took particular exception. He accused Hus of trying to undermine the church.[2] This was, of course, untrue; but there can be no denying that this is where Hus's—like Wyclif's—ecclesiology led. In strict terms he was culpable just because, in strict terms, his definition of the church as the body of the elect excluded any guarantee of the authenticity of the visible church. As we shall see Hus tended in *De ecclesia* to qualify this position; but, taken together with his own disobedience to his superiors, d'Ailly's allegation was not unjustified. It seemed to his audience to be strengthened by article 18 in which Hus had declared that heretics should not be handed over to the secular arm.[3] At this they burst into protests. The session ended with d'Ailly again advising Hus to submit to the Council; he would then be treated with piety and humanity.[4] Alternatively he could persist in his obstinacy and desire a further hearing. Hus once again protested his wish to submit but begged another hearing to explain the charges against him. If his arguments were then not accepted he would defer to the Council. But this is just what the Council refused to do.[5]

After the tumult had subsided d'Ailly told Hus that he must abjure his errors and publicly promise never to uphold them again, but would preach their opposite.[6] The Council had thus reached its decision. Not a dissenting voice was raised. It was then that the full tragedy of Hus becomes apparent. He was presented with the stark decision of abjuring both what he had never held and what he still held, or being branded obdurate and a heretic in wishing to defend himself. It was not a choice but a conflict. Unlike the hero who dies for a cause at the hands of an enemy, Hus was torn between two causes: loyalty to the church and fidelity to his own conscience. To the end he sought to reconcile them. Hence his plea, even after d'Ailly's pronouncement, to be allowed to explain and defend himself. Hus's agonies were those of a reformer who wished to conform, of one who still sought changes within the communion of the church. He had devoted his life to the destruction of heresy. As he wrote at the end: 'God is my witness that I have never taught or preached the errors of which my false witnesses accuse me. My main purpose which I have always pursued in my preaching and all

[1] Ibid., 299. [2] Ibid., 272–3. [3] Ibid., 293–4.

[4] This is dubious; the indications are that had Hus abjured he would have been permanently excluded from all activities, probably imprisoned.

[5] Palacký, *Documenta* 308. [6] Ibid., 309.

my acts and writings has been to root out sin. In this truth of the gospel, which I have taught by pen and word, I gladly die.'[1] No one can doubt it. Yet it was he who had been condemned as the heretic. It was a fate which both Wyclif and Luther escaped, not merely in the penalty but in the agony which it presented.

Hus's last few weeks between 9 June and his burning on 6 July were taken up in examining his conscience and in pouring out his feelings in letters to his friends. It is difficult to read them unmoved.[2] Repeatedly he reverted to the same theme of the need to follow his conscience. To abjure what he had never held, and to retract what he believed, was something he could not do.[3] As he put it in his final effort to explain himself in Constance cathedral on the day of his death, 'I dare not lie before God.'[4]

Hus firmly believed both in his probity and his loyalty to authority. He continued to express himself willing to be convinced; the Council continued to demand unconditional submission. Sigismund had, after the final public hearing on 9 June, authorized the fathers to proceed against Hus as a heretic. He had himself, before Hus returned to his room, sought to gain his submission. Whatever he felt about Hus earlier,[5] he clearly regarded him as a heretic by the end. On 18 June Hus was handed the charges against him in definitive form. They consisted of one list of 30 articles taken from his own writings, and another list of 29 articles made up of witnesses' statements.[6] Thus to the extent that Hus had established the distinction between what he had himself written and what was attributed to him he had gained a point. But it was of little help in upholding his claim to be innocent. The new articles were substantially the same as before: of the previous 39, now reduced to 30, 27 remained and 10 had been withdrawn. Hus duly made his comments and amendments to them, but refused to recant. He treated this as a last attempt to make the fathers grasp his meaning.

[1] Palacký, *Documenta* 323; de Vooght, *L'hérésie* 460.

[2] Printed in *Documenta* 80–153.

[3] Ibid., 126–7. [4] 556–61.

[5] The question of Sigismund's sincerity is likely to remain forever open. Czech writers like Lützow considered Sigismund as duplicity incarnate. Certainly it was tantamount to betrayal not to honour his safe-conduct even if he had not considered its implications at the time that he gave it. On the other hand, he seems to have had an uneasy conscience about Hus's death: he is reported to have blushed when sentence was passed and he was always sensitive to accusations of culpability subsequently.

[6] Palacký, *Documenta* 230–4; Sedlák, *M. Jan Hus* II, 331*–43*; Mansi, *Concilia* 27, 1207 ff.

As for the list of twenty-nine allegations, Hus had always denied them. Thus *impasse* had been reached. An effort to break it was made on 1 July when representatives of the Council came to ask Hus if he would submit to it. Hus in his written reply once more denied that he had held the articles falsely imputed to him and affirmed his willingness to retract those which he had written if their falsity were proved to him.[1] On 5 July, in a last attempt, Hus was called before a concourse of fathers, including d'Ailly and Zarabella. He was offered the concession of abjuring just his own thirty articles. So far as the 29 articles from witnesses were concerned, Hus merely had to condemn them. Hus refused to retract what he had written. The same day Sigismund sent Hus's constant companions, John of Chlum and Wenceslas of Dubá, together with four prelates, to prevail upon Hus; but the words of John of Chlum, in advising him to do what his conscience dictated, must only have strengthened Hus in his resolution.[2]

The following day, 6 July, Hus was taken to the cathedral and there in full view solemnly condemned and degraded.[3] As the charges were read out against him he again protested his innocence amid a clamour to be silent, a command repeated by cardinal Zarabella. A final mortification was the additional charge inserted into the witnesses' articles that he had claimed to be a fourth person of the Godhead.[4] Weeping in despair, Hus was stripped of his priestly insignia. After being solemnly degraded from his order, and his soul pronounced consigned to the devil, he was escorted by soldiers through the town to the funeral pyre outside it. He died singing the *Credo*.

Hus's heresy

That Hus's heresy—if such it was—was not Wyclif's has long been accepted. The living proof is to be found not only in his own writings, which we must now consider, but in his legacy, which we shall discuss afterwards. The difference between the Lollards and the Hussites is the measure of that between Wyclif and Hus; or perhaps more strictly, between England and Bohemia. For, as we have earlier said, Hus was first and foremost a reformer in the tradition of Milíč and Janov. Wyclif entered as an additional element—and complication—after the main lines of the native movement had been formed. It was as much on principle as doctrine that Hus defended Wyclif; Wyclif became treated

[1] Van der Hardt, IV, 430.
[2] Palacký, *Documenta* 316–17.
[3] Ibid., 317–24, 556–61.
[4] Ibid.

as a symbol in the dispute between the reformers and the authorities, to be defended or attacked according to standpoint. It is that which makes his importance for Bohemia both greater and less than a mere mentor. Doctrinally, his influence was secondary; but as an individual he became a rallying point for Hus and his supporters, and a weapon in the hands of their enemies. Without Wyclif Hus would still have been the same reformer, but he might well not have been burned for it. It is in this light that their relationship must be seen.

Hus as a thinker was neither original nor profound. He lacked Wyclif's extremism and Janov's inventiveness. Nor despite his endless disputations in the university was he particularly clear or systematic. Apart from his strictly academic exercises like his *Sentences* and his *Quodlibeta*,[1] most of what he wrote was of a moral and practical nature. Far more than for Wyclif the majority of Hus's works were *pièces d'occasion*. Philosophy as such played little part; like all his kind, he became a realist, but it is misleading to pretend that realism influenced him in reaching his main positions. Hus could have said all that he said without any metaphysics; and in the one sector where Wyclif's realist philosophy impinged directly upon his theology, as opposed to ecclesiology —the eucharist—Hus remained as orthodox as the non-realists.

The charge first raised by Loserth eighty years ago,[2] that Hus plagiarized from Wyclif everything he held, has long been refuted.[3] It arose from Loserth's own misconception of scholasticism, both as a method and in its different systems, and was no doubt fostered by the sudden rediscovery of Wyclif after centuries of oblivion. Whereas Hus's works had been printed at the Reformation,[4] Wyclif's remained as dusty manuscripts until first Lechler[5] and then the Wyclif Society, among whose editors Loserth was foremost, came to their rescue. Yet Loserth was not entirely wrong; there is not merely similarity but often identity between what Hus wrote and Wyclif's words. Hus did copy, often by the page, from Wyclif; but it still did not make him a Wyclifite. On the main theological issues raised by the forty-five articles—the yardstick of Wyclif's teachings throughout the period from 1403 to 1415—Hus remained independent of the English re-

[1] Ed. B. Ryba, Prague 1948.

[2] *Wiclif und Hus* (Munich and Berlin 1925).

[3] References in Spinka, op. cit.; the main scholars concerned were Czech: among them V. Novotný, J. Sedlák, V. Kybal, V. Flajšhans, F. M. Bartoš.

[4] *Mon.*, 2 vols., Nuremberg 1558.

[5] With his edition of the *Trialogus*, Oxford 1869.

former. Loserth failed, in his exultant parallel passages, to distinguish between content and form. It is that which we must now attempt.

Hus's outlook can best be treated in the context of the main issues in which he was involved, since these were for the most part the occasions for his writing. We may begin with the most persistent, the eucharist. In the complaint of the clergy against Hus in 1409 he was accused of having preached remanence as early as 1399, before he had been consecrated a priest. Hus never ceased to deny the charge; and even the most diligent search through all Hus's printed works reveals nothing that can be held against him.[1] He treated the question in a number of sermons and other writings. They included the fourth book of his Commentary on the *Sentences*;[2] his treatise *De sanguine Christi*,[3] published in 1406, the year after Hus had been a member of a commission appointed by Zbyněk to investigate the fraud of the bleeding host in the church of Wilmak; and *De corpore Christi*[4] in 1408. He finally reaffirmed his position in *De cena domini* written in 1415 when imprisoned at Constance.[5] In all of these Hus held to the traditional position of the transubstantiation of the bread and wine into Christ's body and blood. His Commentary on the *Sentences*, written at the very time when the first accusations of remanence were being made against him by the Prague clergy, has been rightly described as a monument to his orthodoxy;[6] in the eleventh distinction of the work he writes of the conversion of the bread and wine, with only their appearances remaining.[7] In *De corpore Christi* he adopted the practice he frequently employed of taking the same text as Wyclif to reach an opposite conclusion: in this case Berengarius's heresy. It lay in maintaining that what had, before consecration, been non-consecrated bread became, after consecration, simply consecrated bread, not Christ's body.[8] He expressed the same viewpoint in *De cena domini* more emphatically, in view of his past experiences, than ever before:

> Lastly I have said above that Christ by his own power and words transubstantiates the bread into his body and the wine into his blood. . . . Wherefore

---

[1] Sedlák, *Studie a texty* I, 451–506; de Vooght, *Hussiana* 263 ff.

[2] Ed. Flajšhans distinctions 8–13.

[3] Ibid., fasc. III, 1–37.

[4] Ed. Flajšhans, I, fasc. II, 3–30.

[5] *Mon.* I, 38r–41v.

[6] De Vooght, *L'hérésie* 119.

[7] Sentences, *Opera Omnia* II, pt. II, 570.

[8] Ecce magna heresis fuit Berengarii, de qua fuit informatus, quia scilicet tenuit quod qui in altero ponitur ante consecrationem est panis non consecratus, sed post consecrationem est solum panis consecratus et non verum corpus Christi; similiter vinum. . . .

I have sung the song approved by the church from the time that I learned to sing (and) I have sung it in the schools and in the churches. Afterwards I have read (it) in the offices and masses, and I have never preached that, in the sacrament of the altar, the substance of the material bread remains, of which assertion the enemies of truth accuse me.[1]

This passage is more pregnant than may at first appear; for in it are also contained the main tenets which Hus never ceased to assert. One was that transubstantiation was due to Christ not the priest: the latter was the instrument, or the occasion, but not the cause or creator, of the bread becoming Christ. To assert otherwise was blasphemy.[2] The second, and more directly provocative statement, was that the bread was Christ's body; but Hus always went on to specify that after consecration it became sacramental bread. Thus he at once echoed Wyclif's insistence upon the identification of Christ's body with bread and distinguished between its natural and sacramental—'supersubstantial'—form. The reason was probably an amalgam of his habitual desire to put an orthodox gloss on Wyclif's words—in this case the insistence on Christ's body as bread—and to refute Zbyněk's unorthodox statement in his decree of 1406 that *nothing* remained after consecration—whereas the bread and wine did so as accidents. But he also seems to have been preoccupied by the real problem which Wyclif had raised: namely, if the bread and wine no longer really subsisted after consecration, but were truly Christ's body, a communicant in eating the host would be physically dismembering and breaking Christ's body. Unlike Wyclif, Hus did not go on to posit cases of the bread being stale or the wine overfermented, which would add insult to Christ's injury. But he clearly regarded the implications of the host's unqualified identification with Christ as comparable to, or even greater than, the error of remanence.[3] In order to obviate it Hus stressed the distinction between Christ's form, which was the sacramental bread, and his substance which inhered within it. Both were Christ, but in eating the host Christ himself remained unscathed. To untutored ears

[1] *Mon.* I, 40r.

[2] In altari quippe sacerdotum manu corpus Christi conficitur, non creatur, non nascitur, sed quod totum est in dextera patris totum est in manu sacerdotis (PRS 116). See also *On Simony* (trans. M. Spinka, in *Advocates of Reform* 199).

[3] Modo maiorem dicit glossa esse heresim tenere quod corpus Christi frangitur. manibus tractatur vel dentibus conteritur; ideo dicit omnia illa esse ad species [i.e, ad sacramenta] referenda, ut sic dicitur: panem et vinum non solum esse sacramentum, sed in veritate ipsum panem (i.e. speciem) panis tractari, frangi et fidelium dentibus atteri (*De corpore Christi*, *Opera omnia* I, fasc. II, 11).

and malicious tongues, the vital distinction between sacramental and natural bread could be lost; and the bread which became Christ's body after consecration taken simply for bread. But on no occasion did Hus ever do so.[1] The words 'sacramental' or 'supersubstantial' were always employed to describe the host after consecration. Thus, as so often, Hus accomplished a neat junction between Wyclif and the tenets of faith. Too neat in this case; Hus was inviting trouble by framing orthodox views in terms taken from Wyclif.

Next, there is the closely allied question of the sacramental powers of sinful priests. It will be recalled that Wyclif never came to any definitive conclusion on the matter; hence, in the strictest sense it is inaccurate to talk of a Wyclifite doctrine here. Yet we also saw that the whole tendency of Wyclif's arguments was towards depreciating sacramental powers in general and those of sinful priests in particular. It is hard to believe that had he felt absolutely free to express his true opinion, Wyclif—after 1381 at least—would not have come down against the powers of sinful priests. Hus, from the outset, showed no equivocation. He granted to all priests the power of consecration but he distinguished between so doing worthily (*digne*) and unworthily (*indigne*). The priest in sin could still officiate at mass or hear confessions, but his power derived from his office and not from personal merit: he therefore acted equivocally.[2] In *De cena domini* Hus claimed that he had

[1] 2⁰ dicitur quod corpus Christi sub speciebus panis continetur realiter continentia potentiali, eo quod corpus Christi presens est in sacramento venerabili, prout confitetur fides solida Christiana. (*Sentences*, Bk. IV, d. 10, 566).

Again: Sciendum etiam quod post verba consecrationis, in ipso sacramento tam diu est corpus et sanguis domini quam diu manet species panis et vini, et non seorsum corpus et seorsum sanguis, sed sub utraque specie manet Christus totus, ut canit ecclesia. Unde corpus Christi est sub specie panis per transsubstantiationem panis in ipsum corpus, et sanguis est concomitanter (*De cena domini*, *Mon* I, 40r). See also *Mon.* I, 164v.

[2] Item credendum quod tam bonus quam malus sacerdos habens fidem rectam circa sacramentum venerabile, et habens intentionem sic facere, ut precipit Christi, et dicens verba in missa secundum institutionem ecclesie conficit, id est virtute verborum sacramentaliter, facit ministerialiter, esse sub specie panis verum corpus Christi. Similiter sub specie vini fiat ministerialiter esse verum sanguinem Christi . . . transsubstantians panem in corpus suum et vinum in sanguinem suum. . . . Dico etiam quod tam bonus quam malus sacerdos conficit. . . . Et ponitur prima questione tertia: sacramentum corporis et sanguinis domini, nec a bono magis, nec a malus minus perficitur sacerdote, quia non merito consecrantis sed verbo perficitur creatoris (ibid., 39r).

Also: Concedimus enim quod malus papa, episcopus vel prelatus est indignus minister sacramentorum per quem deus baptisat vel consecrat. . . . Minister autem

arrived at this position as long ago as 1401, in a sermon on Christ's body, and that he afterwards taught it in the university and in his Commentary on the *Sentences*. His enemies had reported to Alexander V that he had said that a priest in mortal sin could not consecrate; but 'I wrote and write now that any such person does not consecrate worthily and meritoriously, but unworthily before God, and he does so to his own prejudice in despising God's name'.[1] He expressed the same view in distinction 12, Book IV of his Commentary on the *Sentences*, where he said that, to consecrate the host, nothing was needed beyond the required material and a minister who could say the words and had the intention of performing the office.[2] He acknowledged that it would be better for those who were unworthy to celebrate mass not to do so, but this did not disqualify them.[3]

This attitude to sinful priests is closely bound up with—indeed rests upon—another distinction not to be found in Wyclif: between office and merit. For Hus, the very fact that a man was in holy orders meant that his office, no matter how exalted or humble or whatever his own individual condition, carried with it powers to mediate for God. Thus when a sinful priest consecrated the host he did so in virtue of words which came from God.[4] Similarly, while in the strictest sense he

---

ille malus et pestifer non baptisat, non conficit, non consecrat digne, sed indigne in sui damnationem exercet ministerium Jesu Christi. Et sic nostra pars concedit cum scriptura Judam, Caipham, Annam et ceteros huiusmodi fuisse episcopi equivoce, sed vere fures et latrones (*Responsio ad scriptum Stephani Páleč, Mon.* I, 256r).

[1] *Mon.* I, 39v.

[2] Item aliud est posse simpliciter conficere, et aliud ordinatim. Dico ergo de posse simpliciter quod nichil requiritur ultra materiam debitam nisi minister debitus, ad quem requiritur tres conditiones. Prima quod sit sacerdos, etiam quod possit proferre verba consecrationis, et quod habere possit debitam intentionem conficiendi et faciendi quod ecclesia facit; propter defectum conditionis secunde mutus non potest conficere; propter defectum conditionis tertie carens usu rationis non potest conficere. Sed prima conditio est hic propria, quia potest solum sacerdos, et quilibet sacerdos cui competere possunt iste conditiones, scilicet debita prolatio ac intentio. (*Sentences*, Bk. IV, d. 13, 584).

[3] Melius ergo foret toti ecclesie quod non sic missarent in crimine, quia alias ecclesia cum Apostolo non sic quemlibet singulariter et coniunctim singulos existentes in crimine ab illo cibo sacratissimo, qui mors est malis vita bonis. . . . Item contra illud mendacium pono per possibile apud deum quod quilibet sacerdos et omnes simul qui sunt hodie, incidant in peccatum mortale, in quo durent per diem naturalem, quo stante nullus istorum debet missare per supradictam regulam Apostoli, alias oppositum faciens iudicium sibi manducaret et biberet, contraveniens voluntati divini (PRS 173).

[4] *De cena domini, Mon.* I, 39r.

could not give absolution, in a wider sense he had such power as a priest.[1] In each case priests were the instrument in bringing God to the faithful: even if not in themselves proficient, they yet officiated.[2]

This in turn raised the all-important issue of what constituted a true priest and pope. Here, again, Hus's position, while superficially appearing to have much the same outcome as Wyclif's, rested upon a different foundation. It was moral and Janovian, where Wyclif's, in the beginning, was metaphysical: the English scholastic had started from the assumption that anyone not of the elect was, as *prescitus*, excluded from the church, and could not therefore be a true priest. Hus, on the contrary, long before he embraced this notion in 1412, in *De ecclesia*, began from the simple premise of mortal sin as something individual, and distinct from the nature of priesthood. He maintained that distinction throughout his trial at Constance: the office was independent of the qualities (merit) of its bearer. Accordingly a true priest, in Hus's terms, was one who remained true to God. If ultimately Hus consigned him to the same category as Wyclif had—among the *presciti*—their differences in origin continued to assert themselves. The touchstone of Hus's true priest was the practical one of conformity to Christ's precepts. But so long as he remained a priest—within the communion of the visible church and not an excommunicate—he was due the respect of his office.

Thus there were false priests and true priests, but so long as they shared their order in common they both remained priests, the bad equivocally, the good truly priests.[3] This ultimately saved Hus's position from the destructive effects of Wyclif's, for whom the order of priesthood was devoid of intrinsic respect just because there was no means of knowing who was truly of it. In Hus's sense a sinful pope or priest was like Judas; on the one hand a brigand and criminal who *ipso facto* was excluded from membership of Christ; and on the other hand, under the present dispensation, to be treated with the respect due to his office.[4] As Hus said, their position was equivocal. What he omitted to add was that the equivocation here, as elsewhere, was characteristic of his thought, and in no small measure the result of his trying to balance his own predominantly moral predilections against Wyclif's more doctrinaire assumptions.

In most cases Hus saved himself from falling over the brink into heterodoxy; but in his attitude to the hierarchy in general and the pope

[1] *Tractatus responsivus* (ed. S. H. Thomson, Princeton 1927), 21.

[2] PRS 174.

[3] *Responsio ad Páleč*, *Mon.* I, 256v.

[4] Ibid., 256v–258v.

in particular he failed. Some of the most impassioned, and uncomprehending, exchanges at Constance between him and his judges were over his definition of a true priest. So long as he kept within the scriptural and patristic framework, which was his natural milieu, Hus was on firm, if obscure, ground. He could quote Gregory the Great that those who sold and bought the holy offices could not be priests;[1] and Chrisostom that a priest could remain one juridically but not morally;[2] and Jerome that to be a priest was not in itself enough to be a Christian.[3] But when he went on to attack the very conception of the pope as head of the church, or Christ's true successor, he divided from the conciliarists and traditionalists and aligned himself with Wyclif. Where the former in varying ways recognized the pope's headship, Hus from the writing of *De ecclesia* onwards treated him as at best dispensable and at worst a menace to the church.

This work was the summation of Hus's revolt against authority: it was the outcome of his defiance of the pope, and his own archbishop, over acts of disobedience, indulgences, absolution, and crusades, culminating in his own final rejection of papal primacy. Its significance is twofold: it formed the basis for Hus's condemnation in 1415, as the source for most of the articles taken from his writings; and it mirrors both Hus's main theological tenets and their relation to Wyclif's doctrine. This rather than any intrinsic merits of its own is the reason why *De ecclesia* ranks first amongst Hus's treatises. Far from being the finest product of the movement it portrays all Hus's own inconsistence and limitations as a thinker. For all his scholasticism Hus was a moralist who was at his best denouncing abuses in debate or sermon. His most succinct works were his polemics such as his replies to Páleč[4] and Znojmo[5] and his Czech work *On simony*.[6] Since, however, *De ecclesia* runs the gamut of Hus's main positions, it must be examined in some detail.

It falls effectively into two parts:[7] the first concerning the nature of the church, and the second the practical questions in which Hus had been involved. The work was written as a reply to the eight doctors of

[1] *Responsio ad Páleč*, *Mon.* I, 256v. See De Vooght, *Hussiana* 211–38.

[2] De Vooght, *Hussiana* 217.

[3] Ibid., *Mon.* I, 133r–134v.

[4] *Mon.* I, 255v–264r.

[5] Ibid., 265r.–302r.

[6] Translated by M. Spinka in *Advocates of Reform* (*Library of Christian Classics XIV*, 196–278).

[7] It divides at ch. II. The first ten chapters occupy only 89 pages as compared with 147 for the following fourteen chapters.

the theological faculty, led by Páleč and Znojmo, who had put forward their conditions for a reconciliation with Hus at the abortive synod of February 1413. It was in turn answered by Páleč's *De ecclesia*.[1] Hus opens with the different meanings of the church, which he took over from Wyclif, followed by his own definition, also from Wyclif. This ran as follows: 'The holy catholic, that is, universal, church is the body of all the predestined, present, past and future.'[2] This church was the bride of Christ.[3] It was not the first time that Hus had given this definition: it can be traced back to his synodal sermon of 1405.[4] But it was at that time only one of three; and Hus there and elsewhere adhered to the accepted connotation of church as the *congregatio fidelium*. In *De ecclesia*, however, the restricted notion became the only acceptable one. He traced its different ramifications in this world (the militant), in purgatory (the sleeping) and in heaven (the triumphant).[5] Like Wyclif he made it independent of specific place or time, to wherever the just were,[6] all to be finally united in heaven.[7] Its members were joined by the future grace of final salvation and present grace and charity.[8] Christ was the head, and they his mystical body.[9] Parallel to the church of the saved was the congregation of the damned (the *presciti*) who were excluded from the church of Christ. Hus adopted various analogies from the human body to show that though the damned were in the visible church they were not of it.[10] Accordingly membership of the church was from divine, not human, election: that is, through God's predestination of those who persevered to the end in his charity.[11] With St. Augustine, and not always consistently, Hus distinguished between present and future grace to show that those who enjoyed the former did not necessarily continue in it to be saved.[12]

The two main features of Hus's doctrine of the church, both taken over from Wyclif, were the exclusion of the *presciti* from all eternity and Christ's sole headship of the mystic body of the elect.[13] They were

[1] Ed. S. H. Thomson (Cambridge 1956). [2] Ibid., 2. [3] Ibid., 3.

[4] *Mon.* II, 28r; noted in De Vooght, *Hussiana* 9 ff., where he also discusses Hus's letter to Peter.

[5] *De ecclesia* 7. [6] Ibid., 2. [7] Ibid., 8.

[8] Unitas autem ecclesie katholice consistit in unitate predestinationis, cum singula eius membra sunt unum predestinatione et in unitate beatitudinis, cum singuli filii sunt in beatitudine finaliter uniti. In presenti etiam eius unitas consistit in unitate fidei et virtutum et in unitate caritatis . . . (ibid., 10).

[9] Ibid., 12. [10] Ibid., 14–15. [11] Ibid., 17. [12] Ibid., 17–18.

[13] Ibid., 20–23. Et cum par sit ratio de uno prescito sicut de reliquo, sequitur quod nullus prescitus est membrum sancte matris ecclesie katholice. Item impossibile est

the source of his heterodoxy. Like Wyclif he emphasized the indestructibility of the grace of predestination; those to whom it was given could never lose it, even when, like Peter who had denied Christ, they sinned.[1] The damned, on the other hand, were of the devil and nothing could redeem them from final perdition.[2] Hus was aware of the traditional teaching, notably of St. Augustine and Gregory the Great, that the church contained all the faithful, both good and bad, saved and damned; but he explained their exclusion by reference to God's final dispositions.[3] Just as straw always remained straw, so the *presciti* remained *presciti* even if in present grace. For that reason they were never true members of the church.[4]

So far so good. The two bodies have been delineated. But it is when the practical implications are broached that Hus's definitions break down. They do so for the same reasons as Wyclif's did. It is impossible logically both to assert ignorance of who is damned and who is saved and to damn those who contravene Christ's laws. To condemn prelates for worldliness and for being of Antichrist was *ipso facto* to put them among the damned; not to have done so would have undermined Wyclif's entire moral case against the abuses within the church. As we saw in chapter seven, Wyclif's pragmatism, although founded upon his metaphysics, ultimately overcame them. To make sinfulness palpable was to make the *presciti* knowable and so also, by the same token, the saved. Hus, whose initial moral bias was even more pronounced than Wyclif's, can hardly be blamed for having done the same;[5] indeed unless he had stopped in his tracks it is hard to see what else he could have done.

His discussion soon turned into a practical and moral disquisition on the iniquities of the pope and the hierarchy. Theory was to all intents and purposes left behind. The *presciti* became a moral rather than a metaphysical category, which was applied to the erring hierarchy: in

---

Christum umquam non diligere sponsam suam val aliquam eius partem, cum necessario ipsam diligit ut seipsum. Sed impossibile est ut aliquem prescitum sic diligat, ergo impossibile est ut aliquis prescitus sit membrum illius ecclesie (ibid., 23).

[1] *De ecclesia* 27–8.

[2] Ibid., 30.

[3] Ibid., 33.

[4] Ibid., 34–5.

[5] De Vooght, *Hussiana* 30–1, attributes this inconsistency to Hus's wavering between the orthodox and Wyclifian definition of the church. It may be; but Wyclif, as we saw, also adopted the same double standard just because it alone offered a palpable test of loyalty to Christ. Moreover, both Hus and Wyclif based their opposition to the hierarchy on moral and practical grounds—Hus more so than Wyclif.

fact it bears a strong resemblance in essentials to Janov's notion of the communion of the elect as distinct from the mass of the faithful constituting the church. Something of the same kind is also to be found in Jacobellus's defence of Wyclif's Decalogue.[1] Moral purity became the distinguishing mark. Hus went further in this than Wyclif in two respects. The first, as we have said, was his distinction between office and merit, treated at some length in *De ecclesia*;[2] by this, however heinous a prelate's individual mores, his status as a priest upheld him in his authority. The second was a less thoroughgoing application of the Augustinian concepts of present and final grace. Already a chink in Hus's resolution can be seen on page 10 of *De ecclesia*, where he wrote that 'in the present their (the elect's) unity consists in unity of faith and the [theological] virtues and charity'.[3] What, then, becomes of the distinction between present and final grace? Hus seems prepared to accept any evidence of grace as a sign of predestination. The force of predestination is further modified on page 38 where, having stressed that no one without a special revelation has the right to call himself a member of the church,[4] it is stated that laymen are not obliged to believe in their ecclesiastical superiors unless they are true to God.[5] A priest had an obligation to be virtuous: 'If he is manifestly sinful, then it should be supposed, *from his works*, that he is not just, but the enemy of Christ.'[6] This is not of itself to reintroduce the traditional concept of the church as the communion of all believers;[7] it is rather to exclude the *presciti* there and then, without waiting for God's final judgement. Their external bond of pride is more readily recognizable than the nuances between present and final grace.[8]

Hus's doctrine led, in a modified form, to where Wyclif's led: into a denunciation of papal pretensions. It was, however, both more

[1] In Sedlák in *Studie a texty* II, 316–28. [2] 48–52.

[3] Also discussed in de Vooght, *Hussiana* 31. On the other hand see *De ecclesia* 39 where Hus argues that present membership of the church does not necessarily entail true membership of the predestined: Isto ergo modo multi reputative etiam secundum presentem iustitiam dicuntur esse de ecclesia sed non vere secundum predestinationem ad gloriam. [4] Ibid., 36–7.

[5] hic dicitur quod laycus non tenetur credere de suo preposito nisi verum. Patet quia nemo tenetur quicquam credere, nisi ad quod movet eum deus credere, sed deus non movet hominem ad credendum falsum, licet enim ex fide falsa quandoque occasionaliter bonum proveniat, et deus moveat ad substantiam actus. Tamen deus non movet sic hominem, ut fallitur (ibid., 38).

[6] Ibid. [7] As de Vooght asserts, *Hussiana* 31.

[8] *De ecclesia* 40.

moderate and more personal: as much an *apologia pro vita sua* as an attack on the papacy as institution. To take the latter first: Hus was prepared to accept that the pope and cardinals were the most dignified part of the Roman church and to be treated as such so long as they followed Christ.[1] What, however, he in common with Wyclif denied was that the pope and cardinals were the Roman church and in the direct line of descent from Peter and the Apostles. In the first place, the pope and cardinals could err and sin. The egregious example of Agnes, pope Joanna, who for two years and five months had reigned as pope John VIII until her sex had been revealed, was the stock example of papal fallibility employed by Gerson and the conciliarists as well as Wyclif and Hus.[2] In the second place, Hus, like Wyclif, denied that the pope as head of the Roman church was head of the whole Catholic church: he was one local head among many, comparable in position to the patriarch of Antioch or the head of the Alexandrine church.[3] In the third place, Hus once again followed Wyclif in his interpretation of Matthew 16: 18:[4] 'You are Peter, and on this rock I shall build my church.' According to Wyclif, as to Marsilius, the rock referred to Christ and not to Peter.[5] The papal claim to primacy, which was founded upon Peter's pre-eminence, thus fell to the ground. Peter had been chief among the Apostles for his personal virtues[6] and not as Christ's vicar. The pope was not his heir, nor the cardinals the successors of the Apostles.[7] Christ alone was head, and the universal church alone infallible.[8] To say otherwise would be to put man before God.[9] For Hus, as for Wyclif, the papacy was a human institution, the work of the emperor Constantine: the word pope was not to be found in the bible.[10] Thus, in each case, Hus and Wyclif distinguished the place of the pope from the rest of the hierarchy. Ultimately, he could, if necessary, be

[1] Verumtamen inter partes eius in comparatione maioritatis papa et suum collegium sunt pars precipua dignitate, dum tamen sequuntur Christum propinquius, et deserendo fastum et ambitionem primatus serviant matri sue efficacius atque humilius (ibid., 48).

[2] E.g., ibid., 48, 103, 107 f., 141, 233.

[3] Ibid., 48.

[4] Ibid., 57–62.

[5] *De potestate pape* 56 ff. See pp. 532 ff. above.

[6] *De ecclesia*, 66.

[7] Ibid., 110–12.

[8] Unde nec papa est caput nec cardinales corpus totum sancte universalis ecclesie katholice, nam solus Christus est caput illius ecclesie et singuli predestinati simul corpus et quilibet membrum, quia una est persona cum Christo Ihesu ipsa sponsa (ibid., 51–2).

[9] Ibid., 65.

[10] Ibid., 101 ff.

dispensed with, just because he had no foundation in scripture.[1] Christ, not he, was the head of the church; at most he could claim to be Christ's vicar if he remained true to him.

Papal authority was therefore circumscribed by the superior authority of the bible. If Hus made none of the same issue between human traditions and scripture which Wyclif made, he nevertheless insisted that the Fathers and papal decrees should be observed only in so far as they were founded upon the bible. Papal decrees were the mark of fallible men and carried none of the imperative obligation of the bible, which was the word of God. Belief in the former was a matter of opinion to be determined by their consonance with God's law.[2] In reply to the charges of his opponents that his interpretation of the bible was arbitrary, Hus maintained that it was in accordance with the inspiration of the Holy Spirit and the exposition of the Fathers.[3] In his Commentary on the *Sentences* Hus called the bible 'the most certain, profound and worthy' source of all knowledge[4] because its subject was the divine.[5] For that reason the bible must be read, heard and preached as necessary to eternal life.[6] He rejected Páleč's description of the bible as something inanimate; for Hus, on the contrary, it was the book of life, a living presence essential to leading and finding a true Christian life.[7] His own outlook was founded upon it. To a much greater extent than Wyclif he depended upon scriptural citation for his arguments. It went together with his reliance upon the Fathers, pre-eminent among whom were the four doctors, Jerome, Ambrose, Augustine, and Gregory the Great, as well as Chrisostom, Damascene and the pseudo-Denis.[8] Of St. Augustine, he said that he was of greater value

[1] Non tamen dico quod civitas Roma sit sedes apostolica ad tantum necessaria, quod sine ea non possit stare ecclesia Ihesu Christi, nam per possibile destructa Roma ut Sodoma adhuc posset stare ecclesia christiana. Nec etiam est verum quod ubicumque est papa ibi est Roma, quamvis verum est ubicumque fuerit papa dum hic est in terris ibi est auctoritas Petri in papa . . . (ibid., 172–3).

[2] Et isto modo tenetur quilibet christianus credere explicite vel implicite omnem veritatem quam sanctus spiritus posuit in scriptura. Et isto modo non tenetur homo dictis sanctorum preter scripturam nec bullis papalibus credere, nisi quid dixerint ex scriptura vel quod fundaretur implicite in scriptura. Sed potest opinative homo credere bullis, quia tam papa quam sua curia potest falli propter ignorantiam veritatis (ibid., 56). Also ibid., 106, and *Mon.* 1, 262r.

[3] Ibid., 133.

[4] *Sentences* 17–18.

[5] Ibid., 20.

[6] Spiritura sacra debet legi, audiri et predicari propter vitam eternam (ibid.).

[7] quia scriptura est liber vite per se iudicans (*Responsio ad Páleč, Mon.* 1, 262r).

[8] *De ecclesia* 121.

to the church than many of the popes and perhaps all the cardinals that had ever been: he knew more about the law of Christ and had helped to define Catholic doctrine by purging the church of error and heresy.[1] Hus's reverence for the bible and the Fathers is shown in a letter to his disciple, master Martin, written from prison at Constance: 'Live', he wrote, 'according to the law of Christ and diligently seek to preach God's word. . . . Willingly read the bible and especially the New Testament, and where you do not understand turn at once to the expositors. . . .'[2]

This distinction between the authority of the bible and the Fathers, on the one hand, and the hierarchy, on the other, underlay Hus's attitude to the pope. It was the source of his opposition to simony, indulgences, John XXIII's crusade, and his attacks upon general abuses among the clergy. Even less than Wyclif did Hus regard himself as simply a solitary individual pitting his own conscience against the wrongs of the time. Rather he saw himself as upholding the authentic evangel of Christ, confirmed in the writings of the Fathers and the practices of the early church. Unlike Wyclif this solidarity was moral rather than historical: only occasionally did Hus enter into historical excursus and then largely along the lines already taken by Wyclif.[3] For Hus, even more than for Wyclif because of his personal involvement, the central issue became one of obedience. Since the bible spoke for God, and the pope, when he diverged from it, only for himself and other men, in those circumstances to disobey the pope was to obey God. This was Hus's repeated justification for his acts of defiance.[4] As with so much else in comparison with Wyclif, Hus's attitude to the bible was at once more immediate and practical in application, and theoretically more confined. While he refused to submit to the ban of his superiors, he never went to Wyclif's lengths of reviling them or denying them the authority of their office. The bible was above all a mirror of conduct, and he used it to reflect his own as well as the hierarchy's.

With this for his criterion, Hus's view of the authority of pope and

[1] Unde non dubium quin beatus Augustinus plus profuit ecclesie quam multe pape et in doctrina forte plus quam omnes cardinales . . . (ibid.).

[2] Palacký, *Documenta* 119–20.

[3] Usually Ralph Diceto under the name of Cestrensis. *De ecclesia* 103 ff., 144, 146, 166.

[4] E.g., Ex hiis habetur quod devianti pape rebellare est Christo domino obedire, quod potissime provenit in provisionibus, que affectionem sapiunt personalem (ibid., 169).

cardinals was inevitably a restricted one. The pope was at best Christ's vicar, never head of the church on his own account.[1] Since neither he nor the cardinals enjoyed the sanction of the bible, the election of a pope by cardinals was unauthorized.[2] A true pope could only be known through revelation:[3] which in effect was to render any certainty impossible. It was to make living the test and the one to which Hus had recourse.[4] It was also to deny the pope a *plenitudo potestatis* and the cardinals an inherent and immutable place within the hierarchy of the church.[5] In particular Hus refused the title of 'most holy' (*sanctissimus*) to the pope on the grounds that it was exclusive to Christ.[6] This was to figure among the charges brought against him by Gerson at Constance. What was required for recognition of priests as true incumbents of their offices was conformity with Christ's example, namely, the renunciation of worldliness, wealth, pomp and pride.[7] These may be summed up in Hus's four signs of an erring pope: a preference for human over divine laws; worldliness; the selling of benefices; obstruction to the preaching of God's word.[8] The pope who persisted in them was Antichrist, the abomination of desolation.[9] The term was applied

[1] Quomodo ergo doctores sine ostensione scripture docent quod papa sit illius sancte ecclesie et collegium corpus, cum sufficiat fideli christiano cum fide formata et perseverantia pro fide articuli de ecclesia credere katholica, quod sit una universitas fidelium predestinatorum salvanda virtute meriti Christi, qui est caput illius ecclesie sancte katholice, licet non explicite descenderit ad aliquem eius vicarium quem cognosceret capitalem? (ibid., 112).

[2] Nullus ergo sic erat nec sic vocatus fuit papa in primitiva ecclesia ante ecclesie dotationem. . . . Talis enim dignitas et nominatio dicitur a Silvestro pro tempore dotationis ecclesie inchoasse. Et capta ista descriptione pape ex cunctis circumstantiis, quas pretendit, planum est quod nullus prelatus huiusmodi debet esse (*Tractatus responsivus* 146). Also *De ecclesia* 51–2, 64–7, 96–100.

[3] Nullus papa est persona dignissima illius ecclesie katholice preter Christum, igitur nullus papa est caput illius ecclesie preter Christum . . . sequitur quod nullus sine revelatione asseret rationabiliter de se vel alio quod est caput ecclesie particularis sancte, quamvis bene vivendo debet sperare quod sit membrum sancte catholice sponse Christi (*De ecclesia* 107).

[4] E.g., ibid., 115, 129.

[5] Ibid., 101, 107, 110–12, 119–22, 125–8. Also *Responsio ad Znojmo* 275r–v.

[6] E.g., Si officium est pater sanctissimus, videat ipse fictor, et Judas Scarioth fuit tunc episcopus sanctissimus, cum Christus de eo dixit quod sit diabolus. . . . Et cum dicit fictor quod esse papam est nomen officii, tunc sequitur quod ille homo papa malus et prescitus secundum officium est sanctissimus. Et per consequens secundum illud officium est optimus (*Responsio ad Znojmo*, *Mon.* 1, 258r–v). Also, *De ecclesia* 107, 117.

[7] E.g., *De ecclesia* 91, 107, 181. [8] Ibid., 167. [9] E.g., ibid., 103, 140.

widely to all who were guilty—especially the clergy—of these moral failings. As with Janov its mark was worldliness.[1] Hus attached special importance to simony and preaching. The first, the subject of one of his most fiery treatises, was, together with apostasy and blasphemy, one of the three great heresies.[2] Where apostasy was a turning away from God, and blasphemy the defaming of his power by human assertions, such as the glorification of the pope's authority, simony was the overthrowing of God's order.[3] Every heretic was a simoniac in that he had sold his soul to the devil.[4] It was a sin against the Holy Spirit, for a simoniac was a trafficker in holy things: 'the evil consent to an exchange of spiritual for non-spiritual things'.[5] On Hus's definition this meant all priests who received payment for their spiritual ministrations,[6] including all payments to the pope and papal reservations.[7] Far from his office protecting him, the pope, if guilty of simony, was a greater sinner than anyone because of his more exalted status.[8] The pope indeed should be free of temporal dominion and worldly goods, and anyone proving holier than he had a better right to their use.[9] Apart from their immorality such practices made for inefficiency, filling the church with bishops many of whom were 'not even fit to herd swine'.[10] How could a pope know the spiritual qualities of an appointee hundreds of miles away?[11]

Hus's remedy was not wholesale expropriation, but a return to apostolic simplicity, which included the holding of goods in common.[12] Those priests who persisted in leading sinful lives should be shunned and tithes withheld from them.[13] Where revenues were excessive the lay lords should have power of confiscation and in the case of simoniacs should suppress them.[14] As to simony itself, Hus saw the remedy in a return to the ancient practice of election to spiritual offices, to be made in the presence of the people.[15] He certainly regarded simony as the most besetting of all sins and described it in *De ecclesia* as worse than fornication.[16]

Preaching, on the other hand, was obligatory, a mandate by which all priests were bound. It was so imperative that no ban from a superior

[1] E.g., ibid. 129 and ch. XI.
[2] *On Simony* 199 ff.
[3] Ibid.
[4] Ibid.
[5] Ibid., 202.
[6] Ibid., 208.
[7] Ibid., 213 ff.; *De ecclesia* 104–5, 116.
[8] Ibid., 214.
[9] Ibid.
[10] Ibid., 217.
[11] Ibid., 215.
[12] Ibid., 230 ff., 239.
[13] Ibid., 252, 273.
[14] Ibid., 272, 275.
[15] Ibid., 268, 270.
[16] Et cum idem vel maius est iudicium de quancunque maiori spirituali fornicatione . . . (*De ecclesia* 223).

should be allowed to stand in its way.[1] An indication of how imperative Hus considered it to be, is that, of the six of Wyclif's 45 articles which he chose publicly to defend in the summer of 1412, two of them concerned preaching.[2] Article 14 stated that those failing to preach or to hear God's word because of excommunication were traitors to God. Article 15 said that any priest or deacon could preach without papal or episcopal permission. How else, asked Hus, was Antichrist to be combated? God's word was the best way of instructing the ignorant and exposing the false words of the pseudo-prophets and disciples of Antichrist.[3] Preaching, then, as much as living, was the test of a true and holy priest, the pope included.[4]

One of the more radical consequences of Hus's attitude here was over the role of laymen. Although he did not go so far as Wyclif in this direction, he was prepared to allow them to judge their spiritual superiors, and, if the latter were found wanting, to refuse them recognition. In the main this was to take the form of withholding tithes, as we have just seen. Hus advocated this course in his 1412 defence of another of Wyclif's six articles, that tithes were pure alms, which, as freely given, could be as freely withheld.[5] He also went farther when he defended another of the articles in which Wyclif had affirmed that lay lords could freely withdraw the temporal goods of habitually delinquent ecclesiastics.[6] Even allowing for the element of debate and provocation in Hus's position, what he said there was consonant with what he maintained elsewhere. If the priesthood lived a life contrary to Christ it was for laymen to correct them, as in the case of the Czech clergy, whose sinful ways certainly warranted secular intervention.[7] Similarly, Hus denied the priesthood an inherent superiority regardless of their conduct; he opposed the view of a preacher at Pilsen that the worst priest was better than the best layman. It arose from the mistaken assumption that office counted for more than merit.[8] Not only should sinful priests not be obeyed, but they should be corrected.[9] His most radical statement of

[1] Ex isto consequenter sequitur quod sacerdos Christi vivens secundum legem eius, habens scripture notitiam et affectum ad edificandum populum, debet predicare non obstante pretensa excommunicatione. Patet quia predicare verbum dei est mandatam sacerdotibus, teste Petro apostolo, Act. x, 42 (ibid., 190).

[2] In *Mon.* I, 110v–134v.

[3] Ibid., 115v–116r.

[4] *De ecclesia* 158.

[5] *Mon.* I, 125v–128r.

[6] Ibid., 118r–125v.

[7] Ibid., 120v–121r.

[8] Ibid., 146r.

[9] Sed bene sequitur quod nec papa nec alius debet corripi vel corrigi in quantum sequitur caput Christi, sed si episcopus vel confessor vicem Christi gerens attemptat actum luxurie in virgine vel casta coniuge, numquid non debet eum vehementer

this view was in his question, 'Whether Moses the lawgiver was a priest'.[1] Glossing the meaning of the word priest (*sacerdos*) he concluded that every good Christian was a priest because he was holy to God.[2] Conversely not all bishops and priests were good Christians although ordained.[3] For himself, said Hus, he would prefer to be a good Christian than a wicked prelate or pope; for as a good Christian he would be king and priest, and one of Christ's immediate vicars—Moses's own position.[4]

This sense of communion with God was expressed in Hus's definition of the three kinds of Christian communion: through grace, which was the communion of the saints making up the mystic body of Christ; through the sacraments; and through prayer. They were the preserve of the good alone, who could only be excluded by mortal sin.[5] Hus, at this point, seems to have believed that the elect can never be in mortal sin,[6] a different position from Wyclif and one which reflects his more equivocal attitude to the concept of the *congregatio predestinatorum*. Together with this sense of equality before the eyes of God, in merit or in sin, went a leaning towards the equality of orders. Again it was not so pronounced as in Wyclif; it was also counterbalanced by Hus's fundamental insistence upon obedience, in normal circumstances, to superiors. Yet on more than one occasion Hus spoke of priests and deacons as the only two orders in the primitive church.[7] Among the Apostles Christ had made no distinction of grade; they were all equal members of the same college. The division between cardinals, bishops and priests was not of Christ's doing, but came about subsequently. Christ himself wanted all to be equal.[8] Elsewhere, it is true, Hus spoke

---

corripere tamquam Antichristum et sue anime perfidum inimicum? (*De ecclesia* 205). See also 199–200.

[1] J. Sedlák, *M. Jan Hus* II, 107*–116*.

[2] Ex iam dictis patet et etiam ex hoc nomine sacerdos, quod componitur ex greco et latino, quod est sacrum dans (dist. 21. clericos), quod omnis bonus christianus sacerdos, quia est sacrum deo (ibid., 109*).

[3] Et patet quod non omnes episcopi vel sacerdotes sunt boni christiani quamvis sunt in gradu huiusmodi ab hominibus ordinati (ibid., 110*).

[4] Ibid., 111*. [5] *De ecclesia* 212. [6] Ibid., 213.

[7] Cum igitur ex ordinacione Christi tempore apostolorum duo ordines cleri pro sua ecclesia suffecerunt, scilicet dyaconus et sacerdos . . . (ibid., 128).

[8] *Mon.* I, 291r (misnumbered 301r). De Vooght (*Hussiana* 6 and passim) avers that Hus did not uphold the equality of all priests and bishops. It is true that Hus always paid the respect due to office; but, in the widest senses of orders as such, Hus clearly did believe in the ideal equality which he saw in the primitive church.

of pope and cardinals as the *precipua pars* of the church;[1] he constantly asserted the respect due to a priest's office whatever his own state of merit. Hus here never really resolved the conflict between equality and authority. But the weight of his strictures upon the hierarchy and his own decision to disobey his superiors would seem to outweigh his more formal justifications.[2]

More significant were the limitations upon the priesthood as a whole. Civilly, Christ had barred them from litigation and secular authority.[3] This included fighting crusades for the submission of other Christians. But, even more, no priest had the power of unconditionally binding and loosing unless God had done so first.[4] The same applied to excommunication[5] and granting indulgences.[6] The reason was the same as Wyclif's: only a man in mortal sin is cut off from God's communion, or rather cuts himself off. Accordingly, before he could be anathematized he must have already excommunicated himself from God. If he has not, then the sentence is invalid and unjust, and the just man has no cause to fear it.[7] So long as a man participates in God's

[1] E.g., *De ecclesia* 48.

[2] Nullus tamen hiis debet rebellionis erigere calcaneum contra suos prepositos aut vicio inobedience denigrari, sed debemus ipsos supponendo esse nostros legittimos prepositos in omnibus racionibus humiliter obedire, quia sic est voluntas dei nostri patri familias, qui nos in suam vocat vineam (PRS 137–8). But against this must be put the extended justification of disobedience in *De ecclesia*, which, in my view, outweighs anything Hus said on the other side. Indeed, Hus's stand against his superiors must be accounted tantamount to open rebellion.

[3] Dico secundo quod non licet Romano pontifici, nec expedit sibi vel cuicunque episcopo vel clero pro dominatione seculari vel mundi divitiis pugnare (*Mon.* I, 176r).

[4] Tamen impossibile est quod aliquis homo solvat vel ligat hominem nisi de quanto conformatur capiti, fonti et sponso ecclesie, domino nostro Jesu Christo (*Refutatio octo doctorum theologie*, *Mon.* I, 308v).

And: Ideo supponendum est primo quod dictum Salvatoris est necessarium de virtute sermonis eo quod non est possibile sacerdotem quicquam solvere vel ligare, nisi illa solutio vel ligatio sit in celis. . . . (*De ecclesia* 77).

See also, *Mon.* I, 175v, 181r; *De ecclesia* 78–9, 82, 83; *Tractatus responsivus*, 80.

[5] *De ecclesia* 183, 189, 208–16.

[6] *Mon.* I, 174r–175r. Dico tertio quod nemo est capax indulgentie nisi fuerit et quanto fuerit dignus vel dispositus per gratiam apud deum (ibid., 175v).

[7] Ex istis primo sequitur quod nunquam fit nec potest esse excommunicatio a tribus primis communicationibus [i.e. of the saints, the eucharist, prayer] nisi peccatum mortale. Patet quia nunquam aliquis separatur a communione sanctorum que est participacio gratie dei et sacramentorum et suffragiorum ad vitam preparantium nisi per peccatum mortale, quod solum dividit vel separat hominem a communione huiusmodi sicut separat ab ipso deo. Nec etiam potest fieri nisi per peccatum mortale,

grace he is of his communion. The same applies to the remission of sin. It must come from God, since it requires his infinite power and mercy through the giving of the Holy Spirit. Only God can do this.[1] The priest's function is to declare his sentence not himself to pass it.[2] He can only therefore express in time what God has eternally decreed.[3] To claim more for priestly power is blasphemy.[4]

It was on these grounds that Hus opposed the bull of indulgences[5] which led directly to his excommunication. In the first place, although priests have power to declare absolution, they cannot do so in the form of an indulgence without a special revelation from God. In the second place no sinner is capable of receiving an indulgence unless first worthily disposed to do so through God's grace; it therefore demanded God's prior intervention.[6] Accordingly the pope had no power to remit sins for a period of time unless this had been revealed to him. To presume to do so for war or earthly gain was to fly in the face of Christ's precepts.[7] It was also to go against the practice of the early church where none of the Apostles had presumed to give the Holy Spirit.[8] No one was absolved unconditionally; before God remitted sin he first prepared a sinner to be contrite and penitent; without penitence no one could be saved and only God could move a sinner to feel it.[9] The pope then, in offering remission of sins was claiming to do what only God could realize.[10] He was also acting against scripture, where indulgences were not mentioned, and assuming his own salvation when he might be one of the *presciti*.[11]

Hus did not deny the power of the keys: but he took them out of human hands. To pretend that indulgences in the accepted sense, remained, becomes somewhat sophistical. Indeed his own position was

---

eo quod quamdiu homo est in gratia tamdiu est particeps communionis triplicis supradicte secundum presentem iustitiam. Et deus, cum sit iustissimus iudex, non potest dampnificare hominem nisi ex eius demerito in huiusmodi participacione. . . . Secundo sequitur quod nunquam aliquis iudex potest aliquem sic excommunicare, nisi ipse per crimen prius excommunicet seipsum (*De ecclesia* 213).

[1] *De ecclesia* 77–8.

[2] Ibid., 79.

[3] Ibid., 81; see also *Mon.* I, 181r.

[4] et patet quod blasphemia foret presumptio asserere quod homo remittat malevolentiam contra tantum dominum factam, ipso domino non approbante (*De ecclesia* 82).

[5] *Mon.* I, 174r–189r.

[6] Ibid., 175r–v.

[7] Ibid., 176r, 178r.

[8] Ibid., 180v.

[9] Quantumcunque igitur fuerit magnus Christi episcopus non potest quemquam absolvere nisi de quanto contritus et absolutus fuerit apud deum (181r–v).

[10] Ibid., 184r.

[11] Ibid.

founded upon the very assumption that human agencies could be discounted whenever they did not conform to God's decrees; although it was theoretically possible for them to do so, in practice it provided a permanent justification for disobeying superiors. So long as a man participated in God's grace he could not be damned.[1] Since his exclusion, just as his rehabilitation, could only come from God, obedience to superiors could never be absolute.[2] True obedience was to Christ, and demanded grace, whereas to preach obedience to the pope was a mark of Antichrist.[3] With St. Bernard Hus held that obedience must be founded on loyalty to God and freely given.[4] Only then was it meritorious.[5]

Ultimately, then, Hus's position resolved itself into a choice between obeying God or obeying man. He came down unequivocally for God. There was nothing novel in the standpoint, but there was in its application. Hus was able to cite the authorities freely to show that human precepts must only be followed if they accorded with God's.[6] But with Hus this became the justification for defying his superiors. What had been traditionally conceived as harmony between God's mandates and those of the hierarchy Hus saw as opposition: the curia was one more human voice, to disobey which, far from entailing mortal sin, was frequently to obey Christ.[7] This was Hus's defence for having continued to preach after he had been excommunicated.[8] As he explained in his *Exposition of the Decalogue*, written in Czech in 1413:

> Having placed these saints and Christ the God before my eyes, I did not consent to obey pope Alexander and priest Zbyněk, the archbishop, that I should not preach the word of God. . . . The word of God says: 'Preach the word to all the world.' But their commands are contrary: Do not preach the word to all the world. . . . Know accordingly that you are not bound to obey except in such matters as you are bound by obedience to God.[9]

Although Hus added that obedience to God included obedience to evil prelates who obeyed him, in fact he had followed Christ to the exclusion of the pope. That, however unintended, was his offence.

[1] *De ecclesia* 213.

[2] Non enim in infinitum tenetur obedire quis suo privato proposito, sicut garriunt insensati (ibid., 202).

[3] Ibid., 200.

[4] Ibid., 179.

[5] Ibid., 189.

[6] E.g., *De ecclesia* 153 ff., 184–9.

[7] Ibid., 184.

[8] Cum ergo ex iam dictis quilibet predicantis officium de mandato accipit, qui ad sacerdotium accedit, patet quod illud mandatum debet exequi, pretensa excommunicatione non obstante (ibid., 191).

[9] Quoted in Spinka, op. cit., 36.

From what has been said the most radical part of Hus's teaching was his attitude to the church hierarchy. If he owed little to Wyclif on the status of sinful priests and nothing on the eucharist, his opposition to the hegemony of Rome was very much along Wyclifian lines, especially the role of Peter and the headship of Christ. So were his definition of the church, which did not include the hierarchy as such, or the *presciti*; the conception of Antichrist; the limitation upon the powers of priesthood; and his opposition to papal indulgences and crusades. Yet, in nearly every case, they received from Hus nuances which are not to be found in Wyclif. Even the starkest of all his departures from orthodoxy —his view of the church as the *congregatio predestinatorum*—was insensibly modified: present habitual grace, though firmly excluded at the front door, tended to reappear through the back. Nor does the priesthood ever lose its virtual *raison d'être*, which it did with Wyclif. That Hus leaned heavily upon Wyclif both for his ideas and words is undeniable. But in almost every case they underwent modification which changed their original import. The change was almost invariably from extremism to greater moderation, from theory to practice, from metaphysics to morals. If the words remained largely Wyclif's the voice and the attitudes were those of the Czech reformer, who in the tradition of Milíč and Janov began and ended with the state of Christian life here and now. Hus's position was more personal than Wyclif's because he was directly involved in the issues he took up. Where for Wyclif the truth of the bible remained abstract, for Hus it concerned his own conduct. Faith in Christ became a test of conscience, to uphold which he died.[1]

The final balance between the two reformers can best be struck in the list of charges preferred against Hus. It will be recalled that the first act of the commission at Constance was to present Hus with the list of forty-five articles for his responses.[2] To their general surprise, Hus gave qualified assent to only four of them, hedged on another five, and rejected (*non teneo nec tenui*) the remaining thirty-six. The overall discrepancy is a fair reflexion of the divergence between Hus and Wyclif; only in some of Hus's replies to the nine articles in the first two groups was he less than frank. The original resounding defence of Wyclif's six articles and the challenge to the pope had by then become understandably muted.

[1] Ex quo sequitur quod illa stili maxima est contra conscientiam et per consequens contra Christum (*De ecclesia* 235).

[2] In J. Sedlák *M. Jan Hus* II, 305*–10*.

Let us examine them more closely. Of the five articles to which he was prepared to own, two (11 and 13) concerned excommunication. On article 11 Hus agreed that excommunication was first from God and could only be imposed for mortal sin. To article 13 he said it could be correct for a man to continue to preach after he had been excommunicated. Likewise he assented to article 14 that preaching was possible without special licence, in an emergency. He also declared that article 15 on sinful lords and prelates was correct in the sense that they did not hold office worthily. Similarly with article 17, on correction of the clergy: it was permissible if made as friendly advice. On article 16 he refused to affirm or deny what he had publicly upheld in his defence of Wyclif in 1412, and written in his book *On simony*, that secular lords could sequestrate the property of habitually delinquent clergy. He also remained neutral over article 18, that tithes were pure alms; but he opposed their withdrawal. He also refused to commit himself on article 33 blaming Constantine and Sylvester for the endowment of the church —a view which elsewhere he had maintained. Article 8, that a pope who was *prescitus* had no power, shows the tenuousness of Hus's balance between Wyclif's doctrine and his own. He denied that he had ever held the doctrine, even though everything that he wrote in *De ecclesia* on obeying Christ against the blasphemies of Antichrist refutes him; and he went on to distinguish between the pope as *person* and *minister*: by the first as *prescitus* he was damned; by the second he had the power due to his office. This defence was less from dishonesty than a genuine confusion in Hus's own thinking: it shows more strikingly than a mere descriptive enumeration the limits of Wyclif's influence upon Hus. It never extended to the full theoretical foundations of Hus's outlook; this lack of assimilation is largely responsible for Hus's ambiguities in *De ecclesia*, and elsewhere, towards the church. Finally on article 5, which said that there was no mention of the mass in the bible, Hus agreed that while strictly true, Christ's words gave priests the power of celebrating it.

To the remaining articles, Hus's replies were almost always unequivocally negative. He rejected the first three on the eucharist: article 4, that sinful priests cannot administer the sacraments; article 6, that God obeys the devil; article 7, that aural confession is unnecessary; article 9, that Urban VI was the last valid pope; article 10, that it was against scripture for the church to have temporal goods; article 12, that a prelate excommunicating an appellant to the king was a traitor; article 19, on the uselessness of special prayers; articles 20, 21, 23 and

24, 31, 34 and 35, attacking the religious orders; articles 22 and 31, accusing their founders of having sinned because of their foundations; article 26, that the prayers of the *presciti* are worthless; article 27, that everything is from necessity; article 28, that papal reservations are made from cupidity; article 29, on the universities; article 30, that papal excommunication is from Antichrist; articles 32 and 39, that donations to the church are against Christ; article 36, that popes and prelates having possessions are heretics; article 37, that Rome is the synagogue of Satan; article 40, that papal elections were introduced by the devil; article 41, that the supremacy of the church need not be believed; article 42, that it is foolish to believe in indulgences; article 43, against oaths; article 44, that saints Augustine, Benedict and Bernard were damned for having founded orders and having had possessions; and article 45, that all religious orders were indifferently introduced by the devil. Often, as in article 44, Hus's rejection was in the form of an outspoken defence of the opposite position. But this was not an attack on Wyclif, since Hus himself had opposed the condemnation of the 45 articles on the very ground that many of them did not represent Wyclif's real teaching—as they assuredly did not. Nevertheless they show clearly Hus's genuine divergence from Wyclif over the three main areas of the sacraments, sinful priests and the religious orders; and somewhat more superficially over the pope, since the difference here was more a matter of expression, as the subsequent articles from Hus's own works show.

With Hus's virtual denial of the 45 articles, the next stage was the presentation of the 42 articles abstracted by Páleč mainly from Hus's *De ecclesia*.[1] Hus's replies to them were of three kinds; acceptance, rejection, and modification, often of a trivial nature as in his definition of the church in article 1. Hus accepted barely one third as they stood. Of those which he denied for one reason or another, five were manifest fabrications: 17, that popes not following Christ were not to be feared, which should have been the opposite; 19, that no one is a cardinal of any church who does not conform to God's will; 20, that a pope who does not conform to Christ's example is Antichrist; 22, that the pope is the beast of the Apocalypse; 41, that on arrival at the Council of Constance he, Hus, had told the citizens that if he retracted it would be under pressure and should be ignored; 42, that he had written that he had been received with honour by pope and emperor. Others were distortions, such as 27, that Christ had obeyed the devil, which Hus corrected to

[1] Palacký, *Documenta* 204–24; Sedlák, *M. Jan Hus* 311*–17*.

'consented to hear him on his way to Jerusalem'; 24, that a pope who has the greatest possessions is most holy (*sanctissimus*), which should have been the opposite: that his holiness (as to merit) was not from endowment but from following Christ.

As we have seen Páleč's 42 articles were in due course superseded by a new set of 39 articles, made up of 26 from *De ecclesia*, 7 from Hus's treatise against Páleč and 6 from his treatise against Znojmo.[1] Of the 26 articles from *De ecclesia*, only eleven of Páleč's original 42 remained:[2] article (1) that there was only one holy church, the community of all the predestined; (2) that Paul was never a member of the devil, although he committed acts against the church similar to those done by the wicked. Similarly Peter fell into serious perjury, with God's permission, only to arise more strongly: i.e. the predestined remained eternally of God's communion whatever their temporal faults. The others were: (3) No part of the church is ever separated from the rest of it because of the bond of the charity of predestination; (7) Judas was never a true disciple of Christ; (8) The holy and universal church is the *congregatio predestinatorium*; (15) The pope loses his power if he fails to conform to the life and ways of Christ and Peter; (16) The pope is the most holy (*sanctissimus*) not because he holds Peter's place but because of his wealth; (22) A wicked man acts wickedly; a virtuous man virtuously;[3] (23) A priest, living according to Christ's law, knowing the bible and wishing to instruct the people, may preach notwithstanding so-called excommunication; (25) Ecclesiastical censures are anti-Christian, imposed by the clergy for their own exaltation and the people's subjugation if they do not obey . . . they are acts of Antichrist.

[1] Sedlák, ibid., 318*–39*.

[2] In fact only 10, as two of the previous articles (29 and 30) now became joined to form one (no. 10).

[3] De Vooght, *L'hérésie* 372, denies that Hus said this; but Hus himself acknowledged his authorship with the comment 'My words'. They are to be found in *De ecclesia* 176. De Vooght similarly tries (ibid., 296) to defend Hus from Gerson's charge in the last of the twenty articles which the Paris chancellor drew up against him (in Palacký *Documenta* 185–7); article 20 accused Hus of holding that every act performed outside charity was a sin. Literally Hus does not seem to have said this; but in a number of places he came within distance of doing so: e.g. 'Unde totus modus vivendi hominis caritative est virtusosus, et totus modus vivendi hominis preter caritatem est viciosus' (*De ecclesia* 176). Similarly on article 19, as Gerson averred (and in opposition to de Vooght), Hus came very close to preaching that a just man did not need to fear the pope's excommunication. Hus's characteristic equivocations cannot efface the challenge to papal authority which underlies his *De ecclesia*.

Of these eleven only (16) could be called a flagrant travesty of what Hus had said; in view of the commission's sensitivity to Hus's initial protests over most of the other articles, it is hard to understand why this one—so entirely out of keeping with Hus's beliefs—should have been retained.

The remaining articles from *De ecclesia* dealt with the pope (10, 12, 13, 14); the church as the body of the elect (4, 5, 6, 7, 8); the cardinals (17); Peter's headship, or rather the absence of it (9); a sinful priest's equivocal power to administer the sacraments (11); the right of lay lords to coerce erring priests (19); excommunication (21); obedience (20); interdict (26); and one that caused resentment among the hearers at his trial: that convicted heretics should not be handed over to the secular arm (18).

The articles excerpted from Hus's works against Páleč and Znojmo were of a similar nature: on priests and lords in mortal sin; the grace of predestination; sinful popes and priests as brigands; Christ, not Peter, as head of the church; and the non-scriptural derivation of the papal office. There was also Hus's defence of Wyclif's 45 condemned articles. During his trial, Hus argued along the lines which we have already examined in his works. It will be observed how they centred upon his ecclesiology; there was no direct mention of the sacraments, or indulgences, the papal crusade, or tithes and offerings, even though the last issue was raised at his trial. The final lists, of 30 articles[1] from his own writings and 29 from the assertions of witnesses,[2] is clearest confirmation of the distinction between Hus's and Wyclif's teachings, even if we allow that those of the latter were far from being faithfully represented. Compared with the previous 39 articles,[3] 27 of the final 30 were retained; ten were omitted including (16) the travesty of Hus's opinion on the pope's power; one article (13) was the result of telescoping the old articles 10 and 17; and two were entirely new (4 and 30). Since they were the final outcome of six months' deliberation and interrogation by the Council, and the constituted counts on which Hus was finally condemned and burned, a brief résumé may be given, together with Hus's final comments.[4]

Article 1 was that 'the church is the congregation of the predestined'. Hus added the significant words 'in the strict sense according to St. Augustine'. . . . This was to qualify Wyclif's exclusive definition

[1] In Mansi, 27 1209–11. Sedlák, *M. Jan Hus* II, 338*–43*.

[2] Palacký, *Documenta* 230–4.

[3] By Sedlák, op. cit., II, 331*–338*.

[4] Ibid.

and to recognize the traditional position, by which the church could also be understood as *congregationes fidelium* or as special churches like the church of Rome.[1] It was an attempt, it must be admitted, to have the best of both worlds: to locate the true universal and Catholic church exclusively among the elect without discounting the visible church and its hierarchy. The contrast was given point in Hus's comments on the second part of the first article: that the holy universal church is unique, as the number of predestined is unique. After 'unique' Hus added 'which is not part in relation to another in the strict sense'. The church of the elect and of the faithful remained forever distinct.

Article 2 was the same as before: Paul was never of the devil in spite of his sinful acts. Hus added 'non-predestined' to 'member' to show that a predestinate could be temporarily in sin.

Article 3 was that the non-predestined were not part of the church. Hus added 'Catholic, strictly speaking' to the word 'church'.

Article 4 was a totally new one, the relevance of which to Hus is not apparent: the two natures of divinity and humanity are one Christ.

Article 5 was similar to 3: the non-predestined although sometimes in grace are never part of the holy church; and conversely the elect always belong even if without present grace. Hus added the same comment as before 'Catholic, strictly speaking'.

Article 6: The church as the body of the predestined, whether or not in present grace, was an article of faith. Hus added the authority of St. Augustine in support.

Article 7: Peter was not, and is not, head of the holy Catholic church, to which Hus added 'universal in the strict sense'.

Article 8: Priests living sinfully degrade their priestly power and regard the sacraments and attributes of the church as infidels do. Hus added citations from Deut. 37: 5 and Psalm 77: 36–7.

Article 9: The pope owes his position to the emperor, to which Hus added 'so far as his temporal authority and his headship of the four churches'.

Article 10: No one without revelation can claim for himself or another headship of a particular church, or that the pope is head of the Roman church. Hus added the word 'special' to 'revelation'.

Article 11: No pope should be believed head of the Roman church unless God has predestined him. Hus added 'persevering in a meritorious life'.

Article 12: No one takes the place of Christ or St. Peter if he does

[1] Synodal sermon for 1405, *Mon.* II, 128r.

not follow in their ways: for otherwise God will not delegate his power to him. Hus added 'by his office and merit' after 'place'.

Article 13: The pope is not true and manifest successor to Peter, first among the Apostles, if he lives in a way contrary to him; if he is avaricious he is then the successor of Judas. The same held for the cardinals as the successors of the Apostles. Hus again added 'by office and merit' to 'successor'.

Article 14: Those doctors saying that anyone who was subject to ecclesiastical censure, and refused to submit, should be handed over to the secular arm, followed the pontiffs, scribes and pharisees who had handed over Christ. Hus said this referred to the eight doctors of Prague.

Article 15: Ecclesiastical obedience was an ecclesiastical invention and went beyond the express authority of scripture. Hus elucidated this as the distinction between obedience in itself, and explicit obedience to Christ's law; but this did not mean that all obedience to God's law was also obedience to the church. No comment from Hus.

Article 16: The immediate division in human works is between virtuous and vicious. If a man is vicious then he acts viciously; if he is virtuous, he acts virtuously. No comment from Hus.

Article 17: Priests of Christ who live according to this law, and who know the bible and want to instruct the people, should preach notwithstanding pretended excommunication. Again: If the pope or other prelate orders such a priest not to preach, he should not obey.

Hus amplified 'pretended excommunication' with the words 'injurious, illicit, fulminated through malice'.

Article 18: Whoever becomes a priest has the obligation to preach despite pretended excommunication. Hus repeated the same comment, fortified this time by the authority of Augustine, Gregory the Great and Isidore.

Article 19: Ecclesiastical censures, excommunication, suspension and interdict are imposed upon the people by the priesthood for their own exaltation; they increase avarice, protect evil, and prepare the way for Antichrist. Hus agreed.

Article 20: If the pope is sinful, and certainly if he is *prescitus*, then like Judas the Apostle he is a devil, brigand and son of perdition, and not head of the holy Catholic church, to which he does not belong. No comment.

Article 21: The grace of predestination is the bond indissolubly joining the body of the church and each of its members to Christ its head.

Hus added 'persevering finally, according to the merit of his life' to 'the head of the militant church'.

Article 22: A pope or prelate who is sinful or *prescitus* is equivocally called pastor, and really a thief and brigand. Hus added, this was because the title referred exclusively to his *office*, not merit.

Article 23: The pope cannot be called *sanctissimus*, even according to his office, because then the king could also be so called from his office. No comment.

Article 24: If the pope lives contrary to Christ, although duly elected according to human constitution, he attains his office by a way other than Christ's. Even if he should be elected principally by God, as Judas was by Christ, he has still diverged from Christ. Hus amplified briefly, and then declared that this was only a hypothesis and subject to correction.

Article 25: The condemnation of Wyclif's forty-five articles was irrational, iniquitous and a bad deed. No comment.

Article 26: Election *viva voce* by the majority of the electors does not entail legitimate election of the person concerned nor that he is a true and manifest successor or vicar of St. Peter or any other Apostle in ecclesiastical office. Whether the electors have chosen well or badly, belief in the elected must rest on his works. The more he acts meritoriously for the church, the greater his power. Hus gave Agnes's example in support; he also added the words 'by the office and merit of his life' to 'successor or vicar'.

Article 27: There is no evidence of the need for a single spiritual head to govern the church, as can be seen from the absence of one since John XXIII's condemnation. No comment.

Article 28: Christ would govern the church better without such monstrous heads and by means of his own true disciples spread throughout the world. Hus added, 'Like Agnes and John XXIII and others who were heretics.'

Article 29: The Apostles and faithful priests of God diligently regulated the church in all that pertained to salvation, before the office of pope was introduced. They would have continued to do so, until the day of judgement had the pope, as was highly likely, disappeared. Hus noted that papal office referred to temporal power and pre-eminence.

Article 30: No one is civil lord or prelate or bishop while in a state of mortal sin. Hus added: 'according to the merit of his life', citing Osias, Gregory the Great and St. Bernard.

Of the nineteen articles by witnesses little needs to be said. They remained what they had always been—a compound of untruths and half-truths; they all derived from charges concocted by Michael de Causis. The fact, as we have seen, that the commission of the Council was prepared to set them aside and seek Hus's recantation from the thirty articles alone shows their worthlessness as a serious document, even to his judges and prosecutors.

What, then, of the thirty articles? In their final form none can really be said to violate Hus's thought, even if the interpretation put upon them did. They expressed his teaching on the nature of the church, the status of the pope, the conditions for obeying the hierarchy, the obligation to preach and the circumstances in which superiors should be defied. As now constituted there was no mention of the sacraments, the power of binding and loosing, or papal crusades and indulgences. They were an admixture of Wyclifite ecclesiology and moral judgement; and from the doctrinal point of view it was his ecclesiology which made Hus culpable. Whatever his qualifications, his definition of the church gave no inherent place to a pope and no guarantee in the genuine power of its hierarchy. That the qualifications, especially between merit and office, were important, nobody will deny. But, however they are read, the final balance comes down against them.

Nevertheless, even within the context of the time and Hus's own convictions, his execution was unjustifiable. Dietrich of Niem, who attacked him and his followers with such vitriol, had, as we saw, himself come close to Hus's distinction between the visible church and a catholic congregation of the saints. He, d'Ailly, Gerson and Zarabella, his leading prosecutors, had been foremost in upholding the authority of a general council over a pope and giving effect to their beliefs in the deposition of John XXIII on the very grounds, of simony and immorality, which Hus gave for invalidating a pope's power. That Hus went one step further in denying the ultimate necessity for a pope scarcely warranted his death at their hands. Hus himself saw the irony of the situation. As he wrote to Wenceslas of Dubá and John of Chlum, the spiritual men

> who declare themselves to be the holy church and the council thrice holy and infallible, are yet deceived when, after adoring John XXIII on their knees and kissing his feet and calling him most holy, they then condemn him as a dissolute murderer, sodomite, simoniac and heretic. They have therefore cut off the church's head, torn out its heart. . . . Where, then, is the opinion

of master Stanislas [Znojmo] of good memory (may God have mercy on him) and Páleč, and the others with him, who affirmed that the pope is head of the church and its perfectly sufficient governor, the heart of the church and its principle of life, the inexhaustible fount of its authority, the source from which flow the powers of his inferiors, the haven at once indestructible and sufficient for every Christian and where every Christian should seek shelter?[1]

Why, he asked in another letter, did the cardinals elect as pope one who was a heretic, murderer and sodomite? How could they allow him to indulge in simony after he had been elected? Were they not also simoniacs for permitting it? Why had they continued to address him as most holy father? Through fear, replied Hus. The great abomination was envy, cupidity and simony.[2] That Hus should have died for putting into words what other men did in deeds, makes his death a blot upon history as well as a personal tragedy.

The Hussite revolt

The paradoxes of Hus's martyrdom did not end with his death. He had been in essentials the most moderate among the Czech reformers, and yet, with Jerome, burned nearly a year later in May 1416,[3] the one to pay the supreme penalty. Similarly, while he became the symbol and efficient cause of the movement which arose out of his death, he was not its architect. Beyond the general desire for reform and the preaching of God's word, shared by all the reformers, Hus contributed little in tangible doctrine to the movement which he inspired. This was primarily the work of Jacobellus who, always more extreme than Hus, was especially responsible for two of its main characteristics: utraquism and the call for desecularization of the church. Besides advocating the need for communion in two kinds,[4] he, and Nicholas of Dresden, instituted its practice at Prague during 1414.[5] Hus had only come to accept utraquism in the last months of his life and, at first, even then in January 1415, held that it was not indispensable.[6]

[1] Novotný, *Korespondence* 287, 306. Quoted in De Vooght, *L'hérésie* 435.

[2] Ibid., 307–9.

[3] See R. R. Betts, 'Jerome of Prague' in *University of Birmingham Historical Journal*, 1947, 1–91.

[4] Von der Hardt, II, 355 ff.

[5] Ibid., 356; Sedlák, *Studie a texty* II, 145–9.

[6] De Vooght, *L'hérésie* 337, 437; Novotný, *Korespondence*, 104, 236–42.

It was not until after his trial, on 21 June, when it had already been condemned by the Council,[1] that he came out in unqualified support of it.[2]

From 1414 until he died in 1429 Jacobellus remained the guiding spirit in Hussite doctrine. But this did not make him leader of the Bohemian revolt as a whole. Indeed it can only be meaningfully called Hussite at all in the most general sense of having been precipitated by Hus's death. Far from being a united religious movement guided by Hus's teachings and led by his associates,[3] it had at least four main *foci*, each with its distinctive character, from which the struggle was carried on. These were Hus's confrères in the university as his natural successors under Jacobellus and to a lesser degree Christian of Prachatice; the radical popular party composed mainly of citizens from the New Town of Prague; the two brotherhoods of Tabor and, later, Oreb, which were not only far more extreme doctrinally than the Prague theologians, but, as provinces, vied with Prague politically and militarily; and finally the nobles who veered between support for and opposition towards the other elements, at the beginning participating in the struggle against external attack, but ultimately helping in 1434 to destroy the brotherhoods. What united these different groupings were not common tenets of belief but military threats. Whenever the latter momentarily dispersed, dissension broke out. Although, as we shall mention, the Four Articles became the accepted basis of Hussite doctrine, they were more a point of departure for the interminable disputations which went on than a means of unity. For that reason, the history of the Hussite movement is as much military, political, and social, as doctrinal; nor can it really be conceived as heresy in the usual way. Virtually nothing of Hus's ecclesiology passed into it; and its most distinctive religious trait—utraquism—was one which, as we have just said, Hus never actively upheld: this hardly qualified as heresy, since even the Council of Constance had recognized that Christ was its originator, and that it had been practised in the early church.[4] Above all the true Hussites under Jacobellus waged war on the errors and deviations of the Taborites, while a Taborite—the illustrious John Žižka—was as we saw in an earlier chapter the destroyer of the

[1] Mansi, 27, 727–8 on 15 June, 1415.

[2] Novotný, *Korespondence* 294.

[3] For the disparateness of the elements see Joseph Maček, *Villes et compagnes dans le hussitisme* (Czech Academy of Sciences, Prague, n.d.).

[4] Mansi, loc. cit.

Adamites.[1] Consequently, we shall not attempt here to recount the Hussites' history for the generation after Hus's death, ending with the compacts of Basel in 1437. The events have been described often enough.[2] Instead we shall try to depict the doctrinal nature and development of the movement both in the different elements which composed it and as it finally emerged at the end of the Hussite wars proper in 1437.

As we have already suggested the most noteworthy thing about the Hussite reformation was that it was the product of war. For the first time a nation, or more accurately the most important part of it, openly challenged the authority of the church. This action was unique, and the consequences immeasurable. By refusing to accept first the Council of Constance's sentence on Hus, and then its prohibition of communion in both kinds, the Hussite nobles, the university and city of Prague, and the communities which arose at Tabor and Oreb, began the reformation still so often ascribed to Luther a century later. They made the first breach in the church's ecumenicality by physically resisting its authority and by finally compelling recognition of utraquism and the rest of the Four Articles, albeit in a diluted form. That they never turned the break into one of complete separation is hardly to the point. Theirs was a limited operation, which succeeded by refusing to be suppressed. Even if Hus did not lead directly to Luther, or Bohemia to Saxony, the Hussites were the first to achieve reform by revolt against the church. For this reason they deserve to be regarded as reformers, not simply forerunners, and not heretics.

The nobles were the first to raise the standard of revolt against the Council of Constance's decrees. Their letters in the early summer of 1415 demanding Hus's release[3] were followed by a great assembly on 2 September. There, 452 nobles drawn from all parts of Bohemia and Moravia solemnly protested to the Council against Hus's execution and the imputation of heresy to their lands.[4] They then entered into a compact for six years freely to permit preaching on their own estates. They also refused to recognize the Council's decrees, and would obey a new pope only if he acted in accord with God's will; the same applied to bishops. Lastly they invested Prague university with the final

[1] See above.

[2] For general accounts see standard works, e.g. Lützow, Seton-Watson, Denis, Palacký; but especially F. G. Heymann, *John Žižka and the Hussite Revolution* (Princeton 1955), upon which the following account is largely based; Heymann's book is now the outstanding and authoritative work on this subject.

[3] See pp. 650 ff. above.

[4] Palacký, *Documenta* 580–90.

decision on matters of right and wrong.[1] In the following May, after Jerome's death by burning at Constance, the university of Prague issued a eulogy of both martyrs, praising the probity of their lives and their devotion to the faith, and denying utterly that they were heretics.[2]

The inflexibility of the Council must be accounted one of the main causes in the growing alienation of the Czech nobles and masters. The Council fathers now saw every expression of dissent as a sign of heresy; and in their reply to the nobles foolishly accused them and Wenceslas and Sophia of being accomplices (*fautores*) in Hus's heresy: Wenceslas because he had confiscated ecclesiastics' possessions, and Sophia for protecting Hus.[3] All who had signed the nobles' appeal were summoned to Constance to answer the charge of heresy. None went. The Council also tried to act against the university by suspending *sine die* its activities. No notice was taken.[4] Its attempts to prevent the archbishop of Prague, Conrad Vechta, from ordaining Hussite priests—i.e. those who adhered to utraquism—were scarcely more successful: utraquism had been officially recognized by the Czech nobles on 10 March 1417;[5] it was accepted by the majority of the nobles as well as the king and queen at this time. Hence, even where the archbishop of Prague was able to enforce the Council's commands, the many churches under royal or noble control remained immune from interference.

The Council of Constance finally disbanded in April 1418 without having resolved the deadlock between it and the Hussites. Indeed the movement was already taking the classic course of revolution. The moderates, constituted by the nobles and the university, who had initiated it, were increasingly being pushed to the side by the more extreme elements—in this case the Taborites and the citizens of the New Town of Prague. The radicalism of the Taborites is apparent as early as February 1418, and in September a synod at Prague attempted to define the tenets of utraquism in 23 articles drawn up in response to Taborite teachings.

Centred in southern Bohemia, around Bechyně and Sezimovo Uste, the origins of Tabor are far from clear. It was in this region that Hus passed much of his exile between October 1412 and 1414. But how much influence his presence had is problematical, for his outlook was far more faithfully represented by the moderate wing of the Hussites

[1] Palacký, *Documenta* 490–5.
[2] *Mon.* I, 81v–82v.
[3] Palacký, *Documenta* 638–42.
[4] K. Krofta in *Cambridge Medieval History* VIII, 67.
[5] Heymann, *John Žižka*, 59.

under the leadership of the theologians of the university. The outlook of the latter, often known as the Calixtines—from their adherence to the chalice or communion cup—was expressed in the famous Four Articles first issued to the world on 20 April 1420, during Sigismund's offensive against Prague; but they were originally drawn up at a synod there in August 1417,[1] and were also contained in an address to the emperor by a general assembly meeting at Prague in August 1419.[2] As finally defined these were:

First, that the word of God should be preached and proclaimed freely and without impediment by priests throughout the kingdom of Bohemia.

Second, that the holy sacrament of the eucharist should be freely administered in both kinds, bread and wine, to all faithful believers not in mortal sin as Christ himself had instituted it.

Third, that the clergy, who contrary to Christ's precept enjoyed temporal lordship over riches and worldly goods, shall have them withdrawn and be reduced to the evangelical rule and apostolic life of Christ and his disciples.

Fourth, that all mortal sins, and especially public ones and others derogating from God's law, shall be properly and reasonably prohibited and extirpated, wherever found, by those responsible for doing so. These included fornication, murder, lying, theft, usury, and 'superfluous, evil and superstitious arts' among the people; and among the clergy simoniacal exactions for priestly services, as well as immorality, profane behaviour and contentiousness.

This was a programme entirely within the Czech reforming tradition. It went back in essentials to Janov and contained nothing—apart from utraquism—that Hus had not preached for most of his career, although he had never spoken of coercion or expropriation. It is the strongest testimony to the deep-rooted hold of the native reformers and the essentially transitory influence of Wyclif. Doctrinally, only the second point, on utraquism, could be said to conflict with current ecclesiastical teaching, although, even here, the Council of Constance had acknowledged that Christ had instituted communion in both kinds.[3]

[1] Heymann, op. cit., 148; and 70–1 for articles. Lützow, *Master John Hus* 343–4.

[2] Among the many places where the articles can be found are Heymann, op. cit., ch. 10, 148 ff. and 5 (translation of the *Very Pretty Chronicle*); Brezova's Chronicle 374, 391–5; Höfler, *Geschichtsschreiber* VI, 480.

[3] I cannot agree with Heymann's opinion here (*Žižka* 149 f.) that preaching tended to undermine ecclesiastical tradition.

The Articles, however, were primarily practical measures; to have put them into effect would have been tantamount to transforming the church. It was reformation, not dismemberment, which the Hussite party under Jacobellus advocated. The Council of Constance had failed to differentiate between the two, with the result that it helped to unleash, by its repressive measures, a genuinely revolutionary and iconoclastic wave—the Taborites.

As we have said, the earliest official record of Taborite teaching is contained in the twenty-three articles of the synod of Prague of September 1418. These were in the form of an affirmation by the orthodox party in reply to the Taborites.[1] Apart from the first, which followed Jacobellus's controversial line of communion in both kinds for baptized children, they revealed a basic division over the relation of the bible to tradition. The Taborites were fundamentalists very much in the Wyclifite tradition. They wished to confine belief to what was contained explicitly and implicitly in the bible (art. 2), and they regarded both the constitutions and precepts of the church, and the opinions of the *sancti*, as superfluous (arts. 14 and 15). Together with this went a Waldensian desire to sweep away wholesale most of the outward forms and ceremonies of the church: masses, prayers and alms for the dead (arts. 4 and 5); private prayer and prayers to the saints (6 and 7); penances awarded in auricular confession (art. 11); extreme unction (12); ceremonies, customs and rites (16); baptism and benediction and other rites connected with the use of holy water (17); vestments for celebrating mass (18); singing (19); images (20); observances of saints' days, Sundays, fasts and vigils (22, 23). They showed the same affinity with the Waldensians over the status of a priest: a sinful priest should not celebrate mass or baptize, to which the synod in reply offered Hus's distinction between office and merit (9). Recognized priests, on the other hand, were not necessarily alone qualified to celebrate mass (10); superiors need not be obeyed, if they appeared to go against God (13); and priests should labour with the people (23). This was to come near to Wyclif's and the Waldensians' tendency to minimize the difference between priest and layman, even if at the same time the Taborites opposed the handing over of evildoers to the secular arm (art. 8).

Initially the Taborites embraced the most militant millenarianism.[2] It was based upon a series of biblical texts which here, as in everything

[1] Palacký, *Documenta* 677–81.

[2] In Brezova, 397 ff., 414 ff., and 454–61 for 71 articles.

else, underlay Taborism.[1] There was perhaps a touch of Joachism in its emphasis upon an immediate dénouement which would, after the agonies of almost total destruction, usher in an earthly paradise. It also gave echoes of the Adamites' belief[2] in a return to the primal innocence of Adam and Eve. But these were outweighed by the sheer sense of imminent universal destruction. It would occur in 1420[3] and would be preceded by Christ's second coming when he would be disguised as a robber.[4] The period leading up to it would be one not of grace but of retribution by fire and sword in which all the enemies of Christ's law would perish.[5] In striking contrast to Joachim of Fiore, and Franciscan Joachists like Olivi, Christ's followers would not imitate Christ in his mercy and suffering but take the lead in punishing his adversaries.[6] No one, however spiritual, was exempt from this obligation. To fail to drench one's sword in one's enemies' blood was to be cursed; indeed nothing less than washing one's hands in it would suffice.[7] All those wishing to be saved must leave their towns and villages and castles and take to the mountains, as Christ had commanded; those left behind would die there in sin. All but five cities would be desolated: Pilsen, Žatec, Louny, Slaný, and Klatovy, the centres of the new ideas.[8] At the end of this consummation Christ would appear and a great feast (*convivium*) would follow; it would celebrate the coming of the kingdom of the elect, from which all sin would be banished.[9] Here again, there are traces of debased Joachism: the visible and sensible would disappear and the true essence of being would be revealed. Thus the water of baptism and the elements of the eucharist would be superseded by the actual presence of the Holy Spirit;[10] the oil of unction would also become otiose.[11] In the same way the letter of the word, upon which all Taborite beliefs were founded, would be displaced by its spirit, and all written law would come to an end.[12] They also affirmed that the elect would never die physically;[13] that wives would bear children painlessly, and

[1] In Brezova, 417 ff.; they included Matthew 24, 7 and 9; Luke, 21: 31, 32; 21: 21; Revelation 19: 11–13, and 15; Isaiah 19: 18; Jeremiah 50: 40. For a conspectus see Heymann, op. cit., 75–7.

[2] See pp. 399 ff. above.

[3] Brezova 454.

[4] Ibid., 413, 454.

[5] Ibid.

[6] Ibid., 413–14, 454.

[7] Ibid., 414, 454.

[8] Here the key text was from Luke 21, 21: 'Let them which are in Judea flee to the mountains.' Brezova, ibid.; Heymann, 77.

[9] Brezova, op. cit., 416, 455.

[10] Ibid., 416, 459–61.

[11] Ibid., 461, art. 63.

[12] Ibid., 457, art. 27.

[13] Ibid., 455, art. 20.

without physical insemination; they could deny husbands their marital rights and withdraw to the mountains or five cities.[1]

In more immediate matters the views already mentioned in the twenty-three articles were a recurrent theme of Taborism: they constituted an extreme puritanism in all questions of conduct, both ecclesiastical and personal. In particular, even when their chiliasm evaporated with the passing of the year 1420, a chasm continued to separate the Taborites from the Hussites on a number of cardinal issues. First there was the conflict over the standing of church decretals and the writings of the Fathers in relation to the bible: for the Taborites only the bible counted. To a degree far beyond anything Wyclif had maintained, they excluded all non-scriptural sources and human traditions from any binding authority. Nothing but the bible was to be believed;[2] philosophy and the whole of learning were by the same token excluded.[3] Second, there were the eucharist and the sacraments of baptism and unction. Here, too, the Taborites were equally uncompromising, again making definitive what Wyclif had at most implied. Thus they upheld remanence, denied the real presence, and on top of these proscribed the celebration of mass in ceremonial robes: this for long remained one of the main issues between the Taborites and the Hussites.[4] The Taborites, also, as we have seen, denied the power of a sinful priest to administer the sacraments.[5] Third, there was their attack upon all ornaments, images, penances, prayers to the saints,[6] feast days and fasts, and any kind of ostentation. Finally, there was a fundamental divergence over ordination. Just as the Taborites rejected all ecclesiastical tradition, so they broke with the apostolic succession in allowing election of bishops and ordination by the priests themselves.[7] This was to cut the Taborites off from the church of Rome, a step which they took in September 1420, with their appointment as bishop of Nicholas of Pelhřimov.[8] It was one that the Hussites never took; they were saved from the need to resort to such an extreme by the conversion to Hussitism of Conrad of Vechta, archbishop of Prague, in 1421.[9] To the end the Hussites remained part of the Roman church and continued to acknowledge its authority. The Taborites, and their successors the Bohemian Brethren, were, like the Waldensians, a break-away church.

[1] Brezova, op. cit., 458, arts. 29–33.
[2] Ibid., 460, art. 53.
[3] Ibid., arts. 53, 56, 57, 58.
[4] Ibid., 459–60, arts. 37, 38, 39, 40, 42–53.
[5] Ibid., art. 41.
[6] E.g., art. 34, ibid., 458, that all churches dedicated to saints would be destroyed.
[7] Ibid., 461, art. 64.
[8] Heymann, op. cit., 172.
[9] Ibid., 220–1.

In matters of personal conduct the Taborites were correspondingly rigid. They opposed all forms of immorality and levity: in their twelve points presented to the Praguers on 5 August 1420, they demanded the punishment of all fornicators, adulterers, and other proved sinners; the closing of taverns; the banning of usury, oaths and all *spolia* and clerical tribute; the destruction of 'heretical monasteries' and superfluous churches, and the subjection of priests and laymen not to 'pagan and teutonic laws' but to God's law.[1] The general ostentation and splendour of the capital had an unfavourable effect upon the Taborites. Prague was described as Babylon and would suffer the same destruction.[2] In their own lives they advocated abstention from meat-eating,[3] and opposed all possessions.[4]

From this account the distance between the Hussites and the Taborites is clear. The one was, at most, a radical reformation within the church; the other was a new communion outside it. That so much of the history of the Hussite movement revolved round the conflict and friction between the Taborites, and other radical elements (mainly in Prague), on the one hand, and the orthodox Hussite leaders and/or the nobles, on the other, is hardly surprising; nor that ultimately the two brotherhoods were destroyed from within and not by external enemies. We must now briefly follow the events which led to this outcome and the final settlement between the Hussites and the rest of the church.

After the Council of Constance had dissolved in April 1418, without having taken further measures against the Hussites, the new pope Martin V duly repeated its condemnation of Wyclif and Hus. But further action depended upon Wenceslas. For a time he was opposed to outside interference. It was only at the beginning of 1419 that growing pressure from both within—among the Taborites and at Prague—and outside—from the pope and Sigismund—caused him, after much wavering, to intervene. This was due primarily to Sophia. She had supported Hus to the end; but there was now a serious threat to the throne. She accordingly prevailed upon Wenceslas, in February 1419, to ban Hussite services, i.e. communion in both kinds, from all but three churches in Prague. This led to the departure of some Hussite priests for Tabor, as well as Nicholas of Hus, one of Wenceslas's courtiers, who became the first important layman to join the Taborites. Nicholas of Hus was above all a great organizer. His coming to Tabor

[1] Brezova, 397 ff. [2] Ibid., 455, art. 9. [3] Ibid., 462, art. 72.
[4] Ibid., 458, art. 68. They also opposed tithes at first, ibid., 457, art. 22.

was the turning point in its development. Under his leadership a series of great demonstrations was held on the mountains around Prague which turned the Taborites into a mass movement.[1] The first was on 22 July 1419, when 40,000 people were said to have assembled on a hill near Bechyně to which the biblical name of Tabor was given. At this stage it was a purely religious occasion: for worship. But it already constituted a new form of autonomous activity which before long was to become directly political.

This only happened, however, after the beginning of the revolution proper, which took place in Prague. The effect of Wenceslas's ban upon the majority of the Hussite churches was the lifting of the interdict on the city. This entailed reconsecration of the restored churches; and it was on 18 June, at one such ceremony in the church of St. Nicholas in the Old Town, that a large crowd gathered under the fiery John Želivský, former monk and now preacher at the Hussite church of St. Mary in the Snow in the New Town. Like Hus before him, Želivský used his sermons to attack iniquities against God's law. He became the most influential of the Hussite leaders, drawing his support mostly from the poorer strata of the New Town. Wenceslas replied to his demonstration on 6 July by ordering the removal of all Hussites from the government of the New Town. Želivský countered this with a carefully prepared demonstration through the city to the church of St. Stephen, not yet reconsecrated, on 30 July; after delivering a particularly inflammatory sermon, Želivský himself carried the chalice, containing the host, for all to see. Those assembled forcibly entered the church and celebrated mass with communion in both kinds. They then set off on their return to St. Mary in the Snow. On the way they stopped outside the New Town Hall and demanded the release of some recently arrested Hussites. Rejecting the attempted explanations of the councillors, they finally stormed the building and threw out of the window the luckless officials who had failed already to escape.

This first Prague defenestration marked the beginning of the Hussite Revolt. It also meant the death of Wenceslas, who, on hearing the news, suffered a stroke. He managed to call for Sigismund's aid and reach a compromise with the revolutionaries over the election of a new city council before dying from a second attack. The vacancy on the throne opened the way for the development of the revolt. Had Wenceslas lived, or had a son to succeed him, things might have been different. But the fact that his heir was Sigismund, generally regarded

[1] Heymann, op. cit., 62 ff.

as the betrayer of Hus, as well as an alien who could only gain the throne through invasion, fused the demand for religious and political change with a war of survival. As long as invasion, or the threat of it, continued, so did the Hussite revolution. Certainly Želivský now treated Sigismund as the main enemy. In a series of sermons he attacked him as the Great Red Dragon, at once an allusion to the Order of the Dragon which Sigismund had founded, and to the Apocalypse. It gave Želivský the opportunity of sounding the apocalyptic note which was then so prevalent.

The immediate effect of Wenceslas's death, on 16 August, was rioting and attacks on the monasteries. But they gradually subsided by the end of the month. Meanwhile the queen, Sophia, was acting as regent together with Čeněk of Wartenberg, Lord High Burgave of Prague, and so first among the nobles. They agreed to the calling of a general diet at which a series of conditions for acceptance by Sigismund, as successor to Wenceslas, was issued. They were in two parts:[1] a general document on behalf of the whole of the assembled nobles, gentry and townspeople, and a specific list by Prague, evidence of its leading role. It reflected the alliance between the nobles and the city on a minimum Hussite programme, which included the essentials of the Four Articles, and the safeguarding of Hussite freedom of worship. This referred not only to papal bulls but extended to all foreigners and exiles (mostly Germans) none of whom was to be allowed to hold office.

Already the pressures upon Bohemia from the outside world had inflamed nationalist feelings. Sigismund, although born and brought up in Prague, remained to the Hussites 'the Hungarian King'.[2] From our point of view the document is noteworthy above all for its faithfulness to the Czech reforming tradition. It was neither heretical nor extremist but simply concerned to root out from the church the evils of simony, temporal wealth, and secular involvement. At this stage the movement remained in the hands of the moderate Hussites and nobles. It was to these that Sigismund addressed himself. In reply to Sophia's urgent demands for him to come to Prague at once, he temporized, saying that he would come as soon as he could, and meanwhile confirming Sophia as regent, and Wartenberg as chief adviser; he also invested the latter with the Order of the Dragon, a sign of his conciliatoriness.[3]

Sigismund's continuing absence, and refusal to commit himself, allowed time for the more radical Hussite elements to emerge. Among the Taborites, the first mass meeting in July was followed by another

[1] Ibid., 70–1. [2] Ibid. [3] Ibid., 73.

on 17 September, and a third on 1 October on a hill called 'At the Crosses', some 25 miles from Prague.[1] Each was bigger than the last. People came to it from all over Bohemia and even Moravia. Nicholas of Hus had now been joined as leader by Wenceslas of Koranda, a priest from Pilsen. In language of the Apocalypse he urged the brethren forward: 'The time to wander with the pilgrim's staff is over. Now we shall have to march sword in hand.'[2] At this last meeting thousands of Praguers had joined the gathering; together they all marched back to the capital to a joyous welcome. The citizens and the Taborites had made their first junction. Discussions between the two parties followed the next day.[3] It centred around future joint action. Already there was a divergence on ecclesiastical matters. The Taborites pressed for the election of a bishop in the name of God's law; the Praguers, under the university representatives, refused to take a step which would mean a break with Rome. At this stage nothing further happened; but it was only a matter of time before each went its own way.

In the city itself there were similar manifestations of their differences. The Taborites' puritanical leanings were offended by the splendour of the Prague churches and many adornments were smashed. A further mass meeting had been planned for 10 November, but Sophia and Wartenberg took alarm and banned it; Wartenberg, to forestall trouble, brought about an alliance between members of the nobles—both Calixtine and Romanist—and citizens of the Old Town. Nicholas of Hus seems to have been the main object of their precautions.[4] Both sides strengthened their positions, John Žižka, shortly to be the outstanding Hussite captain, for the first time acting for the popular forces of the New Town by taking over the royal fortress of the Vyšehrad, which dominated it.[5] Fighting broke out and continued for about five days without either side gaining a conclusive victory. On 13 November, in face of a greater threat from without, a solemn armistice was declared which lasted until 23 April 1420:[6] each side guaranteed the rights of the other to freedom of worship and protection of their churches and monasteries; and Vyšehrad was handed back to the royalists.

Already outside Prague on 6 November a group of barons and knights was challenging the authority of Wartenberg and his alliance

[1] Heymann, op. cit., 80 ff. [2] Ibid.

[3] *Monumenta conciliorum generalium, saec 15*, I, 387.

[4] Heymann, *Žižka* 81–2.

[5] Ibid., 82. [6] F. Palacký, *Urkundliche Beiträge* I, 11.

with the Hussites; a number of towns went over to them, among them the very important royal city of Kutná Hora. Centred on the silver mines, with a strong German community, it was the main bulwark of anti-Hussitism; all those suspected of being adherents of the Hussite 'heresy' were thrown down the mineshafts, regardless of age or sex. Altogether thousands seem to have perished in this way.[1] In March an attempt by the Royalists to destroy Tabor was defeated by Žižka, who now became its military leader.[2] He proceeded to mould it into the most formidable military force in Central Europe, and the instrument by which the Hussite revolution was saved from outside destruction.

At the end of 1419 Sigismund, having defeated the Turks at the battle of Niš on 4 October, at last entered Bohemia at Brno, where he summoned a meeting of the Bohemian estates for Christmas.[3] Čeněk of Wartenberg was appointed regent in place of Sophia—who resigned—assisted by two other Catholic nobles. The king was sufficiently noncommittal on utraquism for the assembled nobles to do homage to him; next, the representatives of Prague, despite a humiliating reception, agreed to transmit his conditions for a reconciliation, namely the dismantling of the barricades and fortifications. The end of the war appeared to be at hand, needing little but Sigismund's formal entry into Prague and his coronation. The king, however, did not go. He went to Breslau instead. There he quickly showed himself in another light. His previous air of tolerance was replaced by a determination to put down Hussitism. Orders were issued early in 1420 for the renunciation of the Wyclifite creed and a return to the obedience of the Roman church.[4] After a pause for dealing with other matters, Sigismund returned to the attack in March. On the 15th of the month he had a prominent Prague merchant, John Krása (on a visit to Breslau), executed in a particularly brutal way for alleged utterances against the Council of Constance.[5] On the same day he issued a decree for punishment by death of all unrepentant heretics in Bohemia. A papal bull proclaiming a crusade against them had just been issued. Sigismund now chose to put their destruction before his coronation. In the event he failed in the first and had to wait 16 years for the second. Not until within one year of his death did he enter Prague and then mainly on Hussite terms.

[1] Letter to Venetians in ibid., I, 41; Heymann, *Žižka* 87.

[2] Heymann, ibid., 92 ff.

[3] Heymann, 107 ff.

[4] Ibid., 108; *Urkundliche Beiträge* I, 15, 16.

[5] He was dragged along the streets by horses and then burned alive. Heymann, op. cit., 110.

The events which followed belong to Bohemia's political and military history rather than to that of religion and heresy.[1] Briefly, however, Sigismund by his action united for a time all the different elements in Bohemia against him. In April Čeněk of Wartenberg, despite the honours with which Sigismund had plied him, rallied to the Praguers. The latter, with the example of the unfortunate Krása before them, and the pronouncement of the crusade, could only resist if they were not to lose their religious liberty. They accordingly met at the beginning of April; all sections, the Old and New Towns, university masters, Hussite radicals under Želivský, pledged themselves to defend their religion and prepared their dispositions. A call was issued to all cities to send representatives. Wartenberg, for his part, brought over many of the nobles. On 20 April 1420, he and the other leading noble, Ulrich of Rosenberg, having renounced fealty to Sigismund, issued a manifesto calling for the freedom of God's law and the welfare of the Czech people, and defiance against Sigismund. Ten accusations were made against him, including responsibility for Krása's death, the massacres of Kutná Hora and Hus's execution. It then proclaimed the Four Articles.[2]

The effect was to unite the Hussites into a national movement around a defined programme of religious reform and in defence of religious freedom. Throughout Bohemia nobles and cities rallied to Wartenberg's call; and it may well be that, had printing then been in existence to turn the hundreds of copies made of the manifesto into tens of thousands, the Reformation would have become European-wide a century earlier than it was.[3] Decisive military success did not, however, come until July 1420. An alliance which included the Bohemian nobles and the Taborites was not easy to maintain. From early on Wartenberg could not reconcile himself to their revolutionary ways and beliefs; he soon entered into secret negotiations with Sigismund, although he was not prepared to renounce utraquism.[4] As a result 4,000 royalist troops were admitted to Hradčany castle at Prague. Fighting broke out between them and the Praguers, and an armistice was concluded on 12 May 1420. Once more the city seemed about to submit; delegates were sent to Sigismund at Kutná Hora. But he went too far and demanded unconditional surrender.[5]

It was then that the capital turned to the Taborites. They arrived on 20 May under Žižka, several thousand strong.[6] In addition to attending

[1] Heymann, ibid., 112 ff. [2] Ibid., 114–15. [3] Ibid., 157.
[4] Ibid., 118–19. [5] Ibid., 119–21.
[6] One source said 9,000, ibid., 123.

to the military needs, new religious discussions took place between the two parties, which led to the joint adoption of the Four Articles. Representatives from the other brotherhood of Oreb, under their leader Ambrose of Hradec, who had been fighting in eastern Bohemia, were also included.[1] The Four Articles remained the basis of the Hussite creed throughout the rest of the war. On 14 July Žižka defeated the crusading army, perhaps 80,000 strong, on the slopes of Vítkov (St. Vitus) just to the east of the capital. It was the Valmy of the Hussite War. Never again was the capital to face such peril, nor the Hussite cause to be in such jeopardy. Žižka, although vastly outnumbered, had by his new tactics established a military and moral ascendancy which was never to be lost.[2] On 30 October the defence of the capital was finally assured with Sigismund's defeat at the Vyšehrad and the permanent retention of the fortress by the Praguers.[3]

But the danger from without was far from over. Altogether four more crusades were to be launched against Bohemia before peace was made. They all ended ignominiously; but for a period of ten years they presented a continuing threat to the Hussite kingdom. The second crusade was in the Autumn of 1421. This time the crusading army was even larger, numbering perhaps over 100,000.[4] It included the archbishops of Cologne, Trier and Magdeburg as well as the papal legate and some of the most prominent German princes. It started from Cheb at the end of August, and, after unsuccessfully besieging the town of Žatec barring the way to Prague, fled at the beginning of October at the rumour of an approaching Hussite army under Žižka.[5]

Sigismund, however, was preparing to attack in the East from Hungary. Originally he had planned it to make it coincide with the crusaders' offensive from the West, thereby forcing the Hussites to fight a war on two fronts. But the retreat from Žatec spoiled that.

At this time the Hussites were themselves far from united; not only were relations between Prague and Tabor strained but the vacillations and suspicions of the more prominent nobles, like Ulrich of Rosenberg and Čeněk of Wartenberg, towards them made for endemic instability in the Hussite alliance. The year before both men had gone across to Sigismund; and Žižka had spent the Autumn of 1420 in warring against

[1] Ibid., 129. For Oreb, ibid., 131 ff. They took their name from a hill a few miles to the east of Hradek Králové in north-eastern Bohemia.

[2] Heymann, op. cit., 134 ff.; Brezlova 383 ff.

[3] Heymann, op. cit., 178–9.

[4] Ibid., 273.

[5] Ibid., 274–5.

Rosenberg in Southern Bohemia.[1] They had then become reconciled with the Hussites, and participated in the national assembly at Čáslav in June 1421.[2]

The assembly was designed to find a common basis for religious and political unity between Bohemia and Moravia. Sigismund had there been declared deposed, and a council of twenty-one appointed to govern until a successor had been found. Wartenberg had been among the five barons elected to it. Shortly afterwards Wartenberg had commanded an army against the Silesians but his refusal of the opportunity to invade Silesia in pursuit of them had been severely criticized. Now in October 1421 both nobles once more deserted to Sigismund as he prepared a new offensive from Moravia. It ended as ingloriously as the others.[3] Between 21 December and 10 January, Sigismund incurred a series of overwhelming defeats from Žižka at Kutná Hora, Nebovidy, Habry and Německý Brod. Sigismund retired from Bohemia not to return for many years.

Crusading ardour, however, was not yet extinguished. An imperial diet, meeting at Nuremberg at the end of July 1422, approved a third expedition. Leadership of it was solemnly entrusted to Frederick, Elector of Brandenburg, on 4 September;[4] it crossed into Bohemia in early October. By the end of the year, the crusaders had melted away without having fought a battle: for once defeat had been averted by timely retreat. Not until 1427 was another attempt made; by then the Hussite armies had achieved such renown that the crusaders fled before contact could be made. Even so, they did not escape unscathed.[5] The fifth and last crusade took place in 1431, when the papal legate sought to impose by force of arms what negotiations, over the sending of Hussite legates to the Council of Basel, had failed to achieve.[6] This time it ended in headlong flight before the Czech forces at Domažlice.

The failure of the crusades reflected the spiritual bankruptcy of its sponsors. Their attempt to match ideas by armies, and to use force where argument failed, was the confession of defeat from which Hussite victory sprang. Without the challenge of suppression and destruction the army which Žižka fashioned would never have come into being or the alliances between the different Hussite groups been maintained. Not that they were ever stable. After the defeat of Sigismund at Vítkov in July 1420, by the Praguers and the Taborites, the latter presented their twelve points at the beginning of August for a more

[1] Heymann, op. cit., 171 ff. [2] Ibid., 220 ff. [3] Ibid., 291 ff.
[4] Ibid., 344. [5] Ibid., 462. [6] Ibid., 465–6.

radical policy.[1] Among them was the proposal to destroy all monasteries. They tried to put it into effect by burning four monasteries in the capital. This led to increasing tension between the Taborites and radicals under Želivský, on the one hand, and the city authorities and the university doctors, on the other. It was further aggravated by the burning and sacking of the beautiful Cistercian monastery at Zbraslav, where Wenceslas IV was among the many kings buried there; his remains were disinterred and made the object of fun. The Taborites left Prague on 22 August with their differences unresolved. A month later they moved farther apart from the orthodox party when they unilaterally elected Nicholas of Pelhřimov their bishop and elder, thereby breaking away from the authority of Rome and asserting their autonomy from the rest of the Hussites.[2]

Friction between the two groups mounted during the Autumn, due largely to the growing intransigence of Nicholas of Hus who remained in Prague.[3] It was finally agreed to air their differences at a public disputation on 10 December. It was then that the 72 articles, indicting Taborite teaching, were presented by Peter of Mladeňovice, Hus's former companion.[4] After various Taborite replies it was agreed to allow a month for both parties to prepare written statements.[5] It is noteworthy that the close companions of Hus, Jacobellus and Christian of Prachatice, led the attack on Taborite doctrines and were among the staunchest defenders of orthodoxy in such matters as the use of vestments for celebrating mass—one of the great issues between the two sides.

At the same time, other tendencies were becoming apparent at Tabor under Martin Houska. He had defended the 72 Taborite errors at the December disputation. He was arrested at the end of January.[6] He had come, *inter alia*, to deny the whole notion of transubstantiation; Christ's body, through the resurrection, was now in heaven and could not be in the host. The eucharist could therefore only commemorate him; and the bread should be distributed for all the congregation to break, as at

[1] See p. 699 above. Heymann, *Žižka* 166 ff.

[2] Heymann, ibid., 172–3.

[3] He died from a riding accident in December 1421; had this not occurred there may well have been a dénouement between him and the more conservative elements among the Prague citizens.

[4] Heymann, op. cit., 192 ff.

[5] See *Taborite chronicle* 189 ff. in Höfler *Geschichtsschreiber* (*Fontes Rerum Austriacarum* I, Bd. VI).

[6] Heymann, *Žižka* 211 ff.

the Last Supper. To pretend to turn it into the body of Christ was a fraud.[1] This error came to be associated with Pickhartism; but the real Pickharts, in the sense of being Free Spirits, were, as we saw in an earlier chapter, the Adamites whom Žižka destroyed at the end of 1421.[2] The charge seems to have been made against anyone denying transubstantiation and was later levelled against Želivský and Prokop the Bald, Žižka's successor.[3]

These tendencies gradually alienated Žižka from Tabor; in 1423 he transferred to the Orebites in eastern Bohemia.[4] Like Tabor the name Oreb has been given to a hill: in this case near Třebechovice, a few miles east of Hradec Králové.[5] Its leader was the priest Ambrose of Hradec, who became a lifelong friend of Žižka. His cool and balanced personality was reflected in the much less extreme outlook of the Orebites, who, although radical upholders of the law of God, were free from chiliasm. Their main excess was in their anti-monasticism, as shown on their way to the relief of Prague in 1420. At the first all-Hussite synod of Prague in July 1421, Oreb had been put in the eastern of the four regions into which the country was divided.[6] It was to make it into a fit instrument for God's will that Žižka drew up his constitutions for the community and put himself at the head of its soldiers until his death from plague in October 1424.[7]

The Prague synod of 1421 was an attempt to do for the Bohemian church what the assembly of Čáslav had done for the Bohemian kingdom: namely to declare its principles and create a machinery for its government.[8] The former were defined in twenty-three articles. They are striking for their orthodoxy. Like the twenty-three articles of the synod of 1418, doctrinally they were based firmly upon traditional teaching, and morally in the direct line of descent from Hus and Janov. Where they differed from those of three years earlier was in their concern with the Pickhart heresy of the eucharist. Indeed the emphasis was throughout upon the need to follow the rites and customs of the primitive church and teachings of the apostles. Faith in the literal truth of the bible and the Nicene creed were upheld.

On the eucharist there were to be no innovations without good reason. The mass was to be celebrated according to the tradition of the Catholic church with all the customary prayers and ornaments; the real

[1] *Urkundliche Beiträge* I, 204–8.
[2] See pp. 399 ff. above.
[3] Heymann, op. cit., 457 ff.
[4] Ibid., 361 ff.
[5] Ibid., 131 ff.
[6] Ibid., 244.
[7] Ibid., 374 ff.
[8] *Urkundliche Beiträge* 128–34.

presence of Christ was affirmed. Communion was to be given whenever any of the other sacraments were administered. Baptism by water and unction with oil were to be retained. The existing forms of praying, and canonical laws, were obligatory upon all priests as was auricular confession. In their own lives they were not to have civil possessions, or participate in secular offices, or perform their spiritual duties for money; they were to be celibate, and of good and sober conduct. The articles on vestments, the use of oil and water, celibacy and confession, were a rejection of Taborite teachings and caused most dispute.[1] The fact that they were accepted by the majority of the synod, including some Taborites, is evidence of the general desire to conform to the rite of the Catholic church. Four 'supreme governors' were elected to preside over the church: Jacobellus, John of Příbram, Prokop of Pilsen and John Želivský.

The presence of Taborites at Prague soon led to the inevitable friction between them and the citizens. Some of the more outspoken Taborite priests were accused of Pickhartism. They included Prokop the One-eyed, who in September 1421 was executed with Martin Houska for heresy—mainly over the eucharist.[2] Žižka was responsible for these measures as he had been for putting down the Adamites. From this time on, Tabor tended increasingly towards mysticism. It led, among other things, to Žižka's growing alienation from Tabor and his transference to Oreb. The extent of Pickhart influence beyond the Adamites is difficult to estimate. Brezova in his Hussite chronicle lists a score of charges against them.[3] In addition to the rejection of the sacramental character of the eucharist there were the usual recognizable Free Spirit claims to divinity, in being sons of God; Christ himself was relegated to the status of an ordinary man. With this went freedom from all constraint and obedience. They went naked and indulged in the standard excesses engendered by freedom of the spirit. They also attacked and killed priests, and denigrated saints' days and fasts. But the general abhorrence at these beliefs, and the prompt measures against them, allowed them little chance of survival after the final annihilation of the Adamites in October 1421.

Meanwhile in Prague, at about the same time, a struggle was developing between Želivský and Jacobellus, following Želivský's virtual take-over of the city government in October 1421.[4] This was to infringe

[1] Heymann, *Žižka* 245. [2] Ibid., 258.

[3] Höfler, *Geschichtsschreiber* II, 501–3, has a German translation of the Czech articles on pp. 499–501. [4] Heymann, op. cit., 278 ff., 307 ff.

the third of the Four Articles, against priestly involvement in secular affairs. It ended finally on 9 March with the beheading of Želivský and his followers. The execution of the tribune of the people and the instigator of the revolution led to an outcry and the flight of many councillors and nobles responsible for Želivský's death. Želivský's party was restored and many of the Prague masters were banished to Hradec Králové. Tension ceased with the coming of the Polish prince Korybut in May, to take up the post of regent which had been offered to him.[1] It was as short-lived as Korybut's regency. But he remained a faithful supporter of the Hussite cause.[2]

The years 1423 to 1427 were ones of great military success, first under Žižka and then Prokop the Bald. Žižka was the architect of Hussite arms. Blind since childhood in one eye, he became totally blind in 1421, from an arrow wound in the other eye.[3] He, more than anyone else, had also been responsible for gaining ecclesiastical assent to forcible conversion to the Four Articles; in his Cromwellian conviction in the law of God, supported, if necessary, by the sword, he personified the Hussite reformation.[4] When he died of plague in October 1424, besieging Přibyslav, while campaigning in Moravia, his Orebite troops took the name of 'Orphans' to show their loss.[5] He had fought not only against Sigismund and foreign invaders, but increasingly, as leader of the Orebites, against the nobles and the Prague party. During 1423 he defeated first the latter at the battle of Strachův Dvůr[6] in March, and Wartenberg and his followers at Hořice in April.[7]

The changed relations between the brotherhoods can be seen at the diet of St. Gall, 16 October 1423.[8] Neither was represented.[9] Consisting of the conservative Hussites and Catholic nobles, it was designed against Žižka. Its resolutions contained no reference to the Four Articles, and six of the new regency council of the twelve appointed were orthodox Catholic nobles who took communion in only one kind (*sub una*). This was a royal attempt to gain control of Bohemia, and a settlement with Sigismund was clearly envisaged.[10] It was against this combination that Žižka gained one of the most momentous internal victories of the war, at the battle of Malešov 7 June 1424.[11] It decided the military pre-

[1] Heymann, op. cit., 327 ff. [2] Ibid., 357 ff. [3] Ibid., 255–8.

[4] E.g., his constitution for Oreb (Heymann, *Žižka*, appendix x, 492–7; also 375 ff.).

[5] Ibid., 439. [6] Ibid., 389. [7] Ibid., 366.

[8] Ibid., 368. Civil war between Prague and Tabor had broken out over the question of vestments but had ended in a public disputation.

[9] Ibid., 394 ff. [10] Ibid., 398 [11] Ibid., 408 ff.

dominance of the brotherhoods for another decade and probably saved the Hussite revolution.[1] It also led to Prague's loss of control to Žižka of most of the cities of eastern Bohemia.[2] Peace was agreed in September, and a further attempt made at toleration between the Hussites and the Catholic nobles.[3] Immediately afterwards Žižka embarked on a vast new combined expedition to Moravia, where he died.

After his death military leadership soon passed to Tabor under Prokop the Bald, who maintained it from 1426 to his death in 1434. It was he who carried Bohemian arms across the frontier into Germany, gaining a series of overwhelming victories over the Saxons and the Austrians in 1426 and 1427.[4] Internally, also, after the treaty of Vožice in October 1425, greater stability ensued. Jacobellus to his death in 1429 continued to oppose all attempts by the conservatives under John Příbram to return to Roman practices. He was ably seconded by John Rokycana who became effective spiritual head of the Hussite church after Jacobellus.[5] Peter Payne, the former Wyclifite,[6] who from the beginning had identified himself with the Hussite revolt became spokesman for the Orphans. Prokop and Rokycana were firm allies; so that for perhaps the first time there was a firm basis of co-operation between the capital and Tabor. Prokop turned the Taborites again into a skilled fighting force which no enemy dared challenge.

Attempts at negotiation had continued intermittently ever since the war had begun; it was largely owing to Sigismund's vacillations that they had not materialized.[7] A new effort between the emperor and Prokop and Payne was made in 1429 at Bratislava, but foundered over Prokop's and Payne's insistence upon keeping the Four Articles. When Martin V was finally prevailed upon to summon a new general council at Basel for March 1431, the Hussites at first made their attendance conditional upon the participation of the Eastern church where communion in two kinds had always been practised. Even when they dropped this demand, remembering Hus's fate they stood out for firm guarantees of safe-conduct. Negotiations for a time broke down on this issue at Cheb, whereupon the papal legate committed the ultimate futility of summoning the fifth—and last—crusade against the Hussites. After its ritual failure, new talks were opened at Cheb in May 1432. The Czechs ultimately gained their way over adequate safe-conducts and freedom to defend the Four Articles at the Council: their embassy

[1] Ibid., 414.
[2] Ibid.
[3] Ibid., 430 ff.
[4] Ibid., 458 ff.
[5] Ibid., 457.
[6] See ch. VII, pp. 571 ff. above.
[7] Ibid., 463 ff.

was headed by Prokop, Rokycana, Nicholas of Pelhřimov and Peter Payne. A series of long and amicable debates took place on each of the Four Articles over the first three months of 1433.[1] Of their nature they were inconclusive. Both sides decided to go to Prague for a diet there in June 1433. One of the main obstacles was the Hussite insistence upon compulsory communion in both kinds throughout the whole of Bohemia.

Meanwhile during the summer a lightning Hussite campaign was conducted through west Prussia in alliance with Poland.[2] But the decisive event was Prokop's decision to renew the war against the Hussites' enemies by laying siege to their stronghold at Pilsen. This gave the chance for the dormant antagonisms between the conservatives and the radicals once more to become active. A league between the nobles was formed against the brotherhoods and the New Town of Prague, which was stormed on 5 May 1434. At the end of May the two sides engaged in battle at Lipany. The brotherhoods were overwhelmingly defeated and their leaders Prokop the Bald (the Great) and Prokop the Lesser killed. Thus ten years after Mâlešov the nobles had their revenge. They also destroyed the driving force of the Hussite movement, even if it had in late years become mainly military.[3] Nevertheless, Rokycana remained to defend their principles although he now had to admit the more conservative elements like John Příbram and Christian of Prachatice.

The basis of agreement with the Council representatives had been reached before Lipany; it was finally accepted in 1436 and ratified in 1437.[4] The Four Articles formed their foundation; but in a diluted form. Communion was to be given in one kind as well as two to those who chose it. Punishment of mortal sins was confined to those 'whose concern it was'. Preaching was limited to ordained priests and worthy deacons. They were to have no hereditary possessions but the church retained its existing property.

Sigismund had at last accepted these conditions in July 1436 at a joint Bohemian and Moravian diet; and having revoked all bans against the kingdom he entered his long-delayed inheritance at Prague on 16 August. He reigned for sixteen months before he died. His com-

[1] For an illuminating account see E. F. Jacob, 'The Bohemians at the Council of Basel, 1433' in *Prague Essays*, ed. R. W. Seton-Watson (Oxford 1948) 81–123.

[2] Heymann, *Žižka* 466.

[3] Ibid., 468–9.

[4] *Monumenta conciliorum generalium, saec 15*, I, 666 ff. and Jacob, art. cit., 122–3. Also E. Denis, *Huss et la Guerre des Hussites* 495 ff. for text of compacts.

ing marked the return of Bohemia to the communion of the church. The war however continued in less cataclysmic forms for another two generations. The Hussites had remained undefeated, although time modified their achievements. That does not diminish their importance. They were the first movement for reform which challenged the authority of Rome without being destroyed or excluded. For the first time reformation had become distinct from heresy.

Appendix I[1]

John of Brünn's confession

Ego frater Johannes de Brunna ordinis Predicatorum, interrogatus fui a [529] fratre Gallo ejusdem ordinis et inquisitore heretice pravitatis in regno Bohemie, si vellem sub juramento dicere meram veritatem de secta beghardorum et beginarum et (in) libertate spiritus vivencium. Respondi quod libenter dicerem, nam ego fui xx annis beghardus et octo annis vixi[2] in libertate spiritus, et in istam sectam intravi hoc modo. Cum essem in Brunna, habens uxorem legittimam, et cuidam ibidem familiaris essem, quesivi ab eo, qualiter ad vitam perfectam possem pervenire. Qui instruxit me, quod vita beghardorum in paupertate viventium esset[3] perfeccior omni statu in mundo existentium, quia perfeccius veritatem ewangelicam imitarentur, quam quicunque alii, sive sint clerici sive religiosi sive layci; et cum ab eo quererem, quomodo ad illam perfeccionem pervenirem, respondit: 'Vende omnia que habes et da pauperibus, qui in dicta paupertate sunt viventes.' Et cum quererem, quid facerem cum uxore mea, respondit quod nichil tenerer[4] uxori, nisi in quantum michi placeret, et bene possem eam dimittere. Et cum dicerem, quod vellem super hoc habere consultos sacerdotes, respondit quod non, quia ipsi te a proposito averterent, ideo quod maxime odiunt vitam nostram perfectam. Sicque ab eo recepta licencia et ab uxore non obtenta, et venditis omnibus bonis que habui, dedi medietatem uxori, et cum parte mea transsivi Coloniam, et intravi domum pauperem cum predicto Nicolao magistro meo, et hec domus sita est juxta Sanctum Stepphanum in nova civitate, et cum in predicta domo essem, genua flexi ad informacionem magistri mei coram fratribus dicte[5] domus, petens me ex caritate[6] recipi, quibus respondentibus, quod me libenter reciperent per duos vel tres dies, ita mansi cum eis usque mane. Mane autem facto, procurator eorum quesivit a me, quid ego apud pauperes et contemptibiles facerem, utrum paupertatem voluntariam (observare) et ab omnibus contempni vellem. Cui ego humiliter respondi: 'Vere, frater, ego vobiscum desidero manere, quousque me Deus ad statum perfeccionis adduxerit.' Respondit ille: 'Cum sero fratres convenerint, tunc tu debes coram ipsis genu flectere, et ab eis humiliter petere, quod stare cum ipsis te permittant.' Quibus factis dictus procurator una cum

[1] Edited by W. Wattenbach, 'Über die Secte der Brüder vom freien Geiste', SPAW 29 (1887) 517–44. In the notes which follow, Hs stands for Handschrift, i.e. manuscript.

[2] fixi Hs. [3] est Hs. [4] teneret Hs.

[5] dicti Hs. [6] caritati Hs.

[530] aliis fratribus me duxit ad partem secrete, et michi quedam de observanciis dicti ordinis exposuit in hunc modum: 'Frater, si desideras nobiscum manere, tu omnia debes resignare ad manus nostras, pecuniam et quecunque habes, et cum ad fratres veneris, omnia ponas coram ipsis ad mensam. Si ipsi jubent te recedere, non debes (remanere) nec recipere pecuniam supradictam.' Quibus peractis receperunt me ad vitam eorum perfectam. Post hec me instruxit de austeritate ordinis in hunc modum: 'Verus observator paupertatis nichil habet proprium, set debet esse vacuus ab omnibus rebus temporalibus, sicut Christus in cruce.' Cum autem exutus fuissem et nudus coram eis starem et genua flecterem et omnia in manus eorum resignassem.[1] Et cum sic nudus starem, concesserunt michi unam tunicam centum pecias[2] habentem, dicentes: 'Ista tunica induaris sicut Christus pro derisione et contemptu indutus fuit. Et tu sustineas pacienter propter ipsum omnium contemptus, qui tibi propter ipsum fiunt illati, et quanto plus sustinueris,[3] tanto plus sanccior eris. Et si te (aliquis) crastina die per civitatem transseuntem hereticum appellaverit vel truserit vel verberaverit, aut te in aliquo molestaverit, nichil respondeas ei, set omnia pacienter sustineas. Et cum fratre cui adjunctus eris, debes mendicare panem, nec oculos erigas, set in terram defigas et capucio cooperias. Et fratre tuo stante sta, eo ambulante ambula et clamante clama, sicut Christus, qui cum suis apostolis et amicis per civitatem transsibat, non panem mendicando[4] set suam passionem et contemptum ab omnibus querendo. Unde siquis postergante[5] te clamaret: Frater accipe elimosinam! tu redire non debes nec respicere nec ipsum exspectare, set paulatim procedas usque ad te pervenerit. Item si te debilitas vel esuries apprehenderet in via, tu poteris naturam tuam confortare occulte et sub capucio commedendo propter scandalum hominum, sive sit sextis feriis sive aliis diebus (sive) quatuor temporibus, quia pauper Christi nullum[6] facit peccatum cibo naturam suam refocillando, eciam si diebus talibus carnibus uteretur, ut dicit Caritas: Edentes et bibentes que apud vos sunt. Cum autem cum predicto fratre tuo domum redieris, coram ipso genu flexo pedes ejus osculaberis[7] et veniam ab eo postulabis,[8] ut tibi remittat si tu in aliquo offendisti eum in via. Et residentibus fratribus, dicta prius benediccione mense, commedes illud quod tibi apponitur cum silencio. Item cum in ecclesia fueris, supra tua genua debes stare et cooperto capucio, et dictis matutinis tuis sive oraciones tuas,[9] tunc ibidem debes passionem Christi meditare, non discurrendo per ecclesiam, set [531] in uno loco remaneas et Deo perfruendo interius. Item si te contingat semel videre corpus Christi in elevacione, hoc tibi tantum sufficiat, ac si cencies vidisses. Set videre elevacionem, hoc pertinet ad illos simulatores sanctitatis, qui volunt apparere coram hominibus que relinquunt interiora. Item diebus dominicis debent communicare semel vel bis in septimana, si locus fuerit, nam

[1] A lacuna here.
[2] peciis Hs.
[3] sustineris Hs.
[4] manducando Hs.
[5] postergarem Hs.
[6] nullam Hs.
[7] oscularis Hs.
[8] postulaberis Hs.
[9] sic.

hoc decet pauperes Christi, nec oportet eos omnia confiteri sacerdotibus; eciam si in illa nocte cum muliere jacuerint, nullam debent[1] (habere) conscienciam de hiis, quia veritatis paupertas que procedit ex profunditate divina, pro ipsis respondebit. Sacerdotes vero qui hoc non intelligunt, invertunt ipsis pauperibus in perniciem animarum. Si autem sompnus tuam naturam superet, non habeas de hoc conscienciam, quod in domo vel in ecclesia vel infra divinum officium dormias. Et similiter esuriendo commedas ut natura tua recreetur. Si eciam in diebus dominicis ambulando invenias aliquas pecunias in via, non elevabis propter observanciam x preceptorum. Sex[2] aliis vero diebus poteris elevare quidquid inveneris, et ad tuum hospicium reportes. Item si aliquis pauper frater hospes venerit de via, tunc exemplo Christi pedes ejus lavabis et coram ipso genua flectendo eum recipias, et caritatem sibi ministrabis, te[3] ipsius oracionibus recommendando.[4] Item tu debes te exercere in illis operibus, que sunt tibi contraria, ad hoc quod vita tua anichiletur et diminuatur[5] et spiritui totalier subiciatur,[6] quia natura tua est sterilis et sibi ipsi in omnibus operibus anichilatur,[7] et ideo frangi debet et subici divine voluntati, et ut eidem ad meritum obediat et obtineat omnem actum velitum[8] et concupitum. Item si sextis (feriis) videris de mane ova commedere, non scandalizeris neque pro peccato habeas nec sacerdoti confitearis, quia carnem suam in Christi servicio exinanivit et servituti Christi subegit. Item si transsieris per viam, nichil a quocunque debes postulare nec ire ubi elimosina distribuatur aliis, nec debes manum tuam porrigere pro ipsa recipienda elimosina a quacunque creatura. Set si manus Dei permiserit hoc, recipe cum graciarum accione. Item si fueris (missus) pro epistola, debes humiliter ire. Item non debes ad hospicium intrare ambulando per viam, set debes clamando petere hospicium, et si receptus non fueris, debes sub domo[9] dormire. Et si per predones male tractatus fueris exemplo Christi pacienter debes sustinere.'

Quo ad proficientes fuerat sic instructus a predictis fratribus: 'Frater, tu jam perfecisti omnia que ad predictum statum pertinent; jam nunc poteris [532] naturam tuam adjuvare commedendo et bibendo quociens natura tua postulaverit, et illud quod habere poterit, nam necesse est, ut natura exterior, (que) in Christi servicio est annichilata, ut iterum ad idem servicium, quod est interius in mente, restauretur, et ideo poteris commedere quocienscunque tibi placuerit. Item in quadragesima et in parascheven bene poteris commedere carnes vel lacticinia, si habere potueris, quia hoc non facit peccatum, hac de causa, ut naturam in servicio Christi debilitatam restaures, et de hoc nullam conscienciam habeas, nec confitearis sacerdotibus, quia sacerdotes pro fatuis habent tales, qui permittunt divinam naturam et veritatem usque ad

[1] debet consc. Hs.
[2] Set Hs.
[3] et Hs.
[4] recommendendo Hs.
[5] diminuetur Hs.
[6] subicietur Hs.
[7] Perhaps adversatur.
[8] sic.
[9] sic.

sompnum in ipsis operari, ut ad summam libertatem perveniant. Item de jure poteris mentiri et homines decipere qualitercunque poteris, et de hoc non habeas conscienciam, quia liber [spiritus] effectus es a peccatis. Item si frater pecuniam non habuerit, potest licite a peregrinis recipere, et illam expendendo in eternitatem transmittere, nec tenetur eam solvere, quia liber spiritu est, et si solvat, conscienciam coinquinat. Item si in via aliquam pecuniam inveniret, nom tenetur eam reddere, set eam expendere in servicio Christi cum fratribus, quia Deus in sua providencia sic ordinavit, quod ita bene illius est, qui invenit, sicut illius qui perdidit. Si autem ille cujus pecunia fuerat, repeteret, tunc liber spiritu[1] deberet eum cum verbis et verberibus male tractare, dicendo: 'Illa pecunia est ita bene mea sicut tua, quia Deus dedit eam michi, ut eam expenderem, et ad supremum paupertatis gradum transmitterem, et ideo in eternitatem transmisi', et si deprehenderetur, pocius deberet mori vel illum occidere, quam pecuniam reddere: alias a libertate spiritus recederet, a perpetua ad temporalem, quod minime est faciendum. Unde si contigerit eum mori, tunc spiritus ejus transsiret ad vitam eternam sine mora. Item si inveneris in via aliquem infirmum, debes sibi compati et diligenter ministrare, et debes ab eo querere si habet aliquam pecuniam; illam debes ab eo recipere, ne perveniat ad manus sacerdotum, et si pecuniam nollet dare, potes[2] eam violenter recipere et recedere, et postea cum fratribus et sororibus in libertate spiritus expendere et in eternitatem transmittere, et de hoc non habeas conscienciam. Et si homo iste moritur fame, quia ei non plus fecisti nisi ad suum originale (principium) transmisisti, [et] de hoc non habeas conscienciam, nec debes timere dyabolum nec infernum nec purgatorium, quia vere nichil sunt in natura, set excogitata per clericos et sacerdotes ad timorem hominum, set homo habens conscienciam est ipse dyabolus [533] et infernus et purgatorium, se ipsum tormentando. Set liber spiritu[3] omnia ista evadet, quia homo liberatus est per veritatem divinam. Item frater liber spiritu potest predicare hominibus cum ad hospicium recipietur, et si interrogatus fuerit, qua auctoritate predicaret, respondet: 'Si homines possunt a me veritatem audire et addiscere, ita libenter possunt a me recipere sicut a sacerdote, quia spiritu pauper residens in angulo ecclesie ita clare et clarius videt divinam veritatem, quando ille predicat, quam sacerdos in publico populo predicans. Et si frater bycharus[4] deberet predicare in publico, multo clarius predicaret quam sacerdos, quia dictus pauper Christi veritatem hausit de abysso Trinitatis, quam nullus hominum pertranssire poterit nisi liber spiritu.' Si autem dicatur: 'Quomodo scit veritatem illam, cum legere nesciat nec scripturam sacram intelligat?' respondeat quod melius est scripturam videre et veritatem, quam legere. Et si[5] dicatur, quid hoc sit dictum, respondeat[6] quod, qui veritate vivit, est factus liber sui ipsius et a se regressus et se ipsum relinquid et omnem aliam creaturam.

[1] spiritus Hs. [2] potest Hs. [3] spiritus Hs.
[4] beghardus? [5] sic Hs. [6] respondit Hs.

Item si interrogatus fueris: »Quo vadis?« dicas: »Nescio, nisi quo me Deus veritas duxerit, quia mei ipsius potens non sum, set totaliter in eternitate liquefactus.« Si autem queratur, cujus libertatis sis, dicas, quod liber a mea veritate, nullus me inpedire potest nec aliquid creatum. Su autem queratur, quid sit fundamentum libertatis et veritatis, et quomodo potest quis ad istam pervenire, respondeas: »Ego sum de libertate nature, et omnia que natura mea appetit, satisfacio et concedo sufficienter. Eciam si mulierem in sacratissima nocte peterem, ego satisfacio appetitui meo sine omni consciencia, nec debeo habere pro peccato, quia spiritu[1] liber est, et cum hoc sum homo naturalis, et ideo oportet libere satisfacere operibus nature.« Est autem perfecta libertas: omnia que oculus videt et concupiscit, hoc manus assequatur. Et si aliud accedens sibi occurrerit contrarium merito interficere potest, quia per hoc non infrangitur libertas, si homo predictis contrarietatibus resistit. Frater percucientem percuciendo, interficere volentem interficiendo, non de hoc habeas conscienciam, nec sacerdoti confitearis, quia interfectum transmisisti ad suum originale principium, a quo effluxit. Item dicti fratres in spiritu viventes, cum ad perfectum statum libertatis pervenerint, ita totaliter et corporaliter transmutantur, quod unum cum Deo efficiuntur, et Deus totaliter et corporaliter est cum eis, quod angeli in speculo Trinitatis non [534] possunt discernere inter Deum et animam, que in libertate spiritus vixerit, propter prefatam unionem ipsorum. Item frater et soror in libertate spiritus viventes, si simul puerum generaverint,[2] ipsum possunt merito occidere, vel in aquam proicere sicut alium vermem, nec de hoc debet habere conscienciam, nec debet confiteri sacerdotibus, quia eum ad originale principium transmittunt. Et merito possunt dicere sine omni peccato, quod illius sacerdotis sit, et hoc ex perfeccione libertatis spiritus, in qua stant, quia pauperes spiritu nichil habent, unde possunt vivere et illum puerum nutrire, et de hoc non debent[3] (habere) conscienciam. Item si dicunt mendacia vel deceptoria vel dampnosa, quia stantes in illa libertate spiritus non possunt peccare, quia sunt inpeccabiles et in supremo gradu perfeccionis, quod perfecciores fieri non possunt. Item fratres et sorores habent signa inter se, per que mutuo agnoscuntur et agnoscunt se et voluntatem eorum exprimunt, quando convenire volunt, sicut quando ipsa[4] digitum ponit super nasum, tunc frater domum ingrediatur, sive sit in ecclesia sive in platea. Quando autem caput tangit, tunc intrat cameram et parat stratum. Set quando pectus tangit, tunc lectum ascendit, et quociens opus nature et dileccionis fuerit, cum ea perficiet, quia omnia illa in libertate spiritus viventes sine peccato facere possunt. Item si frater et soror stant[5] in predicta libertate, et si communicet de mane et de sero oportunitatem habuerint, potest licite sine omni peccato actum carnalem exercere. Item communicant sepius et frequenter confitentur, ut hominibus bonum exemplum prebeant.[6] Item dicunt, quando moriuntur,

[1] spiritus? [2] generaverit Hs. [3] debet consc. Hs.
[4] ipse Hs. [5] stans Hs. [6] prebeantur Hs.

directe ad celum empyreum volant, eciam (si) sine extrema unccione et communione moriuntur, quia dicunt quod clerici et sacerdotes hoc excogitaverunt. Item dicunt quod (nullus) sit infernus nec dyabolus, et quod Deus non dat se in manibus sacerdotum in transsubstanciacione panis in missa, quia illi non sunt in caritate et gracia; ergo nisi abstractus fuerit ab hominibus, hoc conficere non potest. Et tamen talem nullum vidi sacerdotem, ergo nullus eorum potest consecrare corpus Christi. Item dicunt, quod in pauperibus solum veritas inveniatur, et non in sacerdotibus qui student in vanitate. Item sacerdotes Deum non habent, nec sacerdotes veritatem agnoscunt; ergo pauperes Christi non debent narrare[1] sacerdotibus veritatem, ita quod secreta eorum non debent sacerdotibus revelare in confessione, nec debent clericis obedire. Jejunia et alia bona opera [sacerdotes] non agnoscunt. Item dicunt, quod quando pauper spiritu ab omni creatura [535] est segregatus, tunc transsit in dignitatem, ita quod consors fit divine nature, et sic non indiget honorare sanctos. Item frater si debet communicare et ante missam esuriet, licite possit commedere ante missam et postea communicare, quia sicud spiritus libere agit, sic et caro libere agat opera nature sine omni peccato, sive sit cum una muliere sive cum pluribus, quia natura ita est debilitata, quod oportet eam sustentari, sive fiat [fit] per furtum sive per spolium, quia omnia sunt communia que Deus creavit, cum ipse liber existat. Item si aliquis dicet tibi: »Frater, ego ita bene liber (sum) sicud et tu, quia in eandem naturam nobilitatem habeo,[2] quam habes tu«, respondeas ei: »Si expendisti vitam tuam secundum formam vite Christi, sicut ego feci, tunc liber es vite. Ego vero vitam meam expendi in contemptu paupertatis et sustinui multa propter Christum. Item si intrarem thabernam et commederem et biberem et non haberem unde solverem, possum libere inde exire sine omni peccato. Et si importune a me repeteret ut solverem, possum sine omni peccato repetentem verberare, quia illa bona Deus sibi commisit, ut ea michi ministret, et ego in eternitatem transmitterem.« Eciam si soror ejusdem libertatis eodem die communicasset, et veniret ad fratrem et diceret ei: Frater, rogo caritatem, conjaceas[3] michi, non deberet dicere: Communicavi, set deberet exercere opus nature fortiter bis vel quater, ut satisfaceret nature, nec conscienciam deberet habere de hoc, nec deberet confiteri. Item si actum sodomiticum cum masculo desideraret, debet libere et licite exercere sine omni peccato, quia alias liber spiritu non esset. Item quando frater habet gravia peccata, quando est in statu incipiencium, ille non debet dicere de gravioribus, set solum levia, et hoc ideo, quia sacerdotes qui talia audiunt, possunt ea dicere in domibus suis, quia ipsi sacerdotes non stant in veritate perfeccionis, et ideo non oportet eis omnia revelare. Item dicunt, quod illi qui sunt in vera libertate, nullus potest eis imperare quicquam aut eos excommunicare vel aliquid[4] interdicere, nec papa nec archiepiscopus nec aliquis vivens habet auctoritatem super eos, quia sunt liberi nec subjacent

[1] maeer Hs. [2] sic. [3] coniacias Hs. [4] aliud Hs.

cujuscunque hominis jurisdiccioni,[1] ideo non curant quecunque statuta vel mandata ecclesie.

De confessione.

Ego confiteor, quod illa peccata tenui octo annis, et credidi predicta omnia esse ver2, et exercui predicta, pro peccatis non habendo, quia stabam in libertate spiritus, et ideo quidquid feci, carnes commedendo sextis feriis et in vigiliis apostolorum, luxuriando et homines decipiendo et furando ac percuciendo, numquam habui pro peccatis, nec confessus fui quando volui [536] communicare. Eciam inter ducentos beghardos ac libertatem tenentes[2] vix unus invenitur, qui non tenetur (ad) predictos articulos.

Albert of Brünn's confession

Item Albertus beghardus tenuit, quod qui esset in vera libertate, possit ita bonam missam dicere sub capucio, sicud sacerdos, quia talis homo potest se ita bene conjungere Deo sicut sacerdos in altari. Item quod frequens communicacio[3] corporis Christi et sagwinis vel celebracio multiplex missarum non facit hominem sanctum sive sancciorem, quia videmus quod sacerdotes, qui omni die celebrant,[4] sunt ita mali et pejores quam illi qui raro communicant vel celebrant. Item quod homo qui est liber spiritu, verius fruitur Deo, quam ille qui omni nocte surgit et genu flexo orat. Item quod in elevacione corporis Christi homo non rapitur[5] ad superiora, et ideo quidquid facit homo infra cingulum,[6] non est peccatum. Ego vidi unum beghardum, qui totam noctem jacuit cum una begina in presencia mea in Brunna, et eam communicavit. Item dicunt quod grossi homines sunt qui se cum passione Christi occupant, et illi vocantur in vulgari blochwerg, set dicunt quod homo debet super se ascendere et seipsum speculari, et tunc potest facere quidquid voluerit, et non debet jejunare nec aliqua bona facere, quia illa plus impediunt quam promoveant, nec dedent videre corpus Christi, ubi hoc facere possunt sine scandalo hominum, quia vere credunt, quod omnis liber spiritu ita bene potest[7] habere in cordibus suis corpus Christi, sicut sacerdotes in manibus suis; unde ego audivi ab una begina, que dixit, quod isti sacerdotes faciunt tot deos in ecclesia, quod homo quiescere non potest. Item dicunt, quod infernus nichil aliud est quam[8] hominis propria voluntas, quia ibi non est ignis naturalis; et ergo, quando frangit homo suam propriam voluntatem, eciam frangit proprium infernum. Item dicunt et firmiter credunt, quod omnia peccata carnalia et contra naturam, non est peccatum. Item multi beghardi non credunt articulos in symbolo fidei. Item verbum beghardi forcius est quam verbum sacerdotis qui predicat, quia beghardus

[1] iurisdiccione Hs. [2] tenentibus Hs. [3] excom. Hs.
[4] celebrantur Hs. [5] capitur Hs.
[6] angelum Hs. [7] possunt Hs. [8] quod Hs.

studuit suam doctrinam in libro Trinitatis, set sacerdos in pellibus vitulorum. Item Albertus interrogatus fuit a fratre Gallo ordinis Predicatorum, quid[1] ipsi beghardi habent pro fundamento, quod peccatum sodomiticum non habent pro peccato, nec reputant eciam peccatum. Respondit: Ego tenui et firmiter credidi, quod omnes beghardi credunt, quod homo ad tantam libertatem [537] posset pervenire, quod fit ita liber spiritu, quod mortalia peccata sunt venialia, et hoc delet aqua benedicta, quia si peccata mortalia reputarent peccatum esse, tunc non esset liber spiritu. Et illud peccatum, quod in se mortale est, veniale est. Et ideo quando confitentur, solum venialia confitentur, ac si majora numquam commisissent, et hoc solum faciunt ad complacenciam hominum, ut ab hominibus reputentur sancti. Et in ista libertate spiritus ego frater Johannes de Brunna una cum fratre meo Alberto steti xx annis, et omnia predicta tenui et nunquam peccatum reputavi, nec unquam fuissemus confessi, si non timuissemus homines, et multa alia que non scripta (sunt) in libro hoc.

Hic nota errores in Clementinis c(apite) de he(reticis).

John Hartmann's confession

[538] Nunc sequitur publicum instrumentum predictos continens errores et plures alios etc.

In nomine Domini Amen. Anno ejusdem M⁰ ccc⁰ lxvij,[2] indicione vj. die vj vicesima[3] mensis Decembris, ab hora ix. vel quasi usque ad horam completorii, pontificatus sanctissimi[4] in Christo patris et domini nostri, domini Urbani pape quinti anno vj. in Erdfordia[5] Moguntine[6] dyocesis, in⁰ allodio reverendi in Christo patris ac domini, domini archiepiscopi Moguntini, in estuario majori, in mei notarii ac notariorum publicorum et testium subscriptorum presencia constitutus coram venerabili viro et religioso fratre Waltero Corlink,[7] ordinis Predicatorum, sacre theologie professore[8] et inquisitore heretice pravitatis auctoritate apostolica in certis partibus Almannie deputato, quidam beghardus nomine Johannes[9] Hartmanni de villa Astmansteten dicte dyocesis Moguntine, vel dictus Johannes Spinner [539] inter beghardos, qui prius juravit ad sancta Dei ewangelia de dicenda veritate pro tunc et semper in forma debita et consueta. Interrogatus a dicto Walthero inquisitore, in quo consistat[10] libertas spiritus, respondit, quod in hoc, quod totaliter cessat remorsus consciencie, et quod homo redditur penitus impeccabilis, et sic interrogatus a predicto inquisitore[11] de primo

[1] quod Hs.
[2] Anno Domini M.
[3] M⁰ ccc⁰ vj. xxvj die G.
[4] p. in Chr. sanct. p. d. U. quinti G.
[5] Erfordia G.
[6] Mag. G.
[7] sic.
[8] professori et inquisitoris Hs.
[9] Johannis G.
[10] consistit G.
[11] ab eodem G.

articulo in Clementinis de[1] hereticis 'Ad nostrum', qui incipit 'quod si quis homo in vita presenti', scilicet quando ipse stetit in tali contemplacione, de qua prius dictum[2] est, videlicet in summo gradu perfeccionis, quem ipse in principio habuit, quando in abysso divinitatis fuit, an sit aliqua differencia inter Deum et se, respondit quod in tali perfeccione et summo gradu unus est cum Deo et Deus cum eo, unus absque ulla[3] distinccione, et dixit quod in hoc consistat[4] vera libertas spiritus, sic quod cessat omnis remorsus consciencie et homo talis redditur impeccabilis. Interrogatus an homo in vita presenti, qui stat in tali contemplacione, amplius possit[5] proficere, respondit quod sic stans in libertate amplius proficere non potest, et quod talis homo tantum et talem perfeccionis gradum acquirit, quod redditur penitus inpeccabilis.

Interrogatus de secundo articulo in Clem. qui incipit '2° quod jejunare' etc. dixit quod hominem non oportet jejunare vel orare, postquam gradum perfeccionis hujusmodi fuerit assecutus, et quod sensualitas est ita spiritui et racioni subjecta, quod talis homo licite potest concedere corpori quidquid sibi placet.

Interrogatus de 3° articulo qui incipit '3° quod illi qui sunt' etc. respondit quod illi qui sunt in predicto gradu perfeccionis et spiritu libertatis, non sunt humane subjecti obediencie nec ad aliqua precepta vel statuta ecclesie obligantur, quia veri liberi sunt et talis liber est rex et dominus omnium creaturarum, et[6] omnia sunt sua et potest licite accipere pro usu suo quecunque sibi placent. Et si aliquis in hoc vellet eum impedire, talem impedientem posset talis liber occidere et ab eo auferre bona sua, quia occidendo ipsum remitteret ad originale suum principium, et omnia que delectant eum potest licite facere. Et antequam non perficeret actum ad quem natura sua ipsum inclinaret, pocius deberet una tota terra interfici et perire. Et hoc quod dixit de una terra, dixit de omnibus aliis. Interrogatus an talis liber spiritu licite posset auferre ab aliquo pro usu suo calicem aureum, respondit quod sic, et dixit, quod melius esset huic quod reciperet calicem aureum quam pannum grossum. Item an imperatorem vellet interficere, si [540] prohiberet ipsum aliquam rem recipere pro sua utilitate[7] sibi convenientem, si posset, respondit sub distinccione, quod si imperator non esset liber spiritu, tunc vellet eum interficere. Set si imperator esset perfeccior in libertate spiritus, tunc esset dubium, quod dubium dixit set pro tunc nolle revelare.

Interrogatus de 4° articulo in Clem. qui incipit 'Quarto quod homo ita potest' etc. dixit quod stans in tali gradu perfeccionis, sicut ipse primo fuit, talis potest finalem beatitudinem secundum omnem gradum perfeccionis pro tunc assequi, sicut eam obtinebit in vita beata, si solummodo mortalitas

[1] Clem. qui inc. Ad. n. si quis homo in v. pr. quando G.
[2] q. predictum G. [3] omni M. [4] consisteret G.
[5] non possit G. [6] idest G.
[7] In M. correctly in voluntate.

corporis non esset. Et quod talis liber spiritu ita beatus esset sicud beatus Petrus vel beata virgo Maria in regno celorum vel in vita beata. Interrogatus quando est in tali summo gradu perfeccionis et quando taliter est unum cum Deo sicut dictum est, an hoc sit sine medio quocunque: respondit quod sic, sine medio. Et dixit consequenter, quod nec angeli nec Maria possent[1] discernere inter Deum et ipsum in tali perfeccione. Et dixit quod in tali contemplacione sua transformatus in deitatem ita cum Deo unum efficitur et Deus cum eo, quod nec angeli nec Maria possent discernere inter Deum et ipsum propter perfectam unionem eorum. Et quod in unitate divine essencie et trinitatis trium personarum liber spiritu stans in tali summo gradu, in quo ipse primo stetit, quidquid vult esse in deitate, hoc est; quia si vult esse pater, est pater; si filius, est filius; si spiritus sanctus, est spiritus sanctus in deitate. Et ex hoc dixit, quod filius in divinis esset frater[2] suus et sibi attineret.

Interrogatus de 5⁰ articulo in Clem. qui sic incipit: 'Quinto quod quelibet intellectualis' etc. dixit quod nobilitas spiritus ex effluxu divinitatis et refluxu in deitatem[3] est unum cum Deo, et ibi est pura et vera beatitudo, et talis liber spiritu non indiget lumine glorie elevante ad Deum videndum et eo beate fruendum, quia ibi nulla est distinccio. Item dixit, ubi est tale lumen[4] essenciale, quod est Deus, ibi omne lumen creatum tenebre sunt[5] et obfuscacio, et nulla multitudo est ibi ponenda in divinis et inter talem liberum spiritu.

Interrogatus de 6⁰ articulo qui incipit: 'Sexto quod in actibus' etc. respondit quod talis homo liber redditur inpeccabilis et potest agere quidquid vult et sibi placet. Et si natura inclinaret eum ad actum venereum, potest licite ipsum perficere cum sorore sua carnali vel matre et in quocunque loco sint, eciam [541] in altari. Et dixit quod magis naturale est, talem actum venereum exercere cum sorore sua carnali, quam cum alia muliere, propter conformitatem[6] nature. Et subjunxit, quod perfectus liber a se licenciat virtutes sub tali distinccione, quod homo liber non est sub lege quacunque nec tenetur ad statuta ecclesie nec precepta qualiacunque, quia est liber spiritu, idest ein frŷ geist, quod idem est quod homo liber, et statuta et precepta ecclesie debent saltem tenere grossi homines, idest homines sub lege existentes, quos ipse grossos homines appellat. Item dixit quod per hoc quod cognosceret carnaliter sororem carnalem, ipsa non est minus virgo nec perdit castitatem, set magis casta redditur per concubitum carnalem. Item dixit, quod si cum aliqua puella se permiscuerit, nec ipse nec puella amittunt virginitatem, ymmo si per alios esset violata et amisisset virginitatem, per hoc quod cum homine libero, qui staret in tali gradu perfeccionis, qui cum ipsa coierit, virginitatem amissam recuperabit. Et posuit exemplum de decem viris unam puellam carnaliter cognoscentibus, sic quod unus est grossior alio in proporcione corporum et eciam naturalium, sic quod grossior eam primo haberet, et alii

[1] possunt G. [2] filius G. [3] deitate et essencialiter est G.
[4] t. bonum l. M. [5] tenebra est G. [6] affinitatem M.

consequenter usque ad ultimum, qui est minor vel minimus inter omnes, si talis est liber spiritu et habuerit ipsam ultimus liber spiritu, talis corrupta virginitatem amissam per alios per ipsum liberum spiritu recuperabit. Et subjunxit quod sic est de mulieribus, sicut de vitulis vel bobus, qui creati sunt ad usum hominum quod possunt commedi, sic et mulieres create sunt ut sint ad usum illorum qui sunt in libertate spiritus. Et tunc interrogatus a predicto inquisitore: 'Si essent duo in libertate spiritus, qui ambo vellent unam puellam cognoscere, quis eorum deberet alium precedere?' respondit sicut prius, quod iste qui esset major liber spiritu, deberet cum ea prius coire et tunc alius. Set in essent equi liberi, tunc deberent cum taxillis sortem mittere, et cui sors daret, ille primo cognoscere deberet eam. Interrogatus an Christus fuisset liber spiritu, respondit quod non, quod probavit per ewangelium, quia Christus in passione sua dixit: 'Pater, si possibile est, transseat a me calix iste; non tamen sicut ego volo set sicut tu'. Et addidit quod Christus in die parascheves, postquam mortuus fuit in cruce, tunc primo veram libertatem fuerit assecutus, propter quod et feria sexta a vulgaribus dicitur fritag. Interrogatus an Christus post resurreccionem suam Mariam Magdalenam cognoverit carnaliter, respondit quod ista esset alta et profunda questio sive sentencia, quam non vellet dicere, quamvis bene sciret, subridendo subjungens, quod inquisitor libenter deberet sibi benefacere, quod hoc vellet [542] sibi indicare, quia aliqui hoc tenerent, quod in futura vita fiat permixtio maris et femine, sicut in presenti, quod si non esset, tunc homines vellent libencius in ista vita cum uxoribus suis manere, quam ad futuram vitam anhelare. Item Mariam dixit non fuisse[1] liberam spiritu, quia aliter non tociens suspirasset de absencia filii sui, dicens: 'Eya bone fili, eya bone fili, quando te videbo?'

Item de 7º articulo qui incipit: 'Septimo quod mulieris osculum' etc. dixit, quod actus carnalis ad quem natura hominem inclinat, tali in spiritu libero non est peccatum, set aliqui amplexantur et osculantur mulieres propter hoc solum, quod conversacio eorum sit communis cum hominibus aliis, et ne dicatur de eis proprie, quod ipsi sint gabhardi et nescirent conversari cum hominibus.

Item de 8º articulo qui incipit: 'Octavo quod in elevacione' etc. dixit, quod talis liber spiritu licite potest dimittere[2] omnia statuta ecclesie, et non tenetur ad alia quecunque statuta, et si est in tali contemplacione interiori, non deberet assurgere ad elevacionem corporis Christi, ne impediatur in puritate et altitudine sue contemplacionis, quod se cum exterioribus quovis modo occuparet, nec oportet quod talis perfectus liber spiritu recipiat quecunque sacramenta, nisi in quantum talis homo extravagaretur et vellet se verlustigen, et etiam in tali extravagacione ita bene inveniret Deum in ludo scacorum, sicut in sacramento eukaristie, si in tali ludo inveniret majorem delectacionem. Item dixit, si non esset baptizatus et si nesciretur, non curaret,

[1] esse M. [2] posset obmittere G.

nisi in quantum vellet se verlustigen, et dixit, si paganus esset in tali libertate spiritus, non indigeret de baptismo. Item dixit quod liber spiritu non tenetur confiteri, quia talis est inpeccabilis, nec indiget de quibuscunque aliis sacramentis. Et dixit quod nullus potest exprimere talem veritatem et alluminacionem, nisi qui vere liber est et in se ipso invenit, et ergo multum inquisitor deberet sibi regraciari, quod sibi talia revelavit et eum sic illuminavit, quia plus valet sibi talis illuminacio, quam tota pecunia consulum Erfordensium que est in turri eorum. Interrogatus an talia dixerit ex demencia cordis vel debilitate corporis seu ex aliqua infirmitate,[1] respondit quod nullo istorum modorum, set ex fundo suo talia dixit, quia sic in se invenit, et iste solus talia exprimere potest ex vero fundamento, qui est expertus talia in se ipso, et quod predicatores predicant et docent ex libris, et studio pellium obliviscuntur eorum que docent, set qui intima profunditate divini abyssus[2] [543] talia perspiciunt, illi verissime talia dicere possunt. Et quod a ix annis postquam in tali libertate fuit constitutus, nunquam habuit temporalem corporis passionem nec fuit minutus nec infirmus nec medicinam quamcunque[3] recepit. Interrogatus de palliditate, an sit ex infirmitate aliqua, et qua de causa, respondit quod sit ex infirmitate, set causam non vellet dicere pro presenti. Interrogatus an talia negare posset existens in tali libertate spiritus, respondit quod sic. Si esset constitutus in periculo corporis, ad conservandum corpus suum licite posset negare et tociens quociens oporteret abjurare sine omni peccato, nec jurando nec negando talia mentiretur, set verum diceret. Et posuit exemplum: Si cognovisset sororem suam carnalem carnaliter, et ex hoc accusaretur, licite posset negare et jurare quod non fecit, quia in hoc non dicit falsum in spiritu liber, quia intendit quod non fecit in eternitate. Et non oportet eum dicere de tempore, et sic licite potest decipere inquirentem et[4] accusantem, quia loquitur veritatem ex fundamento libertatis, in quo nullum est falsum nec esse potest. Acta sunt hec Erfordie Mog. dioc. predicto anno ind. pont. die mense hora et loco quibus supra, presentibus honorabilibus et religiosis viris, fratre Johanne Tutilstete ord. Pred. et dicto de Stalberg procuratore monasterii S. Petri in monte Erfordensi ord. S. Benedicti, domino Heinrico advocati, provisore dicti allodii, et d. Heinrico apothecario, perpetuo vicario ecclesie beate Marie virginis Erfordensis, ac Bartholomeo de Vocberstete et Johanne helunci notariis publicis, et aliis fide dignis testibus ad premissa rogatis et requisitis.

Et ego Hermannus Insula, clericus Hildesheymensis dyocesis . . .

[1] inf. corporis M.
[2] sic.
[3] nunquam M.
[4] et non acc. qui M.

Appendix II[1]

Report of the inquisition into the Beguines at Sweydnitz

In nomine domini amen. Sub anno natiuitatis eiusdem M⁰CCC⁰XXXII⁰, [239] Indiccione XV^ma^, in vigilia natiuitatis gloriosissime virginis et matris Marie, que est VII⁰ Idus Septembris[2] hora quasi prime in Sweidnitz Wratislaviensis dyocesis in refectorio domus religiosorum virorum fratrum ordinis Predicatorum in presencia mei notarii subscripti ac honorabilium et reverendorum virorum dominorum Heynrici Schammonis plebani de Putrido ponte, Arnoldi rectoris Capelle leprosorum ante Sweidnittcz, Petri Swarczmanni lectoris, Johannis Lewe, Conradi de Ebirsbach fratrum ordinis Minorum, fratrum Craschonis, Arnoldi, Swen, Johannis, Modilici, de ordine Predicatorum, honorabilis et religiosus vir dominus frater Iohannes de Swenkenfelt, lector Predicatorum ibidem in Sweidnicz inquisitor contra hereticam pravitatem per Wratislaviensem et Lubucensem dyoceses auctoritate apostolica deputatus multorumque aliorum virorum religiosorum, secularium et sapientum tam virorum ac mullierum infrascriptas testes pro testimonio contra Capuciatas moniales coram se fecerat evocari videlicet: Hedwigim de Wratislavia, Adilheyd quandam inclusam, Katherinam de Lipcz, Margaretham pictricem, Cunegundim de Monsterberg, Luttardim de Lipczk, Elizabet de Strigouia, et Iulianam, que coram predicto inquisitore conparentes ad sanctam dei crucem ipsam manualiter tangendo omnes et cingule de veritate dicenda iuraverunt in hunc modum: Ego Hedwigis, ego Adilheildis, ego Katherina, ego Margaretha et ego Cunegundis et ego Lutthardis et ego Elizabeth et ego Iuliana iuramus ad sanctam dei crucem, quod omnem veritatem dicemus, quam scimus de moribus et vita et conversacione Capuciatarum monialium, nec hoc dimittemus causa timoris, amoris, fauoris uel invidie, nec propter aliam aliquam causam. Sic nos deus adiuvet et hec sancta dei crux. Quequedam testes per predictum inquisitorem et me subscriptum notarium sunt examinate diligenter diebus subnotatis.

Prima testis Hedwigis de Wratislavia iurata et interrogata de vita et moribus Capuciatarum, cum quibus aliquando conversata fuit, respondit, quod fuit cum eis in Sweidnitcz non plene per annum et Wratislawie tribus quartalibus annis, dicit eciam interrogata, quod isto anno feria quarta in ebdomada Penthecostes incluse in earum cameris laboraverunt, in diebus quoque dominicis disponunt lanas suas ad operandum per ebdomadam et

[1] Edited by B. Ulanowski in *Scriptores rerum Polonicarum* XIII, vol. 5 (1889) 233–55.

[2] d. 7 Septembris 1332.

in diebus apostolorum fuerunt post prandium et hoc dicunt esse bona opera. [240] Item Hedwigis iurata et interrogata dixit, quod percuciunt se interdum usque ad sanguinem et dicunt, hoc non esse nude, sicut fit, confitendum sed involute, et dicunt quod ille, que sic alias percuciunt non debeant habere aliquam conscienciam de impaciencia, cum sint perfecte et nunquam efficiantur inpacientes, percusse vero adhuc oportet, ut petant veniam a percutientibus. Item iurata et interrogata dixit eas obedienciam habere inter se, cum non sint alicuius ordinis approbati dicuntque ad subditas sibi: oportet vos flecti vel frangi, et mittunt se ad domus suas diuersas involute causam sic dicendo: bona, vade mecum ad talem locum vel ad talem, sicque vadens postea detinetur. Item iurata et interrogata respondit quod capuciate dixerunt ei: Si necessitas infirmitatis te occuparet et quod Corpus Christi non portaretur ad domum nostram, velles tu pocius domum exire et accipere Corpus Christi uel manere in domo et mori sine sacramento Christi; tunc ego dixi: Pocius vellem domum exire et accipere Corpus Christi; Capuciatis respondentibus, quod ipse hoc non facerent, et subiunxerunt: Tu non vales nobis ad paupertatem. — Item Hedwigis interrogata per iuramentum dixit, quod cum esset inter eas, et ut eis interdum videbatur, quod nimiam moram in ecclesia orando protraxisset: Stomachate, dixerunt ei, tu iaces super te, tu fugis te ipsam, du mynst dich selbir, non expedis paupertati. Item Hedwigis iurata et interrogata dicit, quod dicunt et est eorum opinio, quod cum sint in statu perfecto, sompnus, vigilia, cibus et potus, ieiunium, quantum ad meritum sunt equalia, et omnia opera propter deum per eas facta sint equalia, quia esse earum est opus earum. Item Heduigis iurata et interrogata dixit, quod habent camerulam quandam paruam in domo sua, quam nemo ingreditur, nisi sola magistra. Item dicit per iuramentum, quod dicunt velle se ad earum sectam iuuenculas recipere, quas secundum suum possunt informare propositum, non antiquas mulieres, quas ita ut iuuenes informare non possunt, et dicunt: Antiqui canes non possunt bene domari; percuciuntque se cum cordis nodatis et acuatis et corrigiis vsque ad sanguinem et dicunt hoc se facere ideo et fieri debere, ut natura edometur. Item eadem Hedwigis iurata et interrogata dixit se vidisse, quod [non]-nunquam plures earum existentes in stuba in exitu prima prostrauit se circa limen hostii, quam conculcans secunda in exitu prostrauit se iuxta eam, quam conculcans et primam tertia in exitu et sic deinceps conculcauerunt se et prostrauerunt, donec omnes consumerentur. Et ipsa Hedwigis fuit ex eis, que hoc fecerunt, et hoc fuit in Wratislauia. Item Hedwigis iurata et interrogata dicit de certa sciencia, quod docent iuuenculas in recepcione earum nunquam sumere necessitatem cibi, potus, etc. donec perficiantur; perfecte enim effecte, ut dicunt, possunt et debent recuperare, que et quantum prius caruerunt, et nec in vestibus habere dicunt necessitatem. Et si aliqua in bonis vestibus venit ad eas, induunt eam semicinciis auferendo vestes bonas et pro se tanquam pro perfectis vsurpando. Et si qua non wlt dare vestes, tunc dicunt ad eam: tu non vales ad paupertatem. Audiuit eciam ab ipsis, quod dixerunt: homo hic tantum posset profici, quod esset perfectus, et ille, que sunt in tali statu perfeccionis et spiritu libertatis non tenentur alicui obedire. Item Hedwigis iurata et interrogata [dixit], quod cum diceret ad eas: oportet me confiteri, quod nerebam in ebdomada Penthecostes, ipse responderunt, non oportet te hoc confiteri, quia sunt bona opera et dicit, quod earum sit opinio, quod quidquid contra earum voluntatem fit, hoc reputant peccatum. Et dicunt sic Capuciate subditis suis: fac, quod iubemus te et non peccabis, quia non iubemus, quod sit peccatum. Et si subdite earum facerent aliquid de genere bonorum operum contra earum voluntatem, ut ire ad ecclesiam et similia, contra iussum earum, hoc reputant peccatum. Item iurata et interro- [241] gata dixit se frequenter audisse de ore Girdrudis de Ciuitate, que est hic: Sicut deus est deus, ita ipsa esset deus cum deo; et sicut Christus nunquam separatus est a deo, sic nec ipsa; et si quando aliqua impuritas sibi accidit, ipsa se mox deo in pristina puritate conformat, stans in equalitate diuina. Et quando Hedwigis ipsam super hys acuis verbis reprehenderet, alie eam defenderunt. Item Heduigis dicit iurata: quando fuerunt rephrehense, quod tunc dixerunt: Nos videmus in libro vite, sed sacerdotes et predicatores vident in cutibus faccarum. Nos volumus claudere domum nostram et volumus facere, quidquid nobis placet. Item iurata dicit, quod quondam audiuit in Wratislauia, quod quedam dixerunt: Si Christus nasci deberet, adhuc inveniretur ita pura virgo, sicut fuit beata virgo Maria. Item Hedwigis dixit, quod Capuciate ipsam in ecclesia pedibus calcassent propter hoc, quod deponeret contra ipsas, et nominauerunt eam antiquam hereticam et serpentem, dicentes, quod perpetue damnaretur, quod destruere vellet earum bonam vitam. Item Hedwigis eadem iurata et interrogata dixit, quod semel cum Anna ceca iuit ad parrochiam in Sweydnitcz, et hoc non est dimidius annus, volens communicare, sed quia sacerdotes diu protraxerunt, dixit ipsa Hedwigis: Ach deus, quod ita diu protrahunt; Anna dicente: Si non esset bonum conueniencie, nuncquam vellem huc venire ad communicandum. Item dicit, quod vna in Sweidnitcz sit, que vocatur Gerdrudis de Olsna, que publice contra quendam fratrem predicatorem, quando predicauit de hereticis et de eis, insurrexit, et dixit sibi in faciem: Vos menciemini. Item frater Conradus de Ebirsbach ordinis Minorum idem in sua consciencia dixit, quod vna de Capuciatis aput eum fuerit et ipsum rogauerit, quod Hedwigym ad hoc teneret, quod omnino diceret de eis aliquid, nec eas infamaret. Item Hedwigis iurata et interrogata: vtrum causa amoris, fauoris uel invidie testificeretur, respondit, quod non, sed propter deum et iusticiam, et ut fides confirmetur.

Adelheidis secunda testis, quondam inclusa, iurata et interrogata de vita et moribus Capuciatarum, cum quibus conuersata est, respondit, quod fuerit cum eis vno anno minus tribus septimanis, et dicit, quod habent obedienciam inter se et emittunt subditas suas et mittunt in domibus suis, sicut alii religiosi, et ipse me volebant et ego nolui. Item eadem iurata et interrogata dixit, quod est communis modus inter seniores earum, quod diebus dominicis et festiuis operantur opera similia nerendo, suendo et alia opera similia faciendo, incluse tamen et custodem ponendo, ut si quis venerit et pro eis sciscitatus fuerit, respondeant eas esse in ecclesia vel alibi. Et cum super hoc reprehenderetur per ipsam Adelheidim, utpote quia contra ordinacionem facerent ecclesie, stomachando responderunt: Miramur multum, quod ecclesia est ydolum tuum effectum, et quod tot annis non meruisti aput deum, quod esses perfecta, ut sederes domi et operareris opera karitatis. Item dicit iurata, quod est communis modus inter eas, quarum magistra est Heylbig, quod recipiunt iuuenculas ad sectam suam et a iuuentute imbuunt illas doctrina sua, que sic imbute a iuuentute incipiunt (s) tamquam veridicam, et est talis: Quod non oportet confiteri rem aliquam nude, sicut perpetrata est, et reprehenderunt eandem, quia voluit confiteri Predicatoribus vel Minoribus, suadentes ei, ut non confiteretur aliis, preterquam cui ipse confiterentur, dicentes: Tu vilis, vis totum, quod tu scis, inmundis sacerdotibus apportare. Item iurata dixit, quod omnis intencio earum est, ut ostenderent coram hominibus ymaginem sanctitatis, et hoc faciunt propter auariciam, ut, parentes hominibus sancte [242] et bone, ab eis recipiant multas elemosinas et dona; et prohibent subdites suis ire ad parrochiam et ad alias ecclesias, nisi habeant secum per ipsas destinatas pedagogas; et se ipsas preferunt omnibus aliis ordinibus, dicentes in sua secta perfectum esse statum paupertatis et in nullis aliis et omnes alias mulieres, quantumcunque devotas, vituperant et statum adnullant earundem. Item iurata et interrogata dicit hanc doctrinalem proposicionem inter eas: Quidquid libenter faceres, noli facere et omne tibi valde contrarium perfice. Item iurata dicit, quod docent iuvenculas se debere exercitari tali exercicio gravi, per quod deducuntur extra racionem, unde quedam ex eis inventa aput leprosas et propter indiscreta exercicia et castigaciones irracionabiles ad mentis insaniam perducta, et hec cognominatur de Glacz, et interrogata, quare non commederet, quid ibi in affliccione iaceret, respondit: Quia ad tantam perfectionem deuenisset, quod non indigeret commedere nec bibere, quia Christus eam pasceret; et fuit totaliter infatuata et in racione destructa. Item Adelheidis iurata et interrogata dicit se audivisse ab illis, que fuerunt aput eas, quod titulus earum est: unio filiarum Vdillyndis, in qua secta multa sunt statuta: primo quod attrahunt ad sectam suam blandis sermonibus et dulcibus virgines et muliers indifferenter, cuiuscunque status existant uel condicionis, quas suadent vivere secundum eorum iussa et voluntates, nec ecclesie nec ullius iussa curare; secundum est quod docent in earum congregacionis domo manere, in coquina vel in aliis officinis ipsarum, nec sermonem, nec ecclesias adire, asserentes eas credere debere, quod propterea, quia propriam voluntatem dimiserunt et propter opera caritatis, que operantur, dominus deus eis inspirabit, quecunque doctores aliqui seu predicatores in ecclesia docere possunt, dicere uel predicare; et quanto plus, vt eadem iurata retulit, ad que aliqua mirabiliter horret, ad [ea] tanto plus cogitur talis huiusmodi operare, ut earum voluntas frangatur et natura. Et [ad] hoc confirmandum Hedwigis de Wratislauia iurata dixit, quod inter eas existens semel invenit erucam inter olera coctam, quam cum naturaliter horret, incitaverunt eam, ut ipsam comederet et suam naturam vinceret, quod tamen non fecit, sed flendo earum conatum evasit. Item Adelheidis iurata dixit: de catta mortua inuenta in platea per quandam ad earum coaccionem excoriandam, quod cum illa ex horrore nature facere dissimularet, cogerunt eam tandem arvinam, que esse poterat in catta, exprimere, seu excipere et cum ea ipsarum calceos inungere et pellem super forum venalem portare, ut magis vinceretur in ea horror naturalis; et hoc accidit in Stroszburg. Item Adilheydis iurata dixit, quod audivit ab illo genere hominum scilicet a begardis eis familiaribus, cum locuntur de summa Trinitate, quantum possibile est homini de hoc loqui, ut dicunt vnus alium interrogans: scis uel intelligis aliquid de hoc sensu; alter quispiam respondens dicit: scio, et in tantum sanctam Trinitatem in potestate habeo, quod equito eam veluti sellam dextrarii. Item eadem Adilheydis iurata dixit, se scire de certa sciencia, quod cum alique, que dicuntur perfecte inter eas et ad plenum exercitate exeunt ab earum congregacione, ad libertatem, ut dicunt, spiritus veniendo, tunc luxuriantur omni tempore nullam differenciam temporis oportunitate habita faciendo cum Beghardis commeduntque carnes in vigiliis apostolorum et sextis feriis, vbi hoc commode possunt perficere, nec de hoc conteruntur, nec confitentur conscienciam de hoc penitus non habendo, eademque iurata dicit, quod inter tales Beghardos et huiusmodi mulieres portantes ymaginem sanctitatis maxime et artissime paupertatis committuntur opportunitate nacta quasi omnia genera peccatorum Sodomiticorum et inmundiciarum, hec dicit de certa sciencia, quia audivit ab illa, cui talia acciderunt, et eciam de certo ab alys est experta, quod abutuntur [243] se mutuo lateraliter et in anum tangentes se mutuo impudice et lingvas suas in ora sua ad invicem pre delectacione mittentes oportunitate habita eciam in ecclesia sive infra sermonem sive Missam sive alia divina officia celebrata; dicit eciam iurata, quod ad hanc opinionem, quod huiusmodi factum nepharium fiat quasi licitum, induxerunt et inducunt huiusmodi homines scelestos, religiosos aliquos de approbatis ordinibus, prelatosque aliquos seculares ecclesiarum et sacerdotes. Item iurata dixit se hic in Sweydnicz in domo earum Beghardis ministrasse commedere et quod dicti Beghardi volebant postea aliqua ad ipsas loqui ista repellebantur ab aliis huiusmodi verbis: Recede hinc, hic non habes aliquid facere. Item Adelheidis dixit iurata, quod audivisset de ore Gertrudis de Ciuitate, que est inter eas hic, ista verba: Quando deus omnia creauit, tunc ego concreavi sibi omnia uel creavi omnia cum eo, et sum deus cum deo, et sum Christus, et sum plus. Item dixit iurata se audisse a Margaretha de Lichenaw, quod Christus ascendens et lignum sancte Crucis secum in celum assumpsit; ista contradicens, quod non, sed pro salute hominum asserens, quod in terris dimiserit, reprehensa fuit valde, quod esset grossa ancilla, habens sensum, qui non wlt sistere, sed omnia penetratre. Item eadem Adelheidis iurata dixit, quod Gerdrudis de Ciuitate asseruit se portare Eternitatem arietinam, et multis audientibus dixit. Item Anna ceca dixit, ut Adilheydis iurata dicit, se audisse de ore eius, quod infra XXti annos nunquam sit mentita, [neque] posset ad impacienciam incitari, licet multis verbis inpaciencie multas concitet ad impacienciam. Item iurata dicit, quod omnia, ad que coguntur respondere, involute respondent et sub glosis communiter omnes, et hanc doctrinam habeant et capiunt ab eadem Anna ceca et Gertrudi de Olzna. Item iurata et interrogata dicit, quod audivit magistram earum nomine, Helbig, dicentem: Nobilius opus, quod possum facere, est ut portem tynam cum fecibus seu ceruisia ultima per plateas, ut satis ordinem sororibus meis; et illa eadem operatur omni tempore, eciam Pascato, et ad hoc alias inducit, et que nolunt, ipsas persequitur. Item Adilheydis interrogata respondit se audisse a magistra et a Gerdrude de Ciuitate et ab Anna ceca pluries et ab aliis eciam communiter, quod essent in tali statu, quod omnia earum opera esent perfecta et esset oracio apud deum ipsarum vigilare, sicut dormire, commedere et bibere sicut ieiunare, ociari sicut laborare et in ceteris similiter. Item iurata dicit, quod cum in domo earum graviter infirmaretur cupiens communicare petensque, quod sacerdos cum sacra communione vocaretur, ipse ei responderunt: Tu toto anno confiteris et communicas, non sufficit tibi, credis, quod immundum sacerdotem velimus vocare propter te et dare sibi denarios; tu paupertati non tantum profecisti, quod paupertas debeat vel velit facere pro te hoc; at illa cum econtrario responderet: Certe ego desidero sumere corpus Christi, nec sine eo in infirmitate mea esse possum vel valeo; e contrario ille responderunt: Tu debes te dimittere; intendentes, quod deberet sine communione mori. Cumque quedam miserta diceret: Refollicemus pauperculam aliquantulum et infirmam; alie econtrario dixerunt: Dimittas dyabolum mori, ut paupertas expurgetur. De flagellis vero dicit iurata et interrogata, ut Hedwigis. Item Adilheydis iurata dicit, quod audivit ab eis in Aquisgrani, quod asseruerunt Christum habere duo esse: vnum divinitatis et aliud humanitatis; quibus auditis iuvencule earum statim dixerunt: Et nos habiture sumus duplex esse; asserueruntque ibidem vnam in Trinitate personam fore corpus Christi, aliam animam eius, terciam divinitatem ipsius. Suntque ipsa testante talis condicionis, quod quidquid senciunt se intelligere, fidem circa hanc materiam et eius similes concipiunt, firmiter tenent, [244] nullatenusque dimittunt, sic in pertinacibus suis contemptibus, ut frequencius moriendo. Item iurata et interrogata dixit, ut testatur, se ab eis audisse in Sweydnicz asserciones huiusmodi temerarias: Nos sumus, que seruamus decem precepta. Nos sumus, qui sequimur sancti Spiritus consilia. Nos sumus, que vivimus secundum Ewangelium. Nos habemus veram fidem, quam coram regibus et principibus confiteri volumus et probare; dicuntque, quando aliquis incipiet insurgere contra ipsarum sectam, hoc esse signum novissimi diei certissimum et adventus Antechristi et perfeccionis earum consumacionis. Item iurata et interrogata testatur, quod, quando portatur Corpus Christi ad aliquem infirmum, inquirendo prius quo et ad quem portatur infirmum, mittunt illuc ex suis pallidas, exterminatas facies habentes, ut appareant coram hominibus religiose et spiritales, conmittentes eis, ut suadeant infirmis blandis sermonibus et pietatem pretendentibus, ut legent testamenta pro pauperibus, id est pro eis, suggerendo infirmis, quod melius faciunt legando testamenta pro eis, quam si hoc facerent quibuscunque sacerdotibus secularibus uel religiosis; et ad funera mortuorum mittunt similiter et eadem intencione et pro elemosinis tales personas religiosum vultum pretendentes; et addidit, cum esset inter eas et quando invitaretur veluti pauper ad prandium vel ad cenam ab aliquo cive uel civissa oneraverunt eam saccis iubentes eam, ut de cibariis sibi appositis subtraheret et pro eis, que asserunt se pauperes, portaret. Et, quando hoc contradicente consciencia facere noluit, repulerunt eam a loco, vbi prandere solita erat, scilicet ab vxore Hylfriti, civis Sweidnicensis, et aliam sibi substituerunt. Item iurata testatur, quod cum aliqua earum in infirmitate incepit agonizare, tunc loco «Credo» et aliorum bonorum operum, que agonizanti homini preponuntur, ut in fide stabilis perseueret, spem de misericordia dei firmam concipiat, et contricionem offense diuine habeat, replicant sibi omnem defectum et offensas, qus contra eas commisit, dum inter eas viveret. Item eadem iurata Adelheydis dicit, quod Heylbig de Molendino magistra earum dixerit: Quando Christus in celum ascendit, nonne duxit Corpus suum secum, quod hic tantum honoratur; tunc ipsa Adelheyd volebat de hoc instare, tunc Anna ceca prohibuit eam, ne verbis eius responderet. Item, Adelheydis ut dicit iurata, fuit magistra earum per dimidium annum. Item dicit iurata, quod audivit ab illo genere hominum, quod hic homo tantum posset proficere, quod inpeccabilis efficeretur et quod voluntas eius caperetur, sicut beate virginis; dicit eciam, quod iste, que sunt in perfeccione, non sunt humane subiecte obediencie, et deffendunt offertoria et dicunt, quod transcenderunt omnem obedienciam; hee sunt, que ab eis veniunt ad spiritum libertatis. Item dicit iurata, quod Capuciate dicunt, quod se exercere in actibus virtutis est hominis imperfecti, perfecti autem anima licenciat a se omnes virtutes. Item dicunt Capuciate, ut Adelheydis iurata dicit, quod ab intus tantum habent de divinitate et arce contemplacionis sue, quod non opportet assurgere, nec aliquam reverenciam exhibere corpori Christi, quod dicunt figuram esse, nec occupari de passione domini, et alia misteria incarnacionis. Item Adelheydis iurata dicit, quod in Mencz seniores, de secta earum coegerunt iuvenes, ut asseres mortuorum de omnibus ecclesiis domum portaverunt et cum digitis oportuit, quod carnes fetidas de asseribus deponerent, ut propter horrorem domarentur. Et quod iuvenes de ossibus capitum, scilicet de caluariis, commederent et biberent. Item iurata dicit, quod semel ipsa Adelheidis in Sweidnicz communicata fuit sine licencia magistre, tunc dixerunt ei: tu potuisses pocious ranam accepisse in os tuum, quam sine nostra licencia communicasse. Dicit eadem iurata, quod Gertrudis [245] de Ciuitate mutata semper veste sex diebus immediate sequentibus communicata fuit incipiendo in magna quarta feria. Item iurata dixit, quod in Colonia fuit quidam Beghardus, qui cum frigus habuit, ecclesias intrauit, et quascunque potuit ymagines furabatur et ignem de eis calefaciendo se. Item interrogata, vtrum talia timore, odio, vel rancore etc. respondit: amore fidei et veritatis. — Hee due examinate sunt eadem die, quo iuraverunt.

Katherina de Lypcz, tercia testis, que cum Capuciatis in Lypcz dimidio anno conversata fuit, iurata et interrogata de vita et moribus earum respondit, quod laborabant diebus dominicis et festivis, dicentes hoc non esse peccatum, ut pro pauperibus laborarent, nec necessitas coegit eas ad hoc, cum haberent omnia necessaria. Item iurata dixit, quod ibidem asseruerunt, quod sic talibus diebus laborare non esset confitendum, nec de hoc habenda esset consciencia. Item ibidem dixerunt ad eandem, ut iurata et interrogata asseruit: quidquid iubemus te, fac, et non peccabis, quia non iubemus te peccatum, quia deo facimus et congregacioni, quod facimus. Item Katherina iurata dicit, quod cum ibidem diceretur ab aliis, quod paucis plus quam virgini matri concessum esset, quod ad conductum earum in hora mortis Christus adveniret, ceteris vero sancti angeli mitterentur, quod dedignarentur, si ad conductum earum angeli venirent et non Christus in propria persona cum virgine matre, tante sanctitatis essent. Et hoc audivit in Lypcz a quadam nomine Elizabeth de Geytan; dicit quod audivit ab Anna ceca in Sweydnicz, que dicit: Multi sancti sunt in celo, quorum festum peragitur, ita merito festum alicuius hic in terris celebraretur, quia sancti aliqui peccaverunt, inter nos alique sunt, que nuncquam peccaverunt. Item iurata dicit, quod eedem ipsam ibidem docuerunt, quod de negligenciis in ecclesiis in remissione divini servicii commissis et de offensis contra eas commissis, quando diceret coram eis culpam suam, humiliter se prosternendo, et ipse parcerent sibi dicendo: Deus parcat tibi; quod ita esset absoluta, sicut sacerdos eam absolueret, nec hoc indigeret confiteri. Item Katherina iurata de interrogata dicit, ut Adelheydis, se multociens audisse, quod Capuciate dixerunt: si fas esset nos predicare, melius sciremus, quam multi sacerdotes vel doctores, quia ipsi vident in cuttibus faccarum, sed nos videmus ab intus. Item Katherina iurata dixit, quod cum venisset ad eas et mansisset XIIII^or diebus, dixerunt ei: Si iam morereris in voluntate manendi nobiscum, anima tua nunquam intraret purgatorium. Item dicit, quod habeant quibus obediant, dicuntque, quod, que eis non seruent obedienciam, de suo collegio dampnentur, hocque dicunt se habere a deo, quia a papa non habent. Item Katherina iurata et interrogata dicit, ul alie due: Hedwigis et Adelheidis, quod docent iuvenculas, quas ad earum sectam induxerunt: Totum, ad quod inclinamini, non debetis facere et quod abhominabile vobis videtur et contrarium debetis facere et hoc tam in cibo, quam in potu, quam in ieiunio, oracione, in vestibus et in ceteris omnibus. Item Katherina iurata dicit, quod cum ieiuniis, vigiliis et aliis modis se extenuauerint, percuciunt sibi venam in pede dicentes et docentes hoc, quod semper pallor in facie maneat et appareat, et facies exterminata videatur, quod est pro earum intencione conveniens, ut hominibus sancte videantur et religiose. Item iurata et interrogata [dicit, quod] persuadent iuvenculas ad earum sectam receptas domi manere, non adire ecclesias seu sermones, dicentes eas magis mereri, si domi laborant pro sororibus, et quod debeant credere, quod deus docebit et inspirabit eis domi, quidquid predicatur uel docetur in ecclesia, et sint earum oracionibus participes, sicut essent in Ecclesia. Item iurata dixit, quod dicunt: si homo non pecasset, deus nichi- [246] lominus incarnatus fuisset; et si deus esset incarnandus, aliqua de secta earum deberet se sic tenere, quod esset digna fieri mater Christi. Item Katherina eadem iurata et interrogata dixit, quod quandoque mittunt iuvenculas per vias earum castitati et pudicicie periculosas, et si alique timendo periculum sue pudicicie remurmurant, dicunt: Quare times, nichil tibi nocet, si quid tibi in via contingat. Item dicit iurata, quod suaserunt sibi et dixerunt, quod multo melius esset sibi domi laborare pro pauperibus dominicis diebus et festivis, quam in Ecclesia multas venias facere, et orare. Item iurata Katherina dixit, quod diebus dominicis vice balnei procuraverunt sudores pedum et corporis, aliquas herbas pro hoc vsu decoquentes, eisque decoctis vtentes, dicentes hoc hys diebus facere non fore peccatum, sed licitum, quia aliis diebus oportet laborare. Item dicit, quod cum super hys, que inmediate precedunt, haberet, conscienciam, ab eisque quereret, quomodo hoc confiteri deberet, responderunt, quod grossi sacci lanarum, que essent foris in mundo, deberent talia confiteri, ipse nichil facerent, quod confiteri oporteret, quia facerent pro deo et pauperibus. Item Katherina iurata dixit, quod modo isto anno in die sancte Marie Magdalene hic in Swidnicz Sophia filabat, Anna parabat lanam, ut neret eam die sequenti, Girdrudis de Olzna suebat, et modo in die Marie Magdalene est annus, quod ipse me vocaverunt, ut laborarem cum eis, et ego per totum diem ibidem suebam, et tunc dixerunt verba superius posita de sanctis. Item iurata dicit eas multa dicere de beata virgine, que egerit in templo purgando et alia opera servilia faciendo, et si hoc non fecisset, nunquam mater Christi effecta fuisset. Item Katherina iurata dicit: Beghardus de tali secta in Glogovia in ecclesia fratrum dixit ad eam, cum esset ibi sola: Si vicisti te et si superiores virtutes vite vicerunt inferiores, tunc primo perfecta es et de subtili spiritu, adhuc enim es de grosso spiritu, tunc quidquid accideret tibi in caritate dei, non noceret tibi in castitate, non haberes peccatum; et tacte mulieres per ipsos inpudice in mamillis et alibi cum certentur et erubescant, dicunt Beghardi et ipse Capuciate, quod hoc est grossi spiritus signum: non potuisti omnibus diebus vite tue tantum vti de spiritu, quod curialiter te haberes vel exhiberes te ad virum. Item Katherina iurata dixit, quod Capuciate dixerunt, quod earum oraciones valenciores sunt, quam oraciones sacerdotum. Si enim sacerdotes possunt Christum cohercere in panem, tunc nos ipsum possumus cohercere in cor. Et coram (s) oraciones earum precellunt oraciones omnium sacerdotum, quia sine peccato sunt et non faciunt peccatum; hoc audivit in Lypcz. Item interrogata per iuramentum, utrum odio, amore, timore vel rancore testificata sit, dicit, quod non, sed propter hoc, quia audivisset, quod esset bonum propter fidem dicere veritatem.

Margaretha pictrix quarta testis, que fuit inter Capuciatas, conversata fuit in Swidnicz medio anno et tribus septimanis, iurata et interrogata de vita et moribus ipsarum respondit, quod multociens viderit, quod ipse dominicis et festivis diebus laboraverunt, et quod dicunt: Nulla inter ipsas perfici potest, nisi plus prona sit ad faciendum opera pro ipsis sororibus, quam ire ad ecclesiam. Item iurata et interrogata dicit, quod ipsarum magistra vocatur Helbig, sine cuius licencia nusquam vadunt, nec audent ire. Item veniens ad eas Anna ceca precidit sibi crines, coram que et aliis genuflexit, dum sibi hoc fieret. Item iurata et interrogata dixit se audisse ab eis: Si aliquis vel aliqua haberet bolum panis in manu et diceret hec verba confeccionis (s) etc., quo facto reciperet illud intencione communicandi, tantum valeret et sumeret, [247] ac si a sacerdote communicaretur vel reciperet et hoc audivit ab eis in Swidnicz. Item dicit iurata, quod [audivit] ex parte earum, cum esset cum eis, quod dixerunt et asseruerunt aliquas fore inter se, que abdicatis omnibus voluptatibus in tanta subaccione sensualitatis et virium inferiorum sub racione viverent, sicut beata virgo; in tantum fuit beata virgo in corde eius adnullata, quod per sex septimanas nullam habuit deuocionem ab beatam virginem, nisi sicut ad aliam mulierem uel virginem. Item iurata dixit ab eis se audivisse, quod impeccabiles efficerentur peccato mortali. Item dixit iurata, quod asserunt: si esset mos, nos digniores essemus omni die Corpus Christi recipere, quam sacerdotes quicunque. Item dixit, quod docent et dicunt de visu et de cogitacionibus et huiusmodi in civitate vel extra ipsarum domum commissis esse confitendum, sed que intra domum ipsarum accidunt, de huiusmodi vero non, sed terminandum cum sororibus esse excipiendum, coram quibus super huiuscemodi dicunt culpas suas, hec ante manifeste docuerunt et asseruerunt, sed postquam sunt notate, dicunt, quod propter bonum continencie oportet eas aliqua, que non esset necesse, facere. Item dixit, quod asserunt filium beati Angustini ab ipso quesiuisse: Dic pater bone, quam magna est anima; et ille respondit, ut fingunt: Tam magna est, quod omnes sancti et angeli eam implere non possent, sed ipsa in deo omnia impleret; — filius: dic quam pulchra sit; pater: tam pulchra est, quod si sancti et angeli eius pulchritudinem et similitudinem quererent, tanto magis dissimiles essent; — filius: dic, quo vult anima; Augustinus: wlt in bonum finem, vbi efficietur inconprehensibilis, cum bonum comprehendet. Item dixit se audivisse ab eis dicentibus, quod vellent hominem instruere, si temptaretur a concupiscencia, quomodo si esset mulier, evaderet eam absque accessione ad virum; sed oportet semper esse duas. Quibus auditis Margaretha scandalisata hoc male, sive in malum sensum tendencia intellexit, et sensus malus dictorum verborum tali experimento habuit: quia cum ipsa semel esset multum perturbata, ab vna ipsarum fuit brachiis circumdata et talibus verbis allecta, quod mirabiliter fuit carne mota. Tunc circumdans eam dixit: Si velles michi consentire, vellem tibi aliqua secreta aperire, ad que esses apta, quod nuncquam haberes desiderium a nobis recedendi, et hec fuit Anna ceca. Et antique conveniunt in cellario exclusis iuvenculis; quid ibi faciant, ignorat. Item iurata, vtrum assererent secundum articulum, qui ponitur in Clementinis, vel aliquid ei simile, — De hereticis, Ad nostrum,[1] dixit se non audivisse ab eis tam expresse verba, sicut in isto articulo continentur, sed similia verba et appropinquancia huic sensui audivit, ut dixit, et facta consona huic oppinioni suspicatur ex hoc eas facere, quando conveniunt in cellario iuvenculabus exclusis ex nutibus precedentibus et annuicionibus et aliis gesticulacionibus multimodis et ex hoc, quod celant se et occultant se a iuvenculabus et prohibent sibi mutuo, ne revelentur iuvenculabus secreta ipsarum, per quod hoc habet, quod antique nullum ieiunium ecclesie tenent. Item dicit, quod dicunt, quod nunquam potest una ipsarum invita perfici, nisi si eciam innocens inculpatur, reddat se ream confiteaturque nocuisse, hanc dicunt viam compendiosiorem ad perfeccionem, talisque, ut asserunt, vita ipsarum digna efficitur. Item dicit, quod audivit ab eis, quod oportet ecclesie statuta observare et ordinaciones propter bonum conveniencie, ne prodantur, et earum conventiculum perturbetur, et quod dimitterent frequenter divina officia visitare et ecclesias, nisi propter bonum conveniencie, ut homines devocionem ad eas concipiant, ipsisque benefaciant. Item dicit, quando virgines alique inter eas, aut iuvenes mulieres racione pudicicie [248] timent sole per terras discurrere racione studii, ut ipse solite sunt facere, propter dehonestacionis ac oppressionis periculum, leviter hoc ferunt, et ut opinatur et audivit ab una puella inter eas, licet non nude, quod si violarentur, nichil curarent, quia nichil eis noceret. Item dicit, quod vbicunque congregantur Beghardi, semper alique de Sweidnicz aut de Wratislauia concurrunt ad eos pro doctrina et post reditum earum solent dicere de eis subditis suis: Talis homo — nominando eum aut eam — habet cum deo magnam familiaritatem et similitudinem et bene scit loqui de eo, tamquam homo nobilis, et deus bene potest opus suum perfici in eo et consequi. Item circa IVtum articulum in Clementinis, De hereticis, Ad nostrum, interrogata respondit, quod opinantur et dicunt propter vitam suam pauperem apostolis in celo equabuntur, nec aliquo modo eis erunt inferiores. Item dicunt, quod in earum vita quilibet debet [comedere] os porci racione necessitatis, ut quidquid possit habere, commedat collum gruis, ut se caute circumspiciat, quid et coram quo loquatur, et acciput bouis, ut equanimiter omnia sustineat

[1] c. 3. Clem. V. 3.

quecunque a sacerdotibus vel a religiosis ipsis inferantur. Alias enim, ut asserunt, perfici non possunt et reputant magnam inpungnacionem, si quid dicatur contra earum vitam. Item circa V et VI articulos in Clementinis, Ad nostrum, interrogata dicit, quod opinantur et dicunt, quod postquam homo excesserit, subplantaverit, sive subpeditaverit inferiora omnia et mundana, tunc dat se ad approximacionem, nuditatem et puritatem divinam et solam, nec curat amplius, quidquid in inferioribus viribus paciatur, quia spiritus ex hoc stans in arce sua non inficitur, nec mordetur, et tunc licenciant a se virtutum opera, quia tantum valet ex eis tunc dimittere, quantum fecere, et ostendunt se tales amplius, ac si non indigeant ieiunare vel orare. Et si faciunt, faciunt iuvenculabus in exemplum et tales sic, ut dicunt, omnia inferiora excedentibus oportet alias eis, ut dicunt, inferiores in omnibus deseruire necessitatibus, ne in altitudine contemplacionis sue retardentur. Item iurata dicit, quod dicunt, quando deus vult aliquod opus nobile operare in aliquo nobili homine, tunc talis in medio aliorum sedens surgit quantocius sequestrare se, eique similes similiter mox surgunt de medio cum tali homine seque sequestrando ad loca secreta, hocque non solum dicunt, sed eciam faciunt, sequestracione vero facta, quid faciant, ignorat ipsa et alie iuuencule vel neophite inter eas. Item circa VIII acticulum, quod dicunt, quod vel nichil vel quasi oportet nos facere, querere in humanitate, ex quo habemus deum in anima, et si faciunt Corpori Christi reverenciam, faciunt, ne ab hominibus notentur. Et concordancia facta vidit in Colonia opponi, quod ibidem in elevacione Corporis Christi et viri aliqui et femine ipsa notante minime solebant assurgere sive aliquam reverenciam exhibere. Item interrogata, utrum disputaciones et alia huiusmodi de religiosis domibus, que ponuntur in Clementinis, Cum de quibusdam sint inter eas,[1] respondit, quod sic. Item dixit, quod asserunt, quod mulier vel virgo, que confirmatur in vita in secta ipsarum, non est sui ipsius, sicut puer vnius anni, sed est communitatis. Item super 3° articulo per Adilheydim confesso interrogata respondit, quod dicunt et asserunt rem non nude debere confiteri, sicut acta est, sed si aliqua alteri confiteretur, quam cui ipse confitentur, possit esse libencius inacuta. Item dicit ad 4-tum articulum per Adilheydim confessum interrogata respondit ipsum totum esse verum, non debent earum iuuencule, ut docent eas, dicere in confessione: negligens fui vel neglexi divinum officium, nec ex [249] hoc deprehenduntur, si domi maneant, dum diuina misteria peraguntur. Item circa V-tum articulum per Adelheydim confessum interrogata dicit, quod docent talem proposicionem et alie deducunt eam plus, alie minus. Item dicit Beghardos dicere talem similitudinem: Si ego cogitavi facere ymaginem, si melior fit, quam cogitaueram, tunc superauit meam intencionem et meliorata est vltra eam, sic anima lucratur suo exercicio, quod melius, quam deus cogitauerit, efficitur, hoc consequitur ex accione propria

[1] c. 1. Clem. III. 11.

et conatu, meliorque efficitur, quam ex deo emanauerit, et tunc quiescit super arbore quadam, cuius nomen, qualiter ipsum nominent, ignorat. Interrogata, si beguine hanc opinionem sequantur et acceptent, respondit: verbum earum est eciam. Item interrogata de indiscretis exerciciis et doctrina, ut Hedwigis et Adelheydis protestantur, dixit, quod interfuit, quando percusserunt se cum pellibus de hericio et pectinauerunt carnem suam pectinibus fullonum, qui wlgariter Cartȳn dicuntur, verberantes se kathenulis acuatis et corrigiis nodosis et hec docent iuvenculas facere et suadent, de ieiuniis et aliis similiter, donec ex toto incorporantur eis, et tunc ducunt cum eis remissius esse agendum. Infirmis non miserentur, nec magna eciam necessitate vrgente decumbere eas permittunt; exemplum de Katherina de Gorlicz, quam infirmitate graui decumbere prohibuerunt usque ad terciam diem mortis sue; nec permittunt aliquam procurari sacramento corporis Christi, nisi in ea videant signa mortis, que se cognoscere putant. Item interrogata super primum articulum filiarum Vllindis ex ipsarum statutis de unione per Adilheidim confessum, quod ille est titulis earum, ut audivit, eciam licet non expresse audirect ab eis verba et doctrinam, ut Adelheidis testata est, tamen earum opera sunt dictis consona verbis, occupant enim subditas suas diversis laboribus diebus festivis et quandoque iubent, ut locione vasorum, eieccione sordium et aliis huiusmodi, per que impediuntur abstrahere se a divinis officiis et sermonibus, et que mandantur statuta per ecclesiam audire et si nunquam iubentur ire ad ecclesiam, hoc faciunt propter apparenciam, ut sub pelle agnina tegatur mens lupina, ymo quod peius est, quod asserunt et suadent, quod ille, que talia suadent et faciunt pro earum communitate, in caritate sunt deo magis proxime easque credere debere tantum gracie ex hoc percipere, sicut ex ire ad ecclesiam et audire sermones. Item circa illud, quod dixit Adilheidis de Beghardis, quod aliquando equitant secundum Trinitatem, dicit, quod Begine huiusmodi talia dicunt verba, ex quibus simplices magis in errorem labantur, quam edificantur, et scripturas aliquando peruerse exponunt. Exemplum: veri adoratores etc., sic exponunt: debere deum adorare sine labiis et sine lingua, hoc sit adorare in spiritus et veritate, et affirmant aput se quandam oracionem esse magis deo approximare facientem, quam Pater noster. Item interrogata super hoc, quod Adelheydis confessa fuit de inmundiciis, impudiciis ac sodomia exeuncium ab eis et usque ad libertatem spiritus veniencium dicit se talia audivisse ab aliis, sed non vidit, nisi quod suspicabatur talia de quodam cum quadam in osculis et in tactibus impudicis, ac in tenebris frequenter convenerunt et illa iacebat in lecto simulans se oculos dolere. Item interrogata super hoc verbo, quod Adilheydis confessa fuit et audivit a Gerdrude de Ciuitate, quod ipsa cum deo omnia creauit, dixit se frequenter audisse ab aliis de secta illa, sed non a Gerdrude et addit, quod affirmat, quod homo in congregacione divina possit beatam virginem precellere et opinatur se ipsos eam precellere, si tenent paupertatem voluntariam, sicut Christus, quem dicunt se tenere.

Interrogata super hoc, quod dicunt crucem sanctam cum Christo simul in celum ascendisse, ut Adilheydis iurata testatur, respondit, quod audivit eas [250] asserentes, quod Christo in celum ascendente non remanserunt in terra, nisi cruces latronum. Item audivit, ut eciam Adilheidis testatur, ab Anna ceca, quod non sit mentita tot annis et nec ad impacienciam prouocari, et a Gerdrude de Olzna et ab Heilbig de Praga, que est inter eas veluti Custos inter Minores et pecunias superfluas vnius domus, si sunt, defert ad aliam sue secte. Item dicit, ut Adilheidis, quod ad omnia, ad que respondere coguntur, respondent involute etc. Item de hoc, ut Adilheydis de nobiliori opere, quod se Helbig magistra earum asserebat posse facere etc. illius articuli testatur, ut Adilheidis. Item dicit de status earum perfeccione, qui talis est, prout asserunt, quod omnia earum opera sunt perfecta, et quod omnia earum opera sint quedam sublevacio in deum, ut oracio. Item addidit eas asserere, quod nunquam aliquis salutem consequitur, coadiutorio creaturarum, ut predicacionibus et aliis ordinacionibus ecclesiasticis et sacramentis, sed dicunt se ab intro sine aliquo exteriorum creaturarum auxilio qualicunque salutem consequi, et dicunt nunquam posse esse aliquam perfectam in presenti, nisi ad hoc perveniat, quod nullum sustentaculum habeat creature. Item interrogata, vtrum dicerent se non esse impacientes, respondit, quod sic. Item super XII articulo per Katherinam confesso, respondit, quod primam partem non audivit ab eis, sed vltimam, que est fides earum audivit a Gerdrude de Olzna. Interrogata, vtrum talia dixisset odio, timore etc. respondit, quod non, sed causa amoris, iusticie, fidei et veritatis. — Hee due sunt examinate in die Nativitatis beate virginis. Anno quo supra etc.

Cunegundis de Monsterberg quinta testis iurata et interrogata de vita et moribus Capuciatarum respondit, quod cum quereret ab eis in Wratislauia, si essent aliis sororibus meliores, responderunt, quod sic, quia haberent durissimam vitam et plus aliis perfectam. Item iurata dicit, quod suo tempore, quando fuerit inter eas, vni obedierunt, et magistre. Item iurata dicit, quod alias sorores appellant: saccus lanarum et palliatas. Item de flagellis testatur, ut alie. Item iurata dicit, quod XII eciam ebdomadibus fuerit inter eas in Wratislauia et licet pauperes reputarentur et appellarentur aput homines, tamen haberent omnia bona, ut ollas cum butyro et sagimine plenas et alia necessaria, et dicunt, quod melius est mendicare et domi laborare pro sororibus operari opera caritatis, quam in ecclesia orare medio tempore. Et quidquid proprii habent venientes ad eas ab earum proprietate et possessione et potestate deponunt, recedentibus ab eis non reddunt. Vnde sicut in potestate prioris aut Guardiania sunt res subditorum, ita est inter eas; ipsaque Cunegundis cum esset inter eas oportuit, si quandoque voluit extra domum aliqua necessitate ire, licenciam recipere, a magistra semperque metsecundam incedere. Item iurata dicit, quod, quando venit ad eas, oportuit facere promissionem obediencie, propriis renunciare et alia huiusmodi, que solent fieri in religionibus approbatis. Interrogata, utrum odio, amore etc., respondit: non, sed iusticie causa et veritatis.

Luthardis de Lypczke sexta testis iurata et interrogata de moribus et vita Capuciatarum et quanto fuerit inter eas, respondit: quod in Erfordia uno anno et in Lypcz 3-bus quartalibus anni. Item sub iuramento interrogata, respondit, quod magistra earum est Helbig in Sweydnicz. Item iurata et interrogata de titulo earum, quo intytulantur filie Vldillindis in unione respondit, quod Vdillindem bene audivit commendare, quod esset bona soror, et teneret alias ad deum, et non plus. Non testatur odio, amore, sed [251] iusticie causa etc.

Elizabeth de Stregouia septima testis iurata et interrogata de vita et moribus Capuciatarum respondit set in Swidnicz inter eas XI ebdomadibus fuisse. Item dicit, quod oportuit eam obedire eis et omnia vota in seculo per eam facta adnullata asseruerunt ex obediencia eis facta sive promissa. Item iurata dicit, quod ex verbis earum taliter sibi innotuit, quod non indigerent confiteri, si quid consciencie haberent de cibo, sive potu, sive nova vita, quam assumsisset, sed quidquid eis diceretur de hoc, vellent recipere. Item dixit, quod talibus verbis traxerunt eam ad se, per que sibi dabant intelligere, quod assumens vitam earum nunquam intraret purgatorium, et efficeretur superior omnibus viventibus in hoc mundo, swaseruntque sibi, ut oraret exulibus Christi vestigiis, ut daretur sioi gracia intrandi ad congregacionem ipsarum, et si veniret ad eas, vellent eam sanare in corpore et in anima, et postquam venit ad eas in voluntate vitam ipsarum assumendo flexis genibus coram eis, precidebant sibi crines, omnibusque propriis renunciauit, extenuerunt eam ieiuniis, vigiliis ac aliis exerciciis tam irracionabiliter, quod cum prius esset puella speciosa, parvo tempore fuit in tantum destructa, quod vix nuncquam recuperabit, nec de pane dando ei ad saturitatem et carnes nominatas per eas: Gotirschlagen fleysch, id est, per se mortuas, nec muscas abigunt de mensa, in estate, et si aliqua commedens aliquam vometur, dicunt famem, si quam patitur, debere eam pati propter deum. Item Corpus Christi sumere et ecclesias adire non permiserunt eam et alias iuxta ipsarum devocionem, sed iuxta suum beneplacitum, videlicet seniorum Capuciatarum. Item fatetur illam proposicionem: Omne contrarium tibi facito, et ad quidquid non inclinaris, facito; et large exponunt eam secundum eas et dicunt fieri debere, ut natura concuciatur. Item de flagellis dicit, sicut, alie. Item dicit, quod in diebus apostolorum et dominicis aliquando post vesperas, aliquando post conpletorium filabant uel lanam pro nendo parabant, cauendo tunc aduentum hominum, ne notarentur, pro posse suo. Item docent, quod homo debet se reddere culpabilem de quocunque, eciam si innocenter inculpatur. Item solite sunt dicere verba involuta et subtilia, profunda et alta, de Trinitate, que non intelligunt. Item oportuit eam interdum geniculare ante magistram et petere licenciam commedendi de pane ad saturitatem, que diu differens, tandem de modico dedit licenciam, nec aquam recentem bibere permisit sed turbulentam. Item iurata dixit, quod solent habere triplicem cervisiam: optimam, quam bibunt Seniores, quando eis videtur. Et iterum aliam valde bonam, quam bibunt Seniores eciam, et in fine bonam, quam bibit conventus, et postea habent turpem wlgariter nuncupando Glatwircze non coctam, quam dant pauperibus et civissis, dicentes se aliam non habere, quando visitantur per eas ciuissas, ut ipsis conpaciantur, et huiuscemodi occasione multas elemosinas percipunt. Causa iusticie et fidei hec testificatur.

Yliana octaua testis iurata et interrogata de moribus et vita Capuciatarum respondit, quod suprema magistra earum est Heylbig, quod Hedwigis de Wratislauia precidit sibi crines. Item dicit, quod iuvenis Margaretha docuerit eam Credo sic: Credo cum sancto Petro in deum patrem omnipotentem et cum sancto Andrea et in Ihesum Christum filium eius etc. Item dicit, quod Heilbig misit Margaretham de Lichenow in Erfordiam, et hoc audivit ab Hedwige de Wratislauia, et scit pro certo, quod debuit ibi manere vno anno. Dicit eciam, quod omnes tenent obedienciam magistre [252] et sine eius licencia nichil presumunt facere vel exire. Item iurata dixit se vidisse Annam cecam iracundam, Gerdrudim de Olzna inpacientem, tunc, quando licenciauerunt Hedwigim de Wratislauia. Testimonium non fert causa amoris, sed iusticie et fidei et precipue veritatis. — Iste quatuor precedentes examinate sunt in crastino Nativitatis B. M.

Margaretha de Nowo foro, nona testis, que coram inquisitore una cum Elizabeth de Monsterberg, quarum dictum subsequitur, in presencia mei subscripti notarii sanctam dei crucem manualiter tangentes anno, mense, indiccione et loco, quibus supra, III ydus Septembris de veritate dicenda, quemadmodum prime iuraverunt, que ambe examinate sunt eodem die. Margaretha inquit iurata de vita et moribus Capuciatarum respondit, quod per Katherinam quodam ipsa et Agnes de Rechyn, que est in Wratislauia, fuerunt seducte, quod promiserant eam sequi extra terram, primo accepto consilio a suo confessore retractauerunt, tunc ista Katherina, que est etiam modo in Wratislauia dixit ad eas: Vos retractastis et perdidistis tale factum et bonum, quod dubium est, vtrum umquam maneatis aput deum et magis bonum, quam umquam de cutibus boum possint vobis dicere vel tradere, et hoc accidit in Nouo foro. Et illa eadem Katherina, ut Margaretha retulit, non vult petere hospicium, sed indifferenter iacet in platheis et ubicunque. Item Margaretha iurata dixit, quod cum per yemem cum eadem Katherina ad hospicium esset recepta, festivis diebus dormiebat, ferialibus laborabat post omnes missas, cum super hoc reprehenderetur, non indigeo ibi esse, sed grossi homines, quia ego habeo tantum de deo, quod superfluit, et oportet me interim per forum vagari et alibi, ut deum pati possim. Et hoc predicat frater Theodorus de Curia ordinis Minorum, ut sibi dicebatur in Wratislavia.

Elizabet de Monsterberg decima testis, que fuit inter Capuciatas, iurata et interrogata dixit, quod Seniores quandoque sequestrauerunt se ab ea et ab aliis iuvenculabus, sed, quid fecerunt, nescit. Item mortuum pullum sustulit in plathea et asportauit ad eas, cum fuit cum eis, quia hoc credebat fieri. Item dixit, quod bonas tunicas portauerunt ad carnem, sed desuper semicincia.

Getrudis, quondam vxor Zacharie de Putrido ponte, vndecima testis iurata et interrogata dixit, quod vna ex Capuciatis, quam bene novit peperit puerum in domo sua, que cum quesivisset ab ea, quomodo pueros genitos occultarent, Capuciata respondit: Magistra nostra docet nos, quod adfuso rothe, in qua rota solemus lanam nehre, percuciamus eas in capite, sive in cerebro, Item dixit, quod eadem instruxit eam multa sortilegia et incantaciones, pro aliquibus desideriis consequendis et adversitatibus avertendis. Hec iuravit VII Ydus Septembris et fert testimonium vieritatis.

Anno domini M⁰CCC⁰XXXII⁰ indiccione XV⁰, III⁰ Ydus Septembris[1] in Refectorio domus fratrum Predicatorum in Sweydnicz subscripto in presencia mei Notarii subscripti et testium suprascriptorum multorumque aliorum virorum, quam eciam mulierum frater Iohannes de Swenkenfelt inquisitor hereticorum predictus coram se per citacionem subscriptas Capuciatas videlicet Gerdrudim de Olzna, Annam cecam, Gerdrudim de Civitate, Mechildim, Cunegundim, Gelam, [253] Zophiam, Hedwigim et Margaretham fecerat euocari. Que inquam coram ipso comparentes manualiter sanctam dei crucem tangentes iuraverunt, quemadmodum prime testes, iuraveruntque, quod omnem, quam scirent, veritatem vellent de se et aliis dicere.

Et Margaritha prima testis inter Capuciatas iurata et interrogata dixit, quod isto anno feria 4ta post Ramos palmarum venit ad congregacionem earum, quia Anna eius cognata deduxit eam de Gorlicz XII annorum puellam. Item veniendo ad eas in eius recepcione geniculavit coram eis et preciderunt sibi pylos, Margaretha de Lychenow, et receperunt ab ea votum, quod nunquam vellet ab eis recedere, sed obediens esse et paupertatem voluntariam cum eis tenere usque ad mortem. Item interrogata, si plebanus iuberet eam ire ad ecclesiam, aliquid aliudve de genere bonorum operum facere, et magistra prohiberet, — quid faceret, vel cui obediret; respondit, quod magistra prohibente, quod plebanus iuberet, facere non audet. Item secundum eam Heylbig est magistra, que in sui absencia instituit Gerdrudim de Olsna. Item dicit, quod non audet ire ad ecclesiam, nec ad alia

[1] d. 11 Septembris 1332.

officia divina sine licencia magistre vel ea contradicente. Item laboraverunt aliquando, ut asserit, dominicis diebus post vesperas filando lanam et pro nendo parando et repeciendo. Item Credo cum sancto Petro dicit se didicisse ab Anna ceca et vlterius Iulianam instrunxit. Item dicit, quod aliquando dominicis diebus iusserunt eam domi manere aliquibus laboribus ipsam occupantes dixerunt, quod ita bene domi oraret, sicut in ecclesia et tantum mereretur. Item proprium non habent, sed totum, quod habent, in potestate superiorum est. Item dixerunt, quod secta earum esset ordo, quod audiens promisit eam tenere. Item percussit se cum pellibus ericii et pectinauerunt eciam se cum carthonibus, sed alie verberaverunt se cum kathenulis acuatis et corrigiis nodosis. Item videtur sibi, quod audiverit ab eis, quod que in earum secta voluntatem haberet manendi et sic moreretur, quod nunquam intraret purgatorium; et hec examinata est eodem die, quo iuravit.

Gerdrudis de Ciuitate secunda de Capuciatis iurata et interrogata, dicit, quod inter eas XXIV-or annis fuerit. Item interrogata dicit, quod ab aliis sororibus differant, que laborant, quia ipse sunt de voluntaria paupertate, subiunxitque: heu perfecte non tenemus; sectam earum congregacionem nominat, sed dicit, quod non sit ordo. Item dicit, quod earum secta non sit statuta ab ecclesia, nec confirmata. Item iurata dixit, quod in secta nostra ita bene salvari possimus, sicut Predicator vel Minor, si ita bene vivimus et vervamus; dicit, quod nullum inimicum habeat in Sweydnicz. Item iurata et interrogata, utrum haberent inter se magistram dicit: habent inter se ancillam, sine cuius licencia non audent quoquam ire et volentes aliqua vel aliquid facere tunc dicunt: magistra, licencia michi ire ibi vel hoc facere; tunc illa respondet non: si, vult denegare licenciam, addendo: sed rogo te, bona, mane, uel si tibi bonum videtur, vade uel fac. Item dixit se sectam dictam in Sweydnicz [intrasse]. Item iurata dicit, quod nichil proprii habet, sed soror est inter eas, que dispensat bona habita inter eas comportata secundum earum necessitatem, si tamen aliqua causaretur necessitate, quod illi sorori non videretur esse necessitas, non consentiret tali. Item ad omnia interrogata per inquisitorem involute et quasi sub glosis respondit. Item interrogata, utrum nunquam dixisset: quando deus creavit omnia, cum eo omnia concreavi et sum deus cum deo etc. respondit: audivi predicare, sed [254] non multum vlterius docui. Item interrogata, utrum laborasset in feria IIIa Pentecostes, respondit, quod videretur sibi: sic. Item interrogata, utrum hoc fecerit ex necessitate paupertatis, dixit, quod non, sed propter necessitatem suorum. Item confessa est, quod audivit predicare: si homo non peccasset, nichilominus deus incarnatus fuisset, et hoc ulterius affirmavit coram aliis, sed tamen occulte.

Examinata ipso die Zophia tercia capuciata iurata et interrogata dicit, quod fuerit inter eas IVor annis in Sweydnicz; dixit, quod sic attraxerunt eam, quod vita earum esset melior, quam aliarum sororum, et sectam earum dicit congregacionem et non ordinem. Dicit eciam, quod habent magistram, nomen eius dicitur Heylbig, et quidquid ipsa deseruit, hoc non est suum, sed congregacionis, et quando voluerit alicubi ire, tunc oportet, quod a magistra recipiant licenciam. Audivit ab Anna ceca et a Gertrude de Olsna, quod Heilbig alias eciam esset magistra, sed Gertrudis de Olsna modo tenet vices loco Heilbig, que tenet eis capitulum sexta feria, in quo verberat eas cum corrigiis, flectunque genua coram magistra et dicunt culpam suam, tunc magistra parcit eis et tamen postea confitetur sacerdotibus. Interrogata, utrum congregacio earum esset bona, respondit: Magistra dicit, quod sit bona, sed ipsa nescit. Item dicit, quod isto anno feria IIII in ebdomada Pentecostes in camerula sedendo nerehebat. Item quod hoc aliis de secta videbatur non esse peccatum, licet sibi videretur. Item audivit ab eis, quod quicunque moreretur, si non habuerit animum ab eis recedendi, nunquam purgatorium subintraret. Item dixit, quod sine licencia magistre non confitentur, nec recipiunt Corpus Christi. Item a senioribus audivit: tu potes domi aliquid laborare, in quo plus mereretur, quam visitando ecclesiam. Item audivit a senioribus et a mediocribus, quod deus tantum dilexisset hominem, si non peccasset, nichilominus incarnatus fuisset. Item audivit ab eisdem, si propter aliquam causam Corpus Christi ad domum non portaretur, vellent in infirmitate se mittere de domo exportare et communicare et post communionem redire, et antequam domum abiurarent, pocius Corpore Christi perpetue carerent. Item dixerunt ei: Fac, quod te iubebimus et non peccabis, quia non iubemus te peccatum. Hec examinata est die, mense, anno quo supra.

Hedwigis de Strigouia quarta Capuciata, que fuit inter eas vno anno post festum beati Michaelis iurata et interrogata dicit, quod habeant magistram, et suprema est Heilbig, et modo Gerdrudis de Olzna preest, quam tamen non nominant magistram, sed sororem, dicit eciam, quod Gerdrudis de Ciuitate aliquando dixit verba, que non intellexit, quia profunda fuerunt. Item dixit in diebus festivis, aliquando filabant uel nerebant, sed diebus apostolorum et dominicis non audivit eciam ab ipsis: si homo non pecasset, deus tamen fuisset incarnatus. Item dicit, quod audivit a Cunegundi de Friburg, priusquam voluntarium paupertatem et sectam dimitterem, prius vellem mori, sic et sperarem, quod deus esset mecum. Et quidquid Hedwigis deservivit, hoc non fuit suum, sed communitatis. Item Hedwigis fatetur se audisse ex ore Gerdrudis de Olsna super hoc se iacticare, quod in Wratislauia in publico sermone surrexerit de predicanti verbum dei in faciem cunctis audientibus, qui aderant et audire poterant, dixeret: Vos mentimini. Item confitetur, quod congregacio earum non per papam nec per aliquem episcopum est confirmata, et tamen dicit se nescire, utrum in bono statu sit, an non; examinata die supra.

[255] Anna ceca quinta Capuciata iurata et interrogata dicit, quod fuerit inter eas XXVI annis et in Sweydnicz intrauit et magistra earum protunc vocabatur Geze, sed est mortua renunciavitque propriis, sed magistra pronunc est Helbig, que commisit magisterium Gerdrudi de Olzna. Congregacionem pauperum nominat sectam earum. Item dicit, quod titulus earum est in vnione filie Vdillindis. Item interrogata, si congregacio earum sit approbata, dicit, quod non; si approbata esset, diu emisissemus illum, per quem haberemus hoc. Item dicit, quod homo potest ita bene vivere in earum congregacione, quod salvaretur, Item dixit, quod quondam dixerit: Quidam sancti sunt in celo, quorum festum celebratur, aliqui sunt ita sancti in terris; sed si malum est, tunc amplius dimittere volo. Et statim mutavit verba sua dicens, quod nesciat, si umquam dixerit. Item fatetur se dixisse: Multa facimus propter bonum conveniencie, que sic non faceremus. Item dicit se velle portare penitenciam, quam posset preter uel excepta crucis signacione. Hee, tres videlicet Zophia, Hedwigis de Strigouia et Anna Ceca prescripte, examinate sunt II Ydus Septembris anno quo supra.

Nomen notarii publici dicitur: Nicolaus quondam Heynrici de Panckendorff miliario vno a Sweydnicz distans. Signum vero ipsius consuetum tali in forma habetis:

S. N.

Bibliography

I. SOURCES

Manuscript

Manchester: John Rylands Library:
200: Ubertino of Casale: *Arbor vitae*.

Munich: Staatsbibliothek:
CLM 311, 1329, 2714, 2936, 4144, 4386, 5137, 6603, 9558, 14216, 14959, 15177, 16225, 17541, 17796, 17833, 18930, 18931, 22373, 24156.

New York: Pierpont Morgan Library:
272, 402 — Prophetiae super Pontificis.

Paris: Bibliothèque Nationale, Collection Doat:
vols. 27, 28, 34, 35.

Rome: Biblioteca Angelica:
382, Peter John Olivi.
Expositio super Apocalypsim.

Biblioteca Vaticana:
Vat. Lat. 1025, Eckhart (last two) *Questiones Parisienses*.
Borghese 38, Peter John Olivi, *Postilla super Apocalypsim*.
Borghese 357, Borghese 358, Vat. Lat. 4986 — Peter John Olivi, *Questiones de evangelica perfectione*.
Vat. Lat. 1001, Peter John Olivi, *Postilla in Mattheum*.
Vat. Lat. 480, Peter John Olivi, *Super regulam fratrum minorum*.
Vat. Lat. 3824, Arnold of Villanova's works.
Vat. Lat. 5740, Arnold of Villanova, *Expositio super Apocalypsim*.
Borghese 190, *Liber de oneribus*.
Borghese 205, *Epistola Cyrilli* and other Joachist tracts.
Vat. Lat. 11906, Errors and extracts concerning Olivi's *Postilla* on the Apocalypse.

Printed

ABBEVILLE, GERARD OF, *Contra adversarium perfectionis Christianae* (ed. S. Clasen) AFH 31 (1938) 276–329; 32 (1939) 89–200.

ALLEN, H. E., *The English Writings of Richard Rolle* (Oxford 1931).
ALVARUS PELAGIUS, *De Planctu Ecclesiae* 2 vols. (Ulm 1474).
AMOROS, L. 'Aegidii Romani Impugnatio doctrinae Petri Johannis Olivi 1311–12' AFH 27 (1934) 399–451.
—— 'Series condempnationum et processum contra doctrinam et sequaces Petri Johannis Olivi' AFH 24 (1931) 495–512.
Archiv Česky (ed. F. Palacký) 6 vols. (Prague 1840–72).
ARNOLD OF VILLANOVA, *Obres Catalones* 2 vols. (Barcelona 1947).
AUGSBURG, DAVID OF, *Tractatus de inquisitione hereticorum* (ed. W. Preger) ABAW 14 (1879) 181–235.
AUVRAY, L., *Les Registres de Gregoire IX* 4 vols. (Paris 1896–1910).
BALUZE, S. AND MANSI, J. D., *Miscellanea* 4 vols. (Lucca 1761–4).
BALUZE, S., *Vitae paparum Avenionensium* 4 vols. (ed. G. Mollat, Paris 1914–1927).
BÄUMKER, K., *Contra Amauricanos* (Münster i W. 1926).
BAZIRE, J. AND COLLEDGE, E., *The Chastising of God's Children* (Oxford 1957).
BERGER, E., *Les Registres d'Innocent IV* (Paris 1884).
BERLIÈRE, U., 'Trois traités inédits sur les Flagellants de 1349' *Revue Bénédictine* 25 (1908) 334–57.
Bibliotheca Veterum Patrum vol. 25 (Lyons 1677).
BIHL, M., 'De tertio ordine S. Francisci in provincia Germaniae superioris sive Argentinensi syntagma' AFH 14 (1921) 138–98, 442–60; 15 (1922) 349–81; 17 (1924) 237–65; 18 (1925) 63–89.
—— 'Formulae et documenta e chancellaria Fr. Michaelis de Cesena (1316–1328)' AFH 23 (1930) 106–71.
BOGAERT, H. VANDEN, see Pomerius.
BÖHMER, H., *Analekten zur Geschichte des Franciscus von Assisi* (Tübingen, 1961).
BÖHMER, J. F., *Acta Imperii selecta* (Innsbruck 1870).
—— *Regista Imperii* (Innsbruck 1881–2).
BONAGRATIA OF BERGAMO, *Tractatus de Christi et Apostolorum Paupertate* (ed. L. Oliger) AFH 22 (1929) 323–35, 487–511.
BONAVENTURE, St., *Opera Omnia* vol. 8 (Quaracchi 1898).
BREZOVA, L., *De gestis et variis accidentibus regni Boemiae* (*Fontes Rerum Bohemicarum* vol. 5 ed. J. Elmer, Prague 1893).
Bullarium diplomatum et privilegiorum Romanorum Pontificum 24 vols. (ed. A. Tomassetti, Turin, 1857–72).
Bullarii Franciscani Epitome (ed. C. Eubel, Quaracchi 1908).
Bullarium Franciscanum (ed. J. Sbaralea and C. Eubel, Rome 1759–1904).
BURDACH, K. AND PUIR, P., *Briefwechsel des Cola di Rienzo* 5 vols. *Vom Mittelalter zur Reformation* II. (Berlin 1914–29).
Calendar of Close Rolls, Richard II, Henry IV (London 1895–1909).

Calendar of entries in Papal Registers relating to Great Britain and Ireland vols. IV–VI ed. W. H. Bliss and J. A. Twemlow (London 1902–4).
Calendar of Patent Rolls, Richard II, Henry IV (London 1921–32).
CALLEBAUT, A., 'Acta Capituli generalis Mediolani celebrati anno 1285' AFH (1929) 273–91.
CELANO, THOMAS OF, *Legenda S. Francisci* in *Analecta Franciscana* 10 (Quaracchi 1926).
CHIAPPINI, A., 'Communitas responsio Religiosi viri ad Rotulum Fr. Ubertini de Casale' AFH 7 (1914) 654–75 and AFH 8 (1915) 56–80.
Chronica regia Coloniensis (ed. G. Waitz, Hanover 1880).
Chronica 24 generalium. Analecta Franciscana 3 (Quaracchi 1897).
Chronicon Moguntinum (ed. C. Hegel, Hanover 1885).
Chroniken der deutschen Städte vom 14 bis 16 Jahrhunderts (Leipzig 1867–1917).
CLAMANGES, NICHOLAS OF, *De Corruptio ecclesiae statu* in *Fasciculus* II, 555–69.
CLARENO, ANGELO OF, *Expositio Regulae Fratrum Minorum* (ed. L. Oliger, Quaracchi 1912).
—— *Apologia pro vita sua* (ed. V. Doucet AFH 39 (1946) 63–200).
—— *Epistola Excusatoria* ALKG I (1885) 521–33.
—— *Historia septem tribulationum* ALKG II (1886) 106–64, 249–336.
COLLEDGE, E., *The Mediaeval Mystics of England* (London 1962).
Compilatio de novo spiritu in W. Preger, *Geschichte der deutschen Mystik im Mittelalter I* (Leipzig 1874) 461–9.
Concilium Basiliense 8 vols. (Basel 1896–1936).
CONINGTON, RICHARD, *Tractatus de paupertate Fratrum Minorum* (ed. A. Heysse) AFH 23 (1930) 57–107, 340–60.
CONRAD OF GELNHAUSEN, *Tractatus de congregando concilio tempore schismatis.* Martène and Durand, *Thesaurus II*, 1200–26.
CONRAD OF MEGENBERG, *Planctus ecclesiae in Germaniam* in R. Scholz, *Unbekannte kirchenpolitischen Streitschriften*, II, 249–345.
COSMAS OF PRAGUE, *Chronica Boemorum*, MGHS new series 2 (Berlin 1923).
COVILLE, A., *Le traité de la ruine de l'église de Nicholas de Clamanges* (Paris 1936).
D'ACHERY, L., *Spicilegium* 3 vols. (Paris 1723).
D'AILLY, PIERRE, Ecclesiological works in Gerson, *Opera II* (Antwerp 1706).
—— *Tractatus de materia concilii generalis* (ed. F. Oakley, *Pierre d'Ailly*, 244–342).
DELORME, F. M., 'Diffinitiones capituli generalis OFM Narbonensis' AFH 3 (1910) 491–504.
—— 'Textes franciscaines' *Archivio Italiano per la Storia della Pietà* I (1951) 179–218.
DENIFLE, H., 'Das Evangelium Aeternum und die Commission zu Anagni' ALKG I, (1885) 49–142.
—— 'Meister Eckharts Lateinische Schriften' ALKG I (1885) 417–615.

DENIFLE H. AND CHATELAIN, E., *Chartularium Universitatis Parisiensis* 4 vols. (Paris 1889–96).
DIETRICH OF NIEM, *De modis uniendi et reformandi ecclesiam in concilio universali* (ed. H. Heimpel, Leipzig 1933 as *Dialog über Union und Reform der Kirche*).
—— *De scismate, libri tres* (ed. G. Erler, Leipzig 1890).
DIGARD, G., FAUÇON, M., THOMAS, A. AND FAWTIER, R., *Les Registres de Boniface VIII* 4 vols. (Paris 1904–39).
DIGNE, HUGH OF, *De finibus paupertatis* (ed. C. Florovsky) AFH 5 (1912) 277–90.
DÖLLINGER, I. I. VON, *Beiträge zur Sektengeschichte* II (Munich 1890).
DOUAIS, C., *Documents pour servir à l'histoire de l'Inquisition dans le Languedoc* 2 vols. (Paris 1900).
DOUCET, V., 'De operibus manuscriptis Fr. Petri Ioannis Olivi in Bibliotheca Universitatis Patavinae asservatis' AFH 28 (1935) 156–97, 404–42.
DOUIE, D. L., 'Three Treatises on Evangelical Poverty by Fr. Richard Conyngton, Fr. Walter Chatton and an anonymous' AFH 24 (1931) 341–69, 25 (1932) 36–58, 210–40.
DUDIK, B., *Iter Romanum* vol. 2 (Vienna 1855).
DUPLESSIS D'ARGENTRÉ, C., *Collectio judiciorum de novis erroribus* 3 vols. (Paris 1775).
DYMMOK, R., *Liber contra XII errores et hereses Lollardorum* (ed. H. S. Cronin, WS 1922).
ECCLESTON, THOMAS OF, *Tractatus de Adventu Fratrum Minorum in Angliam* ed. A. G. Little (Manchester 1951).
ECKHART, J. G., *Corpus historicum medii aevi*, 2 vols. (Leipzig 1723).
ECKHART, MEISTER JOHANNES, *Die Deutschen Werke* (Stuttgart) Collected edition of all German writings, in progress. *Die Lateinischen Werke* (Stuttgart). Collected edition of all Latin writings, in progress.
EMDEN, A. B., *A Biographical Register of the University of Oxford until A.D. 1500* 3 vols.(Oxford 1957–59) .
ENNEN, L. AND ECKERTZ, G., *Quellen zur Geschichte der Stadt Köln* 6 vols. (Cologne 1869–79).
ESSER, K. AND HARDICK, L., *Die Schriften des hl. Franziskus Von Assisi* (Werl i W. 1951).
EYMERIC, N., *Directorium Inquisitorum* (Rome 1585).
—— *Directorium Inquisitorum* (Venice 1595).
FARAL, E., 'Les Responsiones de Guillaume de St. Amour' *Archives* 18 (1950–1) 337–95.
Fasciculi Zizaniorum, ed. W. W. Shirley, Rolls Series (London 1858).
Fasciculus rerum expetendarum et fugiendarum 2 vols ed. E. Brown (London 1690).
FINKE, H., *Acta Aragonensia* 3 vols. (Berlin–Leipzig 1908–22).

FINKE, H, *Acta Concilii Constantiensis* 4 vols. (Constance 1907–28).
FITZRALPH, RICHARD, *De Pauperie Salvatoris*, Bks. I–IV ed R. L. Poole together with Wyclif's *De dominio divino* (WS London 1890).
Fontes rerum Austriacarum, Abt. 1, *Scriptores* (Vienna 1855–1904).
Fontes rerum Bohemicarum (Prague 1873–92).
Fontes rerum Germanicarum (ed. J. F. Böhmer) 4 vols. (Stuttgart 1843–68).
FORSHALL, J. AND MADDEN, F., *The Wycliffite Bible* (Oxford 1850).
FOXE, J., *Acts and Monuments* 3 vols. (London 1684).
FREDERICQ, P., 'Deux sermons inedits de Jean du Fayt', *Bulletin de l'Academie Royale de Belgique, Classe des Lettres* (1903) 688–713.
—— *Corpus documentorum Inquisitionis haereticae pravitatis Neerlandicae* 4 vols. (Ghent 1889–1900).
FRIEDBERG, E., *Corpus iuris canonici* 2 vols. (Leipzig 1879–81).
FRIES, L., *Geschichte, Namen . . . der Bischöfe von Würzburg* 2 vols. (Würzburg 1848).
FUSSENEGGER, G., 'Littera septem sigillorum' AFH 47 (1954) 45–53.
—— 'Relatio commissionis in concilio Viennensi institutae ad decretalem *Exivi de paradiso* praeparandam' AFH 50 (1957) 145–77.
GAGUIN, R., *Compendium de Francorum gestis* (Paris 1500).
GAY, J., *Les Registres de Nicholas III* (Paris 1898–1938).
GERSON, JOHN CHARLIER, *Opera Omnia* 4 vols. (ed. Du Pin, Antwerp 1706).
—— *Oeuvres complètes* 5 vols. so far (ed. P. Glorieux, Paris 1960–3).
—— *Opera* 3 vols. (Nuremberg 1489).
Gesta archiepiscoporum Magdeburgensium, Continuatio MGHS 14.
GILES OF ROME, *De Postestate ecclesiastica* (ed. R. Scholz, Weimar 1929).
GLASSBERGER, NICHOLAUS, *Chronica. Analecta Franciscana* 2 (Quaracchi 1887).
GOLDAST, M., *Monarchia s. Romani imperii* 3 vols. (Frankfurt 1611–14).
GRETSER, J., *Opera Omnia* vol. 12 (Ingoldstadt 1612).
GUI, BERNARD, *Manuel de l'inquisiteur* 2 vols. (ed. G. Mollat, Paris 1926–7).
—— *Practica inquisitionis haereticae pravitatis* (ed. C. Douais, Paris 1886).
GUIBERT, J. DE, *Documenta ecclesiastica ad perfectionis studium* (Rome 1931).
GUIRAUD, J., *Les Registres d'Urbain IV* 3 vols. (Paris 1901–4); index 1929.
—— *Les Registres de Grégoire X* (Paris 1893–1906).
HARDT, H. VON DER, *Rerum Concilii Oecumenici Constantiensis* 6 vols. (Frankfurt 1697–1700).
HARTZHEIM, J. AND SCHANNAT, J. F., *Concilia Germaniae* 11 vols. (Cologne 1759–90).
HEFELE, J. VON AND LECLERCQ, H., *Histoire de Conciles* 8 vols. (Paris 1907–1921).
HERVAEUS NATALIS, *Liber de paupertate Christi et Apostolorum* ed. J. G. Sikes, *Archives* 12–13 (1937–8) 209–79.
HEYSSE, A., 'Circa materiam de usu paupere' AFH 10 (1917) 103–74.
—— Fr. Richardi de Conington OFM, *Tractatus de paupertate Fratrum*

Minorum et Abbreviatura inde a Communitate extracta AFH 23 (1930) 57–105, 340–60.

HEYSSE, A., 'Anonymi Spiritualis responsio "Beatus Vir" contra "Abbreviaturam" Communitatis' AFH 42 (1949) 213–35.

HILTON, WALTER, *The Scale of Perfection* ed. E. Underhill (London 1923).

HODGSON, P., (ed.) *The Cloud of Unknowing* (London 1934).

HÖFLER, C. A. C. VON, *Geschichtsschreiber der hussitischen Bewegung in Böhmen* in *Fontes Rerum Austriacarum*, Abt. I, *Scriptores*, vols. 2, 6, 7 (Vienna 1856–66).

HUS, J., *Historia et Monumenta Johannis Hus et Hieronymi Pragensis* 2 vols. (Nuremberg 1558).

—— *Tractatus de Ecclesia* ed. H. S. Thomson (Cambridge 1956).

—— *Tractatus Responsivus* ed. H. S. Thomson (Princeton 1927).

—— *Sermones de tempore qui collecta dicuntur* ed. A. Schmidtová (Prague 1959).

—— *Posiciones, recommendaciones, sermones* ed. A. Schmidtová (Prague 1958).

—— *On simony* (ed. and trans. M. Spinka in *Advocates of Reform* (London 1953) 196–276).

INNOCENT III, *Opera Omnia* in J. P. Migne, *Patrologia Latina* vols. 214–16 (Paris 1890).

JAFFÉ, P., *Regesta Romanorum Pontificum* 2 vols. (Leipzig 1885–6).

JANOV, M., *Regulae Veteris et Novi Testamenti* 5 vols. (Prague 1908–26).

JEAN DE BEL, *Chronique* 2 vols. (ed. J. Viard et E. Deprez, Paris 1904–5).

JOACHIM OF FIORE, *Liber Concordiae Novi et Veteris Testamenti* (Venice 1519).

—— *Expositio in Apocalypsim* (Venice 1527).

—— *Psalterium Decem Chordarum* (Venice 1527).

—— *Tractatus super Quatuor Evangelia* ed. E. Buonauiti (Rome 1930).

KNIGHTON, H., *Chronicon* 2 vols. (ed. J. R. Lumby) Rolls Series 92 (London 1889–95).

KÖRNER, H. (Cornerus), *Chronica Novella* in J. G. Eckhart *Corpus Historicum medii aevi* II, 431–1344.

LABERGE, D., 'Fr. Petri Ioannis Olivi OFM, tria scripta sui ipsius apologetica annorum 1283 et 1285' AFH 28 (1935) 115–55, 374–407; 29 (1936) 98–141, 365–95.

LANGENSTEIN, HENRY OF, Ecclesiological works in Gerson *Opera omnia* vol. II (Antwerp 1706).

LANGLAND, W., *The Vision of William concerning Piers the Plowman* 2 vols. (Oxford 1886).

LANGLOIS, E., *Les Registres de Nicholas IV* (Paris 1893).

Legendae S. Francisci Assisiensis saec. 13 et 14 conscriptae in *Analecta Franciscana* 10 (Quaracchi 1926–41).

LEMMENS, L., *Documenta Antiqua Franciscana* (I *Scripta Fratris Leonis*; II *Speculum Perfectionis*, Redactio I) (Quaracchi 1901).

Liber Rogeri Dimmock ed. H. S. Cronin, WS 1922.
LIMBORCH, P., *Liber Sententiarum Inquisitionis Tholosanae* (Amsterdam 1692).
LONGPRÉ, E., 'Questiones inédites de Maître Eckhart O.P. et de Gonsalve de Balboa OFM', *Revue Néoscolastique* 29 (1927) 69–85.
—— 'Le Quolibet de Nicholas de Lyre, OFM' AFH 23 (1930) 42–56
LOOMIS, L. R., *The Council of Constance* ed. J. H. Mundy and K. M. Wood (New York 1961).
LORRIS, GUILLAUME DE AND MEUN, JEAN DE, *Le Roman de la Rose* 5 vols. (ed. E. Langlois, Paris 1914–24).
LOSERTH, G., 'Beiträge zur Geschichte der hussitischen Bewegung' *Archiv für Österreichische Geschichte* 75 (1889) 333–413.
MACCARRONE, M., 'Una questione inedita dell' Olivi sull' infallibilita del Papa', *Rivisita di storia della Chiesa in Italia* 3 (1949) 309–43.
Magdeburger Schoppenchronik, Chroniken der Deutschen Städte vol. 7.
MANSI, J. D., *Sacrorum Conciliorum nova et amplissima collectio* vols. 22–32 (Venice 1778–98).
MARGUERITE OF PORÈTE, *Le Mirourer des Simples Âmes* ed. R. Guarnieri (Rome 1961).
MARSILIUS OF PADUA, *Defensor Pacis* ed. R. Scholz, (Hanover 1932).
MARTÈNE, E. AND DURAND, V., *Thesaurus novus anecdotorum seu collectio monumentorum* 5 vols. (Paris 1717).
—— *Veterum scriptorum et monumentorum amplissima collectio* 9 vols. (Paris 1724–33).
MATILDA OF MAGDEBURG, *Revelations, or the Flowing Light of the Godhead* trans. L. Menzies (London 1953).
MATTHEW OF CRACOW, *De squaloribus Romanae Curiae* in *Fasciculus II* (584–607).
MATTHEW OF PARIS, *Chronica Majora* (ed. H. R. Luard) Rolls Series vol. 6 (London 1882).
MAY, W. H., 'The confession of Prous Boneta', *Essays in Medieval Life and Thought presented in honor of A. P. Evans* (New York 1955) 3–30.
MIGNE, J. P., *Patrologia Latinae cursus completus* (Paris 1844–55).
The Mirror of Simple Souls ed. C. Kirchberger (London 1928).
MOLLAT, G., (ed.) *Lettres communes de Jean XXII* 16 vols. (Paris 1904–1946).
Monumenta conciliorum generalium saeculi 15 3 vols. (Vienna-Basel 1857–1886).
Monumenta Erphesfurtensia saec XII–XIV ed. O. Holder-Egger (Hanover and Leipzig 1899).
Monumenta Germaniae Historica, Legum Sect. IV, vols. 2–8 (Hanover 1896–1926).
Monumenta Germaniae Historica, Scriptores vols. 9, 15, 16, 20 (Hanover 1851–1896).

MOSHEIM, J. L., *De Beghardis et de Beguinabus* (Leipzig 1790).

NETTER OF WALDEN, T., *Doctrinale antiquitatum fidei Ecclesiae Catholicae* 3 vols. (Venice 1757).

NIDER, JOHN, *Formicarius* (Strasbourg 1516).

OCKHAM, WILLIAM OF, *Opera Politica* 3 vols. (Manchester 1940–63).

—— *Breviloquium* in R. Scholz, *Wilhelm von Ockham als politischer Denker*.

—— *Dialogus* in M. Goldast, *Monarchia* II (Frankfurt 1614) 398–957.

—— *Epistola ad Fratres Minores* in *Opera Politica* III, 1–17.

—— *An princeps* in *Opera Politica* I, 223–71.

—— *Octo questiones de potestate pape* in *Opera Politica* I, 1–221.

—— *Opus Nonaginta Dierum* in *Opera Politica* I (288–374) and II.

—— *Tractatus contra Benedictum XII* in *Opera Politica* III, 157–322.

—— *Tractatus contra Joannem* in *Opera Politica* III, 19–156.

—— *De imperatorum et pontificum potestate* ed. C. K. Brampton (Oxford 1927), R. Scholz *Unbekannte kirchenpolitischen Streitschriften* II, 451–80, and W. Mulder in AFH 16 (1923) 469–92, 17 (1924) 72–97.

OLIGER, L., 'Acta Inquisitoris Umbriae Fr. Angeli de Assisio contra stigmata S. Francisci negantem, contra Fraticellos aliosque' AFH 24 (1931) 63–90.

—— *Documenta inedita ad historiam Fraticellorum spectantia* AFH 3–6 (1910–1913); also published as separate work.

—— 'Bonagratia de Bergamo et eius Tractatus de Christi et Apostolorum paupertate' AFH 22 (1929) 292–335, 487–511.

—— 'Fr. Bertrandi de Turre processus contra Spirituales Aquitaniae (1315) et Card. Jacobi de Columna litterae defensiorae Spiritalium Provinciae (1316)' AFH 16 (1923) 323–55.

—— 'Die theologische Question des Johannes Pecham über die volkommener Armut' *Franziskanische Studien* 4 (1917) 127–76.

OLIVI, P. J., *Quaestio de infallibilitate Romani pontificis* (ed. M. Maccarrone) *Rivista di Storia della Chiesa* 3 (1949) 325–42.

—— *De renuntiatione Papae Coelestini V quaestio et epistola* (ed. L. Oliger) AFH 11 (1918) 309–73.

—— 'Epistola ad Conradum de Offida', ibid., 366–73.

—— *Quaestiones in Secundum librum Sententiarum* 3 vols. (ed. B. Jansen, Quaracchi 1922–6).

Oraculum Cyrilli ed. P. Puir in *Das Briefwechsel des Cola di Rienzo* pt. 4, 251–327.

PALACKÝ, F., *Documenta Mag. Joannis Hus* (Prague 1869).

—— *Urkundliche Beiträge zur Geschichte des Hussitenkrieges* 2 vols. (Prague 1872–3).

PATON, L. A., *The Prophecies of Merlin* 2 vols. (New York 1926–7).

PECHAM, J., *Tractatus tres de Paupertate* ed. C. L. Kingsford, A. G. Little, F. Tocco BSFS II (Aberdeen 1910).

PELSTER, F., 'Nikolaus von Lyra und seine Quaestio de usu paupere' AFH 46 (1953) 211–50.

PEZ, H., *Scriptores rerum Austriacarum* 3 vols. (Leipzig & Regensburg 1721–44).

PFEIFFER, F., *Deutsche Mystiker des vierzehnten Jahrhunderts* 2 vols. (Leipzig 1845–57).

POMERIUS, H., *De origine monasterii Viridisvallis* in *Analecta Bollandiana* 4 (1885) 263–322.

POTTHAST, A., *Regesta pontificum Romanorum 1198–1304* 2 vols (Berlin 1874–5).

PUIR, P., *Das Briefwechsel des Cola di Rienzo. Vom Mittelalter zur Reformation* (gen. ed. K. Burdach) II, 5 pts. (Berlin 1912–29).

—— *Cola di Rienzo, Darstellung seines Lebens und seines Geistes* (Vienna 1931).

QUINT, J., *Meister Eckehart. Deutsche Predigten und Traktate* (Munich 1955).

RAINIER SACCONI, *Summa de Catharis et Pauperibus de Lugduno* (1250), in (*a*) A. Dondaine, *Un traité neo-manichéen* (Rome 1939) 64–78; (*b*) *Max. Bib. Vet. Pat.* vol. 25 (Lyons 1677) 262–310.

RAYNALDUS, O., *Annales Ecclesiastici* 15 vols. (Lucca 1747–56).

Register of Henry Chichele ed. E. F. Jacob 4 vols. (Canterbury and York Society 1938–47).

Register of John Trefnant ed. W. W. Capes (Hereford 1914–15).

RIPOLL, T., *Bullarium ordinis Fratrum Praedicatorum* 8 vols. (Rome 1779–90).

Rotuli Parliamentorum vols. 3 and 4 (London 1832).

RUPESCISSA, JOHN OF, (Roquetaillade), *Vade mecum in tribulatione* in *Fasciculus II*, 496–508.

RUYSBROECK, J. VAN, *Oeuvres* (3rd edn. and trans. into French by the Benedictines of Wisques) 6 vols. (Brussels and Paris 1920–38).

RYBA, B., *Quodlibet* (Prague 1948).

SABATIER, P., *Speculum perfectionis seu S. Francisci Assiensis Legenda. Antiquissima auctore Fratre Leone* (Paris 1898).

—— *Le speculum perfectionis ou mémoires de frère Léone sur la seconde partie de la vie de Saint François d'Assise* I BSFS 13 (Manchester 1928): II BSFS 17 (Manchester 1931).

SACKUR, G., *Sibyllinische Texte und Forschungen: Pseudo-Methodius, Adso und die tiburtinische Sibylle* (Halle 1898).

SALIMBENE DE ADAM, *Chronica* ed. O. Holder-Egger, MGHS 32 (Hanover and Leipzig 1905–13).

SCHOLZ, R., *Die Publizistik zur Zeit Philipps des Schönen und Bonifaz VIII* (Stuttgart 1903).

—— *Unbekannte kirchenpolitische Streitschriften aus der Zeit Ludwigs des Bayern* 2 vols. (Rome 1911–14).

SEGARIZZI, A., *Historia fratris Dulcini heresiarche* in Muratori vol. 9, pt. v (Città di Castello 1907) 486–501.

SILVIUS, AENEAS, *Historia Bohemica* (Rome 1475).

Snappe's Formulary ed. H. E. Salter (Oxford 1924).

Statutes of the Realm vol. 2 (London 1816).

STEPHEN OF BOURBON, *Anecdotes historiques* ed. Lecoy de la Marche (Paris 1877).

STOLLE, K., *Memoriale thüringisch-erfurtische Chronik* ed. R. Thiele (Halle 1900).

STRAUCH, P., *Schriften aus Gottesfreundliteratur* 3 vols. (Halle 1927–9).

STUBBS, W., *Select English Charters* (9th edn.) (Oxford 1921).

STUMPF, A., *Historia Flagellentium praecipue in Thuringia*, ed. H. A. Erhard in *Neue Mitteilungen aus dem Gebiet historisch-antiquarischer Forschungen* II, ed. K. E. Förstemann (Halle 1835) 1–37.

SUSO, H., *Deutsche Schriften* ed. K. Bihlmeyer (Stuttgart 1907).

—— *Little Book of Eternal Wisdom* and *Little Book of Truth* (trans. J. M. Clark) (London 1953).

Swester Katrei, Meister Eckeharts Toher von Strâzburc ed. F. Pfeiffer in *Deutsche Mystiker des vierzehnten Jahrhunderts* II 448–75.

TAULER, J., *Predigten* complete edn. by G. Hofmann (Freiburg i Br. 1961).

Theologia Deutsch (published as *Das Buch vom Volkommenen Leben*) 2 vols. ed. R. F. Pfeiffer and K. F. Riedler (Zurich 1947).

THÉRY, G., 'Le Commentaire de Maître Eckhart sur le livre de la Sagesse' *Archives* 3 (1928) 321–443, 4 (1929) 233–394.

THOMSON, H. S., 'Four unpublished *Questions* of John Hus' *Medievalia et Humanistica* 7 (1952) 71–88.

TOCCO, F., *La quisitione della poverta nel secolo 14* (Naples 1914).

—— *Studii Francescani* (Florence 1909).

TONDELLI, L., REEVES, M. E. AND HIRSCH-REICH, B., *Il Libro delle Figure dell' Abbate Gioacchino da Fiore* 2nd edn. (Turin 1953).

TRITHEMIUS, J., *Annales Hirsaugiensis* 2 vols. (St. Gall 1690).

UBERTINO OF CASALE, *Arbor Vitae Crucifixae Jesus* (Venice 1485).

—— *Super Tribus Sceleribus* (ed. A. Heysse) AFH 10 (1917) 103–74 (see also ALKG vols. II and III).

ULANOWSKI, B., (ed.) *Examen testium super vita et moribus Beguinarum . . . in Sweydnitz. Scriptores rerum Polonicarum* 13 (1889) 239–55.

Vaticinia sive Prophetiae Abbatis Joachim et Anselmi Episcopi Marsicani (Venice 1589).

Vaticinium Sibillae Erithreae ed. O. Holder-Egger, *Neues Archiv* 15 (1889) 165–8, 30 (1904) 32–486.

VIDAL, J. M., *Bullaire de l'Inquisition française au XIVe siecle* (Paris 1913).

WADDING, L., *Annales Minorum* (2nd edn.; Rome 1731–45).

WALSINGHAM, THOMAS, *Historia Anglicana* vol. 2 ed. H. T. Riley, (London 1869).

WASMOD VON HOMBURG, *Tractatus contra hereticos Beckardos, Lulhardos et Swestriones* (ed. A. Schmidt) *Archiv für Mittelreinische Kirchengeschichte* 14 (1962) 336–86.

WATTENBACH, W., 'Über die Secte der Brüder vom freien Geiste' SPAW 29 (1887) 517–44.

—— *Über die Inquisition gegen die Waldenser in Pommern und der Mark Brandenburg (Philosophische und historische Abhandlungen der königlichen Akademie der Wissenschaft zur Berlin* 3 (1886) 1–102.

WEILAND, L., *Constitutiones et acta publica imperatorum et regum* MGH (Hanover 1896).

WILKINS, D., *Concilia Magnae Brittanniae et Hiberniae* 4 vols. (London 1737).

WILLIAM OF NANGIS, *Chronicon* with *Continuationes* 2 vols. (Paris 1843).

WINTERTHUR, JOHN OF (Vitoduranus), *Chronica* ed. F. Baethgen MGHS new series III (Berlin 1924; reprinted 1955).

WYCLIF, J., *De apostasia* ed. M. H. Dziewicki (WS 1889).

—— *De civili dominio* I ed. R. L. Poole; II and III (2 pts.) ed. J. Loserth WS (WS 1885, 1900, 1903–4).

—— *De dominio divino* ed. R. L. Poole (WS 1890).

—— *Dialogus sive speculum* ed. A. W. Pollard (WS 1886).

—— *De ecclesia* ed. J. Loserth (WS 1886).

—— *De officio regis* ed. A. W. Pollard and C. Sayle (WS 1887).

—— *De eucharistia* ed. J. Loserth (WS 1892).

—— *De potestate papae* ed. J. Loserth (WS 1907).

—— *De logica* 3 vols. (ed. M. H. Dziewicki, WS 1893–99).

—— *De ente: libri primi tractatus primus et secundus* ed. S. H. Thomson (Oxford 1930).

—— *De ente: librorum duorum excerpta* ed. M. H. Dziewicki (WS 1909).

—— *De ente praedicamentali* ed. R. Beer (WS 1891).

—— *Tractatus de logica* ed M. H. Dziewicki 3 vols. (WS 1894–9).

—— *De compositione hominis* ed. R. Beer (WS 1884).

—— *De veritate sacre scripture* ed. R. Buddensieg 3 vols. (WS 1905–7).

—— *De blasphemia* ed. M. H. Dziewicki (WS 1893).

—— *Opera minora* ed. J. Loserth (WS 1913).

—— *Miscellanea philosophica* ed. M. H. Dziewicki 2 vols. (WS 1901–2).

—— *Polemical Works* ed. R. Buddensieg 2 vols. (WS 1883).

—— *De benedicta incarnacione* ed. E. Harris (WS 1886).

—— *De simonia* ed. M. H. Dziewicki (WS 1898).

—— *Opus evangelicum* 2 vols. (WS 1895–6).

—— *Trialogus* ed. G. V. Lechler (Oxford 1869).

—— *Sermones* ed. J. Loserth 4 vols. (WS 1886–90).

—— *Select English Works* ed. T. A. Arnold 3 vols. (Oxford 1869–71).

—— *The English Works of Wyclif hitherto unprinted* ed. F. D. Matthew (Oxford 1880).

II. SECONDARY WORKS

AEGETER, E., *Les hérésies au moyen âge* (Paris 1939). Slight.

ALATRI, P. M. DA, 'Inquisitori Veneti del Duocento' *Collectanea Franciscana* 30 (1960) 398–452.

—— 'L'Inquisizione Francescana nell' Italia centrale nel sec 13' *Collectanea Franciscana* 22 (1952) 225–50; 23 (1951) 51–165.

ALPHANDÉRY, P., *Les idées morales chez les hetérodoxes au début du XIIIe siècle* (Paris 1903).

—— 'De quelques faits de prophetisme dans les sectes latines anterieures au Joachimisme' *Revue de l'histoire des religions* 52 (1905) 177–218.

—— 'Remarques sur le type sectaire dans l'hérésie médiévale latine' in *Transactions of the Third International Congress for the History of Religions* (Oxford 1908) 334–57.

—— 'Le gnosticisme dans les sectes médiévales latines' *Revue d'histoire et de philosophie religieuses* 7 (1927) 395–411.

ALTMEYER, J. T., *Les précurseurs de la reforme aux Pays-Bas* (Paris 1886).

AMATI, G., 'Processus contra Valdesi in Lombardia superiori, anno 1387' *Archivio Storico Italiano* ser. 3 (1865) pt. 1, 3–51, pt. 2, 3–61.

AMOROS, R. L., 'Aegidii Romani impugnatio Petri Joh. Olivi' AFH 28 (1935) 399–431.

ANAGNINE, E., *Dolcino e il movimento ereticale all inizio del Trecento* (Florence 1964).

ANCELET-HUSTACHE, J., *Master Eckhart and Rhineland Mysticism* (London 1959).

ARMAND HUGON, A. AND GONNET, G., *Bibliografia Valdese* (Torre Pellice 1953).

ASEN, J., 'Die Beginen in Köln' *Annalen des historischen Vereins für den Niederrein* 111 (1927) 80–180, and 112 (1928) 71–148.

ASTON, M. E., 'Lollardy and Sedition, 1381–1431' *Past and Present* 17 (1960) 1–44.

AUW, L. VON, *Angelo Clareno et les Spirituels Franciscains* (Lausanne 1952).

BAETHGEN, F., *Der Engelpapst* (Leipzig 1943).

BALTHASAR, K., *Geschichte des Armutsstreites im Franziskanerorden bis zum Konzil von Vienne* (Münster i. W 1911).

BANGE, W., *Meister Eckharts Lehre von göttlichen und geschöpflichen Sein* (Limburg 1937).

BARACK, K. A., 'Hans Böhm und die Wallfahrt nach Nicklashausen im Jahre 1476' *Archiv des historischen Vereins von Unterfranken und Aschaffenburg* vol. 15, 3 (Würzburg 1855) 1–108.

BARRACLOUGH, G., *Papal Provisions* (Oxford 1935).

BARTOŠ, F. M., 'Hus' Commentary on the Sentences of Peter Lombard' *Communio Viatorum* 3 (1960) 145–57.

Bartoš, F. M., 'Hus, Lollardism and Devotio Moderna' ibid., 247–54.

Bascour, D. H., 'La double rédaction du premier commentaire du Maître Eckhart sur la Genèse' *Recherches* 7 (1935) 294–320.

Baudry, L., 'A propos de G. d'Ockham et de Wyclef' *Archives* 12 (1939) 231–51.

—— 'La Lettre de G. Ockham au chapitre d'Assise' *Revue d'histoire franciscaine* 3 (1926) 185–215.

Becker, M. B., 'Florentine Politics and the Diffusion of Heresy in the Trecento' *Speculum* 34 (1959) 60–75.

'Beghards and Beguines' in *Dictionnaire de Spiritualité* 1, 1329–66.

Behagel, W., *Die Gewerbliche Stellung der Frau in mittelalterlichen Köln* (Berlin 1910).

Belperron, P., *La Croisade contre les Albigeois et l'union du Languedoc à la France (1209–49)* (Paris 1948).

Benrath, G. A., 'Wyclif und Hus' *Zeitschrift für Theologie und Kirche* 62 (1965) 196–216.

Benz, E., 'Creator Spiritus: Die Geistlehre des Joachim von Fiore' *Eranos-Jahrbuch* 25 (1956) 285–355.

—— *Ecclesia Spiritualis* (Stuttgart 1934).

—— 'Die Kategorien der religiösen Geschichtsdeutung Joachims' ZKG 50 (1931) 24–111.

—— 'Die Exzerptsätze der Pariser Professoren aus dem *Evangelium Aeternum*' ZKG 51 (1932) 415–55.

—— 'Die Geschichtstheologie der Franziskaner-Spiritualen des XIII und XIV Jahrhunderts nach neuen Quellen' ZKG 52 (1933) 190–221.

—— 'Thomas von Aquin und Joachim von Fiore' ZKG 53 (1934) 51–116.

Bernard, P. P., 'Jerome of Prague, Austria and the Hussites' *Church History* 27 (1958) 3–22.

—— 'Heresy in 14th century Austria' *Medievalia et Humanistica* 10 (1956) 50–67.

Bettoni, E. *Le doctrine philosofiche di Pier di Giovanni Olivi* (Milan 1959).

Betts, R. R., 'Correnti religiose nazionali ed ereticali dalla fine del sec XIV alla meta del XV' in *Movimenti religiose popolare ed eresie del medioevo* in *10 Congresso Internazionale di Scienze Storiche*, (Rome 4–11 Settembre 1955) *Relazioni* III, 485–513.

—— 'English and Czech Influences on the Hussite Movement' TRHS 21 (1939) 71–102.

—— 'Jerome of Prague' *University of Birmingham Historical Journal* 1 (1947) 1–91.

—— 'The great debate about universals in the universities of the fourteenth century' *Prague Essays*, (Oxford 1948) 69–80. See also p. 632 note 1 above.

—— 'Jan Hus' *History* 24 (1939) 97–112.

BETTS, R. R., 'The Place of the Czech Reform Movement in the History of Europe' *Slavonic Review* 25 (1946–7) 373–90.
—— 'Some Political Ideas of the Early Czech Reformers' *Slavonic Review* 31 (1952) 20–35.
BEUZART, P., *Les hérésies pendant le moyen âge et la reforme jusqu' à la mort de Philippe II (1598) dans la région de Douai, d'Arras et au pays d'Alleu* (Le Puy 1912).
BIERBAUM, M., *Bettelordern und Weltgeistlichkeit an der Universität Paris* (Münster i. W 1920).
BIGNAMI-ODIER, J., 'Les visions de Robert d'Uezès, OP (+1296)' AFP 25 (1955) 258–310.
—— *Études sur Jean de Roquetaillade (Johannes de Rupescissa)* (Paris 1952).
—— 'Travaux récents sur Joachim de Flore' *Le Moyen Âge* 58 (1952) 145–161.
BIHEL, S., 'S. Franciscus fuitne angelus sexti sigilli? (Apoc. 7, 2)' *Antonianum* 2 (1927) 59–90.
BIHL, M., 'Aventures du messager envoyé par les Spirituels de Narbonne et de Béziers au Chapitre Général de Naples en mai 1316' AFH 5 (1912) 777–9.
—— 'Disquisitiones Celanenses' AFH 20 (1927) 433–96, 21 (1928) 3–54, 161–205.
BISCARO, G., 'Guglielma la Boema e i Guglielmiti' *Archivio Storico Italiano Lombardo* 57 (1930) 1–67.
—— 'Inquisitori ed eretici Lombardi (1292–1318)' *Miscellanea di Storia Italiana* 3 serie, 19 (Turin 1922) 445–57.
—— 'Eretici ed inquisitori nella Marca Trevisana (1280–1308) *Archivio Veneto* 5 serie 11 (1932) 148–180.
—— 'Inquisitori ed eretici a Firenze (1319–34)' *Studi medievali*, new series, 2 (1929) 347–75, 3 (1930) 266–87, 6 (1933) 161–207.
BIZET, J. A., *Mystiques allemands du 14e siècle* (Paris 1957).
—— *Henri Suso et le déclin de la scholastique* (Paris 1946).
—— *Suso et le Minnesang* (Paris 1947).
BLOOMFIELD, M. W., 'Joachim of Flora. A critical survey of his canon, teachings, sources, biography, and influence' *Traditio* 13 (1957) 249–311.
—— AND REEVES, M. E., 'The penetration of Joachism into Northern Europe' *Speculum* 29 (1954) 772–93.
BOASE, T. S. R., *Boniface VIII* (London 1933).
BOCK, F., 'Studien zum politischen Inquisitionsprozess Johanns XXII' *Quellen und Forschungen aus italienischen Archiven und Bibliotheken* 26 (1935–6) 21–142; 27 (1936–7) 109–134.
—— 'Der Este-Prozess von 1321' AFP 7 (1937) 41–111.
—— 'Process di Giovanni XXII contra i Ghibellini italiani' *Archivio della Deputazione Romana di Storia Patria* 63 (1940) 129–143.

BOCK, F., 'Das Appellationsschriften König Ludwigs IV in den Jahren 1323/4' *Deutsches Archiv* 4 (1941) 179–205.

BOFFITO, P. G., 'Eretici in Piemonte al tempo del gran scisma (1318–1417)' *Studi e documenti di Storia e Dirito* 18 (1897) 775–92.

BÖHMER, H., 'Waldenser' in PRE 30 (1908) 799–890.

BONDATTI, G., *Giochinismo e Francescanismo nel Dugeno* (S. Maria degli Angeli-Portiuncula 1924).

BORST, A., *Die Katharer* (Stuttgart 1953).

—— 'Neue Funde und Forschungen zur Geschichte der Katharer' *Historische Zeitschrift* 174 (1952) 17–30.

BOUSSET, W., *Beiträge zur Geschichte der Eschatologie* ZKG 20 (1900) 103–31, 262–90.

BRANDT, W. J., 'Church and Society in the Late Fourteenth Century' *Medievalia et Humanistica* 13 (1960) 56–67.

BRECK, A. DU P., 'The Manuscripts of John Wyclyf's *De Trinitate*' (*Medievalia et Humanistica*) 7 (1952) 56–70.

BRÉHIER, E. *La Philosophie du moyen âge* (Paris 1937).

BROCK, P. DE B., *The political and social doctrines of the Unity of the Czech Brethren in the fifteenth and early sixteenth centuries* (Hague 1957).

BROOKE, R. B., *Early Franciscan Government* (Cambridge 1959).

BROWE, P., *Die häufige Kommunion im Mittelalter* (Münster i. W. 1938).

BROWN, S. M., 'Movimenti politico-religiosi a Milano ai tempi della Pataria' *Archivio Storico Lombardo* 6 serie 58 (1931) 227–78.

BRUNNER, G., *Ketzer und Inquisition in der Mark Brandenburg im ausgehenden Mittelalter* (Phil. Diss. Berlin 1904).

BÜCHER, K., *Die Frauenfrage im Mittelalter* (Tübingen 1909).

BÜTTNER, T. AND WERNER, E., *Circumcellion und Adamitem* (Berlin 1959).

BUJNOCH, J., *Hus in Konstanz* (Graz, Vienna, Cologne 1963); translation of Peter Mladoňovice's Chronicle.

BUONAIUTI, E., *Gioacchino da Fiore, i Tempi, la Vita, il Messagio* (Rome 1931).

—— 'Il messagio Giochimita e la Religio francescana' *Religio* (formerly *Ricerchi Religiosi*) 14 (1938) 86–109.

BURDACH, K., (ed.) *Vom Mittelalter zur Renaissance* (Berlin 1893–1937): Vol. II (ed. P. Puir) pt. I *Rienzo und die geistige Wandlungen seiner Zeit*; pts. 2–5 *Briefwechsel des Cola di Rienzo* (Berlin 1913–29); Vol. III pts. 1–3 *Der Dichter des Ackermann aus Böhmen und seiner Zeit* (Berlin 1917–32).

—— *Reformation, Renaissance, Humanismus* (Berlin and Leipzig 1926).

CALLAEY, F., *L'Idéalisme franciscain spirituel au XIVe siècle. Étude sur Ubertin de Casale* (Louvain etc. 1911).

—— 'Episode de l'Inquisition en Toscane (1323–4)' *Mélanges Ch. Moeller I* (Louvain 1914) 327–47.

CAPELLE, G. C., *Autour du décret de 1210 III: Amaury de Bène: étude sur son panthéisme formel* (Paris 1932).

CASSIRER, E., *Individuum und Kosmos in der Philosophie der Renaissance* (Leipzig 1927).

CHARLAND, T. M., *Artes Predicandi* (Paris and Ottawa 1936).

CHENON, E., 'L'hérésie à la Charité-sur-Loire et les débuts de l'Inquisition monastique dans la France du Nord au XIIIe siècle' *Nouvelle Revue historique de droit français et étranger* 40 (1917) 299–345.

CHENU, M-D., 'Orthodoxie et hérésie. Le point de vue du théologien' *Annales* 18 (1963) 75–80.

—— 'Moines, clercs, laics au carrefour de la vie évangélique' RHE 49 (1954) 58–89.

CLARK, J. M., *The Great German Mystics* (Oxford 1949).

—— *The Dance of Death in the Later Middle Ages* (Glasgow 1950).

CLASEN, S., *Der Hl. Bonaventura und das Mendikantentum* (Werl i W. 1940).

COHN, N., *The Pursuit of the Millennium* (London 1957).

COLLITZ, H., 'Das Wort Ketzer' *Neue philologische Mitteilungen* 40 (Helsinki 1939) 213–21.

COMBA, E., *Storia dei Valdesi* (1887; 4th edn. 1950).

COMBES, A., *Jean Gerson, commentateur dionysien* (Paris 1940).

—— *Essai sur la critique de Ruysbroeck par Gerson* 3 vols. (Paris 1945–59).

COMPSTON, H. F. B., 'The Thirty Seven Conclusions of the Lollards' EHR 26 (1911) 738–49.

CONGAR, Y. M-J., 'Aspects ecclésialogiques de la querelle entre mendiants et seculiers dans la seconde moitié du XIIIe siècle et le début du XIVe' *Archives* 36 (1961) 35–151.

Convegni del centro di studi sulla spiritualità medioevali: L'Attesa dell età nuova nella spiritualità della fine medioeva (Todi 1962).

CORVI, A., *Il processo di Bonifacio VIII* (Rome 1948).

COULTON, G. G., *The Inquisition* (London 1929).

—— *The Death Penalty for Heresy, 1184–1921* (London 1924).

—— *Inquisition and Liberty* (London 1938).

CREIGHTON, M., *A History of the Papacy during the period of the Reformation* vols. I and II (London 1907–9).

CROCCO, A., *Gioacchino da Fiore* (Naples 1960).

CROMPTON, J., 'Fasciculi Zizaniorum' *Journal of Ecclesiastical History* 12 (1961) 35–45, 155–65.

CRONIN, H. S., 'The Twelve Conclusions of the Lollards' EHR 22 (1907) 292–304.

CROWDER, C. M. D., 'Le concile de Constance et l'édition de Von der Hardt' RHE 57 (1962) 409–445.

CRUMP, C. G. AND JACOB, E. F., *The Legacy of the Middle Ages* (Oxford 1926).

DAHMUS, J., *The prosecution of John Wyclif* (New Haven 1952).

—— 'John Wyclif and the English Government' *Speculum* 35 (1960) 51–68.

d'Alverny, M. T., 'Les écrits historiques concernant la pauvreté Evangelique' *Positions de theses* Ecole de Chartes (Paris 1928).
—— 'Un fragment du procès des Amauriciens' *Archives* 25/26 (1950–1) 325–26.
Daniels, A., *Eine lateinische Rechtfertigungschrift des Meister Eckhart* (Münster i W. 1923).
Davis, G. W., *The Inquisition at Albi* (New York 1948).
Deanesly, M., *The Lollard Bible* (Cambridge 1920).
Debongnie, P., 'Devotion Moderne' in *Dictionnaire de Spiritualité* 3 727–47.
—— 'Les themès de l'Imitation' RHE 36 (1940) 389–444.
—— and Huijben, J., *L'auteur ou les auteurs de l'Imitation*' (Louvain 1957).
Deeley, A., 'Papal provisions and Royal Rights of Patronage in the early 14th century' EHR 43 (1928) 497–527.
Delacroix, H., *Essai sur le mysticisme speculatif en Allemagne au 14ᵉ siècle* (Paris 1900).
Delaruelle, E., Labande, E-R. and Ourliac, P., *L'Église au temps du Grand Schisme et de la crise conciliaire (1378–1449) Histoire de l'Église* vol. 14, 2 pts. (Paris 1962–4).
Delaruelle, E., 'La pietà popolare nel sec. XI' in *Movimenti religiosi popolari del medioevo, 10 Congresso Internazionale di Scienze Storiche* (Rome 1955), *Relazione III*, 309–32.
—— 'L'influence de saint François d'Assise sur la piété populaire' (ibid.).
—— 'Le Catharisme en Languedoc vers 1200' *Annales du Midi* 72 (1960) 149–67.
—— 'Les Grandes Processions de Pénitents de 1349 et 1399' in *Il movimenti dei disciplinati nel settimo centenario dal suo inizio* (Perugia 1960) 104–45.
Delorme, F. L., 'Un homonyme de St. Antoine de Padoue, inquisiteur dans la Marche de Trévise, vers 1300' AFH 8 (1915) 312–16.
Delpoux, C., 'Le Catharisme en Albigeois, La Croisade et l'Inquisition aux 13ᵉ et 14ᵉ siecles' *Cahiers d'Études Cathares* 18–19 (1954).
—— 'Les Cathars et l'Inquisition dans la région de Béziers' *Cahiers d'Études Cathares* 14 (1953).
Dempf, A., *Sacrum Imperium: Geschichts-und Staatsphilosophie des Mittelalters und der politischen Renaissance* (Munich and Berlin 1929).
—— *Meister Eckhart* (Leipzig 1943).
Denifle, H., 'Die Denkschriften der Colonna gegen Bonifaz VIII und die Cardinäle gegen die Colonna' ALKG iv, 493–529.
—— 'Meister Eckeharts lateinische Schriften und die Grundanschauung seiner Lehre' ALKG ii (1886) 417–615.
Denis, E., *Huss et la Guerre des Hussites* (Paris 1930).
Dickens, A. G., 'A Heresy and the Origins of English Protestantism'. *Britain and the Netherlands* ed. J. S. Bromley and R. H. Kossmann ii (Groningen 1964) 47–66.

DITSCHE, M., 'Zur Herkunft und Bedeutung des Begriffes Devotio Moderna' *Historisches Jahrbuch* 79 (1960) 124–95.

DMITREWSKI, M., 'Notes sur le Catharisme et l'Inquisition dans le Midi de la France' *Annales du Midi* 36 (1924) 294–311; 37 (1925) 190–213.

—— 'Fr. Bernard Délicieux OFM. Sa lutte contre l'Inquisition de Carcassonne et d'Albi. Son procès 1297–1319' AFH 17 (1924) 183–218, 313–37, 457–88; 18 (1925) 3–32.

DÖLLINGER, I. I. VON, 'Der Weissagungsglaube und das Prophetentum in der christlichen Zeit' *Historisches Taschenbuch* 5th series (1871) 259–370.

DOHNA, L. G. ZU, *Reformatio Sigismundi* (Göttingen 1960).

DONCKEL, E., 'Studien über die Prophezeiung des Fr. Telesforus' AFH 26 (1933) 29–104, 282–314.

DONDAINE, A., 'L'origine de l'hérésie médiévale' *Rivista di Storia della Chiesa in Italia* 6 (1952) 47–78.

—— 'Nouvelles sources de l'histoire doctrinale du Néomanichéisme au Moyen Age' *Revue des sciences philosophiques et théologiques* 28 (1939) 465–88.

—— 'Les Actes du concil albigeois de Saint Félix de Caraman' *Miscellanea G. Mercati* 5. *Studi e Testi* 125 (Vatican 1946) 324–55.

'La hiérarchie cathare d'Italie:

I Le *De heresi Catharorum in Lombardia*' AFP 19 (1949) 280–312; 20 (1950) 234–324.

II 'Le *Tractatus de hereticis* d'Anselme d'Alexandrie' 234–77 and 307–324.

III 'Catalogue de l'hiérarchie cathare d'Italie' AFP 20 (1950) 278–306.

—— *Un traité néo-manichéen de XIII*^e^ *siècle. Le Liber de duobus principiis* (Rome 1939).

—— 'Aux origines du Valdéisme. Une profession de foi de Valdès' AFP 16 (1946) 191–235.

—— 'S. Pierre Martyr. Études' AFP 23 (1953) 66–162.

—— 'Durande de Huesca et le polémique anti-cathar' AFP 29 (1959) 228–76.

—— 'Durande de Huesca controversiste' *10 Congresso Internazionale de Scienze Storiche* (Rome 1955) vol. 7 218–22.

—— 'Le Manuel de l'Inquisiteur (1230–1330) 'AFP 17 (1947) 85–194.

DOSSAT, Y., 'Le clergé méridionale à la veille de la croisade albigeoise' *Revue historique et littéraire du Languedoc* 1 (1944) 263–78.

—— 'La societé méridionale à la veille de la croisade albigeoise' (ibid.) 66–87.

—— *Les crises de l'inquisition toulousaine au XIII*^e^ *siècle, 1233–1277* (Bordeaux 1959).

DOUAIS, C., *L'Inquisition: ses origines, sa procédure* (Paris 1906).

—— 'Les sources de l'histoire de l'inquisition dans la midi de la France aux 13e et 14e siècles' *Revue de questions historiques* 30 (1881) 383–459.

DOUAIS, C. 'Le formule "Communicatio Bonorum Virorum Consilio" des sentences inquisitoriales' *Le Moyen Age* II (1898) 157–92.

DOUCET, V., 'Angelus Clarinus ad Alvarum Pelagium, *Apologia pro vita sua*' AFH 39 (1946) 63–200.

DOUIE, D. L., *The nature and the effect of the heresy of the Fraticelli* (Manchester 1932).

—— 'The Conflict between the Seculars and Mendicants at the University of Paris in the Thirteenth Century' Aquinas Soc., Paper 23 (London 1954).

—— 'John XXII and the Beatific Vision' *Dominican Studies* 3 (1950) 334–57.

DUHR, J., 'La confrérie dans la vie de l'Église' RHE 35 (1939) 437–78.

DUPARC, P., 'Confréries du Saint Esprit' *Revue historique du droit français et étranger* 36 (1958) 555–85.

DUPRÉ-THESEIDER, E., *Introduzione alle eresie medioevali* (Bologna 1953).

—— 'Problemi di eresiologia medioevale' BSSV 102 (1958) 3–17.

—— 'Fra Dolcino, storia e mito' ibid. 104, 5–25.

—— 'L'eresia a Bologna nei tempi di Dante (1319–34)' *Studi Medievali* N.S. 2 (1929) 347–75; 3 (1930) 266–87.

DURIEUX, P. F., 'La règle des Frères Mineurs et le Testament de Saint François d'Assise en Langue d'Oc du 14e siècle' *Études Franciscaines* N.S. 11 (1958) 204–27.

DVORNIK, F., *Les Slaves, Byzance et Rome au IXe siècle* (Paris 1926).

EHRLE, F., 'Zur Quellenkunde der alteren Franziskanergeschichte' *Zeitschrift für Katholische Theologie* 7 (1883) 323–52.

—— 'Die Spiritualen, ihr Verhältniss zum Franciscanerorden und zu den Fraticellen' ALKG I (1885) 509–69, II (1886) 106–64, 249–336, III (1887) 553–623, IV (1888) 1–190.

—— 'Zur Vorgeschichte des Concils von Vienne' ALKG II (1886) 353–416, III (1887) 1–195.

—— 'Petrus Johannis Olivi, sein Leben und seine Schriften' ALKG III (1887) 409–552.

—— 'Nikolas Trivet, sein Leben, sein Quodlibet und Questiones Ordinarie' in *Festgabe zum 70 Geburtstage Clemens Bäumkers* (Münster i W. 1923) 1–63.

EMDEN, A. B., *An Oxford Hall in Medieval Times* (Oxford 1927).

EMERTON, E., 'Fra Salimbene and the Franciscan Ideal' *Harvard Theological Review* 8 (1915) 480–503.

EMERY, R. W., *Heresy and Inquisition in Narbonne* (New York 1936).

ERBSTÖSSER, M. AND WERNER, E., *Ideologische Probleme des mittelalterlichen Pleberjetums. Die freigeistige Häresie und ihr sozialen Wurzeln* (Berlin 1960).

ESNAULT, R., 'Tracce ereticali nel medio evo francese' *Religio* 14 (1938) 18–53.

ESPOSITO, M., 'Sur quelques manuscrits de l'ancienne littérature religieuse des Vaudois du Piémont' RHE 46 (1961) 127–59.

—— 'Sur quelques écrits concernant les hérésies et les hérétiques au XIIe et XIIIe siècles' RHE 36 (1940) 143–62.

—— 'Un "Auto da fé" à Chieri en 1412' RHE 42 (1947).

ESSER, K., 'Franziskus von Assisi und die Katharer seiner Zeit' AFH 51 (1958) 225–64.

—— *Das Testament des Heiligen Franziskus von Assisi* (Münster i W. 1949).

—— 'Gestalt und Ideal des Minderbruderordens in seinen Anfangen *Franziskanische Studien* 39 (1957) 1–22.

EVANS, A. P., 'Hunting Subversion in the Middle Ages' *Speculum* 33 (1958) 1–22.

—— 'Social aspects of medieval heresy' *Persecution and Liberty. Essays in honour of G. L. Burr* (New York 1931) 93–116.

FARAL, E., 'Les Responsiones de Guillaume de Saint Amour' *Archives* 25–26 (1951) 337–95.

FAWTIER, R., *Ste Catharine de Sienne* 2 vols. (Paris 1921).

FIERTZ, G. B., 'An unusual trial under the inquisition at Fribourg (Switzerland)' *Speculum* 18 (1943) 340–57.

FINKE, H., *Aus den Tagen Bonifaz VIII* (Münster i W. 1902).

—— *Papsttum und die Untergang der Templerordens* (1907).

—— 'Walderprocess in Regensburg 1395' *Deutsche Zeitschrift für Geschichtswissenschaft* 4 (1892) 345–6.

FLADE, P., *Das Römischen Inquisitionsverfahren in Mitteldeutschland.* (Leipzig 1902).

FLICHE, A. AND MARTIN, R., *Histoire de l'Église* vols. 10–14 (Paris 1950–64).

FLICHE, A., THOUZELLIER, C. AND AZAIS, Y., *La Chrétienté Romaine 1198–1274. Histoire de l'Église* vol. 10 (Paris 1950).

FOBERTI, F., *Gioacchino de Fiore e il gioacchinismo* (Padua 1942).

FOLZ, R., *L'idée de l'Empire en Occident du 5e au 14e siècle* (Paris 1953).

FOREST, A., STEENBERGHEN, F. VAN AND GANDILLAC, M. DE, *Le mouvement doctrinale du IXe au* XIVe *siècle. Histoire de l'Église* vol. 13 (Paris 1953).

FOREVILLE, R., 'Manifestation de lollardisme à Exeter, en 1421' *Le Moyen Age* 69 (1963) 691–706.

FÖRG, L., *Die Ketzerverfolgungen in Deutschland unter Gregor IX* (Berlin 1932).

FOURNIER, P., *Études sur Joachim de Flore* (Paris 1909).

FRÉDEGAND, P., 'Le tiers-ordre de St. François d'Assise' *Études Franciscaines* 32 (1921) 360–82, 468–88, 34 (1922) 66–85, 195–210, 367–91, 538–61.

FREYHAN, R., 'Joachism and the English Apocalypse' *Journal of the Warburg and Courtauld Institutes* 18 (1955) 211–44.

FRIES, G. C., 'Patariner, Begharden und Waldenser in Österreich wärend des Mittelalter' *Österreichische Vierteljahresschrift für Katholisches Theologie* 9 (1872) 209–42.

FRISTEDT, S. L., *The Wycliffite Bible* I (Stockholm 1964).
FRUGONI, A., *Celestiniana* (Rome 1954).
—— 'Iacoponi Francescano' in *Iacoponi e il suo tempo* (Todi 1957) 75–102.
FUMI, L., 'L'inquisizione Romana e lo Stato di Milano' *Archivio Storico Lombardo* Seria 4 No. 13 (1910) 5–124, 285–414; 14 (1910) 145–220.
—— *Eretici e rebelli in Umbria* (Todi 1916).
GANDILLAC, M. DE, 'Tradition et développement de la mystique rhénane' *Mélanges de science religieuse* 3 (1946) 37–60.
GARVIN, N. J. AND CORBETT, J. A., *The 'Summa contra Haereticos' ascribed to Prepositinus of Cremona* (University of Notre Dame 1958).
GAUDEMET, J., *La collation par le roi de France des bénéfices vacants* (Paris 1935).
GEWIRTH, A., *Marsilius of Padua* 2 vols. (vol. 2 English translation of *Defensor Pacis*) (New York 1951–56).
GIBBS, M. AND LANG, J., *Bishops and Reform 1215–72* (Oxford 1934).
GIERKE, O., *Das deutsche Genossenschaft* 4 vols. (Berlin 1868–1914).
GLORIEUX, P., 'Guillaume de Saint Amour' in *Mélanges Mandonnet* I (Paris 1930) 51–81.
—— 'Pierre d'Ailly, Jean XXII et Thierry de Nieheim' *Recherches de théologie ancienne et médiévale* 31 (1964) 100–21.
GODEFROY, P., 'Ubertin de Casale' DTC 15 (ii) 2020–34.
GOLDAMMER, K., 'Der Naumberger Meister und die Häretiker' ZKG 64 (1952/3) 94–128.
GONNET, G., see also Armand Hugon.
—— *Enchiridion fontium Valdensium. Receuil critique des sources concernant les Vaudois au moyen âge du IIIe Concile de Latran au synode du Chanforan (1179–1532)* (Torre Pellice 1958).
—— *Il Valdismo medioevale, Prolegomeni* (Torre Pellice 1942).
—— 'Il movimento valdese in Europa secondo le pui recenti ricerchi (sec. XII–XIV)' BSSV 100 (1956) 21–30.
—— 'Waldensia' *Revue d'histoire et de philosophie religieuses* 33 (1953) 202–54.
—— 'Delle varie tappi e correnti della protesta valdese in Europa, da Lione a Chanforan' BSSV 102 (1957) 19–28.
—— 'Appunti sulle fonti de Valdismo medioevale' ibid. (1944) 33–43, and 82 (1944) 35–46.
—— 'Casi di sincretismo ereticali in Piemonte nei secoli XIV e XV' *Bolletino della Societa di Studi Valdesi* 108 (1960) 3–36.
—— 'I Valdesi d'Austria nella seconda meta del secolo 14' ibid. 111 (1962) 3–41.
—— 'Su alcuni aspetta della crisi religiosa nei secoli 15 e 16' ibid., 97 (1955) 79–91.
—— 'Portata e limiti dell' episcopato Valdesi nel medio evo' ibid., 104 (1958) 27–42.
GRABMANN, M., *Mittelalterliches Geistesleben* 3 vols. (Munich 1926–56).

GRABMANN., M, *Neuaufgefundene Pariser Quaestionen Meister Eckharts und ihre Stellung in seinem geistigen Entwicklungsgange* ABAW 32 no. 7 (1927).
—— (in honour of) *Aus der Geisteswelt des Mittelalters. Studien und Texte* ed. A. Lang, J. Lechner, M. Schmaus (Münster i W. 1935).
GRATIEN, P., *L'Histoire de la fondation et de l'évolution de l'ordre des frères mineurs au 13e siècle* (Paris and Gembloux 1928).
GRAUET, H. VON, 'Zur deutschen Kaisersage' *Historisches Jahrbuch* 13 (1892) 100–43.
GREVEN, J., *Die Anfänge der Beginen* (Münster i W. 1912).
GRUNDMANN, H., *Religiöse Bewegungen im Mittelalter* (Hildesheim 1961). (Together with supplement: *Neue Beiträge zur Geschichte der religiösen Bewegungen im Mittelalter*).
—— 'La mistica tedesca nei suoi reflessi popolari: Il Beghinismo' in *Movimenti religiosi popolari ed eresia del medioevo, 10 Congresso Internazionale di scienze Storiche* (Rome 1955) *Relazioni* III 467–84.
—— 'Kerzergeschichte des Mittelalters' in *Die Kirche in ihrer Geschichte, Ein Handbuch* ed. M. D. Schmidt and E. Wolf II (Göttingen 1963).
—— 'Die geschichtlichen Grundlagen der deutschen Mystik' *Deutsches Vierteljahresschrift für Literaturwissenschaft und Geistesgeschichte* 12 (1934) 400–29.
—— 'Der Typus des Ketzers in mittelalterlicher Anschauung' in *Kultur-und Universalgeschichte, Festschrift für Walter Goetz* (1927) 91–107.
—— *Studien über Joachim von Floris* (Leipzig 1927).
—— 'Kleine Beiträge über Joachim von Fiore' ZKG 48 (1929) 137–65.
—— *Neue Forschungen über Joachim von Floris* (Marburg 1950).
—— 'Dante und Joachim von Fiore' *Deutsches Dante-Jahrbuch* 14 (1932) 210–256.
—— 'Die Papstprophetien des Mittelalters' AKG 29 (1928) 77–138.
—— 'Das Liber de Flore' *Historisches Jahrbuch* 49 (1931) 33–91.
GUERRINI, P., 'Gli umiliati a Brescia' *Miscellanea P. Paschini. Lateranum* N.S. 14 fasc. 1–4, vol. I (Rome 1948) 187–214.
GUI, B., article on in *Histoire Littéraire de France* vol. 35 (Paris 1921) 139–232.
GUILLEMAIN, B., *La cour pontificale à Avignon* (Paris 1963).
GUIRAUD, J., *Histoire de l'Inquisition au moyen âge* 2 vols. (Paris 1935–8).
GWYNN, A., *The English Austria Friars* (Oxford 1940).
—— *Medieval Studies presented to Aubrey Gwynn* (ed. J. Watt et al., Dublin 1961).
HAHN, C., *Geschichte der Waldenser und verwandten Sekten* (Stuttgart 1847).
HAIMERL, F. X., *Mittelalterliche Frömmigkeit im Spiegel der Gebetbuch Literatur Süddeutschlands* (Munich 1952).
HALLER, J., *Papsttum und Kirchenreform* (Berlin 1903).
HAMMERICH, L. L., *The Beginning of the Strife between Richard Fitzralph and the Mendicants* (Copenhagen 1938).

HAMPE, K., 'Stilübung zur Ketzerverfolgung unter Kaiser Friedrich II' in *Festgabe für Friedrich von Bezold* (Bonn-Leipzig 1921) 142–9.

HANRAHAN, T. J., 'John Wyclif's Political Activity' *Mediaeval Studies* 20 (1958) 154–66.

HARDICK, L., 'Pecunia et denarii. Untersuchungen zum Geldverbot in den Regeln der Minderbrüder' *Franziskanische Studien* 43 (1961) 216–43.

HARING, N., 'Berengar's definitions of *Sacramentum* and their influence on medieval sacramentology' *Mediaeval Studies* 10 (1948) 109–46.

HARNACK, A., *History of Dogma* (trans. from third edition) 7 vols. (London 1894–99).

HASKINS, C. H., 'Robert le Bougre and the beginnings of the Inquisition in Northern France' *American Historical Review* 7 (1901–2) 437–57, 631–652; and in *Studies in Mediaeval Culture* (Oxford 1929) 299–345.

HAUCK, A., *Kirchengeschichte Deutschlands* 5 vols. (Leipzig 1954).

HAUPT, H., *Die Religiösen Sekten in Franken vor der Reformation* (Würzburg 1882).

—— 'Konrad Schmidt' in *Allgemeine Deutsche Biographie* 31, 683.

—— 'Beiträge zur Geschichte der Sekte vom freien Geiste und das Beghardentums' ZKG 7 (1885) 504–76.

—— 'Ein Beghardenprozess in Eichstädt vom Jahre 1381' ZKG 5 (1882) 487–98.

—— 'Zwei Traktate gegen Beginen und Begharden' ZKG 12 (1891) 85–90.

—— 'Zur Biographie des Nicolaus von Basel' ZKG 7 (1885) 508–11.

—— 'Beginen und Begharden' RPT vol. 2 516–26.

—— 'Zur Geschichte des Joachimismus' ZKG 7 (1885) 372–425.

—— 'Zur Geschichte der Geissler' ZKG 9 (1888) 114–19.

—— 'Brüder des freien Geistes' RPT vol. 2 567–72.

—— 'Kirchliche Geisselung und Geisslerbrüderschaften' RPT vol. 6 432–44.

—— 'Waldensiana' ZKG 10 (1889) 311–29.

—— 'Deutsche-Böhmische Waldenser', ibid. 14 (1894) 1–18.

—— 'Neue Beiträge zur Geschichte des Mittelalterlichen Waldenserthums' *Historische Zeitschrift* 61 (1889) 39–68.

—— 'Waldenserthum und Inquisition in südöst Deutschland bis zur Mitte des 14 Jahrhunderts' *Deutsche Zeitschrift für Geschichtswissenschaft* I (1889) 285–330, III (1891) 337–411.

—— 'Husitische Propaganda in Deutschland' *Historisches Taschenbuch* 6 (1888) 233–304.

—— 'Johann von Drändorfs Verurteilung durch die Inquisition zu Heidelberg' *Zeitschrift für die Geschichte des Oberrheins* N.F. 15 (1900) 479–93.

HEIMPEL, H., *Dietrich von Niem* (Münster i W. 1932).

HEYMANN, F. G., *John Žižka and the Hussite Revolution* (Princeton 1955).

—— *George of Bohemia* (Princeton 1965).

HEYMANN, F. G., 'The Hussite and Utraquist Church in the Fifteenth and Sixteenth Centuries' *Archiv für Reformationsgeschichte* 52 (1961) 1–16.
—— 'The National Assembly of Čáslav' *Medievalia et Humanistica* 8 (1954) 32–55.
HEYSSE, A., 'Descriptio codicis bibliothecae Laurentiae Florentiae S. Crucis plut 31 sin., cod. 3' AFH 11 (1918) 251–69.
HIGHFIELD, J. R. L., 'The English Hierarchy in the Reign of Edward III' TRHS 6 (1956) 115–38.
HILKA, A., 'Altfranzösische Mystik und Beginentum' *Zeitschrift für Romanische Philologie* 47 (1927) 121–70.
HÖDL, L., 'Die Lehre des Petrus Johannis Olivi von der Universalgewalt des Papstes' *Mitteilungen des Grabmann Instituts der Universität München* 1 (Munich 1958).
HOF, H., *Scintilla Animae* (Lund-Bonn 1952).
HOLDER-EGGER, O., 'Italienische Prophetien des 13 Jahrhunderts' *Neues Archiv* 15 (1890) 143–78, 30 (1904) 324–86, 33 (1907) 95–187.
HÜBNER, E., *Deutsche Geisslerlieder* (Berlin and Leipzig 1931).
HUCK, J. C., *Joachim von Floris und die joachisten Literatur* (Freiburg i Br. 1938).
HUIZINGA, J., *The Waning of the Middle Ages* (London 1955).
HURLEY, M., 'Scriptura sola: Wyclif and his critics' *Traditio* 16 (1960) 275–352.
HYMA, A., *The Brethren of the Common Life* (Michigan 1950).
ILARINO DA MILANO, 'Le eresie popolari del secolo XI nella Europa occidentale' *Studi Gregoriani* 2 (Rome 1947) 43–89.
—— *L'eresia di Ugo Speroni nella confutazione del maestro Vacario. Studi e Testi* 115 (Vatican 1945).
—— 'Il *Liber supra Stella* del piacentino Salvo Burce contro i Catari e altre correnti ereticali' *Aevum* 16 (1942) 272–319; 17 (1943) 90–146; 19 (1945) 281–345.
—— 'La *Manifestatio heresis Catarorum* quam fecit Bonacursus' *Aevum* 12 (1938) 281–333.
—— 'Fr. Gregorio O.P., vescovo di Fano, e la *Disputatio inter Catholicum et Paterinum hereticum*' *Aevum* 14 (1940) 85–140.
—— 'La *summa contra haereticos* di Giacomo Capelli OFM, e un suo *Quaresmale* inedito (sec. XIII)' *Collectanea Franciscana* 10 (1940) 66–82.
—— 'Episodio dell' Inquisizione francescana a Treviso' *Collectanea Franciscana* 5 (1935) 611–620.
—— 'L'Istituzione dell' Inquisizione monastico-papale a Venezia nel sec. XIII' *Collectanea Franciscana* 5 (1935) 177–212.
Il Movimentio dei disciplinati nel settimo centenario dal suo inizio (Perugia 1260). Deputazione di storia patria per l'Umbria. Appendici al Bollettino no. 9 (Perugia 1960).

JACOB, E. F., 'John of Roquetaillade' *Bulletin of John Rylands Library* 39 (1956–7) 75–96.
—— 'The Bohemians at the Council of Basel' in *Prague Essays* ed. W. Seton Watson (Oxford 1948) 81–123.
—— *The Fifteenth Century* (Oxford 1961).
—— *Essays in the Conciliar Epoch* (Manchester 1963).
—— 'Petitions for Benefices from English Universities during the Great Schism' TRHS 4th series 27 (1945) 41–59.
—— 'Reynold Pecock, Bishop of Chichester' British Academy Raleigh Lecture for 1951 (London 1953).
JANSEN, B., 'Die Lehre Olivis über das Verhältnis von Leib und Seele' *Franziskanische Studien* 5 (1918) 153–78, 233–58.
—— 'Die Seelenlehre Olivis und ihr Verurteilung aus dem Vienner Konzil' ibid. (1934) 297–314.
JOHN XXII, 'Jacques Duèse pape sous nom de Jean XXII' *Histoire Littéraire de France* vol. 34 (Paris 1914) 391–630.
JORDAN, E., 'Joachim de Flore' DTC 8 (ii) 1425–58.
JUNDT, A., *Histoire du panthéisme populaire au moyen âge* (Paris 1875).
KAEPPELLI, T., 'Une somme contre les hérétiques de S. Pierre Martyr (?)' AFP 17 (1947) 295–335.
—— 'Un processo contro i Valdesi di Pièmont-Giaveno, Coazze, Valgoie nel 1335' *Rivista di Storia della Chiesa in Italia* 1 (1947) 258–91.
KAEPPELLI, T. AND ZANOVÍC, T., 'Traités anti-Vaudois dans le ms 30 de la bibliothèque des Dominicains de Dubrovnik' AFP 24 (1954) 297–305.
KAMINSKY, H., 'Chiliasm and the Hussite Revolution' *Church History* 26 (1957) 65–103. I cannot agree with the assessment of the Free Spirit 59ff.
—— 'Hussite Radicalism and the origins of Tabor, 1415–18' *Medievalia et Humanistica* 10 (1956) 102–30.
—— 'Wyclifism as the ideology of revolution' *Church History* 32 (1963) 57–74.
KAMPERS, F., *Die Deutsche Kaiseridee im Prophetie und Sage* (Münster i W. 1896).
—— 'Die Geburtsurkunde der abländischen Kaiseridee' *Historisches Jahrbuch* 36 (1915) 233–70.
KÄMPF, H., 'Les Codices latini 4008, 4010 der Vatikanischen Bibliothek (aus der Kanzlei Michaels v. Cesena)' *Quellen u. Forschungen aus italienen Archiven u. Bibliotheken* 26 (1935–6) 143–171.
KANTOROWICZ, E., 'Zu den Rechtsgrundlagen der Kaisersage' *Deutsches Archiv für Erforschungen des Mittelalters* 13 (1957) 115–50.
—— *Frederick The Second. 1194–1250* (London 1957).
KARRER, O., *Meister Eckhart* (Munich 1926).
KELLY, P., 'Poverty and the Rhineland Mystics' *Downside Review* 74 (1956) 48–66.

KELLY, P., 'Meister Eckhart's Doctrine of the Divine Subjectivity' *Downside Review* 76 (1958) 65–103.

KERTZ, K. G., 'Meister Eckhart's Teaching on the Birth of the Divine Word in the Soul' *Traditio* 15 (1959) 327–64.

KERVYN DE LETTENHOVE, B., *Histoire de Flandre* 6 vols. (Brussels 1847–50).

KESTENBERG-GLADSTEIN, R., 'The Third Reich: A fifteenth-century polemic against Joachism and its background' *Journal of the Warburg and Courtauld Institutes* 18 (1955) 245–95.

KNOTH, E., *Ubertin von Casale* (Marburg 1903).

KNOWLES, M. D., *The Religious orders in England* vols. I and II (Cambridge 1948–55).

—— *The English Mystical Tradition* (London 1963).

KOCH, G., *Frauenfrage und Ketzertum im Mittelalter* (Berlin 1962).

KOCH, J., 'Der Prozess gegen die Postille Olivis zur Apokalypse' *Recherches de théologie ancienne et médiévale* 5 (1933) 302–15.

—— 'Die Verurteilung Olivis auf dem Konzil von Vienne und ihre Vorgeschichte' *Scholastik V* (1930) 489–522.

—— 'Philosophische und Theologische Irrtumslisten von 1270–1329' *Mélanges Mandonnet II* (Paris 1930) 305–29.

—— 'Der Prozess gegen Johannes de Polliaco' *Recherches de théol. anc. et méd.* 5 (1933) 391–422.

—— 'Kritischen Studien zum Leben Meister Eckharts' AFP 29 (1959) 5–51, 30 (1960) 5–52.

KÖPSTEIN, H., 'Fragen der hussitischen revolutionären Bewegung' *Zeitschrift fur Geschichtswissenschaft* (Berlin) 11 (1963) 146–67.

—— 'Über den deutschen Hussiter Friedrich Reiser' ibid. 5 (1959) 1068–82.

KROFTA, K., 'Bohemia in the fourteenth century' CMH 7, ch. 6, 155–82.

—— 'Bohemia in the fifteenth century', ibid. 8 ch. 3 65–115.

—— 'John Hus', ibid., 8, ch. 2, 45–64.

KYBAL, V., 'Etude sur les origines du mouvement hussite en Bohême: Matthias de Janov' *Revue Historique* 103 (1910) 1–31.

LAGARDE, G. DE, *La naissance de l'esprit laïque au declin du moyen âge* 6 vols. (St. Paul-Trois-Chateaux 1942–6) new edition appearing; so far vols. 1, 2, 4, 5.

—— 'Marsile de Padoue et Guillaume d'Ockham' *Revue des sciences religieuses* 17 (1937) 168–85, 428–54.

LAMBERT, M. D., *Franciscan Poverty* (London 1961).

LANGLOIS, C. V., 'Marguérite Porete' *Revue Historique* 54 (1894) 295–99.

LEA, H. C., *A History of the Inquisition* 3 vols. (London, New York 1888).

LE BRAS, G., 'Les confréries chrétiennes, problèmes et propositions' *Revue d'Histoire du droit français et étranger* 4th series 19–20 (1940–1) 310–63.

LECLERCQ, J., VANDENBROUCKE, P., BOUYER, L., *La Spritualité du Moyen Age* (Paris 1961).

LEFF, G., *Bradwardine and the Pelagians* (Cambridge 1957).
—— *Gregory of Rimini* (Manchester 1961).
—— 'Faith and reason in the thought of Gregory of Rimini' *Bulletin of John Rylands Library* 42 (1959) 88–112.
—— *Medieval Thought* (London 1958).
—— 'The Changing pattern of thought in the earlier fourteenth century' *Bulletin of the John Rylands Library* 43 (1961) 354–72.
—— 'Heresy and the decline of the medieval church' *Past and Present* 20 (1961) 36–51.
LEMMENS, L., *Der heilige Bonaventura, Kardinal und Kirchenlehrer aus dem Franziskanerordern 1221–74* (Kempten 1909).
—— 'Die Anfänge des Clarissenordens' *Römische Quartelschrift* 16 (1902) 93–124.
LITTLE, A. G., *The Grey Friars in Oxford* (Oxford 1892).
—— *Studies in English Franciscan History* (Manchester 1917).
LIZERAND, G., *Le Dossier de l'Affaire des Templiers* (Paris 1923).
LÖHR, G., 'Mendikanterarmut in Dominikanerordern' *Divus Thomas* 18 (1940) 385–427.
—— *Beiträge zur Geschichte der kölner Dominikanerkloster im Mittelalter* (Leipzig 1920).
LOSERTH, J., *Wiclif und Hus* (Berlin 1925).
LOSSKY, V., *Théologie négative et connaissance de Dieu chez maître Eckhart* (Paris 1960).
LÜCKER, M. A., *Meister Eckhart und die Devotio Moderna* (Leiden 1950).
LUNT, W. E., *Papal Revenues in the Middle Ages* 2 vols. (New York 1934).
—— *Financial Relations of the Papacy with England* 2 vols. (Cambridge Mass. 1939–62).
LÜTZOW, COUNT F., *The Life and Times of Master John Hus* (London 1909).
MACCARRONE, M., 'Riforma e sviluppo della religiosa con Innocenzo III' *Rivista di Storia della Chiesa in Italia* 16 (1962) 29–72.
MAČEK, J., '*Le mouvement hussite en Bohême*' (Prague 1958).
—— 'Villes et compagnes dans le hussitisme' (Czech Academy of Sciences pamphlet, Prague n.d.).
MCDONNELL, E. W., *The Beguines and Beghards in Medieval Culture* (New Jersey 1954).
MCFARLANE, K. B., *John Wycliffe and the Beginnings of English Nonconformity* (London 1952).
MCILWAIN, C. H., *The Growth of Political Thought in the West* (New York 1932).
MCKISACK, M., *The Fourteenth Century* (Oxford 1959).
MARTIN, V., *Les Origines du Gallicanisme* (2 vols. Paris 1909).
MAIER, A., 'Per la storia del processo contro l'Olivi' *Rivista di Storia della Chiesa in Italia* 5 (1951) 326–39.

MAIER, A., 'Zu einigen Problemen der Ockhamforschungen' AFH 46 (1953) 161–94.

MAISONNEUVE, H., *Études sur les origines de l'Inquisition* (Paris 1942; 2nd edn. 1960).

MALLARD, W., 'John Wyclif and the tradition of biblical authority' *Church History* 30 (1961) 50–60.

MANDONNET, P., *Les origines de l'Ordo de Poenitentia* (Fribourg, Switz. 1898).

—— *Siger de Brabant et l'Averroisme latin au XIIIe siècle* 2 vols. (Louvain 1908–11).

MANNING, B. L., 'John Wyclif' in CMH 7, 486–507.

MANSELLI, R., *Studi sulle heresie del sec. XII* (Rome 1953).

—— *La 'Lectura super Apocalipsim' di Pietro di Giovanni Olivi* (Rome 1955).

—— *Spirituali e Beghini in Provenza* (Rome 1958).

—— 'La Religiosità d'Arnaldo da Villanova' *Bulletino dell' Istituto Storico Italiano per il Medio Evo* 63 (1951) 1–100.

—— 'Per la storia dell' eresia catara nella Firenze del tempo di Dante' *Bulletino dell' Istituto Storico Italiano per il Medio Evo* 62 (1950) 123–58.

—— 'Per la storia dell' eresia nel sec. XII' ibid. 67 (1955) 189–264.

—— 'L'Anno 1260 fu anno Giochinitico?' *Il movimento dei disciplinati* (Perugia 1960) 99–108.

—— *L'eresia del male* (Naples 1963).

MARTIN-CHABOT, E., *La chanson de la croisade albigeoise* ed. et trad. E. Martin-Chabot (Paris 1961).

MARTINI, M., *Pierre Valdo. Le pauvre de Lyon. L'épopée vaudoise* (Geneva 1961).

MARX, J., *L'Inquisition en Dauphiné* (Paris 1914).

MATROD, H., 'Les Bégards' *Études Franciscaines* 37 (1925) 5–20, 146–68. Of no value.

MATTHEW, F. D., 'The trial of Richard Wyche' EHR 5 (1890) 539–44.

MAY, K. H., 'Zur Geschichte Konrads von Marburg' *Hessische Jahrbuch für Landesgeschichte* 1 (Marburg/Lahn 1951) 87–109.

MEERSEMAN, G. G., 'Pénitents ruraux communitaires en Italie aux XIIe siècle' RHE 49 (1954) 343–90.

—— *Dossier de l'Ordre de la Pénitence au 13e siècle* (Fribourg, Switz. 1961).

—— 'Disciplinati e Penitenti nel Duecento' *Il movimento dei disciplinati* 43–72.

—— 'Etudes sur les anciennes confréries dominicaines' AFP 20 (1950) 5–113, 21 (1951), 51–196, 22 (1952) 5–176, 23 (1953) 275–308.

MEIER, L., *Die Barfüsserschule zu Erfurt* (Münster i W. 1958).

MENENDEZ PELAYO, M., *Historia de los Heterodoxos Españoles* 3 vols. (Buenos Aires 1948).

MENS, A., *Oorsprong en Betekenis van de Nederlandse Begijnenen en Begardenbeweging* (Louvain 1947).

MERCATI, A., 'Fratre Francesco Bartoli d'Assisi Michaelista e la sua ritrattazione' AFH 20 (1927) 260–304.

MERCATI, G., 'Due ricerchi par la storia degli Umiliati' *Rivista di Storia della Chiesa in Italia* 11 (1957) 167–94.

MIERLO, J. VAN, 'Hadewijch, une mystique flamande au treizième siècle' *Revue d'Ascètique et de Mystique* 5 (1924) 269–89, 381–408.

—— 'Het Begardisme' *Verslagen en Mededeelingen der kon. Vlaamse Academie voor Taal en Letterkunde* (1930), 277–305.

—— 'Was Hadjewijch de Ketterin Blomardinne?' *Dietsche Waranden en Belfort* (Louvain 1908) 267–86.

—— 'Hadewijch an de Ketterin Blommardinne' *Tijdschrift voor neerlandsche Taal-en Letterkunde* 40 (1921) 45–64.

—— 'Hadewijch een gelukzalige Bloemardinne?' *Dietsche Warande en Belfort* 25, III (Louvain 1925) 28–49.

—— 'Over de Ketterin Blommardinne' *Verslagen en Medselingen der kon. Vlaamse Academie* (1927) 425–42.

—— 'Encore Hadewijch et Bloemardinne' *Revue Belge de philologie et d'histoire* 7 (1928) 469–510.

—— 'Les Beguines et Lambert di Beges' RHE 23 (1927) 785–91.

MOHR, W., 'Waldes und das frühe Waldensertum' *Zeitschrift für Religions-und Geistesgeschichte* 9 (Cologne 1957) 337–63.

MOLINIER, C., *L'Inquisition dans la midi de la France* (Paris 1880).

MOLLAT, G., *Les Papes d'Avignon au XIVe siècle* (9th edn., Paris 1950).

MOLNAR, A., 'L'évolution de la théologie hussite' *Revue d'histoire et de philosophie religieuses* 43 (1963) 133–71.

—— 'Le Vaudois et la réforme tchèque' BSSV 103 (1958) 37–51.

—— 'Luc de Prague et les Vaudois d'Italie' BSSV 90 (1949) 40–64.

—— 'Les responses de Jean Huss aux quarante-cinq articles' *Recherches de théologie médiévale et ancienne* 31 (1964) 85–99.

—— 'Deux homélies de Pierre Valdès?' *Communio Viatorum* 4 (1961) 51–8.

—— 'Hus' *De matrimonio* and its Waldensian version' (together with Hus's *De matrimonio*) ibid, 2 (1959) 142–57.

—— 'Želivsky, prédicateur de la révolution' ibid. 324–34.

—— 'Le mouvement préhussite et la fin du temps' ibid. 1 (1958) 27–32.

MORGHERN, R., *Medioevo Christiano* (Bari 1951).

—— 'Osservationi critiche su alcuni questioni fondamentali riguardanti le origini e i caratteri delle eresie medioevali' *Archivio della Deputazione Romana di Storia Patria* 67 (1944) 97–151.

—— 'Movimenti religiosi popolari nel periodo della riforma della chiesa' *10 Congresso Internazionale di Scienze Storiche* (Rome 1955) *Relazioni* III 333–56.

—— 'Le origini dell' eresia medioevale in Occidente' *Ricerchi di storia religiosa* 1 (1954) 1–24.

MORRALL, J. B., 'Ockham and Ecclesiology' *Medieval Studies presented to Aubrey Gwynn*, 481–91.

MORRALL, J. B., *Gerson and the Great Schism* (Manchester 1961).
—— 'Some notes on a recent interpretation of William of Ockham's political philosophy' *Franciscan Studies* (new series) 9 (1949) 335–69.
MORRIS, A., *The Christian Origins of Social Revolt* (London 1949). Of no value for medieval heresy.
MÜLLER, E., *Das Konzil von Vienne, 1311–12* (Münster i W. 1934).
MÜLLER, K., *Die Waldenser und ihrer einzelnen Gruppen* (Gotha 1886).
—— *Die Anfänge des Minoriten-Ordens und Bussbrüderschaften* (Freiburg i Br. 1885).
MUNDY, J. H., *Liberty and Political Power in Toulouse, 1050–1230* (New York 1954).
NANTES, R. DE, *Histoire des Spirituels dans l'Ordre de Saint François* (Paris (1909).
NARDI, B., *Saggi sull' aristotelismo padovano dal secolo 14 al 16* (Florence 1958).
NELLI, R. AND ROCHÉ, D., (eds.) *Spiritualité de l'hérésie: Le Catharisme* (Paris-Toulouse 1953).
NEUMANN, E. G., *Reinisches Beginen und Begardenwesen* (Meisenheim am Glan 1960).
NIEL, F., *Albigeois et Cathars* (Paris 1955).
NIGG, W., *Das Buch der Ketzer* (Zürich 1949): too general to be of value.
NOVOTNÝ, V., 'Les origines du mouvement Hussite en Bohême' *Revue de l'histoire des religions* 89 (1924) 77–90.
OAKLEY, F., 'Pierre d'Ailly and the Absolute Power of God' *Harvard Theological Revue* 56 (1963) 59–73.
—— *The Political Thought of Pierre d'Ailly: the Voluntarist Tradition* (Yale 1964).
ÖDIGER, F. W., *Über die Bildung der Geistlichen im späten Mittelalter* (Leiden 1953).
ODLOZILÍK, O., *Wyclif and Bohemia* (Prague 1937).
—— 'Wyclif's influence upon central and eastern Europe' *Slavonic Review* 7 (1928–9) 634–48.
OLIGER, L., 'Della inquisitione francescana in Toscana e nell' Umbria' *Studi Francescani* 3 (1931).
—— 'Beiträge zur Geschichte der Spiritualen, Fratizellen und Clarener in Mittelitalien' ZKG 45 (1926) 215–42.
—— *De Secta Spiritus Libertatis in Umbria saec. 14* (Rome 1943).
—— 'De origine regularum ordinis S. Clarae' AFH 5 (1912) 181–209, 413–447.
—— 'Spirituels' in DTC 14 (ii) 2522–49.
OPITZ, G., 'Über zwei Codices Zum Inquisitionsprozess' *Quellen und Forschungen aus italienen Archiven u. Bibliotheken* 28 (1937–8) 75–106.
OWST, G. R., *Preaching in Medieval England* (Cambridge 1926).
—— *Literature and the Pulpit in Medieval England* (Cambridge 1933).

PAHNKE, M., 'Eckhartiana II. Neue Texte aus dem Eckhartkreis' ZKG 56 (1937) 87–105.
PALACKÝ, F., *Geschichte von Böhmen* vol. 3 (Prague 1845).
PANTIN, W. A., *The English Church in the 14th century* (Cambridge 1955).
—— 'A Benedictine opponent of John Wyclif' EHR 43 (1928) 73–7.
PARTNER, P. D., '*Camara papae*; Problems of Papal Finance in the Later Middle Ages' *Journal of Ecclesiastical History* 4 (1953) 55–68.
—— *The Papal State under Martin V* (London 1958).
PASZTOR, E., 'Le polemiche sulla *Lectura super Apocalipsim* di Pietro di Giovanni Olivi fino alla sua condanna' *Bulletino dell' Istituto Storico Italiano per il Medio Evo* 70 (1958) 365–424.
PAULUS, N., *Geschichte des Ablasses am Ausgang des Mittelalters* (Paderborn 1923).
—— 'Boniface IX und der Ablasse von Schuld und Strafe' *Zeitschrift für Katholische Theologie* 25 (1901) 338–43.
PELSTER, F., 'Die Quaestio Heinrichs von Harclay über die zweite Ankunft Christi' *Archivio italiano per la storia della pietà* 1 (1951) 25–8.
—— 'Ein Gutachen aus dem Eckehart-Prozess in Avignon' *Aus der Geisteswelt des Mittelalters. Studien und Texte M. Grabmann* (Münster i W. 1935) 1099–1124.
PELZER, A., 'Les 51 articles de Guillaume d'Ockham censurés en Avignon en 1326' RHE 18 (1922) 240–70.
PERROY, E., *L'Angleterre et le Grand Schisme d'Occident (1378–99)* 1 (Paris 1933).
PESCHKE, E., 'Die Bedeutung Wiclefs für die Theologie der Böhmen' ZKG 54 (1935) 464–83.
PHILIPPEN, L. J. M., 'Les Béguines et l' hérésie albigeoise' *Annales de l'Académie Royale d'Archéologie de Belgique* 73 (1925).
PHILLIPS, D., *Beguines in Medieval Strasbourg* (Stanford University, California 1941).
PIERRON, J. B., *Die Katholischen Armen* (Freiburg i Br. 1911).
POU Y MARTI, J. M., *Visionarios, Beguinos, y Fraticellos catalanes (siglos XIII–XV)* (Vichy 1930); originally published *Archivo Ibero-Americano* 11 (1919), 12 (1919), 14 (1920), 15 (1921), 18 (1922), 19 (1923) 20 (1923), 21 (1924), 22 (1924), 23 (1925) 24 (1925), 25 (1926).
POUZET, P., 'Les origines lyonnaises de la secte des Vaudois' *Revue d'Histoire de l'Église de France* 22 (1936) 5–37.
POWER, E., 'The Position of Women' in *Legacy of the Middle Ages* ed. C. G. Crump and E. F. Jacob (Oxford 1926) 401–33.
PRA, M. DAL, *Scoto Eriugena ed il neoplatonismo medievale* (Milan 1951).
—— *Amalrico di Bena* (Milan 1951).
Prague Essays ed. W. Seton-Watson (Oxford 1948).
PREGER, W., *Über das Verhältnis der Taboriten zu den Waldesiern des 14 Jahrhunderts* ABAW 18 (1889) 3–111.

PREGER, W., *Beiträge zur Geschichte der Waldesier im Mittelalter* ABAW 13 (1875) 181–250.
—— *Der Traktat des Davids von Augsburg* ABAW 14 (1878) 181–235; see also under Augsburg, David of, 1(*b*).
—— *Geschichte der deutschen Mystik im Mittelalter* 3 vols. (Leipzig 1874–93).
—— *Beiträge zur Geschichte der religiösen Bewegung in den Niederlanden in der zweiten Hälfte des vierzehnten Jahrhunderts*' ABAW 21 (1894) 1–64.
PREVITÉ-ORTON, C. W., 'Marsilius of Padua' *Proceedings of the British Academy* 21 (1935) 137–83.
—— 'Marsilio of Padua, Doctrines' EHR 38 (1923) 1–21.
QUINT, J., *Meister Eckehart, Deutsche Predigten und Traktate* (Munich 1955).
—— *Textbuch zur Mystik des deutschen Mittelalters* (Halle 1962).
Realencyclopädie für protestantische Theologie und Kirche 21 vols. (1896–1913).
REEVES, M. E., 'Joachimist Expectations in the Order of Augustinian Hermits' *Recherches de théologie ancienne et médiévale* 25 (1958) 112–41.
—— 'The *Liber Figurarum* of Joachim of Fiore' *Mediaeval and Renaissance Studies* 2 (1951) 57–81.
—— 'The Abbot Joachim's disciples and the Cistercian Order' *Sophia* 19 (1951) 355–71.
—— 'Joachimist Influences on the Idea of a Last World Emperor' *Traditio* 17 (1961) 323–70.
—— 'The Arbores of Joachim of Fiore' *Studies in Italian History presented to Miss E. M. Jamison* (Rome) 124–36.
—— AND HIRSCH REICH, B., 'The seven seals in the writing of Joachim of Fiore' *Recherches de théologie ancienne et médiévale* 21 (1954) 211–47.
—— 'The *Figurae* of Joachim of Fiore, Genuine and Spurious Collections' *Mediaeval and Renaissance Studies* 3 (1954) 170–99.
REFFKE, E., Eckhartiana IV, 'Studien zum Problem der Entwicklung Meister Eckharts' ZKG 57 (1938) 19–95.
REICHART, B. M., 'Zur Geschichte der deutschen Dominikaner.' *Römische Quartelschrift* 14 (1900) 79–101, 15 (1901) 124–52.
REID, E. J. B., 'The Lollards at Colchester' EHR 29 (1914) 101–4.
REINMANN, J. G., *The Third Order Secular of St. Francis* (Washington 1948).
RENOUARD, Y., *La papauté à Avignon* (1954).
RICHARDSON, H. G., 'Heresy and the Lay Power under Richard II' EHR 51 (1936) 1–28.
—— 'John Oldcastle in Hiding' EHR 55 (1940) 432–8.
RITTER, G., 'Zur Geschichte des häretischen Pantheismus in Deutschland im 15 Jahrhundert' ZKG 43 (1924) 150–9.
RIVIÈRE, J., *Le problème de l'église et de l'état au temps de Philippe le Bel* (Paris 1926).
ROBERTS, A. E., 'Pierre d'Ailly and the Council of Constance' TRHS 4th series 18 (1935) 123–42.

Robson, J. A., *Wyclif and the Oxford Schools* (Cambridge 1961).
Rosenfeld, H., 'Die mittelalterliche Totentanz' *Beiheft zur Archiv für Kulturgeschichte* 3 (Münster i W. 1954).
Ruh, K., 'Die trinitarische Spekulation in deutschen Mystik und Scholastik' *Zeitschrift für Deutsche Philologie* 72 (1951) 24–53.
Runciman, S., *The Medieval Manichee* (Cambridge 1947). See R. Manselli's critique in *Ricerchi religiosi* (1949) 60–90.
Russell, J. B., *Dissent and Reform in the Early Middle Ages* (University of California 1965).
Russo, F., *Bibliografia giochomita* (Florence 1954); useful but often inaccurate.
—— *Gioacchino da Fiore e le fondazioni Florensi in Calabria* (Naples 1959).
Sabatier, P., *Vie de S. François d'Assise* (Paris 1931).
—— 'L'Originalité de Saint François d'Assise' *Franciscan Essays* 1, BSFS, Extra Series I (Aberdeen 1912) 1–17.
St. Axters, P., *La Spiritualité des Pays-Bas* (Paris 1948).
Salembier, L., *Le grand schisme d'Occident* (5th edn. Paris 1922).
Salvatorelli, L., 'Movimento Francescano e Gioachinismo' *10 Congresso Internazionale di Scienze Storiche* (Rome 1955) Relazioni III 403–48.
Samarin, C. and Mollat, G., *La fiscalité pontificale en France au 14e siècle* (Paris 1905).
Savini, S., *Il Catarismo italiano ed i suoi vescovi nei secoli XIII e XIV* (Florence 1958).
Schaff, D., *John Hus* (New York 1915).
Schiff, O., 'Die Wirsberger. Ein Beitrag zur Geschichte der revolutionären Apokalyptik im 15 Jahrhundert' *Historische Vierteljahresschrift* 26 (1931) 776–86.
Schmidt, C., *Histoire et doctrine de la secte des Cathares ou Albigeois* (Paris–Geneva 1849).
Schnürer, G., *Kirche und Kultur im Mittelalter* vols. 2 and 3 (Paderborn 1929, 1930).
Schönbach, A. E., *Studien zur Geschichte der altdeutschen Predigt III: Das Wirken Bertholds von Regensburg gegen die Ketzer. Sitzungberichte der Akademie den Wissenschaften in Wien, phil-hist. Klasse 147*, 5 (Wien 1909).
Scholz, R., *Wilhelm von Ockham als politischer Denker* (Leipzig 1944).
—— 'Marsilius von Padua und die Genesis der modernen Staatsbewusstseins' *Historische Zeitschrift* 156 (1937) 88–103.
—— 'Zur Beurteilung Bonifaz VIII und seines sittlich-religiösen Characters' *Historische Vierteljahresschrift* 9 (1906) 470–515.
Seeberg, E., 'Eckhartiana I' ZKG 56 (1937) 87–105.
Sedlák, J., *M. Jan Hus* (Prague 1915).
Seppelt, F. X., *Der Kampf der Bettelorden an der Universität von Paris in der Mitte des 13 Jahrhunderts* (Breslau 1908).

SETON, W. W., *Blessed Giles of Assisi* BSFS 8 (Manchester 1918).
SETON-WATSON, R., *A History of the Czechs and Slovaks* (London 1944).
SHANNON, A. C., *The Popes and Heresy in the thirteenth century* (New York 1955).
—— 'The secrecy of witnesses in inquisitorial tribunals' in *Essays in Honor of A. P. Evans* (New York 1955) 59–69.
SHIRLEY, W. W., *Catalogue of the Original Works of John Wyclif* (Oxford 1865, 2nd edn. 1924).
SIEBT, F., 'Die Hussitenzeit als Kulturepoch' *Historische Zeitschrift* 195 (1962) 21–62.
SIGMUND, P. E., 'The influence of Marsilius of Padua on 15th century conciliarism' *Journal of the History of Ideas* 23 (1962) 392–402.
SIKES, J. G., 'John de Pouilli and Peter de la Palu' EHR 49 (1934) 219–40.
SMALLEY, B., *The Study of the Bible in the Middle Ages* (2nd edn. 1952).
—— *The English Friars and Antiquity in the early fourteenth century* (Oxford 1960).
—— 'John Wyclif's Postilla super totam Bibliam' *Bodleian Library Record* 4 (1953) 186–205.
—— 'The Bible and Eternity: John Wyclif's Dilemma' *Journal of the Warburg and Courtauld Institutes* 27 (1965) 73–89.
—— 'Wyclif's *Postilla* on the Old Testament and his *Principium*' in *Essays presented to Daniel Callus* (Oxford 1964) 253–96.
SPÄTLING, L., *De Apostolicis, pseudo apostolicis, apostolinis* (Munich 1947).
SPICQ, P. C., *Esquisse d'une histoire de l'exegèse latine au moyen age* (Paris 1944).
SPINKA, M., 'Paul Kravař and Lollard-Hussite Relations' *Church History* 26 (1956) 16–26.
—— *John Hus and the Czech Reform* (Chicago 1941).
STADTER, E., 'Das Glaubensproblem in seiner Bedeutung für die Ethik bei Petrus Johannis Olivi' *Franziskanische Studien* 42 (1960) 225–96.
—— 'Das Problem der Theologie bei Petrus Johannis Olivi' ibid., 43 (1961) 113–70.
STEENBERGHEN, F. VAN, *Siger de Brabant d'après ses œuvres inédites* 2 vols. (Louvain 1931–42).
—— *Les œuvres et la doctrine de Siger de Brabant* (Louvain 1938).
STEGMÜLLER, F., 'Der *Liber contra Manicheos*' *Mélanges offerts à E. Gilson* (Paris 1959) 563–611.
STEIN, I. H., 'An unpublished fragment of Wyclif's *Confessio*' *Speculum* 8 (1933) 503–10.
STEPHANO, A. DE, *Riformatori ed eretici del medioevo* (Palermo 1938).
—— 'Intorno alle origini e la natura della secta spiritus libertatis' *Archivum Romanicum* 11 (1927) 150–162.
STEPHENSON, G., *Gottheit und Gott in der spekulativen Mystik Meister Eckharts* (Bonn 1954).

TANON, L., *Histoire des Tribunaux de l'inquisition en France* (Paris 1893).
TAUBES, J., *Abendländische Eschatologie* (Berne 1947).
TEETAERT, A., 'Quatre questions inédites de Gerard d'Abbéville pour la défense de la supériorité du clergé seculier' *Archivio Italiano per la Storia della Pietà* I (1951) 85–178.
THÉRY, G., *Autour du décret de 1210* 2 vols. (Vol. I David of Dinant, vol. II Alexander of Aphrodisius) (Paris 1925–6).
—— 'Édition critique des pièces relatives au procès d'Eckhart' *Archives* I (1926) 129–268.
THOMPSON, A. H., *The English Clergy and their Organisation in the Later Middle Ages* (Oxford 1947).
THOMPSON, J. A. F., *The Later Lollards, 1414–1520* (Oxford 1965).
—— 'A Lollard Rising in Kent, 1431 or 1438?' *Bulletin of Institute of Historical Research* 37 (1964) 100–2.
THOMSON, S. H., 'A Note on Peter Payne and Wyclyf' *Medievalia et Humanistica* 16 (1964) 60–3.
—— 'Pre-Hussite heresy in Bohemia' EHR (1933) 23–42.
—— 'Some Latin Works erroneously ascribed to Wyclif' *Speculum* 8 (1933) 245–5.
—— 'A "Lost" Chapter of Wyclif's *Summa de Ente*' *Speculum* 4 (1929) 239–246.
—— 'The Philosophical Basis of Wyclif's Theology' *Journal of Religion* 11 (1931) 86–116.
—— 'Unnoticed Manuscripts and Works of Wyclif' *Journal of Theological Studies* 38 (1937) 24–36, 139–48.
THOUZELLIER, C., 'Hérésie et Croisade au XIIe siècle' RHE 49 (1954) 855–72.
—— *Un traité cathare inédit au début au XIIIe siècle d'après le 'Liber contra Manicheos' de Durand de Huesca* (Louvain 1961).
—— 'La pauvreté, arme contre l'Albigéisme' *Revue de l'histoire des religions* 151 (1957) 79–92.
—— 'Controverses vaudois-cathars à la fin du XIIe siècle' *Archives* (1960) 137–227.
—— *Catharisme et Valdéisme en Languedoc à la fin du 12e siècle et au début du 13e siècle* (Paris 1966).
TIERNEY, B., *The Foundations of Conciliar Theory* (Cambridge 1955).
—— 'Ockham, the Conciliar theory and the Canonists' *Journal of the History of Ideas* 15 (1954) 40–70.
TILLMAN, H., *Papst Innocenz III* (Bonn 1954).
TOCCO, F., *Studi Francescani* (Naples 1909).
—— *L'eresia nel medioevo* (Florence 1886).
—— 'Gli Apostolici di Fra Dolcino.' *Archivio Storico Italiano* ser. 5, 19 (1896) 241–75.
TÖPFER, B., *Das Kommende Reich des Friedens* (Berlin 1964).

Töpfer, B., 'Eine Handschrift des Evangelium Aeternum des Geradino von Borgo San Donnino' *Zeitschrift für Geschichtswissenschaft* 8 (1960).

Trapp, D., 'CLM 27034 Unchristened Nominalism and Wycliffite Realism at Prague in 1381' *Recherches de Théologie ancienne et médiévale* 24 (1957) 320–60.

Troeltsch, E., *The Social Teaching of the Christian Churches* 2 vols. (London 1950).

Turberville, A. S., *Mediaeval Heresy and the Inquisition* (London 1920).

—— ' Heresies and the Inquisition' CMH vol. 6, ch. 20, 699–726.

Ullmann, W., *The Origins of the Great Schism* (London 1948).

Vacandard, E., *L'Inquisition* (2nd edn., Paris 1907).

—— 'L'Inquisition' in DTC 7 (ii) 2016–68.

Valois, N., 'Jacques Duèse, Pape sous nom de Jean XXII' *Histoire Littéraire de la France* 34 (1915) 391–630.

—— *La France et le grand schisme d'Occident* 4 vols. (1896–1902).

Vernet, F., 'Frères du Libre Esprit' DTC vol. 6, 800–809.

Vicaire, M. H., *St. Dominic and his Times* (London 1964).

Vidal, J. M., *Bullaire de l'Inquisition* (Paris 1913).

—— 'Un ascète de sang royal, Philippe de Majorque' *Revue des questions historiques* 88 (1910) 361–403.

—— 'Menet de Robécourt, commissaire de l'inquisition de Carcassonne (1320–40)' *Le Moyen Age* 16 (1903) 425–49.

—— 'Procès d'inquisition contre Adhémar de Mosset, noble roussillonais, inculpé de béguinisme (1332–1334)' *Revue d'histoire de l'église de France* 1 (1910) 682–99, 711–24.

Vinay, V., 'Friedrich Reiser e la diaspora valdese di lingua tedesca nella XV secolo' BSSV 109 (1961) 35–56.

Volpe, G., *Movimenti religiosi e sette ereticali nella società medievale italiana (sec. XI–XIV)* (Florence 1926).

Völter, D., *Die Secte von Schwäbisch-Hall und der Ursprung der deutschen Kaisersage* ZKG 4 (1880) 360–93.

Vooght, P. de, 'Le conciliarisme aux conciles de Constance et de Bâle' *Irenikon* 36 (1963) 61–75; and *Le Concile et les Conciles* (Cerf 1960) 143–81.

—— 'L'hérésie des Taborites sur l'Eucharistie (1418–21)' *Irenikon* 35 (1962) 340–50.

—— *L'hérésie de Jean Huss* (Louvain 1960).

—— *Hussiana* (Louvain 1960).

—— *Les sources de la doctrine chrétienne* (Louvain, Bruges 1954).

—— 'Les indulgences dans la théologie de Jean Wyclif et de Jean Huss' *Recherches de théologie religieuse* 41 (1953) 481–518.

—— 'Wyclif et la *scriptura sola*' *Ephemerides Theologicas Lovanienses* 39 (1963) 50–86.

WACHTEL, A., 'Die Weltgeschichtliche Apocalypse-Auslegung des Minoriten Alexander von Bremen' *Franziskanische Studien* 24 (1937) 201–59, 305–63.

WALZ, A., 'Gottesfreunde um Margarete Ebner' *Historisches Jahrbuch* 72 (1953) 253–65.

WAUGH, W. A. T., 'Sir John Oldcastle' EHR 20 (1905) 434–56, 637–58.

—— 'The Lollard Knights' *Scottish Historical Review* 11 (1914) 55–92.

WEIGEL, H., 'Ein Waldenserverhör in Rothenburg im Jahr 1394' *Beiträge zur bayerischen Kirchengeschichte* 23 (1917) 80–6.

WEISS, K., 'Die Seelenmetaphysik des Meister Eckhart' ZKG 52 (1933) 467–516.

WENTZLAFF-EGGEBERT, F. W., *Deutsche Mystik zwischen Mittelalter und Neuzeit* (Tübingen 1947).

WERNER, E., see also under BÜTTNER and ERBSTÖSSER.

—— *Pauperes Christi* (Leipzig 1956).

—— 'Ideologische Aspekte des deutsch-österreichen Waldensertums im 14 Jahrhundert' *Studi Medievali* 3rd series 4 (1963) 218–37.

—— *Nachrichten über spätmittelalterliche Ketzer aus tschechoslovakischen Archiven und Bibliotheken* (Leipzig 1963).

—— 'Popular ideologies in late medieval Europe: Taborite Chiliasm and its antecedents' *Comparative Studies in Society and History* (1960).

—— AND ERBSTÖSSER, M., 'Sozial-religiöse Bewegungen im Mittelalter' *Wissenschaftliche Zeitschrift der Karl-Marx-Universität* 7 (1957–8) (Leipzig)257–82.

WILKS, M. J., *The Problem of Sovereignty in the Later Middle Ages* (Cambridge 1963).

—— 'Predestination, Property and Power: Wyclif's theory of dominion and grace' *Studies in Church History* 2 (1965) 220–36.

WILMS, H., *Geschichte des deutschen Dominikanerrin 1206–1916* (Dülmen i W. 1920).

WOLFF, P., *Histoire de Toulouse* (Toulouse 1958).

WOOD-LEGH, K., *Church Life under Edward III* (Cambridge 1934).

WORKMAN, H. B., *John Wyclif* 2 vols. (Oxford 1926).

WYNGAERT, A. VON DEN, 'De tertio ordine S. Francisci' AFH 13 (1920) 3–77.

ZIPPEL, W., *Die Mystiker und die deutsche Gesellschaft des 13 und 14 Jahrhunderts* (Düren 1935).

ZUHORN, K., 'Die Beginen in Münster' *Westfalische Zeitschrift* 91 (1935) 1–149.

Index